The Core iOS Developer's Cookbook

The Core iOS Developer's Cookbook

Fifth Edition

Erica Sadun
Rich Wardwell

✦Addison-Wesley

Upper Saddle River, NJ • Boston • Indianapolis • San Francisco
New York • Toronto • Montreal • London • Munich • Paris • Madrid
Cape Town • Sydney • Tokyo • Singapore • Mexico City

For information about buying this title in bulk quantities, or for special sales opportunities (which may include electronic versions; custom cover designs; and content particular to your business, training goals, marketing focus, or branding interests), please contact our corporate sales department at corpsales@pearsoned.com or (800) 382-3419.

For government sales inquiries, please contact governmentsales@pearsoned.com.

For questions about sales outside the U.S., please contact international@pearsoned.com.

Visit us on the web: informit.com/aw

Library of Congress Control Number: 2013953064

ISBN-13: 978-0-321-94810-6
ISBN-10: 0-321-94810-6

Text printed in the United States on recycled paper at RR Donnelley in Crawfordsville, Indiana.

First printing: March 2014

Editor-in-Chief:
Mark Taub

Senior Acquisitions Editor:
Trina MacDonald

Senior Development Editor:
Chris Zahn

Managing Editor:
Kristy Hart

Senior Project Editor:
Betsy Gratner

Copy Editor:
Kitty Wilson

Indexer:
Lisa Stumpf

Proofreader:
Anne Goebel

Technical Reviewers:
Collin Ruffenach
Mike Shields
Ashley Ward

Editorial Assistant:
Olivia Basegio

Cover Designer:
Chuti Prasertsith

Senior Compositor:
Gloria Schurick

❖

Erica Sadun

I dedicate this book with love to my husband, Alberto,
who has put up with too many gadgets and too
many SDKs over the years while remaining both
kind and patient at the end of the day.

❖

❖

Rich Wardwell

I dedicate this book to my wife, Julie, who was relegated
to single-parent status during this endeavor,
and my children, Davis and Anne, who never stopped
asking me to play with them even after countless refusals.

❖

Contents

Preface

Welcome to a new *Core iOS Developer's Cookbook*!

With iOS 7, Apple introduced the most significant changes to its mobile operating system since its inception. This cookbook is here to help you get started developing for the latest exciting release. This revision introduces all the new features and visual paradigms announced at the latest Worldwide Developers Conference (WWDC), showing you how to incorporate them into your applications.

For this edition, the publishing team has split the cookbook material into manageable print volumes. This book, *The Core iOS Developer's Cookbook*, provides solutions for the heart of day-to-day development. It covers all the classes you need for creating iOS applications using standard APIs and interface elements. It provides recipes you need for working with graphics, touches, and views to create mobile applications.

And there's *Learning iOS Development: A Hands-on Guide to the Fundamentals of iOS Programming*, which covers much of the tutorial material that used to comprise the first several chapters of the cookbook. There you'll find all the fundamental how-to you need to learn iOS 7 development from the ground up. From Objective-C to Xcode, debugging to deployment, *Learning iOS Development* teaches you how to get started with Apple's development tool suite.

As in the past, you can find sample code at GitHub. You'll find the repository for this Cookbook at https://github.com/erica/iOS-7-Cookbook, all of it refreshed for iOS 7 after WWDC 2013.

If you have suggestions, bug fixes, corrections, or anything else you'd like to contribute to a future edition, please contact us at erica@ericasadun.com or rich@lifeisrich.org. We thank you all in advance. We appreciate all your feedback, which helps make this a better, stronger book.

—*Erica Sadun and Rich Wardwell, January 2014*

What You'll Need

It goes without saying that, if you're planning to build iOS applications, you're going to need at least one iOS device to test your applications, preferably a new model iPhone or iPad. The following list covers the basics of what you'll need to begin:

- **Apple's iOS SDK**—You can download the latest version of the iOS SDK from Apple's iOS Dev Center (http://developer.apple.com/ios). If you plan to sell apps through the App Store, you need to become a paid iOS developer. This costs $99/year for individuals and $299/year for enterprise (that is, corporate) developers. Registered developers receive certificates that allow them to "sign" and download their applications to their iPhone/ iPod touch or iPad for testing and debugging and to gain early access to prerelease versions of iOS. Free-program developers can test their software on the Mac-based simulator but cannot deploy to devices or submit to the App Store.

- **A modern Mac running Mac OS X Mountain Lion (v 10.8) or, preferably, Mac OS X Mavericks (v 10.9)**—You need plenty of disk space for development, and your Mac should have as much RAM as you can afford to put into it.

- **An iOS device**—Although the iOS SDK includes a simulator for you to test your applications, you really do need to own iOS hardware to develop for the platform. You can tether your unit to the computer and install the software you've built. For real-life App Store deployment, it helps to have several units on hand, representing the various hardware and firmware generations, so that you can test on the same platforms your target audience will use.

- **An Internet connection**—This connection enables you to test your programs with a live Wi-Fi connection as well as with a cellular data service.

- **Familiarity with Objective-C**—To program for the iPhone, you need to know Objective-C 2.0. The language is based on ANSI C with object-oriented extensions, which means you also need to know a bit of C, too. If you have programmed with Java or C++ and are familiar with C, you should be able to make the move to Objective-C.

Your Roadmap to Mac/iOS Development

One book can't be everything to everyone. If we were to pack everything you need to know into this book, you wouldn't be able to pick it up. (As it stands, this book offers an excellent tool for upper-body development. Please don't sue if you strain yourself lifting it.) There is, indeed, a lot you need to know to develop for the Mac and iOS platforms. If you are just starting out and don't have any programming experience, your first course of action should be to take a college-level course in the C programming language. Although the alphabet might start with the letter A, the root of most programming languages, and certainly your path as a developer, is C.

Once you know C and how to work with a compiler (something you'll learn in that basic C course), the rest should be easy. From there, you'll hop right on to Objective-C and learn how to program with that, alongside the Cocoa frameworks. The flowchart in Figure P-1 shows the key titles offered by Pearson Education that can help provide the training you need to become a skilled iOS developer.

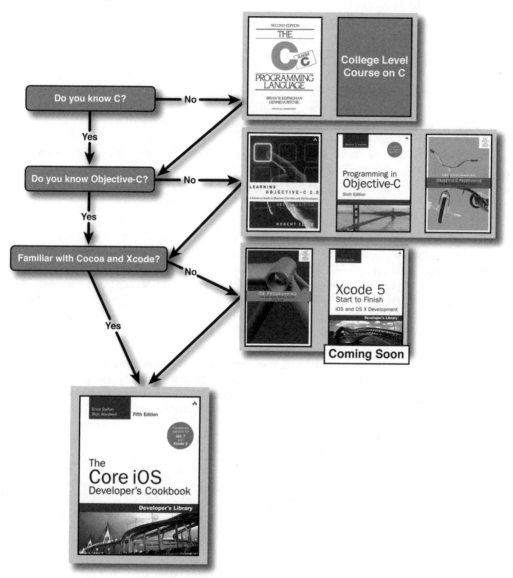

Figure P-1   A roadmap to becoming an iOS developer.

Once you know C, you've got a few options for learning how to program with Objective-C. If you want an in-depth view of the language, you can either read Apple's own documentation or pick up one of these books on Objective-C:

- *Objective-C Programming: The Big Nerd Ranch Guide*, 2nd edition, by Aaron Hillegass and Mikey Ward (Big Nerd Ranch, 2013)

- *Learning Objective-C 2.0: A Hands-on Guide to Objective-C for Mac and iOS Developers*, 2nd edition, by Robert Clair (Addison-Wesley, 2012)

- *Programming in Objective-C 2.0*, 6th edition, by Stephen Kochan (Addison-Wesley, 2012)

With the language under your belt, next up is tackling Cocoa (Mac) or Cocoa Touch (iOS) and the developer tools, otherwise known as Xcode. For that, you have a few different options. Again, you can refer to Apple's own documentation on Cocoa, Cocoa Touch, and Xcode (Apple Developer: developer.apple.com), or if you prefer books, you can learn from the best. Aaron Hillegass, founder of the Big Nerd Ranch in Atlanta (www.bignerdranch.com), is the coauthor of *iOS Programming: The Big Nerd Ranch Guide*, 2nd edition, and author of *Cocoa Programming for Mac OS X*, 4th edition. Aaron's book is highly regarded in Mac developer circles and is the most-recommended book you'll see on the cocoa-dev mailing list.

> **Note**
>
> There are plenty of other books from other publishers on the market, including the bestselling *Beginning iOS 6 Development* by Dave Mark, Jack Nutting, Jeff LaMarche, and Fredrik Olsson (Apress, 2011). Another book that's worth picking up if you're a total newbie to programming is *Beginning Mac Programming* by Tim Isted (Pragmatic Programmers, 2011). Don't just limit yourself to one book or publisher. Just as you can learn a lot by talking with different developers, you will learn lots of tricks and tips from other books on the market.

To truly master Mac or iOS development, you need to look at a variety of sources: books, blogs, mailing lists, Apple's own documentation, and, best of all, conferences. If you get a chance to attend WWDC, you'll know what we're talking about. The time you spend at conferences talking with other developers—and in the case of WWDC, talking with Apple's engineers—is well worth the expense if you are a serious developer.

How This Book Is Organized

This book offers single-task recipes for the most common issues new iOS developers face: laying out interface elements, responding to users, accessing local data sources, and connecting to the Internet. Each chapter groups together related tasks, allowing you to jump directly to the solution you're looking for without having to decide which class or framework best matches that problem.

The Core iOS Developer's Cookbook offers you "cut-and-paste convenience," which means you can freely reuse the source code from recipes in this book for your own applications and then tweak the code to suit the needs of each of your apps.

Here's a rundown of what you'll find in this book's chapters:

- **Chapter 1, "Gestures and Touches"**—On iOS, touch provides the most important way for users to communicate their intent to an application. Touches are not limited to button presses and keyboard interaction. This chapter introduces direct manipulation interfaces, Multi-Touch, and more. You'll see how to create views that users can drag around the screen and read about distinguishing and interpreting gestures, as well as how to create custom gesture recognizers.

- **Chapter 2, "Building and Using Controls"**—Take your controls to the next level. This chapter introduces everything you need to know about how controls work. You'll discover how to build and customize controls in a variety of ways. From the prosaic to the obscure, this chapter introduces a range of control recipes you can reuse in your programs.

- **Chapter 3, "Alerting the User"**—iOS offers many ways to provide users with heads-ups, from pop-up dialogs and progress bars to local notifications, popovers, and audio pings. This chapter shows how to build these indications into your applications and expand your user-alert vocabulary. It introduces standard ways of working with these classes and offers solutions that allow you to use a blocks-based API to easily handle alert interactions.

- **Chapter 4, "Assembling Views and Animations"**—The UIView class and its subclasses populate the iOS device screens. This chapter introduces views from the ground up. This chapter dives into view recipes, exploring ways to retrieve, animate, and manipulate view objects. You'll learn how to build, inspect, and break down view hierarchies and understand how views work together. You'll discover the role that geometry plays in creating and placing views into your interface, and you read about animating views so they move and transform onscreen.

- **Chapter 5, "View Constraints"**—Auto Layout revolutionized view layout in iOS. Apple's layout features make your life easier and your interfaces more consistent. This is especially important when working across members of the same device family with different screen sizes, dynamic interfaces, rotation, or localization. This chapter introduces code-level constraint development. You'll discover how to create relations between onscreen objects and specify the way iOS automatically arranges your views. The outcome is a set of robust rules that adapt to screen geometry.

- **Chapter 6, "Text Entry"**—This chapter introduces text recipes that support a wide range of solutions. You'll read about controlling keyboards, making onscreen elements "text aware," scanning text, formatting text, and so forth. From text fields and text views to iOS's inline spelling checkers, this chapter introduces everything you need to know to work with iOS text in your apps.

- **Chapter 7, "Working with View Controllers"**—In this chapter, you'll discover the various view controller classes that enable you to enlarge and order the virtual spaces your users interact with. You'll learn from how-to recipes that cover page view controllers, split view controllers, navigation controllers, and more.

- **Chapter 8, "Common Controllers"**—The iOS SDK provides a wealth of system-supplied controllers that you can use in your day-to-day development tasks. This chapter introduces some of the most popular ones. You'll read about selecting images from your photo library, snapping photos, and recording and editing videos. You'll discover how to allow users to compose e-mails and text messages and how to post updates to social media such as Twitter and Facebook.

- **Chapter 9, "Creating and Managing Table Views"**—Tables provide a scrolling interaction class that works particularly well both on smaller devices and as a key player on larger tablets. Many iOS apps center on tables due to their simple natural organization features. This chapter introduces tables, explaining how tables work, what kinds of tables are available to you as a developer, and how you can leverage table features in your applications.

- **Chapter 10, "Collection Views"**—Collection views use many of the same concepts as tables but provide more power and more flexibility. This chapter walks you through all the basics you need to get started. Prepare to read about creating side-scrolling lists, grids, one-of-a-kind layouts like circles, and more. You'll learn about integrating visual effects through layout specifications and snapping items into place after scrolling, and you'll discover how to take advantage of built-in animation support to create the most effective interactions possible.

- **Chapter 11, "Documents and Data Sharing"**—Under iOS, applications can share information and data as well as move control from one application to another, using several system-supplied features. This chapter introduces the ways you can integrate documents and data sharing between applications. You'll see how to add these features into your applications and use them smartly to make your apps cooperative citizens of the iOS ecosystem.

- **Chapter 12, "A Taste of Core Data"**—Core Data offers managed data stores that can be queried and updated from your application. It provides a Cocoa Touch–based object interface that brings relational data management out from SQL queries and into the Objective-C world of iOS development. This chapter introduces Core Data. It provides just enough recipes to give you a taste of the technology, offering a jumping-off point for further Core Data learning. You'll learn how to design managed database stores, add and delete data, and query data from your code and integrate it into your UIKit table views and collection views.

- **Chapter 13, "Networking Basics"**—On Internet-connected devices, iOS is particularly suited to subscribing to web-based services. Apple has lavished the platform with a solid grounding in all kinds of network computing services and their supporting technologies. This chapter surveys common techniques for network computing and offers recipes that simplify day-to-day tasks. This chapter introduces the new HTTP system in iOS 7 and provides examples for downloading data, including background downloading. You'll also read about network reachability and web services, including examples of XML parsing and JSON serialization utilizing live services.

- **Chapter 14, "Device-Specific Development"**—Each iOS device represents a meld of unique, shared, momentary, and persistent properties. These properties include the device's current physical orientation, its model name, its battery state, and its access to onboard hardware. This chapter looks at the device from its build configuration to its active onboard sensors. It provides recipes that return a variety of information items about the unit in use.

- **Chapter 15, "Accessibility"**—This chapter offers a brief overview of VoiceOver accessibility to extend your audience to the widest possible range of users. You'll read about adding accessibility labels and hints to your applications and testing those features in the simulator and on the iOS device.

- **Appendix A, "Objective-C Literals"**—This appendix introduces new Objective-C constructs for specifying numbers, arrays, and dictionaries.

About the Sample Code

For the sake of pedagogy, this book's sample code uses a single main.m file. This is not how people normally develop iPhone or Cocoa applications, or, honestly, how they *should* be developing them, but it provides a great way of presenting a single big idea. It's hard to tell a story that requires looking through five or seven or nine individual files at once. Offering a single file concentrates that story, allowing access to that idea in a single chunk.

The examples in this book are not intended as standalone applications. Each is here to demonstrate a single recipe and a single idea. One main.m file with a central presentation reveals the implementation story in one place. Readers can study these concentrated ideas and transfer them into normal application structures, using the standard file structure and layout. The presentation in this book does not produce code in a standard day-to-day best-practices approach. Instead, it reflects a pedagogy that offers concise solutions that you can incorporate into your work as needed.

Contrast this to Apple's standard sample code, where you must comb through many files to build up a mental model of the concepts that are being demonstrated. Those examples are built as full applications, often involving tasks that are related to but not essential to what you need to solve. Finding just the relevant portions is a lot of work, and the effort may outweigh any gains.

In this book, you'll find exceptions to this one-file-with-the-story rule: This book provides standard class and header files when a class implementation is the recipe. Instead of highlighting a technique, some recipes offer these classes and categories (that is, extensions to a preexisting class rather than a new class). For those recipes, look for separate .m *and* .h files, in addition to the skeletal main.m that encapsulates the rest of the story.

For the most part, the examples in this book use a single application identifier: com.sadun. helloworld. This book uses one identifier to avoid clogging up your iOS devices with dozens of examples at once. Each example replaces the previous one, ensuring that your home screen remains relatively uncluttered. If you want to install several examples simultaneously, simply edit the identifier by adding a unique suffix, such as com.sadun.helloworld.table-edits. You can also edit the custom display name to make the apps visually distinct. Your Team Provisioning Profile matches every application identifier, including com.sadun.helloworld. This allows you to install compiled code to devices without having to change the identifier; just make sure to update your signing identity in each project's build settings.

Getting the Sample Code

You'll find the source code for this book at github.com/erica/iOS-7-Cookbook on the open-source GitHub hosting site. There you'll find a chapter-by-chapter collection of source code that provides working examples of the material covered in this book. Recipes are numbered as they are in the book. Recipe 6 in Chapter 5, for example, appears in the 06 subfolder of the C05 folder.

Any project numbered 00 or that has a suffix (like 05b or 02c) refers to material that is used to create in-text coverage and figures. For example, Chapter 9's 00 – Cell Types project helped build Figure 9-2, showing system-supplied table view cell styles. Normally, we delete these extra projects. Early readers of this manuscript requested that we include them in this edition. You'll find a half dozen or so of these extra samples scattered around the repository.

Contribute!

Sample code is never a fixed target. It continues to evolve as Apple updates its SDK and the Cocoa Touch libraries. Get involved. You can pitch in by suggesting bug fixes and corrections as well as by expanding the code that's on offer. GitHub allows you to fork repositories and grow them with your own tweaks and features and to share them back to the main repository. If you come up with a new idea or approach, let us know. Our team is happy to include great suggestions both at the repository and in the next edition of this book.

Getting Git

You can download this book's source code by using the git version control system. Xcode 5 includes robust support for git within the IDE. The git command-line tool is also packaged with the Xcode 5 toolset. Numerous third-party free and commercial git tools are also available.

Getting GitHub

GitHub (http://github.com) is the largest git-hosting site, with more than 150,000 public repositories. It provides both free hosting for public projects and paid options for private projects. With a custom web interface that includes wiki hosting, issue tracking, and an emphasis on social networking for project developers, it's a great place to find new code and collaborate on existing libraries. You can sign up for a free account at the GitHub website, where you can also copy and modify the repository for this book or create your own open-source iOS projects to share with others.

Contacting the Authors

If you have any comments or questions about this book, please drop us an e-mail message at erica@ericasadun.com or rich@lifeisrich.org, or stop by the GitHub repository and contact us there.

Acknowledgments

Erica Sadun

This book would not exist without the efforts of Chuck Toporek, who was my editor and whip cracker for many years and multiple publishers. He is now at Omnigroup and deeply missed. There'd be no cookbook were it not for him. He balances two great skill sets: inspiring authors to do what they think they cannot do and wielding the large "reality trout" of whacking[1] to keep subject matter focused and in the real world. There's nothing like being smacked repeatedly by a large virtual fish to bring a book in on deadline and with compelling content.

Thanks go as well to Trina MacDonald (my terrific editor), Chris Zahn (the awesomely talented development editor), and Olivia Basegio (the faithful and rocking editorial assistant who kept things rolling behind the scenes). Also, a big thank you to the entire Addison-Wesley/Pearson production team, specifically Kristy Hart, Betsy Gratner, Kitty Wilson, Anne Goebel, Lisa Stumpf, Gloria Schurick, and Chuti Prasertsith. Thanks also to the crew at Safari for getting my book up in Rough Cuts and for quickly fixing things when technical glitches occurred.

Thanks to Stacey Czarnowki of Studio B, my agency of many years, and to the recently retired Neil Salkind; to tech reviewers Collin Ruffenach, Mike Shields, and Ashley Ward, who helped keep this book in the realm of sanity rather than wishful thinking; and to all my colleagues, both present and former, at TUAW, Ars Technica, and the Digital Media/Inside iPhone blog.

I am deeply indebted to the wide community of iOS developers, including Jon Bauer, Tim Burks, Matt Martel, Tim Isted, Joachim Bean, Aaron Basil, Roberto Gamboni, John Muchow, Scott Mikolaitis, Alex Schaefer, Nick Penree, James Cuff, Jay Freeman, Mark Montecalvo, August Joki, Max Weisel, Optimo, Kevin Brosius, Planetbeing, Pytey, Michael Brennan, Daniel Gard, Michael Jones, Roxfan, MuscleNerd, np101137, UnterPerro, Jonathan Watmough, Youssef Francis, Bryan Henry, William DeMuro, Jeremy Sinclair, Arshad Tayyeb, Jonathan Thompson, Dustin Voss, Daniel Peebles, ChronicProductions, Greg Hartstein, Emanuele Vulcano, Sean Heber, Josh Bleecher Snyder, Eric Chamberlain, Steven Troughton-Smith, Dustin Howett, Dick Applebaum, Kevin Ballard, Hamish Allan, Oliver Drobnik, Rod Strougo, Kevin McAllister, Jay Abbott, Tim Grant Davies, Maurice Sharp, Chris Samuels, Chris Greening, Jonathan Willing, Landon Fuller, Jeremy Tregunna, Wil Macaulay, Stefan Hafeneger, Scott Yelich, chrallelinder, John Varghese, Andrea Fanfani, J. Roman, jtbandes, Artissimo, Aaron Alexander, Christopher Campbell Jensen, Nico Ameghino, Jon Moody, Julián Romero, Scott Lawrence, Evan K. Stone, Kenny Chan Ching-King, Matthias Ringwald, Jeff Tentschert, Marco Fanciulli, Neil Taylor, Sjoerd van Geffen, Absentia, Nownot, Emerson Malca, Matt Brown, Chris Foresman, Aron Trimble, Paul Griffin, Paul Robichaux, Nicolas Haunold, Anatol Ulrich (hypnocode GmbH), Kristian Glass, Remy "psy" Demarest, Yanik Magnan, ashikase, Shane Zatezalo, Tito Ciuro, Mahipal Raythattha, Jonah Williams of Carbon Five, Joshua Weinberg, biappi, Eric Mock, and everyone at the iPhone developer channels at irc.saurik.com and irc.freenode.net, among many others too numerous to name individually. Their techniques, suggestions, and feedback helped make this book possible. If I have overlooked anyone who helped contribute, please accept my apologies for the oversight.

Special thanks go out to my family and friends, who supported me through month after month of new beta releases and who patiently put up with my unexplained absences and frequent howls of despair. I appreciate you all hanging in there with me. And thanks to my children for their steadfastness, even as they learned that a hunched back and the sound of clicking keys is a pale substitute for a proper mother. My kids provided invaluable assistance over the past few months by testing applications, offering suggestions, and just being awesome people. I try to remind myself on a daily basis how lucky I am that these kids are part of my life.

Rich Wardwell

Although with deadlines mounting I may have versed otherwise, I give my deepest respect and appreciation to Erica for allowing me the honor of participating in the creation of this latest edition of the *Developer's Cookbook*. Through her mentoring and fish slapping, I've learned a great deal and, hopefully, at a minimum, flirted with the high standard that she has set forth.

Without the persistence of Trina MacDonald, our editor, I think I would have given up after the first chapter, screaming into the night. She has directed and encouraged through my frustration with, anxiety about, and ignorance of the book authoring process. I'm also indebted to Olivia Basegio, editorial assistant, and the team of technical editors she expertly arranged and managed. The technical editors' comprehensive efforts resulted in a much better book than we could have ever created on our own, for which I owe a great deal of gratitude: Thank you, Collin Ruffenach, Mike Shields, and Ashley Ward. The production team, including Betsy Gratner and Kitty Wilson, ensured that I appear much more adept at writing than I could ever hope to attain on my own. Many others at Addison-Wesley/Pearson to whom I've never spoken directly had a part; to each I'm immensely thankful for bringing this work to fruition.

A special thanks goes to Bil Moorhead, George Dick, and Daniel Pasco at Black Pixel, who were incredibly understanding as the demands of the book required attention and distraction from my daily responsibilities. It is an honor to work for and with the great folks at Black Pixel.

My parents, Rick and Janet, have been my greatest supporters, encouraging me in all my endeavors, including this one. My in-laws, Steve and Cary, provided a home for us during much of the writing of this book, for which I'm eternally grateful.

Finally, my wife and two children have been the true enablers of this project. I hope to reimburse in full for every honey-do item I neglected and every invite to play that I turned down. Their love and presence made it possible for me to complete this work.

Endnote

[1] No trouts, real or imaginary, were hurt in the development and production of this book. The same cannot be said for countless cans of Diet Coke (Erica) and Diet Mountain Dew (Rich), who selflessly surrendered their contents in the service of this manuscript.

About the Authors

Erica Sadun is the bestselling author, coauthor, and contributor to several dozen books on programming, digital video and photography, and web design, including the widely popular *The iOS 5 Developer's Cookbook*. She currently blogs at TUAW.com and has blogged in the past at O'Reilly's Mac Devcenter, Lifehacker, and Ars Technica. In addition to being the author of dozens of iOS-native applications, Erica holds a Ph.D. in computer science from Georgia Tech's Graphics, Visualization and Usability Center. A geek, a programmer, and an author, she's never met a gadget she didn't love. When not writing, she and her geek husband parent three geeks-in-training, who regard their parents with restrained bemusement when they're not busy rewiring the house or plotting global dominance.

Rich Wardwell is a senior iOS and Mac developer at Black Pixel, with more than 20 years of professional software development experience in server, desktop, and mobile spaces. He has been a primary developer on numerous top-ranking iOS apps in the Apple App Store, including apps for *USA Today* and *Fox News*. Rich has served as a technical editor for *The Core iOS 6 Developer's Cookbook* and *The Advanced iOS 6 Developer's Cookbook*, both by author Erica Sadun, as well as many other Addison-Wesley iOS developer titles. When not knee-deep in iOS code, Rich enjoys "tractor therapy" and working on his 30-acre farm in rural Georgia with his wife and children.

Editor's Note: We Want to Hear from You!

As the reader of this book, you are our most important critic and commentator. We value your opinion and want to know what we're doing right, what we could do better, what areas you'd like to see us publish in, and any other words of wisdom you're willing to pass our way.

You can e-mail or write me directly to let me know what you did or didn't like about this book—as well as what we can do to make our books stronger.

Please note that I cannot help you with technical problems related to the topic of this book, and that due to the high volume of mail I receive, I might not be able to reply to every message.

When you write, please be sure to include this book's title and authors as well as your name and phone or e-mail address. I will carefully review your comments and share them with the authors and editors who worked on the book.

E-mail: trina.macdonald@pearson.com

Mail: Trina MacDonald
          Senior Acquisitions Editor
          Addison-Wesley/Pearson Education, Inc.
          75 Arlington St., Ste. 300
          Boston, MA 02116

Reader Services

Visit our website and register this book at informit.com/register for convenient access to any updates, downloads, or errata that might be available for this book.

1

Gestures and Touches

The touch represents the heart of iOS interaction; it provides the core way that users communicate their intent to an application. Touches are not limited to button presses and keyboard interaction. You can design and build applications that work directly with users' gestures in meaningful ways. This chapter introduces direct manipulation interfaces that go far beyond prebuilt controls. You'll see how to create views that users can drag around the screen. You'll also discover how to distinguish and interpret gestures, which are a high-level touch abstraction, and gesture recognizer classes, which automatically detect common interaction styles like taps, swipes, and drags. By the time you finish reading this chapter, you'll have read about many different ways you can implement gesture control in your own applications.

Touches

Cocoa Touch implements direct manipulation in the simplest way possible. It sends touch events to the view you're interacting with. As an iOS developer, you tell the view how to respond. Before jumping into gestures and gesture recognizers, you should gain a solid foundation in this underlying touch technology. It provides the essential components of all touch-based interaction.

Each touch conveys information: where the touch took place (both the current and previous location), what phase of the touch was used (essentially mouse down, mouse moved, mouse up in the desktop application world, corresponding to finger or touch down, moved, and up in the direct manipulation world), a tap count (for example, single-tap/double-tap), and when the touch took place (through a time stamp).

iOS uses what is called a *responder chain* to decide which objects should process touches. As their name suggests, responders are objects that respond to events, and they act as a chain of possible managers for those events. When the user touches the screen, the application looks for an object to handle this interaction. The touch is passed along, from view to view, until some object takes charge and responds to that event.

At the most basic level, touches and their information are stored in UITouch objects, which are passed as groups in UIEvent objects. Each UIEvent object represents a single touch event, containing single or multiple touches. This depends both on how you've set up your application to respond (that is, whether you've enabled Multi-Touch interaction) and how the user touches the screen (that is, the physical number of touch points).

Your application receives touches in view or view controller classes; both implement touch handlers via inheritance from the `UIResponder` class. You decide where you process and respond to touches. Trying to implement low-level gesture control in non-responder classes has tripped up many new iOS developers.

Handling touches in views may seem counterintuitive. You probably expect to separate the way an interface looks (its view) from the way it responds to touches (its controller). Further, using views for direct touch interaction may seem to contradict Model–View–Controller design orthogonality, but it can be necessary and can help promote encapsulation.

Consider the case of working with multiple touch-responsive subviews such as game pieces on a board. Building interaction behavior directly into view classes allows you to send meaningful semantically rich feedback to your core application code while hiding implementation minutia. For example, you can inform your model that a pawn has moved to Queen's Bishop 5 at the end of an interaction sequence rather than transmit a meaningless series of vector changes. By hiding the way the game pieces move in response to touches, your model code can focus on game semantics instead of view position updates.

Drawing presents another reason to work in the `UIView` class. When your application handles any kind of drawing operation in response to user touches, you need to implement touch handlers in views. Unlike views, view controllers don't implement the all-important `drawRect:` method needed for providing custom presentations.

Working at the `UIViewController` class level also has its perks. Instead of pulling out primary handling behavior into a secondary class implementation, adding touch management directly to the view controller allows you to interpret standard gestures, such as tap-and-hold or swipes, where those gestures have meaning. This better centralizes your code and helps tie controller interactions directly to your application model.

In the following sections and recipes, you'll discover how touches work, how you can respond to them in your apps, and how to connect what a user sees with how that user interacts with the screen.

Phases

Touches have life cycles. Each touch can pass through any of five phases that represent the progress of the touch within an interface. These phases are as follows:

- **`UITouchPhaseBegan`**—Starts when the user touches the screen.
- **`UITouchPhaseMoved`**—Means a touch has moved on the screen.
- **`UITouchPhaseStationary`**—Indicates that a touch remains on the screen surface but that there has not been any movement since the previous event.

- **UITouchPhaseEnded**—Gets triggered when the touch is pulled away from the screen.

- **UITouchPhaseCancelled**—Occurs when the iOS system stops tracking a particular touch. This usually happens due to a system interruption, such as when the application is no longer active or the view is removed from the window.

Taken as a whole, these five phases form the interaction language for a touch event. They describe all the possible ways that a touch can progress or fail to progress within an interface and provide the basis for control for that interface. It's up to you as the developer to interpret those phases and provide reactions to them. You do that by implementing a series of responder methods.

Touches and Responder Methods

All subclasses of the UIResponder class, including UIView and UIViewController, respond to touches. Each class decides whether and how to respond. When choosing to do so, they implement customized behavior when a user touches one or more fingers down in a view or window.

Predefined callback methods handle the start, movement, and release of touches from the screen. Corresponding to the phases you've already seen, the methods involved are as follows:

- **touchesBegan:withEvent:**—Gets called at the starting phase of the event, as the user starts touching the screen.

- **touchesMoved:withEvent:**—Handles the movement of the fingers over time.

- **touchesEnded:withEvent:**—Concludes the touch process, where the finger or fingers are released. It provides an opportune time to clean up any work that was handled during the movement sequence.

- **touchesCancelled:WithEvent:**—Called when Cocoa Touch must respond to a system interruption of the ongoing touch event.

Each of these is a UIResponder method, often implemented in a UIView or UIViewController subclass. All views inherit basic nonfunctional versions of the methods. When you want to add touch behavior to your application, you override these methods and add a custom version that provides the responses your application needs. Notice that UITouchPhaseStationary does not generate a callback.

Your classes can implement all or just some of these methods. For real-world deployment, you will always want to add a touches-cancelled event to handle the case of a user dragging his or her finger offscreen or the case of an incoming phone call, both of which cancel an ongoing touch sequence. As a rule, you can generally redirect a cancelled touch to your touchesEnded:withEvent: method. This allows your code to complete the touch sequence, even if the user's finger has not left the screen. Apple recommends overriding all four methods as a best practice when working with touches.

> **Note**
>
> Views have a mode called *exclusive touch* that prevents touches from being delivered to other views in the same window. When enabled, this property blocks other views from receiving touch events within that view. The primary view handles all touch events exclusively.

Touching Views

When dealing with many onscreen views, iOS automatically decides which view the user touched and passes any touch events to the proper view for you. This helps you write concrete direct manipulation interfaces where users touch, drag, and interact with onscreen objects.

Just because a touch is physically on top of a view doesn't mean that a view has to respond. Each view can use a "hit test" to choose whether to handle a touch or to let that touch fall through to views beneath it. As you'll see in the recipes that follow, you can use clever response strategies to decide when your view should respond, particularly when you're using irregular art with partial transparency.

With touch events, the first view that passes the hit test opts to handle or deny the touch. If it passes, the touch continues to the view's superview and then works its way up the responder chain until it is handled or until it reaches the window that owns the views. If the window does not process it, the touch moves to the `UIApplication` instance, where it is either processed or discarded.

Multi-Touch

iOS supports both single- and Multi-Touch interfaces. Single-touch GUIs handle just one touch at any time. This relieves you of any responsibility to determine which touch you were tracking. The one touch you receive is the only one you need to work with. You look at its data, respond to it, and wait for the next event.

When working with Multi-Touch—that is, when you respond to multiple onscreen touches at once—you receive an entire set of touches. It is up to you to order and respond to that set. You can, however, track each touch separately and see how it changes over time, which enables you to provide a richer set of possible user interaction. Recipes for both single-touch and Multi-Touch interaction follow in this chapter.

Gesture Recognizers

With gesture recognizers, Apple added a powerful way to detect specific gestures in your interface. Gesture recognizers simplify touch design. They encapsulate touch methods, so you don't have to implement them yourself, and they provide a target-action feedback mechanism that hides implementation details. They also standardize how certain movements are categorized, as drags or swipes.

With gesture recognizer classes, you can trigger callbacks when iOS determines that the user has tapped, pinched, rotated, swiped, panned, or used a long press. These detection capabilities simplify development of touch-based interfaces. You can code your own for improved reliability, but a majority of developers will find that the recognizers, as shipped, are robust enough for many application needs. You'll find several recognizer-based recipes in this chapter. Because recognizers all basically work in the same fashion, you can easily extend these recipes to your specific gesture recognition requirements.

Here is a rundown of the kinds of gestures built in to recent versions of the iOS SDK:

- **Taps**—Taps correspond to single or multiple finger taps onscreen. Users can tap with one or more fingers; you specify how many fingers you require as a gesture recognizer property and how many taps you want to detect. You can create a tap recognizer that works with single finger taps, or more nuanced recognizers that look for, for example, two-fingered triple-taps.

- **Swipes**—Swipes are short single- or Multi-Touch gestures that move in a single cardinal direction: up, down, left, or right. They cannot move too far off course from that primary direction. You set the direction you want your recognizer to work with. The recognizer returns the detected direction as a property.

- **Pinches**—To pinch or unpinch, a user must move two fingers together or apart in a single movement. The recognizer returns a scale factor indicating the degree of pinching.

- **Rotations**—To rotate, a user moves two fingers at once, either in a clockwise or counterclockwise direction, producing an angular rotation as the main returned property.

- **Pans**—Pans occur when users drag their fingers across the screen. The recognizer determines the change in translation produced by that drag.

- **Long presses**—To create a long press, the user touches the screen and holds his or her finger (or fingers) there for a specified period of time. You can specify how many fingers must be used before the recognizer triggers.

Recipe: Adding a Simple Direct Manipulation Interface

Before moving on to more modern (and commonly used) gesture recognizers, take time to understand and explore the traditional method of responding to a user's touch. You'll gain a deeper understanding of the touch interface by learning how simple UIResponder touch event handling works.

When you work with direct manipulation, your design focus moves from the UIViewController to the UIView. The view, or more precisely the UIResponder, forms the heart of direct manipulation development. You create touch-based interfaces by customizing methods that derive from the UIResponder class.

Recipe 1-1 centers on touches in action. This example creates a child of UIImageView called DragView and adds touch responsiveness to the class. Because this is an image view, it's important to enable user interaction (that is, set setUserInteractionEnabled to YES). This property affects all the view's children as well as the view itself. User interaction is generally enabled for most views, but UIImageView is the one exception that stumps most beginners; Apple apparently didn't think people would generally use touches with UIImageView.

The recipe works by updating a view's center to match the movement of an onscreen touch. When a user first touches any DragView, the object stores the start location as an offset from the view's origin. As the user drags, the view moves along with the finger—always maintaining the same origin offset so that the movement feels natural. Movement occurs by updating the object's center. Recipe 1-1 calculates x and y offsets and adjusts the view center by those offsets after each touch movement.

Upon being touched, the view pops to the front. That's due to a call in the touchesBegan: withEvent: method. The code tells the superview that owns the DragView to bring that view to the front. This allows the active element to always appear foremost in the interface.

This recipe does not implement touches-ended or touches-cancelled methods. Its interests lie only in the movement of onscreen objects. When the user stops interacting with the screen, the class has no further work to do.

Recipe 1-1 **Creating a Draggable View**

```
@implementation DragView
{
    CGPoint startLocation;
}


- (instancetype)initWithImage:(UIImage *)anImage
{
    self = [super initWithImage:anImage];
    if (self)
    {
        self.userInteractionEnabled = YES;
    }
    return self;
}


- (void)touchesBegan:(NSSet*)touches withEvent:(UIEvent*)event
{
    // Calculate and store offset, pop view into front if needed
    startLocation = [[touches anyObject] locationInView:self];
    [self.superview bringSubviewToFront:self];
}


- (void)touchesMoved:(NSSet*)touches withEvent:(UIEvent*)event
{
    // Calculate offset
```

```
        CGPoint pt = [[touches anyObject] locationInView:self];
        float dx = pt.x - startLocation.x;
        float dy = pt.y - startLocation.y;
        CGPoint newcenter = CGPointMake(
            self.center.x + dx,
            self.center.y + dy);

        // Set new location
        self.center = newcenter;
}
@end
```

Get This Recipe's Code

To find this recipe's full sample project, point your browser to
https://github.com/erica/iOS-7-Cookbook and go to the folder for Chapter 1.

Recipe: Adding Pan Gesture Recognizers

With gesture recognizers, you can achieve the same kind of interaction shown in Recipe 1-1 without working quite so directly with touch handlers. Pan gesture recognizers detect dragging gestures. They allow you to assign a callback that triggers whenever iOS senses panning.

Recipe 1-2 mimics Recipe 1-1's behavior by adding a recognizer to the view when it is first initialized. As iOS detects the user dragging on a `DragView` instance, the `handlePan:` callback updates the view's center to match the distance dragged.

This code uses what might seem like an odd way of calculating distance. It stores the original view location in an instance variable (`previousLocation`) and then calculates the offset from that point each time the view updates with a pan detection callback. This allows you to use affine transforms or apply the `setTranslation:inView:` method; you normally do not move view centers, as done here. This recipe creates a *dx*/*dy* offset pair and applies that offset to the view's center, changing the view's actual frame.

Unlike simple offsets, affine transforms allow you to meaningfully work with rotation, scaling, and translation all at once. To support transforms, gesture recognizers provide their coordinate changes in absolute terms rather than relative ones. Instead of issuing iterative offset vectors, `UIPanGestureRecognizer` returns a single vector representing a translation in terms of some view's coordinate system, typically the coordinate system of the manipulated view's superview. This vector translation lends itself to simple affine transform calculations and can be mathematically combined with other changes to produce a unified transform representing all changes applied simultaneously.

Here's what the `handlePan:` method looks like, using straight transforms and no stored state:

```objc
- (void)handlePan:(UIPanGestureRecognizer *)uigr
{
    if (uigr.state == UIGestureRecognizerStateEnded)
    {
        CGPoint newCenter = CGPointMake(
            self.center.x + self.transform.tx,
            self.center.y + self.transform.ty);
        self.center = newCenter;

        CGAffineTransform theTransform = self.transform;
        theTransform.tx = 0.0f;
        theTransform.ty = 0.0f;
        self.transform = theTransform;

        return;
    }

    CGPoint translation = [uigr translationInView:self.superview];
    CGAffineTransform theTransform = self.transform;
    theTransform.tx = translation.x;
    theTransform.ty = translation.y;
    self.transform = theTransform;
}
```

Notice how the recognizer checks for the end of interaction and then updates the view's position and resets the transform's translation. This adaptation requires no local storage and would eliminate the need for a `touchesBegan:withEvent:` method. Without these modifications, Recipe 1-2 has to store the previous state.

Recipe 1-2   Using a Pan Gesture Recognizer to Drag Views

```objc
@implementation DragView
{
    CGPoint previousLocation;
}

- (instancetype)initWithImage:(UIImage *)anImage
{
    self = [super initWithImage:anImage];
    if (self)
    {
        self.userInteractionEnabled = YES;
        UIPanGestureRecognizer *panRecognizer =
            [[UIPanGestureRecognizer alloc]
                initWithTarget:self action:@selector(handlePan:)];
```

```
        self.gestureRecognizers = @[panRecognizer];
    }
    return self;
}


- (void)touchesBegan:(NSSet *)touches withEvent:(UIEvent *)event
{
    // Promote the touched view
    [self.superview bringSubviewToFront:self];

    // Remember original location
    previousLocation = self.center;
}


- (void)handlePan:(UIPanGestureRecognizer *)uigr
{
    CGPoint translation = [uigr translationInView:self.superview];
    self.center = CGPointMake(previousLocation.x + translation.x,
        previousLocation.y + translation.y);
}
@end
```

Get This Recipe's Code

To find this recipe's full sample project, point your browser to https://github.com/erica/iOS-7-Cookbook and go to the folder for Chapter 1.

Recipe: Using Multiple Gesture Recognizers Simultaneously

Recipe 1-3 builds on the ideas presented in Recipe 1-2, but with several differences. First, it introduces multiple recognizers that work in parallel. To achieve this, the code uses three separate recognizers—rotation, pinch, and pan—and adds them all to the DragView's gestureRecognizers property. It assigns the DragView as the delegate for each recognizer. This allows the DragView to implement the gestureRecognizer:shouldRecognize-SimultaneouslyWithGestureRecognizer: delegate method, enabling these recognizers to work simultaneously. Until this method is added to return YES as its value, only one recognizer will take charge at a time. Using parallel recognizers allows you to, for example, both zoom and rotate in response to a user's pinch gesture.

> **Note**
>
> UITouch objects store an array of gesture recognizers. The items in this array represent each recognizer that receives the touch object in question. When a view is created without gesture recognizers, its responder methods will be passed touches with empty recognizer arrays.

Recipe 1-3 extends the view's state to include scale and rotation instance variables. These items keep track of previous transformation values and permit the code to build compound affine transforms. These compound transforms, which are established in Recipe 1-3's updateTransformWithOffset: method, combine translation, rotation, and scaling into a single result. Unlike the previous recipe, this recipe uses transforms uniformly to apply changes to its objects, which is the standard practice for recognizers.

Finally, this recipe introduces a hybrid approach to gesture recognition. Instead of adding a UITapGestureRecognizer to the view's recognizer array, Recipe 1-3 demonstrates how you can add the kind of basic touch method used in Recipe 1-1 to catch a triple-tap. In this example, a triple-tap resets the view back to the identity transform. This undoes any manipulation previously applied to the view and reverts it to its original position, orientation, and size. As you can see, the touches began, moved, ended, and cancelled methods work seamlessly alongside the gesture recognizer callbacks, which is the point of including this extra detail in this recipe. Adding a tap recognizer would have worked just as well.

This recipe demonstrates the conciseness of using gesture recognizers to interact with touches.

Recipe 1-3 Recognizing Gestures in Parallel

```
@interface DragView : UIImageView <UIGestureRecognizerDelegate>
@end

@implementation DragView
{
    CGFloat tx; // x translation
    CGFloat ty; // y translation
    CGFloat scale; // zoom scale
    CGFloat theta; // rotation angle
}

- (void)touchesBegan:(NSSet *)touches withEvent:(UIEvent *)event
{
    // Promote the touched view
    [self.superview bringSubviewToFront:self];

    // initialize translation offsets
    tx = self.transform.tx;
    ty = self.transform.ty;
    scale = self.scaleX;
    theta = self.rotation;
}
```

```objc
- (void)touchesEnded:(NSSet *)touches withEvent:(UIEvent *)event
{
    UITouch *touch = [touches anyObject];
    if (touch.tapCount == 3)
    {
        // Reset geometry upon triple-tap
        self.transform = CGAffineTransformIdentity;
        tx = 0.0f; ty = 0.0f; scale = 1.0f; theta = 0.0f;
    }
}


- (void)touchesCancelled:(NSSet *)touches withEvent:(UIEvent *)event
{
    [self touchesEnded:touches withEvent:event];
}


- (void)updateTransformWithOffset:(CGPoint)translation
{
    // Create a blended transform representing translation,
    // rotation, and scaling
    self.transform = CGAffineTransformMakeTranslation(
        translation.x + tx, translation.y + ty);
    self.transform = CGAffineTransformRotate(self.transform, theta);

    // Guard against scaling too low, by limiting the scale factor
    if (self.scale > 0.5f)
    {
        self.transform = CGAffineTransformScale(self.transform, scale, scale);
    }
    else
    {
        self.transform = CGAffineTransformScale(self.transform, 0.5f, 0.5f);
    }
}

- (void)handlePan:(UIPanGestureRecognizer *)uigr
{
    CGPoint translation = [uigr translationInView:self.superview];
    [self updateTransformWithOffset:translation];
}

- (void)handleRotation:(UIRotationGestureRecognizer *)uigr
{
    theta = uigr.rotation;
    [self updateTransformWithOffset:CGPointZero];
}
```

```objc
- (void)handlePinch:(UIPinchGestureRecognizer *)uigr
{
    scale = uigr.scale;
    [self updateTransformWithOffset:CGPointZero];
}

- (BOOL)gestureRecognizer:(UIGestureRecognizer *)gestureRecognizer
        shouldRecognizeSimultaneouslyWithGestureRecognizer:
        (UIGestureRecognizer *)otherGestureRecognizer
{
    return YES;
}

- (instancetype)initWithImage:(UIImage *)image
{
    // Initialize and set as touchable
    self = [super initWithImage:image];
    if (self)
    {
        self.userInteractionEnabled = YES;

        // Reset geometry to identities
        self.transform = CGAffineTransformIdentity;
        tx = 0.0f; ty = 0.0f; scale = 1.0f; theta = 0.0f;

        // Add gesture recognizer suite
        UIRotationGestureRecognizer *rot =
            [[UIRotationGestureRecognizer alloc]
                initWithTarget:self
                action:@selector(handleRotation:)];
        UIPinchGestureRecognizer *pinch =
            [[UIPinchGestureRecognizer alloc]
                initWithTarget:self
                action:@selector(handlePinch:)];
        UIPanGestureRecognizer *pan =
            [[UIPanGestureRecognizer alloc]
                initWithTarget:self
                action:@selector(handlePan:)];
        self.gestureRecognizers = @[rot, pinch, pan];
        for (UIGestureRecognizer *recognizer
            in self.gestureRecognizers)
                recognizer.delegate = self;
    }
    return self;
}
@end
```

Get This Recipe's Code

To find this recipe's full sample project, point your browser to https://github.com/erica/
iOS-7-Cookbook and go to the folder for Chapter 1.

Resolving Gesture Conflicts

Gesture conflicts may arise when you need to recognize several types of gestures at the same
time. For example, what happens when you need to recognize both single- and double-taps?
Should the single-tap recognizer fire at the first tap, even when the user intends to enter a
double-tap? Or should you wait and respond only after it's clear that the user isn't about to add
a second tap? The iOS SDK allows you to take these conflicts into account in your code.

Your classes can specify that one gesture must fail in order for another to succeed. Accomplish
this by calling `requireGestureRecognizerToFail:`. This gesture recognizer method takes
one argument, another gesture recognizer. This call creates a dependency between the two
gesture recognizers. For the first gesture to trigger, the second gesture must fail. If the second
gesture is recognized, the first gesture will not be.

iOS 7 introduces new APIs that offer more flexibility in providing runtime failure conditions
via gesture recognizer delegates and subclasses. You implement `gestureRecognizer:`
`shouldRequireFailureOfGestureRecognizer:` and `gestureRecognizer:shouldBe-`
`RequiredToFailByGestureRecognizer:` in recognizer delegates and `shouldRequire-`
`FailureOfGestureRecognizer:` and `shouldBeRequiredToFailByGestureRecognizer:` in
subclasses.

Each method returns a Boolean result. A positive response requires the failure condition specified by the method to occur for the gesture to succeed. These `UIGestureRecognizer` delegate
methods are called by the recognizer once per recognition attempt and can be set up between
recognizers across view hierarchies, while implementations provided in subclasses can define
class-wide failure requirements.

In real life, failure requirements typically mean that the recognizer adds a delay until it can
be sure that the dependent recognizer has failed. It waits until the second gesture is no longer
possible. Only then does the first recognizer complete. If you recognize both single- and
double-taps, the application waits a little longer after the first tap. If no second tap happens,
the single-tap fires. Otherwise, the double-tap fires, but not both.

Your GUI responses will slow down to accommodate this change. Your single-tap responses
become slightly laggy. That's because there's no way to tell if a second tap is coming until time
elapses. You should never use both kinds of recognizers where instant responsiveness is critical to your user experience. Try, instead, to design around situations where that tap means "do
something *now*" and avoid requiring both gestures for those modes.

Don't forget that you can add, remove, and disable gesture recognizers on-the-fly. A single-tap
may take your interface to a place where it then makes sense to further distinguish between
single- and double-taps. When leaving that mode, you could disable or remove the double-tap
recognizer to regain better single-tap recognition. Tweaks like this can limit interface slow-
downs to where they're absolutely needed.

Recipe: Constraining Movement

One problem with the simple approach of the earlier recipes in this chapter is that it's entirely possible to drag a view offscreen to the point where the user cannot see or easily recover it. Those recipes use unconstrained movement. There is no check to test whether the object remains in view and is touchable. Recipe 1-4 fixes this problem by constraining a view's movement to within its parent. It achieves this by limiting movement in each direction, splitting its checks into separate x and y constraints. This two-check approach allows the view to continue to move even when one direction has passed its maximum. If the view has hit the rightmost edge of its parent, for example, it can still move up and down.

> **Note**
>
> iOS 7 introduces UIKit Dynamics, for modeling real-world physical behaviors including physics simulation and responsive animations. By using the declarative Dynamics API, you can model gravity, collisions, force, attachments, springs, elasticity, and numerous other behaviors and apply them to UIKit objects. While this recipe presents a traditional approach to moving and constraining UI objects via gesture recognizers and direct frame manipulation, you can construct a much more elaborate variant with Dynamics.

Figure 1-1 shows a sample interface. The subviews (flowers) are constrained into the black rectangle in the center of the interface and cannot be dragged offscreen. Recipe 1-4's code is general and can adapt to parent bounds and child views of any size.

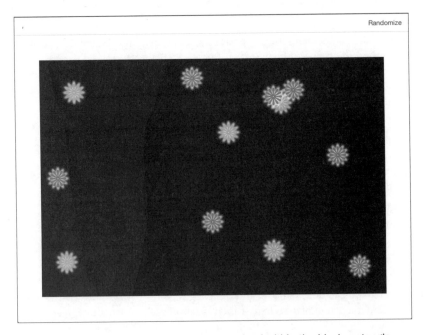

Figure 1-1   The movement of these flowers is constrained within the black rectangle.

Recipe 1-4   **Constrained Movement**

```
- (void)handlePan:(UIPanGestureRecognizer *)uigr
{
    CGPoint translation = [uigr translationInView:self.superview];
    CGPoint newcenter = CGPointMake(
        previousLocation.x + translation.x,
        previousLocation.y + translation.y);

    // Restrict movement within the parent bounds
    float halfx = CGRectGetMidX(self.bounds);
    newcenter.x = MAX(halfx, newcenter.x);
    newcenter.x = MIN(self.superview.bounds.size.width - halfx,
        newcenter.x);

    float halfy = CGRectGetMidY(self.bounds);
    newcenter.y = MAX(halfy, newcenter.y);
    newcenter.y = MIN(self.superview.bounds.size.height - halfy,
        newcenter.y);

    // Set new location
    self.center = newcenter;
}
```

Get This Recipe's Code

To find this recipe's full sample project, point your browser to https://github.com/erica/
iOS-7-Cookbook and go to the folder for Chapter 1.

Recipe: Testing Touches

Most onscreen view elements for direct manipulation interfaces are not rectangular. This
complicates touch detection because parts of the actual view rectangle may not correspond
to actual touch points. Figure 1-2 shows the problem in action. The screen shot on the right
shows the interface with its touch-based subviews. The shot on the left shows the actual view
bounds for each subview. The light gray areas around each onscreen circle fall within the
bounds, but touches to those areas should not "hit" the view in question.

iOS senses user taps throughout the entire view frame. This includes the undrawn area, such
as the corners of the frame outside the actual circles of Figure 1-2, just as much as the primary
presentation. That means that unless you add some sort of hit test, users may attempt to tap
through to a view that's "obscured" by the clear portion of the UIView frame.

Visualize your actual view bounds by setting its background color, like this:

```
dragger.backgroundColor = [UIColor lightGrayColor];
```

This adds the backsplashes shown in Figure 1-2 (left) without affecting the actual onscreen art. In this case, the art consists of a centered circle with a transparent background. Unless you add some sort of test, all taps to any portion of this frame are captured by the view in question. Enabling background colors offers a convenient debugging aid to visualize the true extent of each view; don't forget to comment out the background color assignment in production code. Alternatively, you can set a view layer's border width or style.

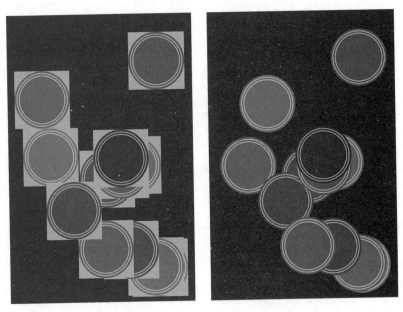

Figure 1-2   The application should ignore touches to the gray areas that surround each circle (left). The actual interface (right) uses a clear background (zero alpha values) to hide the parts of the view that are not used.

Recipe 1-5 adds a simple hit test to the views, determining whether touches fall within the circle. This test overrides the standard UIView's pointInside:withEvent: method. This method returns either YES (the point falls inside the view) or NO (it does not). The test here uses basic geometry, checking whether the touch lies within the circle's radius. You can provide any test that works with your onscreen views. As you'll see in Recipe 1-6, which follows in the next section, you can expand that test for much finer control.

Be aware that the math for touch detection on Retina display devices remains the same as that for older units, using the normalized points coordinate system rather than actual pixels. The extra onboard pixels do not affect your gesture-handling math. Your view's coordinate system remains floating point with subpixel accuracy. The number of pixels the device uses to draw to the screen does not affect UIView bounds and UITouch coordinates. It simply provides a way to provide higher detail graphics within that coordinate system.

> **Note**
>
> Do not confuse the point inside test, which checks whether a point falls inside a view, with the similar-sounding `hitTest:withEvent:`. The hit test returns the topmost view (closest to the user/screen) in a view hierarchy that contains a specific point. It works by calling `pointInside:withEvent:` on each view. If the `pointInside` method returns YES, the search continues down that hierarchy.

Recipe 1-5   Providing a Circular Hit Test

```
- (BOOL)pointInside:(CGPoint)point withEvent:(UIEvent *)event
{
    CGPoint pt;
    float halfSide = kSideLength / 2.0f;

    // normalize with centered origin
    pt.x = (point.x - halfSide) / halfSide;
    pt.y = (point.y - halfSide) / halfSide;

    // x^2 + y^2 = radius^2
    float xsquared = pt.x * pt.x;
    float ysquared = pt.y * pt.y;

    // If the radius < 1, the point is within the clipped circle
    if ((xsquared + ysquared) < 1.0) return YES;
    return NO;
}
```

> **Get This Recipe's Code**
>
> To find this recipe's full sample project, point your browser to https://github.com/erica/iOS-7-Cookbook and go to the folder for Chapter 1.

Recipe: Testing Against a Bitmap

Unfortunately, most views don't fall into the simple geometries that make the hit test from Recipe 1-5 so straightforward. The flowers shown in Figure 1-1, for example, offer irregular boundaries and varied transparencies. For complicated art, it helps to test touches against a bitmap. Bitmaps provide byte-by-byte information about the contents of an image-based view, allowing you to test whether a touch hits a solid portion of the image or should pass through to any views below.

Recipe 1-6 extracts an image bitmap from a `UIImageView`. It assumes that the image used provides a pixel-by-pixel representation of the view in question. When you distort that view (normally by resizing a frame or applying a transform), update the math accordingly. `CGPoints` can be transformed via `CGPointApplyAffineTransform()` to handle scaling and rotation changes. Keeping the art at a 1:1 proportion to the actual view pixels simplifies lookup and avoids any messy math. You can recover the pixel in question, test its alpha level, and determine whether the touch has hit a solid portion of the view.

This example uses a cutoff of 85. This corresponds to a minimum alpha level of 33% (that is, 85 / 255). This custom `pointInside:` method considers any pixel with an alpha level below 33% to be transparent. This is arbitrary. Use any level (or other test, for that matter) that works with the demands of your actual GUI.

Note

Unless you need pixel-perfect touch detection, you can probably scale down the bitmap so that it uses less memory and adjust the detection math accordingly.

Recipe 1-6   Testing Touches Against Bitmap Alpha Levels

```
// Return the offset for the alpha pixel at (x,y) for RGBA
// 4-bytes-per-pixel bitmap data
static NSUInteger alphaOffset(NSUInteger x, NSUInteger y, NSUInteger w)
    {return y * w * 4 + x * 4;}

// Return the bitmap from a provided image
NSData *getBitmapFromImage(UIImage *image)
{
    if (!sourceImage) return nil;

    // Establish color space
    CGColorSpaceRef colorSpace = CGColorSpaceCreateDeviceRGB();
    if (colorSpace == NULL)
    {
        NSLog(@"Error creating RGB color space");
        return nil;
    }

    // Establish context
    int width = sourceImage.size.width;
    int height = sourceImage.size.height;
    CGContextRef context =
        CGBitmapContextCreate(NULL, width, height, 8,
                  width * 4, colorSpace,
                  (CGBitmapInfo) kCGImageAlphaPremultipliedFirst);
    CGColorSpaceRelease(colorSpace);
    if (context == NULL)
    {
```

```objc
        NSLog(@"Error creating context");
        return nil;
    }

    // Draw source into context bytes
    CGRect rect = (CGRect){.size = sourceImage.size};
    CGContextDrawImage(context, rect, sourceImage.CGImage);

    // Create NSData from bytes
    NSData *data =
        [NSData dataWithBytes:CGBitmapContextGetData(context)
                length:(width * height * 4)];
    CGContextRelease(context);

    return data;
}

// Store the bitmap data into an NSData instance variable
- (instancetype)initWithImage:(UIImage *)anImage
{
    self = [super initWithImage:anImage];
    if (self)
    {
        self.userInteractionEnabled = YES;
        data = getBitmapFromImage(anImage);
    }
    return self;
}

// Does the point hit the view?
- (BOOL)pointInside:(CGPoint)point withEvent:(UIEvent *)event
{
    if (!CGRectContainsPoint(self.bounds, point)) return NO;
    Byte *bytes = (Byte *)data.bytes;
    uint offset = alphaOffset(point.x, point.y, self.image.size.width);
    return (bytes[offset] > 85);
}
```

Get This Recipe's Code

To find this recipe's full sample project, point your browser to https://github.com/erica/iOS-7-Cookbook and go to the folder for Chapter 1.

Recipe: Drawing Touches Onscreen

UIView hosts the realm of direct onscreen drawing. Its drawRect: method offers a low-level way to draw content directly, letting you create and display arbitrary elements using Quartz 2D calls. With touch and drawing, you can build concrete, manipulatable interfaces.

Recipe 1-7 combines gestures with drawRect to introduce touch-based painting. As a user touches the screen, the TouchTrackerView class builds a Bezier path that follows the user's finger. To paint the progress as the touch proceeds, the touchesMoved:withEvent: method calls setNeedsDisplay. This, in turn, triggers a call to drawRect:, where the view strokes the accumulated Bezier path. Figure 1-3 shows the interface with a path created in this way.

Figure 1-3   A simple painting tool for iOS requires little more than collecting touches along a path and painting that path with UIKit/Quartz 2D calls.

Although you could adapt this recipe to use gesture recognizers, there's really no point to it. The touches are essentially meaningless; they're only provided to create a pleasing tracing. The basic responder methods (that is, touches began, moved, and so on) are perfectly capable of handling path creation and management tasks.

This example is meant for creating continuous traces. It does not respond to any touch event without a move. If you want to expand this recipe to add a simple dot or mark, you'll have to add that behavior yourself.

Recipe 1-7   **Touch-Based Painting in a** `UIView`

```objc
@implementation TouchTrackerView
{
    UIBezierPath * path;
}


- (instancetype)initWithFrame:(CGRect)frame
{
    self = [super initWithFrame:frame];
    if (self)
    {
        self.multipleTouchEnabled = NO;
    }
    return self;
}


- (void)touchesBegan:(NSSet *)touches withEvent:(UIEvent *)event
{
    // Initialize a new path for the user gesture
    path = [UIBezierPath bezierPath];
    path.lineWidth = IS_IPAD ? 8.0f : 4.0f;

    UITouch *touch = [touches anyObject];
    [path moveToPoint:[touch locationInView:self]];
}


- (void)touchesMoved:(NSSet *)touches withEvent:(UIEvent *)event
{
    // Add new points to the path
    UITouch *touch = [touches anyObject];
    [self.path addLineToPoint:[touch locationInView:self]];
    [self setNeedsDisplay];
}


- (void)touchesEnded:(NSSet *)touches withEvent:(UIEvent *)event
{
        UITouch *touch = [touches anyObject];
        [path addLineToPoint:[touch locationInView:self]];
        [self setNeedsDisplay];
}


- (void)touchesCancelled:(NSSet *)touches
        withEvent:(UIEvent *)event
{
        [self touchesEnded:touches withEvent:event];
}


- (void)drawRect:(CGRect)rect
```

```
{
    // Draw the path
    [path stroke];
}
@end
```

Get This Recipe's Code

To find this recipe's full sample project, point your browser to https://github.com/erica/iOS-7-Cookbook and go to the folder for Chapter 1.

Recipe: Smoothing Drawings

Depending on the device in use and the amount of simultaneous processing involved, capturing user gestures may produce results that are rougher than desired. Touch events are often limited by CPU demands as well as by shaking hands. A smoothing algorithm can offset those limitations by interpolating between points. Figure 1-4 demonstrates the kind of angularity that derives from granular input and the smoothing that can be applied instead.

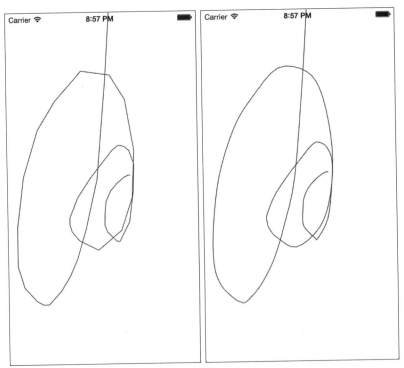

Figure 1-4   Catmull-Rom smoothing can be applied in real time to improve arcs between touch events. The images shown here are based on identical gesture input, with (right) and without (left) smoothing applied.

Catmull-Rom splines create continuous curves between key points. This algorithm ensures that each initial point you provide remains part of the final curve. The resulting path retains the original path's shape. You choose the number of interpolation points between each pair of reference points. The trade-off is between processing power and greater smoothing. The more points you add, the more CPU resources you'll consume. As you can see when using the sample code that accompanies this chapter, a little smoothing goes a long way, even on newer devices. The latest iPad is so responsive that it's hard to draw a particularly jaggy line in the first place.

Recipe 1-8 demonstrates how to extract points from an existing Bezier path and then apply splining to create a smoothed result. Catmull-Rom uses four points at a time to calculate intermediate values between the second and third points, using a granularity you specify between those points.

Recipe 1-8 provides an example of just one kind of real-time geometric processing you might add to your applications. Many other algorithms out there in the world of computational geometry can be applied in a similar manner.

> **Note**
>
> More extensive `UIBezierPath` utilities similar to `getPointsFromBezier` can be found in Erica Sadun's *iOS Drawing: Practical UIKit Solutions* (Addison-Wesley, 2013). For many excellent graphics-related recipes, including more advanced smoothing algorithms, check out the *Graphics Gems* series of books published by Academic Press and available at www.graphicsgems.org.

Recipe 1-8 Creating Smoothed Bezier Paths Using Catmull-Rom Splining

```
#define VALUE(_INDEX_) [NSValue valueWithCGPoint:points[_INDEX_]]

@implementation UIBezierPath (Points)
void getPointsFromBezier(void *info, const CGPathElement *element)
{
    NSMutableArray *bezierPoints = (__bridge NSMutableArray *)info;

    // Retrieve the path element type and its points
    CGPathElementType type = element->type;
    CGPoint *points = element->points;

    // Add the points if they're available (per type)
    if (type != kCGPathElementCloseSubpath)
    {
        [bezierPoints addObject:VALUE(0)];
        if ((type != kCGPathElementAddLineToPoint) &&
            (type != kCGPathElementMoveToPoint))
            [bezierPoints addObject:VALUE(1)];
    }
```

```
        if (type == kCGPathElementAddCurveToPoint)
            [bezierPoints addObject:VALUE(2)];
}

- (NSArray *)points
{
    NSMutableArray *points = [NSMutableArray array];
    CGPathApply(self.CGPath,
        (__bridge void *)points, getPointsFromBezier);
    return points;
}
@end

#define POINT(_INDEX_) \
    [(NSValue *)[points objectAtIndex:_INDEX_] CGPointValue]

@implementation UIBezierPath (Smoothing)
- (UIBezierPath *)smoothedPath:(int)granularity
{
    NSMutableArray *points = [self.points mutableCopy];
    if (points.count < 4) return [self copy];

    // Add control points to make the math make sense
    // Via Josh Weinberg
    [points insertObject:[points objectAtIndex:0] atIndex:0];
    [points addObject:[points lastObject]];

    UIBezierPath *smoothedPath = [UIBezierPath bezierPath];

    // Copy traits
    smoothedPath.lineWidth = self.lineWidth;

    // Draw out the first 3 points (0..2)
    [smoothedPath moveToPoint:POINT(0)];

    for (int index = 1; index < 3; index++)
        [smoothedPath addLineToPoint:POINT(index)];

    for (int index = 4; index < points.count; index++)
    {
        CGPoint p0 = POINT(index - 3);
        CGPoint p1 = POINT(index - 2);
        CGPoint p2 = POINT(index - 1);
        CGPoint p3 = POINT(index);

        // now add n points starting at p1 + dx/dy up
        // until p2 using Catmull-Rom splines
```

```objc
    for (int i = 1; i < granularity; i++)
    {
        float t = (float) i * (1.0f / (float) granularity);
        float tt = t * t;
        float ttt = tt * t;

        CGPoint pi; // intermediate point
        pi.x = 0.5 * (2*p1.x+(p2.x-p0.x)*t +
            (2*p0.x-5*p1.x+4*p2.x-p3.x)*tt +
            (3*p1.x-p0.x-3*p2.x+p3.x)*ttt);
        pi.y = 0.5 * (2*p1.y+(p2.y-p0.y)*t +
            (2*p0.y-5*p1.y+4*p2.y-p3.y)*tt +
            (3*p1.y-p0.y-3*p2.y+p3.y)*ttt);
        [smoothedPath addLineToPoint:pi];
    }

    // Now add p2
    [smoothedPath addLineToPoint:p2];
}

// finish by adding the last point
[smoothedPath addLineToPoint:POINT(points.count - 1)];

return smoothedPath;
}
@end

// Example usage:
// Replace the path with a smoothed version after drawing completes
- (void)touchesEnded:(NSSet *)touches withEvent:(UIEvent *)event
{
    UITouch *touch = [touches anyObject];
    [path addLineToPoint:[touch locationInView:self]];
    path = [path smoothedPath:4];
    [self setNeedsDisplay];
}
```

Get This Recipe's Code

To find this recipe's full sample project, point your browser to https://github.com/erica/
iOS-7-Cookbook and go to the folder for Chapter 1.

Recipe: Using Multi-Touch Interaction

Enabling Multi-Touch interaction in `UIView` instances lets iOS recover and respond to more than one finger touch at a time. Set the `UIView` property `multipleTouchEnabled` to `YES` or override `isMultipleTouchEnabled` for your view. When enabled, each touch callback returns an entire set of touches. When that set's count exceeds 1, you know you're dealing with Multi-Touch.

In theory, iOS supports an arbitrary number of touches. You can explore that limit by running Recipe 1-9 on an iPad, using as many fingers as possible at once. The practical upper limit has changed over time; this recipe modestly demurs from offering a specific number.

When Multi-Touch was first explored on the iPhone, developers did not dream of the freedom and flexibility that Multi-Touch combined with multiple users offered. Adding Multi-Touch to your games and other applications opens up not just expanded gestures but also new ways of creating profoundly exciting multiuser experiences, especially on larger screens like the iPad. Include Multi-Touch support in your applications wherever it is practical and meaningful.

Multi-Touch touches are not grouped. If you touch the screen with two fingers from each hand, for example, there's no way to determine which touches belong to which hand. The touch order is also arbitrary. Although grouped touches retain the same finger order (or, more specifically, the same memory address) for the lifetime of a single touch event, from touch down through movement to release, the correspondence between touches and fingers may and likely will change the next time your user touches the screen. When you need to distinguish touches from each other, build a touch dictionary indexed by the touch objects, as shown in this recipe.

Perhaps it's a comfort to know that if you need it, the extra finger support has been built in. Unfortunately, when you are using three or more touches at a time, the screen has a pronounced tendency to lose track of one or more of those fingers. It's hard to programmatically track smooth gestures when you go beyond two finger touches. So instead of focusing on gesture interpretation, think of the Multi-Touch experience more as a series of time-limited independent interactions. You can treat each touch as a distinct item and process it independently of its fellows.

Recipe 1-9 adds Multi-Touch to a `UIView` by setting its `multipleTouchEnabled` property and tracing the lines that each finger draws. It does this by keeping track of each touch's physical address in memory but without pointing to or retaining the touch object, as per Apple's recommendations.

This is, obviously, an oddball approach, but it has worked reliably throughout the history of the SDK. That's because each `UITouch` object persists at a single address throughout the touch–move–release life cycle. Apple recommends against retaining `UITouch` instances, which is why the integer values of these objects are used as keys in this recipe. By using the physical address as a key, you can distinguish each touch, even as new touches are added or old touches are removed from the screen.

Be aware that new touches can start their life cycle via `touchesBegan:withEvent:` independently of others as they move, end, or cancel. Your code should reflect that reality.

This recipe expands from Recipe 1-7. Each touch grows a separate Bezier path, which is painted in the view's `drawRect` method. Recipe 1-7 essentially starts a new drawing at the end of each touch cycle. That works well for application bookkeeping but fails when it comes to creating a standard drawing application, where you expect to iteratively add elements to a picture.

Recipe 1-9 continues adding traces into a composite picture without erasing old items. Touches collect into an ever-growing mutable array, which can be cleared on user demand. This recipe draws in-progress tracing in a slightly lighter color, to distinguish it from paths that have already been stored to the drawing's stroke array.

Recipe 1-9   Accumulating User Tracings for a Composite Drawing

```
@interface TouchTrackerView : UIView
- (void) clear;
@end

@implementation TouchTrackerView
{
    NSMutableArray *strokes;
    NSMutableDictionary *touchPaths;
}

// Establish new views with storage initialized for drawing
- (instancetype) initWithFrame:(CGRect) frame
{
    self = [super initWithFrame:frame];
    if (self)
    {
        self.multipleTouchEnabled = YES;
        strokes = [NSMutableArray array];
        touchPaths = [NSMutableDictionary dictionary];
    }
    return self;
}

// On clear, remove all existing strokes, but not in-progress drawing
- (void) clear
{
    [strokes removeAllObjects];
    [self setNeedsDisplay];
}

// Start touches by adding new paths to the touchPath dictionary
- (void) touchesBegan:(NSSet *) touches withEvent:(UIEvent *) event
{
```

```
    for (UITouch *touch in touches)
    {
        NSString *key = [NSString stringWithFormat:@"%d", (int) touch];
        CGPoint pt = [touch locationInView:self];

        UIBezierPath *path = [UIBezierPath bezierPath];
        path.lineWidth = IS_IPAD ? 8: 4;
        path.lineCapStyle = kCGLineCapRound;
        [path moveToPoint:pt];

        touchPaths[key] = path;
    }
}
// Trace touch movement by growing and stroking the path
- (void)touchesMoved:(NSSet *)touches withEvent:(UIEvent *)event
{
    for (UITouch *touch in touches)
    {
        NSString *key =
            [NSString stringWithFormat:@"%d", (int) touch];
        UIBezierPath *path = [touchPaths objectForKey:key];
        if (!path) break;

        CGPoint pt = [touch locationInView:self];
        [path addLineToPoint:pt];
    }
    [self setNeedsDisplay];
}


// On ending a touch, move the path to the strokes array
- (void)touchesEnded:(NSSet *)touches withEvent:(UIEvent *)event
{
    for (UITouch *touch in touches)
    {
        NSString *key = [NSString stringWithFormat:@"%d", (int) touch];
        UIBezierPath *path = [touchPaths objectForKey:key];
        if (path) [strokes addObject:path];
        [touchPaths removeObjectForKey:key];
    }
    [self setNeedsDisplay];
}

- (void)touchesCancelled:(NSSet *)touches withEvent:(UIEvent *)event
{
    [self touchesEnded:touches withEvent:event];
}
```

```
// Draw existing strokes in dark purple, in-progress ones in light
- (void)drawRect:(CGRect)rect
{
    [COOKBOOK_PURPLE_COLOR set];
    for (UIBezierPath *path in strokes)
    {
        [path stroke];
    }

    [[COOKBOOK_PURPLE_COLOR colorWithAlphaComponent:0.5f] set];
    for (UIBezierPath *path in [touchPaths allValues])
    {
        [path stroke];
    }
}
@end
```

Get This Recipe's Code

To find this recipe's full sample project, point your browser to https://github.com/erica/iOS-7-Cookbook and go to the folder for Chapter 1.

Note

Apple provides many Core Graphics/Quartz 2D resources on its developer website. Although many of these forums, mailing lists, and source code examples are not iOS-specific, they offer an invaluable resource for expanding your iOS Core Graphics knowledge.

Recipe: Detecting Circles

In a direct manipulation interface like iOS, you'd imagine that most people could get by just pointing to items onscreen. And yet, circle detection remains one of the most requested gestures. Developers like having people circle items onscreen with their fingers. In the spirit of providing solutions that readers have requested, Recipe 1-10 offers a relatively simple circle detector, which is shown in Figure 1-5.

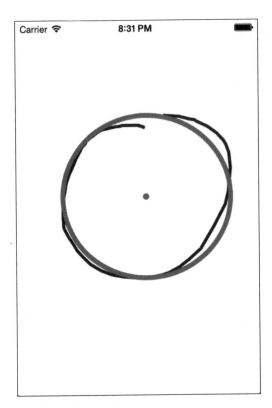

Figure 1-5   The dot and the outer ellipse show the key features of the detected circle.

In this implementation, detection uses a multistep test. A time test checks that the stroke is not lingering. A circle gesture should be quickly drawn. An inflection test checks that the touch does not change directions too often. A proper circle includes four direction changes. This test allows for five. There's a convergence test. The circle must start and end close enough together that the points are somehow related. A fair amount of leeway is needed because when you don't provide direct visual feedback, users tend to undershoot or overshoot where they began. The pixel distance used here is generous, approximately a third of the view size.

The final test looks at movement around a central point. It adds up the arcs traveled, which should equal 360 degrees in a perfect circle. This example allows any movement that falls within 45 degrees for not-quite-finished circles and 180 degrees for circles that continue on a bit wider, allowing the finger to travel more naturally.

Upon these tests being passed, the algorithm produces a least bounding rectangle and centers that rectangle on the geometric mean of the points from the original gesture. This result is assigned to the circle instance variable. It's not a perfect detection system (you can try to fool it when testing the sample code), but it's robust enough to provide reasonably good circle checks for many iOS applications.

Recipe 1-10   **Detecting Circles**

```
// Retrieve center of rectangle
CGPoint GEORectGetCenter(CGRect rect)
{
    return CGPointMake(CGRectGetMidX(rect), CGRectGetMidY(rect));
}


// Build rectangle around a given center
CGRect GEORectAroundCenter(CGPoint center, float dx, float dy)
{
    return CGRectMake(center.x - dx, center.y - dy, dx * 2, dy * 2);
}


// Center one rect inside another
CGRect GEORectCenteredInRect(CGRect rect, CGRect mainRect)
{
    CGFloat dx = CGRectGetMidX(mainRect)-CGRectGetMidX(rect);
    CGFloat dy = CGRectGetMidY(mainRect)-CGRectGetMidY(rect);
    return CGRectOffset(rect, dx, dy);
}


// Return dot product of two vectors normalized
CGFloat dotproduct(CGPoint v1, CGPoint v2)
{
    CGFloat dot = (v1.x * v2.x) + (v1.y * v2.y);
    CGFloat a = ABS(sqrt(v1.x * v1.x + v1.y * v1.y));
    CGFloat b = ABS(sqrt(v2.x * v2.x + v2.y * v2.y));
    dot /= (a * b);

    return dot;
}


// Return distance between two points
CGFloat distance(CGPoint p1, CGPoint p2)
{
    CGFloat dx = p2.x - p1.x;
    CGFloat dy = p2.y - p1.y;

    return sqrt(dx*dx + dy*dy);
}


// Offset in X
CGFloat dx(CGPoint p1, CGPoint p2)
{
    return p2.x - p1.x;
}
```

```objc
// Offset in Y
CGFloat dy(CGPoint p1, CGPoint p2)
{
    return p2.y - p1.y;
}

// Sign of a number
NSInteger sign(CGFloat x)
{
    return (x < 0.0f) ? (-1) : 1;
}

// Return a point with respect to a given origin
CGPoint pointWithOrigin(CGPoint pt, CGPoint origin)
{
    return CGPointMake(pt.x - origin.x, pt.y - origin.y);
}

// Calculate and return least bounding rectangle
#define POINT(_INDEX_) [(NSValue *)[points \
    objectAtIndex:_INDEX_] CGPointValue]

CGRect boundingRect(NSArray *points)
{
    CGRect rect = CGRectZero;
    CGRect ptRect;

    for (NSUInteger i = 0; i < points.count; i++)
    {
        CGPoint pt = POINT(i);
        ptRect = CGRectMake(pt.x, pt.y, 0.0f, 0.0f);
        rect = (CGRectEqualToRect(rect, CGRectZero)) ?
            ptRect : CGRectUnion(rect, ptRect);
    }
    return rect;
}

CGRect testForCircle(NSArray *points, NSDate *firstTouchDate)
{
    if (points.count < 2)
    {
        NSLog(@"Too few points (2) for circle");
        return CGRectZero;
    }

    // Test 1: duration tolerance
    float duration = [[NSDate date]
```

```
        timeIntervalSinceDate:firstTouchDate];
NSLog(@"Transit duration: %0.2f", duration);

float maxDuration = 2.0f;
if (duration > maxDuration)
{
    NSLog(@"Excessive duration");
    return CGRectZero;
}

// Test 2: Direction changes should be limited to near 4
int inflections = 0;
for (int i = 2; i < (points.count - 1); i++)
{
    float deltx = dx(POINT(i), POINT(i-1));
    float delty = dy(POINT(i), POINT(i-1));
    float px = dx(POINT(i-1), POINT(i-2));
    float py = dy(POINT(i-1), POINT(i-2));

    if ((sign(deltx) != sign(px)) ||
        (sign(delty) != sign(py)))
        inflections++;
}

if (inflections > 5)
{
    NSLog(@"Excessive inflections");
    return CGRectZero;
}

// Test 3: Start and end points near each other
float tolerance = [[[UIApplication sharedApplication]
    keyWindow] bounds].size.width / 3.0f;
if (distance(POINT(0), POINT(points.count - 1)) > tolerance)
{
    NSLog(@"Start too far from end");
    return CGRectZero;
}

// Test 4: Count the distance traveled in degrees
CGRect circle = boundingRect(points);
CGPoint center = GEORectGetCenter(circle);
float distance = ABS(acos(dotproduct(
    pointWithOrigin(POINT(0), center),
    pointWithOrigin(POINT(1), center))));
for (int i = 1; i < (points.count - 1); i++)
    distance += ABS(acos(dotproduct(
```

```
            pointWithOrigin(POINT(i), center),
            pointWithOrigin(POINT(i+1), center))));

    float transitTolerance = distance - 2 * M_PI;

    if (transitTolerance < 0.0f) // fell short of 2 PI
    {
        if (transitTolerance < - (M_PI / 4.0f)) // under 45
        {
            NSLog(@"Transit too short");
            return CGRectZero;
        }
    }

    if (transitTolerance > M_PI) // additional 180 degrees
    {
        NSLog(@"Transit too long ");
        return CGRectZero;
    }

    return circle;
}
@end
```

Get This Recipe's Code

To find this recipe's full sample project, point your browser to https://github.com/erica/iOS-7-Cookbook and go to the folder for Chapter 1.

Recipe: Creating a Custom Gesture Recognizer

It takes little work to transform the code shown in Recipe 1-10 into a custom recognizer, but Recipe 1-11 does it. Subclassing UIGestureRecognizer enables you to build your own circle recognizer that you can add to views in your applications.

Start by importing UIGestureRecognizerSubclass.h from UIKit into your new class. The file declares everything you need your recognizer subclass to override or customize. For each method you override, make sure to call the original version of the method by calling the superclass method before invoking your new code.

Gestures fall into two types: continuous and discrete. The circle recognizer is discrete. It either recognizes a circle or fails. Continuous gestures include pinches and pans, where recognizers send updates throughout their life cycle. Your recognizer generates updates by setting its state property.

Recognizers are basically state machines for fingertips. All recognizers start in the possible state (UIGestureRecognizerStatePossible), and then for continuous gestures pass through a series of changed states (UIGestureRecognizerStateChanged). Discrete recognizers either succeed in recognizing a gesture (UIGestureRecognizerStateRecognized) or fail (UIGestureRecognizerStateFailed), as demonstrated in Recipe 1-11. The recognizer sends actions to its target each time you update the state *except* when the state is set to possible or failed.

The rather long comments you see in Recipe 1-11 belong to Apple, courtesy of the subclass header file. They help explain the roles of the key methods that override their superclass. The reset method returns the recognizer back to its quiescent state, allowing it to prepare itself for its next recognition challenge.

The touches began (and so on) methods are called at similar points as their UIResponder analogs, enabling you to perform your tests at the same touch life cycle points. This example waits to check for success or failure until the touches ended callback, and uses the same testForCircle method defined in Recipe 1-10.

Note

As an overriding philosophy, gesture recognizers should fail as soon as possible. When they succeed, you should store information about the gesture in local properties. The circle gesture recognizer should save any detected circle so users know where the gesture occurred.

Recipe 1-11 Creating a Gesture Recognizer Subclass

```
#import <UIKit/UIGestureRecognizerSubclass.h>
@implementation CircleRecognizer


// Called automatically by the runtime after the gesture state has
// been set to UIGestureRecognizerStateEnded. Any internal state
// should be reset to prepare for a new attempt to recognize the gesture.
// After this is received, all remaining active touches will be ignored
// (no further updates will be received for touches that had already
// begun but haven't ended).
- (void)reset
{
    [super reset];

    points = nil;
    firstTouchDate = nil;
    self.state = UIGestureRecognizerStatePossible;
}


// mirror of the touch-delivery methods on UIResponder
// UIGestureRecognizers aren't in the responder chain, but observe
// touches hit-tested to their view and their view's subviews.
```

```objc
// UIGestureRecognizers receive touches before the view to which
// the touch was hit-tested.
- (void)touchesBegan:(NSSet *)touches withEvent:(UIEvent *)event
{
    [super touchesBegan:touches withEvent:event];

    if (touches.count > 1)
    {
        self.state = UIGestureRecognizerStateFailed;
        return;
    }

    points = [NSMutableArray array];
    firstTouchDate = [NSDate date];
    UITouch *touch = [touches anyObject];
    [points addObject: [NSValue valueWithCGPoint:
        [touch locationInView:self.view]]];
}

- (void)touchesMoved:(NSSet *)touches withEvent:(UIEvent *)event
{
    [super touchesMoved:touches withEvent:event];
    UITouch *touch = [touches anyObject];
    [points addObject: [NSValue valueWithCGPoint:
        [touch locationInView:self.view]]];
}

- (void)touchesEnded:(NSSet *)touches withEvent:(UIEvent *)event
{
    [super touchesEnded:touches withEvent: event];
    BOOL detectionSuccess = !CGRectEqualToRect(CGRectZero,
        testForCircle(points, firstTouchDate));
    if (detectionSuccess)
        self.state = UIGestureRecognizerStateRecognized;
    else
        self.state = UIGestureRecognizerStateFailed;
}
@end
```

Get This Recipe's Code

To find this recipe's full sample project, point your browser to https://github.com/erica/iOS-7-Cookbook and go to the folder for Chapter 1.

Recipe: Dragging from a Scroll View

iOS's rich set of gesture recognizers doesn't always accomplish exactly what you're looking for. Here's an example. Imagine a horizontal scrolling view filled with image views, one next to another, so you can scroll left and right to see the entire collection. Now, imagine that you want to be able to drag items out of that view and add them to a space directly below the scrolling area. To do this, you need to recognize downward touches on those child views (that is, orthogonal to the scrolling direction).

This was the puzzle developer Alex Hosgrove encountered while he was trying to build an application roughly equivalent to a set of refrigerator magnet letters. Users could drag those letters down into a workspace and then play with and arrange the items they'd chosen. There were two challenges with this scenario. First, who owned each touch? Second, what happened after the downward touch was recognized?

Both the scroll view and its children own an interest in each touch. A downward gesture should generate new objects; a sideways gesture should pan the scroll view. Touches have to be shared to allow both the scroll view and its children to respond to user interactions. This problem can be solved using gesture delegates.

Gesture delegates allow you to add simultaneous recognition, so that two recognizers can operate at the same time. You add this behavior by declaring a protocol (UIGestureRecognizerDelegate) and adding a simple delegate method:

```
- (BOOL)gestureRecognizer:(UIGestureRecognizer *)gestureRecognizer
    shouldRecognizeSimultaneouslyWithGestureRecognizer:
        (UIGestureRecognizer *)otherGestureRecognizer
{
    return YES;
}
```

You cannot reassign gesture delegates for scroll views, so you must add this delegate override to the implementation for the scroll view's children.

The second question, converting a swipe into a drag, is addressed by thinking about the entire touch lifetime. Each touch that creates a new object starts as a directional drag but ends up as a pan once the new view is created. A pan recognizer works better here than a swipe recognizer, whose lifetime ends at the point of recognition.

To make this happen, Recipe 1-12 manually adds that directional-movement detection, outside the built-in gesture detection. In the end, that working-outside-the-box approach provides a major coding win. That's because once the swipe has been detected, the underlying pan gesture recognizer continues to operate. This allows the user to keep moving the swiped object without having to raise his or her finger and retouch the object in question.

The implementation in Recipe 1-12 detects swipes that move down at least 16 vertical pixels without straying more than 12 pixels to either side. When this code detects a downward swipe, it adds a new DragView (the same class used earlier in this chapter) to the screen and allows it to follow the touch for the remainder of the pan gesture interaction.

At the point of recognition, the class marks itself as having handled the swipe (gestureWasHandled) and disables the scroll view for the duration of the panning event. This gives the child complete control over the ongoing pan gesture without the scroll view reacting to further touch movement.

Recipe 1-12   Dragging Items Out of Scroll Views

```objc
@implementation DragView

#define DX(p1, p2)    (p2.x - p1.x)
#define DY(p1, p2)    (p2.y - p1.y)

const NSInteger kSwipeDragMin = 16;
const NSInteger kDragLimitMax = 12;

// Categorize swipe types
typedef enum {
    TouchUnknown,
    TouchSwipeLeft,
    TouchSwipeRight,
    TouchSwipeUp,
    TouchSwipeDown,
} SwipeTypes;

@implementation PullView
// Create a new view with an embedded pan gesture recognizer
- (instancetype)initWithImage:(UIImage *)anImage
{
    self = [super initWithImage:anImage];
    if (self)
    {
        self.userInteractionEnabled = YES;
        UIPanGestureRecognizer *pan =
            [[UIPanGestureRecognizer alloc] initWithTarget:self
                action:@selector(handlePan:)];
        pan.delegate = self;
        self.gestureRecognizers = @[pan];
    }
}

// Allow simultaneous recognition
- (BOOL)gestureRecognizer:(UIGestureRecognizer *)gestureRecognizer
        shouldRecognizeSimultaneouslyWithGestureRecognizer:
            (UIGestureRecognizer *)otherGestureRecognizer
{
    return YES;
}
```

```objc
// Handle pans by detecting swipes
- (void)handlePan:(UISwipeGestureRecognizer *)uigr
{
    // Only deal with scroll view superviews
    if (![self.superview isKindOfClass:[UIScrollView class]]) return;

    // Extract superviews
    UIView *supersuper = self.superview.superview;
    UIScrollView *scrollView = (UIScrollView *) self.superview;

    // Calculate location of touch
    CGPoint touchLocation = [uigr locationInView:supersuper];

    // Handle touch based on recognizer state

    if(uigr.state == UIGestureRecognizerStateBegan)
    {
        // Initialize recognizer
        gestureWasHandled = NO;
        pointCount = 1;
        startPoint = touchLocation;
    }

    if(uigr.state == UIGestureRecognizerStateChanged)
    {
        pointCount++;

        // Calculate whether a swipe has occurred
        float dx = DX(touchLocation, startPoint);
        float dy = DY(touchLocation, startPoint);

        BOOL finished = YES;
        if ((dx > kSwipeDragMin) && (ABS(dy) < kDragLimitMax))
            touchtype = TouchSwipeLeft;
        else if ((-dx > kSwipeDragMin) && (ABS(dy) < kDragLimitMax))
            touchtype = TouchSwipeRight;
        else if ((dy > kSwipeDragMin) && (ABS(dx) < kDragLimitMax))
            touchtype = TouchSwipeUp;
        else if ((-dy > kSwipeDragMin) && (ABS(dx) < kDragLimitMax))
            touchtype = TouchSwipeDown;
        else
            finished = NO;

        // If unhandled and a downward swipe, produce a new draggable view
        if (!gestureWasHandled && finished &&
            (touchtype == TouchSwipeDown))
        {
```

```
            dragView = [[DragView alloc] initWithImage:self.image];
            dragView.center = touchLocation;
            [supersuper addSubview: dragView];
            scrollView.scrollEnabled = NO;
            gestureWasHandled = YES;
        }
        else if (gestureWasHandled)
        {
            // allow continued dragging after detection
            dragView.center = touchLocation;
        }
    }

    if(uigr.state == UIGestureRecognizerStateEnded)
    {
        // ensure that the scroll view returns to scrollable
        if (gestureWasHandled)
            scrollView.scrollEnabled = YES;
    }
}
@end
```

Get This Recipe's Code

To find this recipe's full sample project, point your browser to https://github.com/erica/iOS-7-Cookbook and go to the folder for Chapter 1.

Recipe: Live Touch Feedback

Have you ever needed to record a demo for an iOS app? There's always compromise involved. Either you use an overhead camera and struggle with reflections and the user's hand blocking the screen or you use a tool like Reflection (http://reflectionapp.com) but you only get to see what's directly on the iOS device screen. These app recordings lack any indication of the user's touch and visual focus.

Recipe 1-13 offers a simple set of classes (called *TOUCHkit*) that provide a live touch feedback layer for demonstration use. With it, you can see both the screen that you're recording and the touches that create the interactions you're trying to present. It provides a way to compile your app for both normal and demonstration deployment. You don't change your core application to use it. It's designed to work as a single toggle, providing builds for each use.

To demonstrate this, the code shown in Recipe 1-13 is bundled in the sample code repository with a standard Apple demo. This shows how you can roll the kit into nearly any standard application.

Enabling Touch Feedback

You add touch feedback by switching on the TOUCHkit feature, without otherwise affecting your normal code. To enable TOUCHkit, you set a single flag, compile, and use that build for demonstration, complete with touch overlay. For App Store deployment, you disable the flag. The application reverts to its normal behavior, and there are no App Store–unsafe calls to worry about:

```
#define USES_TOUCHkit    1
```

This recipe assumes that you're using a standard application with a single primary window. When compiled in, the kit replaces that window with a custom class that captures and duplicates all touches, allowing your application to show the user's touch bubble feedback.

There is one key code-level change you must make, but it's a very small one. In your application delegate class, you define a WINDOW_CLASS to use when building your iOS screen:

```
#if USES_TOUCHkit
#import "TOUCHkitView.h"
#import "TOUCHOverlayWindow.h"
#define WINDOW_CLASS TOUCHOverlayWindow
#else
#define WINDOW_CLASS UIWindow
#endif
```

Then, instead of declaring a UIWindow, you use whichever class has been set by the toggle:

```
WINDOW_CLASS *window;
window = [[WINDOW_CLASS alloc]
    initWithFrame:[[UIScreen mainScreen] bounds]];
```

From here, you can set the window's rootViewController as normal.

Intercepting and Forwarding Touch Events

The key to this overlay lies in intercepting touch events, creating a floating presentation above your normal interface, and then forwarding those events on to your application. A TOUCHkit view lies on top of your interface. The custom window class grabs user touch events and presents them as circles in the TOUCHkit view. It then forwards them as if the user were interacting with a normal UIWindow. To accomplish this, this recipe uses event forwarding.

Event forwarding is achieved by calling a secondary event handler. The TOUCHOverlayWindow class overrides UIWindow's sendEvent: method to force touch drawing and then invokes its superclass implementation to return control to the normal responder chain.

The following implementation is drawn from Apple's Event Handling Guide for iOS. It collects all the touches associated with the current event, allowing Multi-Touch as well as single-touch interactions; dispatches them to TOUCHkit view layer; and then redirects them to the window via the normal UIWindow sendEvent: implementation:

```objc
@implementation TOUCHOverlayWindow
- (void)sendEvent:(UIEvent *)event
{
    // Collect touches
    NSSet *touches = [event allTouches];
    NSMutableSet *began = nil;
    NSMutableSet *moved = nil;
    NSMutableSet *ended = nil;
    NSMutableSet *cancelled = nil;

    // Sort the touches by phase for event dispatch
    for(UITouch *touch in touches) {
        switch ([touch phase]) {
            case UITouchPhaseBegan:
                if (!began) began = [NSMutableSet set];
                [began addObject:touch];
                break;
            case UITouchPhaseMoved:
                if (!moved) moved = [NSMutableSet set];
                [moved addObject:touch];
                break;
            case UITouchPhaseEnded:
                if (!ended) ended = [NSMutableSet set];
                [ended addObject:touch];
                break;
            case UITouchPhaseCancelled:
                if (!cancelled) cancelled = [NSMutableSet set];
                [cancelled addObject:touch];
                break;
            default:
                break;
        }
    }

    // Create pseudo-event dispatch
    if (began)
        [[TOUCHkitView sharedInstance]
            touchesBegan:began withEvent:event];
    if (moved)
        [[TOUCHkitView sharedInstance]
            touchesMoved:moved withEvent:event];
    if (ended)
        [[TOUCHkitView sharedInstance]
            touchesEnded:ended withEvent:event];
    if (cancelled)
        [[TOUCHkitView sharedInstance]
            touchesCancelled:cancelled withEvent:event];
```

```
    // Call normal handler for default responder chain
    [super sendEvent: event];
}
@end
```

Implementing the TOUCHkit Overlay View

The TOUCHkit overlay is a single clear `UIView` singleton. It's created the first time the application requests its shared instance, and the call adds it to the application's key window. The overlay's user interaction flag is disabled, allowing touches to continue past the overlay and on through the responder chain, even after processing those touches through the standard began/moved/ended/cancelled event callbacks.

The touch processing events draw a circle at each touch point, creating a strong pointer to the touches until that drawing is complete. Recipe 1-13 details the callback and drawing methods that handle that functionality.

Recipe 1-13   **Creating a Touch Feedback Overlay View**

```
@implementation TOUCHkitView
{
    NSSet *touches;
    UIImage *fingers;
}


+ (instancetype)sharedInstance
{
    // Create shared instance if it does not yet exist
    if (!sharedInstance)
    {
        sharedInstance = [[self alloc] initWithFrame:CGRectZero];
    }

    // Parent it to the key window
    if (!sharedInstance.superview)
    {
        UIWindow *keyWindow = [UIApplication sharedApplication].keyWindow;
        sharedInstance.frame = keyWindow.bounds;
        [keyWindow addSubview:sharedInstance];
    }

    return sharedInstance;
}


// You can override the default touchColor if you want
- (instancetype)initWithFrame:(CGRect)frame
```

```
{
    self = [super initWithFrame:frame];
    if (self)
    {
        self.backgroundColor = [UIColor clearColor];
        self.userInteractionEnabled = NO;
        self.multipleTouchEnabled = YES;
        touchColor =
            [[UIColor whiteColor] colorWithAlphaComponent:0.5f];
        touches = nil;
    }
    return self;
}

// Basic touches processing
- (void)touchesBegan:(NSSet *)theTouches withEvent:(UIEvent *)event
{
    touches = theTouches;
    [self setNeedsDisplay];
}

- (void)touchesMoved:(NSSet *)theTouches withEvent:(UIEvent *)event
{
    touches = theTouches;
    [self setNeedsDisplay];
}

- (void)touchesEnded:(NSSet *)theTouches withEvent:(UIEvent *)event
{
    touches = nil;
    [self setNeedsDisplay];
}

// Draw touches interactively
- (void)drawRect:(CGRect)rect
{
    // Clear
    CGContextRef context = UIGraphicsGetCurrentContext();
    CGContextClearRect(context, self.bounds);

    // Fill see-through
    [[UIColor clearColor] set];
    CGContextFillRect(context, self.bounds);

    float size = 25.0f; // based on 44.0f standard touch point

    for (UITouch *touch in touches)
```

```
{
    // Create a backing frame
    [[[UIColor darkGrayColor] colorWithAlphaComponent:0.5f] set];
    CGPoint aPoint = [touch locationInView:self];
    CGContextAddEllipseInRect(context,
        CGRectMake(aPoint.x - size, aPoint.y - size, 2 * size, 2 * size));
    CGContextFillPath(context);

    // Draw the foreground touch
    float dsize = 1.0f;
    [touchColor set];
    aPoint = [touch locationInView:self];
    CGContextAddEllipseInRect(context,
        CGRectMake(aPoint.x - size - dsize, aPoint.y - size - dsize,
            2 * (size - dsize), 2 * (size - dsize)));
    CGContextFillPath(context);
}

// Reset touches after use
touches = nil;
}
```

Get This Recipe's Code

To find this recipe's full sample project, point your browser to https://github.com/erica/iOS-7-Cookbook and go to the folder for Chapter 1.

Recipe: Adding Menus to Views

The UIMenuController class allows you to add pop-up menus to any item that acts as a first responder. Normally menus are used with text views and text fields, enabling users to select, copy, and paste. Menus also provide a way to add actions to interactive elements like the small drag views used throughout this chapter. Figure 1-6 shows a customized menu. In Recipe 1-14, this menu is presented after long-tapping a flower. The actions will zoom, rotate, or hide the associated drag view.

This recipe demonstrates how to retrieve the shared menu controller and assign items to it. Set the menu's target rectangle (typically the bounds of the view that presents it), adjust the menu's arrow direction, and update the menu with your changes. The menu can now be set to visible.

Menu items work with standard target-action callbacks, but you do not assign the target directly. Their target is always the first responder view. This recipe omits a canPerformAction:withSender: responder check, but you'll want to add that if some views support certain actions and other views do not. With menus, that support is often tied to the state. For example, you don't want to offer a copy command if the view has no content to copy.

Figure 1-6   Contextual pop-up menus allow you to add interactive actions to first responder views.

Recipe 1-14   **Adding Menus to Interactive Views**

```
- (BOOL)canBecomeFirstResponder
{
    // Menus only work with first responders
    return YES;
}

- (void)pressed:(UILongPressGestureRecognizer *)recognizer
{
    if (![self becomeFirstResponder])
    {
        NSLog(@"Could not become first responder");
```

```
        return;
    }

    UIMenuController *menu = [UIMenuController sharedMenuController];
    UIMenuItem *pop = [[UIMenuItem alloc]
        initWithTitle:@"Pop" action:@selector(popSelf)];
    UIMenuItem *rotate = [[UIMenuItem alloc]
        initWithTitle:@"Rotate" action:@selector(rotateSelf)];
    UIMenuItem *ghost = [[UIMenuItem alloc]
        initWithTitle:@"Ghost" action:@selector(ghostSelf)];
    [menu setMenuItems:@[pop, rotate, ghost]];

    [menu setTargetRect:self.bounds inView:self];
    menu.arrowDirection = UIMenuControllerArrowDown;
    [menu update];
    [menu setMenuVisible:YES];
}

- (instancetype)initWithImage:(UIImage *)anImage
{
    self = [super initWithImage:anImage];
    if (self)
    {
        self.userInteractionEnabled = YES;
        UILongPressGestureRecognizer *pressRecognizer =
            [[UILongPressGestureRecognizer alloc] initWithTarget:self
                action:@selector(pressed:)];
        [self addGestureRecognizer:pressRecognizer];
    }
    return self;
}
```

Get This Recipe's Code

To find this recipe's full sample project, point your browser to https://github.com/erica/iOS-7-Cookbook and go to the folder for Chapter 1.

Summary

UIViews and their underlying layers provide the onscreen components your users see. Touch input lets users interact directly with views via the UITouch class and gesture recognizers. As this chapter has shown, even in their most basic form, touch-based interfaces offer easy-to-implement flexibility and power. You discovered how to move views around the screen and how to bound that movement. You read about testing touches to see whether views should or should not respond to them. You saw how to "paint" on a view and how to attach recognizers to views to interpret and respond to gestures. Here's a collection of thoughts about the recipes in this chapter that you might want to ponder before moving on:

- Be concrete. iOS devices have perfectly good touch screens. Why not let your users drag items around the screen or trace lines with their fingers? It adds to the reality and the platform's interactive nature.

- Users typically have five fingers per hand. iPads, in particular, offer a lot of screen real estate. Don't limit yourself to a one-finger interface when it makes sense to expand your interaction into Multi-Touch territory, screen space allowing.

- A solid grounding in Quartz graphics and Core Animation will be your friend. Using `drawRect:`, you can build any kind of custom `UIView` presentation you want, including text, Bezier curves, scribbles, and so forth.

- If Cocoa Touch doesn't provide the kind of specialized gesture recognizer you're looking for, write your own. It's not that hard, although it helps to be as thorough as possible when considering the states your custom recognizer might pass through.

- Use Multi-Touch whenever possible, especially when you can expand your application to invite more than one user to touch the screen at a time. Don't limit yourself to one-person, one-touch interactions when a little extra programming will open doors of opportunity for multiuser use.

- Explore! This chapter only touches lightly on the ways you can use direct manipulation in your applications. Use this material as a jumping-off point to explore the full vocabulary of the `UITouch` class.

Building and Using Controls

The `UIControl` class is the basis for many iOS interactive elements, such as buttons, text fields, sliders, and switches. These view objects have more in common than just deriving from their ancestor class. Controls all use similar layout paradigms and target-action triggers. Learning to create a single control, no matter how specialized, teaches you how all controls work. Controls may appear visually unique and specialized but use a single design pattern. This chapter introduces controls and their use. You'll discover how to build and customize controls in a variety of ways. This chapter introduces a range of control recipes—from the prosaic to the obscure—you can reuse in your apps.

The `UIControl` Class

In iOS, *controls* refer to the members of a library of prebuilt objects designed for user interaction. Controls consist of buttons and text fields, sliders and switches, along with other Apple-supplied objects. A control's role is to transform user interactions into callbacks. Users touch and manipulate controls and in doing so communicate with your application.

The `UIControl` class lies at the root of the control class tree. Controls are subclasses of `UIView`, from which they inherit all attributes for display and layout. The subclass adds a response mechanism that enhances views with interactivity.

All controls implement ways to dispatch messages when users interact with their interface. Controls send messages using a target-action pattern. When you define a new control, you tell it who receives messages (the *target*), what messages to send (the *action*), and when to send those messages (the triggering condition, such as a user completing a touch within its bounds).

Target-Action

The target-action design pattern offers a low-level way of responding to user interactions. You encounter this pattern almost exclusively with children of the `UIControl` class. With target-action, you tell the control to message a given object when a specific user event takes place. For example, you'd specify which object receives a selector when a user presses a button or adjusts a slider.

You supply an arbitrary selector. The selector is not checked at runtime, so use caution in preparing your code. The compiler will warn you if the selector specified is not declared, hopefully preventing a typo in the selector from going unnoticed and leading to a crash at runtime. The following snippet sets a target-action pair that calls the playSound: selector when a user releases a touch inside a button. If the target (self) does not implement that method, the application crashes at runtime with an undefined method call error:

```
[button addTarget:self action:@selector(playSound:)
    forControlEvents:UIControlEventTouchUpInside];
```

Target-actions do not rely on an established method vocabulary the way delegates do. Unlike with delegates and their required protocols, there are no guarantees about a playSound: implementation. It's up to the developer to make sure that the callback refers to an existing method. A cautious programmer will test a target before assigning a target-action pair with a given selector. Here's an example:

```
if ([someObject respondsToSelector:@selector(playSound:)])
    [button addTarget:someObject action:@selector(playSound:)
        forControlEvents:UIControlEventTouchUpInside];
```

Standard UIControl target-action pairs always pass either zero, one, or two arguments. These optional arguments offer the interaction object (such as a button, slider, or switch that has been manipulated) and a UIEvent object that represents the user's input. Your selector can choose to pass the interaction object or the interaction object and the event. In the preceding example, the selector uses one argument: the UIButton instance that was tapped. This self-reference, where the triggered object is included with the call, enables you to build more general action code that knows which control produced the callback.

Kinds of Controls

System-supplied members of the UIControl family include buttons, segmented controls, switches, sliders, page controls, and text fields. Each of these controls can be found in Interface Builder's (IB's) Object Library (Command-Control-Option-3, View > Utilities > Show Object Library), as shown in Figure 2-1.

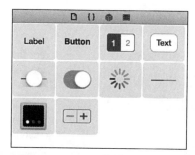

Figure 2-1   Interface Builder provides its available controls in the Object Library. From the top-left, these are labels (`UILabel`), buttons (`UIButton`), segmented controls (`UISegmentedControl`), text fields (`UITextField`), sliders (`UISlider`), switches (`UISwitch`), activity indicators and progress indicators (`UIActivityIndicatorView` and `UIProgressView`, although these are not technically controls), page controls (`UIPageControl`), and steppers (`UIStepper`).

Control Events

Controls respond primarily to three kinds of events: those based on touch, those based on value, and those based on edits. Table 2-1 lists the full range of event types available to controls.

Table 2-1   `UIControl` **Event Types**

Event	Type	Use
`UIControlEventTouchDown`	Touch	A touch down event anywhere within a control's bounds.
`UIControlEventTouchUpInside`	Touch	A touch up event anywhere within a control's bounds. This is the most common event type used for buttons.
`UIControlEventTouchUpOutside`	Touch	A touch up event that falls strictly outside a control's bounds.
`UIControlEventTouchDragEnter` `UIControlEventTouchDragExit`	Touch	Events corresponding to drags that cross into or out from the control's bounds.
`UIControlEventTouchDragInside` `UIControlEventTouchDragOutside`	Touch	Drag events limited to inside the control bounds or to just outside the control bounds.
`UIControlEventTouchDownRepeat`	Touch	A repeated touch down event with a `tapCount` above 1 (for example, a double-tap).

Event	Type	Use
`UIControlEventTouchCancel`	Touch	A system event that cancels the current touch. See Chapter 1, "Gestures and Touches," for more details about touch phases and life cycles.
`UIControlEventAllTouchEvents`	Touch	A mask that corresponds to all the touch events listed so far, used to catch any touch event.
`UIControlEventValueChanged`	Value	A user-initiated event that changes the value of a control such as moving a slider's thumb or toggling a switch.
`UIControlEventEditingDidBegin` `UIControlEventEditingDidEnd`	Editing	Touches inside or outside a `UITextField`. A touch inside begins the editing session. A touch outside ends it.
`UIControlEventEditingChanged`	Editing	An editing change to the contents of a `UITextField`.
`UIControlEventEditingDidEnd-` `OnExit`	Editing	An event that ends an editing session but not necessarily a touch outside its bounds.
`UIControlEventAllEditingEvents`	Editing	A mask of all editing events.
`UIControlEventApplication-` `Reserved`	Application	An application-specific event range (rarely, if ever, used).
`UIControlEventSystemReserved`	System	A system-specific event range (rarely, if ever, used).
`UIControlEventAllEvents`	Touch, value, editing, application, system	A mask of all touch, value, editing, application, and system events.

For the most part, events break down along the following lines. Buttons use touch events; the single `UIControlEventTouchUpInside` event accounts for nearly all button interaction and is the default event created by IB connections. Value events (for example, `UIControlEventValueChanged`) correspond to user-initiated adjustments to segmented controls, switches, sliders, and page controls. Refresh controls for tables also trigger value events. When users switch, slide, or tap those objects, the control value changes. `UITextField` objects trigger editing events. Users cause these events by tapping into (or out from) the text field, or by changing the text field contents.

As with all iOS GUI elements, you can lay out controls in Xcode's IB screen or instantiate them in code. This chapter discusses some IB approaches but focuses more intently on code-based solutions. IB layout, once mastered, remains pretty much the same regardless of the item involved. You place an object into the interface, customize it with inspectors and Auto Layout constraints, and connect it to other IB objects.

Buttons

`UIButton` instances provide simple buttons. Users can tap them to trigger a callback via target-action programming. You specify how the button looks, what art it uses, and what text it displays.

iOS offers two ways to build buttons. You can use a typed button, selected from several prede-signed styles, or build a custom button from scratch. The current iOS SDK offers very limited precooked types. In iOS 7, the entire UI has been redesigned with a flat, minimalistic design. One of the most noteworthy results of this redesign is the deprecation of the timeworn rounded rectangle. The upshot is the addition of a very new style of button, one that is plain (but bolded) text—the `UIButtonTypeSystem` type. In addition, many of the remaining button types no longer have a distinguishing UI.

The typed buttons available are not general purpose. They were added to the SDK primarily for Apple's convenience, not yours. As a rule, Apple does not add UI features that it does not primarily consume itself. Nonetheless, you can use them in your programs as needed if you follow Apple's Human Interface Guidelines (HIG). Figure 2-2 shows the five buttons.

Figure 2-2   iOS SDK offers five typed buttons with three visually distinct interfaces. You can access them in IB or add them to your applications directly with code. The first symbol here represents three buttons: Detail Disclosure, Info Light, and Info Dark. The other two buttons are the Contact Add button and the System button.

- **Detail Disclosure**—This is a blue outlined circle encasing the letter *i*, as seen when you add a detail disclosure accessory to table cells. Detail disclosures are used in tables to lead to a screen that shows details about the currently selected cell. Prior to iOS 7, this button was represented by an encircled chevron.

- **Info Light and Info Dark**—These two buttons are identical to the symbol provided by the detail disclosure, offering a blue outlined, circled *i*—as you see on a Macintosh's Dashboard widget—and they are meant to provide access to an information or settings screen. These are used in many basic applications to flip the view from one side to the other.

- **Contact Add**—This blue outlined circle with a corresponding blue + in its center can be seen in the Mail application for adding new recipients to a mail message.

- **System**—This button provides a transparent background and a text label. The System button contains no bezel or background appearance but can accept a custom image or text title.

Strictly speaking, `UIButtonTypeCustom` is also a "precooked" button in that it adds a label. As it offers no further appearance support, most developers can treat it as a fully custom button.

To use a typed button in code, allocate it, set its frame or Auto Layout constraints, and add a target. Don't worry about adding custom art or creating the overall look of the button. The SDK takes care of all that. For example, here's how to build a simple System button:

```
UIButton *button = [UIButton buttonWithType:UIButtonTypeSystem];
[button setFrame: CGRectMake(0.0f, 0.0f, 80.0f, 30.0f)];
[button setCenter: self.view.center];
[button setTitle:@"Beep" forState:UIControlStateNormal];
[button addTarget:self action:@selector(playSound)
    forControlEvents:UIControlEventTouchUpInside];
[contentView addSubview:button];
```

To build one of the other standard button types, omit the title line. The System button is the only precooked button type that uses a title.

In iOS 7, all `UIViews`, including `UIButtons`, support a `tintColor` property. This property is special: Without any action, subviews will inherit the color from their parent view. In this way, setting `tintColor` on the application's root view can change the tint appearance throughout the application. Set `tintColor` directly on a child view to override the inherited property.

For the typed buttons, `tintColor` allows the replacement of the default blue for a color of your choosing. Throughout the Apple-provided views and controls in iOS 7, `tintColor` is most often used to define a color that signifies interactivity or selection of the view.

Most buttons use the "touch up inside" trigger, where the user's touch ends inside the button's bounds. iOS UI standards allow a user to cancel a button press by moving his or her finger off a button before releasing the finger from the screen. The `UIControlEventTouchUpInside` event choice mirrors that standard.

When using a precooked button, you *must* conform to Apple's mobile HIG on how these buttons can be used. Adding a detail disclosure, for example, to lead to an information page can get your application rejected from the App Store. This might seem a proper extrapolation of the button's role, but if it does not meet the exact wording of how Apple expects the button to be used, it may not pass review. (Obviously, this depends on the reviewer, but you'll be hard pressed to defend an application that violates the HIG.) To avoid potential issues, you might want to use System and custom buttons wherever possible.

Buttons in Interface Builder

Buttons appear by default in the IB library as System button objects (see Figure 2-1). To use them, drag them into your interface. You can then change them to another button type via the Attributes inspector (View > Utility > Show Attributes Inspector, Command-Option-4). A button-type pop-up appears at the top of the inspector. Use this pop-up menu to select the button type you want to use.

If your button uses text, you can enter that text in the Title field. The Image and Background pull-downs let you choose a primary and background image for the button. Each button provides four configuration settings. The four button states are Default (the button in its normal state), Highlighted (when a user is currently touching the button), Selected (an "on" version of the button, for buttons that support toggled states), and Disabled (when the button is unavailable for user interaction).

Changes in the Object Attributes > Button > State Config section apply to the currently selected configuration. You might, for example, use a different button text color for a button in its default state than for its disabled state.

To preview each state, locate the three check boxes in Object Attributes > Control > Content. The Highlighted, Selected, and Enabled options let you set the button state. After previewing, and before you compile, make sure you return the button to the actual state it needs to be in when you first run the application.

Connecting Buttons to Actions

When you Control-drag (right-drag) from a button to an IB object such as the File's Owner view controller in the IB editor, IB presents a pop-up menu of actions to choose from. These actions are polled from the target object's available IBActions. Connecting to an action creates a target-action pair for the button's Touch Up Inside event. You can also Control-drag from the button to your code, and Xcode will add empty function definitions to your implementation file.

Alternatively, you can Control-click (right-click) the button in the document outline, scroll down to Touch Up Inside, and drag from the unfilled dot to the target you want to connect to (in this case, the File's Owner object). The same pop-up menu appears, with its list of available actions.

> **Note**
>
> In IB, you also encounter buttons that look like button views and act like views but are not, in fact, views. Bar button items (UIBarButtonItem) store the properties of toolbar and navigation bar buttons but are not buttons themselves. The toolbars and navigation bars build buttons internally to represent these logical entities.

Recipe: Building Buttons

When using the UIButtonTypeCustom style, you supply all button art. The number of images depends on how you want the button to work. For a simple pushbutton, you might add a single background image and vary the label color to highlight when the button is pushed.

For a toggle-style button, you might use four images: for the "off" state in a normal presentation, the off state when highlighted (that is, pressed), and two more for the "on" state. You choose and design the interaction details, making sure to add local state (the Boolean isOn instance variable in Recipe 2-1) to extend a simple pushbutton to a toggle. If you supply a normal image to buttons and do not specify highlight or disabled images, iOS automatically generates these variants for you.

Recipe 2-1 builds a button that toggles on and off, demonstrating the basic detail that goes into building custom buttons. When tapped, the button switches its art from green (on) to red (off), or from red to green. This allows your (noncolorblind) users to instantly identify a current state. The displayed text reinforces the state setting. Figure 2-3 (left) shows the button created by this recipe.

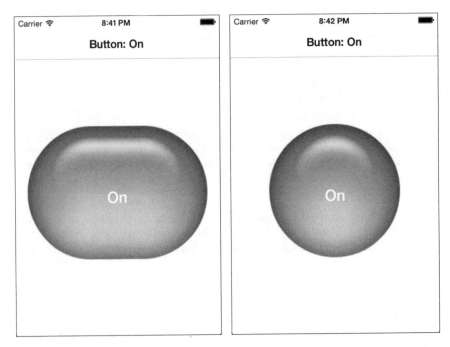

Figure 2-3   Use UIImage stretching to resize art for arbitrary button widths. Set the left cap width to specify where the stretching can take place.

The UIImage resizable image calls in this recipe play an important role in button creation. Resizable images enable you to create buttons of arbitrary width and turn circular art into lozenge-shaped buttons. You specify the caps (that is, the art that should not be stretched). In this case, the cap is 110 pixels wide on the left and right. If you were to change the button width from the 300 pixels used in this recipe to 220, the button would lose the middle stretch, as shown in Figure 2-3 (right).

Buttons can assign image and background image by state. Images set the actual content of the button. Background images provide resizable backdrops over which images and title text may appear. Recipe 2-1 uses background images, letting the button's built-in title field float over the supplied art.

> ### Note
>
> You can round the corners of your views and buttons to different degrees by adjusting layer properties. Adding the Quartz Core framework to your project lets you access view layers, where you can set the layer's cornerRadius property programmatically. Then set the view's clipsToBounds property to YES to achieve that Apple look.

Recipe 2-1   **Building a** UIButton **That Toggles On and Off**

```
#define CAPWIDTH     110.0f
#define INSETS       (UIEdgeInsets){0.0f, CAPWIDTH, 0.0f, CAPWIDTH}
#define BASEGREEN    [[UIImage imageNamed:@"green-out.png"] \
    resizableImageWithCapInsets:INSETS]
#define PUSHGREEN    [[UIImage imageNamed:@"green-in.png"] \
    resizableImageWithCapInsets:INSETS]
#define BASERED      [[UIImage imageNamed:@"red-out.png"]  \
    resizableImageWithCapInsets:INSETS]
#define PUSHRED      [[UIImage imageNamed:@"red-in.png"]  \
    resizableImageWithCapInsets:INSETS]

- (void)toggleButton:(UIButton *)aButton
{
    self.isOn = !self.isOn;
    if (self.isOn)
    {
        [self setBackgroundImage:BASEGREEN
            forState:UIControlStateNormal];
        [self setBackgroundImage:PUSHGREEN
            forState:UIControlStateHighlighted];
        [self setTitle:@"On" forState:UIControlStateNormal];
        [self setTitle:@"On" forState:UIControlStateHighlighted];
    }
    else
    {
```

```objc
        [self setBackgroundImage:BASERED
            forState:UIControlStateNormal];
        [self setBackgroundImage:PUSHRED
            forState:UIControlStateHighlighted];
        [self setTitle:@"Off" forState:UIControlStateNormal];
        [self setTitle:@"Off" forState:UIControlStateHighlighted];
    }
}

+ (instancetype)button
{
    PushButton *button =
        [PushButton buttonWithType:UIButtonTypeCustom];

    // Set up the button alignment properties
    button.contentVerticalAlignment =
        UIControlContentVerticalAlignmentCenter;
    button.contentHorizontalAlignment =
        UIControlContentHorizontalAlignmentCenter;

    // Set the font and color
    [button setTitleColor:
        [UIColor whiteColor] forState:UIControlStateNormal];
    [button setTitleColor:
        [UIColor lightGrayColor] forState:UIControlStateHighlighted];
    button.titleLabel.font = [UIFont boldSystemFontOfSize:24.0f];

    // Set up the art
    [button setBackgroundImage:BASEGREEN
        forState:UIControlStateNormal];
    [button setBackgroundImage:PUSHGREEN
        forState:UIControlStateHighlighted];
    [button setTitle:@"On" forState:UIControlStateNormal];
    [button setTitle:@"On" forState:UIControlStateHighlighted];
    button.isOn = YES;

    // Add action. Client can add one too.
    [button addTarget:button action:@selector(toggleButton:)
        forControlEvents: UIControlEventTouchUpInside];

    return button;
}
```

Multiline Button Text

The button's `titleLabel` property allows you to modify title attributes such as its font and line break mode. Here, the font is set to a very large value (basically ensuring that the text needs to wrap to display correctly) and used with word wrap and centered alignment:

```
button.titleLabel.font = [UIFont boldSystemFontOfSize:36.0f];
[button setTitle:@"Lorem Ipsum Dolor Sit" forState:
    UIControlStateNormal];
button.titleLabel.textAlignment = UITextAlignmentCenter;
button.titleLabel.lineBreakMode = UILineBreakModeWordWrap;
```

By default, button labels stretch from one end of your button to the other. This means that text may extend farther out than you might otherwise want, possibly beyond the edges of your button art. To fix this problem, you can force carriage returns in word wrap mode by embedding new line literals (that is, \n) into the text. This allows you to control how much text appears on each line of the button title.

Adding Animated Elements to Buttons

When working with buttons, you can creatively layer art in front of or behind the buttons. Use the standard `UIView` hierarchy to do this, making sure to disable user interaction for any view that might otherwise obscure your button (`setUserInteractionEnabled:NO`). The image view contents "leak" through to the viewer, enabling you to add live animation elements to the button.

The sample art used in Recipe 2-1 is translucent, allowing you to experiment with this approach. The sample code for this recipe adds optional butterfly art that you can layer behind the button and animate.

Animated elements are particularly helpful when you're trying to show state, such as an operation in progress. They can communicate to users why a button has become unresponsive or creates a different reaction to being pressed. For example, a turbo-enhanced button in a game might provide extra force when tapped. An animated visual helps users identify the change in functionality.

Separating art and text away from button implementation can play other roles in your development. Adding these elements behind or on top of an otherwise empty button allows you to localize both graphic design and phrasing based on your intended deployment without having to redesign the button directly.

Adding Extra State to Buttons

Recipe 2-1 creates a two-state button, providing visuals for on and off states. At times, you may want to implement buttons with further easy-to-distinguish states. Games provide the most common example of this. Many developers implement buttons that typically showcase four states: locked levels, unlocked-but-not-played, unlocked-and-partially-played, and unlocked-and-mastered.

Recipe 2-1 uses a simple Boolean toggle (the `isOn` instance variable) to store the on/off state and to select the art used (in the `toggleButton:` method) based on that state. You can easily expand this example for a wider range of art and button states by storing the state as an integer and providing a switch statement for art selection.

Get This Recipe's Code

To find this recipe's full sample project, point your browser to https://github.com/erica/iOS-7-Cookbook and go to the folder for Chapter 2.

Recipe: Animating Button Responses

There's more to `UIControl` instances than frames and target-action. All controls inherit from the `UIView` class. This means you can use `UIView` animation blocks when working with controls just as you would with standard views. Recipe 2-2 builds a toggle switch that zooms itself whenever a user touches it and returns to its original size when the touch leaves the control.

This recipe creates a livelier interaction element that helps focus greater attention on the control in question.

Note

To add a little flare to your instances, note that buttons support delicious `NSAttributedString` values via `setAttributedTitleForState:`. Recipe 2-4, which follows later in this chapter, updates a segmented control's text color using this method.

Recipe 2-2   **Adding `UIView` Animation Blocks to Controls**

```
- (void) zoomButton: (id) sender
{
    // Slightly enlarge the button
    [UIView animateWithDuration:0.2f animations:^{
        button.transform =
            CGAffineTransformMakeScale(1.1f, 1.1f);}];
}

- (void) relaxButton: (id) sender
{
    // Return the button to its normal size
    [UIView animateWithDuration:0.2f animations:^{
        button.transform = CGAffineTransformIdentity;}];
```

```
}

- (void)toggleButton:(UIButton *)button
{
    self.isOn = !self.isOn;
    if (self.isOn)
    {
        [button setTitle:@"On" forState:UIControlStateNormal];
        [button setTitle:@"On" forState:UIControlStateHighlighted];
        [button setBackgroundImage:BASEGREEN
            forState:UIControlStateNormal];
        [button setBackgroundImage:PUSHGREEN
            forState:UIControlStateHighlighted];
    }
    else
    {
        [button setTitle:@"Off" forState:UIControlStateNormal];
        [button setTitle:@"Off"
            forState:UIControlStateHighlighted];
        [button setBackgroundImage:BASERED
            forState:UIControlStateNormal];
        [button setBackgroundImage:PUSHRED
            forState:UIControlStateHighlighted];
    }
    [self relaxButton:button];
}

+ (instancetype)button
{
    PushButton *button =
        [PushButton buttonWithType:UIButtonTypeCustom];

    // Add actions
    [button addTarget:button action:@selector(toggleButton:)
        forControlEvents: UIControlEventTouchUpInside];
    [button addTarget:button action:@selector(zoomButton:)
        forControlEvents: UIControlEventTouchDown |
            UIControlEventTouchDragInside |
            UIControlEventTouchDragEnter];
    [button addTarget:button action:@selector(relaxButton:)
        forControlEvents: UIControlEventTouchDragExit |
            UIControlEventTouchCancel |
            UIControlEventTouchDragOutside];

    return button;
}
```

Recipe: Adding a Slider with a Custom Thumb

`UISlider` instances provide a control that allows users to choose a value by sliding a knob (called its *thumb*) between its left and right extents. You've seen sliders in the Music application, where the `UISlider` class is used to control volume.

Slider values default to 0.0 for the minimum and 1.0 for the maximum, although you can easily customize these in the IB Attributes inspector or by setting the `minimumValue` and `maximumValue` properties. To stylize the ends of the control, add a related pair of images (`minimumValueImage` and `maximumValueImage`) that reinforce those settings. For example, you might show a snowman on one end and a steaming cup of tea on the other for a slider that controls temperature settings.

You can also set the color of the track before and after the thumb as well as the thumb itself—by adjusting the `minimumTrackTintColor`, `maximumTrackTintColor`, and `thumbTintColor` properties. In iOS 7, setting the `minimumTrackTintColor` to `nil` defaults the area before the thumb to the tint color of the parent view. The other properties revert to their default color when set to `nil`.

The slider's `continuous` property controls whether a slider continually sends value updates as a user drags the thumb. When set to `NO` (the default is `YES`), the slider sends an action event only when the user releases the thumb.

Customizing `UISlider`

In addition to setting minimum and maximum images, the `UISlider` class lets you directly update its thumb component. You can set a thumb to whatever image you like by calling `setThumbImage:forState:`. Recipe 2-3 takes advantage of this option to dynamically build thumb images on-the-fly, as shown in Figure 2-4. The indicator bubble appears above the user's finger as part of the custom-built thumb. This bubble provides instant feedback both textually (the number inside the bubble) and graphically (the shade of the bubble reflects the slider value, moving from black to white as the user drags).

Note

When compositing a `UIView`, iOS creates a bitmap for the view's layer. The performance is approximately the same between using a custom view and using a custom-generated bitmap.

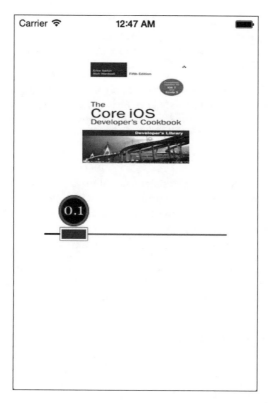

Figure 2-4   Core Graphics/Quartz calls enable this slider's thumb image to dim or brighten based on the current slider value. The text inside the thumb bubble mirrors that value. (As the user slides, the stretched icon adjusts its size to provide additional feedback as a sample of a target-action client in the recipe sample code.)

This kind of dynamically built feedback could be based on any kind of data. You might grab values from onboard sensors or make calls out to the Internet just as easily as you use the user's finger movement with a slider. No matter what live update scheme you use, dynamic updates are certainly graphics intensive—but it's not as expensive as you might fear. The Core Graphics calls are fast, and the memory requirements for the thumb-sized images are minimal.

This particular recipe assigns two thumb images to the slider. The bubble appears only when the slider is in use, for its `UIControlStateHighlighted`. In its normal state, namely `UIControlStateNormal`, only the smaller rectangular thumb appears. Users can tap on the thumb to review the current setting. The context-specific feedback bubble mimics the letter highlights on the standard iOS keyboard.

To accommodate these changes in art, the slider updates its frame at the start and end of each gesture. On being touched (UIControlEventTouchDown), the frame expands by 60 pixels in height. This extra space provides enough room to show the expanded thumb during interaction.

When the finger is removed from the screen (UIControlEventTouchUpInside or UIControlEventTouchUpOutside), the slider returns to its previous dimensions. This restores space to other objects, ensuring that the slider will not activate unless a user directly touches it.

Adding Efficiency

Recipe 2–3 stores a previous value for the slider to minimize the overall computational burden on iOS. It updates the thumb with a new custom image when the slider has changed by at least 0.1, or 10% in value. You can omit this check, if you want, and run the recipe with full live updating. This provided reasonably fast updates even on a first-generation iPod touch unit. On recent iPhones and iPads, it has no performance issues at all.

This recipe also avoids any issues at the ends of the slider—namely when the thumb gets caught at 0.9 and won't update properly to 1.0. In this recipe, a hard-coded workaround for values above 0.98 handles that particular situation by forcing updates.

Recipe 2-3   **Building Dynamic Slider Thumbs**

```
/* Thumb.m */
// Create a thumb image using a grayscale/numeric level
UIImage *thumbWithLevel(float aLevel)
{
    float INSET_AMT = 1.5f;
    CGRect baseRect = CGRectMake(0.0f, 0.0f, 40.0f, 100.0f);
    CGRect thumbRect = CGRectMake(0.0f, 40.0f, 40.0f, 20.0f);

    UIGraphicsBeginImageContext(baseRect.size);
    CGContextRef context = UIGraphicsGetCurrentContext();

    // Create a filled rect for the thumb
    [[UIColor darkGrayColor] setFill];
    CGContextAddRect(context,
        CGRectInset(thumbRect, INSET_AMT, INSET_AMT));
    CGContextFillPath(context);

    // Outline the thumb
    [[UIColor whiteColor] setStroke];
    CGContextSetLineWidth(context, 2.0f);
    CGContextAddRect(context,
        CGRectInset(thumbRect, 2.0f * INSET_AMT, 2.0f * INSET_AMT));
    CGContextStrokePath(context);
```

```objc
    // Create a filled ellipse for the indicator
    CGRect ellipseRect = CGRectMake(0.0f, 0.0f, 40.0f, 40.0f);
    [[UIColor colorWithWhite:aLevel alpha:1.0f] setFill];
    CGContextAddEllipseInRect(context, ellipseRect);
    CGContextFillPath(context);

    // Label with a number
    NSString *numString =
        [NSString stringWithFormat:@"%0.1f", aLevel];
    UIColor *textColor = (aLevel > 0.5f) ?
        [UIColor blackColor] : [UIColor whiteColor];
    UIFont *font = [UIFont fontWithName:@"Georgia" size:20.0f];
    NSMutableParagraphStyle *style =
        [[NSMutableParagraphStyle alloc] init];
    style.lineBreakMode = NSLineBreakByCharWrapping;
    style.alignment = NSTextAlignmentCenter;
    NSDictionary *attr = @{NSFontAttributeName:font,
        NSParagraphStyleAttributeName:style,
        NSForegroundColorAttributeName:textColor};
    [numString drawInRect:CGRectInset(ellipseRect, 0.0f, 6.0f)
        withAttributes:attr];

    // Outline the indicator circle
    [[UIColor grayColor] setStroke];
    CGContextSetLineWidth(context, 3.0f);
    CGContextAddEllipseInRect(context,
        CGRectInset(ellipseRect, 2.0f, 2.0f));
    CGContextStrokePath(context);

    // Build and return the image
    UIImage *theImage = UIGraphicsGetImageFromCurrentImageContext();
    UIGraphicsEndImageContext();
    return theImage;
}

// Return a base thumb image without the bubble
UIImage *simpleThumb()
{
    float INSET_AMT = 1.5f;
    CGRect baseRect = CGRectMake(0.0f, 0.0f, 40.0f, 100.0f);
    CGRect thumbRect = CGRectMake(0.0f, 40.0f, 40.0f, 20.0f);

    UIGraphicsBeginImageContext(baseRect.size);
    CGContextRef context = UIGraphicsGetCurrentContext();

    // Create a filled rect for the thumb
    [[UIColor darkGrayColor] setFill];
```

```
    CGContextAddRect(context,
        CGRectInset(thumbRect, INSET_AMT, INSET_AMT));
    CGContextFillPath(context);

    // Outline the thumb
    [[UIColor whiteColor] setStroke];
    CGContextSetLineWidth(context, 2.0f);
    CGContextAddRect(context,
        CGRectInset(thumbRect, 2.0f * INSET_AMT, 2.0f * INSET_AMT));
    CGContextStrokePath(context);

    // Retrieve the thumb
    UIImage *theImage = UIGraphicsGetImageFromCurrentImageContext();
    UIGraphicsEndImageContext();
    return theImage;
}


/* CustomSlider.m */
// Update the thumb images as needed
- (void)updateThumb
{
    // Only update the thumb when registering significant changes
    if ((self.value < 0.98) &&
        (ABS(self.value - previousValue) < 0.1f)) return;

    // create a new custom thumb image for the highlighted state
    UIImage *customImg = thumbWithLevel(self.value);
    [self setThumbImage:customImg
        forState:UIControlStateHighlighted];
    previousValue = self.value;
}


// Expand the slider to accommodate the bigger thumb
- (void)startDrag:(UISlider *)aSlider
{
    self.frame = CGRectInset(self.frame, 0.0f, -30.0f);
}


// At release, shrink the frame back to normal
- (void)endDrag:(UISlider *)aSlider
{
    self.frame = CGRectInset(self.frame, 0.0f, 30.0f);
}


- (instancetype)initWithFrame:(CGRect)aFrame
{
    self = [super initWithFrame:aFrame];
```

```
    if (self)
    {
        // Initialize slider settings
        previousValue = CGFLOAT_MIN;
        self.value = 0.0f;

        [self setThumbImage:simpleThumb()
            forState:UIControlStateNormal];

        // Create the callbacks for touch, move, and release
        [self addTarget:self action:@selector(startDrag:)
            forControlEvents:UIControlEventTouchDown];
        [self addTarget:self action:@selector(updateThumb)
            forControlEvents:UIControlEventValueChanged];
        [self addTarget:self action:@selector(endDrag:)
            forControlEvents:UIControlEventTouchUpInside |
                UIControlEventTouchUpOutside];
    }
    return self;
}

+ (instancetype)slider
{
    CustomSlider *slider = [[CustomSlider alloc]
        initWithFrame:(CGRect){.size=CGSizeMake(200.0f, 40.0f)}];

    return slider;
}
```

Get This Recipe's Code

To find this recipe's full sample project, point your browser to https://github.com/erica/iOS-7-Cookbook and go to the folder for Chapter 2.

Recipe: Creating a Twice-Tappable Segmented Control

The UISegmentedControl class presents a multiple-button interface, where users can choose one choice out of a group. The control provides two styles of use (not to be confused with UISegmentedControlStyle, which alters the control UI and has been deprecated in iOS 7). In its normal radio-button-style mode, a button once selected remains selected. Users can tap on other buttons, but they cannot generate a new event by retapping their existing choice. The alternative style, provided by the momentary Boolean property, lets users tap on each button as many times as desired but stores no state about a currently selected item. It provides no high-lights to indicate the most recent selection.

Recipe 2-4 builds a hybrid approach. It allows users to see their currently selected option and to reselect that choice if needed. This is not the way segmented controls normally work. There are times, though, when you want to generate a new result on reselection (as in momentary mode) while visually showing the most recent selection (as in radio button mode).

Unfortunately, "obvious" solutions to create this desired behavior don't work. You cannot add target-action pairs that detect `UIControlEventTouchUpInside`. `UIControlEventValueChanged` is the only control event generated by `UISegmentedControl` instances. (You can easily test this yourself by adding a target-action pair for touch events.)

Here is where subclassing comes in to play. It's relatively simple to create a new class based on `UISegmentedControl` that does respond to that second tap. Recipe 2-4 defines that class. Its code works by detecting when a touch has occurred, operating independently of the segmented control's internal touch handlers that are subclassed from `UIControl`.

Segment switches remain unaffected; they'll continue to update and switch back and forth as users tap them. Unlike with the parent class, touches on an already-touched segment continue to do something. In this case, they request that the object's delegate produce the `performSegmentAction` method.

Don't add target-action pairs to your segmented controllers the way you would normally. Since all touch down events are detected, target-actions for value-changed events would add a second callback and trigger twice whenever you switched segments. Instead, implement the delegate callback and let object delegation handle the updates.

Second-Tap Feedback

With the ability to detect a second tap, the user can be provided feedback of a reselection, such as changing the title in the navigation bar. Another alternative is modifying the attributes of the text in the segmented control. UIKit's text attribute feature (first introduced in iOS 5.x) offers an excellent match to this challenge. Segment controls provide optional attributes based on state. The `setTitleTextAttributes:forState:` method lets you introduce a visual flourish limited to the selected segment. Recipe 2-4 uses this method to change the selected text color from white to red after a second tap, and it resets that change after the user selects an alternate segment, as shown in Figure 2-5.

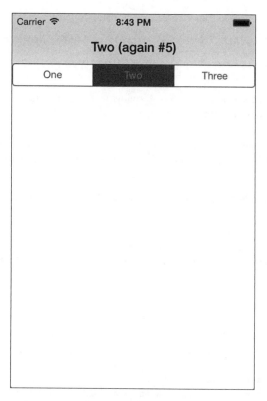

Figure 2-5   By detecting the multiple taps, you can provide the user feedback of this normally unrepresented action on a segmented control. Using attributed strings, text can be decorated to further accent the selection.

Controls and Attributes

Beginning with iOS 6, many UIKit classes, including text fields, text views, labels, buttons, and refresh controls allow you to assign attributed (Core Text–style) strings to their text and title properties:

```
[myButton setAttributedTitle:attributedString forState:UIControlStateNormal]
```

In iOS 7, Apple expanded the vocabulary of text attributes such as font, color, and shadow that can be configured. A full listing of attributes that can be applied to text in an attributed string can be found in the NSAttributedString class reference, under Character Attributes.

For segmented controls and bar items, set attributes by calling setTitleTextAttributes: forState:. Pass an attribute dictionary using the available dictionary keys and values, such as those in the following abbreviated list:

- **NSFontAttributeName**—Provides a UIFont instance.

- **NSForegroundColorAttributeName**—Provides a UIColor instance.

- **NSShadowAttributeName**—Provides an NSShadow instance that can specify shadow offset, blur radius, and shadow color.

- **NSUnderlineStyleAttributeName**—Provides an NSNumber instance that wraps the number of required underlines.

For example, Recipe 2-4 sets a segmented control's text color to white for its selected state. Whenever the control is selected twice in a row, the text color changes from white to red.

Recipe 2-4   Creating a Segmented Control Subclass That Responds to a Second Tap

```
@class SecondTapSegmentedControl;

@protocol SecondTapSegmentedControlDelegate <NSObject>
- (void) performSegmentAction: (SecondTapSegmentedControl *) aDTSC;
@end

@interface SecondTapSegmentedControl : UISegmentedControl
@property (nonatomic, weak)
    id <SecondTapSegmentedControlDelegate> tapDelegate;
@end

@implementation SecondTapSegmentedControl
- (void)touchesEnded:(NSSet *)touches withEvent:(UIEvent *)event
{
    [super touchesEnded:touches withEvent:event];

    if (self.tapDelegate)
        [self.tapDelegate performSegmentAction:self];
}
@end
```

Get This Recipe's Code

To find this recipe's full sample project, point your browser to https://github.com/erica/iOS-7-Cookbook and go to the folder for Chapter 2.

Working with Switches and Steppers

The UISwitch object offers a simple on/off toggle that lets users choose a Boolean value. The switch object contains a single (settable) value property, called on. This property returns either YES or NO, depending on the current state of the control. You can programmatically update a switch's value by changing the property value directly or calling `setOn:animated:`, which offers a way to animate the change:

```
- (void)didSwitch:(UISwitch *)theSwitch
{
    self.title = [NSString stringWithFormat:@"%@"
        theSwitch.on ? @"On" : @"Off"];
}


- (void)viewDidAppear:(BOOL)animated
{
    [super viewDidAppear:animated];
    // Create the switch
    UISwitch *theSwitch = [[UISwitch alloc] init];

    // Trigger on value changes
    [theSwitch addTarget:self action:@selector(didSwitch:)
        forControlEvents:UIControlEventValueChanged];

    [self.view addSubview:theSwitch];

    // Initialize to "off"
    theSwitch.on = NO;
    self.title = @"Off";
}
```

In this example, when the switch updates, it changes the view controller's title. IB offers relatively few options for working with a switch. You can enable it and set its initial value, but beyond that there's not much to customize. A switch produces a value-changed event when a user adjusts it.

> **Note**
>
> Do not name `UISwitch` instances as `switch`. Recall that `switch` is a reserved C word; it is used for conditional statements. This simple oversight has tripped up many iOS developers.

The `UIStepper` class provides an alternative to sliders and switches. Whereas a slider offers a continuous range of values, a switch offers a simple Boolean on/off choice; steppers fall somewhat in the middle. Instances present a pair of buttons, one labeled – and the other labeled +. These iteratively increment or decrement the `value` property.

You generally want to assign a range to the control by setting its `minimumValue` and `maximumValue` to some reasonable bounds so the control ties in more tightly to actual application features such as volume, speed, and other measurable amounts. You do not have to do so, but there are few use cases in which you want to allow user input for unbounded variables. You can make the stepper "wrap" by setting its `wraps` property to YES. When the value exceeds the maximum or falls below the minimum, the `value` wraps around from min to max or max to min, depending on the button pressed.

By default, the stepper autorepeats. That is, it continues to change as long as the user holds one of its buttons. You can disable this by setting the `autorepeat` property to `NO`. The amount the value changes at each tap is controlled by the `stepValue` property. Don't ever set `stepValue` to `0` or a negative number, or you'll raise a runtime exception.

You can configure the interfaces of both switches and steppers with tint color properties and custom artwork. For switches, this includes the `onTintColor`, `tintColor`, and `thumbTintColor` properties for custom coloring and `onImage` and `OffImage` properties for custom artwork. `UIStepper` includes `tintColor` as well as divider, increment, and decrement images that you can configure by state.

Recipe: Subclassing `UIControl`

UIKit provides many prebuilt controls that you can use directly in your applications. There are buttons and switches and sliders and more. But why stop there? You don't have to limit yourself to Apple-supplied items. Why not create your own?

Recipe 2-5 demonstrates how to subclass `UIControl` to build new controls from scratch. This example creates a simple color picker. It lets the user select a color by touching or dragging within the control. As the user traces left and right, the color changes hue. Up and down movements adjust the color's saturation. The brightness and alpha levels for the color are fixed at 100%.

This is a really simple control to work with because there's not much interaction involved beyond retrieving the *x* and *y* coordinates of the touch. It provides a basic example that demonstrates most of the development issues involved in subclassing `UIControl`.

So why build custom controls? First, you can set your own design style. Elements that you place into your interface can and should match your application's aesthetics. If Apple's prebuilt switches, sliders, and other GUI elements don't provide a natural fit into your interface, custom-built controls satisfy your application's needs without sacrificing cohesive design.

Second, you can create controls that Apple didn't provide. From selecting ratings by swiping through a series of stars, or choosing a color from a set of pop-up crayons, custom controls allow your app to interact with the user beyond the system-supplied buttons and switches in the SDK. It's easy to build unique eye-catching interactive elements by subclassing `UIControl`.

Finally, custom controls allow you to add features that you cannot access directly or through subclassing. With relatively little work, you can build your own buttons and steppers from the ground up, which means you can adjust their interaction vocabulary exactly as you wish.

Always keep your custom items visually distinct from system supplied ones. Don't run afoul of HIG issues. When you do use lookalike items, you may want to add a note to Apple when submitting apps to the App Store. Make it clear that you have created a new class rather than using private APIs or otherwise accessing Apple's objects in a manner that's not App Store safe.

Even then, you might be rejected for creating items that could potentially "confuse" the end user.

Creating Controls

The process of building a `UIControl` generally involves four distinct steps. As Recipe 2-5 demonstrates, you begin by subclassing `UIControl` to create a new custom class. In that class, you lay out the visual look of the control in your initialization. Next, you build methods to track and interpret touches, and you finish by generating events and visual feedback.

Nearly all controls offer value of some kind. For example, switches have `isOn`, sliders have a floating-point `value`, and text fields offer `text`. The kinds of values you provide with a custom control are arbitrary. They can be integers, floats, strings, or even (as in Recipe 2-5) colors.

In Recipe 2-5, the control layout is basically a colored rectangle. More complex controls require more complex layout, but even a simple layout like the one shown here can provide all the touch interaction space and feedback needed for a coherent end-user experience.

Tracking Touches

`UIControl` instances use an embedded method set to work with touches. These methods allow the control to track touches throughout their interaction with the control object:

- **`beginTrackingWithTouch:withEvent:`**—Called when a touch enters a control's bounds.
- **`continueTrackingWithTouch:withEvent:`**—Follows the touch with repeated calls as the touch remains within the control bounds.
- **`endTrackingWithTouch:withEvent:`**—Handles the last touch for the event.
- **`cancelTrackingWithEvent:`**—Manages a touch cancellation.

Add your custom control logic by implementing any or all these methods in a `UIControl` subclass. Recipe 2-5 uses the begin and continue methods to locate the user touch and track it until the touch is lifted or otherwise leaves the control.

Dispatching Events

Controls use target-action pairs to communicate changes triggered by events. When you build a new control, you must decide what kind of events your object will generate and add code to trigger those events.

Add dispatching to your custom control by calling `sendActionsForControlEvents:`. This method lets you send an event (for example, `UIControlEventValueChanged`) to your control's targets. Controls transmit these updates by messaging the `UIApplication` singleton. As Apple notes, the application acts as the centralized dispatch point for all messages.

No matter how simple your class, make sure your control vocabulary is as complete as possible. You cannot anticipate exactly how the class will be used in the future. Overdesigning your events provides flexibility for future use. Recipe 2-5 dispatches a wide range of events for what is, after all, a very simple control.

Where you dispatch events depends a lot on the control you end up building. Switch controls, for example, are really only interested in touch up events, which is when their value changes. Sliding controls, in contrast, center on touch movement and require continuing updates as the control tracks finger movement. Adjust your coding accordingly and be mindful of presenting appropriate visual changes during all parts of your touch cycle.

Recipe 2-5 Building a Custom Color Control

```
@implementation ColorControl
- (instancetype)initWithFrame:(CGRect)frame
{
    self = [super initWithFrame:frame];
    if (self)
    {
        self.backgroundColor = [UIColor grayColor];
    }
    return self;
}

- (void)updateColorFromTouch:(UITouch *)touch
{
    // Calculate hue and saturation
    CGPoint touchPoint = [touch locationInView:self];
    float hue = touchPoint.x / self.frame.size.width;
    float saturation = touchPoint.y / self.frame.size.height;

    // Update the color value and change background color
    self.value = [UIColor colorWithHue:hue
        saturation:saturation brightness:1.0f alpha:1.0f];
    self.backgroundColor = self.value;
    [self sendActionsForControlEvents:UIControlEventValueChanged];
}

// Continue tracking touch in control
- (BOOL)continueTrackingWithTouch:(UITouch *)touch
        withEvent:(UIEvent *)event
{
    // Test if drag is currently inside or outside
    CGPoint touchPoint = [touch locationInView:self];
    if (CGRectContainsPoint(self.frame, touchPoint))
    {
        // Update color value
```

```objectivec
        [self updateColorFromTouch:touch];

        [self sendActionsForControlEvents:
            UIControlEventTouchDragInside];
    }
    else
    {
        [self sendActionsForControlEvents:
            UIControlEventTouchDragOutside];
    }

    return YES;
}

// Start tracking touch in control
- (BOOL)beginTrackingWithTouch:(UITouch *)touch
        withEvent:(UIEvent *)event
{
    // Update color value
    [self updateColorFromTouch:touch];

    // Touch Down
    [self sendActionsForControlEvents:UIControlEventTouchDown];

    return YES;
}

// End tracking touch
- (void)endTrackingWithTouch:(UITouch *)touch
        withEvent:(UIEvent *)event
{
    // Test if touch ended inside or outside
    CGPoint touchPoint = [touch locationInView:self];
    if (CGRectContainsPoint(self.bounds, touchPoint))
    {
        // Update color value
        [self updateColorFromTouch:touch];

        [self sendActionsForControlEvents:
            UIControlEventTouchUpInside];
    }
    else
    {
        [self sendActionsForControlEvents:
            UIControlEventTouchUpOutside];
    }
}
```

```
// Handle touch cancel
- (void)cancelTrackingWithEvent:(UIEvent *)event
{
    [self sendActionsForControlEvents:UIControlEventTouchCancel];
}
@end
```

Get This Recipe's Code

To find this recipe's full sample project, point your browser to https://github.com/erica/iOS-7-Cookbook and go to the folder for Chapter 2.

Recipe: Building a Star Slider

Rating sliders allow users to grade items such as movies, software, and so forth by dragging their fingers across a set of images. It's a common task for touch-based interfaces but one that's not well served by a simple `UISlider` instance, with its floating-point values. Instead, a picker like the one built in Recipe 2-6 limits a user's choice to a discrete set of elements, producing a bounded integer value between zero and the maximum number of items shown. As a user's finger touches each star, the control's value updates, and a corresponding event is spawned, allowing your application to treat the star slider like any other `UIControl` subclass.

The art is arbitrary. The example shown in Figure 2-6 uses stars, but there's no reason to limit yourself to stars. Use any art you like, as long as you provide both "on" and "off" images. You might consider hearts, diamonds, smiles, and so on. You can easily update this recipe to provide a starting count of the stars before presentation.

Figure 2-6   Recipe 2-6 creates a custom star slider control that animates each star upon selection. A simple animation block causes the star to zoom out and back as the control's value updates.

In addition to simple sliding, Recipe 2-6 adds animation elements. Upon achieving a new value, a simple animation block is added to the rightmost star to zoom out and back, providing lively feedback to the user in addition to the highlighted visuals. Because the user's finger lays on top of the stars in real use (rather than in the simulator-based screen shot shown in Figure 2-6), the animation uses exaggerated transforms to provide feedback that extends beyond expected finger sizes. Here, the art is quite small, and the zoom goes to 150% of the original size, but you can easily adapt both in your applications to match your needs.

Apart from the minimal layout and feedback elements, Recipe 2-6 follows the same kind of custom UIControl subclass approach used by Recipe 2-5, tracking touches through their life cycle and spawning events at opportune times. The minimal code needed to add the star elements and feedback in this recipe demonstrates how simple UIControl subclassing really is.

Recipe 2-6   **Building a Discrete-Valued Star Slider**

```objc
@implementation StarSlider
- (instancetype)initWithFrame:(CGRect)aFrame
{
    self = [super initWithFrame:aFrame];
    if (self)
    {
        // Lay out five stars, with spacing between and at the ends
        float offsetCenter = WIDTH;
        for (int i = 1; i <= 5; i++)
        {
            UIImageView *imageView = [[UIImageView alloc]
                initWithFrame:CGRectMake(0.0f, 0.0f, WIDTH, WIDTH)];
            imageView.image = OFF_ART;
            imageView.center = CGPointMake(offsetCenter,
                self.intrinsicContentSize.height / 2.0f);
            offsetCenter += WIDTH * 1.5f;
            [self addSubview:imageView];
        }
    }

    // Place on a contrasting background
    self.backgroundColor =
        [[UIColor blackColor] colorWithAlphaComponent:0.25f];

    return self;
}

- (CGSize)intrinsicContentSize
{
    return CGSizeMake(WIDTH * 8.0f, 34.0f);
}

// Handle the value update for the touch point
- (void)updateValueAtPoint:(CGPoint)point
{
    int newValue = 0;
    UIImageView *changedView = nil;

    // Iterate through stars to check against touch point
    for (UIImageView *eachItem in [self subviews])
```

```
    {
        if (point.x < eachItem.frame.origin.x)
        {
            eachItem.image = OFF_ART;
        }
        else
        {
            changedView = eachItem; // last item touched
            eachItem.image = ON_ART;
            newValue++;
        }
    }

    // Handle value change
    if (self.value != newValue)
    {
        self.value = newValue;
        [self sendActionsForControlEvents:
            UIControlEventValueChanged];

        // Animate the new value with a zoomed pulse
        [UIView animateWithDuration:0.15f
            animations:^{changedView.transform =
                CGAffineTransformMakeScale(1.5f, 1.5f);}
            completion:^(BOOL done){[UIView
                animateWithDuration:0.1f
                animations:^{changedView.transform =
                    CGAffineTransformIdentity;}];}];
    }
}

- (BOOL)beginTrackingWithTouch:(UITouch *)touch
        withEvent:(UIEvent *)event
{
    // Establish touch down event
    CGPoint touchPoint = [touch locationInView:self];
    [self sendActionsForControlEvents:UIControlEventTouchDown];

    // Calculate value
    [self updateValueAtPoint:touchPoint];
    return YES;
}

- (BOOL)continueTrackingWithTouch:(UITouch *)touch
        withEvent:(UIEvent *)event
{
    // Test if drag is currently inside or outside
```

```
    CGPoint touchPoint = [touch locationInView:self];
    if (CGRectContainsPoint(self.frame, touchPoint))
        [self sendActionsForControlEvents:
            UIControlEventTouchDragInside];
    else
        [self sendActionsForControlEvents:
            UIControlEventTouchDragOutside];

    // Calculate value
    [self updateValueAtPoint:[touch locationInView:self]];
    return YES;
}

- (void)endTrackingWithTouch:(UITouch *)touch
        withEvent:(UIEvent *)event
{
    // Test if touch ended inside or outside
    CGPoint touchPoint = [touch locationInView:self];
    if (CGRectContainsPoint(self.bounds, touchPoint))
        [self sendActionsForControlEvents:
            UIControlEventTouchUpInside];
    else
        [self sendActionsForControlEvents:
            UIControlEventTouchUpOutside];
}

- (void)cancelTrackingWithEvent:(UIEvent *)event
{
    // Cancelled touch
    [self sendActionsForControlEvents:UIControlEventTouchCancel];
}
@end
```

Get This Recipe's Code

To find this recipe's full sample project, point your browser to https://github.com/erica/iOS-7-Cookbook and go to the folder for Chapter 2.

Recipe: Building a Touch Wheel

This next recipe creates a touch wheel, like the ones used on older model iPods. Touch wheels provide infinitely scrollable input. Users can rotate their finger clockwise or counterclockwise, and the object's value increases or decreases accordingly. Each complete turn around the wheel (that is, a traversal of 360 degrees) corresponds to a value change of 1.0. Clockwise changes are positive; counterclockwise changes are negative. The value accumulates on each touch, although it can be reset; simply assign the control's `value` property back to `0.0`. This property is not a standard part of `UIControl` instances, even though many controls use values.

This recipe computes user changes by casting out vectors from the control's center. The code adds differences in the angle as the finger moves, updating the current value accordingly. For example, three spins around the touch wheel add or subtract 3 to or from the current value, depending on the direction of movement.

This basic wheel defined in Recipe 2-7 tracks touch rotation but does little else. The original iPod scroll wheel offered five click points: in the center circle and at the four cardinal points of the wheel. Adding click support and the associated button-like event support (for `UIControlEventTouchUpInside`) are left as an exercise for you.

Recipe 2-7   Building a Touch Wheel Control

```
@implementation ScrollWheel

// Layout the wheel
- (instancetype)initWithFrame:(CGRect)aFrame
{
    self = [super initWithFrame:aFrame];
    if (self)
    {
        // This control uses a fixed 200x200 sized frame
        CGRect f;
        f.origin = aFrame.origin;
        f.size = self.intrinsicContentSize;
        self.frame = f;

        // Add the touch wheel art
        UIImageView *imageView = [[UIImageView alloc]
            initWithImage:[UIImage imageNamed:@"wheel.png"]];
        [self addSubview:imageView];
    }
    return self;
}


- (BOOL)beginTrackingWithTouch:(UITouch *)touch
        withEvent:(UIEvent *)event
{
    CGPoint point = [touch locationInView:self];

    // Center point of view in own coordinate system
    CGPoint centerPt = CGPointMake(self.bounds.size.width / 2.0f,
        self.bounds.size.height / 2.0f);
```

```objc
    // First touch must touch the gray part of the wheel
    if (!pointInsideRadius(point, centerPt.x, centerPt)) return NO;
    if (pointInsideRadius(point, 30.0f, centerPt)) return NO;

    // Set the initial angle
    self.theta = getAngle([touch locationInView:self], centerPt);

    // Establish touch down
    [self sendActionsForControlEvents:UIControlEventTouchDown];

    return YES;
}

- (CGSize)intrinsicContentSize
{
    return CGSizeMake(200, 200);
}

- (BOOL)continueTrackingWithTouch:(UITouch *)touch
    withEvent:(UIEvent *)event
{

    CGPoint point = [touch locationInView:self];

    // Center point of view in own coordinate system
    CGPoint centerPt = CGPointMake(self.bounds.size.width / 2.0f,
        self.bounds.size.height / 2.0f);

    // Touch updates
    if (CGRectContainsPoint(self.frame, point))
        [self sendActionsForControlEvents:
            UIControlEventTouchDragInside];
    else
        [self sendActionsForControlEvents:
            UIControlEventTouchDragOutside];

    // Falls outside too far, with boundary of 50 pixels?
    if (!pointInsideRadius(point, centerPt.x + 50.0f, centerPt))
        return NO;

    float newtheta = getAngle([touch locationInView:self], centerPt);
    float dtheta = newtheta - self.theta;

    // correct for edge conditions
    int ntimes = 0;
    while ((ABS(dtheta) > 300.0f) && (ntimes++ < 4))
    {
```

```
        if (dtheta > 0.0f)
            dtheta -= 360.0f;
        else
            dtheta += 360.0f;
    }

    // Update current values
    self.value -= dtheta / 360.0f;
    self.theta = newtheta;

    // Send value changed alert
    [self sendActionsForControlEvents:UIControlEventValueChanged];

    return YES;
}

- (void)endTrackingWithTouch:(UITouch *)touch
        withEvent:(UIEvent *)event
{
    // Test if touch ended inside or outside
    CGPoint touchPoint = [touch locationInView:self];
    if (CGRectContainsPoint(self.bounds, touchPoint))
        [self sendActionsForControlEvents:
            UIControlEventTouchUpInside];
    else
        [self sendActionsForControlEvents:
            UIControlEventTouchUpOutside];
}

- (void)cancelTrackingWithEvent:(UIEvent *)event
{
    // Cancel
    [self sendActionsForControlEvents:UIControlEventTouchCancel];
}
@end
```

Get This Recipe's Code

To find this recipe's full sample project, point your browser to https://github.com/erica/iOS-7-Cookbook and go to the folder for Chapter 2.

Recipe: Creating a Pull Control

Imagine a cord at the top of your screen. Pull it hard enough, and it rings a bell or otherwise triggers some sort of event, via a control target-action mechanism. For example, it could roll out a secondary view, start a download, or begin video playback. Recipe 2-8 builds a control that resembles a ribbon. The control updates clients when the interaction, which must start on top of the "ribbon," pulls down far enough to trigger a request. The ribbon winds itself back up afterward, preparing for the next interaction.

Figure 2-7 shows the control built by this recipe, which is attached in this case to the bottom of a secondary view. Tugs bring the view into place and return it offscreen when finished.

Figure 2-7   The ribbon control must be tugged a minimum distance before it triggers and winds back up. Each success sends out a value-changed message to its target-action clients.

Discoverability

Making the ribbon interaction discoverable presents a particular challenge in this recipe. Users might not immediately make the connection between a hanging red shape and a control they can manipulate.

Developer Matthijs Hollemans suggested a simple approach to address this challenge. Until the user interacts with the ribbon, it wiggles slightly a few times, separated by several seconds between each wiggle. The wiggle draws attention to the nature of the control, and the wiggles stop as soon as the user has correctly worked through the control style. A system preference can override this behavior for repeat application uses:

```
- (void)wiggle
{
    if (wiggleCount++ > 3) return;

    // Wiggle slightly
    [UIView animateWithDuration:0.25f animations:^(){
        pullImageView.center = CGPointMake(
            pullImageView.center.x,
            pullImageView.center.y + 10.0f);
    } completion:^(BOOL finished){
        [UIView animateWithDuration:0.25f animations:^(){
            pullImageView.center = CGPointMake(
                pullImageView.center.x,
                pullImageView.center.y - 10.0f);
        }];
    }];

    // Repeat until the count is overridden or it wiggles 3 times
    [self performSelector:@selector(wiggle)
        withObject:nil afterDelay:4.0f];
}
```

Adding accelerometer-based movement is another way to draw user attention to a nonobvious interaction control. Developer Charles Choi recommends allowing the ribbon to respond gently to device movements, offering an alternative mechanism for enhancing the control's discoverability.

With the introduction of motion effects in iOS 7, the implementation for such an interaction has been greatly simplified with a new declarative API. Motion effects, as demonstrated in Listing 2-1, allow the association of accelerometer events from the device with values in your UIKit objects. Simply create an instance of a UIMotionEffect subclass (UIInterpolatingMotionEffect is the only system-supplied option currently), set the keyPath to be modified on the view, and associate the motion effect instance with the targeted view.

Listing 2-1   **Adding Motion Effects**

```
- (void)startMotionEffects
{
    UIInterpolatingMotionEffect *motionEffectX =
        [[UIInterpolatingMotionEffect alloc]
            initWithKeyPath:@"center.x"
            type:UIInterpolatingMotionEffectTypeTiltAlongHorizontalAxis];
    UIInterpolatingMotionEffect *motionEffectY =
        [[UIInterpolatingMotionEffect alloc]
            initWithKeyPath:@"center.y"
            type:UIInterpolatingMotionEffectTypeTiltAlongVerticalAxis];
    motionEffectX.minimumRelativeValue = @-15.0;
    motionEffectX.maximumRelativeValue = @15.0;
    motionEffectY.minimumRelativeValue = @-15.0;
    motionEffectY.maximumRelativeValue = @15.0;
    motionEffectsGroup = [[UIMotionEffectGroup alloc] init];
    motionEffectsGroup.motionEffects =
        @[motionEffectX, motionEffectY];
    [pullImageView addMotionEffect:motionEffectsGroup];
}
```

Take your inspiration from Apple itself. Apple integrates discoverability hints throughout iOS, such as using slide to unlock text that suggests how and what to slide through simple animation.

Testing Touches

Recipe 2-8 limits interactions in two ways. First, the user must touch inside the ribbon art to begin interaction. If the user touches anywhere other than the ribbon, the touch falls through, and the control does not respond to it, even though touches may have begun on top of the control's frame. Second, the recipe tests against the ribbon bitmap to ensure that touches began on a solid (nontransparent) part of the art. As you can see in Figure 2-7, a notch appears at the bottom of the artwork. Touches in this notch won't start a tracking sequence. The recipe compares the touch position with pixels in the art. If the transparency (alpha level) of the art falls below 85 (about 67% transparent), the touch won't connect with the ribbon.

The sample code provided for this recipe does not test for stretched art. It assumes a one-to-one relationship between the art and the onscreen presentation. Because of this, you will either have to drop the transparency test or adapt it for stretched art if you choose to resize this control in any way.

Once the tracking begins, the art follows the touch movement, dragging up or down with the user's finger. If this touch travel exceeds 75 points in this recipe, the control triggers. It sends off a value-changed event to its clients. Strictly speaking, this control does not have a "value," but touch up inside felt like a poor match to the way the control operates.

Upon reaching the trigger point, the continue tracking method returns NO, indicating that tracking has finished, and the control has finished its business for this particular interaction. If the touch travel fails to exceed the threshold or the user stops interacting without reaching that point, the control scrolls back its artwork to the beginning point. This resets the visual presentation, making it ready for the next interaction.

Recipe 2-8   Building a Draggable Ribbon Control

```
- (BOOL)beginTrackingWithTouch:(UITouch *)touch
        withEvent:(UIEvent *)event
{
    // Establish touch down event
    CGPoint touchPoint = [touch locationInView:self];
    CGPoint ribbonPoint = [touch locationInView:pullImageView];

    // Find the data offset in the image
    Byte *bytes = (Byte *) ribbonData.bytes;
    uint offset = alphaOffset(ribbonPoint.x, ribbonPoint.y,
        pullImageView.bounds.size.width);

    // Test for containment and alpha value to disallow touches
    // outside the ribbon and inside the notched area

    if (CGRectContainsPoint(pullImageView.frame, touchPoint) &&
        (bytes[offset] > 85))
    {
        [self sendActionsForControlEvents:UIControlEventTouchDown];
        touchDownPoint = touchPoint;
        return YES;
    }

    return NO;
}

- (BOOL)continueTrackingWithTouch:(UITouch *)touch
        withEvent:(UIEvent *)event
{
    // Once the user has interacted, don't wiggle any more
    wiggleCount = CGFLOAT_MAX;

    // Test for inside/outside touches
    CGPoint touchPoint = [touch locationInView:self];
    if (CGRectContainsPoint(self.frame, touchPoint))
        [self sendActionsForControlEvents:
            UIControlEventTouchDragInside];
    else
```

```
        [self sendActionsForControlEvents:
            UIControlEventTouchDragOutside];

    // Adjust art based on the degree of drag
    CGFloat dy = MAX(touchPoint.y - touchDownPoint.y, 0.0f);
    dy = MIN(dy, self.bounds.size.height - 75.0f);
    pullImageView.frame = CGRectMake(10.0f,
        dy + 75.0f - ribbonImage.size.height,
        ribbonImage.size.width, ribbonImage.size.height);

    // Detect if travel has been sufficient to trigger everything
    if (dy > 75.0f)
    {
        // It has. Play a click, trigger the callback, and roll
        // the view back up.
        [self playClick];
        [UIView animateWithDuration:0.3f animations:^(){
            pullImageView.frame = CGRectMake(10.0f,
                75.0f - ribbonImage.size.height,
                ribbonImage.size.width,
                ribbonImage.size.height);
        } completion:^(BOOL finished){
            [self sendActionsForControlEvents:
                UIControlEventValueChanged];
        }];

        // No more interaction needed or allowed
        return NO;
    }

    // Continue interaction
    return YES;
}

- (void)endTrackingWithTouch:(UITouch *)touch
        withEvent:(UIEvent *)event
{
    // Test if touch ended inside or outside
    CGPoint touchPoint = [touch locationInView:self];
    if (CGRectContainsPoint(self.bounds, touchPoint))
        [self sendActionsForControlEvents:
            UIControlEventTouchUpInside];
    else
        [self sendActionsForControlEvents:
            UIControlEventTouchUpOutside];

    // Roll back the ribbon, regardless of where the touch ended
```

```
    [UIView animateWithDuration:0.3f animations:^(){
        pullImageView.frame = CGRectMake(10.0f,
            75.0f - ribbonImage.size.height,
            ribbonImage.size.width, ribbonImage.size.height);
    }];
}


// Handle cancelled tracking
- (void)cancelTrackingWithEvent:(UIEvent *)event
{
    [self sendActionsForControlEvents:UIControlEventTouchCancel];
}
```

Get This Recipe's Code

To find this recipe's full sample project, point your browser to https://github.com/erica/iOS-7-Cookbook and go to the folder for Chapter 2.

Recipe: Building a Custom Lock Control

We created the lock control you see in Figure 2-8 for a conference after wrapping up the last edition of this *Cookbook*. At that time, numerous people asked for this recipe to be included in the next edition. It's surprisingly easy to build from a UIControl point of view. It consists of four elements: a backdrop, the lock image (which switches to an unlocked version on success), the drag track, and the thumb.

Recipe 2-9 shows the code that creates this control's behavior. In this recipe, interactions have a generous margin. Touches within 20 points of the track and its thumb are considered proper hits. This control is quite Spartan, and the extra space (roughly half the size of a standard fingertip) allows more confident access to the control.

Similarly, users only need to drag over about 75% of the way to complete the action. Again, this margin confirms that the user has intended a full unlock, but it doesn't require frustrating precision. It took a bit of fiddling and user testing to get the "springiness" right; after releasing the thumb, it's pulled back to the left if you haven't finished a successful drag. We ended up using a half second, slightly longer than most interface changes usually take. To compare, a keyboard usually appears in one-third of a second.

Figure 2-8   This simple lock control unlocks and removes itself after the user successfully swipes across at least three-quarters of the way.

Recipe 2-9   **Creating a Lock Control**

```
- (BOOL)beginTrackingWithTouch:(UITouch *)touch
        withEvent:(UIEvent *)event
{
    // Test touches for start conditions
    CGPoint touchPoint = [touch locationInView:self];
    CGRect largeTrack =
        CGRectInset(trackView.frame, -20.0f, -20.0f);
    if (!CGRectContainsPoint(largeTrack, touchPoint))
        return NO;
    touchPoint = [touch locationInView:trackView];
    CGRect largeThumb =
        CGRectInset(thumbView.frame, -20.0f, -20.0f);
    if (!CGRectContainsPoint(largeThumb, touchPoint))
        return NO;
```

```objc
    // Begin tracking
    [self sendActionsForControlEvents:UIControlEventTouchDown];
    return YES;
}

- (BOOL)continueTrackingWithTouch:(UITouch *)touch
        withEvent:(UIEvent *)event
{
    // Strayed too far out?
    CGPoint touchPoint = [touch locationInView:self];
    CGRect largeTrack =
        CGRectInset(trackView.frame, -20.0f, -20.0f);
    if (!CGRectContainsPoint(largeTrack, touchPoint))
    {
        // Reset on failed attempt
        [UIView animateWithDuration:0.2f animations:^(){
            NSLayoutConstraint *constraint =
                [trackView constraintNamed:THUMB_POSITION_TAG];
            constraint.constant = 0;
            [trackView layoutIfNeeded];
        }];
        return NO;
    }

    // Track the user movement by updating the thumb
    touchPoint = [touch locationInView:trackView];
    [UIView animateWithDuration:0.1f animations:^(){
        NSLayoutConstraint *constraint =
            [trackView constraintNamed:THUMB_POSITION_TAG];
        constraint.constant = touchPoint.x;
        [trackView layoutIfNeeded];
    }];
    return YES;
}

- (void)endTrackingWithTouch:(UITouch *)touch
        withEvent:(UIEvent *)event
{
    // Test if touch ended with unlock
    CGPoint touchPoint = [touch locationInView:trackView];
    if (touchPoint.x > trackView.frame.size.width * 0.75f)
    {
```

```
                // Complete by unlocking
                _value = 0;
                self.userInteractionEnabled = NO;
                [self sendActionsForControlEvents:
                    UIControlEventValueChanged];

                // Fade away and remove
                [UIView animateWithDuration:0.5f animations:
                        ^(){self.alpha = 0.0f;}
                    completion:
                        ^(BOOL finished){[self removeFromSuperview];
                }];
        }
        else
        {
            // Reset on failed attempt
            [UIView animateWithDuration:0.2f animations:^(){
                NSLayoutConstraint *constraint =
                    [trackView constraintNamed:
                        THUMB_POSITION_TAG];
                constraint.constant = 0;
                [trackView layoutIfNeeded];
            }];
        }

        if (CGRectContainsPoint(trackView.bounds, touchPoint))
        {
            [self sendActionsForControlEvents:
                UIControlEventTouchUpInside];
        }
        else
        {
            [self sendActionsForControlEvents:
                UIControlEventTouchUpOutside];
        }
}

- (void)cancelTrackingWithEvent:(UIEvent *)event
{
    [self sendActionsForControlEvents:
        UIControlEventTouchCancel];
}
```

Get This Recipe's Code

To find this recipe's full sample project, point your browser to https://github.com/erica/iOS-7-Cookbook and go to the folder for Chapter 2.

Adding a Page Indicator Control

The UIPageControl class provides a line of dots that indicates which item of a multipage view is currently displayed. The dots at the bottom of the SpringBoard home screen present an example of this kind of control in action. Sadly, the UIPageControl class is a disappointment in action. Its instances are awkward to handle, hard to tap, and will generally annoy your users. So when using it, make sure you add alternative navigation options so that the page control acts more as an indicator and less as a control.

Figure 2-9 shows a page control with three pages. Taps to the left or right of the bright-colored current page indicator trigger UIControlEventValueChanged events, launching whatever method you set as the control's action. You can query the control for its new value by calling currentPage and set the available page count by adjusting the numberOfPages property. SpringBoard limits the number of dots representing pages to nine, but your application can use a higher number, particularly in landscape mode.

Figure 2-9 The UIPageControl class offers an interactive indicator for multipage presentations. Taps to the left or right of the active dot enable users to select new pages—at least in theory. The page control is hard to tap, requires excessive user precision, and offers poor response performance.

Recipe: Image Gallery Viewer

Recipe 2-10 uses a UIScrollView instance to display multiple images, as shown in Figure 2-10. Users can scroll through the pictures using swipes, and the page indicator updates accordingly. Similarly, users can tap on the page control, and the scroller animates the selected page into place. This two-way relationship is built by adding a target-action callback to the page control and a delegate callback to the scroller. Each callback updates the other object, providing a tight coupling between the two.

Figure 2-10   In iOS 7, content is king. The only interface elements that are visible include the page control and the iOS status bar, both of which overlay the content.

One common mistake with `UIPageControl` is not sizing the control wide enough to create user navigation tap areas to the right and left of the dots. The intrinsic size of a page control matches closely to the visible size, which severely limits these tap areas. Centering the control without expanding the width creates a page control that is very difficult to use in navigation. Unless the interaction would conflict with other touch elements, expand the page control to the width of its superview through Auto Layout constraints or by setting the frame appropriately.

The design ethos of iOS 7 revolves around content as the primary focus, with limited UI chrome. The images in the gallery fully utilize all of the screen real estate, including under the status bar. Fittingly, the iOS status bar no longer allows translucent or opaque styles, only transparent, providing two styles that toggle the status bar for light and dark content. Change the status bar style by returning a `UIStatusBarStyle` from the `preferredStatusBarStyle` method on your view controller.

The status bar style and the page indicator tint colors could be modified to better suit the underlying picture, based on the average color of the image or a similar metric. This advanced treatment is left as an exercise for you.

> **Note**
>
> The implementation of `UIScrollView` presents unique challenges to arranging UI elements with Auto Layout. Apple provides Technical Note TN2154 (http://developer.apple.com/library/ios/#technotes/tn2154/_index.html), which describes two approaches. Recipe 2-10 uses the *mixed approach*. Auto Layout is addressed in more detail in Chapter 5, "View Constraints."

Recipe 2-10   **An Image Gallery Viewer**

```
@implementation TestBedViewController
{
    PagedImageScrollView *scrollView;
    UIPageControl *pageControl;
}

- (UIStatusBarStyle)preferredStatusBarStyle
{
    return UIStatusBarStyleLightContent;
}

- (void)loadView
{
    self.view = [[UIView alloc] init];
    self.view.backgroundColor = [UIColor blackColor];
    self.navigationController.navigationBarHidden = YES;

    scrollView = [[PagedImageScrollView alloc] init];
```

```objc
    scrollView.delegate = self;
    [self.view addSubview:scrollView];
    PREPCONSTRAINTS(scrollView);
    ALIGN_VIEW_LEFT(self.view, scrollView);
    ALIGN_VIEW_RIGHT(self.view, scrollView);
    ALIGN_VIEW_TOP(self.view, scrollView);
    ALIGN_VIEW_BOTTOM(self.view, scrollView);
    scrollView.images = @[[UIImage imageNamed:@"bird"],
        [UIImage imageNamed:@"ladybug"],
        [UIImage imageNamed:@"flowers"],
        [UIImage imageNamed:@"sheep"]];

    pageControl = [[UIPageControl alloc] init];
    pageControl.numberOfPages = scrollView.images.count;
    pageControl.currentPage = 0;
    pageControl.pageIndicatorTintColor = [UIColor grayColor];
    pageControl.currentPageIndicatorTintColor =
        [UIColor redColor];
    [pageControl addTarget:self
        action:@selector(handlePageControlChange:)
        forControlEvents:UIControlEventValueChanged];
    [self.view addSubview:pageControl];
    PREPCONSTRAINTS(pageControl);
    ALIGN_VIEW_LEFT(self.view, pageControl);
    ALIGN_VIEW_RIGHT(self.view, pageControl);
    ALIGN_VIEW_BOTTOM_CONSTANT(self.view, pageControl, -20);
}

// Update the scrollView after page control interaction
- (void)handlePageControlChange:(UIPageControl *)sender
{
    CGFloat offset =
        scrollView.frame.size.width * pageControl.currentPage;
    [scrollView setContentOffset:CGPointMake(offset, 0)
        animated:YES];
}

// Update the page control after scrolling
- (void)scrollViewDidEndDecelerating:(id)sender
{
    CGFloat distance = scrollView.contentOffset.x /
        scrollView.contentSize.width;
    NSInteger page = distance * pageControl.numberOfPages;
    pageControl.currentPage = page;
}
@end
```

> **Get This Recipe's Code**
>
> To find this recipe's full sample project, point your browser to https://github.com/erica/iOS-7-Cookbook and go to the folder for Chapter 2.

Building Toolbars

It's easy to define and lay out toolbars in code if you've supplied yourself with a few handy macro definitions. The following macros return proper bar button items for the four available styles of items, and you can easily adapt them if you need more control options in your code. These macros are intended for automatic reference counting (ARC) use. If you use manual retain-release (MRR) development, make sure to adapt them with appropriate autorelease calls:

```
#define BARBUTTON(TITLE, SELECTOR) [[UIBarButtonItem alloc] \
    initWithTitle:TITLE style:UIBarButtonItemStylePlain\
    target:self action:SELECTOR]
#define IMGBARBUTTON(IMAGE, SELECTOR) [[UIBarButtonItem alloc] \
    initWithImage:IMAGE style:UIBarButtonItemStylePlain \
    target:self action:SELECTOR]
#define SYSBARBUTTON(ITEM, SELECTOR) [[UIBarButtonItem alloc] \
    initWithBarButtonSystemItem:ITEM \
    target:self action:SELECTOR]
#define CUSTOMBARBUTTON(VIEW) [[UIBarButtonItem alloc] \
    initWithCustomView:VIEW]
```

These styles are text items, image items, system items, and custom view items. Each of these macros provides a `UIBarButtonItem` that can be placed into a `UIToolbar`. Listing 2-2 demonstrates these macros in action, showing how to add each style, including spacers. You can even add a custom view to your toolbars, as Listing 2-2 does. It inserts a `UISwitch` instance as one of the bar button items, as shown in Figure 2-11.

Figure 2-11   Custom toolbar items can include views such as this switch.

The fixed-space bar button item represents the only instance where you need to move beyond these handy macros. You must set the item's `width` property to define how much space the item occupies. Here are a few final pointers:

- **Fixed spaces can have widths.** Of all `UIBarButtonItems`, only `UIBarButtonSystemItemFixedSpace` items can be assigned a width. So create the spacer item, set its width, and only then add it to your items array.

- **Use a single flexible space for left or right alignment.** Adding a single `UIBarButtonSystemItemFlexibleSpace` at the start of an item's list right-aligns all the remaining items. Adding one at the end left-aligns. Use two—one at the start and one at the end—to create center alignments.

- **Take missing items into account.** When hiding a bar button item due to context, when you're not using layout constraints, don't just use flexible spacing to get rid of the item. Instead, replace the item with a fixed-width space that matches the item's original size. Doing so preserves the layout and leaves all the other icons in the same position both before and after the item disappears.

- **Navigation bars support multiple items.** Navigation bars and their navigation items allow you to add arrays of bar button items. You can create a toolbar effect by adding item arrays rather than adding a toolbar directly (for example, `self.navigationItem.rightBarButtonItems = anArray`). All the toolbar hints listed here, including flexible spacers, apply to navigation item layout as well.

Listing 2-2 **Creating Toolbars in Code**

```
@implementation TestBedViewController
- (void)action
{
    // no action actually happens
}

- (void)loadView
{
    self.view = [[UIView alloc] init];
    self.view.backgroundColor = [UIColor whiteColor];
}

- (void)viewDidLoad
{
    [super viewDidLoad];
    UIToolbar *tb = [UIToolbar alloc] init];
    [self.view addSubview:tb];
    PREPCONSTRAINTS(tb);
    ALIGN_VIEW_BOTTOM(self.view, tb);
    ALIGN_VIEW_LEFT(self.view, tb);
    ALIGN_VIEW_RIGHT(self.view, tb);
    NSMutableArray *tbItems = [NSMutableArray array];

    // Set up the items for the toolbar
    [tbItems addObject:
        BARBUTTON(@"Title", @selector(action))];
```

```
    [tbItems addObject:
        SYSBARBUTTON(UIBarButtonSystemItemFlexibleSpace,
            nil)];

    [tbItems addObject:
        SYSBARBUTTON(UIBarButtonSystemItemAdd,
            @selector(action))];

    [tbItems addObject:
        SYSBARBUTTON(UIBarButtonSystemItemFlexibleSpace,
            nil)];

    [tbItems addObject:
        IMGBARBUTTON([UIImage imageNamed:@"star.png"],
            @selector(action))];

    [tbItems addObject:
        SYSBARBUTTON(UIBarButtonSystemItemFlexibleSpace,
            nil)];

    [tbItems addObject:
        CUSTOMBARBUTTON([[UISwitch alloc] init])];

    [tbItems addObject:
        SYSBARBUTTON(UIBarButtonSystemItemFlexibleSpace,
            nil)];

    [tbItems addObject:
        IMGBARBUTTON([UIImage imageNamed:@"moon.png"],
            @selector(action))];

    tb.items = tbItems;
}
@end
```

Summary

This chapter introduces many ways to interact with and get the most from the controls in your applications. Before you move on to the next chapter, here are a few thoughts for you to ponder:

- Just because an item belongs to the UIControl class doesn't mean you can't treat it like a UIView. Give it subviews, resize it, animate it, move it around the screen, or tag it for later.

- Core Graphics and Quartz 2D let you build visual elements as needed. Combine the comfort of the SDK classes with a little real-time wow to add punch to your presentation.

- Use attributed strings and UIKit attribute dictionaries to customize your control's text features. Pick fonts, line and paragraph styling, colors, shadows, and more, as demanded by your design.

- If the iOS SDK hasn't delivered the control you need, consider adapting an existing control or building a new control from scratch.

- Apple provides top-notch examples of UI excellence. Consider mimicking Apple's examples when creating new interaction styles, such as adding confirm buttons to safeguard a delete action.

- IB doesn't always provide the best solution for creating interfaces. With toolbars, you may save time by using Xcode rather than customizing each element by hand in IB.

3

Alerting the User

At times, you need to grab your user's attention. New data might arrive or some status might change. You might want to tell your user that there's going to be a wait before anything more happens—or that the wait is over and it's time to come back and pay attention. iOS offers many ways to provide such a heads-up to the user: from alerts and progress bars to audio pings. In this chapter, you'll discover how to build these indications into your applications and expand your user-alert vocabulary. You'll see real-life examples that showcase these classes and discover how to make sure your user pays attention at the right time.

Talking Directly to Your User through Alerts

Alerts speak to your user. Members of the `UIAlertView` and `UIActionSheet` classes pop up or scroll in above other views to deliver their messages. These lightweight classes add two-way dialog to your apps. Alerts visually "speak" to users and can prompt them to reply. You present your alert, get user acknowledgment, and then dismiss the alert to move on with other tasks.

If you think that an alert is nothing more than a message with an attached OK button, think again. Alert objects provide incredible versatility. You can build progress indicators, allow for text input, make queries, and more. In this chapter's recipes, you'll see how to create a wide range of useful alerts that you can use in your own programs, using the system-supplied alerts as well as some custom ones.

Building Simple Alerts

To create alerts, allocate a `UIAlertView` object. Initialize it with a title and an array of button titles. The title is an `NSString`, as are the button titles. In the button array, each string represents a single button that should be shown.

The method snippet shown here creates and displays the simplest alert scenario. It shows a message with a single OK button. The alert doesn't bother with delegates or callbacks, so its lifetime ends when the user taps a button:

```
- (void)showAlert:(NSString *)theMessage
{
    UIAlertView *av = [[UIAlertView alloc] initWithTitle:@"Title"
        message:theMessage
        delegate:nil
        cancelButtonTitle:@"OK"
        otherButtonTitles:nil];
    [av show];
}
```

Add buttons by introducing them as parameters to `otherButtonTitles:`. Make sure you end your arbitrary list of buttons with `nil`. Adding `nil` tells the method where your list finishes. The following snippet creates an alert with three buttons (Cancel, Option, and OK). Because this code does not declare a delegate, there's no way to recover the alert and determine which of these three buttons was tapped. The alert displays until a user taps, and then it automatically dismisses without any further effect:

```
- (void)showAlert:(NSString *)theMessage
{
    UIAlertView *av = [[UIAlertView alloc] initWithTitle:@"Title"
        message:theMessage
        delegate:nil
        cancelButtonTitle:@"Cancel"
        otherButtonTitles:@"Option", @"OK", nil];
    [av show];
}
```

When working with alerts, space is at a premium. Adding more than two buttons causes the alert to display in multiline mode. Figure 3-1 shows a pair of alerts depicting both two-button (side-by-side display) and three-button (line-by-line display) presentations. Limit the number of alert buttons you add at any time to no more than three or four. Having fewer buttons works better; one or two is ideal. If you need to use more buttons, consider using action sheet objects, which are discussed later in this chapter, rather than alert views.

`UIAlertView` objects provide simple "default" button highlights. These are based on the number of buttons, as shown in Figure 3-1. Two-button alerts highlight the rightmost button. This is defined by the single `otherButtonTitles` in the alert initialization. On alerts with more than two buttons, the bottom button is highlighted. This is usually represented by `cancelButtonTitle`. If you don't supply one, the last button item acts as the default instead. As a rule, Cancel buttons appear at the bottom or left of alerts.

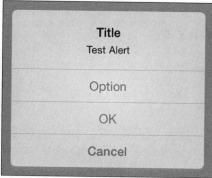

Figure 3-1   Alerts work best with one or two buttons (left). Alerts with more than two buttons stack the buttons as a list, producing a less elegant presentation (right).

Alert Delegates

Need to know if a user tapped OK or Cancel? Alerts use delegates to recover user choices after they've been made, using a simple callback. Delegates should declare the UIAlertViewDelegate protocol. In normal use, you often set the delegate to your primary (active) view controller object.

Delegate methods enable you to react as different buttons are pressed. As you've already seen, you can omit that delegate support if all you need to do is show some message with an OK button.

After the user has seen and interacted with your alert, the delegate receives an alertView: clickedButtonAtIndex: callback. The second parameter passed to this method indicates which button was pressed. Button numbering begins with zero. The Cancel button defaults to button 0. Even though it appears at the left in some views and the bottom in others, its button numbering remains the same unless you adjust the Cancel button index (retrievable via the cancelButtonIndex property). This is not true for action sheet objects, which are discussed later in this chapter.

Here is a simple example of an alert presentation and callback, which prints out the selected button number to the debugging console:

```
@interface TestBedViewController : UIViewController
    <UIAlertViewDelegate>
@end

@implementation TestBedViewController
- (void)alertView:(UIAlertView *)alertView
    clickedButtonAtIndex:(int)index
{
    NSLog(@"User selected button %d\n", index);
}
```

```
- (void)showAlert
{
    UIAlertView *av = [[UIAlertView alloc]
        initWithTitle:@"Alert View Sample"
        message:@"Select a Button"
        delegate:self
        cancelButtonTitle:@"Cancel"
        otherButtonTitles:@"One", @"Two", @"Three", nil];

    // Tag your UIAlertView so it can be distinguished
    // from others in your delegate callbacks.
    av.tag = MAIN_ALERT;
    [av show];
}
@end
```

If your controller works with multiple alerts, tags help identify which alert produced a given callback. Unlike controls that use target-action pairs, all alerts trigger the same methods. Adding an alert-tag-based switch statement lets you differentiate your responses to each alert.

Displaying the Alert

The show instance method tells your alert to appear. When shown, the alert works in a modal fashion. That is, it dims the screen behind it and blocks user interaction with your application outside the alert. This modal interaction continues until your user acknowledges the alert through a button tap, typically by selecting OK or Cancel. When the user does so, control passes to the alert delegate, allowing that delegate to finish working with the alert and respond to the selected button.

The alert properties remain modifiable after creation. You may customize an alert by updating its title or message properties. The message is the optional text that appears below the alert title and above its buttons. You can add more buttons via addButtonWithTitle:.

Kinds of Alerts

The alertViewStyle property allows you to create several alert styles. The default style (UIAlertViewStyleDefault) creates a standard alert, with a title and message text, followed by buttons, as shown in Figure 3-1. It is the bread and butter of the alert world, allowing you to query for button presses such as Yes/No, Cancel/OK, and other simple choices.

iOS offers three more styles, specifically for entering text:

- **UIAlertViewStylePlainTextInput**—This alert style enables users to enter text.
- **UIAlertViewStyleSecureTextInput**—When security is an issue, this alert style allows users to enter text that is automatically obscured as they type it. The text appears as a series of large dots, but the input can be read programmatically by the delegate callback.
- **UIAlertViewStyleLoginAndPasswordInput**—This alert style offers two entry fields, including a plain-text user account login field and an obscured text password field.

When working with text entry alerts, keep your button choices simple. Use no more than two side-by-side buttons—usually OK and Cancel. Too many buttons create improper visuals, with text fields floating off above or to the sides of the alert.

You can recover the text entered in each text field of the alert view. The `textFieldAtIndex:` method takes one argument, an integer index starting at 0, and returns the text field at that index. In real use, the only text field that is not at index 0 is the password field, which uses index 1. After you've retrieved a text field, you can query its contents by using its `text` property, as follows:

```
NSLog(@"%@", [myAlert textFieldAtIndex:0].text);
```

Recipe: Using Blocks with Alerts

Using an alert's delegate callbacks can produce unnecessarily complex code. All your code handling ends up in a common routine. You must implement tagging to differentiate which alert your method must handle. You must vigilantly track which button corresponds to the functionality you wish to execute, such as the alert in Figure 3-2.

Figure 3-2   This alert processes responses in blocks passed at UIAlert button creation instead of in traditional delegate callbacks.

A much simpler solution is to assign the intended implementation when declaring the buttons themselves. Blocks were built just for this task.

Blocks

Blocks are an extension to the C language that were first supported in iOS 4. They are similar in concept to a method or function that can be stored in a variable. C provides a similar mechanism for storing functions: function pointers. Blocks go beyond function pointers by storing a copy of the enclosing scope in addition to the block of executable code.

When a block is defined, a copy of the local stack is created and attached to the block. When the block is finally executed, it has access to this copy of the stack. This is very powerful, allowing a block of code and its surrounding state to be passed to a method. This code can be executed at a future point or within a certain context, such as on another thread or in a certain order.

Block syntax can be a bit perplexing. It inherits much from C function pointers, which for those not familiar can seem a bit unnatural. The caret symbol (^) denotes a block. The general syntax includes a return type, argument list, and the code block itself:

```
^(return type)(argument list) { // code block }
```

The return type can be omitted if void. The argument list can be omitted completely if there are no arguments. The simplest block could then be defined as follows:

```
^{ // your code here }
```

The `typedef` syntax referring to a block is slightly modified from the above:

```
typedef (return type)(^typeName)(argument list);
```

Once a block has been defined, it can then be executed, like this:

```
typedef void (^SomeBlock)(BOOL);
SomeBlock myBlock = ^(BOOL success)
{
    if (success)
        NSLog(@"Successful!");
    else
        NSLog(@"FAILED!");
};
myBlock(YES);
```

This code does very little that could not be done in a standard method call. However, passing blocks as parameters to methods opens up numerous opportunities, such as calling a block while iterating through an array. The unique feature of blocks is the ability to access variables from the enclosing scope. The following example accesses the captured `myBaseNumber`:

```
NSInteger myBaseNumber = 7;
NSArray *numbers = @[@2, @3, @5, @8, @9, @11];
```

```
[numbers enumerateObjectsUsingBlock:^(id obj, NSUInteger idx, BOOL *stop)
{
    NSInteger current = [obj integerValue];
    NSLog(@"%d * %d = %d", myBaseNumber, current, myBaseNumber * current);
}];
```

Blocks can access their captured context even if they have left the scope of that variable.

The ability of blocks to capture their enclosing scope does come with a couple caveats. The stack stored with a block is a copy. Any modifications made to captured variables after the block is declared but before it is run will not be reflected in the block. Any modifications to captured variables in the block will be lost outside the block.

To modify a captured variable from within a block, the variable must be declared with the __block storage type modifier. The variable will reside in storage that is shared between both the enclosing scope of the original code as well as the block. Any changes in one will impact the other.

The second concern with blocks and captured scope is retain cycles.

Retain Cycles and Blocks

When using blocks, be wary of the creation of retain cycles. It is very easy to unintentionally retain self inside a block. This occurs by referencing self directly or by using an ivar, which captures self indirectly.

To avoid the retain cycle, capture a weak variant of self and then assign the weak reference to a strong reference prior to use within the block. Adding the strong reference at the very start of the block ensures that if a strong reference is possible, it endures throughout the entire block scope. Don't forget to check that the strong reference to self is not nil. The following listing avoids issues with retain cycles and nil references:

```
__weak TestBedViewController *weakSelf = self;
[blockAlertView addButtonWithTitle:@"OK" actionBlock:^{
    TestBedViewController *strongSelf = weakSelf;
    if (strongSelf)
    {
        NSString *name = [strongSelf->blockAlertView
            textFieldAtIndex:0].text;
        NSLog(@"Tapped OK after entering: %@", name);
    }
}];
```

Blocks enable clearer APIs and greatly simplified multithreaded programming. This section has only scratched the surface of the capabilities of and uses for blocks. The Apple documentation has a trove of information on blocks and Grand Central Dispatch that are worth exploring.

> **Note**
> Grand Central Dispatch (GCD) is a powerful tool for implementing parallel tasking. Introduced
> with iOS 4, GCD provides a function-based API utilizing blocks for building concurrent code that
> can take advantage of multicore hardware.

While most of Apple's libraries are now fully integrated with blocks, a few classes have not been
modernized. `UIAlert`, for example, desperately calls out for blocks. Once you start using them,
you will see many new opportunities for their use.

Recipe 3-1 adds blocks to button creation on the standard `UIAlertView`, reducing complexity
and centralizing the actions near the button declarations. You no longer need to implement
delegates or the delegate callbacks.

While not provided in this recipe, the existing delegate methods can still be used with a bit of
effort. The `setDelegate` method already saves off the `externalDelegate` for this usage. You
can add proxy methods to `BlockAlertView` to forward each of the `UIAlertView` delegate calls
to the external delegate:

```
- (void)didPresentAlertView:(UIAlertView *)alertView
{
    if ([externalDelegate
        respondsToSelector:@selector(didPresentAlertView:)])
    {
        [externalDelegate didPresentAlertView:alertView];
    }
}
```

When the user taps a button in the alert view, the `BlockAlertView` executes the appropriate
block associated with that button. Another enhancement left to the reader is providing more
control over when that block is run. Currently, the block is executed in the `alertView:`
`clickedButtonAtIndex:` delegate callback of `UIAlertView`. While this may be appropriate,
you might require that the block be executed after the alert dismissal animation completes. You
can add a simple Boolean property to `BlockAlertView` and check to determine which delegate
callback should execute your block.

Recipe 3-1 **Creating Blocks-Based Alerts**

```
@implementation BlockAlertView
{
    __weak id <UIAlertViewDelegate> externalDelegate;
    NSMutableDictionary *actionBlocks;
}

- (instancetype)init
{
    self = [super init];
    if (self)
```

```objc
    {
        self.delegate = self;
        actionBlocks = [[NSMutableDictionary alloc] init];
    }
    return self;
}

- (instancetype)initWithTitle:(NSString *)title
        message:(NSString *)message
{
    return [super initWithTitle:title
        message:message delegate:self cancelButtonTitle:nil
        otherButtonTitles:nil];
}

// Add cancel button to alert with title and block
- (NSInteger)setCancelButtonWithTitle:(NSString *)title
        actionBlock:(AlertViewBlock)block
{
    if (!title) return -1;
    NSInteger index = [self addButtonWithTitle:title
        actionBlock:block];
    self.cancelButtonIndex = index;
    return index;
}

// Add button to alert with title and block
- (NSInteger)addButtonWithTitle:(NSString *)title
        actionBlock:(AlertViewBlock)block
{
    if (!title) return -1;
    NSInteger index = [self addButtonWithTitle:title];
    if (block)
    {
        // Copy moves blocks from stack to heap
        actionBlocks[@(index)] = [block copy];
    }
    return index;
}

- (id<UIAlertViewDelegate>)delegate
{
    return externalDelegate;
}

// If the delegate is self, set on super, otherwise store
// for possible future use to proxy delegate methods.
```

```
- (void) setDelegate: (id) delegate
{
    if (delegate == nil)
    {
        [super setDelegate:nil];
        externalDelegate = nil;
    }
    else if (delegate == self)
    {
        [super setDelegate:self];
    }
    else
    {
        externalDelegate = delegate;
    }
}

#pragma mark - UIAlertViewDelegate

// Execute the appropriate actionBlock.
// View will be automatically dismissed after this call returns
- (void) alertView: (UIAlertView *) alertView
        clickedButtonAtIndex: (NSInteger) buttonIndex
{
    AlertViewBlock actionBlock = actionBlocks[@(buttonIndex)];
    if (actionBlock)
    {
        actionBlock();
    }
}
@end
```

Get This Recipe's Code

To find this recipe's full sample project, point your browser to https://github.com/erica/iOS-7-Cookbook and go to the folder for Chapter 3.

Recipe: Using Variadic Arguments with Alert Views

Methods that can take a variable number of arguments are called *variadic*. You declare such an argument by using an ellipsis (...) after the last parameter. Both NSLog and printf are variadic. You can supply them with a format string along with any number of arguments.

Because most alerts center on text, it's handy to build methods that create alerts from format strings. Recipe 3-2 creates a `say:` method that collects the arguments passed to it and builds a string with them. The string is then passed to an alert view, which is then shown, providing a handy instant display.

The `say:` method does not parse or otherwise analyze its parameters. Instead, it grabs the first argument, uses that as the format string, and passes the remaining items to the `NSString` `initWithFormat:arguments:` method. This builds a string, which is then passed to a one-button alert view as its title.

Defining your own utility methods with variadic arguments lets you skip several steps where you have to build a string with a format and then call a method. With `say:` you can combine this into a single call, as follows:

```
[NotificationAlert say:
    @"I am so happy to meet you, %@", yourName];
```

This recipe, admittedly, uses a very thin example of variadic arguments. They can do a lot more than just get passed along to a string initialization.

Recipe 3-2 Using a Variadic Method for `UIAlertView` Creation

```
+ (void)say:(id)formatstring,...
{
    if (!formatstring) return;

    va_list arglist;
    va_start(arglist, formatstring);
    id statement = [[NSString alloc]
        initWithFormat:formatstring arguments:arglist];
    va_end(arglist);

    UIAlertView *av = [[UIAlertView alloc]
        initWithTitle:statement message:nil
        delegate:nil cancelButtonTitle:@"Okay"
        otherButtonTitles:nil];
    [av show];
}
```

Get This Recipe's Code

To find this recipe's full sample project, point your browser to https://github.com/erica/iOS-7-Cookbook and go to the folder for Chapter 3.

Presenting Lists of Options

`UIActionSheet` instances create simple iOS menus. On the iPhone and iPod touch, they slide choices—basically a list of buttons representing possible actions—onto the screen and wait for the user to respond. On the iPad, they appear in popovers and do not display Cancel buttons. Instead, users cancel actions by tapping outside the popovers.

Action sheets are different from alerts, although both classes derive from the same origins. They were split into separate classes early in iPhone history. Alerts stand apart from the interface and are better used for demanding attention. Menus slide into a view and better integrate with ongoing application work. Cocoa Touch supplies five ways to present menus:

- `showInView:`—On the iPhone and iPod touch, this method slides the menu up from the bottom of the view. On the iPad, the action sheet is centered in the middle of the screen.

- `showFromToolBar:` and `showFromTabBar:`—For the iPhone and iPod touch, when you're working with toolbars, tab bars, or any other kinds of bars that provide those horizontally grouped buttons that you see at the bottom of many applications, these methods align the menu with the top of the bar and slide it out exactly where it should be. On the iPad, the action sheet is centered in the middle of the screen.

- `showFromBarButtonItem:animated:`—On the iPad, this method presents the action sheet as a popover from the specified bar button.

- `showFromRect:inView:animated:`—This method shows the action sheet originating from the rectangle you specify in the coordinates of the view you specify.

> **Note**
>
> Do not use `showInView` with tabbed child view controllers. The action sheet appears properly, but the lower part with the Cancel button becomes unresponsive.

The following snippet shows how to initialize and present a simple `UIActionSheet` instance. Its initialization method introduces a concept that is missing from `UIAlertView`: the Destructive button. Colored in red, a Destructive button indicates an action from which there is no return, such as permanently deleting a file (see Figure 3-3). Its bright red color warns the user about the choice. Use this option sparingly.

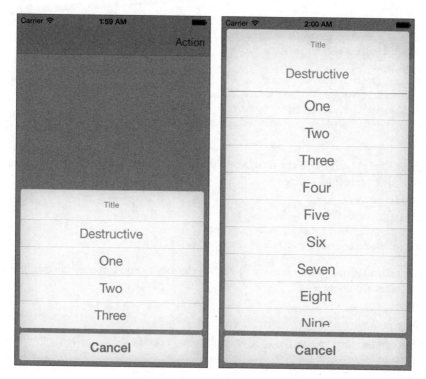

Figure 3-3   On the iPhone and iPod touch, action sheet menus slide in from the bottom of the view. The Destructive menu button appears red and indicates permanent actions with possible negative consequences to your users. Adding many menu items produces the scrolling list on the right.

Action sheet values are returned in button order. In the example on the left in Figure 3-3, the Destructive button is number 0, and the Cancel button is number 4. This behavior contradicts default alert view values, where the Cancel button returns 0. With action sheets, the Cancel button's position sets its number. This may vary, depending on how you add your buttons. In some configurations (no Destructive button), Cancel defaults to the first item as choice 0. You also can check the Cancel button index via the sheet's `cancelButtonIndex` property. This snippet prints the selected button index:

```
- (void)actionSheet:(UIActionSheet *)actionSheet
    didDismissWithButtonIndex:(NSInteger)buttonIndex
{
    self.title = [NSString stringWithFormat:@"Button %d", buttonIndex];
}

- (void)action:(UIBarButtonItem *)sender
{
```

```
    // Destructive = 0, One = 1, Two = 2, Three = 3, Cancel = 4
    UIActionSheet *actionSheet = [[UIActionSheet alloc]
        initWithTitle:@"Title"
        delegate:self
        cancelButtonTitle:@"Cancel"
        destructiveButtonTitle:@"Destructive"
        otherButtonTitles:@"One", @"Two", @"Three", nil];
    [actionSheet showFromBarButtonItem:sender animated:YES];
}
```

Avoid using Cancel buttons on the iPad. Allow users to tap outside the action sheet to cancel interaction after presenting a sheet:

```
UIActionSheet *actionSheet = [[UIActionSheet alloc]
    initWithTitle:theTitle delegate:nil
    cancelButtonTitle:IS_IPAD ? nil : @"Cancel"
    destructiveButtonTitle:nil otherButtonTitles:nil];
```

Canceling an iPad action sheet returns a (default) value of –1. You can override this, but we cannot recommend doing so.

> **Note**
> You can use the same blocks-based approach shown in Recipe 3-1 to conveniently create action sheets similarly to alerts.

Scrolling Menus

As a rough rule of thumb, you can fit a maximum of about 10 buttons (including Cancel) into a portrait orientation and about 5 buttons into landscape on the iPhone and iPod touch. (There's quite a bit more room on the iPad.) Going beyond this number triggers the scrolling presentation shown on the right in Figure 3-3. Notice that the Cancel button is presented below the list, even when scrolling is activated. The Cancel button is always numbered after any previous buttons. As Figure 3-3 demonstrates, this presentation falls fairly low on the aesthetics scale and should be avoided where possible.

Displaying Text in Action Sheets

Action sheets offer many of the same text presentation features as alert views, but they do so with a much bigger canvas. The following snippet demonstrates how to display a message using a UIActionSheet object. It provides a handy way to present a lot of text simultaneously:

```
- (void)show:(id)formatstring,...
{
    if (!formatstring) return;
```

```
va_list arglist;
va_start(arglist, formatstring);
id statement = [[NSString alloc]
    initWithFormat:formatstring arguments:arglist];
va_end(arglist);

UIActionSheet *actionSheet = [[UIActionSheet alloc]
    initWithTitle:statement
    delegate:nil cancelButtonTitle:nil
    destructiveButtonTitle:nil
    otherButtonTitles:@"OK", nil];

[actionSheet showInView:self.view];
}
```

"Please Wait": Showing Progress to Your User

Waiting is an intrinsic part of the computing experience and will remain so for the foresee-able future. It's your job as a developer to communicate that fact to your users. Cocoa Touch provides classes that tell your users to wait for a process to complete. These progress indicators come in two forms: as a spinning wheel that persists for the duration of its presentation and as a bar that fills from left to right as your process moves forward from start to end. The classes that provide these indications are as follows:

- **UIActivityIndicatorView**—This progress indicator is a spinning circle that tells your user to wait without providing specific information about the degree of completion. iOS's activity indicator is small, but its live animation catches the user's eye and is best suited for quick disruptions in a normal application.

- **UIProgressView**—This view presents a progress bar. The bar provides concrete feedback about how much work has been done and how much remains, while occupying a relatively small space. It presents as a thin, horizontal rectangle that fills itself from left to right as progress takes place. This classic user interface (UI) element works best for long delays, where users want to know to what degree the job has finished.

Be aware of blocking. Both of these classes must be used on your main thread, as is the rule with GUI objects. Computationally heavy code can block, keeping views from updating in real time. If your code blocks, your progress view may not update in real time as progress is actually made, getting stuck on its initial value instead.

If you need to display asynchronous feedback, use threading. For example, you may use UIActivityIndicatorView on the main thread and perform computation on a second thread. Your threaded computations can then perform view updates on the main thread to provide a steady stream of progress notifications that will keep your user in sync with the work being done.

Using `UIActivityIndicatorView`

`UIActivityIndicatorView` instances offer lightweight views that display a standard rotating progress wheel. The key word to keep in mind when working with these views is *small*. All activity indicators are tiny and do not look right when zoomed past their natural size.

iOS offers several different styles of the `UIActivityIndicatorView` class.
`UIActivityIndicatorViewStyleWhite` and `UIActivityIndicatorViewStyleGray` are 20-by-20 points in size. The white version looks best against a black background, and the gray looks best against white. It's a thin, sharp style. `UIActivityIndicatorViewStyleWhiteLarge` is meant for use on dark backgrounds. It provides the largest, clearest indicator, at 37-by-37 points in size:

```
UIActivityIndicatorView *aiv = [[UIActivityIndicatorView alloc]
    initWithActivityIndicatorStyle:
        UIActivityIndicatorViewStyleWhiteLarge] ;
```

You can tint an activity indicator by using the `color` property. When you set a color, it overrides the view style but retains the view size (regular or large):

```
aiv.color = [UIColor blueColor] ;
```

You need not center indicators on the screen. Place them wherever they work best for you. As a clear-backed view, the indicator blends over whatever backdrop view lies behind it. The predominant color of that backdrop helps select which color of indicator to use.

For general use, just add the activity indicator as a subview to the window, view, toolbar, or navigation bar you want to overlay. Allocate the indicator and initialize it with a frame or with Auto Layout constraints, preferably centered within whatever parent view you're using. Start the indicator action by sending `startAnimating`. To stop, call `stopAnimating`. Cocoa Touch takes care of the rest, hiding the view when not in use.

Using `UIProgressView`

Progress views enable your users to follow task progress as it happens rather than just saying "Please wait." They present bars that fill over time. The bars indicate the degree to which a task has finished. Progress bars work best for long waits where providing state feedback enables your users to retain the feeling of control.

To create a progress view, allocate a `UIProgressView` instance and set its frame. To use the bar, issue `setProgress:`. This takes one argument, a floating-point number that ranges between 0% (`0.0`, no progress) and 100% (`1.0`, finished). Progress view bars come in two styles: basic white and light gray. The `setStyle:` method chooses the kind you prefer, either `UIProgressViewStyleDefault` or `UIProgressViewStyleBar`. The latter is meant for use in toolbars.

Recipe: Modal Progress Overlays

Although UIAlertView and UIActionSheet provide straightforward communication and interaction with the user, you cannot add your own subviews. To provide a modal progress indicator, you must roll your own alert completely from scratch. Recipe 3-3 uses a simple tinted UIView overlay with a UIActivityIndicatorView.

As shown in Figure 3-4, the overlay view occupies the entire screen size. Using the entire screen lets the overlay fit over the navigation bar. The overlay view must be added to the application window and not, as you might think, to the main UIViewController's view. That view only occupies the space under the navigation bar (the "application frame," in UIScreen terms), allowing continued access to any buttons and other control items in the bar. Filling the window helps block that access.

Figure 3-4   A UIActivityIndicator-augmented modal view provides user feedback during synchronous (blocking) actions. Always provide some way to cancel long-running functions without forcefully quitting the app in your real-world applications.

To prevent any user touches, the overlay sets its `userInteractionEnabled` property to YES. This catches any touch events, preventing them from reaching the GUI below the alert and creating a modal presentation where interaction cannot continue until the alert has finished. You can easily adapt this approach to dismiss an overlay with a touch, but be aware when creating alerts like this that the view does not belong to a view controller. It will not update itself during device orientation changes. If you need to work with a landscape-/portrait-aware system, you can catch the current orientation state before showing the overlay and subscribe to reorientation notifications.

Recipe 3-3   **Presenting and Hiding a Custom Alert Overlay**

```
- (void)removeOverlay:(UIView *)overlayView
{
    [overlayView removeFromSuperview];
}

- (void)action
{
    UIWindow *window = self.view.window;

    // Create a tinted overlay, sized to the window
    UIView *overlayView =
        [[UIView alloc] initWithFrame:window.bounds];
    overlayView.backgroundColor =
        [[UIColor blackColor] colorWithAlphaComponent:0.5f];
    overlayView.userInteractionEnabled = YES;

    // Add an activity indicator
    UIActivityIndicatorView *aiv =
        [[UIActivityIndicatorView alloc]
            initWithActivityIndicatorStyle:
                UIActivityIndicatorViewStyleWhiteLarge];
    [aiv startAnimating];
    [overlayView addSubview:aiv];
    PREPCONSTRAINTS(aiv);
    CENTER_VIEW(overlayView, aiv);

    UILabel *label = [[UILabel alloc] init];
    label.textColor = [UIColor whiteColor];
    label.text = @"Please wait...";
    [overlayView addSubview:label];
    PREPCONSTRAINTS(label);
    CENTER_VIEW_H(overlayView, label);
    CENTER_VIEW_V_CONSTANT(overlayView, label, -44);

    [window addSubview:overlayView];
```

```
    // Use a time delay to simulate a task finishing
    [self performSelector:@selector(removeOverlay:)
        withObject:overlayView afterDelay:5.0f];
}
```

Get This Recipe's Code

To find this recipe's full sample project, point your browser to https://github.com/erica/iOS-7-Cookbook and go to the folder for Chapter 3.

Tappable Overlays

A custom overlay can present information as well as limit interaction. You can easily expand the overlay approach from Recipe 3-3 so that the view dismisses itself on a touch. When tapped, the view removes itself from the screen. This behavior makes the view particularly suitable for showing information in a way normally reserved for the UIAlertView class:

```
@interface TappableOverlay : UIView
@end
@implementation TappableOverlay
- (void)touchesEnded:(NSSet *)touches withEvent:(UIEvent *)event
{
    // Remove this view when it is touched
    [self removeFromSuperview];
}
@end
```

Recipe: Custom Modal Alert View

The simplicity and lack of flexibility of the UIAlertView is often too limiting. While Recipe 3-3 provides a simple modal overlay that is perfect for providing progress during long-running tasks, sometimes you want a fully capable and configurable alert view that doesn't have the artificial restrictions that Apple places on UIAlertView.

Recipe 3-4 provides an alert view that is nearly fully customizable. You can add subviews and configure any element of the UI to meet your needs, including borders, backgrounds, and subview placement. Bypassing the built-in alert allows for custom transition animations. Recipe 3-4 provides a bounce effect during presentation and dismissal. The bounce is implemented with an affine scale transformation, which is covered in more detail in Chapter 5, "View Constraints."

> **Note**
>
> Apple introduced Dynamics, a physics-based animation system, in iOS 7. While this example
> uses a view transform to simulate a bounce in the presentation and dismissal of the alert,
> Dynamics provides a declarative method of adding complex visual interactions.

As shown in Figure 3-5, rather than box you into a specific interface, the alert is a blank slate,
ready for your use. A label and button are provided to get you started.

Figure 3-5   The iOS-supplied alert view can be very limiting. A fully custom alert provides full
customization of both the user interface and interaction.

Frosted Glass Effect

An added flourish to the custom alert is a newly introduced visual effect found in iOS 7 and
highlighted in the Control Center—the frosted glass appearance. Apple provides this effect by
default in a number of UIKit elements: `UITabBar`, `UINavigationBar`, and `UIToolbar`.

Outside the embedded implementation in these bars, no mechanism is available to include this effect in your own views. Apple has provided sample code, a UIImage category, that simulates this effect. Unfortunately, it pales in comparison to the built-in implementation. The category is only a close approximation, and worse, is much slower than the embedded version, rendering it unusable as a live effect.

To work around this limitation, Recipe 3-4 subclasses a UINavigationBar to inherit the superior effect. In the future, Apple will hopefully expose this functionality directly to developers rather than require this subtle hack.

Recipe 3-4   **Custom Alert**

```
@implementation CustomAlert
{
    UIView *contentView;
}


#pragma mark - Utility
- (void)observeValueForKeyPath:(NSString *)keyPath
    ofObject:(id)object change:(NSDictionary *)change
    context:(void *)context
{
    if ([keyPath isEqualToString:@"bounds"])
        contentView.frame = self.bounds;
}


#pragma mark - Instance Creation and Initialization
- (void)internalCustomAlertInitializer
{
    // Add size observer
    [self addObserver:self forKeyPath:@"bounds"
        options:NSKeyValueObservingOptionNew context:NULL];

    // Constrain the size and width based on the initial frame
    self.translatesAutoresizingMaskIntoConstraints = NO;
    CGFloat width = self.bounds.size.width;
    CGFloat height = self.bounds.size.height;
    for (NSString *constraintString in
        @[@"V:[self(==height)]", @"H:[self(==width)]"])
    {
        NSArray *constraints = [NSLayoutConstraint
            constraintsWithVisualFormat:constraintString options:0
            metrics:@{@"width":@(width), @"height":@(height)}
            views:NSDictionaryOfVariableBindings(self)];
        [self addConstraints:constraints];
    }
    [self layoutIfNeeded];
```

```objc
    // Add a content view for auto layout
    contentView = [[UIView alloc] initWithFrame:self.bounds];
    [self addSubview:contentView];
    contentView.autoresizingMask =
        UIViewAutoresizingFlexibleHeight |
        UIViewAutoresizingFlexibleWidth;

    // Add layer styling
    self.layer.borderColor = [UIColor blackColor].CGColor;
    self.layer.borderWidth = 2;
    self.layer.cornerRadius = 20;
    self.clipsToBounds = YES;

    // Create label
    _label = [[UILabel alloc] init];
    [contentView addSubview:_label];
    _label.translatesAutoresizingMaskIntoConstraints = NO;
    _label.numberOfLines = 0;
    _label.textAlignment = NSTextAlignmentCenter;

    // Create button
    _button = [UIButton buttonWithType:UIButtonTypeSystem];
    [contentView addSubview:_button];
    _button.translatesAutoresizingMaskIntoConstraints = NO;

    // Layout subviews on content view
    for (NSString *constraintString in
        @[@"V:|-[_label]-[_button]-|",
          @"H:|-[_label]-|", @"H:|-[_button]-|"])
    {
        NSArray *constraints = [NSLayoutConstraint
            constraintsWithVisualFormat:constraintString
            options:0 metrics:nil
            views:NSDictionaryOfVariableBindings(_button, _label)];
        [contentView addConstraints:constraints];
    }
}

- (instancetype)initWithFrame:(CGRect)frame
{
    if (!(self = [super initWithFrame:frame])) return self;
    [self internalCustomAlertInitializer];
    return self;
}

- (instancetype)initWithCoder:(NSCoder *)aDecoder
{
```

```objc
    if (!(self = [super initWithCoder:aDecoder])) return self;
    [self internalCustomAlertInitializer];
    return self;
}


- (void)dealloc
{
    [self removeObserver:self forKeyPath:@"bounds"];
}


#pragma mark - Presentation and Dismissal
- (void)centerInSuperview
{
    if (!self.superview)
    {
        NSLog(@"Error: Attempting to present without superview");
        return;
    }

    NSArray *constraintArray =
        [self.superview.constraints copy];
    for (NSLayoutConstraint *constraint in constraintArray)
    {
        if ((constraint.firstItem == self) ||
            (constraint.secondItem == self))
                [self.superview removeConstraint:constraint];
    }
    [self.superview addConstraints:CONSTRAINTS_CENTERING(self)];
}


- (void)show
{
    self.transform =
        CGAffineTransformMakeScale(FLT_EPSILON, FLT_EPSILON);
    [self centerInSuperview];

    CustomAnimationBlock expandBlock = ^{self.transform =
        CGAffineTransformMakeScale(1.1f, 1.1f);};
    CustomAnimationBlock identityBlock = ^{self.transform =
        CGAffineTransformIdentity;};
    CustomCompletionAnimationBlock completionBlock =
        ^(BOOL done){[UIView animateWithDuration:0.3f
            animations:identityBlock];};

    [UIView animateWithDuration:0.5f animations:expandBlock
        completion:completionBlock];
}
```

```
- (void)dismiss
{
    CustomAnimationBlock expandBlock = ^{self.transform =
        CGAffineTransformMakeScale(1.1f, 1.1f);};
    CustomAnimationBlock shrinkBlock = ^{self.transform =
        CGAffineTransformMakeScale(FLT_EPSILON, FLT_EPSILON);};
    CustomCompletionAnimationBlock completionBlock =
        ^(BOOL done){[UIView animateWithDuration:0.3f
            animations:shrinkBlock];};

    [UIView animateWithDuration:0.5f animations:expandBlock
        completion:completionBlock];
}
@end
```

Get This Recipe's Code

To find this recipe's full sample project, point your browser to https://github.com/erica/iOS-7-Cookbook and go to the folder for Chapter 3.

Recipe: Basic Popovers

At the time of this writing, popovers remain an iPad-only feature. That may change as Apple introduces new iOS models or ports some of this functionality to the iPhone family of devices. Often you'll want to present information using a popover as an alternative to presenting a modal view. There are several basic rules of popovers that you need to incorporate into your day-to-day development:

- **Always hang onto your popovers.** Create strong local variables that retain your popovers until they are no longer needed. In Recipe 3-5, the variable is reset when the popover is dismissed.

- **Always check for existing popovers and dismiss them.** This is especially important if you create popovers that have different roles in your apps. For example, you may provide popovers for more than one bar button item. Before you present any new popover, dismiss the existing one.

- **Always set your content size.** The default iPad popover is long and thin and may not appeal to your design aesthetics. Setting the `preferredContentSize` property of your view controllers allows you to specify the dimensions the popover should use.

- **Always provide an iPhone option.** Don't sacrifice functionality when changing platforms. Instead, provide an iPhone-family alternative, usually a modally presented controller instead of a popover.

- **Never add a Done button to popovers.** Although you normally add a Done button to a modal presentation, skip it in a popover. Users tap outside the popover to dismiss it, so a Done button is redundant.

> **Note**
>
> As of the initial release of iOS 7, Apple's documentation states that popovers no longer present a graphical arrow pointing to the source of the popover. The `popoverArrowDirection` property on `UIPopoverController` is documented as having been deprecated. However, the arrow is still visible and the methods are not marked as deprecated in the provided SDK headers. This inconsistency in the documentation is likely a holdover from an abandoned design change that will be resolved in a future update.

Recipe 3-5   **Basic Popovers**

```
- (void)popoverControllerDidDismissPopover:
    (UIPopoverController *)popoverController
{
    // Stop holding onto the popover
    popover = nil;
}


- (void)action:(id)sender
{
    // Always check for existing popover
    if (popover)
        [popover dismissPopoverAnimated:YES];

    // Retrieve the nav controller from the storyboard
    UIStoryboard *storyboard =
        [UIStoryboard storyboardWithName:@"Storyboard"
            bundle:[NSBundle mainBundle]];
    UINavigationController *controller =
        [storyboard instantiateInitialViewController];

    // Present either modally or as a popover
    if (IS_IPHONE)
    {
        [self.navigationController
            presentViewController:controller
            animated:YES completion:nil];
    }
    else
    {
        // No Done button on iPads
        UIViewController *vc = controller.topViewController;
```

```
        vc.navigationItem.rightBarButtonItem = nil;

        // Set the preferred content size to iPhone-sized
        vc.preferredContentSize =
            CGSizeMake(320.0f, 480.0f - 44.0f);

        // Create and deploy the popover
        popover = [[UIPopoverController alloc]
            initWithContentViewController:controller];
        [popover presentPopoverFromBarButtonItem:sender
            permittedArrowDirections:UIPopoverArrowDirectionAny
            animated:YES];
    }
}
```

Get This Recipe's Code

To find this recipe's full sample project, point your browser to https://github.com/erica/iOS-7-Cookbook and go to the folder for Chapter 3.

Recipe: Local Notifications

Local notifications alert the user when your application is not running. They offer a simple way to schedule an alert that presents itself at a specific date and time. Unlike push notifications, local notifications do not require any network access and do not communicate with remote servers. As their name suggests, they are handled entirely on a local level.

Local notifications are meant to be used with schedules, such as calendar and to-do list utilities. You can also use them with multitasking applications to provide updates when the application is not running in the foreground. For example, a location-based app might pop up a notification to let a user know that the app has detected that the user is near the local library and that books are ready to be picked up.

The system does not present local notifications when the application is active, only when it's suspended or running in the background. Recipe 3-6 forces the app to quit as it schedules the notification for 5 seconds in the future to allow the notification to appear properly. Don't *ever* do this in App Store applications; we've done it here for demonstration purposes. If you don't force the app to close, you'll miss the notification.

As with push notifications, tapping the action button relaunches the application, moving control back into the `application:didFinishLaunchingWithOptions:` method.
If you retrieve the options dictionary, the notification object can be found via the `UIApplicationLaunchOptionsLocalNotificationKey` key.

Some developers have used this relaunching capability to add features to the notification center, with varied success. The idea works like this: If you add a local notification, a tap will launch the app to perform some task such as tweeting. Thus, you are essentially offering features "through" the notification center. Apple doesn't always respond well to those who use its center in nonstandard ways; your success will most certainly vary as Apple adjusts its policies to these clever but unsanctioned uses.

Best Practices

Don't spam your users. Just because local notifications don't require opt-in doesn't mean that you should abuse them for marketing. Here's a rule of thumb: If a notification doesn't deliver information that your user specifically requested, don't send it. (This goes for push notifications as well. When users opt in, they're not opting in for spam.)

An unsolicited notification is not the user experience you should be aiming for. When your notification arrives in the middle of dinner or at 3 in the morning, you fail to win hearts, reviews, and customers.

Excess notifications are wrong, regardless of whether users can switch on "do not disturb" features. Apple regularly refuses applications that send ads through push notifications; you should note this for local notifications as well. Notification abuse is the easiest way to find your app, and your personal reputation, dragged through the mud.

And, as a final point, make sure to spell-check your notifications.

Recipe 3-6   **Scheduling Local Notifications**

```
- (void)action:(id)sender
{
    UIApplication *app = [UIApplication sharedApplication];

    // Remove all prior notifications
    NSArray *scheduled = [app scheduledLocalNotifications];
    if (scheduled.count)
        [app cancelAllLocalNotifications];

    // Create a new notification
    UILocalNotification* alarm =
        [[UILocalNotification alloc] init];
    if (alarm)
    {
        alarm.fireDate =
            [NSDate dateWithTimeIntervalSinceNow:5.0f];
        alarm.timeZone = [NSTimeZone defaultTimeZone];
        alarm.repeatInterval = 0;
        alarm.alertBody = @"Five Seconds Have Passed";
        [app scheduleLocalNotification:alarm];
```

```
        // Force quit. Never do this in App Store code.
        exit(0);
    }
}
```

Get This Recipe's Code

To find this recipe's full sample project, point your browser to https://github.com/erica/iOS-7-Cookbook and go to the folder for Chapter 3.

Alert Indicators

When an application accesses the Internet from behind the scenes, it's polite to let your user know what's going on. You don't have to create a full-screen alert because Cocoa Touch provides a simple application property that controls a spinning network activity indicator in the status bar. Figure 3-6 shows this indicator in action, to the right of the Wi-Fi indicator and to the left of the current time display.

Figure 3-6   The network activity indicator is controlled by a `UIApplication` property.

The following snippet demonstrates how to access this property, which requires you to do little more than toggle the indicator on or off:

```
- (void)action:(id)sender
{
    // Toggle the network activity indicator
    UIApplication *app = [UIApplication sharedApplication];
    app.networkActivityIndicatorVisible =
        !app.networkActivityIndicatorVisible;
}
```

In a real-world deployment, you normally perform network activities on a secondary thread. At the same time, all UI updates must occur on the main thread. Using GCD, as in this code snippet, enables you to request GUI updates from other threads:

```
dispatch_async(dispatch_get_main_queue(), ^{
    // set activity indicator here
});
```

You might want to keep count of network operations in your application and enable the indicator only when at least one is active.

Badging Applications

If you've used iOS for any time, you've likely seen the small red badges that appear over applications on the home screen. These might indicate the number of missed phone calls or unread e-mails that have accumulated since the user last opened Phone or Mail.

To set an application badge from within a program, set the `applicationIconBadgeNumber` property to a positive integer. To hide badges, set `applicationIconBadgeNumber` to 0.

Remove your badges predictably, such as on opening the application. Users expect that opening an application will clear the badge on the SpringBoard.

Recipe: Simple Audio Alerts

Audio alerts "speak" directly to your users. They produce instant feedback—for users who are not hearing impaired. Fortunately, Apple built basic sound playback into the Cocoa Touch SDK through System Audio services.

The alternatives include using Audio Queue calls or `AVAudioPlayer`. Audio Queue playback is time-consuming to program and involves much more complexity than simple alert sounds need. In contrast, you can load and play system audio with just a few lines of code. `AVAudioPlayer` also has drawbacks. It interferes with iPod audio. In contrast, System Audio can perform a sound without interrupting any music that's currently playing, although that may admittedly not be the result you're looking for, as alerts can get lost in the music.

Alert sounds work best when they're kept short—preferably 30 seconds or shorter, according to Apple. System Audio plays PCM and IMA audio only. That means limiting your sounds to AIFF, WAV, and CAF formats.

System Sounds

To build a system sound, call `AudioServicesCreateSystemSoundID` with a file URL pointing to the sound file. This call returns an initialized system sound object, which you can then play at will. Just call `AudioServicesPlaySystemSound` with the sound object. That single call does all the work:

```
AudioServicesPlaySystemSound(mySound);
```

When iPod audio is playing, the system sound generally plays back at the same volume, without fading, so users may miss your alert. You can check the current playback state by testing as follows:

```
if ([MPMusicPlayerController iPodMusicPlayer].playbackState ==
    MPMusicPlaybackStatePlaying)
```

If the music player is playing, you may choose to pause the existing music playback, substitute a visual element, or consider using an alert as described later in this chapter to add vibration to your sound. To access the MPMusicPlayerController, make sure you import the MediaPlayer module. Modules are discussed in more detail in the following section.

Add an optional system sound completion callback to notify your program when a sound finishes playing by calling AudioServicesAddSystemSoundCompletion(). Unless you use short sounds that are chained one after another, this is a step you can generally skip.

Clean up your sounds by calling AudioServicesDisposeSystemSoundID with the sound in question. This frees the sound object and all its associated resources.

Modules for System Frameworks

To use these system sound services, you must include the Audio Toolbox framework and headers. In iOS 7, Apple introduced modules support to Xcode, simplifying the process of adding system frameworks and headers to your code.

In the past, including support for a system framework required adding the framework to your application target and using the #include macro to include the header in your source code. With modules, a sole @import at the top of your source file will include the headers and Auto Link the framework into your project:

```
@import AudioToolbox;
```

Modules make it easier to add Apple-provided frameworks to your project. However, their primary purpose is to increase the performance of compilation and code indexing. Modules include a database of all symbols in the framework for quick lookup. Apple has anecdotally shown modules to improve build times and code indexing 200% or more, depending on the project.

Modules are enabled by default on new projects created with Xcode 5. Use modules on existing projects by selecting Enable Modules in the project Build Settings.

All system frameworks are available as modules. Unfortunately, there is no method currently available to convert your own frameworks into modules.

Vibration

As with audio sounds, vibration immediately grabs a user's attention. What's more, vibration works for nearly all users, including those who are hearing or visually impaired. Vibration is available, however, only on the iPhone platform at this time. Plus, it should be used sparingly. It puts a great drain on the device battery.

Using the same System Audio services, you can vibrate as well as play a sound. All you need is the following one-line call to accomplish it, as used in Recipe 3-7:

```
AudioServicesPlaySystemSound(kSystemSoundID_Vibrate);
```

You cannot vary the vibration parameters. Each call produces a short 1- to 2-second buzz. On platforms without vibration support (such as the iPod touch and iPad), this call does nothing—but does not produce an error:

```
- (void)vibrate
{
    // Vibrate only works on iPhones
    AudioServicesPlaySystemSound (kSystemSoundID_Vibrate);
}
```

Alerts

Audio Services provides a vibration/sound mashup called an alert sound, which you invoke as follows:

```
AudioServicesPlayAlertSound(mySound);
```

This call, which is also demonstrated in Recipe 3-7, plays the requested sound and, possibly, vibrates or plays an additional alert. On iPhones, when the user has set Settings > Sounds > Vibrate on Ring, it vibrates the phone. This vibration provides a tactile response to the user even if the sound volume is low or muted by the user, obscuring the audio portion of the alert.

iPad units and second-generation and later iPod touch units play the sound sans vibration (because it is unavailable on those units) through the onboard speaker. First-generation iPod touches (see if you can find one these days!) play a short alert melody in place of the sound on the device speaker while playing the requested audio through to the headphones.

iOS automatically lowers any currently playing music during alert playback. This property of alerts can be a useful alternative to system sounds when music playback has been detected.

Delays

The first time you play back a system sound on iOS, you might encounter delays. You may want to play a silent sound on application initialization to avoid a delay on subsequent playback.

Note

When testing on iPhones, make sure you have not enabled the silent ringer switch on the left side of the unit. Audio Services alerts do not play when that switch is enabled. This oversight has tripped up many iPhone developers. If your alert sounds must always play, consider using the AVAudioPlayer class.

Disposing of System Sounds

Don't forget to dispose of system sounds. Your `dealloc` method is a natural place to wrap up matters at an object's end of life. Always consider the life cycle of your sounds and find an approach to manage the disposal of the sound.

For many applications, a few sounds can persist for the duration of an object's (or even an application's) lifetime without placing a burden on memory. For others, you'll want to clean up after yourself as soon as the sound is played. Make sure to design sound disposal into your applications and ensure that you dispose of resources when you're done with them.

In recent versions of Xcode, the iOS simulator offers full sound playback.

Recipe 3-7   Playing Sounds, Alerts, and Vibrations Using Audio Services

```
@implementation SoundPlayer

void _systemSoundDidComplete(SystemSoundID ssID,
    void *clientData)
{
    AudioServicesDisposeSystemSoundID(ssID);
}


+ (void)playAndDispose:(NSString *)sound
{
    NSString *sndpath = [[NSBundle mainBundle]
        pathForResource:sound ofType:@"wav"];
    if ((!sndpath) ||
        (![[NSFileManager defaultManager]
            fileExistsAtPath:sndpath]))
    {
        NSLog(@"Error: %@.wav not found", sound);
        return;
    }

    CFURLRef baseURL =
        (CFURLRef)CFBridgingRetain(
            [NSURL fileURLWithPath:sndpath]);

    SystemSoundID sysSound;
    AudioServicesCreateSystemSoundID(baseURL, &sysSound);
    CFRelease(baseURL);

    AudioServicesAddSystemSoundCompletion(sysSound, NULL,
        NULL, systemSoundDidComplete, NULL);
```

```
    if ([MPMusicPlayerController iPodMusicPlayer].playbackState
        == MPMusicPlaybackStatePlaying)
        AudioServicesPlayAlertSound(sysSound);
    else
        AudioServicesPlaySystemSound(sysSound);
}

@end
```

Get This Recipe's Code

To find this recipe's full sample project, point your browser to https://github.com/erica/iOS-7-Cookbook and go to the folder for Chapter 3.

Summary

This chapter introduces ways for your application to reach out and interact directly with your user instead of the other way around. You've learned how to build alerts—visual, auditory, and tactile—that grab your user's attention and can request immediate feedback. Use these examples to enhance the interactive appeal of your programs and leverage some unique iPhone-only features. Here are a few thoughts to carry away from this chapter:

- Alerts take users into the moment. They're designed to elicit responses while communicating information. While the system alerts are fairly rigid, they are quick and easy to implement. And, as you saw in this chapter, custom alerts can be very powerful interface components that provide a lot of flexibility and customization.

- When a task will take a noticeable amount of time, be courteous to your user by displaying some kind of progress feedback. iOS offers many ways to do this, from heads-up displays (HUDs) to status bar indicators and beyond. You might need to divert the non-GUI elements of your task to a new thread to avoid blocking. It's also courteous to provide a way for the user to cancel out of the operation, if possible.

- Use local notifications sparingly. Never display them unless there's a compelling reason the user would *want* them to be displayed. It's very easy to alienate a user and get your app kicked off a device by overusing local notification alerts.

- System-supplied features do not and should not match every application's design needs. Whenever possible, build custom alerts and menus that fit with your app, using `UIView` instances and animation.

- Audio feedback, including beeps and vibration, can enhance your programs and make your interaction richer. When using system sound calls, your sounds play nicely with iPod functionality and won't ruin the ongoing listening experience. At the same time, don't be obnoxious. Use alert sounds sparingly and meaningfully to avoid annoying your users.

4

Assembling Views and Animations

The `UIView` class and its subclasses populate the iOS device screens. This chapter introduces views from the ground up. You'll learn how to build, inspect, and break down view hierarchies and understand how views work together. You'll discover the role geometry plays in creating and placing views in your interface, and you'll read about animating views so they move and transform onscreen.

Chapter 5, "View Constraints," introduces Auto Layout, a view layout system that leverages a *declarative* constraint-based model. In declarative programming, a developer describes to the SDK how an application or interface behaves, and the system expresses those rules at runtime. You describe your interface by using constraint rules. Constraints produce the geometry and layout of your views.

Whether you work with Auto Layout or not, understanding the foundational geometry of views is critical to building user interfaces.

View Hierarchies

A tree-based hierarchy orders what you see on your iOS screen. Starting with the main window, views are laid out in a specifically hierarchical way. All views may have children, called *subviews*. Each view, including the window, owns an ordered list of these subviews. Views might own many subviews; they might own none. Your application determines how views are laid out and who owns whom.

Subviews display in order, always from back to front. This works something like a stack of animation cels—the transparent sheets used to create cartoons. Only the parts of the sheets that have been painted show through. The clear parts allow any visual elements behind the sheet to be seen. Views, too, can have clear and painted parts and can be layered to build a complex presentation.

Figure 4-1 shows a little of the layering used in a typical window. Here the window owns a `UINavigationController`-based hierarchy. The elements layer together. The window (represented by the empty, rightmost element) owns a navigation bar with its buttons and title label, and a table with its own subviews. These items stack together to build the GUI.

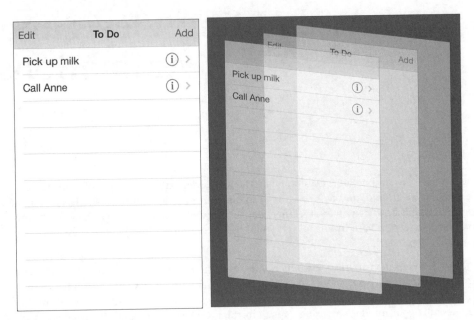

Figure 4-1   Subview hierarchies combine to build complex GUIs.

Listing 4-1 shows the view hierarchy of the window in Figure 4-1. The tree starts from the top `UIWindow` and shows the classes for each of the child views. If you trace your way down the tree, you can see the navigation bar (at level 2) with its two buttons (each at level 3) and the table view (level 4) with its two cells (each at level 6). Some of the items in this listing are private classes, automatically added by the SDK when laying out views. For example, `UILayoutContainerView` is never used directly by developers. It's part of the SDK `UIWindow` implementation.

The only parts missing from this listing are the dozen or so line separators for the table, omitted for space considerations. Each separator is a `UITableViewSeparatorView` instance. The separators belong to `UITableView` and would normally display at a depth of 5.

Listing 4-1   **To-Do List View Hierarchy**

```
--[ 1] UILayoutContainerView
----[ 2] UINavigationTransitionView
------[ 3] UIViewControllerWrapperView
--------[ 4] UITableView
----------[ 5] UITableViewWrapperView
------------[ 6] UITableViewCell
--------------[ 7] UITableViewCellScrollView
----------------[ 8] UITableViewCellContentView
------------------[ 9] UILabel
----------------[ 8] UITableViewCellDetailDisclosureView
------------------[ 9] UIButton
--------------------[10] UIImageView
------------------[ 9] UIImageView
------------[ 6] UITableViewCell
--------------[ 7] UITableViewCellScrollView
----------------[ 8] UITableViewCellContentView
------------------[ 9] UILabel
----------------[ 8] UITableViewCellDetailDisclosureView
------------------[ 9] UIButton
--------------------[10] UIImageView
------------------[ 9] UIImageView
----------[ 5] UIImageView
----------[ 5] UIImageView
----[ 2] UINavigationBar
------[ 3] _UINavigationBarBackground
--------[ 4] _UIBackdropView
----------[ 5] _UIBackdropEffectView
----------[ 5] UIView
--------[ 4] UIImageView
------[ 3] UINavigationItemView
--------[ 4] UILabel
------[ 3] UINavigationButton
--------[ 4] UIButtonLabel
------[ 3] UINavigationButton
--------[ 4] UIButtonLabel
------[ 3] _UINavigationBarBackIndicatorView
```

Recipe: Recovering a View Hierarchy Tree

Each view knows both its parent (aView.superview) and its children (aView.subviews). You can build a view tree, like the one shown in Listing 4-1, by recursively walking through a view's subviews. Recipe 4-1 builds a visual tree by noting the class of each view and increasing the indentation level every time it moves down from a parent view to its children. The results are stored in a mutable string and returned to the calling method.

The code shown in Recipe 4-1 was used to create the tree shown in Listing 4-1. You can use this method to duplicate the results of Listing 4-1, or you can copy it to other applications to view their hierarchies.

Note

UIView includes a "secret" method—recursiveDescription—provided by the UIDebugging category on UIView. Documented in the Apple Tech Note at https://developer.apple.com/library/ios/technotes/tn2239/_index.html, it recursively iterates through child views, appending the description of each view and providing a similar if less configurable and readable output to Recipe 4-1. As a private method, it is easily accessible only from the debugger. Using trickery to access this method from within your code will likely lead to your app being rejected by the App Store and is highly discouraged. Recipe 4-1 provides a cleaner, flexible option without this significant restriction.

Recipe 4-1   **Extracting a View Hierarchy Tree**

```
// Recursively travel down the view tree, increasing the
// indentation level for children
- (void)dumpView:(UIView *)aView atIndent:(int)indent
    into:(NSMutableString *)outString
{
    // Add the indentation dashes
    for (int i = 0; i < indent; i++)
        [outString appendString:@"--"];

    // Follow that with the class description
    [outString appendFormat:@"[%2d] %@\n", indent,
        [[aView class] description]];

    // Recurse through each subview
    for (UIView *view in aView.subviews)
        [self dumpView:view atIndent:indent + 1 into:outString];
}

// Start the tree recursion at level 0 with the root view
- (NSString *)displayViews:(UIView *)aView
{
    NSMutableString *outString = [NSMutableString string];
    [self dumpView:aView atIndent:0 into:outString];
    return outString;
}
```

Get This Recipe's Code

To find this recipe's full sample project, point your browser to https://github.com/erica/iOS-7-Cookbook and go to the folder for Chapter 4.

Exploring XIB and Storyboard Views

Many Xcode users create views and view controllers in Interface Builder (IB), using storyboards and XIB files rather than building them directly in code. The following snippet demonstrates how to use Recipe 4-1 to deconstruct views loaded from these resources:

```
UIView *sampleView = [[[NSBundle mainBundle]
    loadNibNamed:@"Sample" owner:self options:NULL] objectAtIndex:0];
if (sampleView)
{
    NSMutableString *outstring = [NSMutableString string];
    [self dumpView:sampleView atIndent:0 into:outstring];
    NSLog(@"Dumping sample view: %@", outstring);
}


UIStoryboard *storyboard = [UIStoryboard
    storyboardWithName:@"Sample" bundle:[NSBundle mainBundle]];
UIViewController *vc = [storyboard instantiateInitialViewController];
if (vc.view)
{
    NSMutableString *outstring = [NSMutableString string];
    [self dumpView:vc.view atIndent:0 into:outstring];
    NSLog(@"Dumping sample storyboard: %@", outstring);
}
```

The sample code for Recipe 4-1 includes sample XIB and storyboard files. You can edit them yourself and test the view by dumping code to see how the underlying structure matches the presentation you create in IB.

Recipe: Querying Subviews

A view stores an array of its children. Retrieve the array via the `subviews` property. The child views are always drawn after the parent, in the order in which they appear in the `subviews` array. These views draw in order from back to front, and the `subviews` array mirrors that drawing pattern. Views that appear later in the array are drawn after views that appear earlier.

The `subviews` property returns just those views that are immediate children of a given view. At times, you might want to retrieve a more exhaustive list of subviews, including the children's children. Recipe 4-2 introduces `allSubviews()`, a simple recursive function that returns a full list of subviews for any view. Call this function with a view's window (via `view.window`) to return a complete set of views appearing in the `UIWindow` that hosts that view. This list is useful when you want to search for a particular view, such as a specific slider or button.

Although it is not typical, iOS applications may include several windows, each of which can contain many views, some of which may be displayed on an external screen. Recover an exhaustive list of all application views by iterating through each available window. The `allApplicationViews()` function in Recipe 4-2 does exactly that. A call to [[UIApplication sharedApplication] windows] returns the array of application windows. The function iterates through these, adding their subviews to the collection.

In addition to knowing its subviews, each view knows the window it belongs to. The view's window property points to the window that owns it. Recipe 4-2 also includes a simple function called pathToView() that returns an array of superviews, from the window down to the view in question. It does this by calling superview repeatedly until arriving at a window instance.

Views can also check their superview ancestry in another way. The isDescendantOfView: method on UIView determines whether a view lives within another view, even if that view is not its direct superview. This method returns a simple Boolean value. YES means the view descends from the view passed as a parameter to the method.

Recipe 4-2   Subview Utility Functions

```
// Return an exhaustive descent of the view's subviews
NSArray *allSubviews(UIView *aView)
{
    NSArray *results = aView.subviews;
    for (UIView *eachView in aView.subviews)
    {
        NSArray *subviews = allSubviews(eachView);
        if (subviews)
            results = [results arrayByAddingObjectsFromArray:subviews];
    }
    return results;
}


// Return all views throughout the application
NSArray *allApplicationViews()
{
    NSArray *results = [[UIApplication sharedApplication] windows];
    for (UIWindow *window in
        [UIApplication sharedApplication].windows)
    {
        NSArray *subviews = allSubviews(window);
        if (subviews) results =
            [results arrayByAddingObjectsFromArray:subviews];
    }
    return results;
}

// Return an array of parent views from the window down to the view
NSArray *pathToView(UIView *aView)
{
    NSMutableArray *array = [NSMutableArray arrayWithObject:aView];
    UIView *view = aView;
    UIWindow *window = aView.window;
```

```
    while (view != window)
    {
        view = [view superview];
        [array insertObject:view atIndex:0];
    }
    return array;
}
```

Get This Recipe's Code

To find this recipe's full sample project, point your browser to https://github.com/erica/iOS-7-Cookbook and go to the folder for Chapter 4.

Managing Subviews

The UIView class offers numerous methods that help build and manage views. These methods let you add, order, remove, and query the view hierarchy. As shown in Figure 4-1, this hierarchy controls the order of views. Updating the way views relate to each other changes the layout your users see in the app. Here are some approaches for typical view-management tasks.

Adding Subviews

You call addSubview: on a parent to add new subviews. This method adds a subview frontmost within the parent view, placed above any existing views. To insert a subview into the view hierarchy at a particular location other than the front, the SDK offers a trio of utility methods:

- insertSubview:atIndex:

- insertSubview:aboveSubview:

- insertSubview:belowSubview:

These methods control where view insertion happens. The insertion can remain relative to another view, or it can move into a specific index of the subviews array. The above and below methods add subviews in front of or behind a given child, respectively. Insertion increases the index of any subsequent views and does not replace any existing views.

Reordering and Removing Subviews

Applications often reorder and remove views as users interact with the screen. The iOS SDK offers several easy ways to do this, allowing you to change the view order and contents:

- Use [parentView exchangeSubviewAtIndex:i withSubviewAtIndex:j] to exchange the positions of two views.

- Move subviews to the front or back by using `bringSubviewToFront:` and `sendSubviewToBack:`.

- To remove a subview from its parent, call `[childView removeFromSuperview]`. If the child view had been onscreen, it disappears.

When you reorder, add, or remove views, the screen automatically redraws to show the new view presentation.

View Callbacks

When the view hierarchy changes, callbacks can be sent to the views in question. The iOS SDK offers six callback methods. These methods may help your application keep track of views that are moving and changing parents:

- **didAddSubview:**—Is sent to a parent view after it has successfully added a child view via `addSubview:` or one of the other subview insertion methods listed earlier. It lets subclasses of `UIView` perform additional actions when new views are added.

- **didMoveToSuperview:**—Informs views that they've been reparented to a new superview. A view may want to respond to that new parent in some way. When a view is removed from its superview, the new parent is `nil`.

- **willMoveToSuperview:**—Is sent before a move occurs.

- **didMoveToWindow:**—Provides the callback equivalent of `didMoveToSuperview` but when the view moves to a new `Window` hierarchy instead of to just a new superview. You most typically use this when working with external displays with AirPlay.

- **willMoveToWindow:**—Is sent before a move occurs.

- **willRemoveSubview:**—Informs the parent view that a child view is about to be removed.

These methods are rarely used, but when needed, they're almost always lifesavers, allowing you to add behavior without having to know in advance what kind of subview or superview class is being used. The window callbacks are used primarily for displaying overlay views in a secondary window, such as alerts, and input views, such as keyboards.

Tagging and Retrieving Views

The iOS SDK offers a built-in search feature that lets you retrieve subviews by tagging them. A tag is just a number, usually a positive integer, that identifies a view. Assign tags using a view's `tag` property (for example, `myView.tag = 101`). In IB, you can set a view's tag in the Attributes inspector. As Figure 4-2 shows, you specify the tag in the View section.

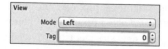

Figure 4-2   Set the tag for any view in IB's Attributes inspector.

Tags are arbitrary. The only "reserved" tag is 0, which is the default property setting for all newly created views. It's up to you to decide how you want to tag your views and which values to use. You can tag any instance that is a child of UIView, including windows and controls. So if you have many buttons and switches, adding tags helps tell them apart when users trigger them. You can add to your callback methods a simple switch statement that looks at the tag and determines how to react.

Apple rarely tags subviews. The only instance we have ever found of view tagging has been in UIAlertViews, where the buttons use tags of 1, 2, and so forth, but it has been several years since that happened. (Apple probably left this tagging in there as a mistake.) If you worry about conflicting with Apple tags, start your numbering at 10 or 100, or some other number higher than any value Apple might use.

Using Tags to Find Views

Tags let you avoid passing user interface elements around your program by making them directly accessible from any parent view. The viewWithTag: method recovers a tagged view from a child hierarchy. The search is recursive, so the tagged item need not be an immediate child of the view in question. You can search from the window with [window viewWithTag:101] and find a view that is several branches down the hierarchy tree. When more than one view uses the same tag, viewWithTag: returns the first item it finds.

The only challenge about using viewWithTag: is that it returns a UIView object. This means you often have to cast it to the proper type before you can use it. For example, you can retrieve a label and set its text like this:

```
UILabel *label = (UILabel *)[self.view.window viewWithTag:101];
label.text = @"Hello World";
```

Recipe: Naming Views by Object Association

Although tagging offers a handy approach to identifying views, some developers may prefer to work with names rather than numbers. Using names adds an extra level of meaning to your view identification schemes. Instead of referring to "the view with a tag of 101," a switch named Ignition Switch can describe its role and add a level of self-documentation missing from a plain number:

```
// Toggle switch
UISwitch *s = (UISwitch *)[self.view viewNamed:@"Ignition Switch"];
[s setOn:!s.isOn];
```

It's easy to extend UIView to add a nametag property and retrieve views by name. The secret lies in Objective-C's runtime *associated object* functions. If you've ever written class categories, you might be thinking, "But if I add new storage, won't I need to subclass?" Associated objects don't require new instance variables. Instead, they provide a way to use key/value pairs outside an object's direct storage, associating that object with information stored elsewhere.

Recipe 4-3 creates a UIView nametag category. It consists of a single property (nametag), which is supported by associated objects and a method (viewNamed:) that works to find any subview by name. The method descends the view hierarchy with a recursive depth-first search and returns the first subview whose name matches a search string.

Naming Views in Interface Builder

Using a named view approach allows you to retrieve subviews without having to declare IBOutlet instance variables. (Whether this is a net benefit to code readability and maintainability is beyond the scope of this section.) Consider the code you saw earlier in this section that toggles a switch from within an interface. You can add that name (Ignition Switch) as a custom runtime attribute in IB.

Figure 4-3 shows how you do this. Select any view and open the Identity Inspector (View > Utilities > Show Identity Inspector). Locate the User Defined Runtime Attributes section and click + to add a new attribute. Set the Key Path to nametag (to match the property defined in Recipe 4-3's UIView class category), Type to String, and Value to the view's new name. Save your changes. You can then use the category's viewNamed: method to retrieve the switch via code and toggle its state.

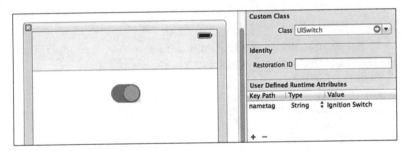

Figure 4-3   Set the tag for any view in IB's Attributes inspector. You may assign user-defined runtime attributes for any Key-value coded (KVC) object value. These values are set at the time the XIB file loads.

> **Note**
>
> You can name a view's layer directly, without associated objects. CALayer instances offer a name property, which helps identify layers when you're working with them. To use layers, import the Quartz Core module in your source and access each layer via view.layer.

Recipe 4-3 **Naming Views**

```objc
#import <objc/runtime.h>
@implementation UIView (NameExtensions)

// Static variable's address acts as the key
// Thanks, Oliver Drobnik
static const char nametag_key;

- (id)nametag
{
    return objc_getAssociatedObject(self, (void *) &nametag_key);
}


- (void)setNametag:(NSString *)theNametag
{
    objc_setAssociatedObject(self, (void *) &nametag_key,
        theNametag, OBJC_ASSOCIATION_RETAIN_NONATOMIC);
}

- (UIView *)viewWithNametag:(NSString *)aName
{
    if (!aName) return nil;

    // Is this the right view?
    if ([self.nametag isEqualToString:aName])
        return self;

    // Recurse depth first on subviews
    for (UIView *subview in self.subviews)
    {
        UIView *resultView = [subview viewNamed:aName];
        if (resultView) return resultView;
    }

    // Not found
    return nil;
}

- (UIView *)viewNamed:(NSString *)aName
{
    if (!aName) return nil;
    return [self viewWithNametag:aName];
}
@end
```

> **Get This Recipe's Code**
>
> To find this recipe's full sample project, point your browser to https://github.com/erica/iOS-7-Cookbook and go to the folder for Chapter 4.

View Geometry

While direct control of view geometry is less necessary now than it used to be, thanks to Apple's introduction of Auto Layout, these tasks continue to play a fundamental role in some situations when working with views. Some of Apple's new APIs, such as the ones that introduce view physics, do not play nicely with Auto Layout. Because of this, you should master the basic ways you interact and adjust view geometry.

Geometric properties define where each view appears, what their sizes are, and how they are oriented. These properties remain valid, even when using Auto Layout; under Auto Layout, they are managed by the constraint system. You can still query and view these properties to retrieve information about where a view has been placed and what geometric transformations have been applied to it.

When working with dynamic views, views with short life spans, and ones whose geometry changes during presentation, you may need to step away from constraints and focus on immediate handling of the basic layout associated with each view. The `UIView` class provides two built-in properties that define these layout aspects.

Every view uses a `frame` to define its boundaries. The frame specifies the outline of the view: its location, width, and height within the coordinate system of its parent view. The associated `bounds` and `center` properties, respectively, define the frame rectangle within the view's *own* coordinate system and the geometric center of the frame in the parent's coordinate system. These three properties are tightly integrated.

If you change a view's frame, the view updates to match the new frame. If you use a bigger width, the view stretches. If you use a new location, the view moves. The view's frame delineates each view's outline. View sizes are not limited to their superview size or even the screen size. A view can be smaller or larger than the screen. It can also be smaller or larger than its parent. When a subview is larger, the subview's visible area overflows the edges of the parent. You can use `clipToBounds` on the parent view to restrict the child from displaying outside the parent's bounds.

Views also use a `transform` property that updates a view's presentation, via affine transformations. These are mathematical equations that adjust a view's 2D geometry. A view might be stretched or squashed by applying a transform, or it might be rotated away from vertical. Together, the frame and transform fully define a view's core geometry.

Frames

A frame rectangle refers to the outline of a view in terms of its parent's coordinate system. Frames use a CGRect structure, which is defined as part of the Core Graphics framework, as its CG prefix suggests. A CGRect is made up of an origin (a CGPoint, *x* and *y*) and a size (a CGSize, width and height). When you create views outside Auto Layout, you normally allocate them and initialize them with a frame. Here's an example:

```
CGRect rect = CGRectMake(0.0f, 0.0f, 320.0f, 416.0f);
myView = [[UIView alloc] initWithFrame:rect];
```

Views provide two fundamental CGRect properties, which are closely tied together: frame and bounds. Frames are different from bounds in terms of their coordinate system. Frames are defined with respect to the parent's system. Bounds are defined with respect to the view's own coordinate system. For that reason, a view's bounds typically use a zero origin. Its coordinate system normally begins at the top-left corner. For some views, like scroll views, bounds may extend beyond their visual frame.

Rectangle Utility Functions

As you've seen, the CGRectMake() function creates its new rectangle using four parameters: the origin's x and y locations, the width of the rectangle, and the height. This method is a critical utility for creating frames. You may want to be aware of several other convenience functions, in addition to CGRectMake(), that help you work with rectangles and frames:

- NSStringFromCGRect(aCGRect) converts a CGRect structure to a formatted string. This function makes it easy to log a view's frame when you're debugging.

- CGRectFromString(aString) recovers a rectangle from its string representation. It is useful when you've stored a view's frame as a string in user defaults and want to convert that string back to a CGRect.

- Although not a function, [NSValue valueWithCGRect:rect] returns a new Objective-C value object that stores the passed rectangle. You can then add the object to dictionaries and arrays as needed. The CGRectValue method retrieves the rectangular structure from the NSValue object. Variations on this approach exist for most Core Graphics types, including points, sizes, and affine transforms.

- CGRectInset(aRect, xinset, yinset) enables you to create a smaller or larger rectangle that's centered on the same point as the source rectangle. Use a positive inset for smaller rectangles, and use a negative inset for larger ones.

- CGRectOffset(aRect, xoffset, yoffset) returns a rectangle that's offset from the original rectangle by *x* and *y* amounts that you specify. This is handy for moving frames around the screen and for creating easy drop-shadow effects.

- CGRectGetMidX(aRect) and CGRectGetMidY(aRect) recover the *x* and *y* coordinates in the center of a rectangle. These functions make it very convenient to recover the midpoints of bounds and frames.

- `CGRectIntersectsRect(rect1, rect2)` lets you know whether rectangle structures intersect. Use this function to know when two rectangular objects overlap. You can retrieve the actual intersection via `CGRectIntersection(rect1, rect2)`. This returns the null rectangle if the two rects do not intersect. (Use `CGRectIsNull(rect)` to check.) The related `CGRectContainsPoint(rect, point)` returns `true` when a provided point is located within the (non-null) rectangle.

- Compare rectangles using `CGRectEqualToRect(rect1, rect2)`. This function checks whether two rectangles are equal in both their size and position. Similar methods include `CGSizeEqualToSize(size1, size2)` and `CGPointEqualToPoint(point1, point2)`, which allow you to compare `CGSize` and `CGPoint` instances.

- Other handy utilities include `CGRectDivide()`, which splits a source rectangle into two components, and `CGRectApplyAffineTransform(rect, transform)`, which applies an affine transform to a rectangle and returns the smallest rectangle that can contain the results.

- `CGRectZero` is a rectangle constant located at `(0,0)` whose width and height are zero. You can use this constant when you're required to create a frame but are unsure what that frame size or location will be at the time of creation. Similar constants are `CGPointZero` and `CGSizeZero`.

Points and Sizes

The `CGRect` structure is made up of two substructures: `CGPoint`, which defines the rectangle's origin, and `CGSize`, which defines its bounds. Points refer to locations defined with x and y coordinates; sizes have width and height. Use `CGPointMake(x, y)` to create points. `CGSizeMake(width, height)` creates sizes. Although these two structures appear to be the same (two floating-point values), the iOS SDK differentiates between them semantically. Points refer to locations. Sizes refer to extents. You cannot set `myFrame.origin` to a size.

Since `CGRect`, `CGPoint`, and `CGSize` are all structs, you can use a range of flexible struct initializations:

```
CGPoint origin = {0, 0};
CGSize size = {100, 200};
CGRect rect1 = CGRectMake(0, 0, 100, 200);
CGRect rect2 = {{0, 0}, {100, 200}};
CGRect rect3 = {origin, size};
CGRect rect4 = {origin, {100, 200}}
CGRect rect5 = {.size.width = 100, .size.height = 200, .origin = {0, 0}};
```

All of these `CGRect`s are identical.

As with rectangles, you can convert the other structs to and from strings. `NSStringFromCGPoint()`, `NSStringFromCGSize()`, `CGPointFromString()`, and `CGSizeFromString()` perform these functions. You can also transform points and sizes to and from dictionaries.

Transforms

The iOS SDK includes affine transformations as part of its Core Graphics implementation. Affine transforms allow points in one coordinate system to transform into another coordinate system. These functions are widely used in both 2D and 3D animations. The version used with UIKit views uses a 3-by-3 matrix to define UIView transforms, making it a 2D-only solution. 3D transforms use a 4-by-4 matrix and are the default for Core Animation layers. With affine transforms, you can scale, translate, and rotate your views in real time. You do so by setting a view's transform property. Here's an example:

```
float angle = theta * (PI / 100.0);
CGAffineTransform transform = CGAffineTransformMakeRotation(angle);
myView.transform = transform;
```

The transform is always applied with respect to the view's center. So when you apply a rotation like this, the view rotates around its center. If you need to rotate around another point, you must first translate the view to the desired point, then rotate, and then return from that translation. There are ways around this, involving working directly with the view's layer property, but that approach is beyond the scope of this chapter.

To revert any changes, set the transform property to the identity transform. This restores the view back to the last settings for its frame:

```
myView.transform = CGAffineTransformIdentity;
```

> **Note**
>
> On iOS, the y coordinate starts at the top and increases downward. This is similar to the coordinate system in PostScript but opposite the Quartz coordinate system historically used on the Mac. On iOS, the origin is in the top-left corner, not the bottom left. iOS continues to move many features originally grounded in Quartz and Core Graphics into the UIKit world. This migration reduces the number of times you need to flip your coordinate system when laying out text or processing images.

Coordinate Systems

As mentioned earlier, views live in two worlds. The frame and center of a view are defined in the coordinate system of its parents. The bounds and subviews of a view are defined in their own coordinate system. The iOS SDK offers several utilities that allow you to move between these coordinate systems, as long as the views involved live within the same UIWindow. To convert a point from another view into your own coordinate system, use convertPoint:fromView:. Here's an example:

```
myPoint = [myView convertPoint:somePoint fromView:otherView];
```

If the original point indicated the location of some object, the new point retains that location but gives the coordinates with respect to myView's origin. To go the other way, use convertPoint:toView: to transform a point into another view's coordinate system. Similarly, `convertRect:toView:` and `convertRect:fromView:` work with `CGRect` structures rather than `CGPoint` ones.

Be aware that the coordinate system for an iOS device may not match the pixel system used to display that system. The discrete 640×960-pixel Retina display on the iPhone 4S, for example, is addressed through a continuous 320×480 coordinate system in the SDK, defined as *points*. Although you can supply higher-quality art to fill those pixels on Retina display units, any locations you specify in points in your code access the coordinate based on the resolution of the lower pixel–density units. The position (160.0, 240.0) in points remains approximately in the center of the 3.5-inch iPhone or iPod touch screens, regardless of pixel density. That center point moves to (160.0, 284.0) on 4-inch iPhones and iPod touches, which use Retina displays.

> **Note**
>
> The `UIScreen` class provides a property called `scale` that defines the relationship between a display's pixel density and its point system. A screen's scale is used to convert from the logical coordinate space of the view system (measured in points and approximately equal to 1/160 inch) to the physical pixel coordinates. Retina displays use a scale of 2.0, and non-Retina displays use a scale of 1.0.

Recipe: Working with View Frames

When you change a view's frame manually (rather than letting Auto Layout do the dirty work), you update its size (that is, its width and height) and its location. For example, you might move a frame as follows:

```
CGRect initialRect = CGRectMake(0.0f, 0.0f, 100.0f, 100.0f);
myView = [[UIView alloc] initWithFrame:initialRect];
[topView addSubview:myView];
myView.frame = CGRectMake(0.0f, 30.0f, 100.0f, 100.0f);
```

This code creates a subview located at (0.0, 0.0) and then moves it down to (0.0, 30.0).

This approach for moving views is fairly uncommon. The iOS SDK does not expect you to move views by changing frames. Instead, it focuses on a view's position. The preferred way to do this is by setting the view's `center`. This is a view property, which you can set directly:

```
myView.center = CGPointMake(160.0f, 55.0f);
```

Although you might expect the SDK to offer a way to move a view by updating its origin, no such option exists. It's easy enough to build your own view class category. Retrieve the view frame, set the origin to the requested point, and then update the frame with the change. This snippet creates a new origin property that lets you retrieve and change the view's origin:

```
- (void)setOrigin:(CGPoint)aPoint
{
    CGRect newFrame = self.frame;
```

```
    newFrame.origin = aPoint;
    self.frame = newFrame;
}
```

Because this extension uses such an obvious property name, if Apple eventually implements the features shown here, your code may break due to name overlap. In the examples in this book, we widely use obvious names. This makes code snippets easier to read and reduces any cognitive burden in recognizing what is being demonstrated. Avoid using obvious names in your production code. Using your personal or company initials as a prefix helps distinguish in-house material.

When you move a view, you don't need to worry about things such as rectangular sections having been exposed or hidden. iOS takes care of the redrawing. This lets you treat your views like tangible objects and delegate rendering issues to Cocoa Touch.

Adjusting Sizes

In the simplest usage patterns, a view's frame and bounds control its size. A frame, as you've already seen, defines the location of a view in its parent's coordinate system. If the frame's origin is set to (0.0, 30.0), the view appears in the superview flush with the left side of the view and offset 30 points from the top. On non-Retina displays, this corresponds to 30 pixels down; on Retina displays, it is 60 pixels down.

Bounds define a view within its own coordinate system. Therefore, the origin for a view's bounds (that is, `myView.bounds`) is normally (0.0, 0.0). For most views, the size matches the normal extent—that is, the frame's `size` property. (This isn't always true for some classes, like `UIScrollView`, whose extent may exceed the visual display.)

You can change a view's size by adjusting either its frame or its bounds. In practical terms, you're updating the size component of those structures. As with moving origins, it's simple to create your own view utility method to do this directly:

```
- (void)setSize:(CGSize)aSize
{
    CGRect newbounds = self.bounds;
    newbounds.size = aSize;
    self.bounds = newbounds;
}
```

When a displayed view's size changes, the view itself updates live. Depending on how the elements within the view are defined and the class of the view itself, subviews may shrink or move to fit, or they may get cropped, depending on a number of flags and whether views are participating in the Auto Layout system:

- The `autoresizesSubviews` property determines whether a view automatically resizes its subviews when it updates its bounds.

- A view's `autoresizingMask` property defines how a view reacts to changes in its parent's bounds. If a view participates in a constraint system, this mask is ignored, and the view will be adjusted by iOS's Auto Layout system.

- The `clipsToBounds` flag determines whether subviews are visible outside a view's bounds. When clipped, only material within the parent's bounds are shown. You can use `sizeToFit` on a view so that it resizes to enclose all its subviews.

- The `contentMode` property is related to other view-resizing properties but specifies how a view's layer (its content bitmap) adjusts when its bounds update. This property, which can be set to a number of scaling, centering, and fitting choices, is best seen when working with image views.

> **Note**
>
> Bounds are affected by a view's transform, a mathematical component that changes the way the view appears. Do not manipulate a view's frame when working with transforms because doing so may not produce expected results. (Some workarounds follow later in this chapter.) For example, after a transform, the frame's origin may no longer correspond mathematically to the origin of the bounds. The normal order of updating a view is to set its frame or bounds, then set its center, and then set its transforms, if applicable.

Sometimes, you need to resize a view before adding it to a new parent. For example, you might have an image view to place into an alert view. To fit that view into place without changing its aspect ratio, you can use a method like this to ensure that both the height and width scale appropriately:

```
- (void) fitInSize: (CGSize) aSize
{
    CGFloat scale;
    CGRect newframe = self.frame;

    if (newframe.size.height > aSize.height)
    {
        scale = aSize.height / newframe.size.height;
        newframe.size.width *= scale;
        newframe.size.height *= scale;
    }

    if (newframe.size.width > aSize.width)
    {
        scale = aSize.width / newframe.size.width;
        newframe.size.width *= scale;
        newframe.size.height *= scale;
    }
    self.frame = newframe;
}
```

CGRects and Centers

As you've seen, UIView instances use a CGRect structure, composed of an origin and a size, to define their frame. A CGRect structure contains no references to a center point. At the same time, UIViews depend on their center property to update a view's position when you move a view to a new point. Unfortunately, Core Graphics doesn't use centers as a primary rectangle concept. As far as centers are concerned, the built-in utilities in Core Graphics are limited to recovering a rectangle's midpoint along the x- or y-axis.

You can bridge this gap by constructing functions that coordinate between the origin-based CGRect struct and center-based UIView objects. Such a function retrieves the center from a rectangle by building a point from the x and y midpoints. It takes one argument, a rectangle, and returns its center point:

```
CGPoint CGRectGetCenter(CGRect rect)
{
    CGPoint pt;
    pt.x = CGRectGetMidX(rect);
    pt.y = CGRectGetMidY(rect);
    return pt;
}
```

Moving a rectangle by its center point is another function that may prove helpful, and one that mimics the way UIViews work. Suppose, for example, that you need to move a view to a new position but need to keep it inside its parent's frame. To test before you move, you could use a function like this to offset the view frame to a new center:

```
CGRect CGRectMoveToCenter(CGRect rect, CGPoint center)
{
    CGRect newrect = CGRectZero;
    newrect.origin.x = center.x-(rect.size.width/2.0);
    newrect.origin.y = center.y-(rect.size.height/2.0);
    newrect.size = rect.size;
    return newrect;
}
```

You could then test that offset frame against the parent (use CGRectContainsRect()) and ensure that the view won't stray outside its container.

Often you need to center one view in another. You can retrieve a rectangle that corresponds to a centered subrectangle by passing the outer view's bounds when adding a subview (the subview coordinate system needs to start with 0, 0) or its frame when adding a view to the outer view's parent:

```
CGRect CGRectCenteredInRect(CGRect subRect, CGRect mainRect)
{
    CGFloat xOffset = CGRectGetMidX(mainRect)-CGRectGetMidX(subRect);
    CGFloat yOffset = CGRectGetMidY(mainRect)-CGRectGetMidY(subRect);
    return CGRectOffset(rect, xOffset, yOffset);
}
```

Other Geometric Elements

As you've seen, it's convenient to use a view's origin and size as well as its `center` property, which allows you to work more natively with Core Graphics calls. You can build on this idea to expose other properties of the view, including its `width` and `height`, as well as basic geometry, such as its `left`, `right`, `top`, and `bottom` points. In some ways, this breaks Apple's design philosophy. It exposes items that normally fall into structures without reflecting the structures. At the same time, it can be argued that these elements are true view properties. They reflect fundamental view characteristics and deserve to be exposed as properties.

Recipe 4-4 provides a full view frame utility category for `UIView`, which lets you make the choice about whether to expose these properties. These properties do not take transforms into account.

> **Note**
>
> While Auto Layout is rendering many of the utility methods in this recipe less critical than in the past, these methods still provide great value, both when you fall back to manual layout or even occasionally when you're using Auto Layout.

Recipe 4-4   `UIView` **Frame Geometry Category**

```
@interface UIView (ViewFrameGeometry)
@property CGPoint origin;
@property CGSize size;

@property (readonly) CGPoint midpoint;

// topLeft is synonymous with origin so not included here
@property (readonly) CGPoint bottomLeft;
@property (readonly) CGPoint bottomRight;
@property (readonly) CGPoint topRight;

@property CGFloat height;
@property CGFloat width;
@property CGFloat top;
@property CGFloat left;
@property CGFloat bottom;
@property CGFloat right;

- (void)moveBy:(CGPoint)delta;
- (void)scaleBy:(CGFloat)scaleFactor;
- (void)fitInSize:(CGSize)aSize;
@end

@implementation UIView (ViewGeometry)
```

```objc
// Retrieve and set the origin
- (CGPoint)origin
{
    return self.frame.origin;
}

- (void)setOrigin:(CGPoint)aPoint
{
    CGRect newFrame = self.frame;
    newFrame.origin = aPoint;
    self.frame = newFrame;
}

// Retrieve and set the size
- (CGSize)size
{
    return self.frame.size;
}

- (void)setSize:(CGSize)aSize
{
    CGRect newFrame = self.frame;
    newFrame.size = aSize;
    self.frame = newFrame;
}

// Query other frame locations

- (CGPoint)midpoint
{
    // midpoint is with respect to a view's own coordinate system
    // versus its center, which is with respect to its parent
    CGFloat x = CGRectGetMidX(self.bounds);
    CGFloat y = CGRectGetMidY(self.bounds);
    return CGPointMake(x, y);
}

- (CGPoint)bottomRight
{
    CGFloat x = self.frame.origin.x + self.frame.size.width;
    CGFloat y = self.frame.origin.y + self.frame.size.height;
    return CGPointMake(x, y);
}

- (CGPoint)bottomLeft
{
    CGFloat x = self.frame.origin.x;
```

```objc
    CGFloat y = self.frame.origin.y + self.frame.size.height;
    return CGPointMake(x, y);
}

- (CGPoint)topRight
{
    CGFloat x = self.frame.origin.x + self.frame.size.width;
    CGFloat y = self.frame.origin.y;
    return CGPointMake(x, y);
}


// Retrieve and set height, width, top, bottom, left, right
- (CGFloat)height
{
    return self.frame.size.height;
}

- (void)setHeight:(CGFloat)newHeight
{
    CGRect newFrame = self.frame;
    newFrame.size.height = newHeight;
    self.frame = newFrame;
}

- (CGFloat)width
{
    return self.frame.size.width;
}

- (void)setWidth:(CGFloat)newWidth
{
    CGRect newFrame = self.frame;
    newFrame.size.width = newWidth;
    self.frame = newFrame;
}

- (CGFloat)top
{
    return self.frame.origin.y;
}

- (void)setTop:(CGFloat)newTop
{
    CGRect newFrame = self.frame;
    newFrame.origin.y = newTop;
    self.frame = newFrame;
}
```

```
- (CGFloat)left
{
    return self.frame.origin.x;
}

- (void)setLeft:(CGFloat)newLeft
{
    CGRect newFrame = self.frame;
    newFrame.origin.x = newLeft;
    self.frame = newFrame;
}

- (CGFloat)bottom
{
    return self.frame.origin.y + self.frame.size.height;
}

- (void)setBottom:(CGFloat)newBottom
{
    CGFloat delta = newBottom -
        (self.frame.origin.y + self.frame.size.height);
    CGRect newFrame = self.frame;
    newFrame.origin.y += delta;
    self.frame = newFrame;
}

- (CGFloat)right
{
    return self.frame.origin.x + self.frame.size.width;
}

- (void)setRight:(CGFloat)newRight
{
    CGFloat delta = newRight-
        (self.frame.origin.x + self.frame.size.width);
    CGRect newFrame = self.frame;
    newFrame.origin.x += delta;
    self.frame = newFrame;
}
@end
```

Get This Recipe's Code

To find this recipe's full sample project, point your browser to https://github.com/erica/iOS-7-Cookbook and go to the folder for Chapter 4.

Recipe: Retrieving Transform Information

Affine transforms enable you to change an object's geometry by mapping that object from one view coordinate system into another. The iOS SDK fully supports standard affine 2D transforms. With them, you can scale, translate, rotate, and skew your views however your heart desires and your application demands.

Transforms are defined in Core Graphics and consist of calls such as `CGAffineTransformMakeRotation()` and `CGAffineTransformScale()`. These build and modify 3-by-3 transform matrices. After these are built, use `UIView`'s `transform` property to assign 2D affine transformations to `UIView` objects.

For example, you might apply a rotation transform directly. This removes any existing transform and replaces it with a simple rotation. The functions with `Make` in their name create new transforms:

```
theView.transform = CGAffineTransformMakeRotation(radians);
```

Or you might add a scaling transform onto whatever transformations have already been applied to the view. The functions without the word `Make` take a transform as their first parameter and return an updated transform after applying a transformation according to the function arguments:

```
CGAffineTransform scaled = CGAffineTransformScale(theView.transform,
    scaleX, scaleY);
theView.transform = scaled;
```

Retrieving Transform Properties

When working with transforms, iOS can provide an affine representation of the transform associated with a view. This representation will not, however, tell you exactly how much the view has been scaled or rotated. Recipe 4-5 addresses this problem by calculating the scale and rotation via a simple `UIView` category.

An affine matrix is stored in iOS as a structure of six fields: a, b, c, d, tx, and ty. Figure 4-4 shows how these values relate to their positions in the standard affine matrix. Simple math allows you to derive scaling and rotation from these, as shown in Recipe 4-5. Note how you can retrieve the tx and ty values directly from the transform. If linear algebra isn't in your wheelhouse, don't worry; you really don't have to understand how these transforms work in order to use them successfully.

In addition to answering the questions "What is the view's current rotation?" and "By how much is it scaled?" you often need to perform math that relates the current geometry post-transform to the parent coordinate system. To do this, you need to be able to specify where elements appear onscreen.

$$\begin{bmatrix} a & b & 0 \\ c & d & 0 \\ t_x & t_y & 1 \end{bmatrix}$$

Figure 4-4   The `CGAffineTransform` structure holds an affine transformation matrix by defining six key values in its fields (left). After applying an affine transform, a view's origin may no longer coincide with its frame's origin (right).

A view's center makes the transition from pre-transform to post-transform without incident. The value may change, especially after scaling, but the property remains meaningful, regardless of what transform has been applied. The center property always refers to the geometric center of the view's frame in the parent's coordinate system.

The frame is not so resilient. After rotation, a view's origin may be completely decoupled from the view. Look at Figure 4-4 (right). It shows a rotated view on top of its original frame (the smaller of the two outlines) and the updated frame (the larger outline). The circles indicate the view's origin before and after rotation.

After the transform is applied, the frame updates to the minimum bounding box that encloses the view. Its new origin (the top-left corner of the outside view) has essentially nothing to do with the updated view origin (the circle at the top-middle). iOS does not provide a way to retrieve that adjusted point.

Recipe 4-5 introduces several methods that perform the math for you. It establishes properties that return a transformed view's corners: top left, top right, bottom left, and bottom right. These coordinates are defined in the parent view; if you want to add a new view on top of the top circle in Figure 4-4 (right), you place its center at `theView.transformedTopLeft`.

The recipe also offers the `originalFrame` method, which returns the inner (original) frame shown in Figure 4-4, even when a transform has been applied. It does so in a rather ham-fisted way, but it works.

Testing for View Intersection

By reader request, Recipe 4-5 adds code to check whether two transformed views intersect. The code also works with views that have not been transformed so that you can use it with any two views, although it's a bit pointless to do so. (You can use the `CGRectIntersectsRect()` function for simple untransformed frames.) This custom intersection method works best for views whose frames do not represent their underlying geometry, like the one shown in Figure 4-4.

The `intersectsView:` method applies an axis separation algorithm for convex polygons. For each edge of each view, it tests whether all the points in one view fall on one side of the edge and whether all the points of the other view fall on the other side. This test is based on the half plane function, which returns a value indicating whether a point is on the left or right side of an edge.

As soon as it finds an edge that satisfies this condition, the `intersectsView:` method returns NO. The views cannot geometrically intersect if there's a line that separates all the points in one object from all the points in the other.

If all eight tests fail (four edges on the first view, four edges on the second), the method concludes that the two views do intersect. It returns YES.

Recipe 4-5   Retrieving Transform Values

```
@implementation UIView (Transform)
- (CGFloat)xScale
{
    CGAffineTransform t = self.transform;
    return sqrt(t.a * t.a + t.c * t.c);
}

- (CGFloat)yScale
{
    CGAffineTransform t = self.transform;
    return sqrt(t.b * t.b + t.d * t.d);
}

- (CGFloat)rotation
{
    CGAffineTransform t = self.transform;
    return atan2f(t.b, t.a);
}

- (CGFloat)tx
{
    CGAffineTransform t = self.transform;
    return t.tx;
}

- (CGFloat)ty
{
    CGAffineTransform t = self.transform;
    return t.ty;
}

// The following three methods move points into and out of the
// transform coordinate system whose origin is at the view center

- (CGPoint)offsetPointToParentCoordinates:(CGPoint)aPoint
{
    return CGPointMake(aPoint.x + self.center.x,
        aPoint.y + self.center.y);
```

```
}

- (CGPoint)pointInViewCenterTerms:(CGPoint)aPoint
{
    return CGPointMake(aPoint.x - self.center.x, aPoint.y - self.center.y);
}

- (CGPoint)pointInTransformedView:(CGPoint)aPoint
{
    CGPoint offsetItem = [self pointInViewCenterTerms:aPoint];
    CGPoint updatedItem = CGPointApplyAffineTransform(
        offsetItem, self.transform);
    CGPoint finalItem =
        [self offsetPointToParentCoordinates:updatedItem];
    return finalItem;
}

// Return the original frame without transform
- (CGRect)originalFrame
{
    CGAffineTransform currentTransform = self.transform;
    self.transform = CGAffineTransformIdentity;
    CGRect originalFrame = self.frame;
    self.transform = currentTransform;

    return originalFrame;
}

// These four methods return the positions of view elements
// with respect to the current transform

- (CGPoint)transformedTopLeft
{
    CGRect frame = self.originalFrame;
    CGPoint point = frame.origin;
    return [self pointInTransformedView:point];
}

- (CGPoint)transformedTopRight
{
    CGRect frame = self.originalFrame;
    CGPoint point = frame.origin;
    point.x += frame.size.width;
    return [self pointInTransformedView:point];
}

- (CGPoint)transformedBottomRight
```

```
{
    CGRect frame = self.originalFrame;
    CGPoint point = frame.origin;
    point.x += frame.size.width;
    point.y += frame.size.height;
    return [self pointInTransformedView:point];
}


- (CGPoint)transformedBottomLeft
{
    CGRect frame = self.originalFrame;
    CGPoint point = frame.origin;
    point.y += frame.size.height;
    return [self pointInTransformedView:point];
}


// Determine if two views intersect, with respect to any
// active transforms

// After extending a line, determine which side of the half
// plane defined by that line, a point will appear
BOOL halfPlane(CGPoint p1, CGPoint p2, CGPoint testPoint)
{
    CGPoint base = CGPointMake(p2.x - p1.x, p2.y - p1.y);
    CGPoint orthog = CGPointMake(-base.y, base.x);
    return (((orthog.x * (testPoint.x - p1.x)) +
        (orthog.y * (testPoint.y - p1.y))) >= 0);
}


// Utility test for testing view points against a proposed line
BOOL intersectionTest(CGPoint p1, CGPoint p2, UIView *aView)
{
    BOOL tlTest = halfPlane(p1, p2, aView.transformedTopLeft);
    BOOL trTest = halfPlane(p1, p2, aView.transformedTopRight);
    if (tlTest != trTest) return YES;

    BOOL brTest = halfPlane(p1, p2, aView.transformedBottomRight);
    if (tlTest != brTest) return YES;

    BOOL blTest = halfPlane(p1, p2, aView.transformedBottomLeft);
    if (tlTest != blTest) return YES;

    return NO;
}


// Determine whether the view intersects a second view
// with respect to their transforms
```

```
- (BOOL)intersectsView:(UIView *)aView
{
    if (!CGRectIntersectsRect(self.frame, aView.frame)) return NO;

    CGPoint A = self.transformedTopLeft;
    CGPoint B = self.transformedTopRight;
    CGPoint C = self.transformedBottomRight;
    CGPoint D = self.transformedBottomLeft;

    if (!intersectionTest(A, B, aView))
    {
        BOOL test = halfPlane(A, B, aView.transformedTopLeft);
        BOOL t1 = halfPlane(A, B, C);
        BOOL t2 = halfPlane(A, B, D);
        if ((t1 != test) && (t2 != test)) return NO;
    }
    if (!intersectionTest(B, C, aView))
    {
        BOOL test = halfPlane(B, C, aView.transformedTopLeft);
        BOOL t1 = halfPlane(B, C, A);
        BOOL t2 = halfPlane(B, C, D);
        if ((t1 != test) && (t2 != test)) return NO;
    }
    if (!intersectionTest(C, D, aView))
    {
        BOOL test = halfPlane(C, D, aView.transformedTopLeft);
        BOOL t1 = halfPlane(C, D, A);
        BOOL t2 = halfPlane(C, D, B);
        if ((t1 != test) && (t2 != test)) return NO;
    }
    if (!intersectionTest(D, A, aView))
    {
        BOOL test = halfPlane(D, A, aView.transformedTopLeft);
        BOOL t1 = halfPlane(D, A, B);
        BOOL t2 = halfPlane(D, A, C);
        if ((t1 != test) && (t2 != test)) return NO;
    }

    A = aView.transformedTopLeft;
    B = aView.transformedTopRight;
    C = aView.transformedBottomRight;
    D = aView.transformedBottomLeft;

    if (!intersectionTest(A, B, self))
    {
        BOOL test = halfPlane(A, B, self.transformedTopLeft);
        BOOL t1 = halfPlane(A, B, C);
```

```
            BOOL t2 = halfPlane(A, B, D);
            if ((t1 != test) && (t2 != test)) return NO;
    }
    if (!intersectionTest(B, C, self))
    {
            BOOL test = halfPlane(B, C, self.transformedTopLeft);
            BOOL t1 = halfPlane(B, C, A);
            BOOL t2 = halfPlane(B, C, D);
            if ((t1 != test) && (t2 != test)) return NO;
    }
    if (!intersectionTest(C, D, self))
    {
            BOOL test = halfPlane(C, D, self.transformedTopLeft);
            BOOL t1 = halfPlane(C, D, A);
            BOOL t2 = halfPlane(C, D, B);
            if ((t1 != test) && (t2 != test)) return NO;
    }
    if (!intersectionTest(D, A, self))
    {
            BOOL test = halfPlane(D, A, self.transformedTopLeft);
            BOOL t1 = halfPlane(D, A, B);
            BOOL t2 = halfPlane(D, A, C);
            if ((t1 != test) && (t2 != test)) return NO;
    }

    return YES;
}
@end
```

Get This Recipe's Code

To find this recipe's full sample project, point your browser to https://github.com/erica/iOS-7-Cookbook and go to the folder for Chapter 4.

Display and Interaction Traits

In addition to physical screen layout, the UIView class provides properties that control how your view appears and whether users can interact with it. Every view uses an opaqueness factor (alpha) that ranges between opaque and transparent. Adjust this by issuing [myView setAlpha:value] or setting the myView.alpha property where the alpha values fall between 0.0 (fully transparent) and 1.0 (fully opaque). This is a great way to fade views in and out. Use the hidden property to hide views entirely without animation.

You can assign a color to the background of any view. For example, the following property colors your view red:

```
myView.backgroundColor = [UIColor redColor];
```

This property affects different view classes in different ways, depending on whether those views contain subviews that block the background. Create a transparent background by setting the view's background color to clear, as shown here:

```
myView.backgroundColor = [UIColor clearColor];
```

Every view offers a background color property, regardless of whether you can see the background. Using bright, contrasting background colors is a great way to visualize the true extents of views. When you're new to iOS development, coloring in views provides you a concrete sense of what is and is not onscreen and where each component is located.

Not all colors are solid tints. The UIColor class lets you use tiled patterns just as you would use solid colors. The colorWithPatternImage: method returns a UIColor instance built from a pattern image you supply. This method helps build textures that you can use to color views.

The userInteractionEnabled property controls whether users can touch and interact with a given view. For most views, this property defaults to YES. For UIImageView, it defaults to NO, which can cause a lot of grief among beginning developers. They often place a UIImageView as their backsplash and don't understand why their switches, text entry fields, and buttons do not work. Make sure to enable the property for any view that needs to accept touches, whether for itself or for its subviews, which may include buttons, switches, pickers, and other controls. If you're experiencing trouble with items that seem unresponsive to touch, check the userInteractionEnabled property value for that item and for its parents.

Disable this property for any display-only view you layer over your interaction area. To show a noninteractive overlay clock, for example, via a transparent full-screen view, disable its interaction by assigning its userInteractionEnabled flag to NO. This allows touches to pass through the view and fall below to the actual interaction area of your application. A view with its userInteractionEnabled flag set to NO only stops the flagged view from receiving the touches; these touches will continue through the view to any underlying views. To create a please-wait-style blocker, make sure to enable user interaction for your overlay. This catches user taps and prevents users from accessing your primary interface behind that overlay.

You may also want to disable interaction during transitions to ensure that user taps do not trigger actions as views are being animated. Unwanted touches can be problematic, particularly for games and puzzles.

UIView Animations

UIView animation is one of the odd but lovely perks of working with iOS as a development platform. It enables you to create a moving expression of visual changes when updating views, producing smooth animated results that enhance the user experience. Best of all, this occurs without requiring you to do much work.

UIView animations are perfect for building a visual bridge between a view's current and changed states. With them, you emphasize visual change and create an animation that links together those changes. Changes that can be animated include the following:

- **Changes in location**—Moving a view around the screen by updating its center

- **Changes in size**—Updating the view's frame and bounds

- **Changes in stretching**—Updating the view's content stretch regions

- **Changes in transparency**—Altering the view's alpha value

- **Changes in color**—Updating a view's background color

- **Changes in rotation, scaling, and translation**—Basically, any affine transforms you apply to a view

Animations underwent a profound redesign between the 3.x and 4.x SDKs. Starting with the 4.x SDK, developers were offered a way to use the new Objective-C blocks paradigm to simplify animation tasks. Although you can still work with the original animation transaction techniques, the new alternatives provide a much easier approach, and the Apple documentation specifically discourages the old-style approach.

> **Note**
>
> Most Apple-native animations last about one-third or one-half second. When working with helper views (playing supporting roles that are similar to Apple's keyboard or alerts), you may want to match your animation durations to these timings. Call `[UIApplication statusBarOrientationAnimationDuration]` to retrieve a standard time interval.

Building Animations with Blocks

Blocks constructs simplify the creation of basic animation effects in your code. Consider the following snippet, which produces a fade-out effect for a view with a single statement in an embedded block:

```
[UIView animationWithDuration: 1.0f
    animations:^{contentView.alpha = 0.0f;}];
```

Adding a completion block lets you tidy up after your animation finishes. The following snippet fades out the content view and then removes it from its superview when the animation completes:

```
[UIView animationWithDuration: 1.0f
    animations:^{contentView.alpha = 0.0f;}
    completion:^(BOOL done){[contentView removeFromSuperview];}];
```

When you need to add further options to your animations, a full-service blocks-based method (`animateWithDuration:delay:options:animations:completion:`) provides both a way to pass animation options (as a mask) and to delay the animation (allowing a simple approach to animation "chaining").

When working with animation constants, be sure to use the modern `UIViewAnimationOptions` varieties, which have the word `Options` in their names. Older constants like `UIViewAnimationCurveEaseInOut` will not work with post-iOS 4.x calls.

Occasionally, it is necessary to ensure that a view property change is excluded from an animation. This is particularly useful when you aren't sure where your view changes will be called, such as from within a developer-created animation block or certain system methods that are already within an animation block. In iOS 7, Apple provides the `performWithoutAnimation:` method on `UIView`, which accepts a block, much like the animation methods. Any view property changes inside the block will be excluded from animation, even when called from an encapsulating animation block.

Recipe: Fading a View In and Out

At times, you want to add information to your screen that overlays your view but does not of itself do anything. For example, you might show a top-scores list or some instructions or provide a context-sensitive tooltip. Recipe 4-6 demonstrates how to use a `UIView` animation block to fade a view into and out of sight. This recipe follows the most basic animation approach. It creates a view animation block that sets the `alpha` property.

Note how this code controls the behavior of the right bar button item. When tapped, it is immediately disabled until the animation concludes. The animation's completion block reenables the button and flips the button text and callback selector to the opposite state. This allows the button to toggle the animation from on to off and from off to back on.

Recipe 4-6   **Animating Transparency Changes to a View's** `Alpha` **Property**

```
- (void)fadeOut:(id)sender
{
    self.navigationItem.rightBarButtonItem.enabled = NO;
    [UIView animateWithDuration:1.0f
            animations:^{
                // Here's where the actual fade out takes place
                imageView.alpha = 0.0f;
            }
            completion:^(BOOL done){
                self.navigationItem.rightBarButtonItem.enabled = YES;
                self.navigationItem.rightBarButtonItem =
                    BARBUTTON(@"Fade In", @selector(fadeIn:));
            }];
}
```

```
- (void)fadeIn:(id)sender
{
    self.navigationItem.rightBarButtonItem.enabled = NO;
    [UIView animateWithDuration:1.0f
            animations:^{
                // Here's where the fade in occurs
                imageView.alpha = 1.0f;
            }
            completion:^(BOOL done){
                self.navigationItem.rightBarButtonItem.enabled = YES;
                self.navigationItem.rightBarButtonItem =
                    BARBUTTON(@"Fade Out", @selector(fadeOut:));
            }];
}
```

Get This Recipe's Code

To find this recipe's full sample project, point your browser to https://github.com/erica/iOS-7-Cookbook and go to the folder for Chapter 4.

Recipe: Swapping Views

The UIView animation block doesn't limit you to a single change. Place as many animation differences as needed in an animation block. Recipe 4-7 combines size transformations with transparency changes to create a more compelling animation. It does this by adding several directives simultaneously to the animation block. This recipe performs five actions at a time. It zooms and fades one view into place while zooming out and fading away another and then exchanges the two in the subview array list.

You'll want to prepare the back object for its initial animation by shrinking it and making it transparent. When the swap: method first executes, that view will be ready to appear and zoom to size. As with Recipe 4-6, the completion block reenables the bar button on the right, allowing successive presses.

Recipe 4-7   **Combining Multiple View Changes in Animation Blocks**

```
@implementation TestBedViewController
- (void)swap:(id)sender
{
    self.navigationItem.rightBarButtonItem.enabled = NO;
    [UIView animateWithDuration:1.0f
      animations:^{
        frontObject.alpha = 0.0f;
        backObject.alpha = 1.0f;
```

```
        frontObject.transform = CGAffineTransformMakeScale(0.25f, 0.25f);
        backObject.transform = CGAffineTransformIdentity;
        [self.view exchangeSubviewAtIndex:0
            withSubviewAtIndex:1];
    }
  completion:^(BOOL done){
        self.navigationItem.rightBarButtonItem.enabled = YES;

        // Swap the view references
        UIImageView *tmp = frontObject;
        frontObject = backObject;
        backObject = tmp;
    }];
}
```

Get This Recipe's Code

To find this recipe's full sample project, point your browser to https://github.com/erica/iOS-7-Cookbook and go to the folder for Chapter 4.

Recipe: Flipping Views

Transitions extend `UIView` animation blocks to add even more visual flair. Several transition styles do just what their names suggest. You can flip views to their backs and curl views up and down in the manner of the Maps application. Recipe 4-8 demonstrates how to include these transitions in your interfaces.

Here's a list of the set of transitions in iOS 7.0. You can see that there are four flips, two curls, a cross dissolve, and a "do nothing" no-op choice:

- `UIViewAnimationOptionTransitionNone`

- `UIViewAnimationOptionTransitionFlipFromLeft`

- `UIViewAnimationOptionTransitionFlipFromRight`

- `UIViewAnimationOptionTransitionFlipFromTop`

- `UIViewAnimationOptionTransitionFlipFromBottom`

- `UIViewAnimationOptionTransitionCurlUp`

- `UIViewAnimationOptionTransitionCurlDown`

- `UIViewAnimationOptionTransitionCrossDissolve`

Recipe 4-8 uses the block-based `transitionFromView:toView:duration:options:completion:` API. This method replaces a view by removing it from its superview and adding the new view to the initial view's parent. It animates this over the supplied duration, using the transition specified in the options flags. Recipe 4-8 uses a flip-from-left transition, although you can use any of the other transitions as desired.

The related `transitionWithView:duration:options:animations:completion:` method provides even more flexibility. It takes an animations block as a parameter, allowing for a completely custom transition. You can use it to create shrink/grow, flip, and other complex view transition animations.

If you use constraints (see Chapter 5), you must redefine them as well. Removing a subview invalidates and removes from the superview all constraints that refer to that view.

Recipe 4-8   Using Transitions with `UIView` Animations

```
- (void)flip:(id)sender
{
    self.navigationItem.rightBarButtonItem.enabled = NO;
    UIView *toView = fromPurple ? maroon : purple;
    UIView *fromView = fromPurple ? purple : maroon;
    [UIView transitionFromView: fromView
            toView: toView
            duration: 1.0f
            options: UIViewAnimationOptionTransitionFlipFromLeft
            completion: ^(BOOL done){
                self.navigationItem.rightBarButtonItem.enabled = YES;
                fromPurple = !fromPurple;
                CENTER_VIEW(self.view, toView);
            }];
}
```

Get This Recipe's Code

To find this recipe's full sample project, point your browser to https://github.com/erica/iOS-7-Cookbook and go to the folder for Chapter 4.

Recipe: Using Core Animation Transitions

In addition to `UIView` animations, iOS supports Core Animation as part of its Quartz Core framework. The Core Animation API offers highly customizable animation solutions for your iOS applications. Specifically, it offers built-in transitions that provide the same kind of view-to-view changes available in Recipe 4-8, as well as a vast wealth of other fundamental animation possibilities that are beyond the scope of this chapter.

> **Note**
>
> With each release of iOS, Apple has continually added more Core Animation functionality to UIKit directly. iOS 7 introduced key frame animation to `UIView`—a feature that previously required Core Animation.

Core Animation transitions expand your `UIView` animation vocabulary with just a few small differences in implementation. `CATransitions` work on layers rather than on views. Layers are the Core Animation rendering surfaces associated with `UIViews`. When working with Core Animation, you apply `CATransitions` to a view's default layer (`myView.layer`) rather than to the view itself.

With these transitions, you don't set your parameters through `UIView` the way you do with `UIView` animation. Create a Core Animation object, set its parameters, and then add the parameterized transition to the layer:

```
CATransition *animation = [CATransition animation];
animation.delegate = self;
animation.duration = 1.0f;
animation.type = kCATransitionMoveIn;
animation.subtype = kCATransitionFromTop;

// Perform some kind of view exchange or removal here

[myView.layer addAnimation:animation forKey:@"move in"];
```

An animation uses both a type and a subtype. The type specifies the kind of transition used. The subtype sets its direction. Together the type and subtype tell how the views should act when you apply the animation to them.

Core Animation transitions are distinct from the `UIViewAnimationTransitions` discussed in previous recipes. Cocoa Touch offers four types of Core Animation transitions, which are highlighted in Recipe 4-9. The available types are cross-fades, pushes (one view pushes another offscreen), reveals (one view slides off another), and covers (one view slides onto another). The last three types enable you to specify the direction of motion for the transition by using subtypes. For obvious reasons, cross-fades do not have a direction, and they do not use subtypes.

Because Core Animation is part of the Quartz Core framework, you must use `@import QuartzCore` in your code when using these features.

> **Note**
>
> Apple's Core Animation features 2D and 3D routines built around Objective-C classes. These classes provide graphics rendering and animation for your iOS and Mac applications. Core Animation avoids many low-level development details associated with, for example, direct Open GL, while retaining the simplicity of working with hierarchical view layers.

Recipe 4-9   **Animating Transitions with Core Animation**

```
- (void)animate:(id)sender
{
    // Set up the animation
    CATransition *animation = [CATransition animation];
    animation.delegate = self;
    animation.duration = 1.0f;

    switch ([(UISegmentedControl *)self.navigationItem.titleView
                selectedSegmentIndex])
    {
        case 0:
            animation.type = kCATransitionFade;
            break;
        case 1:
            animation.type = kCATransitionMoveIn;
            break;
        case 2:
            animation.type = kCATransitionPush;
            break;
        case 3:
            animation.type = kCATransitionReveal;
            break;
        default:
            break;
    }
    animation.subtype = kCATransitionFromLeft;

    // Perform the animation
    [self.view exchangeSubviewAtIndex:0 withSubviewAtIndex:1];
    [self.view.layer addAnimation:animation forKey:@"animation"];
}
```

Get This Recipe's Code

To find this recipe's full sample project, point your browser to https://github.com/erica/iOS-7-Cookbook and go to the folder for Chapter 4.

Recipe: Bouncing Views as They Appear

Apple often uses two animation blocks, one called after another finishes, to add bounce to animations. For example, a view might zoom into a view a bit more than needed and then use a second animation to bring that enlarged view down to its final size. Bounces add a little more life to your animation sequences, providing an extra physical touch.

When calling one animation after another, be sure that the animations do not overlap. The easiest way to ensure this is to use a nested set of animation blocks with chained animations in the completion blocks. Recipe 4-10 uses this approach to bounce views slightly larger than their end size and then shrink them back down to the desired frame.

This recipe uses two simple `typedef`s to simplify the declaration of each animation and completion block. Notice that the animation block stages that do the work of scaling the view in question are defined in order. The first block shrinks the view, the second one zooms it extra large, and the third restores it to its original size.

The completion blocks go the opposite way. Because each block depends on the one before it, you must create them in reverse order. Start with the final side effects and work your way back to the original. In Recipe 4-10, `bounceLarge` depends on `shrinkBack`, which in turn depends on `reenable`. This reverse definition can be a bit tricky to work with, but it certainly beats laying out all your code in nested blocks.

The sample project for this recipe contains an additional helper class (`AnimationHelper`), which wraps the behavior you see in Recipe 4-10 in a slightly less-awkward package. As Recipe 4-10 demonstrates, trying to layout an animation sequence backward, so each bit can be referenced by the item that called it, gets very clumsy very fast.

The helper class builds the whole block sequence and returns animation blocks similar to those in Recipe 4-10, which are ready to be executed and contain embedded completion blocks.

Recipe 4-10   **Bouncing Views**

```
typedef void (^AnimationBlock)(void);
typedef void (^CompletionBlock)(BOOL finished);

- (void)bounce
{
    // Prepare for animation
    self.navigationItem.rightBarButtonItem.enabled = NO;
    bounceView.transform = CGAffineTransformMakeScale(0.0001f, 0.0001f);
    bounceView.center = RECTCENTER(self.view.bounds);

    // Define the three stages of the animation in forward order
    AnimationBlock makeSmall = ^(void){
        bounceView.transform = CGAffineTransformMakeScale(0.01f, 0.01f);};
    AnimationBlock makeLarge = ^(void){
        bounceView.transform = CGAffineTransformMakeScale(1.15f, 1.15f);};
    AnimationBlock restoreToOriginal = ^(void) {
        bounceView.transform = CGAffineTransformIdentity;};

    // Create the three completion links in reverse order
    CompletionBlock reenable = ^(BOOL finished) {
        self.navigationItem.rightBarButtonItem.enabled = YES;};
    CompletionBlock shrinkBack = ^(BOOL finished) {
```

```
    [UIView animateWithDuration:0.3f
        animations:restoreToOriginal completion:reenable];};
CompletionBlock bounceLarge = ^(BOOL finished){
    [NSThread sleepForTimeInterval:0.5f]; // wee pause
    [UIView animateWithDuration:0.3f
        animations:makeLarge completion:shrinkBack];};

// Start the animation
[UIView animateWithDuration: 0.1f
    animations:makeSmall completion:bounceLarge];
}
```

Get This Recipe's Code

To find this recipe's full sample project, point your browser to https://github.com/erica/iOS-7-Cookbook and go to the folder for Chapter 4.

Recipe: Key Frame Animations

While nested animation blocks and completion blocks can be used to create fairly advanced animations, the complexity can become overwhelming quickly. In iOS 7, Apple introduced key frame animations to UIKit, powerful animations that are suited for advanced needs. These animations vastly simplify creating complex effects such as the bounce in Recipe 4-10. Key frame animations previously required diving into Core Animation, but now, this powerful animation tool is available directly from `UIView`.

In traditional key frame animation, you provide the important frames of the animation sequence and their expected timestamps within the animation, and the system is responsible for rendering all the *in-between* frames to provide for a smooth animation. The simplest form of key frame animation is simply providing the start and end frames and letting the animation system handle the rest.

To use key frame animation with `UIView`, begin a key frame animation block with `animateKeyframesWithDuration:delay:options:animations:completion:`. Within the animation block, set each important reference frame—or, in this case, each animatable `UIView` property—along with the start time and duration of that specific frame with `addKeyframeWithRelativeStartTime:relativeDuration:animations:`. The key frame animation blocks will animate in sequence at the appropriate times and durations.

One critical difference from between key frame and other animation methods: With key frame animation, start times and durations range between 0.0 and 1.0, indicating the percentage of progress through the animation. 0.0 represents the beginning of the overall animation, and 1.0 represents the end of the complete animation. For a 2-second animation, a start time of 0.5 corresponds to 1 full second into the animation.

Recipe 4-11 replicates the functionality of Recipe 4-10, this time using key frame animations. No helper class is required, and the code is significantly easier to write, understand, and manage.

Recipe 4-11   **Key Frame Animation**

```
- (void)bounce
{
    // Prepare for animation
    self.navigationItem.rightBarButtonItem.enabled = NO;
    bounceView.transform = CGAffineTransformMakeScale(0.0001f, 0.0001f);
    bounceView.center = RECTCENTER(self.view.bounds);

    // Begin the key frame animation
    [UIView animateKeyframesWithDuration:0.6
        delay:0.0
        options:UIViewKeyframeAnimationOptionCalculationModeCubic
        animations:^{
            // Implied first key frame - current view (tiny)
            // Second key frame - make view big
            [UIView addKeyframeWithRelativeStartTime:0.0
                relativeDuration:0.5
                animations:^{
                    bounceView.transform =
                        CGAffineTransformMakeScale(1.15f, 1.15f);
                }];

            // Third key frame - shrink to normal
            [UIView addKeyframeWithRelativeStartTime:0.5
                relativeDuration:0.5
                animations:^{
                    bounceView.transform =
                        CGAffineTransformIdentity;
                }];
        }
        completion:^(BOOL finished) {
            [self enable:YES];
        }];
}
```

Get This Recipe's Code

To find this recipe's full sample project, point your browser to https://github.com/erica/iOS-7-Cookbook and go to the folder for Chapter 4.

Recipe: Image View Animations

In addition to displaying static pictures, the `UIImageView` class supports built-in animation sequences. After loading an array of image cels, you can tell instances to animate them. Recipe 4-12 shows how.

Start by creating an array populated by individual images loaded from files and assign this array to the `UIImageView` instance's `animationImages` property. Set `animationDuration` to the total loop time for displaying all the images in the array. Finally, begin animating by sending the `startAnimating` message. (There's a matching `stopAnimating` method available for use as well.)

After you add the animating image view to your interface, you can place it into a single location, or you can animate it just as you would animate any other `UIView` instance.

Recipe 4-12   **Using** `UIImageView` **Animation**

```
NSMutableArray *butterflies = [NSMutableArray array];

// Load the butterfly images
for (int i = 1; i <= 17; i++)
    [butterflies addObject:[UIImage imageWithContentsOfFile:
        [[NSBundle mainBundle]
            pathForResource: [NSString stringWithFormat:@"bf_%d", i]
            ofType:@"png"]]];

// Create the view
UIImageView *butterflyView = [[UIImageView alloc]
    initWithFrame:CGRectMake(40.0f, 300.0f, 100.0f, 51.0f)];

// Set the animation cells and duration
butterflyView.animationImages = butterflies;
butterflyView.animationDuration = 0.75f;
[butterflyView startAnimating];

// Add the view to the parent
[self.view addSubview:butterflyView];
```

Get This Recipe's Code

To find this recipe's full sample project, point your browser to https://github.com/erica/iOS-7-Cookbook and go to the folder for Chapter 4.

Summary

UIViews provide the components your users see and interact with. As this chapter shows, even in their most basic form, UIViews offer incredible flexibility and power. You have discovered how to use views to build up elements on a screen, retrieve views by tag or name, and introduce eye-catching animation. Here's a collection of thoughts about the recipes you saw in this chapter that you might want to consider before moving on:

- When you're dealing with multiple views, hierarchy should always remain in your mind. Use your view hierarchy vocabulary to take charge of your views and always present the proper visual context to your users.

- Don't let the Core Graphics/UIKit center dichotomy stand in your way. Use functions that help you move between these structures to produce the results you need, especially when you're working with simple views that don't use transforms.

- Make friends with tags, whether numeric or custom nametags. They provide immediate access to views in the same way that a program's symbol table provides access to variables. They are not evil or wrong, and they can play a useful role in your development vocabulary.

- Take control of transforms. They're just math. Transforms shouldn't keep you from retrieving information about your views, whether determining the current rotation or scaling value, or the position of your view's corners. Transforms provide incredible power in many iOS development arenas, and the recipes in this chapter add tweaks that ensure that the information and control you need are ready to use when you need them.

- Blocks are wonderful. Use them to simplify your life, your code, and your animations.

- Animate everything. Animations don't have to be loud, splashy, or badly designed. The iOS SDK's strong animation support enables you to add smooth transitions between user tasks. The iOS experience is characterized by subtle, short, smooth transitions.

- Much of this chapter focuses on direct view hierarchies and placement, for when you take charge of view layout yourself. Read about declarative constraints and Auto Layout in Chapter 5 for a better, more powerful way to manage your view layouts.

View Constraints

Auto Layout revolutionizes the way developers create user interfaces (UIs). It provides a flexible and powerful system that describes how views and their content relate to each other and to the superviews they occupy. In contrast to the manually managed frame geometry, springs and struts of the past, this technology offers incredible control over layout and a wider range of customization. Apple is driving developers to adopt this technology with new device screen sizes and new APIs that vary the UI dynamically at runtime. Before the advent of Auto Layout, handling these scenarios was difficult or even impossible.

With Auto Layout, laying out views is as straightforward as describing the relationships between views and letting iOS do the hard work of placing the views appropriately. In addition, when you define relationships and dynamic layout properties of views rather than hard code origins and sizes, view objects will behave and react correctly to orientation changes, differing device sizes or aspect ratios, and even the varying sizes of labels due to localization or the preferences of the user with Dynamic Type.

This chapter introduces code-level Auto Layout constraint development. Constraints define how views relate to one another and to the windows and superviews they occupy. iOS processes these constraints to define the actual frame geometry of each view.

> **Note**
>
> Auto Layout is a deep and expansive topic that can easily fill an entire book. It is covered only cursorily here. For a comprehensive look at Auto Layout with vastly deeper analysis and examples, including use within Interface Builder (IB), take a look at the latest edition of Erica Sadun's *Auto Layout Demystified*, also published by Addison-Wesley.

What Are Constraints?

Constraints are rules that allow you to describe your view layout to iOS. They limit how views relate to each other and specify how they may be laid out. With constraints, you can say "these items are always lined up in a horizontal row" or "this item resizes itself to match the height of that item." Constraints provide a layout language that you add to views to describe geometric relationships.

iOS takes charge of meeting those demands via a constraint satisfaction system. The rules must make sense. A view cannot be both to the left *and* to the right of another view. One of the key challenges when working with constraints is ensuring that the rules are rigorously consistent. When your rules fail, they fail loudly. Xcode provides you with verbose logging that explains what may have gone wrong.

Another key challenge is making sure your rules are specific enough. An underconstrained interface can create unexpected results when faced with many possible layout solutions. You might request that one view lie to the right of the other, but unless you tell the system otherwise, you might end up with the right view at the top of the screen and the left view at the bottom—because that one rule doesn't say anything about vertical orientation.

Constraints allow you to design resolution-independent apps. A constraint-based application built for the 4-inch iPhone before the introduction of a future magical 5-inch iPhone should require no code updates to work on the new device.

For apps that will be localized, use constraints instead of creating individual XIBs for each language. One constraint-based XIB can adapt to multiple localizations.

Constraints can be declared both visually in IB and programmatically in your application source code. Xcode 5 introduced numerous Auto Layout improvements in IB. The IB approach is simple to use and easy to lay out. This chapter focuses on code. It offers code-centered examples that help you craft common view constraints in Objective-C.

Constraint Attributes

Constraints use a limited geometric vocabulary consisting of attributes and relations. Attributes are the "nouns" of the constraint system, describing positions within a view's alignment rectangle. Alignment rectangles will be described in detail shortly, but for the moment, you can think of them as being closely related to the view's frame. Relations are "verbs," specifying how the attributes compare to each other.

The attribute nouns speak to physical geometry. Constraints offer the following view attribute vocabulary:

- `left`, `right`, `top`, and `bottom`—The edges of a view's alignment rectangle on the left, right, top, and bottom of the view. These correspond to a view's minimum X, maximum X, minimum Y, and maximum Y values.

- `leading` and `trailing`—The leading and trailing edges of the view's alignment rectangle. In left-to-right (English-like) systems, these correspond to "left" (leading) and "right" (trailing). In right-to-left linguistic environments like Arabic or Hebrew, these roles flip: Right is leading, and left is trailing.

  When internationalizing your applications, always prefer leading and trailing over left and right. This allows your interfaces to flip properly when using right-to-left languages, like Arabic and Hebrew.

- `width` and `height`—The width and height of the view's alignment rectangle.

- **centerX** and **centerY**—The *x*-axis and *y*-axis centers of the view's alignment rectangle.

- **baseline**—The alignment rectangle's baseline, typically a fixed offset above its bottom attribute.

The relation verbs compare values. Constraint math is limited to three relations: setting equality or setting lower and upper bounds for comparison. You can use the following layout relations:

- **Less-than inequality**—NSLayoutRelationLessThanOrEqual

- **Equality**—NSLayoutRelationEqual

- **Greater-than inequality**—NSLayoutRelationGreaterThanOrEqual

You might not think that these three relations would give you much to work with. However, these three relations cover all the ground needed for user interface layout. They offer ways to set specific values and apply maximum and minimum limits.

Constraint Math

All constraints, regardless of how they are created, are essentially equations or inequalities in the following form:

$$y \ (relation) \ m * x + b$$

If you have a math background, you may have seen a form more like this, with *R* referring to the relation between *y* and the computed value on the right side:

$$y \ R \ m * x + b$$

y and *x* are view attributes of the kind you just read about above, such as width or centerY or top. Here, *m* is a constant scaling factor, and *b* is a constant offset. For example, you might say, "View B's left side should be placed 15 points to the right of View A's right side." The relation equation that results is something like this:

$$View \ B's \ left = View \ A's \ right + 15$$

Here, the relation is equality, the constant offset (*b*) is 15, and the scaling factor, or multiplier (*m*), is 1. We've taken care here to keep the equation above from looking like code because, as you'll see, you do not use code directly to declare your constraints in Objective-C.

Constraints do not have to use strict equalities. They can use inequality relations as well. For example, you might say, "View B's left side should be placed *at least* 15 points to the right of View A's right side," or

$$View \ B's \ left >= View \ A's \ right + 15$$

Offsets lets you place fixed gaps between items, and multipliers let you scale. Scaling is especially useful when laying out grid patterns, letting you multiply by the height of a view rather than just add a fixed distance to the next view.

The Laws of Constraints

Although you can think of constraints as hard "math," they're actually just preferences. iOS finds a layout solution that best matches your constraints; this solution may not always be unique. Here are a few basic facts about constraints:

- **Constraints are relationships, not directional.** You don't have to solve the right side to calculate the left side.

- **Constraints have priorities.** Priorities range numerically from 0 to 1,000. The Auto Layout system uses priorities to sort constraints. Higher priorities are always satisfied before lower priorities. A priority of 99 is always considered after a priority of 100. During layout, the system iterates through any constraints you have added, attempting to satisfy them all. Priorities come into play when deciding which constraint has less sway. The 99 priority constraint will be broken in favor of the 100 priority constraint if the two come into conflict.

  The highest priority you can assign is "required" (that is, `UILayoutPriorityRequired`) (value 1,000), which is also the default. A required priority should be satisfied exactly— for example, "This button is exactly this size." So, when you assign a different priority, you're actually attenuating that constraint's sway within the overall layout system.

  Even required priorities may be overridden when constraints come into conflict. Don't be shocked if your 100×100 view ends up being presented at 102×107 if your constraints aren't perfectly balanced. Table 5-1 details several priority presets and their values.

Table 5-1   **Priority Constants**

Type	Value
`UILayoutPriorityRequired` (default)	1,000
`UILayoutPriorityDefaultHigh`	750
`UILayoutPriorityDefaultLow`	250
`UILayoutPriorityFittingSizeLevel`	50

- **Constraints don't have any natural "order" outside priorities.** All constraints of the same priority are considered at the same time. If you need some constraint to take precedence, assign it a higher priority than the others.

- **Constraints can be approximated.** Optional constraints try to optimize their results. Consider the constraint "View 2's top edge should be at the same position as View 1's bottom edge." The constraint system attempts to squeeze these two views together by minimizing their distance. If other constraints prevent them from touching, the system places them as close as it can, minimizing the absolute distance between the two attributes.

- **Constraints can have cycles.** As long as all items are satisfied, it doesn't matter which elements refer to which. Don't sweat the cross-references. In this declarative system, circular references are okay, and you will not encounter infinite looping issues.

- **Constraints are animatable.** You can use `UIView` animation to gradually change from one set of constraints to another. In the animation block, call `layoutIfNeeded` after changing your constraints, and the views will animate from the previous constrained layout to the new layout.

- **Constraints can refer to view siblings.** You can align the center point of one view's subview with the center point of an entirely different view as long as both views have a common view ancestor. For example, you might create a complex text entry view and align its rightmost button's right attribute with the right attribute of an embedded image view below it. There's just one limitation here, which follows next.

- **Constraints should not cross bounds systems.** Don't cross into and out of scroll views, collection views, and table views for alignment. If there's some sort of content view with its own bounds system, you avoid hopping out of that to an entirely different bounds system in another view. Doing so may not crash your app, but it's not a good idea, and it's not well supported by Auto Layout.

- **Auto Layout may not play nicely with transforms.** Exercise care when mixing transforms with Auto Layout, especially those that include rotation.

- **Auto Layout does not work with iOS 7 UIKit Dynamics.** You can use Auto Layout *inside* any view that's affected by dynamic behaviors, but you cannot combine Auto Layout view placement with dynamic animator management.

- **Auto Layout works with iOS 7 motion effects.** The visual changes applied by `UIMotionEffect` instances won't disturb your underlying layout as they only affect the view's layer.

- **Constraints can fail at runtime.** If your constraints cannot be resolved (see the examples at the end of this chapter) and come into conflict, the runtime system chooses which constraints to disregard so it can present whatever view layout it can. This is usually ugly and nearly always not the visual presentation you intended. Auto Layout sends exhaustive descriptions of what went wrong to your Xcode console. Use these reports to fix your constraints and bring them into harmony with each other.

- **Badly formed constraints will interrupt application execution.** Unlike constraint conflicts, which produce error messages but allow your application to continue running, some constraint calls will actually crash your application through unhandled exceptions. For example, if you pass a constraint format string such as `@"V[view1]-|"` (which is missing a colon after the letter *V*) to a constraint creation method, you'll encounter a runtime exception:

```
Terminating app due to uncaught exception 'NSInvalidArgumentException', reason:
'Unable to parse constraint format'
```

This error cannot be detected during compilation; you must carefully check your format strings by hand. Designing constraints in IB helps avoid bad-typo scenarios.

- **A constraint must refer to at least one view.** You can create a constraint without any items and compile that code without warnings, but the code will raise an exception at runtime.

- **Beware of invalid attribute pairings.** You cannot legally match a view's left edge to another view's height. Invalid pairings raise runtime exceptions. Specifically, you shouldn't mix size attributes with edge attributes. You can generally guess which pairs are problematic because they make no sense.

> **Note**
>
> Working with constraints adds all sorts of wonderful and new ways to crash your apps at runtime. Take extreme care when developing and testing your constraint-based application and build tests to ensure that you check their operations in as many scenarios as possible. Let's hope that someone builds a constraint validator to catch, at least, simple typos like `@"H:[myView"`, a visual format constraint that is missing a closing square bracket.

Constraints and Frames

Auto Layout constraints work with the same underlying frame geometry introduced in Chapter 4, "Assembling Views and Animations." Constraints on views ultimately resolve to a frame. Much of the power of Auto Layout revolves around properly handling views with dynamic and varied content when laying out the UI. `UIView` supports two additional properties—intrinsic content size and alignment rectangles—that extend beyond the traditional frame geometry, allowing Auto Layout to construct the appropriate relationships between views.

Intrinsic Content Size

Under Auto Layout, a view's content plays as important a role in its layout as its constraints. This is expressed through each view's `intrinsicContentSize`. This method describes the minimum space needed to express the full content of the view without squeezing or clipping that data. It derives from the natural properties of the content each view presents.

For an image view, for example, this corresponds to the size of the image it presents. A larger image requires a larger intrinsic content size. For a label, this varies with its font and the amount of text. As the font changes, the label's intrinsic content height varies. As the text length grows or shrinks in conjunction with the selected font, the label's intrinsic content width adjusts to match.

A view's intrinsic size allows Auto Layout to best match a view's frame to its natural content. Avoiding an underconstrained or ambiguous layout generally requires setting two attributes in each axis. When a view has an intrinsic content size, that size accounts for one of the two attributes. You can, for example, place a text-based control or an image view in the center of its parent, and its layout will not be ambiguous. The intrinsic content size plus the location combine for a fully specified placement. In reality, the intrinsic content size is resolved to actual constraints by the layout system.

When you change a view's contents, call `invalidateIntrinsicContentSize` to let Auto Layout know to recalculate at its next layout pass.

Compression Resistance and Content Hugging

Two properties impact how Auto Layout considers the intrinsic content size. As the name suggests, *compression resistance* refers to the way a view protects its content. A view with a high compression resistance fights against shrinking. It won't allow that content to clip. The *content hugging* priority refers to the way a view prefers to avoid extra padding around its core content or stretching of that core content (as with an image view that uses a scaled content mode). These priorities can be set for each axis on a view (via `setContentCompressionResistance-Priority:forAxis:` and `setContentHuggingPriority:forAxis:`).

Alignment Rectangles

Constraints take a different approach to frames than do traditional manual layout. Frames describe where to place views on the screen and how big those views will be. When laying out views, constraints use a related geometric element called an *alignment rectangle*.

As developers create complex views, they may introduce visual ornamentation such as shadows, exterior highlights, reflections, and engraving lines. As they do, these features usually become attached as subviews or sublayers. As a consequence, a view's frame, its full extent, grows as items are added.

Unlike frames, a view's alignment rectangle is limited to a core visual element. Its size remains unaffected as new items join the primary view. Consider Figure 5-1 (left). It depicts a view with an attached shadow and badge, which is placed behind and offset from the main element. When laying out this view, you want Auto Layout to focus on aligning just the core element.

Figure 5-1   A view's alignment rectangle (center) refers strictly to the core visual element to be aligned, without embellishments.

The center image in Figure 5-1 shows the view's alignment rectangle. This rectangle excludes all ornamentation, such as a drop shadow and badge. It's the part of the view you want Auto Layout to consider when it does its work.

Contrast this with the rectangle shown in the right image in Figure 5-1. This version includes all the visual ornamentation, extending the view's bounds beyond the area that should be considered for alignment. This rectangle encompasses all the view's visual elements. These ornaments could potentially throw off a view's alignment features (for example, its center, bottom, and right) if they were considered during layout.

By laying out views based on alignment rectangles instead of the frame, Auto Layout ensures that key information like a view's edges and center are properly considered during layout.

Declaring Alignment Rectangles

When building ornamented views, such as image views with built-in shadows, you should report geometry details to Auto Layout. Implementing the `alignmentRectForFrame:` method allows your views to declare accurate alignment rectangles when they use ornamentation such as shadows or reflections.

This method takes one argument: a frame. This argument refers to the destination frame that the view will inhabit; think of the rectangle on the right in Figure 5-1. That frame will encompass the entire view, including any ornamentation attached to the view. It's up to you to provide an accurate representation of the alignment rectangle with respect to that destination frame and your view's embedded elements.

Your method returns a `CGRect` value that specifies the rectangle for your view's core visual geometry, as the center rectangle in Figure 5-1 does. This is typically the main visual object's frame and excludes any ornamentation views you have added as subviews or into your view's layer as sublayers.

When planning for arbitrary transformations, make sure to implement `frameForAlignment-Rect:` as well. This method describes the inverse relationship, producing the resulting fully ornamented frame (for example, Figure 5-1, right image) when passed a constrained alignment rectangle (for example, Figure 5-1, center image). You extend the bounds to include any ornamentation items in your view, scaling them to the alignment rectangle passed to this method.

Creating Constraints

The `NSLayoutConstraint` class lets you create constraints in two ways. You can use a rather long method call to constrain one item's attribute to another, explaining how these attributes relate, or you can apply a rather nifty visual formatting language to specify how items are laid out along vertical and horizontal lines.

This section demonstrates both approaches, allowing you to see what they look like and how they are used. Remember this: Regardless of how you build your constraints, they all produce "*y* relation *mx + b*" results. All constraints are members of the `NSLayoutConstraint` class, no matter how you create them.

Basic Constraint Declarations

The `NSLayoutConstraint`'s class method `constraintWithItem:attribute:relatedBy:`
`toItem:attribute:multiplier:constant:` (*gesundheit!*) creates a single constraint at a time.
These constraints relate one item to another.

The creation method produces a strict *view.attribute R view.attribute * multiplier + constant* relation, where *R* is an equal-to (==), a greater-than-or-equal-to (>=), or a less-than-or-equal-to (<=)
relation.

Consider the following example:

```
[self.view addConstraint:
    [NSLayoutConstraint
        constraintWithItem:textfield
        attribute:NSLayoutAttributeCenterX
        relatedBy:NSLayoutRelationEqual
        toItem:self.view
        attribute:NSLayoutAttributeCenterX
        multiplier:1.0f
        constant:0.0f]];
```

This call adds a new constraint to a view controller's view (`self.view`). It horizontally center-aligns a text field within this view. It does this by setting an equality relation (`NSLayoutRelationEqual`) between the two views' horizontal centers
(`NSLayoutAttributeCenterX` attributes). The multiplier here is 1, and the offset
constant is 0. This relates to the following equation:

$$[textfield]'s\ centerX = ([self.view]'s\ centerX * 1) + 0$$

It basically says, "Please ensure that my view's center and the text field's center are co-aligned
at their *X* positions." The `UIView`'s `addConstraint:` method adds that constraint to the view,
where it is stored with any other constraints in the view's `constraints` property.

Visual Format Constraints

The preceding section shows you how to create single constraint relations. A second
`NSLayoutConstraint` class method builds constraints using a text-based visual format
language. Think of it as ASCII art for Objective-C nerds. Here's a simple example:

```
[self.view addConstraints: [NSLayoutConstraint
    constraintsWithVisualFormat:@"V:[leftLabel]-15-[rightLabel]"
    options:0
    metrics:nil
    views:NSDictionaryOfVariableBindings(leftLabel, rightLabel)]];
```

This request creates all the constraints that satisfy the relation or relations specified in the visual format string. These strings, which you will see in many examples in following sections, describe how views relate to each other along the horizontal (H) or vertical (V) axis. This example basically says, "Ensure that the right label appears 15 points below the left label."

Note several things about how this constraints formatting example is created:

- The axis is specified first as a prefix, either `H:` or `V:`.

- The variable names for views appear in square brackets in the strings.

- The fixed spacing appears between the two as a number constant, `-15-`.

- This example does not use any format options (the `options` parameter), but here is where you would specify whether the alignment is done left to right, right to left, or according to the leading-to-trailing direction for a given locale, discussed earlier in this chapter.

- The metrics dictionary, also not used in this example, lets you supply constant numbers into your constraints without having to create custom formats. For example, if you want to vary the spacing between these two text labels, you could replace `15` with a metric name (for example, `labelOffset` or something like it) and pass that metric's value in a dictionary. Set the name as the key, the value as an `NSNumber`. Passing dictionaries (for example, `@{@"labelOffset", @15}`) is a lot easier than creating a new format `NSString` instance for each width you might use.

- The `views:` parameter does not, despite its name, pass an array of views. It passes a dictionary of variable bindings. This dictionary associates variable name strings with the views they represent. This indirection allows you to use developer-meaningful symbols like `leftLabel` and `rightLabel` in your format strings.

Building constraints with formats strings always creates an array of results. Some format strings are quite complex, and others are simple. It's not always easy to guess how many constraints will be generated from each string. Be aware that you will need to add the entire collection of constraints to satisfy the format string that you processed.

Variable Bindings

When working with visual constraints, the layout system needs to be able to associate view names like `leftLabel` and `rightLabel` with the actual views they represent. Enter variable bindings, via a handy macro defined in `NSLayoutConstraint.h`, which is part of the UIKit headers.

The `NSDictionaryOfVariableBindings()` macro accepts an arbitrary number of local variable arguments. As you can see in the earlier example, these need not be terminated with a nil. The macro builds a dictionary from the passed variables, using the variable names as keys and the actual variables as values. For example, this function call:

```
NSDictionaryOfVariableBindings(leftLabel, rightLabel)
```

builds this dictionary:

```
@{@"leftLabel":leftLabel, @"rightLabel":rightLabel}
```

If you'd rather not use the variable bindings macro, you can easily create a dictionary by hand and pass it to the visual format constraints builder.

Format Strings

The format strings you pass to create constraints follow a basic grammar, which is specified as follows:

```
(<orientation>:)? (<superview><connection>)? <view>(<connection><view>)*
(<connection><superview>)?
```

The question marks refer to optional items, and the asterisk refers to an item that may appear zero or more times. Although daunting to look at, these strings are actually quite easy to construct. The next sections offer an introduction to format string elements and provide copious examples of their use.

Orientation

You start with an optional orientation—either H: for horizontal or V: for vertical alignment. This specifies whether the constraint applies left and right or up and down. If omitted, the orientation defaults to horizontal. Consider this constraint: "H:[view1][view2]". It says to place View 2 directly to the right of View 1. The H specifies the alignment that the constraint follows. Figure 5-2 (left) shows an interface that uses this rule.

The following is an example of a vertical layout: "V:|[view1]-20-[view2]-20-[view3]". It leaves a gap of 20 points below View 1 before placing View 2, followed again by a 20-point gap before View 3. Figure 5-2 (right) shows what this might look like.

Without further constraints, these views are severely underconstrained. Auto Layout will do what it thinks you want, but it's often wrong. In the left image, you should also constrain the vertical layout. In this case, both views are aligned to the top of the superview. In the image to the right, the horizontal layout should be specified—aligning each view to the left, abutting the superview.

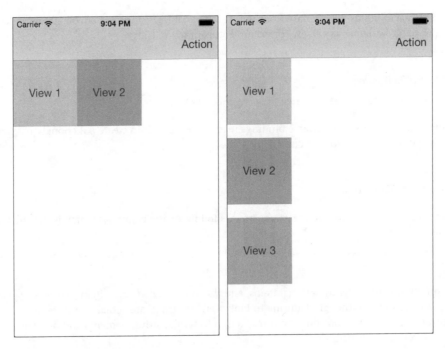

Figure 5-2   Layout results for `"H:[view1][view2]"` (left) and `"V:|[view1]-20-[view2]-20-[view3]"` (right).

Here are the horizontal and vertical constraints, respectively, that were used in separate executions to create the images shown in Figure 5-2:

```
[self.view addConstraints:[NSLayoutConstraint
    constraintsWithVisualFormat:@"H:[view1][view2]"
    options:0 metrics:nil
    views:NSDictionaryOfVariableBindings(view1, view2)]];
```

and:

```
[self.view addConstraints:[NSLayoutConstraint
    constraintsWithVisualFormat:@"V:|[view1]-20-[view2]-20-[view3]"
    options:0 metrics:nil
    views:NSDictionaryOfVariableBindings(view1, view2, view3)]];
```

Note the use of the vertical bar (|) near the beginning in the format string above. The vertical bar always refers to the superview. You see it only at the beginning or ending of format strings. At the beginning, it appears just after the horizontal or vertical specifier (`"V:|..."` or `"H:|..."`). At the end, it appears just before the terminal quote (`"...|"`). In iOS 7, skipping the vertical bar in this example will cause the views to appear under the status and navigation bars.

> **Note**
>
> During debugging, you can use the `constraintsAffectingLayoutForAxis:` view method to retrieve all the constraints that affect either the horizontal or vertical layout access. Do not ship code with this method. It is not intended for deployment use, and Apple makes it clear that it is not App Store–safe.

Connections

Place connections between view names to specify the way a layout flows. An empty connection (in other words, one that has been omitted) means "follow on directly."

The first constraint you saw for Figure 5-2, `"H:[view1][view2]"`, uses an empty connection. There's nothing specified between the square brackets of View 1 and the brackets of View 2. This tells the constraint to place View 2 directly to the right of View 1.

A hyphen (-) indicates a small fixed space. The constraint `"H:[view1]-[view2]"` uses a hyphen connection. This constraint leaves a standard (as defined by Apple) gap between View 1 and View 2, as shown in Figure 5-3.

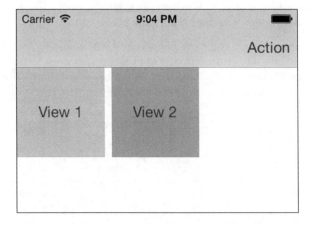

Figure 5-3   `"H:[view1]-[view2]"` adds a spacer connection.

Place a numeric constant between hyphens to set an exact gap size. The constraint `"H:[view1]-30-[view2]"` adds a 30-point gap between the two views, as shown in Figure 5-4. This is visibly wider than the small default gap produced by the single hyphen.

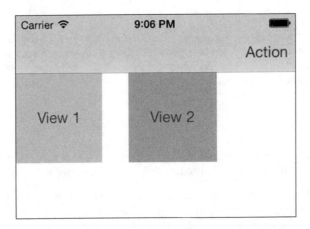

Figure 5-4   `"H:[view1]-30-[view2]"` uses a fixed-size gap of 30 points, producing a noticeably wider space.

The format `"H:|[view1]-[view2]|"` specifies a horizontal layout that starts with the super-view. The superview is immediately followed by the first view, then a spacer, the second view, and then the superview, which you can see in Figure 5-5.

This constraint left-aligns View 1 and right-aligns View 2 with the superview. To accomplish this, something has to give. Either the left view or the right view must resize to meet these constraints. When we ran the test app for this edition, it happened to be View 1 that adjusted, which is what you see in Figure 5-5. In the previous edition, it happened to be View 2.

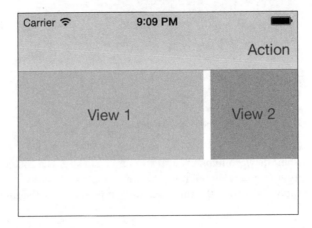

Figure 5-5   `"H:|[view1]-[view2]|"` tells both views to hug the edges of their superview. With a fixed-size gap between them, at least one of the views must resize to satisfy the constraint.

Often, you don't want to bang up right against the superview edges. A similar constraint, `"H:|-[view1]-[view2]-|"`, leaves an edge inset between the edges of the superview and the start of View 1 and end of View 2 (see Figure 5-6).

These gaps follow standard IB/Cocoa Touch layout rules and have not yet been exposed in specifics via the iOS API. The inset gaps at the edges are normally slightly larger than the default view-to-view gaps. You can see the gap size differences in the view layout created from this constraint in Figure 5-6.

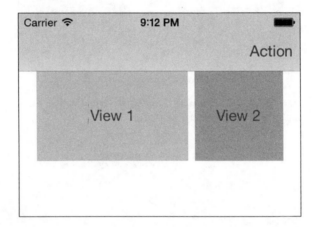

Figure 5-6   `"H:|-[view1]-[view2]-|"` introduces edge insets between the views and their superviews.

If your goal is to add a flexible space between views, there's a way to do that, too. Add a relation rule between the two views (for example, `"H:|-[view1]-(>=0)-[view2]-|"`) to allow the two views to retain their sizes and be separate while maintaining gaps at their edges with the superview, as shown in Figure 5-7. This rule, which equates to "at least 0 points distance," provides a more flexible way to let the views spread out. It is recommended to use a small number here so that you don't inadvertently interfere with a view's other geometry rules.

These constraints are not, of course, limited to just one or two views. You can easily stick in a third, fourth, or more. Consider this constraint: `"H:|-[view1]-[view2]-(>=5)-[view3]-|"`. It adds a third view, separated from the other two views by a flexible space. Figure 5-8 shows what this might look like.

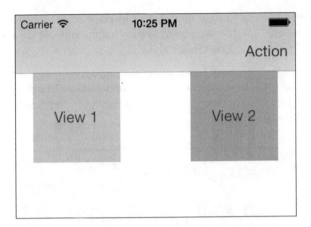

Figure 5-7   `"H:|-[view1]-(>=0)-[view2]-|"` uses a flexible space between the two views, allowing them to separate, while maintaining their sizes.

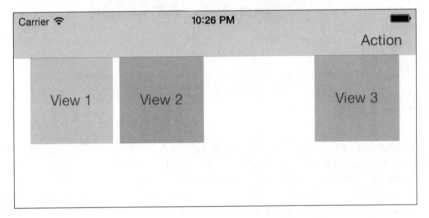

Figure 5-8   `"H:|-[view1]-[view2]-(>=5)-[view3]-|"` demonstrates a rule that includes three views.

Predicates

The last two examples in the previous section uses relationship rules with comparisons. These are also called *predicates*, an affirmation of the way a relation works between view elements. Predicates appear in parentheses. For example, you might specify that the size of a view is at least 50 points by using the following format:

```
[view1(>=50)]
```

This predicate relates to a single view. Notice that it is included within the view's square brackets rather than as part of a connection between views. You're not limited to a single request. For example, you might use a similar approach to let a view's size range between 50 and 70 points. When adding compound predicates, separate the parts of your rule with commas:

```
[view1(>=50, <=70)]
```

Relative relation predicates allow your views to grow. If you want your view to expand across a superview, tell it to size itself to some value greater than zero. The following rule stretches a view horizontally across its superview, allowing only for edge insets at each side:

```
H:|-[view1(>=0)]-|
```

Figure 5-9 shows what this constraint looks like when rendered.

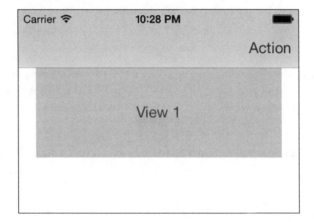

Figure 5-9   "`H:|-[view1(>=0)]-|`" adds a flexibility predicate to the view, letting it stretch across its parent. Edge insets offset it slightly from the superview's sides.

When using an equality relationship (`==`), you can skip the double-equals in your format predicates. For example `[view1(==120)]` is equivalent to `[view1(120)]`, and `[view1]-(==50)-[view2]` is the same as `[view1]-50-[view2]`.

Metrics

When you don't know a constant's value (like 120 or 50) a priori, use a metrics dictionary to provide the value. This dictionary is passed as one of the parameters to the constraint creation method. Here is an example of a format string that uses a metric stand-in:

```
[view1(>=minwidth)]
```

The `minwidth` stand-in must map to an `NSNumber` value in the passed metric dictionary. For more examples of metric use, refer to Recipe 5-2's `constrainSize:` method. It demonstrates how to use metrics, using values from an associated dictionary in its constraints.

View-to-View Predicates

Predicates aren't limited to numeric constants. You can relate a view's size to another view, for example, to ensure that it's no bigger than that view in the layout. This example limits View 2's extent to no bigger than that of View 1, along the axis that the constraint is currently using:

```
[view2(<=view1)]
```

You can't do a lot more with format strings and view-to-view comparisons. If you want to establish more complex relationships, like those between centers, tops, and heights, skip the visual format strings and use the item constraint constructor instead.

Priorities

Each constraint may specify an optional priority by adding an at sign (@) and a number or metric. For example, you can say that you want a view to be 500 points wide but that the request has a relatively low priority:

```
[view1(500@10)]
```

You place priorities after predicates. Here's an example of a layout format string with an embedded priority:

```
[view1]-(>=50@30)-[view2]
```

Format String Summary

Table 5-2 summarizes format string components used to create constraints with the `constraintsWithVisualFormat:options:metrics:views:` class method of `NSLayoutConstraint`.

Table 5-2   **Visual Format Strings**

Type	**Format**	**Example**
Horizontal or vertical arrangement	`H:` `V:`	`V:[view1]-15-[view2]` Puts View 2's top 15 points below View 1's bottom.
Views	`[item]`	`[view1]` The view bindings dictionary matches the bracketed name to a view instance.

Type	Format	Example
Superview	`|`	`H:|[view1]|` Make View 1's width size to that of the superview.

Relations	`==`
	 `<=`
	 `>=`
		`H:[view1]-(>=20)-[view2]`
		 Set View 2's leading edge at least 20 points from View 1's trailing edge.

Metrics	`metric`	`H:[view1(<=someWidth)]`
		 `V:[view1]-mySpacing-[view2]`
		 Metrics are keys. `someWidth` and `mySpacing` must map to `NSNumber` values in the passed metrics dictionary.

Flush alignment	`[item][item]`	`H:[view1][view2]` Sets View 1's trailing edge flush with View 2's leading edge.
Flexible space	`[item]-(>=0)-[item]`	`[view1]-(>=0)-[view2]` Views can stretch apart as needed, "at least zero points apart."
Fixed space	`[item]-[item]`	`[view1]-[view2]` Leave a small system-defined fixed space (8 points) between the two views.
Custom Fixed space	`[item]-gap-[item]`	`V:[view1]-20-[view2]` Set View 1's bottom 20 points from view 2's top.
Fixed width or height	`[item(size)]` `[item(==size)]`	`[view1(50)]` Set View 1's extent to exactly 50 points along this axis.

Minimum and maximum width/height	`[item(>=size)]`
	 `[item(<=size)]`
		`[view1(>=50)]`
		 `[view1(<=50)]`
		 Limit View 1's minimum or maximum size for this axis.

Match width/height with another view	`[item(==item)]`
	 `[item(<=item)]`
	 `[item(>=item)]`
		`[view1(==view2)]`
		 Matches View 1 to View 2's size along the axis.

Flush with superview	`|[item]` `[item]|`	`V:|[view1]` Set View 1's top flush with the superview's top.

Type	Format	Example
Inset from superview	`|-[item]` `[item]-|`	`|-[view1]` Place a fixed space (20 points) between the superview and View 1 along this axis.
Custom inset from super-view	`|-gap-[item]` `[item]-gap-|`	`H:|-15-[view1]` Insets the view from the superview by 15 points on the leading edge.
Priority (from 0 to 1000)	`@value`	`[view1(<=50@20)]` Gives View 1 a maximum size of 50 points along this axis, with a very low priority (20).

Aligning Views and Flexible Sizing

It is supremely easy to align views with constraints:

- The four format strings `"H:|[self]"`, `"H:[self]|"`, `"V:|[self]"`, and `"V:[self]|"`, respectively, produce left, right, top, and bottom alignment.

- Add a predicate with a sizing relation, and these format strings become stretch to left, stretch to right, and so on: `"H:|[self(>0)]"`, `"H:[self(>0)]|"`, `"V:|[self(>0)]"`, and `"V:[self(>0)]|"`.

- A second vertical pipe adds full-axis resizing, allowing views to stretch from left to right or top to bottom: `"H:|[self(>0)]|"` or `"V:|[self(>0)]|"`.

- Add edge indicators to inset the stretches: `"H:|-[self(>0)]-|"` or `"V:|-[self(>0)]-|"`.

Constraint Processing

The display of a view's content proceeds through multiple phases. Prior to Auto Layout, two phases were provided: the layout phase and the rendering phase. Auto Layout augments the traditional two phases by inserting a third phase to kick off the process—the constraint phase.

The layout phase allows a developer to modify the frame geometry of the view's subviews by implementing the `layoutSubviews` method. When iOS determines the view's layout to be invalid, this method will be called, and you can update the manual layout of your subviews. You can also request a relayout by calling `setNeedsLayout` or `layoutIfNeeded`. The first method is a polite request that allows iOS to coalesce multiple layout requests and call `layoutSubviews` at an appropriate time in the future. The second method is more demanding, resulting in a nearly immediate call to `layoutSubviews`.

The rendering phase allows for complete control over the drawing of the view's UI by implementing the `drawRect:` method. When the view's display is invalidated, the method will be called, allowing for low-level drawing into the view. If the rendering needs to be changed, you can request the view to be redrawn with `setNeedsDisplay` or `setNeedsDisplayInRect:`, triggering a call to `drawRect:`.

With Auto Layout, the *constraints phase* occurs prior to the preceding phases. This phase allows for the creation or updating of Auto Layout constraints through implementation of the `updateConstraints` method. Much like the layout phase, the constraints phase can be invalidated by iOS or manually, using the similarly named and behaving `setNeedsUpdate-Constraints` and `updateConstraintsIfNeeded` methods.

Importantly, any view that overrides `updateConstraints` should also call `[super update-Constraints]` as the final step before returning from the method. After the constraints phase completes, Auto Layout has appropriately calculated the frame geometry of all the subviews in the view.

When any of the above phases resolves, the next phase is triggered. The constraints phase triggers the layout phase, which triggers the rendering phase.

The progression of phases provides a somewhat unexpected opportunity. The layout phase occurs after the constraint phase has calculated and set all the frame geometry based on the assigned constraints. Once in the layout phase, you can make changes to a view's frame geometry that may contradict the directions set forth by your constraints. You can even use the constraint-generated geometry to make decisions on the final layout of a view. Since the constraints have already been calculated, changing the frame geometry will "stick" until the next constraints phase. Be careful that your layout pass does not make constraint changes and trigger an infinite loop of layout and update constraint calls.

Most of the time, these hooks are not needed. On rare occasions when they're required, the level of flexibility and control provided is empowering.

Managing Constraints

All constraints belong to the `NSLayoutConstraint` class, regardless of how they are created. When working with constraints, you can add them to your views either one by one, using `addConstraint:`, or in arrays by using the `addConstraints:` instance method (notice the *s* at the end of the name). In day-to-day work, you often deal with collections of constraints that are stored in arrays.

A constraint always has a natural home in the nearest common ancestor of the views involved in the constraint. A constraint must be installed on a common ancestor of every view referenced. A self-installing category method on `NSLayoutConstraint` can programmatically determine the natural and correct view for installation. This is left as an exercise for the reader.

Constraints can be added and removed at any time. The two methods, `removeConstraint:` and `removeConstraints:`, enable you to remove one or an array of constraints from a given view. Because these methods work on objects, they might not do what you expect them to do when you attempt to remove constraints.

Suppose, for instance, that you build a center-matching constraint and add it to your view. You cannot then build a second version of the constraint with the same rules and expect to remove the first by using a standard removeConstraint: call. They are equivalent constraints, but they are not the *same* constraint. Here's an example of this conundrum:

```
[self.view addConstraint:
    [NSLayoutConstraint constraintWithItem:textField
        attribute:NSLayoutAttributeCenterX
        relatedBy:NSLayoutRelationEqual
        toItem:self.view
        attribute:NSLayoutAttributeCenterX
        multiplier:1.0f constant:0.0f]];
[self.view removeConstraint:
    [NSLayoutConstraint constraintWithItem:textField
        attribute:NSLayoutAttributeCenterX
        relatedBy:NSLayoutRelationEqual
        toItem:self.view
        attribute:NSLayoutAttributeCenterX
        multiplier:1.0f constant:0.0f]];
```

Executing these two method calls ends up as follows: The self.view instance contains the original constraint, and the attempt to remove the second constraint is ignored. Removing a constraint not held by the view has no effect.

You have two choices for resolving this. First, you can hold onto the constraint when it's first added by storing it in a local variable. Here's what that would look like, more or less:

```
NSLayoutConstraint *myConstraint =
    [NSLayoutConstraint constraintWithItem:textField
        attribute:NSLayoutAttributeCenterX
        relatedBy:NSLayoutRelationEqual
        toItem:self.view
        attribute:NSLayoutAttributeCenterX
        multiplier:1.0f constant:0.0f];
[self.view addConstraint:myConstraint];

// later
[self.view removeConstraint:myConstraint];
```

Or you can use a method (see Recipe 5-1) that compares constraints and removes a constraint that numerically matches the one you pass.

Knowing whether your constraints will be static (used for the lifetime of your view) or dynamic (updated as needed) helps you decide which approach you need. If you think you might need to remove a constraint in the future, either hold on to it via a local variable so that you can later remove it from your view or use workarounds like the one detailed in Recipe 5-1.

Here are some basic points you need to know about managing constraints:

- You can add constraints to and remove constraints from view instances. The core methods are `addConstraint:` (`addConstraints:`), `removeConstraint:` (`removeConstraints:`), and `constraints`. The last of these returns an array of constraints stored by the view.

- Constraints are not limited to container views. Nearly any view can work with constraints. (A class method, `requiresConstraintBasedLayout`, specifies whether classes depend on constraints to operate properly.)

- If you want to code a subview with constraints, switch off the subview's `translatesAutoresizingMaskIntoConstraints` property. You'll see this in action in the sample code for this chapter and further discussed in the "Debugging Your Constraints" section toward the end of this chapter.

Recipe: Comparing Constraints

All constraints use a fixed structure in the following form, along with an associated priority:

*view1.attribute (relation) view2.attribute * multiplier + constant*

Each element of this equation is exposed through a constraint's object properties—namely `priority`, `firstItem`, `firstAttribute`, `relation`, `secondItem`, `secondAttribute`, `multiplier`, and `constant`. These properties make it easy to compare two constraints.

Views store and remove constraints as objects. If two constraints are stored in separate memory locations, they're considered unequal, even if they describe the same conditions. To allow your code to add and remove constraints on-the-fly without storing those items locally, use comparisons.

Recipe 5-1 introduces three methods. The `constraint:matches:` method compares the properties in two constraints to determine whether they match. Note that only the equation is considered, not the priority (although you can easily add this if you want), because two constraints describing the same conditions are essentially equivalent, regardless of the priority a developer has assigned to them.

The two other methods, `constraintMatchingConstraint:` and `removeMatching-Constraint:`, respectively, help locate the first matching constraint stored within a view and remove that matching constraint.

In Recipe 5-1, a view is bounced from the top and bottom of its superview by removing a matched constraint and replacing it with a new constraint. In this case, it might be easier to store this constraint as an instance variable for simple removal at a future point. That said, the ability to retrieve and remove a similar constraint can be very useful when working with many constraints or removing specific constraints dynamically.

> **Note**
>
> Recipe 5-1 implements a `UIView` class category. This category is used and expanded throughout this chapter to provide a set of utility methods you can use in your own applications.

Recipe 5-1   **Comparing Constraints**

```objc
@implementation UIView (ConstraintHelper)
 // This ignores any priority, looking only at y (R) mx + b
- (BOOL)constraint:(NSLayoutConstraint *)constraint1
    matches:(NSLayoutConstraint *)constraint2
{
    if (constraint1.firstItem != constraint2.firstItem) return NO;
    if (constraint1.secondItem != constraint2.secondItem) return NO;
    if (constraint1.firstAttribute != constraint2.firstAttribute) return NO;
    if (constraint1.secondAttribute != constraint2.secondAttribute) return NO;
    if (constraint1.relation != constraint2.relation) return NO;
    if (constraint1.multiplier != constraint2.multiplier) return NO;
    if (constraint1.constant != constraint2.constant) return NO;

    return YES;
}

// Find first matching constraint (priority ignored)
- (NSLayoutConstraint *)constraintMatchingConstraint:
    (NSLayoutConstraint *)aConstraint
{
    for (NSLayoutConstraint *constraint in self.constraints)
        if ([self constraint:constraint matches:aConstraint])
            return constraint;

    for (NSLayoutConstraint *constraint in self.superview.constraints)
        if ([self constraint:constraint matches:aConstraint])
            return constraint;
    return nil;
}

// Remove constraint
- (void)removeMatchingConstraint:(NSLayoutConstraint *)aConstraint
{
    NSLayoutConstraint *match =
        [self constraintMatchingConstraint:aConstraint];
    if (match)
    {
        [self removeConstraint:match];
        [self.superview removeConstraint:match];
```

```
      }
  }
  @end
```

Animating Constraints

Recipe 5-1 moves a view by removing a constraint that aligns the view to the top or bottom and adding an inverse constraint. The following snippet from Recipe 5-1 moves the view from the top to the bottom:

```
NSLayoutConstraint * constraintToMatch =
    [NSLayoutConstraint constraintWithItem:view1
        attribute:NSLayoutAttributeTop
        relatedBy:NSLayoutRelationEqual toItem:self.view
        attribute:NSLayoutAttributeTop multiplier:1.0f constant:0];
[self.view removeMatchingConstraint: constraintToMatch];

NSLayoutConstraint * updatedConstraint =
    [NSLayoutConstraint constraintWithItem:view1
        attribute:NSLayoutAttributeBottom
        relatedBy:NSLayoutRelationEqual toItem:self.view
        attribute:NSLayoutAttributeBottom multiplier:1.0f constant:0];
[self.view addConstraint:updatedConstraint];

[self.view layoutIfNeeded];
```

The `layoutIfNeeded` in the final line forces Auto Layout to reprocess the constraints and render the updated view. Unfortunately, this transition occurs abruptly. Animating the change in constraints is actually quite simple. All that is required is calling `layoutIfNeeded` from within an animation block:

```
[UIView animateWithDuration:0.3 animations:^{
    [self.view layoutIfNeeded];
}];
```

The view will now animate from the top to bottom and back in the same manner as if you specified the actual origin values within the animation block manually.

Recipe: Creating Fixed-Size Constrained Views

When working with constraints, start thinking about your views in a new way. You don't just set a frame and expect the view to stay where and how big you left it. Constraint layout uses an entirely new set of assumptions.

Here's how you might have written a utility method to create a label before Auto Layout:

```
- (UILabel *)createLabelTheOldWay:(NSString *)title
{
    UILabel *label = [[UILabel alloc]
        initWithFrame:CGRectMake(0.0f, 0.0f, 100.0f, 100.0f)];
    label.textAlignment = NSTextAlignmentCenter;
    label.text = title;

    return label;
}
```

With Auto Layout, you approach code-level view creation in a new way. Your code adds constraints that adjust the item's size and position instead of building a fixed frame and setting its center.

Disabling Autoresizing Constraints

Autoresizing refers to the struts-and-springs layout tools used in IB and to the autoresizing flags, like UIViewAutoresizingFlexibleWidth, used in code. When you lay out a view's resizing behavior with these approaches, that view should not be referred to in any constraints you define.

When you move into the constraints world, you start by disabling a view property that automatically translates autoresizing masks into constraints. As a rule, you either enable this, allowing the view to participate in the constraint system via its autoresizing mask, or you disable it entirely and manually add your own constraints.

The constraints-specific property in question is translatesAutoresizingMaskInto-Constraints. Setting this to NO ensures that you can add constraints without conflicting with the automated system. This is pretty important. If you fail to disable the property and start using constraints, you'll generate constraint conflicts. The autoresizing constraints won't coexist peacefully with ones you write directly. Here's an example of a runtime error message that results:

```
2012-06-24 15:34:54.839 HelloWorld[64834:c07] Unable to simultaneously satisfy
constraints.
Probably at least one of the constraints in the following list is one you don't
want. Try this: (1) look at each constraint and try to figure out which you don't
expect; (2) find the code that added the unwanted constraint or constraints and
fix it. (Note: If you're seeing NSAutoresizingMaskLayoutConstraints that you don't
understand, refer to the documentation for the UIView property
```

```
translatesAutoresizingMaskIntoConstraints)
(
    "<NSLayoutConstraint:0x6ec9430 H:[UILabel:0x6ec5210(100)]>",
    "<NSAutoresizingMaskLayoutConstraint:0x6b8e2a0
        h=--& v=--& H:[UILabel:0x6ec5210(0)]>"
)
Will attempt to recover by breaking constraint
<NSLayoutConstraint:0x6ec9430 H:[UILabel:0x6ec5210(100)]>
Break on objc_exception_throw to catch this in the debugger.
```

Choosing between autoresizing layout and constraints layout is an important part of your coding work.

Starting Within View Bounds

The first method in Recipe 5-2, `constrainWithinSuperviewBounds`, requests that a view be placed entirely within its superview's bounds. It creates four constraints to ensure this. One requires that the view's left side be at or to the right of the superview's left side, another that the view's top be at or below the superview's top, and so forth.

The reason for creating this method is that in a loosely constrained system, it's entirely possible that your views will disappear offscreen with negative origins. This method basically says, "Please respect the (0,0) origin and the size of the superview when placing my subviews."

In most real-world development, this set of constraints is not normally necessary. Such constraints are particularly useful, however, when you're first getting started and want to explore constraints from code. They allow you to test small constraint systems while ensuring that the views you're exploring remain visible so that you can see how they relate to each other.

In addition, as you get up to speed with constraints, you'll probably want to add some sort of debugging feedback to let you know where your views end up once your primary view loads and your constraints fire. Consider adding the following loop to your `viewDidAppear:` method:

```
- (void)viewDidAppear:(BOOL)animated
{
    [super viewDidAppear:animated];
    for (UIView *subview in self.view.subviews)
        NSLog(@"View (%d) location: %@",
            [self.view.subviews indexOfObject:subview],
                NSStringFromCGRect(subview.frame));
}
```

Constraining Size

Recipe 5-2's second method, `constrainSize:`, fixes a view's extent to the `CGSize` you specify. This is a common task when working with constraints. You cannot just set the frame the way you're used to setting it. And, again, remember that your constraints are requests, not specific layouts. If your constraints are not well formed, your 100-point-wide text field may end up 107 points wide in deployment—or worse.

You can define constraints that request a specific width or height for a given view, but the sizes for the two constraints can't be known ahead of time. The method is meant for use across a wide variety of views. Therefore, the sizes are passed to the constraint as *metrics*. Metrics basically act as numeric constraint variables.

These particular constraints use two metric names: `"theHeight"` and `"theWidth"`. The names are completely arbitrary. As a developer, you specify the strings, which correspond to keys in the `metrics:` parameter dictionary. You pass this dictionary as an argument in the constraint-creation call. When working with metrics, each key must appear in the passed dictionary, and its value must be an `NSNumber`.

The two constraints in this method set the desired horizontal and vertical sizes for the view. The format strings (`"H:[self(theWidth)]"` and `"V:[self(theHeight)]"`) tell the constraint system how large the view should be along each axis.

A third method, `constrainPosition:`, builds constraints that fix the origin of a view within its superview. Note the use of the constant to create offsets in this method.

Putting It Together

Using these tools, we can replace the old label-creation method above with a much more powerful variant that uses Auto Layout:

```
- (UILabel *)createLabelWithTitle:(NSString *)title
    onParent:(UIView *)parentView
{
    UILabel *label = [[UILabel alloc] init];
    label.textAlignment = NSTextAlignmentCenter;
    label.text = title;

    // Add label to parent view so constraints can be added
    [parentView addSubview:label];

    // Turn off automatic translation of autoresizing masks into constraints
    label.translatesAutoresizingMaskIntoConstraints = NO;

    // Add constraints
    [label constrainWithinSuperviewBounds];

    [label constrainSize:CGSizeMake(100, 100)];
```

```
    [label constrainPosition:CGPointMake(50, 50)];

    return label;
}
```

Before adding constraints that relate the label above and its superview, the label must be added as a subview to the parent view. Adding constraints to views or relating views that are not in the same view hierarchy will result in unexpected behavior at best or, more likely, a runtime crash. This may require a slight reordering in your view instantiation, such as the variations above that include adding the label to the parent view.

No matter how you restructure your view generation, maintain the following order: Create your views, add them to their parent view, disable the automatic translation of autoresizing masks, and, finally, apply the necessary constraints.

Recipe 5-2   Basic Size Constraints

```
@implementation UIView (ConstraintHelper)
- (void)constrainWithinSuperviewBounds
{
    if (!self.superview) return;

    // Constrain the top, bottom, left, and right to
    // within the superview's bounds
    [self.superview addConstraint:[NSLayoutConstraint
        constraintWithItem:self attribute:NSLayoutAttributeLeft
        relatedBy:NSLayoutRelationGreaterThanOrEqual
        toItem:self.superview attribute:NSLayoutAttributeLeft
        multiplier:1.0f constant:0.0f]];
    [self.superview addConstraint:[NSLayoutConstraint
        constraintWithItem:self attribute:NSLayoutAttributeTop
        relatedBy:NSLayoutRelationGreaterThanOrEqual
        toItem:self.superview attribute:NSLayoutAttributeTop
        multiplier:1.0f constant:0.0f]];
    [self.superview addConstraint:[NSLayoutConstraint
        constraintWithItem:self attribute:NSLayoutAttributeRight
        relatedBy:NSLayoutRelationLessThanOrEqual
        toItem:self.superview attribute:NSLayoutAttributeRight
        multiplier:1.0f constant:0.0f]];
    [self.superview addConstraint:[NSLayoutConstraint
        constraintWithItem:self attribute:NSLayoutAttributeBottom
        relatedBy:NSLayoutRelationLessThanOrEqual
        toItem:self.superview attribute:NSLayoutAttributeBottom
        multiplier:1.0f constant:0.0f]];
}

- (void)constrainSize:(CGSize)aSize
```

```
{
    NSMutableArray *array = [NSMutableArray array];

    // Fix the width
    [array addObjectsFromArray:[NSLayoutConstraint
        constraintsWithVisualFormat:@"H:[self(theWidth@750)]"
        options:0 metrics:@{@"theWidth":@(aSize.width)}
        views:NSDictionaryOfVariableBindings(self)]];

    // Fix the height
    [array addObjectsFromArray:[NSLayoutConstraint
        constraintsWithVisualFormat:@"V:[self(theHeight@750)]"
        options:0 metrics:@{@"theHeight":@(aSize.height)}
        views:NSDictionaryOfVariableBindings(self)]];

    [self addConstraints:array];
}

- (void)constrainPosition:(CGPoint)aPoint
{
    if (!self.superview) return;

    NSMutableArray *array = [NSMutableArray array];

    // X position
    [array addObject:[NSLayoutConstraint constraintWithItem:self
        attribute:NSLayoutAttributeLeft relatedBy:NSLayoutRelationEqual
        toItem:self.superview attribute:NSLayoutAttributeLeft
        multiplier:1.0f constant:aPoint.x]];

    // Y position
    [array addObject:[NSLayoutConstraint constraintWithItem:self
        attribute:NSLayoutAttributeTop relatedBy:NSLayoutRelationEqual
        toItem:self.superview attribute:NSLayoutAttributeTop
        multiplier:1.0f constant:aPoint.y]];

    [self.superview addConstraints:array];
}
@end
```

Get This Recipe's Code

To find this recipe's full sample project, point your browser to https://github.com/erica/iOS-7-Cookbook and go to the folder for Chapter 5.

Recipe: Centering Views

To center views, associate their center properties (centerX and centerY) with the corresponding properties in their container. Recipe 5-3 introduces a pair of methods that retrieve a view's superview and apply the equality relation between their centers.

Notice that these constraints are added to a parent view and not the child view. This is because constraints cannot reference views outside their own subtree. Here's the error that's generated if you attempt to do otherwise:

```
2012-06-24 16:09:14.736 HelloWorld[65437:c07] *** Terminating app due to uncaught
 exception 'NSGenericException', reason: 'Unable to install constraint on view.
Does the constraint reference something from outside the subtree of the view?
That's illegal. constraint:<NSLayoutConstraint:0x6b6ebf0 UILabel:0x6b68e40.centerY
== UIView:0x6b64a00.centerY> view:<UILabel: 0x6b68e40; frame = (0 0; 0 0); text =
'View 1'; clipsToBounds = YES; userInteractionEnabled = NO; layer = <CALayer:
0x6b67220>>'
libc++abi.dylib: terminate called throwing an exception
```

Here are a couple of simple rules:

- When creating constraints, add them to the superview when the superview is mentioned, as either the first or second item of the constraint.

- When working with format strings, add to the superview when the string contains the superview vertical pipe symbol anywhere.

Recipe 5-3   Centering Views with Constraints

```
@implementation UIView (ConstraintHelper)
- (void)centerHorizontallyInSuperview
{
    if (!self.superview) return;

    [self.superview addConstraint:[NSLayoutConstraint
        constraintWithItem:self attribute:NSLayoutAttributeCenterX
        relatedBy:NSLayoutRelationEqual
        toItem:self.superview attribute:NSLayoutAttributeCenterX
        multiplier:1.0f constant:0.0f]];
}

- (void)centerVerticallyInSuperview
{
    if (!self.superview) return;

    [self.superview addConstraint:[NSLayoutConstraint
        constraintWithItem:self attribute:NSLayoutAttributeCenterY
        relatedBy:NSLayoutRelationEqual
```

```
            toItem:self.superview attribute:NSLayoutAttributeCenterY
            multiplier:1.0f constant:0.0f]];
}
@end
```

Get This Recipe's Code

To find this recipe's full sample project, point your browser to https://github.com/erica/iOS-7-Cookbook and go to the folder for Chapter 5.

Recipe: Setting Aspect Ratio

Constraint multipliers, the m of the $y = m * x + b$ equation, can help set aspect ratios for your views. Recipe 5-4 demonstrates how to do this by relating a view's height (y) to its width (x) and setting the m value to the aspect. Recipe 5-4 builds an NSLayoutRelationEqual relationship between the width and height of a view, using the aspect ratio as the multiplier.

The recipe applies its aspect updates by managing a fixed constraint, which it stores locally in an NSLayoutConstraint variable called aspectConstraint. Each time the user toggles the aspect from 16:9 to 4:3 or back, this recipe removes the previous constraint and creates and then stores another one. It builds this new constraint by setting the appropriate multiplier and then adds it to the view.

To allow the view's sides some flexibility, while keeping the view reasonably large, the createLabel method in this recipe does two things. First, it uses width and height predicates. These request that each side exceed 300 points in length. Second, it prioritizes its requests. These priorities are high (750) but not required (1000), so the constraint system retains the power to adjust them as needed. The outcome is a system that can change aspects in real time and dynamically change its layout definition at runtime.

For readability, the aspect ratio constraint creation is embedded in the code in Recipe 5-4, but it can easily be added to the ConstraintHelper category.

Aspect ratio constraints can also be used for great effect with images to maintain the natural image aspect ratio. A view's content mode may not sufficiently preserve its natural image aspect. Utilize the size property provided by UIImage to build a natural aspect ratio constraint by dividing its width by its height.

Recipe 5-4   **Creating Aspect Ratio Constraints**

```
- (UILabel *)createLabelWithTitle:(NSString *)title onParent:(UIView *)parentView
{
    UILabel *label = [[UILabel alloc] init];
    label.textAlignment = NSTextAlignmentCenter;
    label.text = title;
```

```objc
    label.backgroundColor = [UIColor greenColor];
    [parentView addSubview:label];

    // Turn off automatic translation of autoresizing masks into constraints
    label.translatesAutoresizingMaskIntoConstraints = NO;

    // Add constraints
    [label constrainWithinSuperviewBounds];
    [label addConstraints:[NSLayoutConstraint
        constraintsWithVisualFormat:@"H:[label(>=theWidth@750)]"
        options:0 metrics:@{@"theWidth":@300.0}
        views:NSDictionaryOfVariableBindings(label)]];
    [label addConstraints:[NSLayoutConstraint
        constraintsWithVisualFormat:@"V:[label(>=theHeight@750)]"
        options:0 metrics:@{@"theHeight":@300.0}
        views:NSDictionaryOfVariableBindings(label)]];
    [label centerInSuperview];

    return label;
}


- (void)toggleAspectRatio
{
    if (aspectConstraint)
        [self.view removeConstraint:aspectConstraint];

    if (useFourToThree)
        aspectConstraint = [NSLayoutConstraint
            constraintWithItem:view1
            attribute:NSLayoutAttributeWidth
            relatedBy:NSLayoutRelationEqual toItem:view1
            attribute:NSLayoutAttributeHeight
            multiplier:(4.0f / 3.0f) constant:0.0f];

    else
        aspectConstraint = [NSLayoutConstraint
            constraintWithItem:view1
            attribute:NSLayoutAttributeWidth
            relatedBy:NSLayoutRelationEqual toItem:view1
            attribute:NSLayoutAttributeHeight
            multiplier:(16.0f / 9.0f) constant:0.0f];

    [self.view addConstraint:aspectConstraint];
    useFourToThree = !useFourToThree;
}
```

> **Get This Recipe's Code**
>
> To find this recipe's full sample project, point your browser to https://github.com/erica/iOS-7-Cookbook and go to the folder for Chapter 5.

Recipe: Responding to Orientation Changes

A device's screen geometry may influence how you want to lay out interfaces. For example, a landscape aspect ratio may not provide enough vertical range to fit in all your content. Consider Figure 5-10. The portrait layout places the iTunes album art on top of the album name, the artist name, and a Buy button, with the album price. The landscape layout moves the album art to the left and places the album name, artist, and Buy button in the lower-right corner.

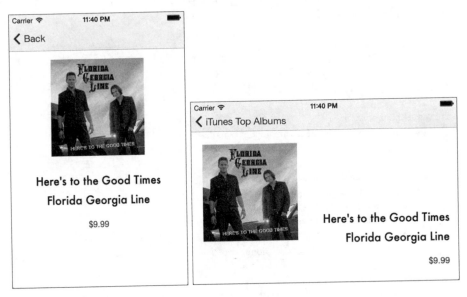

Figure 5-10   The same content in portrait and landscape layouts.

To accomplish this, your layout constraints must be orientation aware. The `updateView-ControllerConstraints` method in Recipe 5-5 refreshes your constraints, based on the current orientation. This includes removing all existing constraints and setting new constraints. Call this method in `willAnimateRotationToInterfaceOrientation:duration:`. This creates a smooth visual update that matches the animation of the rest of the interface. In addition, this rotation method occurs after the view controller's `interfaceOrientation` property has been set to the new orientation (unlike `willRotateToInterfaceOrientation:`

`duration:`). When interface orientation is evaluated in the update method to generate the appropriate constraints, it will be set correctly.

Recipe 5-5 uses a number of constraint macros that are detailed near the end of the chapter.

Recipe 5-5   **Updating View Constraints**

```
- (void)updateViewControllerConstraints
{
    [self.view removeConstraints:self.view.constraints];

    NSDictionary *bindings = NSDictionaryOfVariableBindings(
        imageView, titleLabel, artistLabel, button);

    if (IS_IPAD ||
        UIDeviceOrientationIsPortrait(self.interfaceOrientation) ||
        (self.interfaceOrientation == UIDeviceOrientationUnknown))
    {
        for (UIView *view in @[imageView,
            titleLabel, artistLabel, button])
        {
            CENTER_VIEW_H(self.view, view);
        }
        CONSTRAIN_VIEWS(self.view, @"V:|-80-[imageView]-30-\
            [titleLabel(>=0)]-[artistLabel]-15-[button]-(>=0)-|",
            bindings);
    }
    else
    {
        // Center image view on left
        CENTER_VIEW_V(self.view, imageView);

        // Lay out remaining views
        CONSTRAIN(self.view, imageView, @"H:|-[imageView]");
        CONSTRAIN(self.view, titleLabel, @"H:[titleLabel]-15-|");
        CONSTRAIN(self.view, artistLabel, @"H:[artistLabel]-15-|");
        CONSTRAIN(self.view, button, @"H:[button]-15-|");
        CONSTRAIN_VIEWS(self.view, @"V:|-(>=0)-[titleLabel(>=0)]\
            -[artistLabel]-15-[button]-|", bindings);

        // Make sure titleLabel doesn't overlap
        CONSTRAIN_VIEWS(self.view,
            @"H:[imageView]-(>=0)-[titleLabel]", bindings);
    }
}

// Catch rotation changes
```

```
- (void)willAnimateRotationToInterfaceOrientation:
    (UIInterfaceOrientation)toInterfaceOrientation
    duration:(NSTimeInterval)duration
{
    [super willAnimateRotationToInterfaceOrientation:
        toInterfaceOrientation duration:duration];
    [self updateViewControllerConstraints];
}
```

Get This Recipe's Code

To find this recipe's full sample project, point your browser to https://github.com/erica/iOS-7-Cookbook and go to the folder for Chapter 5.

Debugging Your Constraints

The most common problems you encounter when adding constraints programmatically are ambiguous and unsatisfiable layouts. Expect to spend a lot of time at the Xcode debugging console and don't be surprised when you see a large dump of information that starts with the phrase "Unable to simultaneously satisfy constraints."

iOS does its best at runtime to let you know which constraints could not be satisfied and which constraints it has to break in order to proceed. Often, it suggests a list of constraints that you should evaluate to see which item is causing the problem. This usually looks something like this:

```
Probably at least one of the constraints in the following list is one you don't
want. Try this: (1) look at each constraint and try to figure out which you don't
expect; (2) find the code that added the unwanted constraint or constraints and
fix it. (Note: If you're seeing NSAutoresizingMaskLayoutConstraints that you don't
understand, refer to the documentation for the UIView property
translatesAutoresizingMaskIntoConstraints)
(
    "<NSAutoresizingMaskLayoutConstraint:0x6e5bc90 h=-&- v=-&-
UILayoutContainerView:0x6e540f0.height == UIWindow:0x6e528a0.height>",
    "<NSAutoresizingMaskLayoutConstraint:0x6e5a5e0 h=-&- v=-&-
UINavigationTransitionView:0x6e55650.height ==
UILayoutContainerView:0x6e540f0.height>",
    "<NSAutoresizingMaskLayoutConstraint:0x6e592f0 h=-&- v=-&-
UIViewControllerWrapperView:0x6bb90d0.height ==
UINavigationTransitionView:0x6e55650.height - 64>",
    "<NSAutoresizingMaskLayoutConstraint:0x6e57b90 h=-&- v=-&-
UIView:0x6baef20.height == UIViewControllerWrapperView:0x6bb90d0.height>",
    "<NSAutoresizingMaskLayoutConstraint:0x6e5cd40 h=--- v=---
V:[UIWindow:0x6e528a0(480)]>",
```

```
    "<NSAutoresizingMaskLayoutConstraint:0x6bbe890 h=--& v=--&
UILabel:0x6bb3730.midY ==>",
    "<NSLayoutConstraint:0x6bb8cc0 UILabel:0x6bb3730.centerY ==
UIView:0x6baef20.centerY>"
)
```

If you get a message like this, most likely, you have forgotten to switch off `translatesAutoresizingMaskIntoConstraints` for one of your views. If you see an `NSAutoresizingMaskLayoutConstraint` listed, and it's associated with, for example, a `UILabel` that you're laying out (as is the case here), this is a big hint about where your problem lies. The two constraints that are causing the issue are highlighted in the preceding snippet.

In other cases, you might have required constraints that are simply in conflict with each other because one contradicts what the other one is saying. In the dump above, constraints required a view be both center-aligned and left-aligned. To keep going, the layout system had to make a choice. It decided to cancel the *y*-centering requirement, allowing the view to align with the top of its parent:

```
Will attempt to recover by breaking constraint
<NSLayoutConstraint:0x6e94250 UILabel:0x6b90e00.centerY ==
UIView:0x6b8ca50.centerY>
```

Although constraint dumps can be scary, certain strategies lend a hand. First, when working in code, develop your constraints a little at a time. This helps you determine when things start to break. Second, consider using the macros from the upcoming Listing 5-1. There's no reason to clutter up your code with "align with superview" and "set size to *n* by *m*" over and over again. Finally, if you're not required to set your constraints in code, consider using the IB tools provided to make your visual layout life easier.

Recipe: Describing Constraints

When developing and debugging constraints, you may find it useful to produce human-readable descriptions of arbitrary `NSLayoutConstraint`s. Recipe 5-6 builds concise strings that describe constraints as equations, as follows:

- `(1000)[UILabel:6bb32a0].right <= [self].right`
- `(750)[self].width == ([self].height * 1.778)`
- `(750)[UILabel:6bb32a0].leading == ([UILabel:6ed2e70].trailing + 60.000)`

This recipe transforms constraint instances into these textual presentations. It does so in the context of the view whose constraints are being considered (and hence the references to self and superview, in addition to specific subviews that are listed by class and memory address).

Notice that not every constraint includes two items. A constraint may refer only to itself (as in the second example, which sets its width as a multiplier of its height). In these cases, the `item2` property is invariably `nil`.

Recipe 5-6   **Describing Constraints**

```objc
@implementation UIView (ConstraintHelper)

// Return a string that describes an attribute
- (NSString *)nameForLayoutAttribute:(NSLayoutAttribute)anAttribute
{
    switch (anAttribute)
    {
        case NSLayoutAttributeLeft: return @"left";
        case NSLayoutAttributeRight: return @"right";
        case NSLayoutAttributeTop: return @"top";
        case NSLayoutAttributeBottom: return @"bottom";
        case NSLayoutAttributeLeading: return @"leading";
        case NSLayoutAttributeTrailing: return @"trailing";
        case NSLayoutAttributeWidth: return @"width";
        case NSLayoutAttributeHeight: return @"height";
        case NSLayoutAttributeCenterX: return @"centerX";
        case NSLayoutAttributeCenterY: return @"centerY";
        case NSLayoutAttributeBaseline: return @"baseline";
        case NSLayoutAttributeNotAnAttribute: return @"not-an-attribute";
        default: return @"unknown-attribute";
    }
}

// Return a name that describes a layout relation
- (NSString *)nameForLayoutRelation:(NSLayoutRelation)aRelation
{
    switch (aRelation)
    {
        case NSLayoutRelationLessThanOrEqual: return @"<=";
        case NSLayoutRelationEqual: return @"==";
        case NSLayoutRelationGreaterThanOrEqual: return @">=";
        default: return @"unknown-relation";
    }
}

// Describe a view in its own context
- (NSString *)nameForItem:(id)anItem
{
    if (!anItem) return @"nil";
    if (anItem == self) return @"[self]";
    if (anItem == self.superview) return @"[superview]";
    return [NSString stringWithFormat:@"[%@:%d]", [anItem class], (int) anItem];
}

// Transform the constraint into a string representation
```

```objc
- (NSString *)constraintRepresentation:(NSLayoutConstraint *)aConstraint
{
    NSString *item1 = [self nameForItem:aConstraint.firstItem];
    NSString *item2 = [self nameForItem:aConstraint.secondItem];
    NSString *relation =
        [self nameForLayoutRelation:aConstraint.relation];
    NSString *attr1 =
        [self nameForLayoutAttribute:aConstraint.firstAttribute];
    NSString *attr2 =
        [self nameForLayoutAttribute:aConstraint.secondAttribute];

    NSString *result;

    if (!aConstraint.secondItem)
    {
        result = [NSString stringWithFormat:@"(%4.0f) %@.%@ %@ %0.3f",
            aConstraint.priority, item1, attr1,
            relation, aConstraint.constant];
    }
    else if (aConstraint.multiplier == 1.0f)
    {
        if (aConstraint.constant == 0.0f)
            result = [NSString stringWithFormat:@"(%4.0f) %@.%@ %@ %@.%@",
                aConstraint.priority, item1, attr1,
                relation, item2, attr2];
        else
            result = [NSString stringWithFormat:
                @"(%4.0f) %@.%@ %@ (%@.%@ + %0.3f)",
                aConstraint.priority, item1, attr1, relation,
                item2, attr2, aConstraint.constant];
    }
    else
    {
        if (aConstraint.constant == 0.0f)
            result = [NSString stringWithFormat:
                @"(%4.0f) %@.%@ %@ (%@.%@ * %0.3f)",
                aConstraint.priority, item1, attr1, relation,
                item2, attr2, aConstraint.multiplier];
        else
            result = [NSString stringWithFormat:
                @"(%4.0f) %@.%@ %@ ((%@.%@ * %0.3f) + %0.3f)",
                aConstraint.priority, item1, attr1, relation,
                item2, attr2, aConstraint.multiplier,
                aConstraint.constant];
    }

    return result;
```

```
}

- (void)showConstraints
{
    NSString *viewName = [NSString stringWithFormat:
        @"[%@:%d]", [self class], (int) self];
    NSLog(@"View %@ has %d constraints",
        viewName, self.constraints.count);
    for (NSLayoutConstraint *constraint in self.constraints)
        NSLog(@"%@", [self constraintRepresentation:constraint]);
    printf("\n");
}

@end
```

| **Get This Recipe's Code**
| To find this recipe's full sample project, point your browser to https://github.com/erica/iOS-
| 7-Cookbook and go to the folder for Chapter 5.

Constraint Macros

Constraints provide reliable components for view layout. That said, in their native form, constraints are both overly verbose and fundamentally redundant. You end up implementing the same complex hard-to-read calls over and over again.

Debugging constraints is a real pain. Simple typos take too much effort, and constraints tend to be the same from app to app. A repository of predefined macros saves time and increases the readability and reliability of the view layout sections. Instead of centering a view inside another view and having to debug that layout each time you implement it, a single CENTER_VIEW macro does the job consistently each time.

Creating macros, as shown in Listing 5-1, shifts the work from producing exact constraint definitions to ensuring that constraints are consistent and sufficient across each entire view. These two conditions should form the focus of your view layout work.

Macros

Listing 5-1 shows a comprehensive set of macro definitions. These have been tested and are used in many recipes in this book, although they approach constraints in a fairly simple manner. Note that these macros do not return the constraints but actually add the constraints to the appropriate view. If you need to maintain access to newly created constraints for later removal, you can easily add macros that return the constraints or use the functionality in Recipe 5-1 to locate and remove constraints.

Another addition is not included in Listing 5-1 due to space limitations but is occasionally handy: variants that accept constraint constants. Such a variant can be particularly useful when aligning views to their parent and is trivial to add to your constraint macros library. You need to gauge the level of complexity and flexibility you need to expose in your constraint code and amend as necessary.

For the macro-averse, possible alternatives include using a function library or creating a constraint category on UIView. Decide what works best for your code style and layout needs and then build and refine your utility library over time.

Listing 5-1   **Constraint Macros**

```
// Prepare Constraint Compliance
#define PREPCONSTRAINTS(VIEW) \
    [VIEW setTranslatesAutoresizingMaskIntoConstraints:NO]

// Add a visual format constraint
#define CONSTRAIN(PARENT, VIEW, FORMAT) \
    [PARENT addConstraints:[NSLayoutConstraint \
        constraintsWithVisualFormat:(FORMAT) options:0 metrics:nil \
        views:NSDictionaryOfVariableBindings(VIEW)]]
#define CONSTRAIN_VIEWS(PARENT, FORMAT, BINDINGS) \
    [PARENT addConstraints:[NSLayoutConstraint  \
        constraintsWithVisualFormat:(FORMAT) options:0 metrics:nil \
        views:BINDINGS]]

// Stretch across axes
#define STRETCH_VIEW_H(PARENT, VIEW) \
    CONSTRAIN(PARENT, VIEW, @"H:|["#VIEW"(>=0)]|")
#define STRETCH_VIEW_V(PARENT, VIEW) \
    CONSTRAIN(PARENT, VIEW, @"V:|["#VIEW"(>=0)]|")
#define STRETCH_VIEW(PARENT, VIEW) \
    {STRETCH_VIEW_H(PARENT, VIEW); STRETCH_VIEW_V(PARENT, VIEW);}

// Center along axes
#define CENTER_VIEW_H(PARENT, VIEW) \
    [PARENT addConstraint:[NSLayoutConstraint \
        constraintWithItem:VIEW attribute: NSLayoutAttributeCenterX \
        relatedBy:NSLayoutRelationEqual \
        toItem:PARENT attribute:NSLayoutAttributeCenterX \
        multiplier:1.0f constant:0.0f]]
#define CENTER_VIEW_V(PARENT, VIEW) \
    [PARENT addConstraint:[NSLayoutConstraint \
        constraintWithItem:VIEW attribute: NSLayoutAttributeCenterY \
        relatedBy:NSLayoutRelationEqual \
        toItem:PARENT attribute:NSLayoutAttributeCenterY \
        multiplier:1.0f constant:0.0f]]
```

```
#define CENTER_VIEW(PARENT, VIEW) \
    {CENTER_VIEW_H(PARENT, VIEW); CENTER_VIEW_V(PARENT, VIEW);}


// Align to parent
#define ALIGN_VIEW_LEFT(PARENT, VIEW) \
    [PARENT addConstraint:[NSLayoutConstraint \
        constraintWithItem:VIEW attribute: NSLayoutAttributeLeft \
        relatedBy:NSLayoutRelationEqual \
        toItem:PARENT attribute:NSLayoutAttributeLeft \
        multiplier:1.0f constant:0.0f]]
#define ALIGN_VIEW_RIGHT(PARENT, VIEW)
    [PARENT addConstraint:[NSLayoutConstraint \
        constraintWithItem:VIEW attribute: NSLayoutAttributeRight \
        relatedBy:NSLayoutRelationEqual \
        toItem:PARENT attribute:NSLayoutAttributeRight \
        multiplier:1.0f constant:0.0f]]
#define ALIGN_VIEW_TOP(PARENT, VIEW)
    [PARENT addConstraint:[NSLayoutConstraint \
        constraintWithItem:VIEW attribute: NSLayoutAttributeTop \
        relatedBy:NSLayoutRelationEqual \
        toItem:PARENT attribute:NSLayoutAttributeTop \
        multiplier:1.0f constant:0.0f]]
#define ALIGN_VIEW_BOTTOM(PARENT, VIEW) \
    [PARENT addConstraint:[NSLayoutConstraint \
        constraintWithItem:VIEW attribute: NSLayoutAttributeBottom \
        relatedBy:NSLayoutRelationEqual \
        toItem:PARENT attribute:NSLayoutAttributeBottom \
        multiplier:1.0f constant:0.0f]]


// Set Size
#define CONSTRAIN_WIDTH(VIEW, WIDTH) \
    [VIEW addConstraint:[NSLayoutConstraint constraintWithItem:VIEW \
        attribute:NSLayoutAttributeWidth \
        relatedBy:NSLayoutRelationEqual toItem:nil \
        attribute:NSLayoutAttributeNotAnAttribute \
        multiplier:1.0f constant:WIDTH]];
#define CONSTRAIN_HEIGHT(VIEW, HEIGHT) \
    [VIEW addConstraint:[NSLayoutConstraint constraintWithItem:VIEW \
        attribute:NSLayoutAttributeHeight \
        relatedBy:NSLayoutRelationEqual toItem:nil \
        attribute:NSLayoutAttributeNotAnAttribute \
        multiplier:1.0f constant:HEIGHT]];


#define CONSTRAIN_SIZE(VIEW, HEIGHT, WIDTH) \
    {CONSTRAIN_WIDTH(VIEW, WIDTH); CONSTRAIN_HEIGHT(VIEW, HEIGHT);}
```

```
// Set Aspect
#define CONSTRAIN_ASPECT(VIEW, ASPECT) \
    [VIEW addConstraint:[NSLayoutConstraint \
        constraintWithItem:VIEW attribute:NSLayoutAttributeWidth \
        relatedBy:NSLayoutRelationEqual \
        toItem:VIEW attribute:NSLayoutAttributeHeight \
        multiplier:(ASPECT) constant:0.0f]]

// Item ordering
#define CONSTRAIN_ORDER_H(PARENT, VIEW1, VIEW2) \
    [PARENT addConstraints: [NSLayoutConstraint \
        constraintsWithVisualFormat: (@"H:["#VIEW1"]->=0-["#VIEW2"]")\
        options:0 metrics:nil \
        views:NSDictionaryOfVariableBindings(VIEW1, VIEW2)]]
#define CONSTRAIN_ORDER_V(PARENT, VIEW1, VIEW2) \
    [PARENT addConstraints:[NSLayoutConstraint \
        constraintsWithVisualFormat:(@"V:["#VIEW1"]->=0-["#VIEW2"]")
        options:0 metrics:nil
        views:NSDictionaryOfVariableBindings(VIEW1, VIEW2)]]
```

Summary

This chapter provides an introduction to iOS's Auto Layout features. Before you move on to the next chapter, here are a few thoughts to take along with you:

- You may be still thinking in terms of struts, springs, and flexible sizes, but Apple's Auto Layout system offers better control and tremendous power, with more extensible tools.

- IB provides an excellent set of layout tools. However, constraint-based interfaces in code are viable and easy to use. The layout system gives you excellent control over your views, regardless of whether you specify your constraints visually or programmatically.

- One of the great things about working with constraints is that you move away from specific-resolution solutions for your interfaces. Yes, your user experience on a tablet is likely to be quite different from that on a member of the iPhone family, but at the same time, these new tools let you design for different window (and possibly screen) sizes within the same mobile family. There's a lot of flexibility and power hidden within these simple rules.

- Start incorporating visual ornaments such as shadows into your regular design routine. Alignment rectangles ensure that your user interfaces will set up properly, regardless of any secondary view elements you add to your frames.

- Reserve visual format strings for general view layout and use view-to-view relations for detail specifics. Both approaches play important roles, and neither should be omitted from your design playbook.

6

Text Entry

Some might disparage the utility of text entry on a family of touch-based devices. After all, users can already convey a whole lot of information by using simple gestures. However, text plays an important role, especially as mobile users move away from the office and home for their daily computing interactions. Users need to enter and read characters onscreen for many reasons. Text allows users to sign in to accounts, view and reply to e-mail, specify URLs and read the web pages they refer to, and more. Apple's brilliant predictive keyboard transforms text entry into a simple and fairly reliable process; its classes and frameworks offer powerful ways to present and manipulate text from your applications.

iOS 7 could easily be considered the "text" update. Apple shed the heavy textures, user interface (UI) chrome, and shadows, now centering attention on the content. In many if not most cases, that content is text. This design focus, combined with the most significant update to the text layout and rendering engine since iOS's inception with the new Text Kit technology, reveals how important text is to the iOS ecosystem.

From presentation to input, Text Kit brings foundational changes to the text system. You have complete control over text rendering, including many attributes such as kerning and line spacing that previously required delving into the dark magic known as Core Text. The UIKit text and text entry controls are now built on top of Text Kit. Text Kit, in turn, is built on top of Core Text.

While a full investigation of the offerings of Text Kit is beyond the scope of this book, the flexibility and power provided are welcomed and worth exploring.

This chapter introduces text recipes that support a wide range of solutions. You'll read about controlling keyboards, making onscreen elements "text-aware," scanning text, formatting text, and editing text. This chapter provides handy recipes for common problems that you'll encounter while working with text entry.

Recipe: Dismissing a `UITextField` Keyboard

A commonly asked question about smaller devices and the `UITextField` control is "How do I dismiss the keyboard after the user finishes typing?" There's no built-in way to automatically detect that a user has stopped typing and then respond. Yet when users finish editing the contents of a `UITextField`, the keyboard really should go away. The iPad offers a keyboard-dismissal button, but the iPhone and iPod touch do not.

Fortunately, it takes little work to respond to the end of text field edits, regardless of platform. You do so by allowing users to tap Done and then resign first responder status. Resigning first responder moves the keyboard out of sight, as Recipe 6-1 shows. Here are a few key points about implementing this approach:

- **Setting the return key type to `UIReturnKeyDone` replaces the word *Return* with the word *Done*.** You can do this in Interface Builder's (IB's) Attributes inspector or by assignment to the text field's `returnKeyType` property. Using a Done-style return key tells the user *how* to finish editing rather than just relying on the fact that users have used a similar approach on nonmobile systems. Figure 6-1 shows a keyboard with a Done key.

Figure 6-1   Setting the name of the Return Key to Done (left) tells a user how to finish editing the field. Specify this directly in code or use IB's text field Attributes inspector to customize the way the text field looks and acts.

- **Be the delegate.** You set the text field's `delegate` property to your view controller, either in code or in IB by right-clicking the text field and making the assignment there. Make sure your view controller declares and implements the `UITextFieldDelegate` protocol.

- **Implement the `textFieldShouldReturn:` method.** This method catches all return key presses, no matter how they are named. Use this method to resign first responder and hide the keyboard until the user touches another text field or text view.

> **Note**
>
> You can also use `textFieldShouldReturn:` to perform an action when the return key is pressed in addition to dismissing the keyboard.

Your code needs to handle each of these points to create a smooth interaction process for your `UITextField` instances.

Preventing Keyboard Dismissal

Just as you can take charge of keyboard dismissal, your code can also block that action. View controllers can force keyboards to remain onscreen when the current responder does not support text. To make this happen, override the `disablesAutomaticKeyboardDismissal` method. The method returns a Boolean value that allows or disallows keyboard dismissal.

Text Trait Properties

Text fields implement the `UITextInputTraits` protocol. This protocol provides eight properties that you set to define the way the field handles text input:

- **`autocapitalizationType`**—Defines the text autocapitalization style. Available styles use sentence capitalization, word capitalization, all caps, and no capitalization. Avoid capitalizing when entering user names and passwords. Use word capitalization for proper names and street address entry fields.

- **`autocorrectionType`**—Specifies whether the text is subject to iOS's autocorrect feature. When this property is enabled (set to `UITextAutocorrectionTypeYes`), iOS suggests replacement words to the user. Most developers disable autocorrection for user name and password fields, so iOS doesn't accidentally correct myFacebookAccount to, for example, myofacial count.

- **`spellCheckingType`**—Determines whether to enable spell checking as the user types. Enable it with `UITextSpellCheckingTypeYes` and disable it with `UITextSpellCheckingTypeNo`. Spell checking is different from autocorrection, which updates items in-place as users type. Spell checking detects and underlines misspelled items in text views, providing a visual hint for corrective replacement. By default, spell checking is enabled whenever autocorrection is active.

- **keyboardAppearance**—Provides two keyboard presentation styles: a light look (the default) and a dark look.

- **keyboardType**—Lets you specify the keyboard that appears when a user interacts with a field or text view. iOS provides nearly a dozen varieties. These types include standard ASCII, numbers and punctuation, PIN-based number entry (0–9), phone number entry (0–9, #, *), decimal number entry (0–9, and .), URL-optimized (prominent ., /, and .com), e-mail-optimized (prominent @ and .), and Twitter-optimized (prominent @ and #).

  Each keyboard has advantages and disadvantages in terms of the mix of characters it presents. The e-mail keyboard, for example, is meant to support address entry. It includes the @ symbol, along with text. The Twitter keyboard offers easy access to the hashtag (#) symbol as well as the user ID (@) symbol.

- **enablesReturnKeyAutomatically**—Helps control whether the return key is disabled when there's no text in an entry field or view. If you set this property to YES, the return key becomes enabled after the user types at least one character.

- **returnKeyType**—Specifies the text shown on the keyboard's return key. You can choose from the default (Return), Go, Google, Join, Next, Route, Search, Send, Yahoo, Done, and Emergency Call. Choose a value that matches the action the user performs when completing a task.

- **secureTextEntry**—Toggles a text-hiding feature that is meant to provide more secure text entry. When this property is enabled, you can see the last character typed, but all other characters are shown as a series of dots. Switch on this feature for password text fields.

Other Text Field Properties

In addition to the standard text traits, text fields offer other properties that control how the field is presented. Here are ones you should know about:

- **Placeholder**—Figure 6-2 shows a field's placeholder text. This text appears in light gray when the text field is empty. It provides a user prompt that describes the target content for that field. Use the placeholder to provide usage hints such as User Name or E-mail address, as demonstrated in Figure 6-2.

Figure 6-2   Placeholder text appears inside text fields in a light gray color when the field is empty. Any text added to the field obscures the placeholder. You can set this text by using IB's text field Attributes inspector or by editing the `placeholder` property for the field object.

- **Border style**—Text fields allow you to control the type of borderStyle displayed around the text area. You can choose from a simple line, a bezel, and a rounded rectangle presentation (used in Figure 6-2). These are best seen in IB, where the Attributes inspector lets you toggle between the styles.

- **Clear button**—The text field clear button appears as an *X* at the right side of the entry area. Set clearButtonMode to specify if and when this button appears: always (UITextFieldViewModeAlways), never (UITextFieldViewModeNever), while editing (UITextFieldViewWhileEditing), or unless editing is ongoing (UITextFieldViewModeUnlessEditing). Always gives the greatest control to the user.

Recipe 6-1   **Using the Done Key to Dismiss a Text Field Keyboard**

```
// Dismiss the keyboard when the user taps Done
- (BOOL)textFieldShouldReturn:(UITextField *)textField
{
    [textField resignFirstResponder];
    return YES;
}


- (void)viewDidLoad
{
    [super viewDidLoad];

    // Update all text fields, including those defined in IB,
    // setting delegate, return key type, and other useful traits
    for (UIView *view in self.view.subviews)
    {
        if ([view isKindOfClass:[UITextField class]])
        {
            UITextField *aTextField = (UITextField *)view;
            aTextField.delegate = self;

            aTextField.returnKeyType = UIReturnKeyDone;
            aTextField.clearButtonMode =
                UITextFieldViewModeWhileEditing;

            aTextField.borderStyle = UITextBorderStyleRoundedRect;
            aTextField.contentVerticalAlignment =
                UIControlContentVerticalAlignmentCenter;
            aTextField.autocorrectionType =
                UITextAutocorrectionTypeNo;

            aTextField.font =
                [UIFont fontWithName:@"Futura" size:12.0f];
            aTextField.placeholder = @"Placeholder";
```

```
      }
    }
}
```

Recipe: Dismissing Text Views with Custom Accessory Views

Custom accessory views allow you to present material whenever the keyboard is shown onscreen. Common uses include adding custom buttons and other controls such as font and color pickers that affect text as the user types or additional navigation through forms. Recipe 6-2 adds two buttons: one that clears already-typed text and another that dismisses the keyboard. Figure 6-3 shows the keyboard with these add-ons.

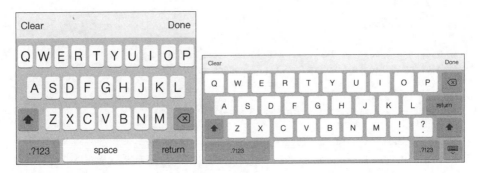

Figure 6-3   Accessory input views allow you to add custom view elements to standard iOS keyboard presentations. Here, a pair of buttons augment iPhone and iPad keyboards.

Each accessory view is associated with a given responder (a descendent of the `UIResponder` class), such as a text field or text view. Add accessories by setting the `inputAccessoryView` property for the view. Recipe 6-2 uses a simple toolbar as its accessory view, providing extra functionality with minimal coding.

Adding a Done button to the toolbar provides the same kind of user control for text views (large, scrolling, multiline text editing views) as Recipe 6-1 offers for text fields (one-line text-input controls). The difference is that this approach allows text views to continue using the return key to add carriage returns to text for paragraph breaks.

> **Note**
>
> One of this book's tech reviewers writes that he can never remember which is a text view and which is a text field. To this, I reply, "A view is two; a field is sealed." Text views can use any number of lines (including two or more). Text fields are single-line text entry controls, limited to a styled bounding border.
>
> iOS developer Phil Mills offers a more amusing mnemonic: "Take my text field...please." Text fields are, as he points out, one-liners.

Recipe 6-2's Done button resigns first responder status in its callback method. This button is not required for iPad users whose keyboard automatically includes a dismiss button, but it does no harm as used here. If you want to filter out the Done button when a universal application is run on the iPad, check the current user interface idiom. The following macro gives you a simple way to test for an iPad:

```
#define IS_IPAD (UI_USER_INTERFACE_IDIOM() == UIUserInterfaceIdiomPad)
```

Always be aware that Apple may introduce new iOS device form factors, with more space or less space available to users, so try to code accordingly, especially when working with screen-consuming features like accessory views. There's really not much you can do on that account with the current two idioms (iPhone and iPad), but it's worth inserting notes into code in places that could see changes in the future.

Recipe 6-2   Adding Custom Buttons to Keyboards

```
@implementation TestBedViewController
{
    UITextView *textView;
    UIToolbar *toolBar;
}


// Remove text from text view
- (void)clearText
{
    [textView setText:@""];
}


// Dismiss keyboard by resigning first responder
- (void)leaveKeyboardMode
{
    [textView resignFirstResponder];
}


- (UIToolbar *)accessoryView
{
    // Create toolbar with Clear and Done
    toolBar = [[UIToolbar alloc] initWithFrame:
```

```
            CGRectMake(0.0f, 0.0f, self.view.frame.size.width, 44.0f)];
        toolBar.tintColor = [UIColor darkGrayColor];

        // Set up the items as Clear - flexspace - Done
        NSMutableArray *items = [NSMutableArray array];
        [items addObject:BARBUTTON(@"Clear", @selector(clearText))];
        [items addObject:SYSBARBUTTON(UIBarButtonSystemItemFlexibleSpace, nil)];
        [items addObject:BARBUTTON(@"Done", @selector(leaveKeyboardMode))];
        toolBar.items = items;

        return toolBar;
}

- (void)loadView
{
        self.view = [[UIView alloc] init];
        self.view.backgroundColor = [UIColor whiteColor];

        // Create text view and add the custom accessory view
        textView = [[UITextView alloc] initWithFrame:self.view.bounds];
        textView.font = [UIFont fontWithName:@"Georgia"
            size:(IS_IPAD) ? 24.0f : 14.0f];
        textView.inputAccessoryView = [self accessoryView];

        // Use constraints to fill application bounds
        [self.view addSubview:textView];
        PREPCONSTRAINTS(textView);
        STRETCH_VIEW(self.view, textView); }
@end
```

Get This Recipe's Code

To find this recipe's full sample project, point your browser to https://github.com/erica/iOS-7-Cookbook and go to the folder for Chapter 6.

Recipe: Adjusting Views Around Keyboards

By necessity, iOS keyboards are large. They occupy a good portion of the screen whenever they are in use. Because of that, you'll want to adjust your text fields and text views so the keyboard does not block them when it appears onscreen. Figure 6-4 demonstrates this problem.

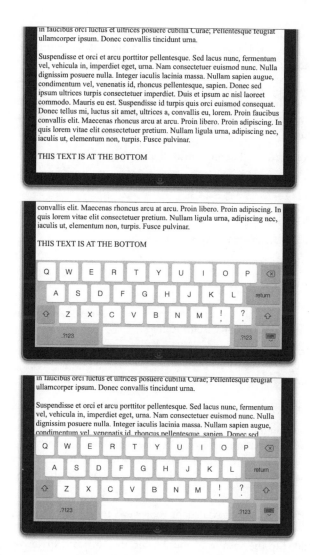

Figure 6-4   Keyboards occupy a large portion of the iOS device screen. If you do not force views to resize themselves and/or shift up on the screen when a keyboard appears, the keyboards will obscure onscreen material that should remain visible. You cannot see the bottom text in the last image because the text view extends behind the keyboard and reaches all the way to the bottom of the screen.

The top image shows the source text view, before it becomes first responder. The middle image demonstrates what users *expect* to happen—namely that the entire view remains accessible by touch even when the keyboard is onscreen. The bottom image demonstrates what happens when you do *not* resize or reposition views. In this case, roughly one-third of a screen of text view material becomes inaccessible. Users cannot see the final line of text, let alone edit it in any meaningful manner. The keyboard prevents any touches from getting through to the last paragraph or so of text.

Mitigate the keyboard's presence by allowing views to resize or shift around it. When the keyboard appears, views that continue to require interaction should adjust themselves out of the way so that they don't overlap. To accomplish this, your application must subscribe to keyboard notifications.

iOS offers several notifications that are transmitted using the standard `NSNotificationCenter`, as follows:

- `UIKeyboardWillShowNotification`
- `UIKeyboardDidShowNotification`
- `UIKeyboardWillChangeFrameNotification`
- `UIKeyboardWillHideNotification`
- `UIKeyboardDidHideNotification`

Listen for these by adding your class as an observer. The following snippet listens for the "will hide" notification and uses a target-selector callback:

```
[[NSNotificationCenter defaultCenter] addObserver:self
    selector:@selector(keyboardWillHide:)
    name:UIKeyboardWillHideNotification object:nil];
```

You can also handle notification updates via a blocks-based API.

The two notifications you'll usually want to listen for are "will show" and "will hide," which offer opportune times for you to react to the keyboard arriving onscreen or preparing to leave. Each notification provides a `userInfo` dictionary that supplies the end frame for the keyboard, using the `UIKeyboardFrameEndUserInfoKey` key. You are not granted direct access to the keyboard itself.

Retrieving the keyboard `frame` lets you adapt your views to the keyboard's presence. Recipe 6-3 adds a keyboard spacer view that adjusts its constraints to accommodate the height of the keyboard. When added to the bottom of your layout, the keyboard spacer view listens to and manages keyboard events and resizes appropriately. When you constrain your text view with the spacer, the text view will adjust appropriately as the spacer resizes:

```
// Create a spacer
KeyboardSpacingView *spacer =
    [KeyboardSpacingView installToView:self.view];

// Place the spacer under the text view
CONSTRAIN(self.view, @"V:|[textView][spacer]|",
    NSDictionaryOfVariableBindings(textView, spacer));
```

This implementation is fully hardware-aware and properly adjusts for optional input accessory views.

Recipe 6-3   **Creating a Dedicated Keyboard Spacer**

```
@implementation KeyboardSpacingView
{
    NSLayoutConstraint *heightConstraint;
}

// Listen for keyboard
- (void)establishNotificationHandlers
{
    // Listen for keyboard appearance
    [[NSNotificationCenter defaultCenter]
        addObserverForName:UIKeyboardWillShowNotification
        object:nil queue:[NSOperationQueue mainQueue]
        usingBlock:^(NSNotification *note)
    {
        // Fetch keyboard frame
        NSDictionary *userInfo = note.userInfo;
        NSTimeInterval duration =
            [userInfo[UIKeyboardAnimationDurationUserInfoKey]
                doubleValue];
        CGRect keyboardEndFrame = [self.superview
            convertRect:[userInfo[UIKeyboardFrameEndUserInfoKey]
                CGRectValue]
            fromView: self.window];

        // Adjust to window
        CGRect windowFrame = [self.superview
            convertRect:self.window.frame fromView:self.window];
        CGFloat heightOffset = (windowFrame.size.height -
            keyboardEndFrame.origin.y) -
            self.superview.frame.origin.y;

        // Update and animate height constraint
        heightConstraint.constant = heightOffset;
        [UIView animateWithDuration:duration animations:^{
            [self.superview layoutIfNeeded];
        }];
    }];

    // Listen for keyboard exit
    [[NSNotificationCenter defaultCenter]
        addObserverForName:UIKeyboardWillHideNotification object:nil
        queue:[NSOperationQueue mainQueue]
```

```objc
            usingBlock:^(NSNotification *note)
    {
        // Reset to zero
        NSDictionary *userInfo = note.userInfo;
        NSTimeInterval duration =
            [userInfo[UIKeyboardAnimationDurationUserInfoKey]
                doubleValue];
        heightConstraint.constant = 0;
        [UIView animateWithDuration:duration animations:^{
            [self.superview layoutIfNeeded];
        }];
    }];
}


// Stretch sides and bottom of spacer to superview
- (void)layoutView
{
    self.translatesAutoresizingMaskIntoConstraints = NO;
    if (!self.superview) return;
    for (NSString *constraintString in @[@"H:|[view]|", @"V:[view]|"])
    {
        NSArray *constraints = [NSLayoutConstraint
            constraintsWithVisualFormat:constraintString options:0
            metrics:nil views:@{@"view":self}];
        [self.superview addConstraints:constraints];
    }
    heightConstraint = [NSLayoutConstraint constraintWithItem:self
        attribute:NSLayoutAttributeHeight
        relatedBy:NSLayoutRelationEqual toItem:nil
        attribute:NSLayoutAttributeNotAnAttribute multiplier:1.0f
        constant:0.0f];
    [self addConstraint:heightConstraint];
}


+ (instancetype)installToView:(UIView *)parent
{
    if (!parent) return nil;
    KeyboardSpacingView *view = [[self alloc] init];
    [parent addSubview:view];

    [view layoutView];
    [view establishNotificationHandlers];
    return view;
}

@end
```

> **Get This Recipe's Code**
>
> To find this recipe's full sample project, point your browser to https://github.com/erica/iOS-7-Cookbook and go to the folder for Chapter 6.

Recipe: Creating a Custom Input View

A custom input view replaces the keyboard with a view of your design whenever a text view or text field becomes first responder. You can add custom input views to nontext views as well as to text views. Recipe 6-4 focuses on the text scenario.

When you set a responder's `inputView` property, the view that is assigned to that property replaces the system keyboard. The easiest way to demonstrate this feature is to create a colored view and assign it to the `inputView` property. Consider the following code snippet. It creates two text fields. The code assigns the second field's `inputView` property to a basic `UIView` instance that has a purple background:

```
// Create two standard text fields
UITextField *textField1 = [[UITextField alloc] init];
textField1.borderStyle = UITextBorderStyleRoundedRect;
[self.view addSubview:textField1];
PREPCONSTRAINTS(textField1);
CONSTRAIN_SIZE(textField1, 30, 200);
CENTER_VIEW_H(self.view, textField1);
ALIGN_VIEW_TOP_CONSTANT(self.view, textField1, 40);

UITextField *textField2 = [[UITextField alloc] init];
textField2.borderStyle = UITextBorderStyleRoundedRect;
[self.view addSubview:textField2];
PREPCONSTRAINTS(textField2);
CONSTRAIN_SIZE(textField2, 30, 200);
CENTER_VIEW_H(self.view, textField2);
ALIGN_VIEW_TOP_CONSTANT(self.view, textField2, 80);

// Create a purple view to be used as the input view
UIView *purpleView = [[UIView alloc] initWithFrame:
    CGRectMake(0.0f, 0.0f, self.view.frame.size.width, 120.0f)];
purpleView.backgroundColor = COOKBOOK_PURPLE_COLOR;

// Assign the input view
textField2.inputView = purpleView;
```

Figure 6-5 shows this snippet's results. When the first text field becomes first responder, the system-supplied keyboard scrolls onscreen; when the second field is selected, the purple view appears instead.

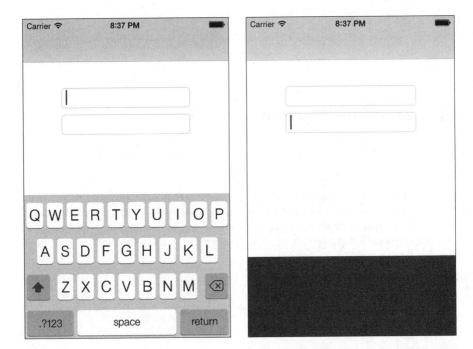

Figure 6-5   Otherwise identical, these two text fields produce different results upon becoming first responder. The top field (left image) presents a standard keyboard. The solid-color view assigned to the bottom field's `inputView` property (right image) replaces the system keyboard.

Because the purple view offers no interactive elements, there's not much you can do. You cannot enter text; you cannot dismiss the "keyboard." You can only marvel at the functionality of displaying a custom view. Reselect the top text field to switch back to the standard keyboard.

For the most part, custom input views are not used for text input in real-life coding. Although input views play an important role in other design patterns, especially gaming, their utility for text is fairly limited. That's because the `inputAccessoryView` property expands keyboard options without sacrificing built-in keys. Further, the range of keyboard options now includes numeric and decimal entry (added in iOS 4.1). These were the prevailing requirements for designing custom keyboards in early iOS releases.

Where do custom input views make sense when working with text? For those willing to spend time and effort developing their own keyboards, taking into account the various platforms and orientations, not to mention Shift modifier keys, input views provide complete control over the user experience. You create a fully customized skinnable input element that replaces the system keyboard with a look and feel uniquely suited to your design. This requires a huge amount of work, at many levels.

Recipe 6-4 provides a barebones example of a custom text-input view. Instead of character entry, it offers two buttons: One types Hello, and the other types World (see Figure 6-6). When tapped, each button inserts the word into its attached text view.

Figure 6-6   The custom keyboard attached as this text view's input view allows users to enter Hello and World—and that's all.

The challenge in creating a custom text-input view like this lies in how the text changes propagate back to the first responder. iOS offers no direct link or property that tells a custom input view who its owner is, nor can you use simple superview properties. Because of this challenge, you might want to implement a simple class extension to UIView to recover the current first responder:

```
@interface UIView (FirstResponderUtility)
+ (UIView *)currentResponder;
@end

@implementation UIView (FirstResponderUtility)
- (UIView *)findFirstResponder
{
    if ([self isFirstResponder]) return self;

    for (UIView *view in self.subviews)
```

```
    {
        UIView *responder = [view findFirstResponder];
        if (responder) return responder;
    }
    return nil;
}

+ (UIView *)currentResponder
{
    UIWindow *keyWindow =
        [[UIApplication sharedApplication] keyWindow];
    return [keyWindow findFirstResponder];
}
@end
```

> **Note**
>
> In the preceding code snippet, the class method, `currentResponder`, is named to marginally avoid conflict with private APIs.
>
> `firstResponder` is an actual unpublished method. When adding category methods to Apple's classes in production code (rather than sample code, which this is), a good rule of thumb is to prefix all method names with your initials, your company's initials, or some other unique identifier. This ensures that your method names do not overlap with Apple's or (importantly) with any methods Apple might add in the future. To enhance readability and recognition of method names in samples, this book does not follow this advice.

Recipe 6-4 builds a custom `UIToolbar` as an input view that displays two options (Hello and World). When tapped, the toolbar inserts a string into the first responder's text. It retrieves the first responder if this has not yet been set. Then it checks that the responder is a kind of `UITextView`. Only then does it insert the new text.

Certain truths are universally acknowledged regarding input views. First, the owner of a presented input view is always first responder. Second, that owner is a subview of the application's key window. You can leverage these facts in code, although you'll probably want to expand the minimal error condition checking shown in Recipe 6-4, particularly with regard to the reuse of the `responderView` instance variable.

Recipe 6-4   Creating a Custom Input View

```
@interface InputToolbar : UIToolbar
@end

@implementation InputToolbar
{
    UIView *responderView;
}
```

```objectivec
- (void)insertString:(NSString *)string
{
    if (!responderView || ![responderView isFirstResponder])
    {
        responderView = [UIView currentResponder];
        if (!responderView) return;
    }

    if ([responderView isKindOfClass:[UITextView class]])
    {
        UITextView *textView = (UITextView *) responderView;
        NSMutableString *text =
            [NSMutableString stringWithString:textView.text];
        NSRange range = textView.selectedRange;
        [text replaceCharactersInRange:range withString:string];
        textView.text = text;
        textView.selectedRange =
            NSMakeRange(range.location + string.length, 0);
    }
    else
        NSLog(@"Cannot insert %@ in unknown class type (%@)",
            string, [responderView class]);
}


// Perform the two insertions
- (void)hello:(id)sender {[self insertString:@"Hello "];}
- (void)world:(id)sender {[self insertString:@"World "];}

// Initialize the bar buttons on the toolbar
- (instancetype)initWithFrame:(CGRect)aFrame
{
    self = [super initWithFrame: aFrame;
    if (self)
    {
        NSMutableArray *theItems = [NSMutableArray array];
        [theItems addObject:SYSBARBUTTON(
            UIBarButtonSystemItemFlexibleSpace, nil)];
        [theItems addObject:BARBUTTON(
            @"Hello", @selector(hello:))];
        [theItems addObject:SYSBARBUTTON(
            UIBarButtonSystemItemFlexibleSpace, nil)];
        [theItems addObject:BARBUTTON(
            @"World", @selector(world:))];
        [theItems addObject:SYSBARBUTTON(
            UIBarButtonSystemItemFlexibleSpace, nil)];
        self.items = theItems;
```

```
    }
    return self;
}
@end
```

Recipe: Making Text-Input-Aware Views

While only a few views support text input by default, with a bit of effort, you can add keyboard support to almost any view. The key is the simple `UIKeyInput` protocol. By combining it with a little first responder manipulation, you can update any view to offer text input.

Recipe 6-5 illustrates how to transform a standard `UIToolbar` into a view that accepts keyboard entry, letting users type text directly into the toolbar, as shown in Figure 6-7. As the user types, the toolbar text updates, even properly handling the Delete key.

Figure 6-7   Adding the `UIKeyInput` protocol to a toolbar transforms the view into one that can accept and display keyboard input, including deletions.

This recipe requires several features. First, the toolbar must declare the UIKeyInput protocol. This protocol announces that the view implements simple text entry and can display the system keyboard (or a custom keyboard, if desired) when it becomes first responder.

Second, the toolbar must retain state—that is, the string being entered must be stored. Saving the string as a retained mutable property allows the toolbar to know what text it is currently working with and to display that text to the user.

Next, the toolbar must be able to become first responder. It does so in two ways: by implementing canBecomeFirstResponder (returning YES) and by catching touches to detect when it should assume that role. Adding a touch handler allows the toolbar to become the first responder when a user touches the view.

Finally, it must implement the three required UIKeyInput protocol methods: hasText, insertText:, and deleteBackward. These methods do exactly what their names imply. The hasText method returns YES whenever the view has any text available. The other two methods insert text at the current insertion point (always at the end for this recipe) and delete one character at a time from the end of the displayed text.

By declaring the protocol, becoming first responder, and handling both the string state and the input callbacks, Recipe 6-5 provides a robust way to add basic text entry to standard UIView elements. You can extend these same text features to many other classes, including labels, navigation bars, buttons, and so forth, to use in your applications as needed.

Recipe 6-5 Adding Keyboard Input to Nontext Views

```
@interface KeyInputToolbar: UIToolbar <UIKeyInput>
@end

@implementation KeyInputToolbar
{
    NSMutableString *string;
}

// Is there text available that can be deleted
- (BOOL)hasText
{
    if (!string || !string.length) return NO;
    return YES;
}

// Reload the toolbar with the string
- (void)update
{
    NSMutableArray *theItems = [NSMutableArray array];
    [theItems addObject:SYSBARBUTTON(UIBarButtonSystemItemFlexibleSpace, nil)];
    [theItems addObject:BARBUTTON(string, @selector(becomeFirstResponder))];
    [theItems addObject:SYSBARBUTTON(UIBarButtonSystemItemFlexibleSpace, nil)];
```

```
        self.items = theItems;
}


// Insert new text into the string
- (void)insertText:(NSString *)text
{
    if (!string) string = [NSMutableString string];
    [string appendString:text];
    [self update];
}


// Delete one character
- (void)deleteBackward
{
    // Super caution, even if hasText reports YES
    if (!string)
    {
        string = [NSMutableString string];
        return;
    }

    if (!string.length)
        return;

    // Remove a character
    [string deleteCharactersInRange:NSMakeRange(string.length - 1, 1)];
    [self update];
}


// When becoming first responder, send out a notification to that effect.
// Can be used to add a Done button in the navigation bar
- (BOOL)becomeFirstResponder
{
    BOOL result = [super becomeFirstResponder];
    if (result)
        [[NSNotificationCenter defaultCenter]
            postNotification:[NSNotification notificationWithName:
                @"KeyInputToolbarDidBecomeFirstResponder" object:nil]];
    return result;
}


- (BOOL)canBecomeFirstResponder
{
    return YES;
}


- (void)touchesBegan:(NSSet *)touches withEvent:(UIEvent *)event;
```

```
{
    [self becomeFirstResponder];
}
@end
```

Get This Recipe's Code

To find this recipe's full sample project, point your browser to https://github.com/erica/iOS-7-Cookbook and go to the folder for Chapter 6.

Recipe: Adding Custom Input Views to Nontext Views

Although custom input views can be applied to text views and text fields, they are more valuable in other use cases. Input doesn't have to be about text. In fact, by taking the system keyboard out of the equation, custom input views can range to whatever kind of scenario you need.

Think of input views as context-sensitive graphical menus that appear only when a particular view class becomes first responder. When you tap a warrior, perhaps a set of weapons scrolls onscreen, including a bow, a mace, and a sword. The user can select the kind of attack the warrior should apply. Or think of a graphics layout program. When a circle, square, or line is tapped, maybe an onscreen palette is revealed that lets users set the stroke width, the stroke color, and the fill. The only limit to the utility of custom input is your imagination.

Recipe 6-6 demonstrates how a custom input view can affect a nontext view. It combines the code from Recipes 6-4 and 6-5, creating both an input-aware view (`ColorView`), which can become first responder with a touch, and an input view (`InputToolbar`) that affects the display of that primary view. In this example, the base view's role is limited to displaying a color. The toolbar controls what color that is.

Because there's no other way to transfer first responder control, the input view also offers a Done button, which allows the user to dismiss the keyboard, thus resigning first responder from the big color view.

Adding Input Clicks

Use the `UIDevice` class to add input clicks to your custom input accessory views. The `playInputClick` method plays the standard system keyboard click and can be called when you respond to user input taps.

Adopt the `UIInputViewAudioFeedback` protocol in the accessory input class and add an `enableInputClicksWhenVisible` delegate method that always returns `YES`. This defers audio playback to the user's preferences, which are set in Settings > Sounds. To hear these clicks, the user must have enabled keyboard click feedback. If the user has not done so, your calls to `playInputClick` are simply ignored.

Recipe 6-6   Creating a Custom Input Controller for a Nontext View

```objc
@interface ColorView : UIView
@property (strong) UIView *inputView;
@end


// Key Input Aware View
@implementation ColorView

// UITextInput protocol
- (BOOL)hasText {return NO;}
- (void)insertText:(NSString *)text {}
- (void)deleteBackward {}

// First responder support
- (BOOL)canBecomeFirstResponder {return YES;}
- (void)touchesBegan:(NSSet *)touches
    withEvent:(UIEvent *)event {[self becomeFirstResponder];}

// Initialize with user interaction allowed
- (instancetype)initWithFrame:(CGRect)aFrame
{
    self = [super initWithFrame:aFrame];
    if (self)
    {
        self.backgroundColor = COOKBOOK_PURPLE_COLOR;
        self.userInteractionEnabled = YES;
    }
    return self;
}
@end


// Color input toolbar
@interface InputToolbar : UIToolbar <UIInputViewAudioFeedback>
@end

@implementation InputToolbar
- (BOOL)enableInputClicksWhenVisible
{
    return YES;
}

- (void)updateColor:(UIColor *)aColor
{
    [UIView currentResponder].backgroundColor = aColor;
    [[UIDevice currentDevice] playInputClick];
}
```

```
// Color updates
- (void)light:(id) sender {
    [self updateColor:[COOKBOOK_PURPLE_COLOR
        colorWithAlphaComponent:0.33f]];}
- (void)medium:(id)sender {
    [self updateColor:[COOKBOOK_PURPLE_COLOR
        colorWithAlphaComponent:0.66f]];}
- (void)dark:(id)sender {
    [self updateColor:COOKBOOK_PURPLE_COLOR];}

// Resign first responder on pressing Done
- (void)done:(id)sender
{
    [[UIView currentResponder] resignFirstResponder];
}

// Create a toolbar with each option available
- (instancetype)initWithFrame:(CGRect)aFrame
{
    self = [super initWithFrame:aFrame];
    if (self)
    {
        NSMutableArray *theItems = [NSMutableArray array];
        [theItems addObject:BARBUTTON(@"Light", @selector(light:))];
        [theItems addObject:SYSBARBUTTON(
            UIBarButtonSystemItemFlexibleSpace, nil)];
        [theItems addObject:BARBUTTON(@"Medium", @selector(medium:))];
        [theItems addObject:SYSBARBUTTON(
            UIBarButtonSystemItemFlexibleSpace, nil)];
        [theItems addObject:BARBUTTON(@"Dark", @selector(dark:))];
        [theItems addObject:SYSBARBUTTON(
            UIBarButtonSystemItemFlexibleSpace, nil)];
        [theItems addObject:BARBUTTON(@"Done", @selector(done:))];
        self.items = theItems;
    }
    return self;
}
@end
```

Get This Recipe's Code

To find this recipe's full sample project, point your browser to https://github.com/erica/iOS-7-Cookbook and go to the folder for Chapter 6.

Recipe: Building a Better Text Editor (Part I)

Undo support and persistence help create better text editors in your application. These features ensure that your users can reverse mistakes and pick up their work from where they left off. Accomplishing them requires surprisingly little programming, as demonstrated in Recipe 6-7.

Text views provide built-in support that works hand-in-hand with select, cut, copy, and paste. The undo manager understands these actions, and possible user messages might include Undo Paste, Redo Cut, and so forth. All the view controller needs to do is instantiate an undo manager; it leaves the rest of the work to the built-in objects.

Recipe 6-7 adds Undo and Redo buttons to the keyboard accessory view. These buttons must be updated each time the text view contents change. To accomplish this, the view controller becomes the text view's delegate and implements the `textViewDidChange:` delegate method. Buttons are enabled or disabled accordingly.

This recipe uses persistence to store the text contents between application launches. It archives its contents to file in the `performArchive` method. The application delegate calls this method right before the application is due to suspend and also each time the text view resigns first responder status to better ensure that the data remains fresh and up to date between application sessions:

```
- (void) applicationWillResignActive:(UIApplication *)application
{
    [tbvc archiveData];
}
```

On launch, any data in that file is read in to initialize the text view instance during the view controller setup.

Recipe 6-7   Adding Undo Support and Persistence to Text Views

```
#define SYSBARBUTTON(ITEM, SELECTOR) [[UIBarButtonItem alloc] \
    initWithBarButtonSystemItem:ITEM target:self action:SELECTOR]
#define SYSBARBUTTON_TARGET(ITEM, TARGET, SELECTOR) \
    [[UIBarButtonItem alloc] initWithBarButtonSystemItem:ITEM \
    target:TARGET action:SELECTOR]

// Store data out to file
- (void)archiveData
{
    [textView.text writeToFile:DATAPATH atomically:YES
        encoding:NSUTF8StringEncoding error:nil];
}

// Update the undo and redo button states
- (void)textViewDidChange:(UITextView *)textView
{
```

```
    [self loadAccessoryView];
}


// Choose which items to enable and disable on the toolbar
- (void) loadAccessoryView
{
    NSMutableArray *items = [NSMutableArray array];
    UIBarButtonItem *spacer =
        SYSBARBUTTON(UIBarButtonSystemItemFixedSpace, nil);
    spacer.width = 40.0f;

    BOOL canUndo = [textView.undoManager canUndo];
    UIBarButtonItem *undoItem = SYSBARBUTTON_TARGET(
        UIBarButtonSystemItemUndo, self, @selector(undo));
    undoItem.enabled = canUndo;
    [items addObject:undoItem];
    [items addObject:spacer];

    BOOL canRedo = [textView.undoManager canRedo];
    UIBarButtonItem *redoItem = SYSBARBUTTON_TARGET(
        UIBarButtonSystemItemRedo, self, @selector(redo));
    redoItem.enabled = canRedo;
    [items addObject:redoItem];
    [items addObject:spacer];

    [items addObject:SYSBARBUTTON(UIBarButtonSystemItemFlexibleSpace, nil)];
    [items addObject:BARBUTTON(@"Done", @selector(leaveKeyboardMode))];

    toolbar.items = items;
}


// Call undo on the undoManager and update toolbar buttons
- (void) undo
{
    [textView.undoManager undo];
    [self loadAccessoryView];
}


// Call redo on the undoManager and update toolbar buttons
- (void) redo
{
    [textView.undoManager redo];
    [self loadAccessoryView];
}


// Return a plain accessory view
- (UIToolbar *) accessoryView
```

```
{
    toolbar = [[UIToolbar alloc]
        initWithFrame:CGRectMake(0.0f, 0.0f, 100.0f, 44.0f)];
    toolbar.tintColor = [UIColor darkGrayColor];
    return toolbar;
}


- (void)loadView
{
    self.view = [[UIView alloc] init];

    // Load any existing string
    if ([[NSFileManager defaultManager] fileExistsAtPath:DATAPATH])
    {
        NSString *string =
            [NSString stringWithContentsOfFile:DATAPATH
                encoding:NSUTF8StringEncoding error:nil];
        textView.text = string;
    }

    // Subscribe to keyboard frame changes and update layout
    [[NSNotificationCenter defaultCenter] addObserver:self
        selector:@selector(updateTextViewBounds:)
        name:UIKeyboardDidChangeFrameNotification object:nil];
}
```

Get This Recipe's Code

To find this recipe's full sample project, point your browser to https://github.com/erica/iOS-7-Cookbook and go to the folder for Chapter 6.

Recipe: Building a Better Text Editor (Part II)

Starting with iOS 6, text views and text fields work with attributed text strings (that is, strings that support styles, not just plain-text ones). This allows you to create highly featured text views and fields with multiple fonts, styles, and colors.

Much of this functionality prior to iOS 7 leaned heavily on Core Text for anything more than simple styles. With Text Kit, that support has been simplified and expanded. For simple text editors, it takes very little work to add support for basic styles: bold, italic, and underline.

Enabling Attributed Text

To handle style requests, you must change a flag that lets your text view work with attributed (in other words, styled) text. Set the `allowsEditingTextAttributes` property to YES. Upon doing so, several things happen:

- The text view begins updating its `attributedText` property. This property enables you to retrieve the text view's contents as an attributed string.

- The view begins responding to a series of special `UIResponder` methods that toggle boldface, italic, and underline for selected text. These methods are detailed in the next section.

- The view's interactive user-interface menu starts to show new options, allowing users to style the current selection using bold, italic, and underline.

Controlling Attributes

In iOS 6, `NSObject` offers methods to control several text attributes. These methods are intended for use by `UIResponder` subclasses and are part of the `UIResponderStandardEditActions` informal protocol. This protocol declares common editing commands for the iOS user interface.

The methods of interest include `toggleBoldFace:`, `toggleItalics:`, and `toggleUnderline:`. These three methods apply styles to the current text selection or, if the styles have already been applied, remove them.

To allow these updates, you just tell the responder (in this case, a text view) to enable text attribute editing. The text view or text field in question does all the heavy lifting. You can implement these calls with nothing more than bar button actions.

Recipe 6-8 demonstrates how to build these features into your iOS application. Figure 6-8 shows the interface built by this recipe.

Figure 6-8   The `UIResponderStandardEditActions` protocol defines common text editing commands, which you wrap into your user interface. The keyboard accessory view offers one-button access in addition to the BIU options that automatically appear in the system menu. The accessory view allows you to select all (Sel) or apply (or remove) bold (B), italic (I), and underline (U).

Other Responder Functionality

Notice the Sel option on the accessory bar, to the left of the BIU (bold, italic, and underline) choices. This bar button adds a Select All feature via the same `UIRespondersStandardEditActions` protocol used for style toggles. Editing methods include the following:

- `copy:`, `cut:`, `delete:` and `paste:` for basic edits
- `select:` and `selectAll:` for selections
- `toggleBoldFace:`, `toggleItalics:`, and `toggleUnderline:` for style updates

This protocol also lets you control the direction of writing through the `makeTextWriting-DirectionLeftToRight:` and `makeTextWritingDirectionRightToLeft:` methods.

Recipe 6-8   **Enhanced Text Editor**

```objc
// Handy bar button macros
#define BARBUTTON(TITLE, SELECTOR) [[UIBarButtonItem alloc] \
    initWithTitle:TITLE style:UIBarButtonItemStylePlain \
    target:self action:SELECTOR]
#define BARBUTTON_TARGET(TARGET, TITLE, SELECTOR) \
    [[UIBarButtonItem alloc] initWithTitle:TITLE \
    style:UIBarButtonItemStylePlain target:TARGET action:SELECTOR]
#define SYSBARBUTTON(ITEM, SELECTOR) [[UIBarButtonItem alloc] \
    initWithBarButtonSystemItem:ITEM target:self action:SELECTOR]
#define SYSBARBUTTON_TARGET(ITEM, TARGET, SELECTOR) \
    [[UIBarButtonItem alloc] initWithBarButtonSystemItem:ITEM \
        target:TARGET action:SELECTOR]

// Choose which items to enable and disable on the toolbar
- (void)loadAccessoryView
{
    NSMutableArray *items = [NSMutableArray array];

    BOOL canUndo = [textView.undoManager canUndo];
    UIBarButtonItem *undoItem = SYSBARBUTTON_TARGET(
        UIBarButtonSystemItemUndo, self, @selector(undo));
    undoItem.enabled = canUndo;
    [items addObject:undoItem];

    BOOL canRedo = [textView.undoManager canRedo];
    UIBarButtonItem *redoItem = SYSBARBUTTON_TARGET(
        UIBarButtonSystemItemRedo, self, @selector(redo));
    redoItem.enabled = canRedo;
    [items addObject:redoItem];

    // Add select all
    [items addObject:SYSBARBUTTON(UIBarButtonSystemItemFlexibleSpace, nil)];
    [items addObject:BARBUTTON_TARGET(textView, @"Sel", @selector(selectAll:))];

    // Add style buttons
    [items addObject:SYSBARBUTTON(UIBarButtonSystemItemFlexibleSpace, nil)];
    [items addObject:BARBUTTON_TARGET(textView,
        @"B", @selector(toggleBoldface:))];
    [items addObject:BARBUTTON_TARGET(textView,
        @"I", @selector(toggleItalics:))];
    [items addObject:BARBUTTON_TARGET(textView,
        @"U", @selector(toggleUnderline:))];
```

```
    [items addObject:SYSBARBUTTON(UIBarButtonSystemItemFlexibleSpace, nil)];
    [items addObject:BARBUTTON(@"Done", @selector(leaveKeyboardMode))];

    toolbar.items = items;
}
```

Get This Recipe's Code

To find this recipe's full sample project, point your browser to https://github.com/erica/iOS-7-Cookbook and go to the folder for Chapter 6.

Recipe: Text-Entry Filtering

You might sometimes want to ensure that a user enters only a certain subset of characters. For example, you might want to create a numeric-only text field that does not handle letters. Although you can use predicates to test the final entry against a regular expression (the NSPredicate class's MATCH operator supports regex values and is demonstrated in Recipe 6-10), for filtered data, it's easier to check each new character as it is typed against a legal set.

A UITextField delegate can catch those characters as they are typed and decide whether to add each character to the active text field. The optional textField:shouldChangeCharacters-InRange:replacementString: delegate method returns either YES, allowing the newly typed character(s), or NO, disallowing it (or them). In practice, this works on a character-by-character basis, being called after each user keyboard tap. However, with iOS's pasteboard support, the replacement string could theoretically be longer when text is pasted to a text field.

Recipe 6-9 looks for any disallowed characters within the new string. When it finds them, it rejects the entry, leaving the text field unedited. It would entirely reject a paste of mixed allowed and disallowed text.

This recipe considers four scenarios: text entry that is alphabetic only, numeric, numeric with an allowed decimal point, and a mix of alphanumeric characters. You can adapt this example to any set of legal characters you want.

The third entry type, numbers with a decimal point, uses a little trick to ensure that only one decimal point gets typed. Once it finds a period character in the associated text field, it switches the characters it accepts from a set with the period to a set without it. Users can sneak around this by using paste. Even if you feel that it's unlikely for users to do so, design against the possibility. Disallow pasting by overriding your text field's canPerformAction:withSender: method to specifically exclude this action.

The following snippet ensures that users cannot paste into a text field. It returns NO when queried about the paste: action. Similar guards offer selection (select and select all) when the field has text to select (hasText). The cut and copy options mandate that the user selection include a valid nonempty selection range:

```
@interface LimitedTextField : UITextField
@end
@implementation LimitedTextField
- (BOOL)canPerformAction:(SEL)action withSender:(id)sender
{
    UITextRange *range = self.selectedTextRange;
    BOOL hasText = self.text.length > 0;

    if (action == @selector(cut:)) return !range.empty;
    if (action == @selector(copy:)) return !range.empty;
    if (action == @selector(select:)) return hasText;
    if (action == @selector(selectAll:)) return hasText;
    if (action == @selector(paste:)) return NO;

    return NO;
}
@end
```

The lesson is this: Never underestimate the user's ability to thwart your design when you leave openings to do so.

Recipe 6-9   Filtering User Text Entry

```
#define ALPHA @"ABCDEFGHIJKLMNOPQRSTUVWXYZabcdefghijklmnopqrstuvwxyz "

@implementation TestBedViewController
- (BOOL)textField:(UITextField *)aTextField
    shouldChangeCharactersInRange:(NSRange)range
    replacementString:(NSString *)string
{
    NSMutableCharacterSet *cs =
        [NSMutableCharacterSet
            characterSetWithCharactersInString:@""];

    switch (segmentedControl.selectedSegmentIndex)
    {
        case 0:
            [cs addCharactersInString:ALPHA];
            break;
        case 1:
            [cs formUnionWithCharacterSet:
                [NSCharacterSet decimalDigitCharacterSet]];
            break;
        case 2:
            [cs formUnionWithCharacterSet:
                [NSCharacterSet decimalDigitCharacterSet]];
```

```
                    // permit one decimal only
                    if ([textField.text rangeOfString:@"."].location
                        == NSNotFound)
                        [cs addCharactersInString:@"."];
                    break;
            case 3:
                [cs addCharactersInString:ALPHA];
                [cs formUnionWithCharacterSet:
                    [NSCharacterSet decimalDigitCharacterSet]];
                break;
            default:
                break;
    }

    NSString *filtered =
        [[string componentsSeparatedByCharactersInSet:[cs invertedSet]]
            componentsJoinedByString:@""];
    BOOL basicTest = [string isEqualToString:filtered];
    return basicTest;
}


- (void)segmentChanged:(UISegmentedControl *)seg
{
    // Reset text on segment change
    textField.text = @"";
}

- (void)loadView
{
    self.view = [[UIView alloc] init];
    self.view.backgroundColor = [UIColor whiteColor];

    // Create a testbed text field to work with
    textField = [[UITextField alloc] init];
    textField.placeholder = @"Enter Text";
    [self.view addSubview:textField];

    PREPCONSTRAINTS(textField);
    CONSTRAIN(self.view, textField, @"V:|-30-[textField]");
    CONSTRAIN(self.view, textField, @"H:|-[textField(>=0)]-|");

    textField.delegate = self;
    textField.returnKeyType = UIReturnKeyDone;
    textField.clearButtonMode = UITextFieldViewModeAlways;
    textField.borderStyle = UITextBorderStyleRoundedRect;
    textField.autocorrectionType = UITextAutocorrectionTypeNo;
```

```
    // Add segmented control with entry options
    segmentedControl = [[UISegmentedControl alloc] initWithItems:
            [@"ABC 123 2.3 A2C" componentsSeparatedByString:@" "]];
    segmentedControl.selectedSegmentIndex = 0;
    [segmentedControl addTarget:self action:@selector(segmentChanged:)
        forControlEvents:UIControlEventValueChanged];
    self.navigationItem.titleView = segmentedControl;
}
@end
```

Get This Recipe's Code

To find this recipe's full sample project, point your browser to https://github.com/erica/iOS-7-Cookbook and go to the folder for Chapter 6.

Recipe: Detecting Text Patterns

Recipe 6-9 introduces ways to limit users to entering legal characters. From there, it's just a short hop to matching user input against a variety of legal patterns. Consider a floating-point number. It might be described as an optional sign followed by a whole component followed by an optional decimal and then a fractional component. Or maybe the whole component should be optional but the sign mandatory.

Unfortunately, there are many standard ways of describing things, and those ways increase exponentially when you expand from simple numbers to phone numbers, e-mail addresses, and URLs. Apple has taken care of many of these for you, with its built-in data detector classes, but it often helps to know how to roll your own.

Rolling Your Own Expressions

Some standards organizations have published descriptions of exactly what makes up a legal value. Enterprising developers have transformed many of those descriptions into fairly portable regular expressions. Consider the following regular expression definition of a floating-point number:

```
^[+-]?[0-9]+[\.]?[0-9]*$
```

It's not a perfect definition, but for many purposes, it's a pretty good one—and a flexible one to boot. It accepts a pretty good range of floating-point numbers with optional signs at the start. Admittedly, as presented, it won't accept –.75, but it will also not accept –., which I think offers a fair compromise because –0.75 isn't too hard for the user to guess. Alternatively, you could use a set of regular expression checks and accept any positive result that occurs out of that set—for example, adding in floating points that do not require a whole portion but do require a decimal point to start, followed by one or more digits:

```
^[+-]?\.[0-9]+$
```

NSPredicate instances can compare NSString text to a regular expression, detecting when users have entered a valid floating-point number. Here's an example:

```
NSPredicate *fpPredicate = [NSPredicate predicateWithFormat:
    @"SELF MATCHES '^[+-]?[0-9]+[\\.]?[0-9]*$'"];
BOOL match = [fpPredicate evaluateWithObject:string];
```

It is, as already stated, a bit harder to detect phone numbers, e-mail addresses, and other more sophisticated entry types. Here's a naïve go at the phone number problem, using U.S. numbers, in the form of a regular expression:

```
^[\(]?([2-9][0-9]{2})[\)]?[-.\. ]?([2-9][0-9]{2})[-.\. ]?([0-9]{4})$
```

This regular expression offers optional parentheses, although there is no way to check that they balance; you could, however, accomplish that with some simple additional Objective-C coding. This regular expression ensures that both the area code and the phone number prefix don't start with 0 or 1, and it allows the user to enter optional spacers between the numbers (a space, a dash, or a period). In other words, for one line of description, it's a pretty okay but not spectacular definition of phone numbers.

Recipe 6-10 uses this regular expression to determine when a user has entered a phone number. Upon receiving a positive match, it updates the navigation bar's title to acknowledge success. This recipe demonstrates how you can perform real-time filtering and pattern matching to detect a particular pattern and provide a way to act on positive results.

Enumerating Regular Expressions

The NSRegularExpression class offers a block-based enumeration approach to finding matches within a string. Use this approach to apply updates to given ranges. When you work with attributed text, you can apply color or font hints to just the elements that match the regex. This is similar to a text view's spell checker, which adds underline to highlight misspelled words.

To roll your own, create a regular expression. Enumerate it over a string (typically one found in a text view of some sort) and use each range to create some kind of visual update. With attributed strings, it's easier than ever to add visual feedback to text view contents:

```
// Check for matches
NSRegularExpression *regex = [NSRegularExpression
    regularExpressionWithPattern:@"REGEXHERE"
    options:NSRegularExpressionCaseInsensitive error:nil];

// Enumerate over a string
[regex enumerateMatchesInString:text options:0 range:fullRange
```

```
    usingBlock:^(NSTextCheckingResult *match,
        NSMatchingFlags flags, BOOL *stop){
        NSRange range = match.range;
        // Perform some action on the range
}];
```

Data Detectors

The NSDataDetector class is a subclass of NSRegularExpression. Data detectors allow you to search for well-defined data types, including dates, addresses, URL links, phone numbers, and transit information, using Apple's fully tested algorithms instead of trying to create your own regular expressions. Even better, they're localized!

Take the same approach shown previously for enumerating regular expressions. This code snippet searches for links (URLs) and phone numbers:

```
NSError *error = NULL;
NSDataDetector *detector = [NSDataDetector dataDetectorWithTypes:
    NSTextCheckingTypeLink|NSTextCheckingTypePhoneNumber
    error:&error];

// Enumerate over a string
[detector enumerateMatchesInString:text options:0 range:fullRange
    usingBlock:^(NSTextCheckingResult *match,
        NSMatchingFlags flags, BOOL *stop){
            NSRange range = match.range;
            // Perform some action on the range
}];
```

The checks are built around the NSTextCheckingResult class. This class describes items that match the data detector's content discovery. The kinds of data detectors supported by iOS are going to grow over time. For now, they are limited to dates (NSTextCheckingTypeDate), addresses (NSTextCheckingTypeAddress), links (NSTextCheckingTypeLink), phone numbers (NSTextCheckingTypePhoneNumber), and transit info like flight information (NSTextCheckingTypeTransitInformation). Hopefully, this list will expand to include common stock symbols, UPS/FedEx shipping numbers, and other easily recognized patterns.

Using Built-in Type Detectors

UITextViews and UIWebViews offer built-in data type detectors, including phone numbers, HTTP links, and so forth. Set the dataDetectorTypes property to allow the view to automatically convert pattern matches into clickable URLs that are embedded into the view's text. Legal types include addresses, calendar events, links, and phone numbers. Use UIDataDetectorTypeAll to match all supported types or use UIDataDetectorTypeNone to disable pattern matching.

Useful Websites

When working with regular expressions, you may want to check out a number of handy websites to assist with your work:

- The Regular Expression Library (http://regexlib.com) site has indexed thousands of regular expressions from contributors around the world.

- Go to Regex Pal (http://regexpal.com) to test your regular expressions via an interactive JavaScript tool.

- Use the txt2re generator (http://txt2re.com) to build code that extracts elements from source strings that you provide. It supports output in C as well as several other language destinations.

> **Note**
>
> With Text Kit in iOS 7, an alternative approach to using the UITextField delegate used in Recipes 6-9 and 6-10 is subclassing NSTextStorage and overriding the processEditing method.

Recipe 6-10   Detecting Text Patterns Using Predicates and Regular Expressions

```
@implementation TestBedViewController
{
    UITextField *textField;
    UISegmentedControl *segmentedControl;
}

- (void)updateStatus:(NSString *)string
{
    // This is a predicate matching U.S. telephone numbers
    NSPredicate *telePredicate = [NSPredicate predicateWithFormat:
        @"SELF MATCHES \
        '^[\\(]?([2-9][0-9]{2})[\\)]?[-.\\. ]?([2-9][0-9]{2})\
        [-.\\. ]?([0-9]{4})$'"];
    BOOL match = [telePredicate evaluateWithObject:string];
    self.title = match ? @"Phone Number" : nil;
}

- (BOOL)textField:(UITextField *)aTextField
    shouldChangeCharactersInRange:(NSRange)range
    replacementString:(NSString *)string
{
    NSString *newString = [textField.text
        stringByReplacingCharactersInRange:range withString:string];
```

```objc
    if (!string.length)
    {
        [self updateStatus:newString];
        return YES;
    }

    NSMutableCharacterSet *cs = [NSMutableCharacterSet
        characterSetWithCharactersInString:@""];
    [cs formUnionWithCharacterSet:
        [NSCharacterSet decimalDigitCharacterSet]];
    [cs addCharactersInString:@"()-. "];

    // Legal characters check
    NSString *filtered = [[string componentsSeparatedByCharactersInSet:
        [cs invertedSet]] componentsJoinedByString:@""];
    BOOL basicTest = [string isEqualToString:filtered];

    // Test for phone number
    [self updateStatus:basicTest ? newString : textField.text];

    return basicTest;
}

- (void)loadView
{
    self.view = [[UIView alloc] init];

    textField = [[UITextField alloc] initWithFrame:
        CGRectMake(0.0f, 0.0f, 300.0f, 30.0f)];
    textField.placeholder = @"Enter Phone Number";
    [self.view addSubview:textField];

    PREPCONSTRAINTS(textField);
    CONSTRAIN(self.view, textField, @"V:|-30-[textField]");
    CONSTRAIN(self.view, textField, @"H:|-[textField(>=0)]-|");

    textField.delegate = self;
    textField.returnKeyType = UIReturnKeyDone;
    textField.clearButtonMode = UITextFieldViewModeAlways;
    textField.borderStyle = UITextBorderStyleRoundedRect;
    textField.autocorrectionType = UITextAutocorrectionTypeNo;
}
@end
```

> **Get This Recipe's Code**
>
> To find this recipe's full sample project, point your browser to https://github.com/erica/iOS-7-Cookbook and go to the folder for Chapter 6.

Recipe: Detecting Misspelling in a `UITextView`

The `UITextChecker` class provides a way to automatically scan text for misspellings. To use this class, you must first set the target language—for example, `en` for English, `en_US` for U.S. English, or `fr_CA` for Canadian French. The language codes use a combination of ISO 639-1 and optional ISO 3166-1 regions. So, while you can choose to use a general English dictionary (`en`), you can also differentiate between usage in the United States (`en_US`), Australia (`en_AU`), and the United Kingdom (`en_GB`). Query `UITextChecker` for an array of available languages from which to pick.

The `UITextChecker` class also allows you to learn new words (`learnWord:`) and forget words (`unlearnWord:`) to customize the onboard dictionary to the user's need. Learned words are used across languages; so, when you add a person's name, that name is available universally. Checker objects can also set words to ignore using instance methods.

Recipe 6-11 demonstrates how to incorporate a text checker into your application by iteratively selecting each misspelled word. To do this, you need to control range selection for the text view. To select text in a `UITextView`, it must already be first responder. Check the responder status and update the view if needed:

```
if (![textView isFirstResponder])
    [textView becomeFirstResponder];
```

Then calculate a range you want to select, making sure to take the content length into account, and set the `selectedRange` property for the text view:

```
textView.selectedRange = NSMakeRange(offset, length);
```

Because a text view must be editable, as well as the first responder, the keyboard appears onscreen while you perform any range selection. Because the user can edit any material you have onscreen, code for cases in which user edits may disrupt your application.

Recipe 6-11   **Searching for Misspellings**

```
@implementation TestBedViewController

- (void)nextMisspelling:(id)sender
{
    if (![textView isFirstResponder])
        [textView becomeFirstResponder];

    NSRange entireRange = NSMakeRange(0, textView.text.length);
```

```
    // Scan for a new word from the current offset
    NSRange range = [textChecker
        rangeOfMisspelledWordInString:textView.text
        range:entireRange
        startingAt:textOffset
        wrap:YES language:@"en"];

    // Skip forward each time a new misspelling is found / select the word
    if (range.location != NSNotFound)
    {
        textOffset = range.location + range.length;
        textView.selectedRange = range;
    }
    else
        textOffset = 0;
}

@end
```

Get This Recipe's Code

To find this recipe's full sample project, point your browser to https://github.com/erica/iOS-7-Cookbook and go to the folder for Chapter 6.

Spell Checker Protocol

Using `UITextChecker`, you can add a handy little protocol to `NSString` for checking the spelling correctness of any string (see Listing 6-1).

Listing 6-1   **Spell Checker Protocol**

```
@implementation NSString (SpellCheck)
- (BOOL)isSpelledCorrectly
{
    UITextChecker *checker = [[UITextChecker alloc] init];
    NSRange checkRange = NSMakeRange(0, self.length);
    NSString *language = [[NSLocale currentLocale]
        objectForKey:NSLocaleLanguageCode];
    NSRange range = [checker rangeOfMisspelledWordInString:self
        range:checkRange startingAt:0 wrap:NO language:language];
    return (range.location == NSNotFound);
}
@end
```

Searching for Text Strings

It takes little work to adapt Recipe 6-11 to search for text. To implement search, add a text field to your navigation bar and change the bar button to Find. Use NSString's rangeOfString:options:range: method to locate the desired string. Be careful: The string you search for must not be nil. After finding the range of your target text (and assuming that the location is not NSNotFound), you can scroll the text view to the right position by calling scrollRangeToVisible:. Pass the range returned by the string method.

> **Note**
>
> NSNotFound is a constant used to indicate that a range was not successfully located. Check the location field after a search to ensure that a valid value was set.

Summary

This chapter introduces many ways to creatively use text in your iOS applications. In this chapter, you've read about controlling the keyboard and resizing views to accommodate text entry. You've discovered how to create custom input views and how to filter text and test it for valid entry. Before you leave this chapter, here are a few final thoughts to take away:

- Don't assume that your users will or will not be using Bluetooth keyboards. Test your applications with hardware as well as software text entry.

- Although accessory views provide a wonderful way to add extra functionality to your text-input chores, don't overdo the accessories. Keyboards on the iPhone and iPod touch already cover an overwhelming portion of the screen. Adding accessory views further diminishes user space. Where possible, go spartan and minimal in your accessory design.

- Never assume that a user will use shake-to-undo, a feature of questionable value. Provide undo/redo support directly in your application's GUI, where the user can immediately recognize what to do rather than have to recall that Apple added that obscure feature and that it's available for use. Shake-to-undo should always supplement other undo/redo support, not replace it. Undo/redo buttons are a best-use scenario for accessory views.

- Even though you might not be able to construct a perfect regular expression to test user input, don't discount regular expressions that are good enough to cover most cases. And don't forget that you can always use more than one regular expression in sequence to test different approaches to the same problem.

- Check out the new features offered in Text Kit. Text Kit is much more approachable than Core Text and brings substantial functionality and flexibility to text rendering and text input.

7

Working with View Controllers

View controllers simplify view management for many iOS applications. Each view controller owns a hierarchy of views, which presents a complete element of a unified interface. View controllers enable you to build applications that centralize many tasks, including orientation changes and responding to user actions. This chapter looks at using view controller–based classes and how to apply them to real-world situations for both iPhone/iPod and iPad design scenarios.

View Controllers

As their name suggests, view controllers provide the *controller* component of iOS's Model–View–Controller design pattern. Each view controller manages a set of views that comprise a single user-interface component within an application. View controllers coordinate view loading and appearance as well as participate in responding to user interactions.

View controllers also harmonize with the device and underlying operating system. When a user rotates the device, for example, the view controller may update its views' layout. When the OS encounters a low-memory scenario, controllers respond to memory warnings.

In short, view controllers provide central management. They negotiate with a range of orthogonal development requirements sourced from views, models, iOS, and the device itself.

View controllers also centralize presentation metaphors. The ability to layer view controllers in containers extends the paradigm to exciting custom designs. The most common styles of system-supplied parent/child view controllers include navigation controllers that allow users to move their attention from view to view, page view controllers that present virtual books, tab controllers that offer pushbutton access to multiple child controllers, and split view controllers that offer master-list/detail presentations.

View controllers aren't views. They are classes with no visual representation except through the views they manage. View controllers help your views live in a larger application design environment.

The iOS SDK offers many view controller classes. These classes range from general to specific. Here's a quick guide to a subset of the view controllers you'll encounter while building your iOS application interfaces.

The `UIViewController` Class

`UIViewController` is the parent class for view controllers and the one you use to manage your primary views. It is the workhorse of view controllers. You may spend a large part of your time customizing subclasses of this one class. The basic `UIViewController` class manages each primary view's lifetime from start to finish and takes into account the changes that the view must react to along the way.

`UIViewController` instances are responsible for configuring how a view looks and what subviews it displays. Often they rely on loading that information from XIB or storyboard files. Instance methods let you manually create the view layout in code (`loadView`) or add behavior after a view finishes loading (`viewDidLoad`).

Reacting to views being displayed or dismissed is another job that view controllers handle. These are the realities of belonging to a larger application. Methods such as `viewWillAppear:` and `viewWillDisappear:` let you finish any bookkeeping associated with your view management. You might preload data in anticipation of being presented or clean up once a view will no longer be shown onscreen.

Each of the tasks mentioned here specifies how a view fits into an enveloping application. The `UIViewController` mediates between views and these external demands, allowing the view to change itself to meet these needs.

Navigation Controllers

As the name suggests, navigation controllers allow you to drill up and down through tree-based view hierarchies, which is an important primary interface design strategy on smaller members of the iOS device family and a supporting one on tablets. Navigation controllers create the translucent navigation bars that appear at the top of many standard iOS applications.

Navigation controllers let you push new views into place onto a stored stack and automatically generate Back buttons that show the title of the calling view controller. All navigation controllers use a "root" view controller to establish the top of their navigation tree, letting those Back buttons lead you back to the primary view. On tablets, you can use a navigation controller–based interface to work with bar button–based menu items, to present popover presentations, or to integrate with `UISplitViewController` instances for a master/detail presentation experience.

Handing off responsibility to a navigation controller lets you focus design work on creating individual view controller screens. You don't have to worry about specific navigation details other than telling the navigation controller which view to move to next. The history stack and the navigation buttons are handled for you.

Tab Bar Controllers

The `UITabBarController` class lets you control parallel presentations in your application. These are like stations on a radio. A tab bar helps users select which view controller to "tune in to," without there being a specific navigation hierarchy. Each parallel world operates independently, and each can have its own navigation hierarchy. You build the view controller or navigation controller that inhabits each tab, and Cocoa Touch handles the multiple-view details.

For example, when tab bar instances offer more than a certain number of view controller choices at a time (five on the iPhone family of devices, more on tablets), users can customize them through the More > Edit screen. The More > Edit screen lets users drag their favorite controllers down to the button bar at the bottom of the screen. No extra programming is involved. You gain editable tabs for free. All you have to do is request them via the `customizableViewControllers` property.

Split View Controllers

Meant for use on tablet applications, the `UISplitViewController` class offers a way to encapsulate a persistent set of data (typically a table) and associate that data with a detail presentation. You can see split views in action in the iPad's Mail application. When used in landscape orientation, a list of messages appears on the left; individual message content appears on the right. The detail view (the message content in Mail) on the right is subordinate to the master view (Mail's message list) on the left. Tapping a message updates the right-side view with its contents.

In portrait orientation, the master view is normally hidden. It is accessed via a popover, which is reached by tapping the left button of the split view's top bar or via a swipe gesture (in iOS 5.1 and later).

Page View Controllers

Like navigation controllers, tab view controllers, and split view controllers, page view controllers are containers for other view controllers. They manage pages of content using either a book-like page curling presentation or a scrolling style. When using the page curling style, you set the book's "spine," typically along the left or top of the view. Build your "book" by adding individual content view controllers. Each "page" transitions to the next using page curls or pans.

Popover Controllers

Specific to tablets, popover controllers create transient views that pop over other existing interface content. These controllers present information without taking over the entire screen, the
way that modal views normally do. The popovers are usually invoked by tapping a bar button
item in the interface (although they can be created using other interaction techniques) and are
dismissed either by interacting with the content they present or by tapping outside their main
view.

Popovers are populated with view controller instances. Build the view controller and assign it
as the popover's `contentViewController` property before presenting the popover. This allows
popovers to present any range of material that you can design into a standard view controller,
offering exceptional programming flexibility.

> **Note**
>
> Starting in iOS 5, you can subclass `UINavigationBar` and incorporate custom presentations
> into your app's navigation interfaces. Use the `initWithNavigationBarClass:`
> `toolbarClass:` initialization method.

Developing with Navigation Controllers and Split Views

The `UINavigationController` class offers one of the most important ways of managing
interfaces on a device that has limited screen space. It creates a way for users to navigate up
and down a hierarchy of interface presentations to create a virtual GUI that's far larger than
the device. Navigation controllers fold their GUIs into a neat tree-based scheme. Users travel
through that scheme using buttons and choices that transport them around the tree. You see
navigation controllers in the Contacts application and in Settings, where selections lead to new
screens and Back buttons move to previous ones.

Several standard GUI elements reveal the use of navigation controllers in applications, as
shown in Figure 7-1 (left). These include their large navigation bars that appear at the top of
each screen, the backward-pointing button at the top left that appears when the user drills
into hierarchies, and option buttons at the top right that offer other application functionality
such as editing. Many navigation controller applications are built around scrolling lists, where
elements in a list lead to new screens, indicated by the disclosure indicator (gray chevron) and
the detail disclosure button (encircled *i*) found on the right side of each table cell.

The iPad, with its large screen size, doesn't require the kind of space-saving shortcuts that
navigation controllers leverage on iPhone-family devices. Tablet applications can use navigation controllers directly, but the `UISplitViewController` shown in Figure 7-1 (right) offers a
presentation that's better suited for the more expansive device.

Notice the differences between the iPhone implementation on the left and the iPad implementation on the right of Figure 7-1. The iPad's split view controller contains no chevrons. When
items are tapped, their data appears on the same screen, using the large right-side detail area.

The iPhone, lacking this space, presents chevrons which indicate that new views will be pushed onscreen. Each approach takes device-specific design into account in its presentation.

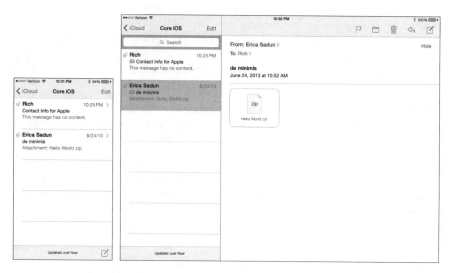

Figure 7-1   The iPhone's navigation controller (left) uses gray chevrons to indicate that detail views will be pushed onscreen when their parents are selected. On the iPad (right), split view controllers use the entire screen, separating navigation elements from detail presentations.

Both the iPhone-family and iPad Inbox views use similar navigation controller elements. These include the Back button (< iCloud), an options button (Edit), and the description in the title bar (the current folder, Core iOS). Each element is created using the navigation controller API to present a hierarchy of e-mail accounts and mailboxes.

The difference lies at the bottom of the navigation tree, at the level of individual messages that form the leaves of the data structure. The iPhone-family standard uses chevrons to indicate leaves. When selected, these leaf view controllers are pushed onto the navigation stack. They join the other view's controllers that trace a user's progress through the interface. The iPad doesn't push its leaves. It presents them in a separate view and omits chevrons that otherwise indicate that users have reached the extent of the hierarchy traversal.

iPhone-style navigation controllers play roles as well on the iPad. When iPad applications use standard (iPhone-style) navigation controllers, they usually do so in narrow contexts such as transient popover presentations, where the controller is presented onscreen in a small view with a limited lifetime. Otherwise, iPad applications are encouraged to use the split view approach that occupies the entire screen.

Using Navigation Controllers and Stacks

Every navigation controller owns a root view controller. This controller forms the base of its stack. You can programmatically push other controllers onto the stack as the user makes choices while navigating through the model's tree. Although the tree itself may be multidimensional, the user's path (essentially his history) is always a straight line representing the choices already made to date. Moving to a new choice extends the navigation breadcrumb trail and automatically builds a Back button each time a new view controller gets pushed onto the stack.

Users can tap a Back button to pop controllers off the stack. The name of each button is the title of the most recent view controller. As you return through the stack of previous view controllers, each Back button indicates the view controller that can be returned to. Users can pop back until they reach the root. Then they can go no further. The root is the base of the tree, and you cannot pop beyond that root.

This stack-based design lingers even when you plan to use just one view controller. You might want to leverage the `UINavigationController`'s built-in navigation bar to build a simple utility that uses a two-button menu, for example. This would disregard any navigational advantage of the stack. You still need to set that one controller as the root via `initWithRootViewController:`.

Pushing and Popping View Controllers

Add new items onto the navigation stack by pushing a new controller with `pushViewController:animated:`. Each view controller provides a `navigationController` property. This property points to the navigation controller that this controller is participating in. The property is `nil` if the controller is not pushed onto a navigation stack.

Use the `navigationController` property to push a new view controller onto the navigation stack and call the push method on the navigation controller. When pushed, the new controller slides onscreen from the right (assuming that you set `animated` to `YES`). A left-pointing Back button appears, leading you one step back on the stack. The Back button uses a chevron along with the title of the previous view controller on the navigation stack. Replace the chevron with a custom image by setting the `backIndicatorImage` property. Always use caution when overriding Apple standard elements. Be sure to maintain the spirit of the Apple Human Interface Guidelines (HIG).

You might push a new view for many reasons. Typically, these involve navigating to specialty views such as detail views or drilling down a file structure or preferences hierarchy. You can push controllers onto the navigation controller stack after your user taps a button, a table item, or a disclosure accessory.

There's little reason to ever subclass `UINavigationController`. Perform push requests and navigation bar customization (such as setting up a bar's title or buttons) inside `UIViewController` subclasses. Customization gets passed up to the navigation controller from the child controllers.

For the most part, you don't access the navigation controller directly. The exceptions to this rule include managing the navigation bar's buttons, changing the bar's look, and initializing with a custom navigation bar class. You might change a bar style or its tint color by accessing the `navigationBar` property directly, as follows:

```
self.navigationController.navigationBar.barStyle =
    UIBarStyleBlack;
```

Be aware that in iOS 7, Apple added `barTintColor` to tint the bar background instead of `tintColor`. The `tintColor` property is repurposed to tint bar button items.

Bar Buttons

To add new buttons, you modify your `navigationItem`, which provides a representational class that describes the content shown on the navigation bar, including its left and right bar button items and its title view. Here's how you can assign a button to the bar:

```
self.navigationItem.rightBarButtonItem = [[UIBarButtonItem alloc]
    initWithTitle:@"Action" style:UIBarButtonItemStylePlain target:self
    action:@selector(performAction:)];
```

To remove a button, assign the item to `nil`. Bar button items are not views. They are classes that contain titles, styles, and callback information that navigation items and toolbars use to build actual buttons in to interfaces. iOS does not provide you with access to the button views built by bar button items and their navigation items.

Starting in iOS 5, you can add multiple bar button items to the left and right. Assign an array to the `rightBarButtonItems` (notice the s) or `leftBarButtonItems` properties for the navigation item:

```
self.navigationItem.rightBarButtonItems = barButtonArray;
```

Edge-to-Edge Layout

The design focus of iOS 7 is your application's content—more specifically, your user's content. Borders and shadows have been removed and transparency has been added in navigation bars and other UI elements. This change significantly impacts the layout of your views, especially when you're using a navigation bar.

Beginning with iOS 7, all view controllers use full-screen layout. The `wantsFullScreenLayout` property on `UIViewController` has been deprecated, and setting it to `NO` will likely lead to very unexpected layout. With full-screen layout, the view controller will size its view to fill the entire screen, passing fully under the translucent system status bar. In addition, by default, all bars in iOS 7 are now translucent to further reveal the underlying content.

The flowing of content under bars will shift your content in ways that are foreign in previous versions. You must actively include the area underneath the status bar and your own bars in your layout.

To provide more control over placement, `UIViewController` now provides a number of new layout properties. Manage status bar visibility at the view controller level by implementing `prefersStatusBarHidden` in your subclasses and returning an appropriate Boolean. Many of the new properties allow the positioning or sizing of views based on the currently displayed bars.

For view controllers, you can now specify which edges of the view should be extended under translucent bars by setting `edgesForExtendedLayout`. By default, this property is `UIRectEdgeAll`—which means all your edges will extend through the translucent elements as shown in Figure 7-2 (left). You can also specify any specific edge(s) or `UIRectEdgeNone`, stopping the content view edge when it reaches the bar, as shown in Figure 7-2 (right). By default, `edgesForExtendedLayout` also includes opaque bars. Set `extendedLayoutIncludesOpaque-Bars` to `NO` to alter this behavior.

 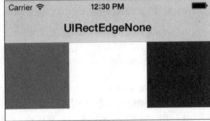

Figure 7-2   In iOS 7, `edgesForExtendedLayout` on `UIViewController` controls the edge of the view used for layout. `UIRectEdgeAll`, the default, extends the edge through the translucent bars (left). `UIRectEdgeNone` stops the edge at the extent of the bars (right).

Scroll views are also impacted by the system status bar and developer-implemented bars (navigation bar, toolbar, and tab bar). By default, `UIScrollViews` automatically adjust their content insets to handle these bar elements. To turn off this behavior and manually manage the scroll view insets, set `automaticallyAdjustsScrollViewInsets` to `NO`.

Finally, to assist in laying out content within your views, iOS 7 provides the `topLayoutGuide` and `bottomLayoutGuide` properties. These properties indicate the top and bottom bar edges in your view controller's view. The location represented depends on the visible bars.

For `topLayoutGuide`:

- Status bar but no navigation bar visible—bottom of the status bar.
- Navigation bar visible—bottom of the navigation bar.
- No status or navigation bar visible—top of the screen.

For `bottomLayoutGuide`:

- Toolbar or tab bar visible—top of the toolbar or tab bar.
- No toolbar or tab bar visible—bottom of the screen.

Use these properties to create relative constraints, positioning your subviews relative to the bar edges regardless of the frame location or foreknowledge of bar visibility. Use them with Auto Layout constraints both in Interface Builder (IB) or in your layout code. Outside of Auto Layout, use guides in frame-based positioning. Reference the offset value in the guide's `length` property.

Recipe: The Navigation Item Class

The objects that populate the navigation bar are put into place using the `UINavigationItem` class, which is a class that stores information about those objects. Navigation item properties include the left and right bar button items, the title shown on the bar, the view used to show the title, and any Back button used to navigate back from the current view.

This class enables you to attach buttons, text, and other UI objects in three key locations: the left, the center, and the right of the navigation bar. Typically, this works out to be a regular button on the right, some text (usually the `UIViewController`'s title) in the middle, and a Back-style button on the left. But you're not limited to this layout. You can add custom controls to any of three locations: the left, the center (title area), and the right. You might build navigation bars with search fields in the middle instead, or segment controls, toolbars, pictures, and more. Further, you can add multiple items to the left and right button arrays. It's all easy to modify.

Titles and Back Buttons

The central title area is especially customizable. You can assign a title to the navigation item like this:

```
self.navigationItem.title = @"My Title"
```

This is equivalent to setting the view controller's `title` property directly. The simplest way to customize the actual title is to use the `title` property of the child view controller rather than the navigation item:

```
self.title = @"Hello";
```

When assigned, the navigation controller uses the title to establish the Back button's "go back" text. If you push a new controller on top of a controller titled `"Hello"`, the Back button indicates that it links to `"Hello"`.

You could also replace the text-based title with a custom view such as a control. This code adds a custom segmented control, but this could be an image view, a stepper, or anything else:

```
self.navigationItem.titleView =
    [[UISegmentedControl alloc] initWithItems:items];
```

Macros

Macros simplify your work when building bar buttons because the creation task is so repetitive. The following macro creates a basic button item:

```
#define BARBUTTON(TITLE, SELECTOR) [[UIBarButtonItem alloc] \
    initWithTitle:TITLE style:UIBarButtonItemStylePlain \
    target:self action:SELECTOR]
```

You supply it with a title and a selector to call. Each call to this macro specifies only the title and selector, tightening up the code's readability:

```
self.navigationItem.rightBarButtonItem =
    BARBUTTON(@"Push", @selector(push:));
```

This version of the macro assumes that the target is "self", which is quite common, although you could easily adapt this. The following macro adds a target that you specify:

```
#define BARBUTTON_TARGET(TITLE, TARGET, SELECTOR) \
    [[UIBarButtonItem alloc] initWithTitle:TITLE \
    style:UIBarButtonItemStylePlain target:TARGET action:SELECTOR]
```

The vocabulary of bar buttons you use varies by your particular application demands. It's easy to create macros for system items provided by Apple, image items created from picture resources, and custom view items, which can embed controls and other non-bar button elements.

Recipe 7-1 combines these features to demonstrate how controller titles and navigation items build together during drilling. It offers a super-simple interface: You select the title for the next item you want to push onto the navigation stack, and then you push it on. This allows you to see how the navigation controller stack grows using default behavior.

Recipe 7-1   **Basic Navigation Drilling**

```
// Array of strings
- (NSArray *)fooBarArray
{
    return [@"Foo*Bar*Baz*Qux" componentsSeparatedByString:@"*"];
}

// Push a new controller onto the stack
- (void)push:(id)sender
{
    NSString *newTitle =
        [self fooBarArray][seg.selectedSegmentIndex];

    UIViewController *newController =
        [[TestBedViewController alloc] init];
    newController.edgesForExtendedLayout = UIRectEdgeNone;
```

```
    newController.title = newTitle;

    [self.navigationController
        pushViewController:newController animated:YES];
}


- (void)loadView
{
    self.view = [[UIView alloc] init];
    self.view.backgroundColor = [UIColor whiteColor];

    // Establish a button to push new controllers
    self.navigationItem.rightBarButtonItem =
        BARBUTTON(@"Push", @selector(push:));

    // Create a segmented control to pick the next title
    seg = [[UISegmentedControl alloc] initWithItems:
        [self fooBarArray]];
    seg.selectedSegmentIndex = 0;
    [self.view addSubview:seg];
    PREPCONSTRAINTS(seg);

    UILabel *label =
        [self labelWithTitle:@"Select Title for Pushed Controller"];
    [self.view addSubview:label];
    PREPCONSTRAINTS(label);

    id topLayoutGuide = self.topLayoutGuide;
    CONSTRAIN(self.view, label, @"H:|-[label(>=0)]-|");
    CONSTRAIN(self.view, seg, @"H:|-[seg(>=0)]-|");
    CONSTRAIN_VIEWS(self.view,
        @"V:[topLayoutGuide]-[label]-[seg]",
        NSDictionaryOfVariableBindings(seg, label, topLayoutGuide));
}
```

Get This Recipe's Code

To find this recipe's full sample project, point your browser to https://github.com/erica/iOS-7-Cookbook and go to the folder for Chapter 7.

Recipe: Modal Presentation

With normal navigation controllers, you push your way along views, stopping occasionally to pop back to previous views. That approach assumes that you're drilling your way up and down a set of data that matches the tree-based view structure you're using. Modal presentation offers another way to show a view controller.

After you send the `presentViewController:animated:completion:` message to a view controller, the specified view controller appears on the screen and takes control until it's dismissed with `dismissViewControllerAnimated:completion:`. This enables you to add special-purpose dialogs to your applications that go beyond alert views.

Typically, modal controllers prompt users to pick data such as contacts from Contacts or photos from Photos or perform a short-lived task such as sending e-mail or setting preferences. Use modal controllers in any setting where it makes sense to perform a limited-time task that lies outside the normal scope of the active view controller.

Modal presentations can use four transition styles:

- **Slide**—This transition style slides a new view over the old.
- **Flip**—This transition style turns a view over to the "back" of the presentation.
- **Fade**—This transition style dissolves the new view into visibility.
- **Curl**—This transition style makes the primary view curl up out of the way to reveal the new view beneath it.

Set these styles in the `modalTransitionStyle` property of the presented view controller. The standard, `UIModalTransitionStyleCoverVertical`, slides the modal view up and over the current view controller. When dismissed, it slides back down.

`UIModalTransitionStyleFlipHorizontal` performs a back-to-front flip from right to left. It looks as if you're revealing the back side of the currently presented view. When dismissed, it flips back, left to right.

`UIModalTransitionStyleCrossDissolve` fades the new view in over the previous one. On dismissal, it fades back to the original view.

Use `UIModalTransitionStylePartialCurl` to curl up content (in the way the Maps application does) to reveal a modal settings view "underneath" the primary view controller.

On the iPhone and iPod touch, modal controllers always fully take over the screen. The iPad offers more nuanced presentations. The iPad offers five presentation styles set by the `modalPresentationStyle` property:

- **Full screen**—A full-screen presentation (`UIModalPresentationFullScreen`) is the default on the iPhone, where the new modal view completely covers both the screen and any existing content. This is the only presentation style that is legal for curls; any other presentation style raises a runtime exception, crashing the application.
- **Page sheet**—In the page sheet style (`UIModalPresentationPageSheet`), coverage defaults to a portrait aspect ratio, so the modal view controller completely covers the screen in portrait mode and partially covers the screen in landscape mode, as if a portrait-aligned piece of paper were added to the display.

- **Form sheet**—The form sheet style (`UIModalPresentationFormSheet`) display covers a small center portion of the screen, allowing you to shift focus to the modal element while retaining the maximum visibility of the primary application view.

- **Current context**—This is the presentation style of the view's parent view controller (`UIModalPresentationCurrentContext`).

- **Custom**—This custom presentation style (`UIModalPresentationCustom`), managed by the Custom Transitions API, was added in iOS 7.

These styles are best experienced in landscape mode to visually differentiate the page-sheet presentation from the full-screen one.

> **Note**
>
> iOS 7 introduces a model for creating custom transitions between view controllers to augment those provided by the system. Custom transitions provide nearly unlimited flexibility in creating creative transitions that can be used nearly anywhere that view controllers currently transition, including modal presentation and navigation controller stack changes.

Presenting a Custom Modal Information View

Presenting a modal controller branches off from your primary navigation path, introducing a new interface that takes charge until your user explicitly dismisses it. You present a modal controller like this:

```
[self presentViewController:someControllerInstance animated:YES completion:nil];
```

The controller that is presented can be any kind of view controller subclass, as well. In the case of a navigation controller, the modal presentation can have its own navigation hierarchy built as a chain of interactions. Use the completion block to finish up any tasks you need to perform after the view controller has animated into place.

Always provide a Done option of some kind to allow users to dismiss the controller. The easiest way to accomplish this is to present a navigation controller and add a bar button to its navigation items with an action:

```
- (IBAction)done:(id)sender
{
    [self dismissViewControllerAnimated:YES completion:nil];
}
```

Storyboards simplify the creation of modal controller elements. Drag in a navigation controller instance, along with its paired view controller, and add a Done button to the provided navigation bar. Set the view controller's class to your custom modal type and connect the Done button to the done: method. Name your navigation controller in the Attributes inspector so that you can use that identifier to load it.

You can either add the modal components to your primary storyboard or create them in a separate file. Recipe 7-2 loads a custom file (Modal~DeviceType.storyboard), but you can just as easily add the elements in your MainStoryboard_DeviceType file.

Recipe 7-2 provides the key pieces for creating modal elements. The presentation is performed in the application's main view controller hierarchy. Here, users select the transition and presentation styles from segmented controls, but these are normally chosen in advance by the developer and set in code or in IB. This recipe offers a toolbox that you can test on each platform, using each orientation to explore how each option looks.

> ### Note
>
> As of the initial iOS 7 release, a well-reported issue exists in the full-screen flip transition presented in Recipe 7-2. The navigation bar contents drop abruptly into position at the end of the animation. Hopefully, this issue will be resolved in a future iOS release.

Recipe 7-2   **Presenting and Dismissing a Modal Controller**

```
// Presenting the controller
- (void)action:(id)sender
{
    // Load info controller from storyboard
    UIStoryboard *storyBoard = [UIStoryboard
        storyboardWithName:
            (IS_IPAD ? @"Modal~iPad" : @"Modal~iPhone")
        bundle:[NSBundle mainBundle]];
    UINavigationController *navController =
        [storyBoard instantiateViewControllerWithIdentifier:
            @"infoNavigationController"];

    // Select the transition style
    int styleSegment =
        [segmentedControl selectedSegmentIndex];
    int transitionStyles[4] = {
        UIModalTransitionStyleCoverVertical,
        UIModalTransitionStyleCrossDissolve,
        UIModalTransitionStyleFlipHorizontal,
        UIModalTransitionStylePartialCurl};
    navController.modalTransitionStyle =
        transitionStyles[styleSegment];

    // Select the presentation style for iPad only
    if (IS_IPAD)
    {
```

```objc
        int presentationSegment =
            [iPadStyleControl selectedSegmentIndex];
        int presentationStyles[3] = {
            UIModalPresentationFullScreen,
            UIModalPresentationPageSheet,
            UIModalPresentationFormSheet};

        if (navController.modalTransitionStyle ==
            UIModalTransitionStylePartialCurl)
        {
            // Partial curl with any non-full-screen presentation
            // raises an exception
            navController.modalPresentationStyle =
                UIModalPresentationFullScreen;
            [iPadStyleControl setSelectedSegmentIndex:0];
        }
        else
            navController.modalPresentationStyle =
                presentationStyles[presentationSegment];
    }

    [self.navigationController presentViewController:navController
        animated:YES completion:nil];
}


- (void)loadView
{
    self.view = [[UIView alloc] init];
    self.view.backgroundColor = [UIColor whiteColor];
    self.navigationItem.rightBarButtonItem =
        BARBUTTON(@"Action", @selector(action:));

    segmentedControl =
        [[UISegmentedControl alloc] initWithItems:
            [@"Slide Fade Flip Curl"
                componentsSeparatedByString:@" "]];
    [segmentedControl setSelectedSegmentIndex:0];
    self.navigationItem.titleView = segmentedControl;

    if (IS_IPAD)
    {
        NSArray *presentationChoices =
            [NSArray arrayWithObjects:@"Full Screen",
                @"Page Sheet", @"Form Sheet", nil];
        iPadStyleControl =
            [[UISegmentedControl alloc] initWithItems:
                presentationChoices];
```

```
        [iPadStyleControl setSelectedSegmentIndex:0];
         [self.view addSubview:iPadStyleControl];
        PREPCONSTRAINTS(iPadStyleControl);
        CENTER_VIEW_H(self.view, iPadStyleControl);
        id topLayoutGuide = self.topLayoutGuide;
        CONSTRAIN_VIEWS(self.view,
            @"V:[topLayoutGuide]-[iPadStyleControl]",
            NSDictionaryOfVariableBindings(topLayoutGuide,
                iPadStyleControl));
    }
}
```

Get This Recipe's Code

To find this recipe's full sample project, point your browser to https://github.com/erica/iOS-7-Cookbook and go to the folder for Chapter 7.

Recipe: Building Split View Controllers

Using split view controllers is the preferred way to present hierarchically driven navigation on the iPad. Such a controller generally consists of a table of contents on the left and a detail view on the right, although the class (and Apple's guidelines) is not limited to this presentation style. The heart of the class consists of the notion of an organizing section (master) and a presentation section (detail), both of which can appear onscreen simultaneously in landscape orientation, and whose organizing section optionally converts to a popover in portrait orientation. (You can override this default behavior by implementing `splitViewController:shouldHideViewController:inOrientation:` in your delegate, letting your split view show both sections in portrait mode.)

Figure 7-3 shows the very basic split view controller built by Recipe 7-3 in landscape (left) and portrait (right) orientations. This controller sets the color of the detail view by selecting an item from the list in the root view. In landscape, both views are shown at once. In portrait orientation, the user must tap the upper-left button on the detail view to access the root view as a popover or use an optional swipe gesture. When programming for this orientation, be aware that the popover can interfere with detail view, as it is presented over that view; design accordingly.

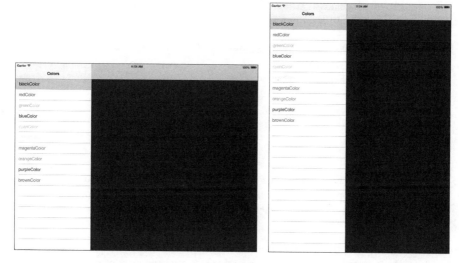

Figure 7-3   At their simplest, split view controllers consist of an organizing pane and a detail view pane. The organizing pane, which you see in this figure, is normally hidden in portrait orientation (right). Users view it via a popover accessed from a navigation bar button or invoke it with a swipe gesture.

The code in Recipe 7-3 builds three separate objects: the master and detail view controllers and the split view controller that owns the first two. The split view controller always contains two children, the master at index 0 and the detail at index 1.

You'll want to add the master and detail controllers to navigation controller shells, to provide a consistent interface. In the case of the detail controller, this provides a home for the bar button in portrait orientation. The following method builds the two child view controllers, embeds them into navigation controllers, adds them to a view controller array, and returns a new split view controller that hosts those views:

```
- (UISplitViewController *)splitViewController
{
    // Create the navigation-embedded root (master) view
    ColorTableViewController *rootVC =
        [[ColorTableViewController alloc] init];
    rootVC.title = @"Colors"; // make sure to set the title
    UINavigationController *rootNav =
        [[UINavigationController alloc]
            initWithRootViewController:rootVC];

    // Create the navigation-run detail view
    DetailViewController *detailVC =
        [DetailViewController controller];
    UINavigationController *detailNav =
```

```
        [[UINavigationController alloc]
            initWithRootViewController:detailVC];

    // Add both to the split view controller
    UISplitViewController *svc =
        [[UISplitViewController alloc] init];
    svc.viewControllers = @[rootNav, detailNav];
    svc.delegate = detailVC;

    return svc;
}
```

The master view controller is often some kind of table view controller, as is the one in Recipe 7-3. What you see here is pretty much as bare bones as tables get. It is a list of color items (specifically, UIColor method names), each one with a cell title that is tinted to match that color.

When an item is selected, the controller uses its built-in splitViewController property to send a request to its detail view. This property returns the split view controller that owns the root view. From there, the controller can retrieve the split view's delegate, which has been assigned to the detail view. By casting that delegate to the detail view controller's class, the root view can affect the detail view more meaningfully. In this extremely simple example, the selected cell's text tint is applied to the detail view's background color.

> **Note**
>
> Make sure you set the root view controller's title property. It is used to set the text for the button that appears in the detail view in portrait mode.

Recipe 7-3's DetailViewController class is about as skeletal an implementation as you can get. It provides the most basic functionality you need to provide a detail view implementation with split view controllers. This consists of the will-hide/will-show method pair that adds and hides that all-important bar button for the detail view.

When the split view controller converts the master view controller into a popover controller in portrait orientation, it passes that new controller to the detail view controller. It is the detail controller's job to retain and handle that popover until the interface returns to landscape orientation. In this skeletal class definition, a strong property holds onto the popover for the duration of portrait interaction.

Recipe 7-3 **Building Detail and Master Views for a Split View Controller**

```
@interface DetailViewController : UIViewController
    <UIPopoverControllerDelegate, UISplitViewControllerDelegate>
@property (nonatomic, strong)
    UIPopoverController *popoverController;
@end
```

```objc
@implementation DetailViewController
+ (instancetype)controller
{
    DetailViewController *controller =
        [[DetailViewController alloc] init];
    controller.view.backgroundColor = [UIColor blackColor];
    return controller;
}

// Called upon going into portrait mode, hiding the normal table view
- (void)splitViewController:(UISplitViewController*)svc
    willHideViewController:(UIViewController *)aViewController
    withBarButtonItem:(UIBarButtonItem*)barButtonItem
    forPopoverController:(UIPopoverController*)aPopoverController
{
    barButtonItem.title = aViewController.title;
    self.navigationItem.leftBarButtonItem = barButtonItem;
    self.popoverController = aPopoverController;
}

// Called upon going into landscape mode
- (void)splitViewController:(UISplitViewController*)svc
    willShowViewController:(UIViewController *)aViewController
    invalidatingBarButtonItem:(UIBarButtonItem *)barButtonItem
{
    self.navigationItem.leftBarButtonItem = nil;
    self.popoverController = nil;
}

// Use this to avoid the popover hiding in portrait.
// When omitted, you get the default behavior.
/* - (BOOL)splitViewController:(UISplitViewController *)svc
    shouldHideViewController:(UIViewController *)vc
    inOrientation:(UIInterfaceOrientation)orientation
{
    return NO;
}*/
@end


@interface ColorTableViewController : UITableViewController
@end

@implementation ColorTableViewController
+ (instancetype)controller
{
    ColorTableViewController *controller =
```

```
        [[ColorTableViewController alloc] init];
    controller.title = @"Colors";
    return controller;
}


- (NSInteger)numberOfSectionsInTableView:(UITableView *)tableView
{
    return 1;
}


- (NSArray *)selectors
{
    return @[@"blackColor", @"redColor", @"greenColor", @"blueColor",
        @"cyanColor", @"yellowColor", @"magentaColor", @"orangeColor",
        @"purpleColor", @"brownColor"];
}


- (NSInteger)tableView:(UITableView *)tableView
    numberOfRowsInSection:(NSInteger)section
{
    return [self selectors].count;
}


- (UITableViewCell *)tableView:(UITableView *)tableView
    cellForRowAtIndexPath:(NSIndexPath *)indexPath
{
    UITableViewCell *cell =
        [tableView dequeueReusableCellWithIdentifier:@"generic"];
    if (!cell) cell = [[UITableViewCell alloc]
        initWithStyle: UITableViewCellStyleDefault
        reuseIdentifier:@"generic"];

    // Set title and color
    NSString *item = [self selectors][indexPath.row];
    cell.textLabel.text = item;
    cell.textLabel.textColor =
        [UIColor performSelector:NSSelectorFromString(item)
            withObject:nil];

    return cell;
}


- (void)tableView:(UITableView *)tableView
    didSelectRowAtIndexPath:(NSIndexPath *)indexPath
{
    // On selection, update the main view background color
    UINavigationController *nav =
```

```
        [self.splitViewController.viewControllers lastObject];
    UIViewController *controller = [nav topViewController];
    UITableViewCell *cell = [tableView cellForRowAtIndexPath:indexPath];
    controller.view.backgroundColor = cell.textLabel.textColor;
}
@end
```

Get This Recipe's Code

To find this recipe's full sample project, point your browser to https://github.com/erica/iOS-7-Cookbook and go to the folder for Chapter 7.

Recipe: Creating Universal Split View/Navigation Apps

Recipe 7-4 modifies Recipe 7-3's split view controller to provide a functionally equivalent application that runs properly on both iPhone and iPad platforms. Accomplishing this takes several steps that add to Recipe 7-3's code base. You do not have to remove functionality from the split view controller approach, but you must provide alternatives in several places.

Recipe 7-4 uses a macro to determine whether the code is being run on an iPad- or iPhone-style device. It leverages the UIKit user interface idiom as follows:

```
#define IS_IPAD (UI_USER_INTERFACE_IDIOM() == UIUserInterfaceIdiomPad)
```

This macro returns YES when the device characteristics are iPad-like rather than iPhone-like (such as on the iPhone or iPod touch). First introduced in iOS 3.2, which introduced the iPad as a new hardware platform, idioms allow you to perform runtime checks in your code to provide interface choices that fit with the deployed platform.

In an iPhone deployment, the detail view controller code remains identical to Recipe 7-3, but to be displayed, it must be pushed onto the navigation stack rather than shown side by side in a split view. The navigation controller is set up as the primary view for the application window rather than the split view. A simple check at application launch lets your code choose which approach to use:

```
- (UINavigationController *)navWithColorTableViewController
{
    ColorTableViewController *rootVC =
        [[ColorTableViewController alloc] init];
    rootVC.title = @"Colors";
    UINavigationController *nav = [[UINavigationController alloc]
        initWithRootViewController:rootVC];
    return nav;
}


- (BOOL)application:(UIApplication *)application
```

```
            didFinishLaunchingWithOptions:(NSDictionary *)launchOptions
{
    window = [[UIWindow alloc] initWithFrame:
        [[UIScreen mainScreen] bounds]];

    UIViewController * rootVC = nil;
    if (IS_IPAD)
        rootVC = [self splitViewController];
    else
        rootVC = [self navWithColorTableViewController];

    rootVC.edgesForExtendedLayout = UIRectEdgeNone;
    window.rootViewController = rootVC;
    [window makeKeyAndVisible];
    return YES;
}
```

The rest of the story lies in the two methods of Recipe 7-4, within the color-picking table view controller. Two key checks decide whether to show disclosure accessories and how to respond to table taps:

- On the iPad, disclosure indicators should never be used at the last level of detail presentation. On the iPhone, they indicate that a new view will be pushed on selection. Checking for deployment platform lets your code choose whether to include these accessories in cells.

- When you're working with the iPhone, there's no option for using split views, so your code must push a new detail view onto the navigation controller stack. Compare this to the iPad code, which only needs to reach out to an existing detail view and update its background color.

In real-world deployment, these two checks would likely expand in complexity beyond the details shown in this simple recipe. You'd want to add a check to your model to determine whether you are, indeed, at the lowest level of the tree hierarchy before suppressing disclosure accessories. Similarly, you might need to update or replace presentations in your detail view controller.

Recipe 7-4 **Adding Universal Support for Split View Alternatives**

```
- (UITableViewCell *)tableView:(UITableView *)tableView
    cellForRowAtIndexPath:(NSIndexPath *)indexPath
{
    UITableViewCell *cell =
        [tableView dequeueReusableCellWithIdentifier:@"generic"];
    if (!cell) cell = [[UITableViewCell alloc]
        initWithStyle:UITableViewCellStyleDefault
        reuseIdentifier:@"generic"];
```

```
    NSString *item = [self selectors][indexPath.row];
    cell.textLabel.text = item;
    cell.textLabel.textColor =
        [UIColor performSelector:NSSelectorFromString(item)
            withObject:nil];

    cell.accessoryType = IS_IPAD ?
        UITableViewCellAccessoryNone :
        UITableViewCellAccessoryDisclosureIndicator;

    return cell;
}

- (void)tableView:(UITableView *)tableView
    didSelectRowAtIndexPath:(NSIndexPath *)indexPath
{
    UITableViewCell *cell =
        [tableView cellForRowAtIndexPath:indexPath];

    if (IS_IPAD)
    {
        UINavigationController *nav =
            [self.splitViewController.viewControllers lastObject];
        UIViewController *controller = [nav topViewController];
        controller.view.backgroundColor = cell.textLabel.textColor;
    }
    else
    {
        DetailViewController *controller =
            [DetailViewController controller];
        controller.view.backgroundColor = cell.textLabel.textColor;
        controller.title = cell.textLabel.text;

        [self.navigationController
            pushViewController:controller animated:YES];
    }
}
```

Get This Recipe's Code

To find this recipe's full sample project, point your browser to https://github.com/erica/iOS-7-Cookbook and go to the folder for Chapter 7.

Recipe: Tab Bars

On the iPhone and iPod touch, the `UITabBarController` class allows users to move between multiple view controllers and to customize the bar at the bottom of the screen. This is best seen in the music application. It offers one-tap access to different views and a More button that leads to user selection and editing of the bottom bar. Tab bars are not recommended for use as a primary design pattern on the iPad, although Apple supports their use when needed, especially in split views and popovers.

With tab bars, you don't push views the way you do with navigation bars. Instead, you assemble a collection of controllers (they can individually be `UIViewControllers`, `UINavigationControllers`, or any other kind of view controllers) and add them to a tab bar by setting the bar's `viewControllers` property. Cocoa Touch does the rest of the work for you. Set `allowsCustomizing` to `YES` to enable end-user reordering of the bar.

Recipe 7-5 creates 11 simple view controllers of the `BrightnessController` class. This class sets the background to a specified gray level—in this case, from 0% to 100%, in steps of 10%. Figure 7-4 (left) shows the interface in its default mode, with the first four items and a More button displayed.

Users may reorder tabs by selecting the More option and then tapping Edit. This opens the configuration panel shown in Figure 7-4 (right). These 11 view controllers offer options a user can navigate through and select from. Note that the navigation bar in Figure 7-4 (right) has not been converted to the standard flat UI appearance as of the iOS 7 release.

Note that the translucent navigation bar background tint is black throughout the entire interface. Apple provides the `UIAppearance` protocol, which allows you to customize UI properties for all instances of a given class. Recipe 7-5 uses this functionality to tint its navigation bar's background black:

```
[[UINavigationBar appearance] setBarTintColor:[UIColor blackColor]];
```

> **Note**
>
> Starting with iOS 7, `tintColor` no longer tints the background of bars, such as the navigation bar. To tint the background, use the `barTintColor` property.

This recipe adds its 11 controllers twice. The first time it assigns them to the list of view controllers available to the user:

```
tabBarController.viewControllers = controllers;
```

The second time it specifies that the user can select from the entire list when interactively customizing the bottom tab bar:

```
tabBarController.customizableViewControllers = controllers;
```

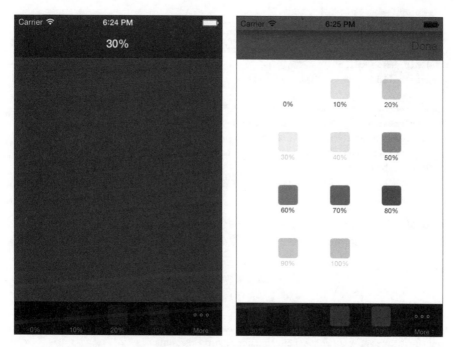

Figure 7-4   Tab bar controllers allow users to pick view controllers from a bar at the bottom of the screen (left) and customize the bar from a list of available view controllers (right).

The second line is optional; the first is mandatory. After setting up the view controllers, you can add all or some to the customizable list. If you don't, you still can see the extra view controllers by tapping the More button, but users won't be able to include them in the main tab bar on demand.

Tab art appears inverted in color on the More screen. According to Apple, this is the expected and proper behavior. Apple has no plans to change this. It does provide an interesting view contrast when your 100% black swatch appears as pure white on that screen. In addition, in iOS 7, the icon and text for items are now tinted with the inherited tintColor for the application.

Recipe 7-5   Creating a Tab Bar View Controller

```
#pragma mark - BrightnessController
@interface BrightnessController : UIViewController
@end

@implementation BrightnessController
{
    int brightness;
```

```
}

// Create a swatch for the tab icon using standard Quartz
// and UIKit image calls
- (UIImage*)buildSwatch:(int)aBrightness
{
    CGRect rect = CGRectMake(0.0f, 0.0f, 30.0f, 30.0f);
    UIGraphicsBeginImageContext(rect.size);
    UIBezierPath *path = [UIBezierPath
            bezierPathWithRoundedRect:rect cornerRadius:4.0f];
    [[[UIColor blackColor]
        colorWithAlphaComponent:(float) aBrightness / 10.0f] set];
    [path fill];

    UIImage *image = UIGraphicsGetImageFromCurrentImageContext();
    UIGraphicsEndImageContext();

    return image;
}

// The view controller consists of a background color
// and a tab bar item icon
- (BrightnessController *)initWithBrightness:(int)aBrightness
{
    self = [super init];
    brightness = aBrightness;
    self.title = [NSString stringWithFormat:@"%d%%",
        brightness * 10];
    self.tabBarItem =
        [[UITabBarItem alloc] initWithTitle:self.title
            image:[self buildSwatch:brightness] tag:0];
    self.view.autoresizesSubviews = YES;
    self.view.autoresizingMask =
        UIViewAutoresizingFlexibleWidth |
        UIViewAutoresizingFlexibleHeight;
    return self;
}

// Tint the background
- (void)loadView
{
    self.view = [[UIView alloc] init];
    self.view.backgroundColor =
        [UIColor colorWithWhite:(brightness / 10.0f) alpha:1.0f];
}

+ (id)controllerWithBrightness:(int)brightness
```

```
{
    BrightnessController *controller =
        [[BrightnessController alloc]
            initWithBrightness:brightness];
    return controller;
}
@end

#pragma mark - Application Setup
@interface TestBedAppDelegate : NSObject
     <UIApplicationDelegate, UITabBarControllerDelegate>
@property (nonatomic, strong) UIWindow *window;
@end

@implementation TestBedAppDelegate
{
    UITabBarController *tabBarController;
}

- (void)applicationDidFinishLaunching:(UIApplication *)application
{
    // Globally use a black tint for nav bars
    [[UINavigationBar appearance]
        setBarTintColor:[UIColor blackColor]];

    // Build an array of controllers
    NSMutableArray *controllers = [NSMutableArray array];
    for (int i = 0; i <= 10; i++)
    {
        BrightnessController *controller =
            [BrightnessController controllerWithBrightness:i];
        UINavigationController *nav =
            [[UINavigationController alloc]
                initWithRootViewController:controller];
        nav.navigationBar.barStyle = UIBarStyleBlackTranslucent;
        [controllers addObject:nav];
    }

    tabBarController = [[UITabBarController alloc] init];
    tabBarController.tabBar.barTintColor = [UIColor blackColor];
    tabBarController.tabBar.translucent = NO;
    tabBarController.viewControllers = controllers;
    tabBarController.customizableViewControllers = controllers;
    tabBarController.delegate = self;

    _window = [[UIWindow alloc]
        initWithFrame:[[UIScreen mainScreen] bounds]];
```

```
    _window.tintColor = COOKBOOK_PURPLE_COLOR;
    tabBarController.edgesForExtendedLayout = UIRectEdgeNone;

    _window.rootViewController = tabBarController;
    [_window makeKeyAndVisible];
    return YES;
}
@end
```

Get This Recipe's Code

To find this recipe's full sample project, point your browser to https://github.com/erica/iOS-7-Cookbook and go to the folder for Chapter 7.

Remembering Tab State

On iOS, persistence is golden. When starting or resuming your application from termination or interruption, always return users to a state that closely matches where they left off. This lets your users continue whatever tasks they were involved with and provides a user interface that matches the previous session. Listing 7-1 introduces an example of doing exactly that.

This update to Recipe 7-5 stores both the current tab order and the currently selected tab, and it does so whenever those items are updated. When a user launches the application, the code searches for previous settings and applies them if they are found.

To respond to updates, a tab bar delegate must declare the UITabBarControllerDelegate protocol. The approach used here depends on two delegate methods. The first, tabBar-Controller:didEndCustomizingViewControllers:changed:, provides the current array of view controllers after the user has customized them with the More > Edit screen. This code captures their titles (10%, 20%, and so on) and uses that information to relate a name to each view controller.

The second delegate method is tabBarController:didSelectViewController:. The tab bar controller calls this method each time a user selects a new tab. By capturing the selectedIndex, this code stores the controller number relative to the current array.

In this example, these values are stored using iOS's built-in user defaults system, NSUserDefaults. This preferences system works very much like a large mutable dictionary. Set values for keys by using setObject:forKey:, as shown here:

```
[[NSUserDefaults standardUserDefaults] setObject:titles
    forKey:@"tabOrder"];
```

Then retrieve them with objectForKey:, like so:

```
NSArray *titles = [[NSUserDefaults standardUserDefaults]
    objectForKey:@"tabOrder"];
```

Synchronizing your settings ensures that the stored defaults dictionary matches your changes:

```
[[NSUserDefaults standardUserDefaults] synchronize];
```

When the application launches, it checks for previous settings describing the last selected tab order and selected tab. If it finds them, it uses these settings to set up the tabs and select a tab to make active. Because the titles contain the information about what brightness value to show, this code converts the stored title from text to a number and divides that number by 10 to send to the initialization method.

Most applications aren't based on such a simple numeric system. If you use titles to store your tab bar order, make sure you name your view controllers meaningfully and in a way that lets you match a view controller with the tab ordering.

> **Note**
>
> You could also store an array of the view tags as NSNumbers or, better yet, use the NSKeyedArchiver class. Archiving lets you rebuild views using state information that you store on termination. Another option is the state preservation system introduced in iOS 6.

Listing 7-1 **Storing Tab State to User Defaults**

```
@implementation TestBedAppDelegate
{
    UITabBarController *tabBarController;
}

- (void)tabBarController:(UITabBarController *)tabBarController
    didEndCustomizingViewControllers:(NSArray *)viewControllers
    changed:(BOOL)changed
{
    // Collect and store the view controller order
    NSMutableArray *titles = [NSMutableArray array];
    for (UIViewController *vc in viewControllers)
        [titles addObject:vc.title];

    [[NSUserDefaults standardUserDefaults] setObject:titles
        forKey:@"tabOrder"];
    [[NSUserDefaults standardUserDefaults] synchronize];
}

- (void)tabBarController:(UITabBarController *)controller
    didSelectViewController:(UIViewController *)viewController
{
    // Store the selected tab
    NSNumber *tabNumber =
        [NSNumber numberWithInt:[controller selectedIndex]];
```

```objc
    [[NSUserDefaults standardUserDefaults]
        setObject:tabNumber forKey:@"selectedTab"];
    [[NSUserDefaults standardUserDefaults] synchronize];
}


- (BOOL)application:(UIApplication *)application
    didFinishLaunchingWithOptions:(NSDictionary *)launchOptions
{
    // Globally use a black tint for nav bars
    [[UINavigationBar appearance]
        setBarTintColor:[UIColor blackColor]];

    NSMutableArray *controllers = [NSMutableArray array];
    NSArray *titles = [[NSUserDefaults standardUserDefaults]
        objectForKey:@"tabOrder"];

    if (titles)
    {
        // titles retrieved from user defaults
        for (NSString *theTitle in titles)
        {
            BrightnessController *controller =
                [BrightnessController controllerWithBrightness:
                    ([theTitle intValue] / 10)];
            UINavigationController *nav =
                [[UINavigationController alloc]
                    initWithRootViewController:controller];

            nav.navigationBar.barStyle = UIBarStyleBlackTranslucent;
            [controllers addObject:nav];
        }
    }
    else
    {
        // generate all new controllers
        for (int i = 0; i <= 10; i++)
        {
            BrightnessController *controller =
                [BrightnessController controllerWithBrightness:i];
            UINavigationController *nav =
                [[UINavigationController alloc]
                    initWithRootViewController:controller];
            nav.navigationBar.barStyle = UIBarStyleBlackTranslucent;
            [controllers addObject:nav];
        }
    }
```

```
    tabBarController = [[UITabBarController alloc] init];
    tabBarController.tabBar.barTintColor = [UIColor blackColor];
    tabBarController.tabBar.translucent = NO;
    tabBarController.viewControllers = controllers;
    tabBarController.customizableViewControllers = controllers;
    tabBarController.delegate = self;

    // Restore any previously selected tab
    NSNumber *tabNumber = [[NSUserDefaults standardUserDefaults]
        objectForKey:@"selectedTab"];
    if (tabNumber)
        tabBarController.selectedIndex = [tabNumber intValue];

    _window = [[UIWindow alloc]
        initWithFrame:[[UIScreen mainScreen] bounds]];
    _window.tintColor = COOKBOOK_PURPLE_COLOR;
    tabBarController.edgesForExtendedLayout = UIRectEdgeNone;

    _window.rootViewController = tabBarController;
    [_window makeKeyAndVisible];
    return YES;
}
@end
```

Recipe: Page View Controllers

The UIPageViewController class builds a book-like interface that uses individual view
controllers as its pages. Users swipe from one page to the next or tap the edges to move to
the next page or previous page. You can create a book-looking layout with pages, as shown in
Figure 7-5 (left), or use a flat scrolling presentation, as shown in Figure 7-5 (right). The scrolling
presentation offers an optional page indicator presentation, which is shown here at the bottom
of the view.

All of a controller's pages can be laid out in a similar fashion, as in Figure 7-5, or each page can
provide a unique user interaction experience. Apple precooked all the animation and gesture
handling into the class for you. You provide the content, implementing delegate and data
source callbacks.

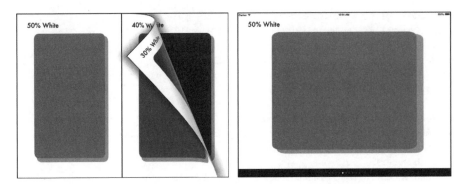

Figure 7-5   The `UIPageViewController` class creates virtual "books" from individual view controllers. View your books in paged (left) or scrolling (right) presentations.

Book Properties

Your code customizes a page view controller's look and behavior. Key properties specify how many pages display simultaneously, the content used for the reverse side of each page, and more. Here's a rundown of those Apple-specified properties:

- The `transitionStyle` property controls how one view controller transitions to the next. At this writing, the only transition styles supported by the page view controller are the page curl, as shown in Figure 7-5 (left), `UIPageViewControllerTransitionStylePageCurl`, and the scrolling presentation, `UIPageViewControllerTransitionStyleScroll`. This latter style was introduced in iOS 6.

- The controller's `doubleSided` property determines whether content appears on both sides of a page, as shown in Figure 7-5 (left), or just one side (right). Reserve the double-sided presentation for side-by-side layout when showing two pages simultaneously. If you don't, you'll end up making half your pages inaccessible. The controllers on the "back" of the pages will never move into the primary viewing space. The book layout is controlled by the book's spine.

- The `spineLocation` property can be set at the left or right, top or bottom, or center of the page. The three spine constants are `UIPageViewControllerSpineLocationMin`, corresponding to top or left, `UIPageViewControllerSpineLocationMax` for the right or bottom, and `UIPageViewControllerSpineLocationMid` for the center. The first two of these produce single-page presentations; the last, with its middle spine, is used for two-page layouts. Return one of these choices from the `pageViewController:spineLocationForInterfaceOrientation:` delegate method, which is called whenever the device reorients, to let the controller update its views to match the current device orientation.

- Set the `navigationOrientation` property to specify whether the spine goes left/right or top/bottom. Use either `UIPageViewControllerNavigationOrientationHorizontal` (left/right) or `UIPageViewControllerNavigationOrientationVertical` (top/bottom). For a vertical book, the pages flip up and down rather than employing the left and right flips normally used.

Wrapping the Implementation

Like table views, a page view controller uses a delegate and data source to set the behavior and contents of its presentation. Unlike with table views, it's simplest to wrap these items into a custom class to hide their details from applications. The code needed to support a page view implementation is rather quirky—but highly reusable. A wrapper lets you turn your attention away from fussy coding details to specific content-handling concerns.

In the standard implementation, the data source is responsible for providing page controllers on demand. It returns the next and previous view controllers in relationship to a given one. The delegate handles reorientation events and animation callbacks, setting the page view controller's controller array, which always consists of either one or two controllers, depending on the view layout. As Recipe 7-6 demonstrates, it's a bit of a mess to implement, but once built, it's something you really don't need to spend much time coming back to.

Recipe 7-6 creates a `BookController` class. This class numbers each page, hiding the next/previous implementation details and handling all reorientation events. A custom delegate protocol (`BookDelegate`) becomes responsible for returning a controller for a given page number when sent the `viewControllerForPage:` message. This simplifies implementation so that the calling app has only to handle a single method, which it can do by building controllers by hand or by pulling them from a storyboard.

To use the class defined in Recipe 7-6, you establish the controller, declare it as a child view controller, and add its view as a subview. Adding `BookController` as a child view controller ensures that it receives orientation and memory events. This type of view controller relationship will be discussed in more detail in the next recipe. Finally, the initial page number is set. Here's what that code might look like:

```
- (void)viewDidLoad
{
    [super viewDidLoad];
    if (!bookController)
        bookController = [BookController bookWithDelegate:self
            style:BookLayoutStyleBook];
    bookController.view.frame = self.view.bounds;

    [self addChildViewController:bookController];
    [self.view addSubview:bookController.view];
    [bookController didMoveToParentViewController:self];

    [bookController moveToPage:0];
}
```

The book controller creation convenience method also takes a second argument: a style. Recipe 7-6 allows developers to build four styles of books: a traditional book, a vertical book, and two scrolling styles:

```
typedef enum
{
    BookLayoutStyleBook, // side by side in landscape
    BookLayoutStyleFlipBook, // side by side in portrait
    BookLayoutStyleHorizontalScroll,
    BookLayoutStyleVerticalScroll,
} BookLayoutStyle;
```

The standard book presents one page in portrait (spine vertical and to the left) and a side-by-side presentation in landscape (spine vertical in the middle). This corresponds to a standard Western-style book, with page movement going left to right.

The "flip"-style book uses a horizontal spine. In landscape mode, the spine is at the top, with one page shown at a time. In portrait, that extends to two pages, with the horizontal spine in the middle, halfway between top and bottom.

The two scroll layouts allow you to scroll horizontally and vertically through individual pages. You cannot use multipage (side-by-side) layout with scrolling.

The tear-down process in viewWillDisappear allows the book controller to retire from its superview:

```
- (void)viewWillDisappear:(BOOL)animated
{
    [super viewWillDisappear:animated];
    [bookController willMoveToParentViewController:nil];
    [bookController.view removeFromSuperview];
    [bookController removeFromParentViewController];
}
```

Exploring the Recipe

Recipe 7-6 handles its delegate and data source duties by tagging each view controller's view with a page number. It uses this number to know exactly which page is presented at any time and to delegate another class, BookDelegate, to produce a view controller by index.

The page controller itself always stores zero, one, or two pages in its view controller array. Zero pages means the controller has not yet been properly set up. One page is used for spine locations on the edge of the screen, two pages for a central spine. If the page count does not exactly match the spine setup, you will encounter a rather nasty runtime crash.

The controllers presented in those pages are produced by the two data source methods, which implement the before and after callbacks. In the page controller's native implementation, controllers are defined strictly by their relationship to each other, not by an index. This recipe replaces those relationships with a simple number, asking its delegate for the page at a given index.

Here, given the orientation, the `useSideBySide:` method determines where to place the spine and thus how many controllers show simultaneously. This implementation sets landscape as side by side and portrait as one page. You may want to change this for your applications. For example, you might use only one page on the iPhone, regardless of orientation, to enhance text readability.

Recipe 7-6 allows both user- and application-based page control. Users can swipe and tap to new pages, or the application can send a `moveToPage:` request. This allows you to add external controls in addition to the page view controller's gesture recognizers.

The direction that the page turns is set by comparing the new page number against the old. This recipe uses a Western-style page turn, where higher numbers are to the right and pages flip to the left. You may want to adjust this as needed for countries in the Middle East and Asia.

Recipe 7-6 continually stores the current page to system defaults, so it can be recovered when the application is relaunched. It also notifies its delegate when the user has turned to a given page.

Building a Presentation Index

Page view controllers' scrolling layouts allow you to add an optional index (utilizing a page control). Any book that uses the scrolling layout style (`UIPageViewControllerTransitionStyleScroll`) can implement two data source methods. iOS uses them to build the indicator at the bottom of the scrolling book that you saw in Figure 7-5 (right).

As you can see from this snippet, the implementation since its inception is a bit wobbly:

```
- (NSInteger)presentationIndexForPageViewController:
    (UIPageViewController *)pageViewController
{
    // Slightly borked in iOS 6 & 7
    // return [self currentPage];
    return 0;
}


- (NSInteger)presentationCountForPageViewController:
    (UIPageViewController *)pageViewController
{
    if (bookDelegate &&
       [bookDelegate respondsToSelector:@selector(numberOfPages)])
       return [bookDelegate numberOfPages];

    return 0;
}
```

Apple's documentation states that `presentationIndexForPageViewController` should return the index of the selected item. Unfortunately, this leads to madness (and crashes). Returning `0` from the presentation index and the number of pages for the presentation count produces the most stable indicator. The page count used here is deferred to the book's delegate, via an optional method called `numberOfPages`.

Note that you are not limited to a one-to-one correlation between your index and your page count and current page number. For a large book, you can imagine dividing this number down somewhat, so each page dot corresponds to 5 or 10 pages, showing progress through the book without an exact page correspondence.

Note

Apple enables you to access a page view controller's gesture recognizers to allow or disallow touch-based page turns based on a touch's location on a page. Don't do it. First, this approach is not valid for scroll-based controllers. Second, adding recognizer delegate methods tends to mess up app stability.

Recipe 7-6   Creating a Page View Controller Wrapper

```
// Define a custom delegate protocol for this wrapper class
@protocol BookControllerDelegate <NSObject>
- (id)viewControllerForPage:(NSInteger)pageNumber;
@optional
- (NSInteger)numberOfPages; // for scrolling layouts
- (void)bookControllerDidTurnToPage:(NSNumber *)pageNumber;
@end

// A book controller wraps the page view controller
@interface BookController : UIPageViewController
    <UIPageViewControllerDelegate, UIPageViewControllerDataSource>
+ (instancetype)bookWithDelegate:
    (id<BookControllerDelegate>)theDelegate
        style:(BookLayoutStyle)aStyle;
- (void)moveToPage:(NSUInteger)requestedPage;
- (int)currentPage;

@property (nonatomic, weak)
    id <BookControllerDelegate> bookDelegate;
@property (nonatomic, assign) NSUInteger pageNumber;
@property (nonatomic) BookLayoutStyle layoutStyle;
@end

#pragma mark - Book Controller
@implementation BookController
```

```
#pragma mark Utility
// Page controllers are numbered using tags
- (NSInteger)currentPage
{
    NSInteger pageCheck = ((UIViewController *)[self.viewControllers
        objectAtIndex:0]).view.tag;
    return pageCheck;
}


#pragma mark Presentation indices for page indicator (Data Source)
- (NSInteger)presentationIndexForPageViewController:
    (UIPageViewController *)pageViewController
{
    // Slightly borked in iOS 6 & 7
    // return [self currentPage];
    return 0;
}


- (NSInteger)presentationCountForPageViewController:
    (UIPageViewController *)pageViewController
{
    if (_bookDelegate && [_bookDelegate
            respondsToSelector:@selector(numberOfPages)])
        return [_bookDelegate numberOfPages];

    return 0;
}


#pragma mark Page Handling
// Update if you'd rather use some other decision strategy
- (BOOL)useSideBySide:(UIInterfaceOrientation)orientation
{
    BOOL isLandscape =
        UIInterfaceOrientationIsLandscape(orientation);

    // Each layout style determines whether side by side is used
    switch (_layoutStyle)
    {
        case BookLayoutStyleHorizontalScroll:
        case BookLayoutStyleVerticalScroll: return NO;
        case BookLayoutStyleFlipBook: return isLandscape;
        default: return isLandscape;
    }
}

// Update the current page, set defaults, call the delegate
- (void)updatePageTo:(NSUInteger)newPageNumber
```

```
{
    _pageNumber = newPageNumber;

    [[NSUserDefaults standardUserDefaults]
        setInteger:_pageNumber forKey:DEFAULTS_BOOKPAGE];
    [[NSUserDefaults standardUserDefaults] synchronize];

    SAFE_PERFORM_WITH_ARG(bookDelegate,
        @selector(bookControllerDidTurnToPage:),
        @(_pageNumber));
}

// Request view controller from delegate
- (UIViewController *)controllerAtPage:(NSInteger)aPageNumber
{
    if (_bookDelegate && [_bookDelegate respondsToSelector:
        @selector(viewControllerForPage:)])
    {
        UIViewController *controller =
            [_bookDelegate viewControllerForPage:aPageNumber];
        controller.view.tag = aPageNumber;
        return controller;
    }
    return nil;
}

// Update interface to the given page
- (void)fetchControllersForPage:(NSUInteger)requestedPage
    orientation:(UIInterfaceOrientation)orientation
{
    BOOL sideBySide = [self useSideBySide:orientation];
    NSInteger numberOfPagesNeeded = sideBySide ? 2 : 1;
    NSInteger currentCount = self.viewControllers.count;

    NSUInteger leftPage = requestedPage;
    if (sideBySide && (leftPage % 2))
        leftPage = floor(leftPage / 2) * 2;

    // Only check against current page when count is appropriate
    if (currentCount && (currentCount == numberOfPagesNeeded))
    {
        if (_pageNumber == requestedPage) return;
        if (_pageNumber == leftPage) return;
    }

    // Decide the prevailing direction, check new page against the old
    UIPageViewControllerNavigationDirection direction =
```

```
            (requestedPage > _pageNumber) ?
            UIPageViewControllerNavigationDirectionForward :
            UIPageViewControllerNavigationDirectionReverse;

    // Update the controllers, never adding a nil result
    NSMutableArray *pageControllers = [NSMutableArray array];
    SAFE_ADD(pageControllers, [self controllerAtPage:leftPage]);
    if (sideBySide)
        SAFE_ADD(pageControllers,
            [self controllerAtPage:leftPage + 1]);
    [self setViewControllers:pageControllers
        direction:direction animated:YES completion:nil];
    [self updatePageTo:leftPage];
}


// Entry point for external move request
- (void)moveToPage:(NSUInteger)requestedPage
{
    // Thanks Dino Lupo
    [self fetchControllersForPage:requestedPage
        orientation:(UIInterfaceOrientation)
            self.interfaceOrientation];
}


#pragma mark Data Source
- (UIViewController *)pageViewController:
        (UIPageViewController *)pageViewController
    viewControllerAfterViewController:
        (UIViewController *)viewController
{
    [self updatePageTo:_pageNumber + 1];
    return [self controllerAtPage:(viewController.view.tag + 1)];
}


- (UIViewController *)pageViewController:
        (UIPageViewController *)pageViewController
    viewControllerBeforeViewController:
        (UIViewController *)viewController
{
    [self updatePageTo:_pageNumber - 1];
    return [self controllerAtPage:(viewController.view.tag - 1)];
}


#pragma mark Delegate Method
- (UIPageViewControllerSpineLocation)pageViewController:
        (UIPageViewController *)pageViewController
    spineLocationForInterfaceOrientation:
```

```
            (UIInterfaceOrientation)orientation
{
    // Always start with left or single page
    NSUInteger indexOfCurrentViewController = 0;
    if (self.viewControllers.count)
        indexOfCurrentViewController =
            ((UIViewController *)[self.viewControllers
                objectAtIndex:0]).view.tag;
    [self fetchControllersForPage:indexOfCurrentViewController
        orientation:orientation];

    // Decide whether to present side by side
    BOOL sideBySide = [self useSideBySide:orientation];
    self.doubleSided = sideBySide;

    UIPageViewControllerSpineLocation spineLocation = sideBySide ?
            UIPageViewControllerSpineLocationMid :
            UIPageViewControllerSpineLocationMin;
    return spineLocation;
}

// Return a new book controller
+ (instancetype)bookWithDelegate:(id)theDelegate
    style:(BookLayoutStyle)aStyle
{
    // Determine orientation
    UIPageViewControllerNavigationOrientation orientation =
        UIPageViewControllerNavigationOrientationHorizontal;
    if ((aStyle == BookLayoutStyleFlipBook) ||
        (aStyle == BookLayoutStyleVerticalScroll))
        orientation = UIPageViewControllerNavigationOrientationVertical;

    // Determine transitionStyle
    UIPageViewControllerTransitionStyle transitionStyle =
        UIPageViewControllerTransitionStylePageCurl;
    if ((aStyle == BookLayoutStyleHorizontalScroll) ||
        (aStyle == BookLayoutStyleVerticalScroll))
        transitionStyle = UIPageViewControllerTransitionStyleScroll;

    // Pass options as a dictionary. Keys are spine location (curl)
    // and spacing between vc's (scroll).
    BookController *bc = [[BookController alloc]
        initWithTransitionStyle:transitionStyle
        navigationOrientation:orientation
        options:nil];
```

```
        bc.layoutStyle = aStyle;
        bc.dataSource = bc;
        bc.delegate = bc;
        bc.bookDelegate = theDelegate;

        return bc;
}
@end
```

Get This Recipe's Code

To find this recipe's full sample project, point your browser to https://github.com/erica/iOS-7-Cookbook and go to the folder for Chapter 7.

Recipe: Custom Containers

Apple's split view controller was groundbreaking in that it introduced the notion that more than one controller could live onscreen at a time. Until the split view, the rule was one controller with many views at a time. With the split view, several controllers coexist onscreen, all of them independently responding to orientation and memory events.

Apple exposed this multiple-controller paradigm to developers in the iOS 5 SDK, allowing developers to design a parent controller and add child controllers to it. Events are passed from parent to child as needed. This allows you to build custom containers, outside the Apple-standard set of containers such as tab bar and navigation controllers.

Recipe 7-7 builds a reusable container that can hold either one or two children. When loaded with two child view controllers, it lets you flip from one to the other and back. It has quite a lot of conditionality built in. That's because it can be used as a standalone view controller, as a child view controller itself, and as a modal view controller. Imagine the following situations.

As with a navigation controller, you can create this flip view controller directly and set it as your primary window's root view controller. In that case, it has no further relationship with any hierarchy. It merely manages its children. You can also use it as a child of some other container, such as in a tab bar controller presentation, a split view controller, and so forth. When used in that way, it acts as both a parent of its children and as a child of the container that holds it. Finally, you can present the controller directly. The flip view container must behave as a solid citizen in all these situations. The controller therefore has two tasks. First, it must manage its children using standard UIKit calls. Second, it must be aware of how it is participating in the view hierarchy. This recipe adds a navigation bar so a Done button becomes available to end users.

Adding and Removing a Child View Controller

In the simplest scenario, adding a child to a container controller takes three steps:

1. Call `addChildViewController:` on the parent and pass the child as the argument (for example, `[self addChildViewController:childvc]`).

2. Add the child controller's view as a subview (for example, `[self.view addSubview:childvc.view]`).

3. Call `didMoveToParentViewController:` on the child with the parent as its argument (for example, `[childvc didMoveToParentViewController:self]`).

To remove a child view controller, the steps are almost (but not quite) mirrored:

1. Call `willMoveToParentViewController:` on the child, passing `nil` as the argument (for example, `[childvc willMoveToParentViewController:nil]`).

2. Remove the child controller's view (for example, `[childvc.view removeFromSuperview]`).

3. Call `removeFromParentViewController` on the child (for example, `[childvc removeFromParentViewController]`).

Transitioning Between View Controllers

UIKit offers a simple way to animate view features when you move from one child view controller to another. You provide a source view controller, a destination, and a duration for the animated transition. You can specify the kind of transition in the options. Supported transitions include page curls, dissolves, and flips. This method creates a simple curl from one view controller to the next:

```
- (void)action:(id)sender
{
    [redController willMoveToParentViewController:nil];
    [self addChildViewController:blueController];

    [self transitionFromViewController:redController
        toViewController:blueController
        duration:1.0f
        options:UIViewAnimationOptionLayoutSubviews |
            UIViewAnimationOptionTransitionCurlUp
        animations:^(void){}
        completion:^(BOOL finished){
            [redController.view removeFromSuperview];
            [self.view addSubview:blueController.view];

            [redController removeFromParentViewController];
            [blueController didMoveToParentViewController:self];
```

```
            }
        ];
}
```

You can use the same approach to animate `UIView` properties without the built-in transitions. For example, this method re-centers and fades out the red controller while fading in the blue. These are all animatable `UIView` features and are changed in the `animations:` block:

```
- (void)action:(id)sender
{
    [redController willMoveToParentViewController:nil];
    [self addChildViewController:blueController];

    blueController.view.alpha = 0.0f;
    [self transitionFromViewController:redController
        toViewController:blueController
        duration:2.0f
        options:UIViewAnimationOptionLayoutSubviews
        animations:^(void){
            redController.view.center = CGPointMake(0.0f, 0.0f);
            redController.view.alpha = 0.0f;
            blueController.view.alpha = 1.0f;
        }
        completion:^(BOOL finished){
            [redController.view removeFromSuperview];
            [self.view addSubview:blueController.view];

            [redController removeFromParentViewController];
            [blueController didMoveToParentViewController:self];
        }
    ];
}
```

Using transitions and view animations is an either/or scenario. Either set a transition option *or* change view features in the animations block. Otherwise, they conflict, as you can easily confirm for yourself. Use the completion block to remove the old view and move the new view into place.

Although simple to implement, this kind of transition is not meant for use with Core Animation. If you want to add Core Animation effects to your view-controller-to-view-controller transitions, think about using a custom segue instead. Segues are covered in the following recipe.

As mentioned in Recipe 7-2, a third option is available for animating transitions between `UIViewControllers` in iOS 7: The custom transitions API allows you to create advanced animations that can even interact dynamically with the user.

Recipe 7-7   **Creating a View Controller Container**

```objectivec
- (void) viewDidDisappear: (BOOL) animated
{
    [super viewDidDisappear:animated];
    if (!controllers.count)
    {
        NSLog(@"Error: No root view controller");
        return;
    }

    // Clean up the child view controller
    UIViewController *currentController =
        (UIViewController *)controllers[0];
    [currentController willMoveToParentViewController:nil];
    [currentController.view removeFromSuperview];
    [currentController removeFromParentViewController];
}

- (void) flip: (id) sender
{
    // Please call only with two controllers
    if (controllers.count < 2) return;

    // Determine which item is front, which is back
    UIViewController *front = (UIViewController *)controllers[0];
    UIViewController *back =  (UIViewController *)controllers[1];

    // Select the transition direction
    UIViewAnimationOptions transition = reversedOrder ?
        UIViewAnimationOptionTransitionFlipFromLeft :
        UIViewAnimationOptionTransitionFlipFromRight;

    // Hide the info button until after the flip
    infoButton.alpha = 0.0f;

    // Prepare the front for removal, the back for adding
    [front willMoveToParentViewController:nil];
    [self addChildViewController:back];

    // Perform the transition
    [self transitionFromViewController: front
        toViewController:back duration:0.5f options:transition
        animations:nil completion:^(BOOL done){

        // Bring the Info button back into view
        [self.view bringSubviewToFront:infoButton];
```

```
        [UIView animateWithDuration:0.3f animations:^(){
            infoButton.alpha = 1.0f;
        }];

        // Finish up transition
        [front removeFromParentViewController];
        [back didMoveToParentViewController:self];

        reversedOrder = !reversedOrder;
        controllers = @[back, front];
    }];
}


- (void)viewWillAppear:(BOOL)animated
{
    [super viewWillAppear:animated];
    if (!controllers.count)
    {
        NSLog(@"Error: No root view controller");
        return;
    }

    UIViewController *front = controllers[0];
    UIViewController *back = nil;
    if (controllers.count > 1) back = controllers[1];

    [self addChildViewController:front];
    [self.view addSubview:front.view];
    [front didMoveToParentViewController:self];

    // Check for presentation and for "flippability"
    BOOL isPresented = self.isBeingPresented;

    // Clean up instance if re-use
    if (navbar || infoButton)
    {
        [navbar removeFromSuperview];
        [infoButton removeFromSuperview];
        navbar = nil;
    }

    // When presented, add a custom navigation bar.
    // iPhone navbar height must consider status bar.
    CGFloat navbarHeight = IS_IPHONE ? 64.0 : 44.0;
    if (isPresented)
    {
        navbar = [[UINavigationBar alloc] init];
```

```
        [self.view addSubview:navbar];
        PREPCONSTRAINTS(navbar);
        ALIGN_VIEW_TOP(self.view, navbar);
        ALIGN_VIEW_LEFT(self.view, navbar);
        ALIGN_VIEW_RIGHT(self.view, navbar);
        CONSTRAIN_HEIGHT(navbar, navbarHeight);
    }


    // Right button is Done when VC is presented
    self.navigationItem.leftBarButtonItem = nil;
    self.navigationItem.rightBarButtonItem = isPresented ?
        SYSBARBUTTON(UIBarButtonSystemItemDone,
            @selector(done:)) : nil;


    // Populate the navigation bar
    if (navbar)
        [navbar setItems:@[self.navigationItem] animated:NO];


    // Size the child VC view(s)
    CGFloat verticalOffset =
        (navbar != nil) ? navbarHeight : 0.0f;
    CGRect destFrame = CGRectMake(0.0f, verticalOffset,
        self.view.frame.size.width,
        self.view.frame.size.height - verticalOffset);
    front.view.frame = destFrame;
    back.view.frame = destFrame;


    // Set up info button
    if (controllers.count < 2) return; // our work is done here


    // Create the "i" button
    infoButton = [UIButton buttonWithType:UIButtonTypeInfoLight];
    infoButton.tintColor = [UIColor whiteColor];
    [infoButton addTarget:self action:@selector(flip:)
        forControlEvents:UIControlEventTouchUpInside];


    // Place "i" button at bottom right of view
    [self.view addSubview:infoButton];
    PREPCONSTRAINTS(infoButton);
    ALIGN_VIEW_RIGHT_CONSTANT(self.view, infoButton,
        -infoButton.frame.size.width);
    ALIGN_VIEW_BOTTOM_CONSTANT(self.view, infoButton,
        -infoButton.frame.size.height);
}
@end
```

Recipe: Segues

When you use storyboards, IB provides a set of standard segues to transition between your view controllers. With custom containers come their little brother, custom segues. Just as tab and navigation controllers provide a distinct way of transitioning between child view controllers, you can build custom segues that define transition animations unique to your class.

IB doesn't provide a lot of support for custom containers with custom segues, so it's best to develop your segue presentations in code for now. Here's how you might implement code to move a view controller to a new view:

```
// Informal custom delegate method
- (void)segueDidComplete
{
    // Retrieve the two vc's
    UIViewController *source =
        [childControllers objectAtIndex:vcIndex];
    UIViewController *destination =
        [childControllers objectAtIndex:nextIndex];

    // Reparent as needed
    [destination didMoveToParentViewController:self];
    [source removeFromParentViewController];

    // Update the bookkeeping
    vcIndex = nextIndex;
    pageControl.currentPage = vcIndex;
}


// Transition to new view using custom segue
- (void)switchToView:(int)newIndex
    goingForward:(BOOL)goesForward
{
    if (vcIndex == newIndex) return;
    nextIndex = newIndex;

    // Segue to the new controller
    UIViewController *source =
        [childControllers objectAtIndex:vcIndex];
    UIViewController *destination =
        [childControllers objectAtIndex:newIndex];
```

```
    // Start the reparenting process
    [source willMoveToParentViewController:nil];
    [self addChildViewController:destination];

    RotatingSegue *segue = [[RotatingSegue alloc]
        initWithIdentifier:@"segue"
        source:source destination:destination];
    segue.goesForward = goesForward;
    segue.delegate = self;
    [segue perform];
}
```

Here, the code identifies the source and destination child controllers, builds a segue, sets its parameters, and tells it to perform. An informal delegate method is called back by that custom segue on its completion. Recipe 7-8 shows how the segue is built. In this example, it creates a rotating cube effect that moves from one view to the next. Figure 7-6 shows the segue in action.

Figure 7-6   Custom segues allow you to create visual metaphors for your custom containers. Recipe 7-8 builds a "cube" of view controllers that can be rotated from one to the next. The switches on each controller update the art alpha value from translucent to solid and back.

The segue's goesForward property determines whether the rotation moves to the right or left around the virtual cube. Although this example uses four view controllers, as you saw in the code that laid out the child view controllers, that's a limitation of the metaphor, not of the code itself, which will work with any number of child controllers. You can just as easily build three- or seven-sided presentations with this, although you are breaking an implicit "reality" contract with your user if you do so. To add more (or fewer) sides, you should adjust the animation geometry in the segue away from a cube to fit your virtual *n*-hedron.

Recipe 7-8   **Creating a Custom View Controller Segue**

```objc
@implementation RotatingSegue
{
    CALayer *transformationLayer;
    UIView __weak *hostView;
}


// Return a shot of the given view
- (UIImage *)screenShot:(UIView *)aView
{
    // Arbitrarily dims to 40%. Adjust as desired.
    UIGraphicsBeginImageContext(hostView.frame.size);
    [aView.layer renderInContext:UIGraphicsGetCurrentContext()];
    UIImage *image =
        UIGraphicsGetImageFromCurrentImageContext();
    CGContextSetRGBFillColor(UIGraphicsGetCurrentContext(),
        0, 0, 0, 0.4f);
    CGContextFillRect(UIGraphicsGetCurrentContext(),
        hostView.frame);
    UIGraphicsEndImageContext();
    return image;
}


// Return a layer with the view contents
- (CALayer *)createLayerFromView:(UIView *)aView
    transform:(CATransform3D)transform
{
    CALayer *imageLayer = [CALayer layer];
    imageLayer.anchorPoint = CGPointMake(1.0f, 1.0f);
    imageLayer.frame = (CGRect){.size = hostView.frame.size};
    imageLayer.transform = transform;
    UIImage *shot = [self screenShot:aView];
    imageLayer.contents = (__bridge id) shot.CGImage;

    return imageLayer;
}
```

```objc
// On starting the animation, remove the source view
- (void)animationDidStart:(CAAnimation *)animation
{
    UIViewController *source =
        (UIViewController *) super.sourceViewController;
    [source.view removeFromSuperview];
}

// On completing the animation, add the destination view,
// remove the animation, and ping the delegate
- (void)animationDidStop:(CAAnimation *)animation
    finished:(BOOL)finished
{
    UIViewController *dest =
        (UIViewController *) super.destinationViewController;
    [hostView addSubview:dest.view];
    [transformationLayer removeFromSuperlayer];
    if (_delegate &&
        [_delegate respondsToSelector:
            @selector(segueDidComplete)])
    {
        [_delegate segueDidComplete];
    }
}

// Perform the animation
- (void)animateWithDuration:(CGFloat)aDuration
{
    CAAnimationGroup *group = [CAAnimationGroup animation];
    group.delegate = self;
    group.duration = aDuration;

    CGFloat halfWidth = hostView.frame.size.width / 2.0f;
    float multiplier = goesForward ? -1.0f : 1.0f;

    // Set the x, y, and z animations
    CABasicAnimation *translationX = [CABasicAnimation
        animationWithKeyPath:@"sublayerTransform.translation.x"];
    translationX.toValue =
        [NSNumber numberWithFloat:multiplier * halfWidth];

    CABasicAnimation *translationZ = [CABasicAnimation
        animationWithKeyPath:@"sublayerTransform.translation.z"];
    translationZ.toValue = [NSNumber numberWithFloat:-halfWidth];

    CABasicAnimation *rotationY = [CABasicAnimation
        animationWithKeyPath:@"sublayerTransform.rotation.y"];
```

```
    rotationY.toValue =
        [NSNumber numberWithFloat: multiplier * M_PI_2];

    // Set the animation group
    group.animations = [NSArray arrayWithObjects:
        rotationY, translationX, translationZ, nil];
    group.fillMode = kCAFillModeForwards;
    group.removedOnCompletion = NO;

    // Perform the animation
    [CATransaction flush];
    [transformationLayer addAnimation:group forKey:kAnimationKey];
}

- (void)constructRotationLayer
{
    UIViewController *source =
        (UIViewController *) super.sourceViewController;
    UIViewController *dest =
        (UIViewController *) super.destinationViewController;
    hostView = source.view.superview;

    // Build a new layer for the transformation
    transformationLayer = [CALayer layer];
    transformationLayer.frame = hostView.bounds;
    transformationLayer.anchorPoint = CGPointMake(0.5f, 0.5f);
    CATransform3D sublayerTransform = CATransform3DIdentity;
    sublayerTransform.m34 = 1.0 / -1000;
    [transformationLayer setSublayerTransform:sublayerTransform];
    [hostView.layer addSublayer:transformationLayer];

    // Add the source view, which is in front
    CATransform3D transform = CATransform3DMakeIdentity;
    [transformationLayer addSublayer:
        [self createLayerFromView:source.view
            transform:transform]];

    // Prepare the destination view either to the right or left
    // at a 90/270 degree angle off the main
    transform = CATransform3DRotate(transform, M_PI_2, 0, 1, 0);
    transform = CATransform3DTranslate(transform,
        hostView.frame.size.width, 0, 0);
    if (!goesForward)
    {
        transform =
            CATransform3DRotate(transform, M_PI_2, 0, 1, 0);
        transform =
```

```
            CATransform3DTranslate(transform,
                hostView.frame.size.width, 0, 0);
        transform =
            CATransform3DRotate(transform, M_PI_2, 0, 1, 0);
        transform =
            CATransform3DTranslate(transform,
                hostView.frame.size.width, 0, 0);
    }
    [transformationLayer addSublayer:
        [self createLayerFromView:dest.view
            transform:transform]];
}

// Standard UIStoryboardSegue perform
- (void)perform
{
    [self constructRotationLayer];
    [self animateWithDuration:0.5f];
}
@end
```

Get This Recipe's Code

To find this recipe's full sample project, point your browser to https://github.com/erica/iOS-7-Cookbook and go to the folder for Chapter 7.

Segues and IB

Starting in the iOS 6 SDK, you can apply custom segues in your storyboards. You'll need to tie those segues to some action item, such as a button or bar button press, or similar actionable element. Figure 7-7 shows how custom segues are listed in IB. The "rotating" segue is from Recipe 7-8.

What's more, segues can be "unwound." Unwinding allows you to move back from a new view controller to its logical parent, using a custom segue you provide. You achieve this by implementing a few methods:

- Specify whether you can unwind with `canPerformUnwindSegueAction:fromViewController:withSender:`.

- Return a view controller to `viewControllerForUnwindSegueAction:fromViewController:withSender:`. This controller will be the unwinding destination.

- Supply the required unwinding segue instance via `segueForUnwindingToViewController:fromViewController:identifier:`. Typically, you'll want your unwind to animate in the reverse direction from your original segue.

Finally, you can now allow or disallow any segue by implementing `shouldPerformSegue-WithIdentifier:sender:`. You return either `YES` or `NO`, depending on whether you want the identified segue to proceed.

Figure 7-7   Storyboards allow you to apply custom segues in IB. IB scans for `UIStoryboardSegue` child classes. Here, IB lists the custom "rotating" segue along with system-supplied options.

Summary

This chapter shows many view controller classes in action. You've learned how to use them to handle view presentation and user navigation for various device deployment choices. With these classes, you have discovered how to expand virtual interaction space and create multipage interfaces, as demanded by applications, while respecting the HIG on the platform in question. Before moving on to the next chapter, here are a few points to consider about view controllers:

- Use navigation trees to build hierarchical interfaces. They work well for looking at file structures or building a settings tree. When you think "disclosure view" or "preferences," consider pushing a new controller onto a navigation stack or using a split view to present them directly.

- Don't be afraid to use conventional UI elements in unconventional ways, as long as you respect the overall Apple HIG. You can apply innovative approaches for `UINavigationController` that don't involve any navigation. The tools are there for you to use.

- Be persistent. Let your users return to the same GUI state that they last left from. `NSUserDefaults` provides a built-in system for storing information between application runs. Use these defaults to re-create the prior interface state. The State Preservation and Restoration API introduced in iOS 6 provides another path for persisting large portions of your UI state.

- Go universal. Let your code adapt itself for various device deployments rather than force your app into an only-iPhone or only-iPad design. This chapter touches on some simple runtime device detection and interface updates that you can easily expand for more challenging circumstances. Universal deployment isn't just about stretching views and using alternate art and XIB files. It's also about detecting when a device influences the *way* you interact in addition to the look of the interface.

- When working with custom containers, don't be afraid of using storyboards directly. You do not have to build and retain an array of all your controllers simultaneously. Storyboards offer direct access to all your elements. As with the new page view controller class, just load the controllers you need, when you need them.

8

Common Controllers

The iOS SDK provides a wealth of system-supplied controllers that you can use in your day-to-day development tasks. This chapter introduces some of the most popular ones. You'll read about selecting images from your device library, snapping photos, and recording and editing videos. You'll discover how to allow users to compose e-mails and text messages, and how to post updates to social services like Twitter and Facebook. Each controller offers a way to leverage prepackaged iOS system functionality. Here's the know-how you need to get started using them.

Image Picker Controller

The `UIImagePickerController` class enables users to select images from a device's media library and to snap pictures with its camera. It is somewhat of a living fossil; its system-supplied interface was created back in the early days of iPhone OS. Over time, as Apple rolled out devices with video recording (iOS 3.1) and front and rear cameras (iOS 4), the class evolved. It introduced photo and video editing, customizable camera view overlays, and more.

Image Sources

The image picker works with three sources:

- **`UIImagePickerControllerSourceTypePhotoLibrary`**—This source contains all images synced to iOS. Material in this source includes images snapped by the user (Camera Roll), from photo streams, from albums synced from computers, copied via the camera connection kit, and so on.

- **`UIImagePickerControllerSourceTypeSavedPhotosAlbum`**—This source refers only to the Camera Roll, which consists of pictures and videos captured by the user on units with cameras or to the Saved Photos album for noncamera units. Photo stream items captured on other devices also sync into the Camera Roll.

- **UIImagePickerControllerSourceTypeCamera**—This source enables users to shoot pictures with a built-in iPhone camera. The source provides support for front and back camera selection and both still and video capture.

Although you might want more nuanced access to iCloud and to shared and individual photo streams, for now you can access your entire library, just the Camera Roll, or just the Camera. Submit your enhancement suggestions to http://bugreport.apple.com.

Presenting the Picker on iPhone and iPad

Figure 8-1 shows the image picker presented on an iPhone and iPad, using a library source. The UIImagePickerController class is designed to operate in a modal presentation on iPhone-like devices (left) or a popover on tablets (right).

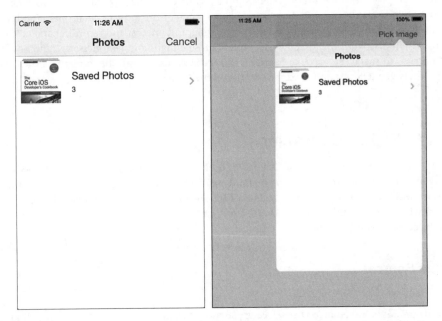

Figure 8-1 The core image picker allows users to select images from pictures stored in the media library.

On iPhone-like devices, present the picker modally. On the iPad, embed pickers into popovers instead. Never push image pickers onto an existing navigation stack. On older versions of iOS, doing so would create a second navigation bar under the primary one. On modern versions of iOS, it throws a nasty exception: "Pushing a navigation controller is not supported by the image picker".

Recipe: Selecting Images

In its simplest role, the image picker enables users to browse their library and select a stored photo. Recipe 8-1 demonstrates how to create and present a picker and retrieve an image selected by the user. Before proceeding with general how-to, you need to know about two key how-to's.

How To: Adding Photos to the Simulator

Before running this recipe on a Mac, you might want to populate the simulator's photo collection. You can do this in two ways. First, you can drop images onto the simulator from Finder. Each image opens in Mobile Safari, where you can then tap-and-hold and choose Save Image to copy the image to your photo library.

Once you set up your test photo collection as you like, navigate to the Application Support folder in your home library on your Mac. Open the iPhone Simulator folder and then the folder for the iOS version you're currently using (for example, 7.0). Inside, you'll find a Media folder. The path to the Media folder will look something like this: /Users/(*Your Account*)/ Library/Application Support/iPhone Simulator/(*OS Version*)/Media.

Back up the newly populated Media folder to a convenient location. Creating a backup enables you to restore it in the future without having to re-add each photo individually. Each time you reset the simulator's contents and settings, this material gets deleted. Having a folder on hand that's ready to drop in and test with can be a huge time saver.

Alternatively, purchase a copy of Ecamm's PhoneView (http://ecamm.com). PhoneView offers access to a device's Media folder through the Apple File Connection (AFC) service. Connect an iPhone or iPad, launch the application, and then drag and drop folders from PhoneView to your Mac. Make sure you check Show Entire Disk in PhoneView preferences to see all the relevant folders.

Using PhoneView, copy the DCIM, PhotoData, and Photos folders from a device to a folder on your Macintosh. Once copied, quit the simulator and add the copied folders into the ~/Library/ Application Support/iPhone Simulator/(*OS Version*)/Media destination. When you next launch the simulator, your new media will be waiting for you in the Photos app.

The Assets Library Module

This recipe uses the assets library module. Be sure to add it to your source file with `@import AssetsLibrary`.

Using the assets library may sound complicated, but there are strong underlying reasons why this is a best practice for working with image pickers. An image picker may return an asset URL without providing a direct image to use. Recipe 8-1 assumes that this is a possibility and offers a method to load an image from the assets library (loadImageFromAssetURL:into:). A typical URL looks something like this:

```
assets-library://asset/asset.JPG?id=553F6592-43C9-45A0-B851-28A726727436&ext=JPG
```

This URL provides direct access to media.

Fortunately, Apple has now moved past an extremely annoying assets library issue. Historically, iOS queried the user for permission to use his or her location—permissions that users would often deny. Apps would get stuck because you cannot force the system to ask again. Beginning with iOS 6, the message properly states that the app would like to access a user's photos rather than location, hopefully leading users to grant access. Determine your authorization situation by querying the class's authorizationStatus. You can reset these granted privileges by opening Settings > Privacy and updating service-based permissions (like location and photo access) on an app-by-app basis.

Unfortunately, as of the initial release of iOS 7, Apple added a nasty bug related to asset library authorization on the iPad. A crash occurs when returning from the permission request if you display a picker in a popover. Restarting the app resolves the issue but provides a poor first-run experience. A workaround is to request asset library access prior to displaying the popover:

```
// Force authorization for asset library
[assetsLibrary enumerateGroupsWithTypes:ALAssetsGroupAll
    usingBlock:^(ALAssetsGroup *group, BOOL *stop) {
        // If authorized, catch the final iteration and display popover
        if (group == nil)
        {
            dispatch_async(dispatch_get_main_queue(), ^{
                popover = [[UIPopoverController alloc]
                    initWithContentViewController:
                        viewControllerToPresent];
                popover.delegate = self;
                [popover presentPopoverFromBarButtonItem:
                        self.navigationItem.rightBarButtonItem
                    permittedArrowDirections:
                        UIPopoverArrowDirectionAny
                    animated:YES];
            });
        }
        *stop = YES;
    } failureBlock:nil];
```

With the procedural details addressed, the next section introduces the image picker itself.

Presenting a Picker

Create an image picker by allocating and initializing it. Next, set its source type to the library (all images) or Camera Roll (captured images). Recipe 8-1 sets the photo library source type, allowing users to browse through all library images.

```
UIImagePickerController *picker = [[UIImagePickerController alloc] init];
picker.sourceType = UIImagePickerControllerSourceTypePhotoLibrary;
```

An optional editing property (allowsEditing) adds a step to the interactive selection process. When enabled, it allows users to scale and frame the image they picked before finishing their selection. When it is disabled, any media selection immediately redirects control to the next phase of the picker's life cycle.

Be sure to set the picker's delegate property. The delegate property conforms to the UINavigationControllerDelegate and UIImagePickerControllerDelegate protocols; it receives callbacks after a user has selected an image or cancelled selection. When using an image picker controller with popovers, declare the UIPopoverControllerDelegate protocol as well.

When working on iPhone-like devices, always present the picker modally; check for the active device at runtime. The following test (iOS 3.2 and later) returns true when run on an iPhone and false on an iPad:

```
#define IS_IPHONE (UI_USER_INTERFACE_IDIOM() == UIUserInterfaceIdiomPhone)
```

The following snippet shows the typical presentation patterns for image pickers:

```
if (IS_IPHONE)
{
    [self presentViewController:picker animated:YES completion:nil];
}
else
{
    if (popover) [popover dismissPopoverAnimated:NO];
    popover = [[UIPopoverController alloc]
        initWithContentViewController:picker];
    popover.delegate = self;
    [popover presentPopoverFromBarButtonItem:
            self.navigationItem.rightBarButtonItem
        permittedArrowDirections:UIPopoverArrowDirectionAny
        animated:YES];
}
```

Handling Delegate Callbacks

Recipe 8-1 considers the following three possible image picker callback scenarios:

- The user has successfully selected an image.
- The user has tapped Cancel (only available on modal presentations).
- The user has dismissed the popover that embeds the picker by tapping outside it.

The last two cases are simple. For a modal presentation, dismiss the controller. For a popover, remove any local references holding onto the instance. Processing a selection takes a little more work.

Pickers finish their lives by returning a custom information dictionary to their assigned delegate. This info dictionary contains key/value pairs related to the user's selection. Depending on the way the image picker has been set up and the kind of media the user selects, the dictionary may contain few or many of these keys.

For example, when working with images on the simulator dropped in via Safari, expect to see nothing more than a media type and a reference URL. Images shot on a device and then edited through the picker may contain all six keys listed here:

- **UIImagePickerControllerMediaType**—Defines the kind of media selected by the user—normally `public.image` for images or `public.movie` for movies. Media types are defined in the Mobile Core Services framework. Media types are primarily used in this context for adding items to the system pasteboard.

- **UIImagePickerControllerCropRect**—Returns the portion of the image selected by the user as an `NSValue` that stores a `CGRect`.

- **UIImagePickerControllerOriginalImage**—Offers a `UIImage` instance with the original (unedited) image contents.

- **UIImagePickerControllerEditedImage**—Provides the edited version of the image, containing the portion of the picture selected by the user. The `UIImage` returned is small, sized to fit the device screen.

- **UIImagePickerControllerReferenceURL**—Specifies a file system URL for the selected asset. This URL always points to the original version of an item, regardless of whether a user has cropped or trimmed an asset.

- **UIImagePickerControllerMediaMetadata**—Offers metadata for a photograph taken within the image picker.

Recipe 8-1 uses several steps to move from the info dictionary contents to produce a recovered image. First, it checks whether the dictionary contains an edited version. If it does not find this, it accesses the original image. If that fails, it retrieves the reference URL and tries to load it through the assets library. Normally, at the end of these steps, the application has a valid image instance to work with. If it does not, it logs an error and returns.

Finally, don't forget to dismiss modally presented controllers before wrapping up work in the delegate callback.

> **Note**
>
> When it comes to user interaction zoology, `UIImagePickerController` is a cow. It is slow to load. It eagerly consumes application memory and spends extra time chewing its cud. Be aware of these limitations when designing your apps and do not tip your image picker.

Recipe 8-1 **Selecting Images**

```objc
#define IS_IPHONE (UI_USER_INTERFACE_IDIOM() == \
    UIUserInterfaceIdiomPhone)

// Dismiss the picker
- (void)performDismiss
{
    if (IS_IPHONE)
        [self dismissViewControllerAnimated:YES completion:nil];
    else
    {
        [popover dismissPopoverAnimated:YES];
        popover = nil;
    }
}


// Present the picker
- (void)presentViewController:
    (UIViewController *)viewControllerToPresent
{
    if (IS_IPHONE)
    {
        [self presentViewController:viewControllerToPresent
            animated:YES completion:nil];
    }
    else
    {
        // Workaround to an Apple crasher when asking for asset
        // library authorization with a popover displayed
        ALAssetsLibrary * assetsLibrary =
            [[ALAssetsLibrary alloc] init];
        ALAuthorizationStatus authStatus;

        if (NSFoundationVersionNumber >
                NSFoundationVersionNumber_iOS_6_0)
            authStatus = [ALAssetsLibrary authorizationStatus];
        else
            authStatus = ALAuthorizationStatusAuthorized;

        if (authStatus == ALAuthorizationStatusAuthorized)
        {
            popover = [[UIPopoverController alloc]
                initWithContentViewController:viewControllerToPresent];
            popover.delegate = self;
            [popover presentPopoverFromBarButtonItem:
                    self.navigationItem.rightBarButtonItem
                permittedArrowDirections:UIPopoverArrowDirectionAny
```

```objc
                    animated:YES];
        }
        else if (authStatus == ALAuthorizationStatusNotDetermined)
        {
            // Force authorization
            [assetsLibrary enumerateGroupsWithTypes:ALAssetsGroupAll
                usingBlock:^(ALAssetsGroup *group, BOOL *stop){
                // If authorized, catch the final iteration
                // and display popover
                if (group == nil)
                {
                    dispatch_async(dispatch_get_main_queue(), ^{
                        popover = [[UIPopoverController alloc]
                            initWithContentViewController:
                                viewControllerToPresent];
                        popover.delegate = self;
                        [popover presentPopoverFromBarButtonItem:
                                self.navigationItem.rightBarButtonItem
                            permittedArrowDirections:
                                UIPopoverArrowDirectionAny
                            animated:YES];
                    });
                }
                *stop = YES;
            } failureBlock:nil];
        }
    }
}


// Popover was dismissed
- (void)popoverControllerDidDismissPopover:
    (UIPopoverController *)aPopoverController
{
    popover = nil;
}


// Retrieve an image from an asset URL
- (void)loadImageFromAssetURL:(NSURL *)assetURL
    into:(UIImage **)image
{
    ALAssetsLibrary *library = [[ALAssetsLibrary alloc] init];
    ALAssetsLibraryAssetForURLResultBlock resultsBlock =
        ^(ALAsset *asset)
    {
        ALAssetRepresentation *assetRepresentation =
            [asset defaultRepresentation];
        CGImageRef cgImage =
```

```
            [assetRepresentation CGImageWithOptions:nil];
        CFRetain(cgImage); // Thanks, Oliver Drobnik
        if (image) *image = [UIImage imageWithCGImage:cgImage];
        CFRelease(cgImage);
    };
    ALAssetsLibraryAccessFailureBlock failureBlock =
        ^(NSError *__strong error)
    {
        NSLog(@"Error retrieving asset from url: %@",
            error.localizedFailureReason);
    };

    [library assetForURL:assetURL
        resultBlock:resultsBlock failureBlock:failureBlock];
}


// Update image and for iPhone, dismiss the controller
- (void)imagePickerController:(UIImagePickerController *)picker
    didFinishPickingMediaWithInfo:(NSDictionary *)info
{
    // Use the edited image if available
    UIImage __autoreleasing *image =
        info[UIImagePickerControllerEditedImage];

    // If not, grab the original image
    if (!image)
        image = info[UIImagePickerControllerOriginalImage];

    // If still no luck, check for an asset URL
    NSURL *assetURL = info[UIImagePickerControllerReferenceURL];
    if (!image && !assetURL)
    {
        NSLog(@"Cannot retrieve an image from the selected item. Giving up.");
    }
    else if (!image)
    {
        // Retrieve the image from the asset library
        [self loadImageFromAssetURL:assetURL into:&image];
    }

    // Display the image
    if (image)
        imageView.image = image;

    if (IS_IPHONE)
        [self performDismiss];
}
```

```
// iPhone-like devices only: dismiss the picker with cancel button
- (void)imagePickerControllerDidCancel:
    (UIImagePickerController *)picker
{
    [self performDismiss];
}

- (void)pickImage
{
    if (popover) return;

    // Create and initialize the picker
    UIImagePickerController *picker =
        [[UIImagePickerController alloc] init];
    picker.sourceType =
        UIImagePickerControllerSourceTypePhotoLibrary;
    picker.allowsEditing = editSwitch.isOn;
    picker.delegate = self;

    [self presentViewController:picker];
}
```

Get This Recipe's Code

To find this recipe's full sample project, point your browser to https://github.com/erica/iOS-7-Cookbook and go to the folder for Chapter 8.

Recipe: Snapping Photos

In addition to selecting pictures, the image picker controller enables you to snap photos with a device's built-in camera. Because cameras are not available on all iOS units (specifically, older iPod touch and iPad devices), begin by checking whether the device running the application supports camera usage:

```
if ([UIImagePickerController isSourceTypeAvailable:
    UIImagePickerControllerSourceTypeCamera]) ...
```

The rule is this: Never offer camera-based features for devices that don't have cameras. Although iOS 7 was deployed only to camera-ready devices, no one but Apple knows what hardware will be released in the future. As unlikely as it sounds, Apple could introduce new models without cameras. Until Apple says otherwise, assume that the possibility exists for a noncamera system, even under modern iOS releases. Further, assume that this method will accurately report state for camera-enabled devices whose source has been disabled through some future system setting.

Setting Up the Picker

You instantiate a camera version of the image picker the same way you create a picture selection one. Just change the source type from the library or Camera Roll to the camera:

```
picker.sourceType = UIImagePickerControllerSourceTypeCamera;
```

As with other modes, you can allow or disallow image editing as part of the photo-capture process by setting the allowsEditing property.

Although the setup with UIImagePickerControllerSourceTypeCamera is the same as with UIImagePickerControllerSourceTypePhotoLibrary, the user experience differs slightly (see Figure 8-2). The camera picker offers a preview that displays after the user taps the camera icon to snap a photo. This preview lets users retake the photo or use the photo as is. Once they tap Use, control passes to the next phase. If you've enabled image editing, the user will be able to edit the image. If not, control moves to the standard "did finish picking" method in the delegate.

Figure 8-2   The camera version of the image picker controller offers a distinct user experience for snapping photos.

Most modern devices offer more than one camera. All iOS 7–capable devices ship with both a rear- and front-facing camera. Even among the iOS 6–supported devices, only the iPhone 3GS has a single camera. Assign the `cameraDevice` property to select which camera you want to use. The rear camera is always the default.

The `isCameraDeviceAvailable:` class method queries whether a specific camera device is available. This snippet checks to see whether the front camera is available, and if it is, selects it:

```
if ([UIImagePickerController isCameraDeviceAvailable:
    UIImagePickerControllerCameraDeviceFront])
    picker.cameraDevice = UIImagePickerControllerCameraDeviceFront;
```

Here are a few more points about the camera or cameras that you can access through the `UIImagePickerController` class:

- You can query the device's ability to use flash by using the `isFlashAvailableForCameraDevice:` class method. Supply either the front or back device constant. This method returns YES for available flash, or otherwise NO.

- When a camera supports flash, you can set the `cameraFlashMode` property directly to auto (`UIImagePickerControllerCameraFlashModeAuto`, which is the default), to always used (`UIImagePickerControllerCameraFlashModeOn`), or always off (`UIImagePickerControllerCameraFlashModeOff`). Selecting off disables the flash regardless of ambient light conditions.

- Choose between photo and video capture by setting the `cameraCaptureMode` property. The picker defaults to photo-capture mode. You can test what modes are available for a device by using `availableCaptureModesForCameraDevice:`. This returns an array of NSNumber objects, each of which encodes a valid capture mode, either photo (`UIImagePickerControllerCameraCaptureModePhoto`) or video (`UIImagePickerControllerCameraCaptureModeVideo`).

Displaying Images

When working with photos, keep image size in mind. Snapped pictures, especially those from high-resolution cameras, can be quite large, even in the age of Retina displays. Those captured from front-facing video cameras use lower-quality sensors and are much smaller.

Content modes provide an in-app solution to displaying large images. They allow image views to scale their embedded images to available screen space. Consider using one of the following modes:

- The `UIViewContentModeScaleAspectFit` mode ensures that the entire image is shown with the aspect ratio retained. The image may be padded with empty rectangles on the sides or the top and bottom to preserve that aspect.

- The `UIViewContentModeScaleAspectFill` mode displays as much of the image as possible, while filling the entire view. Some content may be clipped so that the entire view's bounds are filled.

Saving Images to the Photo Album

Save a snapped image (or any `UIImage` instance, actually) to the photo album by calling `UIImageWriteToSavedPhotosAlbum()`. This function takes four arguments. The first is the image to save. The second and third arguments specify a callback target and selector, typically your primary view controller and `image:didFinishSavingWithError:contextInfo:`. The fourth argument is an optional context pointer. Whatever selector you use, it must take three arguments: an image, an error, and a pointer to the passed context information.

Recipe 8-2 uses the `UIImageWriteToSavedPhotosAlbum()` function to demonstrate how to snap a new image, allow user edits, and then save the image to the photo album.

Recipe 8-2 **Snapping Pictures**

```
// "Finished saving" callback method
- (void)image:(UIImage *)image
    didFinishSavingWithError:(NSError *)error
    contextInfo:(void *)contextInfo;
{
    // Handle the end of the image write process
    if (!error)
        NSLog(@"Image written to photo album");
    else
        NSLog(@"Error writing to photo album: %@",
            error.localizedFailureReason);
}


// Save the returned image
- (void)imagePickerController:(UIImagePickerController *)picker
    didFinishPickingMediaWithInfo:(NSDictionary *)info
{
    // Use the edited image if available
    UIImage __autoreleasing *image =
        info[UIImagePickerControllerEditedImage];

    // If not, grab the original image
    if (!image)
        image = info[UIImagePickerControllerOriginalImage];

    // If still no luck, check for an asset URL
    NSURL *assetURL = info[UIImagePickerControllerReferenceURL];
    if (!image && !assetURL)
    {
        NSLog(@"Cannot retrieve an image from selected item. Giving up.");
    }
    else if (!image)
    {
```

```
            NSLog(@"Retrieving from Assets Library");
            [self loadImageFromAssetURL:assetURL into:&image];
    }

    if (image)
    {
        // Save the image
        UIImageWriteToSavedPhotosAlbum(image, self,
            @selector(image:didFinishSavingWithError:contextInfo:),
            NULL);
        imageView.image = image;
    }

    [self performDismiss];
}

- (void)loadView
{
    self.view = [[UIView alloc] init];
    self.view.backgroundColor = [UIColor whiteColor];

    imageView = [[UIImageView alloc] init];
    imageView.contentMode = UIViewContentModeScaleAspectFit;
    [self.view addSubview:imageView];
    PREPCONSTRAINTS(imageView);
    STRETCH_VIEW(self.view, imageView);

    // Only present the "Snap" option for camera-ready devices
    if ([UIImagePickerController isSourceTypeAvailable:
        UIImagePickerControllerSourceTypeCamera])
        self.navigationItem.rightBarButtonItem =
            SYSBARBUTTON(UIBarButtonSystemItemCamera,
                @selector(snapImage)));

    // Set up title view with Edits: ON/OFF
    editSwitch = [[UISwitch alloc] init];
    UILabel * editLabel =
        [[UILabel alloc] initWithFrame:CGRectMake(0, 0, 40, 13)];
    editLabel.text = @"Edits";
    self.navigationItem.leftBarButtonItems =
        @[[[UIBarButtonItem alloc] initWithCustomView:editLabel],
          [[UIBarButtonItem alloc] initWithCustomView:editSwitch]];

}
```

Recipe: Recording Video

Even in the age of ubiquitous cameras on iOS 7, exercise caution regarding not just the availability but also the kinds of cameras provided by each device. When recording video, your application should check whether a device supports camera-based video recording.

This is a two-step process. It isn't sufficient to only check for a camera, such as those in the first-generation and 3G iPhones (in contrast to early iPad and iPod touch models, which shipped without cameras). Only the 3GS and newer units provided video-recording capabilities and, however unlikely, future models could ship without cameras or with still cameras.

That means you perform two checks: first, that a camera is available, and second, that the available capture types include video. This method returns a Boolean value indicating whether the device running the application is video-ready:

```
- (BOOL)videoRecordingAvailable
{
    // The source type must be available
    if (![UIImagePickerController isSourceTypeAvailable:
        UIImagePickerControllerSourceTypeCamera])
    return NO;

    // And the media type must include the movie type
    NSArray *mediaTypes = [UIImagePickerController
        availableMediaTypesForSourceType:
        UIImagePickerControllerSourceTypeCamera]
    return [mediaTypes containsObject:(NSString *)kUTTypeMovie];
}
```

This method searches for a movie type (kUTTypeMovie, aka `public.movie`) in the results for the available media types query. Uniform Type Identifiers (UTIs) are strings that identify abstract types for common file formats such as images, movies, and data. UTIs are discussed in further detail in Chapter 11, "Documents and Data Sharing." These types are defined in the Mobile Core Services module. Be sure to import the module in your source file:

```
@import MobileCoreServices;
```

Creating the Video-Recording Picker

Recording video is almost identical to capturing still images with the camera. Recipe 8-3 allocates and initializes a new image picker, sets its delegate, and presents it:

```
UIImagePickerController *picker =
    [[UIImagePickerController alloc] init];
picker.sourceType = UIImagePickerControllerSourceTypeCamera;
picker.videoQuality = UIImagePickerControllerQualityTypeMedium;
picker.mediaTypes = @[(NSString *)kUTTypeMovie]; // public.movie
picker.delegate = self;
```

Choose the video quality you want to record. As you improve quality, the data stored per second increases. Select from high (`UIImagePickerControllerQualityTypeHigh`), medium (`UIImagePickerControllerQualityTypeMedium`), low (`UIImagePickerController-QualityTypeLow`), or VGA (`UIImagePickerControllerQualityType640x480`).

As with image picking, the video version allows you to set an `allowsEditing` property, as discussed in Recipe 8-5.

Saving the Video

The info dictionary returned by the video picker contains a `UIImagePickerController-MediaURL` key. This media URL points to the captured video, which is stored in a temporary folder within the app sandbox. Use the `UISaveVideoAtPathToSavedPhotosAlbum()` function to store the video to your library.

This save method takes four arguments: the path to the video you want to add to the library, a callback target, a selector with three arguments (basically identical to the selector used during image save callbacks), and an optional context. The save method calls the target with that selector after it finishes its work, allowing you to check for success.

Recipe 8-3   **Recording Video**

```
- (void)video:(NSString *)videoPath
    didFinishSavingWithError:(NSError *)error
    contextInfo:(void *)contextInfo
{
    if (!error)
        self.title = @"Saved!";
    else
        NSLog(@"Error saving video: %@",
            error.localizedFailureReason);
}

- (void)saveVideo:(NSURL *)mediaURL
{
    // check if video is compatible with album
    BOOL compatible =
        UIVideoAtPathIsCompatibleWithSavedPhotosAlbum(
            mediaURL.path);
```

```
    // save
    if (compatible)
        UISaveVideoAtPathToSavedPhotosAlbum(
            mediaURL.path, self,
            @selector(video:didFinishSavingWithError:contextInfo:),
            NULL);
}

- (void)imagePickerController:(UIImagePickerController *)picker
    didFinishPickingMediaWithInfo:(NSDictionary *)info
{
    [self performDismiss];

    // Save the video
    NSURL *mediaURL =
        info[UIImagePickerControllerMediaURL];
    [self saveVideo: mediaURL];
}

- (void)recordVideo
{
    if (popover) return;
    self.title = nil;

    // Create and initialize the picker
    UIImagePickerController *picker =
        [[UIImagePickerController alloc] init];
    picker.sourceType = UIImagePickerControllerSourceTypeCamera;
    picker.videoQuality = UIImagePickerControllerQualityTypeMedium;
    picker.mediaTypes = @[(NSString *)kUTTypeMovie];
    picker.delegate = self;

    [self presentViewController:picker];
}
```

Get This Recipe's Code

To find this recipe's full sample project, point your browser to https://github.com/erica/iOS-7-Cookbook and go to the folder for Chapter 8.

Recipe: Playing Video with Media Player

The MPMoviePlayerViewController and MPMoviePlayerController classes simplify video display in your applications. Part of the Media Player framework, these classes allow you to embed video into your views or to play movies back, full screen. With the ready-built full-feature video player shown in Figure 8-3, you do little more than supply a content URL. The player provides the Done button, the time scrubber, the aspect control, and the playback controls, plus the underlying video presentation.

Figure 8-3   The Media Player framework simplifies adding video playback to your applications. This class allows off-device streaming video as well as fixed-size local assets. Supported video standards include H.264 Baseline Profile Level 3.0 video (up to 640×480 at 30fps) and MPEG-4 Part 2 video (Simple Profile). Most files with .mov, .mp4, .mpv, and .3gp extensions can be played. Audio support includes AAC-LC audio (up to 48KHz) and MP3 (MPEG-1 Audio Layer 3, up to 48KHz) stereo.

Recipe 8-4 builds on the video recording introduced in Recipe 8-3. It adds playback after each recording by switching the Camera button in the navigation bar to a Play button. Once the video finishes playing, the button returns to Camera. This recipe does not save any videos to the library, so you can record, play, and record, play, ad infinitum.

The image picker supplies a media URL, which is all you need to establish the player. Recipe 8-4 instantiates a new player and sets two properties. The first enables AirPlay, letting you stream the recorded video to an AirPlay-enabled receiver like Apple TV or a commercial application like Reflector (http://reflectorapp.com). The second sets the playback style to show the video full screen. It then presents the movie.

The two movie player classes consist of a presentable view controller and the actual player controller, which the view controller owns as a property. This is why Recipe 8-4 makes so many mentions of `player.moviePlayer`. The view controller class is quite small and easy to launch. The real work takes place in the player controller.

Movie players use notifications rather than delegates to communicate with applications. You subscribe to these notifications to determine when the movie starts playing, when it finishes, and when it changes state (as in pause/play). Recipe 8-4 observes two notifications: when the movie becomes playable and when it finishes.

After the movie loads and its state changes to playable, Recipe 8-4 starts playback. The movie appears full screen and continues playing until the user taps Done or the movie finishes. In either case, the player generates a finish notification. At that time, the app returns to recording mode, presenting its Camera button to allow the user to record the next video sequence.

This recipe demonstrates the basics for playing video in iOS. You are not limited to video you record yourself. The movie player controller is agnostic about its video source. You can set the content URL to a file stored in your sandbox or even point it to a compliant resource on the Internet.

Note

If your movie player opens and immediately closes, check your URLs to make sure they are valid. Do not forget that local file URLs need `fileURLWithPath:`, whereas remote ones can use `URLWithString:`.

Recipe 8-4   **Video Playback**

```
#define SYSBARBUTTON(ITEM, SELECTOR) [[UIBarButtonItem alloc] \
    initWithBarButtonSystemItem:ITEM target:self action:SELECTOR]

- (void)playMovie
{
    // Prepare movie player and play
    MPMoviePlayerViewController *player =
        [[MPMoviePlayerViewController alloc]
            initWithContentURL:mediaURL];
    player.moviePlayer.allowsAirPlay = YES;
    player.moviePlayer.controlStyle = MPMovieControlStyleFullscreen;

    [self.navigationController
        presentMoviePlayerViewControllerAnimated:player];

    // Handle the end of movie playback
    [[NSNotificationCenter defaultCenter]
        addObserverForName:MPMoviePlayerPlaybackDidFinishNotification
        object:player.moviePlayer queue:[NSOperationQueue mainQueue]
        usingBlock:^(NSNotification *notification){
            // Return to recording mode
            self.navigationItem.rightBarButtonItem =
                SYSBARBUTTON(UIBarButtonSystemItemCamera,
            @selector(recordVideo));
```

```
                    // Stop listening to movie notifications
                    [[NSNotificationCenter defaultCenter]
                        removeObserver:self];

            }];

        // Wait for the movie to load and become playable
        [[NSNotificationCenter defaultCenter]
            addObserverForName:MPMoviePlayerLoadStateDidChangeNotification
            object:player.moviePlayer queue:[NSOperationQueue mainQueue]
            usingBlock:^(NSNotification *notification) {

                // When the movie sets the playable flag, start playback
                if ((player.moviePlayer.loadState &
                    MPMovieLoadStatePlayable) != 0)
                    [player.moviePlayer performSelector:@selector(play)
                        withObject:nil afterDelay:1.0f];

        }];
}

// After recording any content, allow the user to play it
- (void)imagePickerController:(UIImagePickerController *)picker
    didFinishPickingMediaWithInfo:(NSDictionary *)info
{
    [self performDismiss];

    // recover video URL
    mediaURL = info[UIImagePickerControllerMediaURL];
    self.navigationItem.rightBarButtonItem =
        SYSBARBUTTON(UIBarButtonSystemItemPlay,
            @selector(playMovie));
}
```

Get This Recipe's Code

To find this recipe's full sample project, point your browser to https://github.com/erica/iOS-7-Cookbook and go to the folder for Chapter 8.

Recipe: Editing Video

Enabling an image picker's `allowsEditing` property for a video source activates the yellow editing bars you've seen in the built-in Photos app. (Drag the grips at either side to see them in action.) During the editing step of the capture process, users drag the ends of the scrubbing track to choose the video range they want to use.

Surprisingly, the picker does not trim the video itself. Instead, it returns four items in the info dictionary:

- `UIImagePickerControllerMediaURL`

- `UIImagePickerControllerMediaType`

- `_UIImagePickerControllerVideoEditingStart`

- `_UIImagePickerControllerVideoEditingEnd`

The media URL points to the untrimmed video, which is stored in a temporary folder within the sandbox. The video start and end points are `NSNumbers`, containing the offsets the user chose with those yellow edit bars. The media type is `public.movie`.

If you save the video to the library (as shown in Recipe 8-3), it stores the unedited version, which is not what your user expects or you want. The iOS SDK offers two ways to edit video. Recipe 8-5 demonstrates how to use the AV Foundation framework to respond to the edit requests returned by the video image picker. Recipe 8-6 shows you how to pick videos from your library and use `UIVideoEditorController` to edit.

AV Foundation and Core Media

This recipe requires access to two very specialized modules. The AV Foundation module provides an Objective-C interface that supports media processing. Core Media uses a low-level C interface to describe media properties. Together these provide an iOS version of the Mac's QuickTime media experience. Import both modules in your source file for this recipe.

Recipe 8-5 begins by recovering the media URL from the image picker's info dictionary. This URL points to the temporary file in the sandbox created by the image picker. The recipe creates a new AV asset URL from that. Next, it creates the export range, the times within the video that should be saved to the library. It does this by using the Core Media `CMTimeRange` structure, building it from the info dictionary's start and end times. The `CMTimeMakeWithSeconds()` function takes two arguments: a time and a scale factor. This recipe uses a factor of 1, preserving the exact times.

An export session allows your app to save data back out to the file system. This session does not save video to the library; that is a separate step. The session exports the trimmed video to a local file in the sandbox tmp folder, alongside the originally captured video. To create an export session, allocate it and set its asset and quality.

Recipe 8-5 saves the trimmed video to a new path. This path is identical to the one it read from but with "-trimmed" added to the core filename. The export session uses this path to set its output URL, uses the export range to specify what time range to include, and selects a QuickTime movie output file type. Then it's ready to process the video. The export session asynchronously performs the file export, using the properties and contents of the passed asset.

When the trimmed movie is complete, save it to the central media library. Recipe 8-5 does so in the export session's completion block.

Recipe 8-5   **Trimming Video with AV Foundation**

```
- (void)trimVideo:(NSDictionary *)info
{
    // recover video URL
    NSURL *mediaURL =
        info[UIImagePickerControllerMediaURL];
    AVURLAsset *asset =
        [AVURLAsset URLAssetWithURL:mediaURL options:nil];

    // Create the export range
    CGFloat editingStart =
        [info[@"_UIImagePickerControllerVideoEditingStart"]
            floatValue];
    CGFloat editingEnd =
        [info[@"_UIImagePickerControllerVideoEditingEnd"]
            floatValue];
    CMTime startTime = CMTimeMakeWithSeconds(editingStart, 1);
    CMTime endTime = CMTimeMakeWithSeconds(editingEnd, 1);
    CMTimeRange exportRange =
        CMTimeRangeFromTimeToTime(startTime, endTime);

    // Create a trimmed version URL: file:originalpath-trimmed.mov
    NSString *urlPath = mediaURL.path;
    NSString *extension = urlPath.pathExtension;
    NSString *base = [urlPath stringByDeletingPathExtension];
    NSString *newPath = [NSString stringWithFormat:
        @"%@-trimmed.%@", base, extension];
    NSURL *fileURL = [NSURL fileURLWithPath:newPath];

    // Establish an export session
    AVAssetExportSession *session = [AVAssetExportSession
        exportSessionWithAsset:asset
        presetName:AVAssetExportPresetMediumQuality];
    session.outputURL = fileURL;
    session.outputFileType = AVFileTypeQuickTimeMovie;
    session.timeRange = exportRange;

    // Perform the export
    [session exportAsynchronouslyWithCompletionHandler:^(){
        if (session.status ==
            AVAssetExportSessionStatusCompleted)
                [self saveVideo:fileURL];
        else if (session.status ==
```

```
        AVAssetExportSessionStatusFailed)
            NSLog(@"AV export session failed");
    else
        NSLog(@"Export session status: %d", session.status);
    }];
}
```

Get This Recipe's Code

To find this recipe's full sample project, point your browser to https://github.com/erica/iOS-7-Cookbook and go to the folder for Chapter 8.

Recipe: Picking and Editing Video

You can use the image picker class to select videos as well as images, as demonstrated in Recipe 8-6. All it takes is a little editing of the media types property. Set the picker source type as normal, to either the photo library or the saved photos album, but restrict the media types property. The following snippet shows how to set the media types to request a picker that presents video assets only:

```
picker.sourceType =  UIImagePickerControllerSourceTypePhotoLibrary;
picker.mediaTypes = @[(NSString *)kUTTypeMovie];
```

Once the user selects a video, Recipe 8-6 enters edit mode. Always check that the video asset can be modified. Call the UIVideoEditorController class method canEditVideoAtPath:. This returns a Boolean value that indicates whether the video is compatible with the editor controller:

```
if (![UIVideoEditorController canEditVideoAtPath:vpath]) ...
```

If it is compatible, allocate a new video editor. The UIVideoEditorController class provides a system-supplied interface that allows users to interactively trim videos. Set its delegate and videoPath properties and present it. (This class can also be used to re-encode data to a lower quality via the videoQuality property.)

The editor uses a set of delegate callbacks that are similar but not identical to the ones used by the UIImagePickerController class. Callbacks include methods for success, failure, and user cancellation:

- videoEditorController:didSaveEditedVideoToPath:
- videoEditorController:didFailWithError:
- videoEditorControllerDidCancel:

Cancellation occurs only when the user taps the Cancel button within the video editor. Tapping outside a popover dismisses the editor but doesn't invoke the callback. For both cancellation and failure, Recipe 8-6 responds by resetting its interface, allowing users to pick another video.

A success callback occurs when a user has finished editing the video and taps Use. The controller saves the trimmed video to a temporary path and calls the did-save method. Do not confuse this "saving" with storing items to your photo library; this path resides in the application sandbox's tmp folder. If you do nothing with the data, iOS deletes it the next time the device reboots. Once past this step, Recipe 8-6 offers a button to save the trimmed data into the shared iOS photo album, using the save-to-library feature introduced in Recipe 8-3.

Recipe 8-6   Using the Video Editor Controller

```
// The edited video is now stored in the local tmp folder
- (void)videoEditorController:(UIVideoEditorController *)editor
    didSaveEditedVideoToPath:(NSString *)editedVideoPath
{
    [self performDismiss];

    // Update the working URL and present the Save button
    mediaURL = [NSURL URLWithString:editedVideoPath];
    self.navigationItem.leftBarButtonItem =
        BARBUTTON(@"Save", @selector(saveVideo));
    self.navigationItem.rightBarButtonItem =
        BARBUTTON(@"Pick", @selector(pickVideo));
}


// Handle failed edit
- (void)videoEditorController:(UIVideoEditorController *)editor
    didFailWithError:(NSError *)error
{
    [self performDismiss];
    mediaURL = nil;
    self.navigationItem.rightBarButtonItem =
        BARBUTTON(@"Pick", @selector(pickVideo));
    self.navigationItem.leftBarButtonItem = nil;
    NSLog(@"Video edit failed: %@", error.localizedFailureReason);
}


// Handle cancel by returning to Pick state
- (void)videoEditorControllerDidCancel:
    (UIVideoEditorController *)editor
{
    [self performDismiss];
    mediaURL = nil;
    self.navigationItem.rightBarButtonItem =
        BARBUTTON(@"Pick", @selector(pickVideo));
    self.navigationItem.leftBarButtonItem = nil;
```

```
    }

    // Allow the user to edit the media with a video editor
    - (void)editMedia
    {
        if (![UIVideoEditorController canEditVideoAtPath:mediaURL.path])
        {
            self.title = @"Cannot Edit Video";
            self.navigationItem.rightBarButtonItem =
                BARBUTTON(@"Pick", @selector(pickVideo));
            return;
        }

        UIVideoEditorController *editor =
            [[UIVideoEditorController alloc] init];
        editor.videoPath = mediaURL.path;
        editor.delegate = self;
        [self presentViewController:editor];
    }


    // The user has selected a video. Offer an edit button.
    - (void)imagePickerController:(UIImagePickerController *)picker
        didFinishPickingMediaWithInfo:(NSDictionary *)info
    {
        [self performDismiss];

        // Store the video URL and present an Edit button
        mediaURL = info[UIImagePickerControllerMediaURL];
        self.navigationItem.rightBarButtonItem =
            BARBUTTON(@"Edit", @selector(editMedia));
    }
```

Get This Recipe's Code

To find this recipe's full sample project, point your browser to https://github.com/erica/iOS-7-Cookbook and go to the folder for Chapter 8.

Recipe: E-mailing Pictures

The Message UI framework allows users to compose e-mail and text messages within applications. As with camera access and the image picker, first check whether a user's device has been enabled for these services. A simple test allows you to determine when mail is enabled:

```
[MFMailComposeViewController canSendMail]
```

When mail capabilities are enabled, users can send their photographs via instances of `MFMailComposeViewController`. Texts are sent through `MFMessageComposeViewController` instances.

Recipe 8-7 uses this composition class to create a new mail item populated with the user-snapped photograph. The mail composition controller works best as a modally presented client on both the iPhone family and iPad. Your primary view controller presents it and waits for results via a delegate callback.

Creating Message Contents

The composition controller's properties allow you to programmatically build a message including to/cc/bcc recipients and attachments. Recipe 8-7 demonstrates the creation of a simple HTML message with an attachment. Properties are almost universally optional. Define the subject and body contents via `setSubject:` and `setMessageBody:`. Each method takes a string as its argument.

Leave To Recipients unassigned to greet the user with an unaddressed message. The times you'll want to prefill this field include adding call-home features such as Report a Bug or Send Feedback to the Developer or when you allow the user to choose a favorite recipient in your settings.

Creating the attachment requires slightly more work. To add an attachment, you need to provide all the file components expected by the mail client. Supply data (via an `NSData` object), a MIME type (a string), and a filename (another string). Retrieve the image data using the `UIImageJPEGRepresentation()` function. This function can take time to work, so expect slight delays before the message view appears.

This recipe uses a hard-coded MIME type of `image/jpeg`. If you want to send other data types, you can query iOS for MIME types via typical file extensions. Use `UTTypeCopyPreferredTagWithClass()`, which is defined in the Mobile Core Services framework, as shown in the following method:

```
#import <MobileCoreServices/UTType.h>
- (NSString *) mimeTypeForExtension: (NSString *) ext
{
    // Request the UTI for the file extension
    CFStringRef UTI = UTTypeCreatePreferredIdentifierForTag(
        kUTTagClassFilenameExtension,
        (__bridge CFStringRef) ext, NULL);
    if (!UTI) return nil;

    // Request the MIME file type for the UTI,
    // may return nil for unrecognized MIME types
    NSString *mimeType = (__bridge_transfer NSString *)
        UTTypeCopyPreferredTagWithClass(UTI, kUTTagClassMIMEType);
    CFRelease(UTI);
```

```
    return mimeType;
}
```

This method returns a standard MIME type based on the file extension passed to it, such as .jpg, .png, .txt, .html, and so on. Always test to see whether this method returns `nil` because the iOS's built-in knowledge base of extension-MIME type matches is limited. Alternatively, search the Internet for the proper MIME representations and add them to your project by hand.

The e-mail uses a filename you specify to name the transmitted data you send. Use any name you like. Here, the name is set to pickerimage.jpg. Because you're just sending data, there's no true connection between the content you send and the name you assign:

```
[mcvc addAttachmentData:UIImageJPEGRepresentation(image, 1.0f)
    mimeType:@"image/jpeg" fileName:@"pickerimage.jpg"];
```

Note

When you use the iOS mail composer, attachments appear at the end of sent mail. Apple does not provide a way to embed images inside the flow of HTML text. This is due to differences between Apple and Microsoft representations.

Recipe 8-7   **Sending Images by E-mail**

```
- (void)mailComposeController:
        (MFMailComposeViewController*)controller
    didFinishWithResult:(MFMailComposeResult)result
    error:(NSError*)error
{
    // Wrap up the composer details
    [self performDismiss];
    switch (result)
    {
        case MFMailComposeResultCancelled:
            NSLog(@"Mail was cancelled");
            break;
        case MFMailComposeResultFailed:
            NSLog(@"Mail failed");
            break;
        case MFMailComposeResultSaved:
            NSLog(@"Mail was saved");
            break;
        case MFMailComposeResultSent:
            NSLog(@"Mail was sent");
            break;
        default:
            break;
    }
}
```

```
}

- (void)sendImage
{
    UIImage *image = imageView.image;
    if (!image) return;

    // Customize the e-mail
    MFMailComposeViewController *mcvc =
        [[MFMailComposeViewController alloc] init];
    mcvc.mailComposeDelegate = self;

    // Set the subject
    [mcvc setSubject:@"Here's a great photo!"];

    // Create a prefilled body
    NSString *body = @"<h1>Check this out</h1>\
<p>I snapped this image from the\
<code><b>UIImagePickerController</b></code>.</p>";
    [mcvc setMessageBody:body isHTML:YES];

    // Add the attachment
    [mcvc addAttachmentData:UIImageJPEGRepresentation(image, 1.0f)
        mimeType:@"image/jpeg" fileName:@"pickerimage.jpg"];

    // Present the e-mail composition controller
    [self presentViewController:mcvc];
}
```

Get This Recipe's Code

To find this recipe's full sample project, point your browser to https://github.com/erica/iOS-7-Cookbook and go to the folder for Chapter 8.

Recipe: Sending a Text Message

It's even easier to send a text from your applications than to send an e-mail. This particular controller is shown in Figure 8-4. As with mail, first ensure that the capability exists on the iOS device and declare the `MFMessageComposeViewControllerDelegate` protocol:

```
[MFMessageComposeViewController canSendText]
```

Monitor the availability of text support, which may change over time, by listening for the `MFMessageComposeViewControllerTextMessageAvailabilityDidChangeNotification` notification.

Figure 8-4   The message compose view controller.

Recipe 8-8 creates the new controller and sets its messageComposeDelegate and its body. If you know the intended recipients, you can prepopulate that field by passing an array of phone number strings. Present the controller however you like and wait for the delegate callback, where you dismiss it.

In iOS 7, the message composer now supports attachments. Be sure to check for availability with the MFMessageComposeViewController class method canSendAttachments before adding yours. Recipe 8-8 adds an image to the message, if supported.

Recipe 8-8   Sending Texts

```
- (void)messageComposeViewController:
        (MFMessageComposeViewController *)controller
   didFinishWithResult:(MessageComposeResult)result
{
    [self performDismiss];

    switch (result)
    {
```

```
            case MessageComposeResultCancelled:
                NSLog(@"Message was cancelled");
                break;
            case MessageComposeResultFailed:
                NSLog(@"Message failed");
                break;
            case MessageComposeResultSent:
                NSLog(@"Message was sent");
                break;
            default:
                break;
        }
}

- (void)sendMessage
{
    MFMessageComposeViewController *mcvc =
        [[MFMessageComposeViewController alloc] init];
    mcvc.messageComposeDelegate = self;

    if ([MFMessageComposeViewController canSendAttachments])
        [mcvc addAttachmentData:
            UIImagePNGRepresentation([UIImage
                imageNamed:@"BookCover"])
            typeIdentifier:@"png" filename:@"BookCover.png"];

    mcvc.body = @"I'm reading the iOS Developer's Cookbook";
    [self presentViewController:mcvc];
}

- (void)loadView
{
    self.view = [[UIView alloc] init];
    self.view.backgroundColor = [UIColor whiteColor];
    if ([MFMessageComposeViewController canSendText])
        self.navigationItem.rightBarButtonItem =
            BARBUTTON(@"Send", @selector(sendMessage));
    else
        self.title = @"Cannot send texts";
}
```

Get This Recipe's Code

To find this recipe's full sample project, point your browser to https://github.com/erica/
iOS-7-Cookbook and go to the folder for Chapter 8.

Recipe: Posting Social Updates

The Social framework offers a unified API for integrating applications with social networking services. The framework currently supports Facebook, Twitter, and the China-based Sina Weibo and Tencent Weibo. As with mail and messaging, start by testing whether the service type you want to support is supported:

```
[SLComposeViewController isAvailableForServiceType:SLServiceTypeFacebook]
```

If it is, you can create a composition view controller for that service:

```
SLComposeViewController *fbController = [SLComposeViewController
    composeViewControllerForServiceType:SLServiceTypeFacebook];
```

You customize a controller with images, URLs, and initial text. Recipe 8-9 demonstrates the steps to create the interface shown in Figure 8-5.

> **Note**
>
> With the introduction of `SLComposeViewController` in iOS 6, the original `TWTweetComposeViewController` introduced in iOS 5 was deprecated. While the APIs are nearly identical, the deprecated version has quirks worth avoiding. Use the `SLComposeViewController` variant when Twitter sharing is needed.

Figure 8-5   Composing Twitter messages.

Recipe 8-9   **Posting Social Updates**

```objc
- (void)postSocial:(NSString *)serviceType
{
    // Establish the controller
    SLComposeViewController *controller = [SLComposeViewController
        composeViewControllerForServiceType:serviceType];

    // Add text and an image
    [controller addImage:[UIImage imageNamed:@"BookCover"]];
    [controller setInitialText:
        @"I'm reading the iOS Developer's Cookbook"];

    // Define the completion handler
    controller.completionHandler =
        ^(SLComposeViewControllerResult result){
        switch (result)
        {
            case SLComposeViewControllerResultCancelled:
                NSLog(@"Cancelled");
                break;
            case SLComposeViewControllerResultDone:
                NSLog(@"Posted");
                break;
            default:
                break;
        }
    };

    // Present the controller
    [self presentViewController:controller];
}

- (void)postToFacebook
{
    [self postSocial:SLServiceTypeFacebook];
}

- (void)postToTwitter
{
    [self postSocial:SLServiceTypeTwitter];
}

- (void)loadView
{
```

```
    self.view = [[UIView alloc] init];
    self.view.backgroundColor = [UIColor whiteColor];
    if ([SLComposeViewController
        isAvailableForServiceType:SLServiceTypeFacebook])
        self.navigationItem.leftBarButtonItem =
            BARBUTTON(@"Facebook", @selector(postToFacebook));
    if ([SLComposeViewController
        isAvailableForServiceType:SLServiceTypeTwitter])
        self.navigationItem.rightBarButtonItem =
            BARBUTTON(@"Twitter", @selector(postToTwitter));
}
```

Get This Recipe's Code

To find this recipe's full sample project, point your browser to https://github.com/erica/iOS-7-Cookbook and go to the folder for Chapter 8.

Data Sharing and Viewing

The previous recipes represent individualized methods of sharing information via e-mail, text message, and specific social networks. iOS provides controllers that simplify the sharing and viewing of data for a vastly larger set of data types and sharing targets. UIActivityViewController centralizes the sharing of data, including many built-in activities, such as e-mail, social sharing, printing, and many more, as well as the ability to extend the controller to your own custom activities. QLPreviewController allows the viewing of many types of data that your app likely could not handle itself. Both of these classes are covered fully in Chapter 11.

Summary

This chapter introduces a number of ready-to-use controllers that you can prepare and present to good effect. System-supplied controllers simplify programming for common tasks like tweeting and sending e-mail. Here are a few parting thoughts about the recipes you just encountered:

- You can roll your own versions of a few of these controllers, but why bother? System-supplied controllers are the rare cases where enforcing your own design takes a back seat to a consistency of user experience across applications. When a user sends an e-mail, he or she expects that e-mail compose screen to look basically the same, regardless of application. Go ahead and leverage Apple system services to mail, tweet, and interact with the system media library.

- The image picker controller has grown to be a bit of a Frankenclass. It has long deserved a proper refresh and redesign. From controlling sources at a fine grain to reducing its memory overhead, the class deserves some loving attention from Apple. Now that so many great media processing classes have made the jump to iOS, we'd love to see better integration with AV Foundation, Core Media, and other key technologies—and not just through a visual controller. Although preserving user privacy is critical, it would be nice if the library opened up a more flexible range of APIs (with user-directed permissions, of course).

- The Social framework can do a lot more than post Facebook updates and tweets. The class lets you submit authenticated and unauthenticated service requests using appropriate security. Use the Accounts framework along with Social to retrieve login information for placing credentialed requests.

9

Creating and Managing Table Views

Tables provide a scrolling list–based interaction class that works particularly well for small GUI elements. Many apps that ship natively with the iPhone and iPod touch center on table-based navigation, including Contacts, Settings, and iPod. On these smaller iOS devices, limited screen size makes using tables, with their scrolling and individual item selection, an ideal way to deliver information and content in a simple, easy-to-manipulate form. On the larger iPad, tables integrate with larger detail presentations, providing an important role in split view controllers. In this chapter, you'll discover how iOS tables work, what kinds of tables are available to you as a developer, and how you can use table features in your own programs.

iOS Tables

A standard iOS table consists of a simple vertical scrolling list of individual cells. Users may scroll or flick their way up and down until they find an item they want to interact with. On iOS, tables are ubiquitous. Several built-in iOS apps are based entirely on table views, and they form the core of numerous third-party applications.

Most tables you see in iOS are built using `UITableView` and customized with options provided by its delegate and data source protocols. In addition to a standard scrolling list of cells, which provides the most generic table implementation, you can create specialized tables with custom art, background, labels, and more.

Specialized tables include the kind of tables you see in the Preferences application, with their white cells over a gray background; tables with sections and an index, such as the ones used in the Contacts application; and related classes of wheeled tables, such as those used to set appointment dates and alarms. And, when you need to move beyond tables and their scrolling lists to more grid-like presentations, you can use the related class of collection views, which are introduced in Chapter 10, "Collection Views."

No matter what type of table you use, they all work in the same general way. Tables are built around the Model–View–Controller (MVC) paradigm. They present cells provided from a data source and respond to user interactions by calling well-defined delegate methods.

A data source provides a class with on-demand information about a table's contents. It represents the underlying data model and mediates between that model and the table's view. A data source tells the table about its structure. For example, it specifies how many sections to use and how many items each section includes. Data sources provide individual table cells on-demand and populate those cells with model data that matches each cell's position within the table.

Data sources express a table's model; delegates act as controllers. Delegates manage user interactions, letting applications respond to changes in table selections and user-directed edits. For example, users might tap on a new cell to select it, reorder a cell to a new position, or add and delete cells. Delegates monitor these user interaction requests, react by allowing and disallowing them, and update the data model in response to successful actions.

The view, data source, and delegate work together to express an MVC development pattern. This pattern is not limited to table views. You see this view/data source/delegate approach used in a number of key iOS classes. Picker views, collection views, and page view controllers all use data sources and delegates.

Delegation

Table view data sources and delegates are examples of delegation, assigning responsibility for specific activities and information to a secondary object. Several UIKit classes use delegation to respond to user interactions and to provide content. For example, when you set a table's delegate, you tell it to pass along any interaction messages and let that delegate take responsibility for them.

Table views provide a good example of delegation. When a user taps on a table row, the `UITableView` instance has no built-in way of responding to that tap. The class is general purpose, and it provides no native semantics for taps. Instead, it consults its delegate—usually a view controller class—and passes along the selection change. You add meaning to the tap at a point of time completely separate from when Apple created the table class. Delegation allows classes to be created without specific meaning while ensuring that application-specific handlers can be added at a later time.

The `UITableView` delegate method `tableView:didSelectRowAtIndexPath:` provides a typical delegation example. A delegate object defines this method and specifies how the app should react to a selection change initiated by the user. You might display a menu or navigate to a subview or place a check mark on the tapped row. The response depends entirely on how you implement the delegated selection change method. None of this was known at the time the table class was implemented.

To set an object's delegate or data source, assign its `delegate` or `dataSource` property. This instructs your application to redirect interaction callbacks to the assigned object. You let Objective-C know that your object implements the delegate methods by declaring the protocol or protocols it implements in the class declaration. This declaration appears in angle brackets (for example, `<UITableViewDelegate>` or `<UITableViewDataSource>`), to the right of the class inheritance. When declaring multiple protocols, separate them with commas within a single set of angle brackets (for example, `<UITableViewDelegate, UITableViewDataSource>`). A class that declares a protocol is responsible for implementing all required methods associated with that protocol and may implement any or all of the optional methods as well.

Creating Tables

iOS includes two primary table classes: a prebuilt controller class (`UITableViewController`) and a direct view (`UITableView`). The controller offers a view controller subclass customized for tables. It includes an established table view that takes up the entire controller view, and it eliminates repetitive tasks required for working with table instances. Specifically, it declares all the necessary protocols and defines itself as its table's delegate and data source. When using a table view outside the controller class, you need to perform these tasks manually. The table view controller takes care of them for you.

Table Styles

On the iPhone, tables come in two formats: plain table lists and grouped tables. Plain tables, by default, display on a simple white background with transparent cells. The iOS Settings application uses the grouped style, which displays on a light gray background with each subsection appearing over a white background.

Changing styles requires nothing more than initializing the table view controller with a different style. You can do this explicitly when creating a new instance. This cannot be changed after initialization. Here's an example:

```
myTableViewController = [[UITableViewController alloc]
    initWithStyle:UITableViewStyleGrouped];
```

When using controllers from XIBs and storyboards, adjust the Table View > Style property in the Attributes inspector.

Laying Out the View

`UITableView` instances are, as the name suggests, views that present interactive tables on the iOS screen. The `UITableView` class descends from the `UIScrollView` class. This inheritance provides the up and down scrolling capabilities for the table. Like other views, `UITableView` instances define their boundaries through frames, and they can be children or parents of other views. To create a table view, you allocate it, initialize it with a frame or constrain it with Auto Layout, and then add all the bookkeeping details by assigning data source and delegate objects.

`UITableViewControllers` take care of the view layout work for you. The class creates a standard view controller and populates it with a single `UITableView`, sets its frame to allow for any navigation bars or toolbars, and so on. You can access that table view via the `tableView` instance variable.

Assigning a Data Source

`UITableView` instances rely on an external source to feed either new or existing table cells on demand. Cells are small views that populate the table, adding row-based content. This external source is called a *data source* and refers to the object whose responsibility it is to return a cell on request to a table.

The table's `dataSource` property sets an object to act as a table's source of cells and other layout information. That object declares and must implement the `UITableViewDataSource` protocol. In addition to returning cells, a table's data source specifies the number of sections in the table, the number of cells per section, any titles associated with the sections, cell heights, an optional table of contents, and more. The data source defines how the table looks and the content that populates it.

Typically, the view controller that owns the table view acts as the data source for that view. When working with `UITableViewController` subclasses, you need not declare the protocol because the parent class implicitly supports that protocol and automatically assigns the controller as the data source.

Serving Cells

The table's data source populates the table with cells by implementing the `tableView:cellForRowAtIndexPath:` method. Any time the table's `reloadData` method is invoked, the table starts querying its data source to load the onscreen cells into your table. Your code can call `reloadData` at any time to force the table to reload its contents.

Data sources provide table cells based on an index path, which is passed as a parameter to the cell request method. Index paths, objects of the `NSIndexPath` class, describe the path through a data tree to a particular node—namely their section and their row. You can create an index path by supplying a section and row:

```
NSIndexPath *myIndexPath = [NSIndexPath indexPathForRow:5 inSection:0];
```

In tables, use sections to split data into logical groups and rows to index members within each group. It's the data source's job to associate an index path with a concrete `UITableViewCell` instance and return that cell on demand.

Registering Cell Classes

Register any cell type you work with early in the creation of your table view. Registration allows cell dequeuing methods to automatically create new cells for you. Typically, you register cells in your initializer or in `loadView` or `viewDidLoad` methods. Be sure that this registration takes place before the first time your table attempts to load its data. Each table view instance registers its own types. You supply an arbitrary string identifier, which you use as a key when requesting new cells.

You can register by class (starting in iOS 6) or by XIBs (iOS 5 and later). Here are examples of both approaches:

```
[self.tableView registerClass:[UITableViewCell class]
    forCellReuseIdentifier:@"table cell"];
[self.tableView registerNib:
    [UINib nibWithNibName:@"CustomCell" bundle:[NSBundle mainBundle]]
        forCellReuseIdentifier:@"custom cell"];
```

Register as many kinds of cells as you need. You are not limited to one type per table. Mix and match cells within a table however your design demands.

Dequeuing Cells

Your data source responds to cell requests by building cells from code, or it can load its cells from Interface Builder (IB) sources. Here's a minimal data source method that returns a cell at the requested index path and labels it with text derived from its data model:

```
- (UITableViewCell *)tableView:(UITableView *)aTableView
    cellForRowAtIndexPath:(NSIndexPath *)indexPath
{
    UITableViewCell *cell = [self.tableView
        dequeueReusableCellWithIdentifier:@"cell"
        forIndexPath:indexPath];
    cell.textLabel.text =
        [dataModel objectAtIndexPath:indexPath].text;
    return cell;
}
```

If you're an established iOS developer, you'll appreciate this: You no longer need to check to see whether the queue already has an existing cell of the type you requested. The queue now transparently creates and initializes new instances as needed.

Use the dequeuing mechanism to request cells. As cells scroll off the table and out of view, the table caches them into a queue, ready for reuse. This mechanism returns any available table cells stored in the queue; when the queue runs dry, the mechanism creates and returns new instances.

Registering cells for reuse provides each instance with an identifier tag. The table searches for that type and pops them off the queue as needed. This saves memory and provides a fast, efficient way to feed cells when users scroll quickly through long lists onscreen.

Assigning a Delegate

Like many other Cocoa Touch interaction objects, `UITableView` instances use delegates to respond to user interactions and implement meaningful responses. Your table's delegate can respond to events such as the table scrolling, user edits, or row selection changes. Delegation allows the table to hand off responsibility for reacting to these interactions to the object you specify, typically the controller object that owns the table view.

If you're working directly with a `UITableView`, assign the `delegate` property to a responsible object. The delegate declares the `UITableViewDelegate` protocol. As with data sources, you can skip setting the delegate and declaring the protocol when working with `UITableViewController` or its custom subclass.

Recipe: Implementing a Basic Table

A basic table implementation consists of little more than a set of data used to label cells and a few methods. Recipe 9-1 provides about as basic a table as you can imagine. It creates the flat (nonsectioned) table shown in Figure 9-1. Each cell includes a text label and an image consisting of the cell's row number inside a box.

Users can tap on cells. When they do so, the controller's title updates to match the selected item. A Deselect button tells the table to remove the current selection and reset the title; a Find button moves the selection into view, even if it's been scrolled offscreen.

This implementation attempts to scroll the "found" selection to the top (`UITableViewScrollPositionTop`), space permitting. Zulu, the last item in this table, cannot scroll any higher than the bottom of the view because you simply run out of table after its cell.

Figure 9-1   Recipe 9-1 builds this basic table view.

Data Source Methods

To display a table, even a basic flat one like the one that Recipe 9-1 builds, every table data source must implement three core instance methods. These methods define how the table is structured and provide content for the table:

- **numberOfSectionsInTableView**—Tables can display their data in sections or as a single list. For flat tables, return 1. This indicates that the entire table should be presented as one single list. For sectioned lists, return a value of 2 or higher.

- **tableView:numberOfRowsInSection:**—This method returns the number of rows for a given section. For Recipe 9-1's flat list, this method returns the number of rows for the entire table. For more complex lists, you need to provide a way to report back per section. Core Data provides especially simple sectioned table integration, as you'll read about in Chapter 12, "A Taste of Core Data." As with all counting in iOS, section ordering starts with 0 as the first section.

- **`tableView:cellForRowAtIndexPath:`**—This method returns a cell to the calling table. Use the index path's `row` and `section` properties to determine which cell to provide and make sure to take advantage of reusable cells where possible to minimize memory overhead.

Responding to User Touches

Recipe 9-1 responds to the user in the `tableView:didSelectRowAtIndexPath:` delegate method. This recipe's implementation updates the view controller's title and enables both bar buttons for searching and deselecting. These buttons remain enabled as long as there's a valid selection. If the user chooses the Deselect option, this code calls `deselectRowAtIndexPath: animated:` and disables both buttons.

> **Note**
>
> When you want a table cell to ignore user touches, set the cell's `selectionStyle` property to `UITableViewCellSelectionStyleNone`. This disables the gray overlay that displays on the selected cell. The cell is still selected but will not highlight on selection in any way. If selecting the cell produces some kind of side effect other than presenting information, this may not be the best approach.

Recipe 9-1 **Building a Basic Table**

```
@implementation TestBedViewController
{
    UIFont *imageFont;
    NSArray *items;
}


// Number of sections
- (NSInteger)numberOfSectionsInTableView:(UITableView *)aTableView
{
    return 1;
}


// Rows per section
- (NSInteger)tableView:(UITableView *)aTableView
    numberOfRowsInSection:(NSInteger)section
{
    return items.count;
}


// Return a cell for the index path
- (UITableViewCell *)tableView:(UITableView *)aTableView
    cellForRowAtIndexPath:(NSIndexPath *)indexPath
```

```
{
    UITableViewCell *cell = [self.tableView
        dequeueReusableCellWithIdentifier:@"cell"
        forIndexPath:indexPath];

    // Cell label
    cell.textLabel.text = items[indexPath.row];

    // Cell image
    NSString *indexString =
        [NSString stringWithFormat:@"%02d", indexPath.row];
    cell.imageView.image =
        stringImage(indexString, imageFont, 6.0f);

    return cell;
}


// On selection, update the title and enable find/deselect
- (void)tableView:(UITableView *)aTableView
    didSelectRowAtIndexPath:(NSIndexPath *)indexPath
{
    UITableViewCell *cell =
        [self.tableView cellForRowAtIndexPath:indexPath];
    self.title = cell.textLabel.text;
    self.navigationItem.rightBarButtonItem.enabled = YES;
    self.navigationItem.leftBarButtonItem.enabled = YES;
}


// Deselect any current selection
- (void)deselect
{
    NSArray *paths = [self.tableView indexPathsForSelectedRows];
    if (!paths.count) return;

    NSIndexPath *path = paths[0];
    [self.tableView deselectRowAtIndexPath:path animated:YES];
    self.navigationItem.rightBarButtonItem.enabled = NO;
    self.navigationItem.leftBarButtonItem.enabled = NO;

    self.title = nil;
}


// Move to the selection
- (void)find
{
    [self.tableView scrollToNearestSelectedRowAtScrollPosition:
        UITableViewScrollPositionTop animated:YES];
```

```
}

// Set up table
- (void)viewDidLoad
{
    [super viewDidLoad];
    self.view.backgroundColor = [UIColor whiteColor];

    self.navigationItem.rightBarButtonItem =
        BARBUTTON(@"Deselect", @selector(deselect));
    self.navigationItem.leftBarButtonItem =
        BARBUTTON(@"Find", @selector(find));
    self.navigationItem.rightBarButtonItem.enabled = NO;
    self.navigationItem.leftBarButtonItem.enabled = NO;

    imageFont = [UIFont fontWithName:@"Futura" size:18.0f];

    [self.tableView registerClass:[UITableViewCell class]
        forCellReuseIdentifier:@"cell"];
    items = [@"Alpha Bravo Charlie Delta Echo Foxtrot Golf \
        Hotel India Juliet Kilo Lima Mike November Oscar Papa \
        Quebec Romeo Sierra Tango Uniform Victor Whiskey Xray \
        Yankee Zulu" componentsSeparatedByString:@" "];
}
@end
```

Get This Recipe's Code

To find this recipe's full sample project, point your browser to https://github.com/erica/iOS-7-Cookbook and go to the folder for Chapter 9.

Table View Cells

The UITableViewCell class offers four utilitarian base styles, which are shown in Figure 9-2. This class provides two text label properties: a primary textLabel and a secondary detailTextLabel, which is used for creating subtitles. The four styles are as follows:

- **UITableViewCellStyleDefault**—This cell offers a single left-aligned text label and an optional image. When images are used, the label is pushed to the right, decreasing the amount of space available for text. You can access and modify detailTextLabel, but it is not shown onscreen.

- **UITableViewCellStyleValue1**—This cell style offers a large black primary label on the left side of the cell and a slightly smaller, gray subtitle detail label to its right.

- **UITableViewCellStyleValue2**—This kind of cell consists of a small primary label on the left, displayed with the current `tintColor`, and a small black subtitle detail label to its right. The small width of the primary label means that most text will be cut off by an ellipsis. This cell does not support images.

- **UITableViewCellStyleSubtitle**—This cell pushes the standard text label up a bit to make way for the smaller detail label beneath it. Both labels display in black. Like the default cell, the subtitle cell offers an optional image.

Figure 9-2   Cocoa Touch provides four standard cell types, several of which support optional images.

Selection Style

Tables enable you to set the `selectionStyle` for the selected cell. In iOS 7, despite the name, `UITableViewCellSelectionStyleBlue` and `UITableViewCellSelectionStyleGray` both result in a light gray background for the selected cell. If you'd rather not show a selection, use `UITableViewCellSelectionStyleNone`. The cell can still be selected, but the gray background will not display.

Adding Custom Selection Traits

When a user selects a cell, Cocoa Touch helps you emphasize the cell's selection. Customize a cell's selection behavior by updating its traits to stand out from its fellows. There are two ways to do this.

The `selectedBackgroundView` property allows you to add controls and other views to just the currently selected cell. This works in a similar manner to the accessory views that appear when a keyboard is shown. You might use the selected background view to add a preview button or a purchase option to the selected cell.

The cell label's `highlightedTextColor` property lets you choose an alternative text color when the cell is selected.

Recipe: Creating Checked Table Cells

Accessory views expand normal `UITableViewCell` functionality. Check marks create interactive one-of-*n* or *n*-of-*n* selections, as shown in Figure 9-3. With these kinds of selections, you can ask your users to pick what they want to have for dinner or choose which items they want to update.

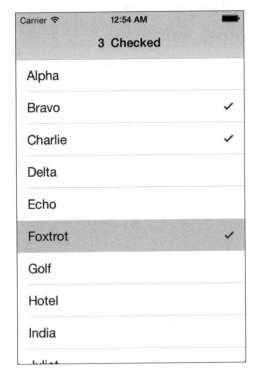

Figure 9-3   Check mark accessories offer a convenient way of making one-of-*n* or *n*-of-*n* selections from a list.

To check an item, use the `UITableViewCellAccessoryCheckmark` accessory type. Unchecked items use the `UITableViewCellAccessoryNone` variation. You set these by assigning the cell's `accessoryType` property.

Cells have no "memory" to speak of other than their last presentation state. They do not know how an application last used them. They are views and nothing more. Therefore, if you reuse cells without tying those cells to some sort of data model, you can end up with unexpected and unintentional results. This is a natural consequence of the MVC design paradigm.

Consider the following scenario. Say you create a series of cells, each of which owns a toggle switch. Users can interact with that switch and change its value. A cell that scrolls offscreen, landing on the reuse queue, could therefore show an already toggled state for a table element the user hasn't yet touched.

To fix this problem, always check your cell state against a stored model and fully configure your cell in `cellForRowAtIndexPath:`. This keeps the view consistent with your application data and avoids lingering "dirty" state from the cell's last use. It's the cell that's being toggled, not the logical item associated with the cell. Reused cells may remain checked or unchecked at next use, so always set the accessory to match the model state, not the cell state.

Recipe 9-2 builds a simple state dictionary to store the on/off state for each index path. Its data source returns cells initialized to match that dictionary. You can easily expand this recipe to store its state to user defaults so it persists between runs. This simple-to-add enhancement is left as an exercise for the reader.

Recipe 9-2 **Accessory Views and Stored State**

```
// Return a cell populated with data model state for the index path
- (UITableViewCell *)tableView:(UITableView *)aTableView
    cellForRowAtIndexPath:(NSIndexPath *)indexPath
{
    UITableViewCell *cell = [self.tableView
        dequeueReusableCellWithIdentifier:@"cell"
        forIndexPath:indexPath];

    // Cell label
    cell.textLabel.text = items[indexPath.row];
    BOOL isChecked =
        ((NSNumber *)stateDictionary[indexPath]).boolValue;
    cell.accessoryType = isChecked ?
        UITableViewCellAccessoryCheckmark :
        UITableViewCellAccessoryNone;

    return cell;
}


// On selection, update the title
- (void)tableView:(UITableView *)aTableView
```

```
    didSelectRowAtIndexPath:(NSIndexPath *)indexPath
{
    UITableViewCell *cell =
        [self.tableView cellForRowAtIndexPath:indexPath];

    // Toggle the cell checked state
    BOOL isChecked =
        !((NSNumber *)stateDictionary[indexPath]).boolValue;
    stateDictionary[indexPath] = @(isChecked);
    cell.accessoryType = isChecked ?
        UITableViewCellAccessoryCheckmark :
        UITableViewCellAccessoryNone;

    // Count the checked items
    int numChecked = 0;
    for (NSUInteger row = 0; row < items.count; row++)
    {
        NSIndexPath *path =
            [NSIndexPath indexPathForRow:row inSection:0];
        isChecked =
            ((NSNumber *)stateDictionary[path]).boolValue;
        if (isChecked) numChecked++;
    }

    self.title = [@[@(numChecked).stringValue, @" Checked"]
        componentsJoinedByString:@" "];
}
```

Get This Recipe's Code

To find this recipe's full sample project, point your browser to https://github.com/erica/
iOS-7-Cookbook and go to the folder for Chapter 9.

Working with Disclosure Accessories

Disclosures refer to the gray, right-facing chevrons and tintColor-imbued info button found
on the right of table cells. Disclosures help you link from a cell to a view that supports that cell.
In the Contacts list and Calendar applications on the iPhone and iPod touch, these chevrons
connect to screens that help you customize contact information and set appointments. Figure
9-4 shows a table view example where each cell displays a disclosure control, showing the two
available types.

On the iPad, you should consider using a split view controller rather than disclosure accessories. The greater space on the iPad display allows you to present both an organizing list and its detail view at the same time, a feature that the disclosure chevrons attempt to mimic on the smaller iPhone units.

The disclosure accessories play two roles:

- The `UITableViewCellAccessoryDetailDisclosureButton` is an actual button—an encircled *i* along with a gray chevron. The button responds to touches and is intended to indicate that tapping leads to a full interactive detail view.

- The gray chevron of `UITableViewCellAccessoryDisclosureIndicator` does not track touches and should lead your users to a further options view—specifically, options about that choice.

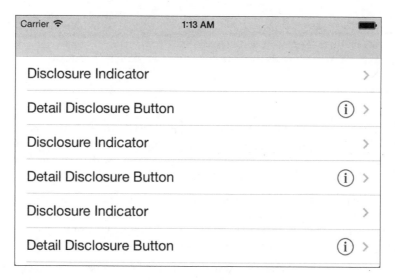

Figure 9-4   The right-pointing chevrons and encircled info buttons indicate disclosure controls, allowing you to link individual table items to another view.

You see these two accessories in play in the Settings application on the iPhone. The disclosure indicator for the Wi-Fi networks enables you to proceed to the Wi-Fi screen. In the Wi-Fi screen, the detail disclosures lead to specific details about each Wi-Fi network: its IP address, subnet mask, router, DNS info, and so forth.

You find disclosure indicators whenever one screen leads to a related submenu. When working with submenus, stick to the simple gray chevron. Remember this rule of thumb: Submenus use gray chevrons, and object customization uses the info button. Respond to cell selection for disclosure indicators and to accessory button taps for detail disclosure buttons.

The following snippet sets `accessoryType` for each cell to `UITableViewCellAccessoryDetailDisclosureButton`. It also sets `editingAccessoryType` to `UITableViewCellAccessoryNone`:

```
- (UITableViewCell *)tableView:(UITableView *)tableView
    cellForRowAtIndexPath:(NSIndexPath *)indexPath
{
    UITableViewCell *cell =
        [tableView dequeueReusableCellWithIdentifier:@"CustomCell"];
    cell.accessoryType =
        UITableViewCellAccessoryDetailDisclosureButton;
    cell.editingAccessoryType = UITableViewCellAccessoryNone;

    return cell;
}


// Respond to accessory button taps
-(void)tableView:(UITableView *)tableView
    accessoryButtonTappedForRowWithIndexPath:(NSIndexPath *)indexPath
{
    // Do something here
}
```

To handle user taps on the detail disclosure button, the `tableView:accessoryButtonTappedForRowWithIndexPath:` method enables you to determine the row that was tapped and implement some appropriate response. In real life, you'd move to a view that explains more about the selected item and enables you to choose from additional options.

Gray disclosure indicators use a different approach. Because these accessories are not buttons, they respond to cell selection rather than the accessory button tap. Add your logic to `tableView:didSelectRowAtIndexPath:` to push the disclosure view onto your navigation stack or by presenting a modal view controller or an alert view.

Neither disclosure accessory changes the way the rest of the cell works. Even when sporting accessories, you can select cells, edit cells, and so forth. Accessories add an extra interaction modality; they don't replace the ones you already have.

Recipe: Table Edits

Bring your tables to life by adding editing features. Table edits transform a static information display into an interactive scrolling control that invites your user to add and remove data. Although the bookkeeping for working with table edits is moderately complex, the same techniques easily transfer from one app to another. Once you master the basic elements of entering and leaving edit mode and supporting undo, you can use these items over and over.

Recipe 9-3 introduces a table that responds meaningfully to table edits. This example creates a scrolling list of random images. Users create new cells by tapping Add and remove cells either by swiping or entering edit mode (by tapping Edit) and using the round red remove controls (see Figure 9-5).

In day-to-day use, every iOS user quickly becomes familiar with the small red circles used to delete cells from tables. Many users also pick up on basic swipe-to-delete functionality. This recipe also adds move controls, those triplets of small gray, horizontal lines that allow users to drag items to new positions. Users leave edit mode by tapping Done.

Adding Undo Support

Cocoa Touch offers the `NSUndoManager` class to provide a way to reverse user actions. By default, every application window provides a shared undo manager. You can use this shared manager or create your own.

All children of the `UIResponder` class can find the nearest undo manager in the responder chain. This means that if you use the window's undo manager in your view controller, the controller automatically knows about that manager through its `undoManager` property. This is enormously convenient because you can add undo support in your main view controller, and all your child views basically pick up that support for free.

The manager can store an arbitrary number of undo actions. You may want to specify how deep that stack goes. The bigger the stack, the more memory you use. Many applications allow 3, 5, or 10 levels of undo when memory is tight. Each action can be complex, involving groups of undo activities, or the action can be simple, as in the examples shown in Recipe 9-3.

This recipe uses an undo manager to support user undo and redo actions for adding, deleting, and moving cells. Undo and Redo buttons enable users to move through their edit history. In this recipe, these buttons are enabled when the undo manager supplies actions to support their use.

Implementing Undo

Recipe 9-3 handles both adding and deleting items by using the same method, `updateItem-AtIndexPath:withObject:`. The method works like this: It inserts any non-nil object at the index path. When the passed object is `nil`, it instead deletes the item at that index path.

This might seem like an odd way to handle requests, because it involves an extra method and extra steps, but there's an underlying motive. This approach provides a unified foundation for undo support, allowing simple integration with undo managers.

The method, therefore, has two jobs to do. First, it prepares an undo invocation. That is, it tells the undo manager how to reverse the edits it is about to apply. Second, it applies the actual edits, making its changes to the `items` array and updating the table and bar buttons.

The `setBarButtonItems` method controls the state of the Undo and Redo buttons. This method checks the active undo manager to see whether the undo stack provides undo and redo actions. If so, it enables the appropriate buttons.

Although we're not fans of shake-to-undo, this recipe does support it. Its `viewDidLoad` method sets the `applicationSupportsShakeToEdit` property of the application delegate. Also note the first responder calls added to provide undo support. The table view becomes the first responder as it appears and resigns it when it disappears.

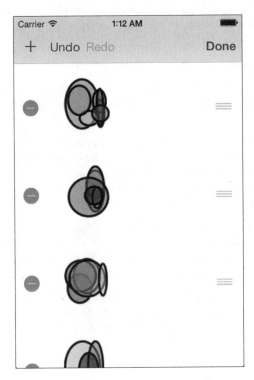

Figure 9-5   Round red remove controls allow your users to interactively delete items from a table.

Displaying Remove Controls

The table displays remove controls with a single call: `[self.tableView setEditing:YES animated:YES]`. This updates the table's `editing` property and presents the round remove controls shown in Figure 9-5 on each cell. The animation is optional but recommended. As a rule, use animations in your iOS interfaces to lead your users from one state to the next so that they're prepared for the mode changes that happen onscreen.

Recipe 9-3 uses a system-supplied Edit/Done button (`self.editButtonItem`) and implements `setEditing:animated:` to move the table into and out of an editing state. When a user taps the Edit or Done button (it toggles back and forth), this method updates the edit state and the navigation bar's buttons.

Handling Delete Requests

On row deletion, the table communicates with your application by issuing a `tableView:commitEditingStyle:forRowAtIndexPath:` callback. A table delete removes an item from the visual table but does not alter the underlying data. Unless you manage the item removal from your data source, the "deleted" item will reappear on the next table refresh. This method offers the place for you to coordinate with your data source and respond to the row deletion that the user just performed.

Delete an item from the data structure that supplies the data source methods (in this recipe, through an `NSMutableArray` of image items) and handle any real-world action such as deleting files, removing contacts, and so on, that occur as a consequence of the user's edit.

Recipe 9-3 animates its cell deletions. The `beginUpdates` and `endUpdates` method pair allows simultaneous animation of table operations such as adding and deleting rows.

Swiping Cells

Swiping is a clean method for removing items from your `UITableView` instances. To enable swipes, simply provide the commit-editing-style method. The table takes care of the rest.

To swipe, users drag swiftly from the right side of the cell to the left. The rectangular delete confirmation appears to the right of the cell, but the cells do *not* display the round remove controls on the left.

After users swipe and confirm, the `tableView:commitEditingStyle:forRowAtIndexPath:` method applies data updates just as if the deletion had occurred in edit mode.

Reordering Cells

You empower your users when you allow them to directly reorder the cells of a table. Figure 9-5 shows a table that displays the reorder control's stacked gray lines. Users can apply this interaction to sort to-do items by priority, choose which songs should go first in a playlist, and so on. iOS ships with built-in table reordering support that's easy to add to your applications.

Like swipe-to-delete, cell reordering support is contingent on the presence or absence of a single method. The `tableView:moveRowAtIndexPath:toIndexPath` method synchronizes your data source with the onscreen changes, similar to committing edits for cell deletion. Adding this method instantly enables reordering.

Adding Cells

Recipe 9-3 uses an Add button to create new content for the table. This button takes the form of a system bar button item, which displays as a plus sign. (See the top-left corner of Figure 9-5.) The `addItem:` method in Recipe 9-3 appends a new random image at the end of the `items` array.

Recipe 9-3   Editing Tables

```objc
@implementation TestBedViewController
{
    NSMutableArray *items;
}


#pragma mark Data Source
// Number of sections
- (NSInteger)numberOfSectionsInTableView:(UITableView *)aTableView
{
    return 1;
}


// Rows per section
- (NSInteger)tableView:(UITableView *)aTableView
    numberOfRowsInSection:(NSInteger)section
{
    return items.count;
}


// Return a cell for the index path
- (UITableViewCell *)tableView:(UITableView *)aTableView
    cellForRowAtIndexPath:(NSIndexPath *)indexPath
{
    UITableViewCell *cell = [self.tableView
        dequeueReusableCellWithIdentifier:@"cell"
        forIndexPath:indexPath];
    cell.imageView.image = items[indexPath.row];
    return cell;
}


#pragma mark Edits
- (void)setBarButtonItems
{
    // Expire any ongoing operations
    if (self.undoManager.isUndoing ||
        self.undoManager.isRedoing)
    {
        [self performSelector:@selector(setBarButtonItems)
            withObject:nil afterDelay:0.1f];
        return;
    }

    UIBarButtonItem *undo = SYSBARBUTTON_TARGET(
        UIBarButtonSystemItemUndo, self.undoManager,
        @selector(undo));
    undo.enabled = self.undoManager.canUndo;
```

```objc
    UIBarButtonItem *redo = SYSBARBUTTON_TARGET(
        UIBarButtonSystemItemRedo, self.undoManager,
        @selector(redo));
    redo.enabled = self.undoManager.canRedo;
    UIBarButtonItem *add = SYSBARBUTTON(
        UIBarButtonSystemItemAdd, @selector(addItem:));

    self.navigationItem.leftBarButtonItems = @[add, undo, redo];
}


- (void)setEditing:(BOOL)isEditing animated:(BOOL)animated
{
    [super setEditing:isEditing animated:animated];
    [self.tableView setEditing:isEditing animated:animated];

    NSIndexPath *path = [self.tableView indexPathForSelectedRow];
    if (path)
        [self.tableView deselectRowAtIndexPath:path animated:YES];

    [self setBarButtonItems];
}

- (void)updateItemAtIndexPath:(NSIndexPath *)indexPath
    withObject:(id)object
{
    // Prepare for undo
    id undoObject =
        object ? nil : items[indexPath.row];
    [[self.undoManager prepareWithInvocationTarget:self]
        updateItemAtIndexPath:indexPath withObject:undoObject];

    // You cannot insert a nil item. Passing nil is a delete request.
    [self.tableView beginUpdates];
    if (!object)
    {
        [items removeObjectAtIndex:indexPath.row];
        [self.tableView deleteRowsAtIndexPaths:@[indexPath]
            withRowAnimation:UITableViewRowAnimationTop];
    }
    else
    {
        [items insertObject:object atIndex:indexPath.row];
        [self.tableView insertRowsAtIndexPaths:@[indexPath]
            withRowAnimation:UITableViewRowAnimationTop];
    }
    [self.tableView endUpdates];
```

```objc
        [self performSelector:@selector(setBarButtonItems)
            withObject:nil afterDelay:0.1f];
}


- (void)addItem:(id)sender
{
    // add a new item
    NSIndexPath *newPath =
        [NSIndexPath indexPathForRow:items.count inSection:0];
    UIImage *image = blockImage(IMAGE_SIZE);
    [self updateItemAtIndexPath:newPath withObject:image];

}

- (void)tableView:(UITableView *)aTableView
    commitEditingStyle:(UITableViewCellEditingStyle)editingStyle
    forRowAtIndexPath:(NSIndexPath *)indexPath
{
    // delete item
    [self updateItemAtIndexPath:indexPath withObject:nil];
}

// Provide re-ordering support
- (void)tableView:(UITableView *)tableView
    moveRowAtIndexPath:(NSIndexPath *)oldPath
    toIndexPath:(NSIndexPath *)newPath
{
    if (oldPath.row == newPath.row) return;

    [[self.undoManager prepareWithInvocationTarget:self]
        tableView:self.tableView moveRowAtIndexPath:newPath
        toIndexPath:oldPath];

    id item = [items objectAtIndex:oldPath.row];
    [items removeObjectAtIndex:oldPath.row];
    [items insertObject:item atIndex:newPath.row];

    if (self.undoManager.isUndoing || self.undoManager.isRedoing)
    {
        [self.tableView beginUpdates];
        [self.tableView deleteRowsAtIndexPaths:@[oldPath]
            withRowAnimation:UITableViewRowAnimationLeft];
        [self.tableView insertRowsAtIndexPaths:@[newPath]
            withRowAnimation:UITableViewRowAnimationLeft];
        [self.tableView endUpdates];
    }
```

```
    [self performSelector:@selector(setBarButtonItems)
        withObject:nil afterDelay:0.1f];
}

#pragma mark First Responder for undo support
- (BOOL)canBecomeFirstResponder
{
    return YES;
}


- (void)viewDidAppear:(BOOL)animated
{
    [super viewDidAppear:animated];
    [self becomeFirstResponder];
}


- (void)viewWillDisappear:(BOOL)animated
{
    [super viewWillDisappear:animated];
    [self resignFirstResponder];
}


#pragma mark View Setup
- (void)viewDidLoad
{
    [super viewDidLoad];
    self.view.backgroundColor = [UIColor whiteColor];

    [self.tableView registerClass:[UITableViewCell class]
        forCellReuseIdentifier:@"cell"];
    self.tableView.rowHeight = IMAGE_SIZE + 20.0f;
    self.tableView.separatorStyle =
        UITableViewCellSeparatorStyleNone;
    self.navigationItem.rightBarButtonItem = self.editButtonItem;

    items = [NSMutableArray array];

    // Provide shake to undo support
    [UIApplication sharedApplication].applicationSupportsShakeToEdit = YES;
    [self setBarButtonItems];
}
@end
```

Get This Recipe's Code

To find this recipe's full sample project, point your browser to https://github.com/erica/iOS-7-Cookbook and go to the folder for Chapter 9.

Recipe: Working with Sections

Many iOS applications use sections as well as rows. Sections provide another level of structure to lists, grouping items together into logical units. The most commonly used section scheme is alphabetic, although you are certainly not limited to organizing your data this way. You can use any section scheme that makes sense for your application.

Figure 9-6 shows a table that uses sections to display grouped names. Each section presents a separate header (that is, "Crayon names starting with . . . "), and an index on the right offers quick access to each of the sections. Notice that there are no sections listed for *K*, *Q*, *X*, and *Z* in the index because those sections are empty. You generally want to omit empty sections from the index.

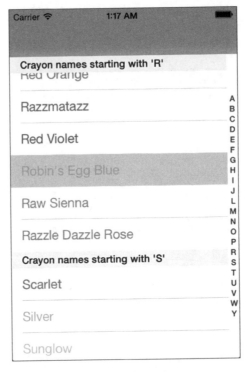

Figure 9-6   Sectioned tables present headers and an index to help users find information as quickly as possible.

Building Sections

When working with groups and sections, think two dimensionally. Section arrays let you store and access the members of data in a section-by-section structure. Implement this approach by creating an array of arrays. A section array can store one array for each section, which in turn contains the titles for each cell.

Predicates help you build sections from a list of strings. The following method alphabetically retrieves items from a flat array. The `beginswith` predicate matches each string that starts with the given letter:

```
- (NSArray *)itemsInSection:(NSInteger)section
{
    NSPredicate *predicate = [NSPredicate predicateWithFormat:
        @"SELF beginswith[cd] %@", [self firstLetter:section]];
    return [crayonColors.allKeys
        filteredArrayUsingPredicate:predicate];
}
```

Add these results iteratively to a mutable array to create a two-dimensional sectioned array from an initial flat list:

```
sectionArray = [NSMutableArray array];
for (int i = 0; i < 26; i++)
    [sectionArray addObject:[self itemsInSection:i]];
```

To work, this particular implementation relies on two things: first, that the words are already sorted (each subsection adds the words in the order they're found in the array); and second, that the sections match the words. Entries that start with punctuation or numbers won't work with this loop. You can trivially add an "other" section to take care of these cases, which this (simple) sample omits.

Although, as mentioned, alphabetic sections are useful and probably the most common grouping, you can use any kind of structure you like. For example, you might group people by departments, gems by grades, or appointments by date. No matter what kind of grouping you choose, an array of arrays provides the table view data source that best matches sectioned tables.

From this initial startup, it's up to you to add or remove items using this two-dimensional structure. As you can easily see, creation is simple, but maintenance gets tricky. Here's where Core Data really helps out. Instead of working with multileveled arrays, you can query your data store on any object field and sort it as desired. Chapter 12 introduces using Core Data with tables. And as you will read in that chapter, it greatly simplifies matters. For now, this example continues to use a simple array of arrays to introduce sections and their use.

Counting Sections and Rows

To create sectioned tables, customize two key data source methods:

- **`numberOfSectionsInTableView:`**—This method specifies how many sections appear in your table, establishing the number of groups to display. When using a section array, as recommended here, return the number of items in the section array—that is, `sectionArray.count`. If the number of items is known in advance (26 in this case, even though some sections have no items), you can hard-code that number, but it's better to code more generally where possible.

■ `tableView:numberOfRowsInSection:`—This method is called with a section number. Specify how many rows appear in that section. With the recommended data structure, just return the count of items at the *n*th subarray:

```
sectionArray[sectionNumber].count
```

Returning Cells

Sectioned tables use both row and section information to find cell data. Earlier recipes in this chapter use a flat array with a row number index. Tables with sections must use the entire index path to locate both the section and row index for the data populating a cell. This method, from a crayon handler helper class, first retrieves the current items for the section and then pulls out the specific item by row. Recipe 9-4 details the helper class methods that work with an array-of-arrays section data source:

```
// Color name by index path
- (NSString *)colorNameAtIndexPath:(NSIndexPath *)path
{
    if (path.section >= sectionArray.count)
        return nil;
    NSArray *currentItems = sectionArray[path.section];

    if (path.row >= currentItems.count)
        return nil;
    NSString *crayon = currentItems[path.row];

    return crayon;
}
```

A similar method retrieves the color:

```
// Color by index path
- (UIColor *)colorAtIndexPath:(NSIndexPath *)path
{
    NSString *crayon = [self colorNameAtIndexPath:path];
    if (crayon)
        return crayonColors[crayon];
    return nil;
}
```

Here is the data source method that uses these calls to return a cell with the proper color and name:

```
// Return a cell for the index path
- (UITableViewCell *)tableView:(UITableView *)aTableView
    cellForRowAtIndexPath:(NSIndexPath *)indexPath
```

```
{
    UITableViewCell *cell =
        [self.tableView dequeueReusableCellWithIdentifier:@"cell"
            forIndexPath:indexPath];

    // Retrieve the crayon name
    NSString *crayonName = [crayons colorNameAtIndexPath:indexPath];

    // Update the cell
    cell.textLabel.text = crayonName;

    // Tint the title
    if ([crayonName hasPrefix:@"White"])
        cell.textLabel.textColor = [UIColor blackColor];
    else
        cell.textLabel.textColor = [crayons colorAtIndexPath:indexPath];

    return cell;
}
```

Creating Header Titles

It takes little work to add section headers to your grouped table. The optional `tableView:`
`titleForHeaderInSection:` method supplies the titles for each section. It's passed an integer.
In return, you supply a title. If your table does not contain any items in a given section or
when you're only working with one section, return `nil`:

```
// Return the header title for a section
- (NSString *)tableView:(UITableView *)aTableView
    titleForHeaderInSection:(NSInteger)section
{
    NSString *sectionName = [crayons nameForSection:section];
    if (!sectionName) return nil;
    return [NSString stringWithFormat:
        @"Crayon names starting with '%@'", sectionName];
}
```

If you aren't happy using titles, you can return custom header views instead.

Customizing Headers and Footers

Sectioned table views are extremely customizable. Both the `tableHeaderView` property and
the related `tableFooterView` property can be assigned to any type of view, each with its own
subviews. So you might add labels, text fields, buttons, and other controls to extend the table's
features.

Headers and footers aren't just one each per table. Each section offers a customizable header and footer view as well. You can alter heights or swap elements out for custom views. The optional `tableView:heightForHeaderInSection:` (or the `sectionHeaderHeight` property) and `tableView:viewForHeaderInSection:` methods let you add individual headers to each section. Corresponding methods exist for footers as well as headers.

Creating a Section Index

Tables that implement `sectionIndexTitlesForTableView:` present the kind of index view that appears on the right in Figure 9-6. This method is called when the table view is created, and the array that is returned determines what items are displayed onscreen. Return `nil` to skip an index. Apple recommends adding section indexes only to plain table views—that is, table views created using the default plain style of `UITableViewStylePlain` and not grouped tables:

```
// Return an array of section titles for index
- (NSArray *)sectionIndexTitlesForTableView:(UITableView *)aTableView
{
    NSMutableArray *indices = [NSMutableArray array];
    for (int i = 0; i < crayons.numberOfSections; i++)
    {
        NSString *name = [crayons nameForSection:i];
        if (name) [indices addObject:name];
    }
    return indices;
}
```

Although this example uses single-letter titles, you are certainly not limited to those items. You can use words or, if you're willing to work out the Unicode equivalents, symbols, including emoji items, that are part of the iOS character library. Here's how you could add a small yellow smile:

```
[indices addObject:@"\ue057"];
```

Handling Section Mismatches

Touching the table index scrolls the table based on the user touch offset. As mentioned earlier in this section, this particular table does not display sections for K, Q, X, and Z. These missing letters can cause a mismatch between a user selection and the results displayed by the table.

To remedy this, implement the optional `tableView:sectionForSectionIndexTitle:` method. This method's role is to connect a section index title (that is, the one returned by the `sectionIndexTitlesForTableView:` method) with a section number. This overrides any order mismatches and provides an exact one-to-one match between a user index selection and the section displayed:

```
#define ALPHA @"ABCDEFGHIJKLMNOPQRSTUVWXYZ"
- (NSInteger)tableView:(UITableView *)tableView
    sectionForSectionIndexTitle:(NSString *)title
    atIndex:(NSInteger)index
{
    return [ALPHA rangeOfString:title].location;
}
```

Delegation with Sections

As with data source methods, the trick to implementing delegate methods in a sectioned table involves using the index path `section` and `row` properties. These properties provide the double access needed to find the correct section array and then the item within that array for this example:

```
// On selecting a row, update the navigation bar tint
- (void)tableView:(UITableView *)aTableView
    didSelectRowAtIndexPath:(NSIndexPath *)indexPath
{
    UIColor *color = [crayons colorAtIndexPath:indexPath];
    self.navigationController.navigationBar.barTintColor = color;
}
```

Recipe 9-4   **Supporting a Table with Sections**

```
/* CrayonHandler.m */
// Return an array of items that appear in each section
- (NSArray *)itemsInSection:(NSInteger)section
{
    NSPredicate *predicate = [NSPredicate predicateWithFormat:
        @"SELF beginswith[cd] %@", [self firstLetter:section]];
    return [[crayonColors allKeys] filteredArrayUsingPredicate:predicate];
}


// Count of available sections
- (NSInteger)numberOfSections
{
    return sectionArray.count;
}


// Number of items within a section
- (NSInteger)countInSection:(NSInteger)section
{
    return [sectionArray[section] count];
}
```

```objc
// Return the letter that starts each section member's text
- (NSString *)firstLetter:(NSInteger)section
{
    return [[ALPHA substringFromIndex:section] substringToIndex:1];
}


// The one-letter section name
- (NSString *)nameForSection:(NSInteger)section
{
    if (![self countInSection:section])
        return nil;
    return [self firstLetter:section];
}


// Color name by index path
- (NSString *)colorNameAtIndexPath:(NSIndexPath *)path
{
    if (path.section >= sectionArray.count)
        return nil;
    NSArray *currentItems = sectionArray[path.section];

    if (path.row >= currentItems.count)
        return nil;
    NSString *crayon = currentItems[path.row];

    return crayon;
}

// Color by index path
- (UIColor *)colorAtIndexPath:(NSIndexPath *)path
{
    NSString *crayon = [self colorNameAtIndexPath:path];
    return crayonColors[crayon];
}
```

Get This Recipe's Code

To find this recipe's full sample project, point your browser to https://github.com/erica/iOS-7-Cookbook and go to the folder for Chapter 9.

Recipe: Searching Through a Table

A search display controller is a kind of controller that enables user-driven searches. These controllers allow users to filter a table's contents in real time, providing instant responsiveness to a user-driven query. It's a great feature that lets users interactively find what they're looking for, with the results updating as each new character is entered into the search field.

You create these controllers by initializing them with a search bar instance and a content controller, normally a table view, whose data source is searched. Recipe 9-5 demonstrates the steps involved in creating and using a search display controller in an application.

Searches are best built around predicates, enabling you to filter arrays to retrieve matching items with a simple method call. Here is how you might search through a flat array of strings to retrieve items that match the text from a search bar. The `[cd]` after `contains` refers to case-insensitive and diacritic-insensitive matching. Diacritics are small marks that accompany a letter, such as the dots of an umlaut (¨) or the tilde (~) above a Spanish *n*:

```
NSPredicate *predicate =
    [NSPredicate predicateWithFormat:@"SELF contains[cd] %@",
        searchBar.text];
filteredArray = [[crayonColors allKeys]
    filteredArrayUsingPredicate:predicate];
```

The search bar in question should appear at the top of the table as its header view, as in Figure 9-7 (left). The same search bar is assigned to the search display controller, as shown in the following code snippet:

```
self.tableView.tableHeaderView = searchBar;
searchController = [[UISearchDisplayController alloc]
    initWithSearchBar:searchBar contentsController:self];
```

Search bars in iOS 7 now support a style property for configuring the presentation: `UISearchBarStyleProminent`, `UISearchBarStyleMinimal`, and `UISearchBarStyleDefault`. The prominent style, which is the default, provides a translucent background with an opaque search field, matching the style found in previous versions of iOS. The minimal style removes the background and provides a translucent search field. When users tap in the search box, the view shifts, and the search bar moves up to the navigation bar area, as shown in Figure 9-7 (right). A search results table view is presented, temporarily supplanting the original table. The search bar and results table view remain until the user taps Cancel, returning the user to the unfiltered table display.

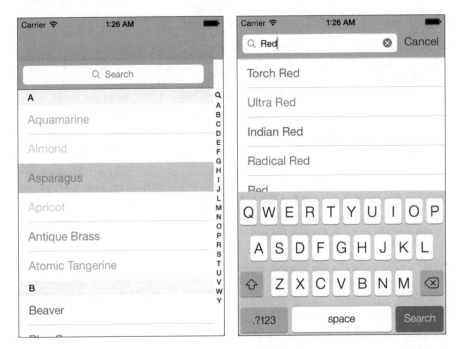

Figure 9-7   The user must scroll to the top of the table to initiate a search. The search bar appears as the first item in the table in its header view (left). Once the user taps within the search bar and makes it active, the search bar jumps into the navigation bar and presents a filtered list of items based on the search criteria (right).

Creating a Search Display Controller

Search display controllers help manage the display of data owned by another controller (in this case, a standard `UITableViewController`). A search display controller presents a subset of that data in its own table view, usually by filtering that data source through a predicate. You initialize a search display controller by providing it with a search bar and a contents controller.

Set up the search bar's text trait features as you would normally do but do not set a delegate. The search bar works with the search display controller without explicit delegation on your part.

When setting up the search display controller, make sure you set both its search results data source and delegate, as shown here. These usually point back to the primary table view controller subclass, which is where you adjust your normal data source and delegate methods to comply with the searchable table:

```
// Create a search bar
searchBar = [[UISearchBar alloc]
    initWithFrame:CGRectMake(0.0f, 0.0f, width, 44.0f)];
searchBar.autocorrectionType = UITextAutocorrectionTypeNo;
searchBar.autocapitalizationType = UITextAutocapitalizationTypeNone;
searchBar.keyboardType = UIKeyboardTypeAlphabet;
self.tableView.tableHeaderView = searchBar;

// Create the search display controller
searchController = [[UISearchDisplayController alloc]
    initWithSearchBar:searchBar contentsController:self];
searchController.searchResultsDataSource = self;
searchController.searchResultsDelegate = self;
```

Registering Cells for the Search Display Controller

When dequeuing, register cell types for each table view in your application. That includes the search display controller's built-in table. Forgetting this step and assuming you can dequeue a cell from `self.tableView` sets you up for a rather nasty crash. Here's how you might register cell classes for both tables:

```
// Register cell classes
[self.tableView registerClass:[UITableViewCell class]
    forCellReuseIdentifier:@"cell"];
[searchController.searchResultsTableView registerClass:[UITableViewCell class]
    forCellReuseIdentifier:@"cell"];
```

A new issue in iOS 7 requires a change in the timing of cell class registration. When retrieving the cells in the `tableView:cellForRowAtIndexPath:` data source method, the search table provided is freshly created; any previously created registrations are lost. The easiest way to resolve this is to register your cell class at the very beginning of the method. This doesn't feel like an efficient approach, but it ensures the availability of the cell class registration until Apple provides a more elegant method.

As you can see in the recipe code, workarounds are used for cases where iOS confuses which table it's requesting cells for.

Building Searchable Data Source Methods

The number of items displayed in a table changes as users search. A shorter search string generally matches more items than a longer one. You report the current number of rows for each table. The number of rows changes as the user updates text in the search field. To detect whether the table view controller or the search display controller is currently in charge, check the passed table view parameter. Adjust the row count accordingly:

```
- (NSInteger)tableView:(UITableView *)aTableView
    numberOfRowsInSection:(NSInteger)section
{
    if (aTableView == searchController.searchResultsTableView)
        return [crayons filterWithString:searchBar.text];
    return [crayons countInSection:section];
}
```

Use a predicate to report the count of items that match the text in the search box. Predicates provide an extremely simple way to filter an array and return only items that match a search string. The predicate used here performs a case-insensitive `contains` match. Each string that contains the text in the search field returns a positive match, allowing that string to remain part of the filtered array. Alternatively, you might want to use `beginswith` to avoid matching items that do not start with that text. The following method performs the filtering, stores the results, and returns the count of items that it found:

```
- (NSInteger)filterWithString:(NSString *)filter
{
    NSPredicate *predicate = [NSPredicate predicateWithFormat:
        @"SELF contains[cd] %@", filter];
    filteredArray = [[crayonColors allKeys]
        filteredArrayUsingPredicate:predicate];
    return filteredArray.count;
}
```

When providing cells, it is especially critical to check the requesting table view. Cell registration calls must be sent to the appropriate table, and, conversely, cells must be dequeued and initialized from the expected table. The following method returns cells retrieved from either the standard set or the filtered set:

```
- (UITableViewCell *)tableView:(UITableView *)aTableView
    cellForRowAtIndexPath:(NSIndexPath *)indexPath
{
    [aTableView registerClass:[UITableViewCell class]
        forCellReuseIdentifier:@"cell"];
    UITableViewCell *cell =
        [aTableView dequeueReusableCellWithIdentifier:@"cell"
            forIndexPath:indexPath];

    NSString *crayonName;
    if (aTableView == self.tableView)
    {
        crayonName = [crayons colorNameAtIndexPath:indexPath];
    }
    else
    {
        if (indexPath.row < crayons.filteredArray.count)
            crayonName = crayons.filteredArray[indexPath.row];
```

```
    }

    cell.textLabel.text = crayonName;
    cell.textLabel.textColor = [crayons colorNamed:crayonName];
    if ([crayonName hasPrefix:@"White"])
        cell.textLabel.textColor = [UIColor blackColor];

    return cell;
}
```

Delegate Methods

Search awareness is not limited to data sources. Determining the context of a user tap is critical for providing the correct response in delegate methods. As with the previous data source methods, this delegate method checks the callback's table view parameter to determine which table view was active. Based on the selected table and index, it picks a color with which to tint both the search bar and the navigation bar:

```
// Respond to user selections by updating tint colors
- (void)tableView:(UITableView *)aTableView
    didSelectRowAtIndexPath:(NSIndexPath *)indexPath
{
    UIColor *color = nil;
    if (aTableView == self.tableView)
        color = [crayons colorAtIndexPath:indexPath];
    else
    {
        if (indexPath.row < crayons.filteredArray.count)
        {
            NSString *colorName =
                crayons.filteredArray[indexPath.row];
            if (colorName)
                color = [crayons colorNamed:colorName];
        }
    }
    self.navigationController.navigationBar.barTintColor = color;
    searchBar.barTintColor = color;
}
```

Using a Search-Aware Index

Recipe 9-5 highlights some of the other ways to adapt a sectioned table to accommodate search-ready tables. When you support search, the first item added to a table's section index should be the UITableViewIndexSearch constant. Intended for use only in table indexes, and only as the first item in the index, this option adds the small magnifying glass icon that indicates that the table supports searches. Use it to provide a quick jump to the beginning of the list. Update `tableView:sectionForSectionIndexTitle:atIndex:` to catch user requests. The `scrollRectToVisible:animated:` call used in this recipe manually moves the search bar into place when a user taps the magnifying glass. Otherwise, users would have to scroll back from section 0, which is the section associated with the letter *A*.

Add a call in `viewWillAppear:` to scroll the search bar offscreen when the view first loads. This allows your table to start with the bar hidden from sight, ready to be scrolled up to or jumped to as the user desires.

Finally, respond to cancelled searches by proactively clearing the search text from the bar.

Recipe 9-5   **Using Search Features**

```
// Add Search to the index
- (NSArray *)sectionIndexTitlesForTableView:
    (UITableView *)aTableView
{
    if (aTableView == searchController.searchResultsTableView)
        return nil;

    // Initialize with the search magnifying glass
    NSMutableArray *indices = [NSMutableArray
        arrayWithObject:UITableViewIndexSearch];

    for (int i = 0; i < crayons.numberOfSections; i++)
    {
        NSString *name = [crayons nameForSection:i];
        if (name) [indices addObject:name];
    }

    return indices;
}


// Handle both the search index item and normal sections
- (NSInteger)tableView:(UITableView *)tableView
    sectionForSectionIndexTitle:(NSString *)title
    atIndex:(NSInteger)index
{
    if (title == UITableViewIndexSearch)
    {
        [self.tableView scrollRectToVisible:searchBar.frame
            animated:NO];
        return -1;
    }
    return [ALPHA rangeOfString:title].location;
}
```

```
// Handle the Cancel button by resetting the search text
- (void)searchBarCancelButtonClicked:(UISearchBar *)aSearchBar
{
    [searchBar setText:@""];
}


// Titles only for the main table
- (NSString *)tableView:(UITableView *)aTableView
    titleForHeaderInSection:(NSInteger)section
{
    if (aTableView == searchController.searchResultsTableView)
        return nil;
    return [crayons nameForSection:section];
}


// Upon appearing, scroll away the search bar
- (void)viewDidAppear:(BOOL)animated
{
    [super viewDidAppear:animated];
    NSIndexPath *path =
        [NSIndexPath indexPathForRow:0 inSection:0];
    [self.tableView scrollToRowAtIndexPath:path
        atScrollPosition:UITableViewScrollPositionTop
        animated:NO];
}
```

Get This Recipe's Code

To find this recipe's full sample project, point your browser to https://github.com/erica/iOS-7-Cookbook and go to the folder for Chapter 9.

Recipe: Adding Pull-to-Refresh to Your Table

Pull-to-refresh is a widely used app feature that has become popular in the App Store over the past few years. It lets you refresh tables by pulling down their tops enough to indicate a request. It is so intuitive to use that many wondered why Apple didn't add it to its UITableViewController class. In iOS 6, though, Apple created a highly stylized and stretchable animated refresh control. With iOS 7, the stretchable control was replaced with a more traditional activity indicator with a slightly expanded animation to provide feedback on the state of the control (see Figure 9-8).

The new UIRefreshControl class provides an extremely handy control that initiates a table view's refresh. Recipe 9-6 demonstrates how to add it to your applications. Create a new instance and assign it to a table view controller's refreshControl property. The control appears directly in the table view, without requiring any further work. When the user pulls down the table view, the pull control is displayed and triggered.

To activate the refresh control programmatically, start a refresh event with `beginRefreshing`. The refresh control turns into an animated progress wheel. When the new data has been prepared, end the refreshing (`endRefreshing`) and reload the table view.

Descending from `UIControl`, instances use target-action to send a custom selector to clients when activated. For some reason, it updates with a value-changed event. Surely, it's long past time for Apple to introduce a `UIControlEventTriggered` event for stateless control triggers like this one.

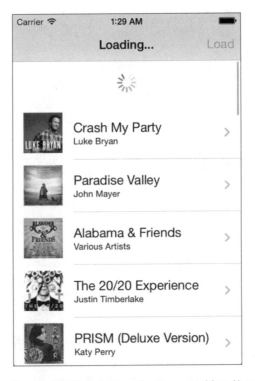

Figure 9-8   You can easily add a pull-to-refresh option to your tables. Users pull down to request updated data.

Using pull-to-refresh allows your applications to delay performing expensive routines. For example, you might hold off fetching new information from the Internet or computing new table elements until the user triggers a request for those operations. Pull-to-refresh places your user in control of refresh operations and provides a great balance between information-on-demand and computational overhead.

The `DataManager` class referred to in Recipe 9-6 loads its data asynchronously, using an operation queue:

```
- (void)loadData
{
    NSString *rss = @"http://itunes.apple.com/us/rss/topalbums/limit=30/xml";
    NSOperationQueue *queue = [[NSOperationQueue alloc] init];
    [queue addOperationWithBlock:
     ^{
         root = [[XMLParser sharedInstance] parseXMLFromURL:
             [NSURL URLWithString:rss]];
         [[NSOperationQueue currentQueue] addOperationWithBlock:^{
             [self handleData];
         }];
     }];
}
```

This approach ensures that data loading won't block the main thread. The refresh control's progress wheel won't be hindered, and the user will be free to interact with other UI elements in your app. After the fetch completes, move control back to the main thread:

```
if (delegate &&
    [delegate respondsToSelector:@selector(dataIsReady:)])
    [delegate performSelectorOnMainThread:@selector(dataIsReady:)
        withObject:self waitUntilDone:NO];
```

Recipe 9-6 offers a Load button in addition to the refresh control. Most applications skip this redundancy, but Recipe 9-6 includes it to show how it would interact with the refresh control. When the user taps Load, you still need to perform the refresh control's `startRefreshing` and `endRefreshing` methods. This ensures that the refresh control operates synchronously with the manual reload.

Recipe 9-6 Building Pull-to-Refresh into Your Tables

```
- (void)dataIsReady:(id)sender
{
    // Update the title
    self.title = @"iTunes Top Albums";

    // Reenable the bar button item
    self.navigationItem.rightBarButtonItem.enabled = YES;

    // Stop refresh control animation and update the table
    [self.refreshControl endRefreshing];
    [self.tableView reloadData];
}

- (void)loadData
```

```
{
    // Provide user status update
    self.title = @"Loading...";

    // Disable the bar button item
    self.navigationItem.rightBarButtonItem.enabled = NO;

    // Start refreshing
    [self.refreshControl beginRefreshing];

    [manager loadData];
}

- (void)viewDidLoad
{
    [super viewDidLoad];
    self.tableView.rowHeight = 72.0f;
    [self.tableView registerClass:[UITableViewCell class]
        forCellReuseIdentifier:@"generic"];

    // Offer a bar button item and...
    self.navigationItem.rightBarButtonItem =
        BARBUTTON(@"Load", @selector(loadData));

    // Alternatively, use the refresh control
    self.refreshControl = [[UIRefreshControl alloc] init];
    [self.refreshControl addTarget:self action:@selector(loadData)
        forControlEvents:UIControlEventValueChanged];

    // This custom data manager asynchronously (nonblocking) loads
    // data in a secondary thread
    manager = [[DataManager alloc] init];
    manager.delegate = self;
}
```

Get This Recipe's Code

To find this recipe's full sample project, point your browser to https://github.com/erica/iOS-7-Cookbook and go to the folder for Chapter 9.

Recipe: Adding Action Rows

Action rows (aka drawer cells) slide open to expose extra cell-specific functionality when users tap the cell associated with them. You may have seen this kind of functionality in commercial apps such as Tweetbot (http://tapbots.com). Recipe 9-7 builds an action row table featuring a pair of buttons in each of its drawers (see Figure 9-9). When tapped, the Title button sets the title on the navigation bar to the cell text; the Alert button displays the same string in a pop-up alert. iOS developer Bilal Sayed Ahmad (@Demonic_BLITZ on Twitter) suggested adding this recipe to the *Cookbook*, and this code is inspired from a sample project he created.

Figure 9-9   Action rows offer cell-specific actions that slide open when a user selects a cell. In this example, the user has tapped the Romeo cell and disclosed a hidden drawer with the Title and Alert buttons.

Recipe 9-7 works by adding a phantom cell to its table view. All other cells adjust around its presence. The implementation starts by adjusting the method that reports the number of rows per section. The drawer lives at `actionRowPath`. When the phantom cell is present, the number of cells increases by one. When it is hidden, the data source simply reports the normal count of its items.

The `viewDidLoad` method registers two cell types: one for standard rows and one for the action row. The data source returns a custom cell when passed a path it recognizes as the custom index.

The action cell has other quirks. It cannot be selected. Recipe 9-7's `tableView:willSelectRowAtIndexPath:` method ensures this by returning `nil` when passed the action row path.

Most of this implementation work takes place in the `tableView:didSelectRowAtIndexPath:` method. It moves the action drawer around by changing its path and performing table updates. Here, the code considers three possible states: The drawer is closed and a new cell is tapped, the drawer is open and the same cell is tapped, and the drawer is open and a different cell is tapped.

The action row path is always `nil` whenever the drawer is shut. When a cell is tapped, the method sets a path for the new drawer directly after the tapped cell. If the user taps the associated cell above the drawer when it is open, the drawer "closes," and the path is set back to `nil`. When the user taps a different cell, this method adjusts its math, depending on whether the new cell is below the old action drawer or above it.

The `beginUpdates` and `endUpdates` method pair used here allows simultaneous animation of table operations. Use this block to smoothly introduce all the row changes created by moving, adding, and removing the action drawer.

Recipe 9-7   **Adding Action Drawers to Tables**

```objc
// Rows per section
- (NSInteger)tableView:(UITableView *)aTableView
    numberOfRowsInSection:(NSInteger)section
{
    return items.count + (self.actionRowPath != nil);
}

// Return a cell for the index path
- (UITableViewCell *)tableView:(UITableView *)aTableView
    cellForRowAtIndexPath:(NSIndexPath *)indexPath
{
    if ([self.actionRowPath isEqual:indexPath])
    {
        // Action Row
        CustomCell *cell = (CustomCell *)[self.tableView
            dequeueReusableCellWithIdentifier:@"action"
            forIndexPath:indexPath];
        [cell setActionTarget:self];
        return cell;
    }
    else
    {
        // Normal cell
        UITableViewCell *cell = [self.tableView
            dequeueReusableCellWithIdentifier:@"cell"
            forIndexPath:indexPath];
```

```objc
        // Adjust item lookup around action row if needed
        NSInteger adjustedRow = indexPath.row;
        if (_actionRowPath &&
            (_actionRowPath.row < indexPath.row))
                adjustedRow--;
        cell.textLabel.text = items[adjustedRow];

        cell.textLabel.textColor = [UIColor blackColor];
        cell.selectionStyle = UITableViewCellSelectionStyleGray;
        return cell;
    }
}


- (NSIndexPath *)tableView:(UITableView *)tableView
    willSelectRowAtIndexPath:(NSIndexPath *)indexPath
{
    // Only select normal cells
    if([indexPath isEqual:self.actionRowPath]) return nil;
    return indexPath;
}

// Deselect any current selection
- (void)deselect
{
    NSArray *paths = [self.tableView indexPathsForSelectedRows];
    if (!paths.count) return;

    NSIndexPath *path = paths[0];
    [self.tableView deselectRowAtIndexPath:path animated:YES];
}

// On selection, update the title and enable find/deselect
- (void)tableView:(UITableView *)aTableView
    didSelectRowAtIndexPath:(NSIndexPath *)indexPath
{
    NSArray *pathsToAdd;
    NSArray *pathsToDelete;

    if ([self.actionRowPath.previous isEqual:indexPath])
    {
        // Hide action cell
        pathsToDelete = @[self.actionRowPath];
        self.actionRowPath = nil;
        [self deselect];
    }
    else if (self.actionRowPath)
    {
```

```
        // Move action cell
        BOOL before = [indexPath before:self.actionRowPath];
        pathsToDelete = @[self.actionRowPath];
        self.actionRowPath = before ? indexPath.next : indexPath;
        pathsToAdd = @[self.actionRowPath];
    }
    else
    {
        // New action cell
        pathsToAdd = @[indexPath.next];
        self.actionRowPath = indexPath.next;
    }

    // Animate the deletions and insertions
    [self.tableView beginUpdates];
    if (pathsToDelete.count)
        [self.tableView deleteRowsAtIndexPaths:pathsToDelete
            withRowAnimation:UITableViewRowAnimationNone];
    if (pathsToAdd.count)
        [self.tableView insertRowsAtIndexPaths:pathsToAdd
            withRowAnimation:UITableViewRowAnimationNone];
    [self.tableView endUpdates];
}


// Set up table
- (void)viewDidLoad
{
    [super viewDidLoad];
    self.tableView.rowHeight = 60.0f;
    self.tableView.backgroundColor =
        [UIColor colorWithWhite:0.75f alpha:1.0f];

    [self.tableView registerClass:[UITableViewCell class]
        forCellReuseIdentifier:@"cell"];
    [self.tableView registerClass:[CustomCell class]
        forCellReuseIdentifier:@"action"];
    items = [@"Alpha Bravo Charlie Delta Echo Foxtrot Golf \
        Hotel India Juliet Kilo Lima Mike November Oscar Papa \
        Quebec Romeo Sierra Tango Uniform Victor Whiskey Xray \
        Yankee Zulu" componentsSeparatedByString:@" "];
}
```

Get This Recipe's Code

To find this recipe's full sample project, point your browser to https://github.com/erica/iOS-7-Cookbook and go to the folder for Chapter 9.

Coding a Custom Group Table

If alphabetic section list tables are the M. C. Eschers of the iPhone table world, with each section block precisely fitting into the negative spaces provided by other sections in the list, then freeform group tables are the Marc Chagalls. Every bit is drawn as a freeform, handcrafted work of art.

It's relatively easy to code up all the tables you've seen so far in this chapter once you've mastered the knack. Perfecting group table coding (which devotees usually call *preferences table* because that's the kind of table used in the Settings application) remains an illusion.

Building group tables in code is all about the collage—handcrafting a look, piece by piece. Creating a presentation like this in code involves a lot of detail work.

Creating Grouped Preferences Tables

There's nothing special involved in terms of laying out a new `UITableViewController` for a preferences table. You allocate it. You initialize it with the grouped table style. That's pretty much the end of it. It's the data source and delegate methods that provide the challenge. Here are the methods you need to define:

- `numberOfSectionsInTableView:`—All preferences tables contain groups of items. Each group is visually contained in an edge-to-edge white background, contrasting with the gray background of the containing table. Return the number of groups you'll be defining as an integer.

- `tableView:titleForHeaderInSection:`—Add the title for each section into this optional method. Return an `NSString` with the requested section name.

- `tableView:numberOfRowsInSection:`—Each section may contain any number of cells. Have this method return an integer indicating the number of rows (that is, cells) for that group.

- `tableView:heightForRowAtIndexPath:`—Tables that use flexible row heights cost more in terms of computational intensity. If you need to use variable heights, implement this optional method to specify what those heights will be. Return the value by section and by row.

- `tableView:cellForRowAtIndexPath:`—This is the standard cell-for-row method you've seen throughout this chapter. What sets it apart is its implementation. Instead of using one kind of cell, you'll probably want to create different kinds of reusable cells (with different reuse tags) for each cell type. Make sure you manage your reuse queue carefully and use as many IB-integrated elements as possible.

- `tableView:didSelectRowAtIndexPath:`—You provide case-by-case reactions to cell selection in this optional delegate method, depending on the cell type selected.

> **Note**
>
> The open-source llamasettings project at Google Code (http://llamasettings.googlecode.com) automatically produces grouped tables from property lists meant for iPhone settings bundles. It allows you to bring settings into your application without forcing your user to leave the app. The project can be freely added to commercial iOS SDK applications without licensing fees.

Recipe: Building a Multiwheel Table

Sometimes you'd like your users to pick from long lists or from several lists simultaneously. This is where `UIPickerView` instances really excel. `UIPickerView` objects produce tables offering individually scrolling "wheels," as shown in Figure 9-10. Users interact with one or more wheels to build their selection.

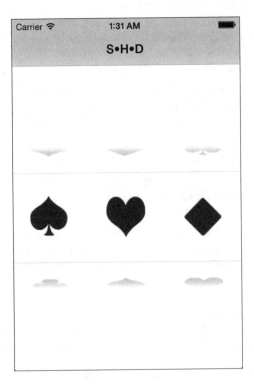

Figure 9-10   `UIPickerView` instances enable users to select from independently scrolling wheels.

These tables, although superficially similar to standard `UITableView` instances, use distinct data and delegate protocols:

- **There is no `UIPickerViewController` class.** `UIPickerView` instances act as subviews to other views. They are not intended to be the central focus of an application view. You can place a `UIPickerView` instance onto another view.
- **Picker views use numbers, not objects.** Components (that is, the wheels) are indexed by numbers and not by `NSIndexPath` instances. It's a more informal class than `UITableView`.

You can supply either title strings or views via the data source. Picker views can handle both approaches.

Creating the `UIPickerView`

When creating the picker, don't forget to assign the delegate and data source. Without this support, you cannot add data to the view, define its features, or respond to selection changes. Your primary view controller should implement the `UIPickerViewDelegate` and `UIPickerViewDataSource` protocols.

Data Source and Delegate Methods

Implement three key data source methods for your `UIPickerView` to make it function properly at a minimum level. These methods are as follows:

- `numberOfComponentsInPickerView:`—Return the number of columns, as an integer.
- `pickerView:numberOfRowsInComponent:`—Return the maximum number of rows per wheel, as an integer. The number of rows does not need to be identical. You can have one wheel with many rows and another with very few.
- `pickerView:titleForRow:forComponent` or `pickerView:viewForRow:forComponent:reusingView:`—These methods specify the text or view used to label a row on a given component.

In addition to these data source methods, you might want to supply one further delegate method. This method responds to a user's wheel selection:

- `pickerView:didSelectRow:inComponent:`—Add any application-specific behavior to this method. If needed, you can query `pickerView` to return the `selectedRowInComponent:` for any of the wheels in your view.

Using Views with Pickers

Picker views use a basic view-reuse scheme, caching the views supplied to it for possible reuse. When the final parameter for the `pickerView:viewForRow:forComponent:reusingView:` method is not `nil`, you can reuse the passed view by updating its settings or contents. Check for the view and allocate a new one only if one has not been supplied.

The height need not match the actual view. Implement `pickerView:rowHeightForComponent:` to set the row height used by each component. Recipe 9-8 uses a row height of 120 points, providing plenty of room for each image and laying the groundwork for the illusion that the picker could be continuous rather than having a starting point and an ending point.

Notice the high number of components: 1 million. The reason for this high number lies in a desire to emulate real cylinders. Normally, picker views have a first element and a last, and that's where they end. This recipe takes another approach, asking "What if the components were actual cylinders, so the last element were connected to the first?" To emulate this, the picker in this recipe uses a much higher number of components than any user will ever be able to access. It initializes the picker to the middle of that number by calling `selectRow:inComponent:Animated:`. The image shown at each component "row" is derived by the modulo of the actual reported row and the number of individual elements to display (in this case, `% 4`). Although the code knows that the picker actually has 1 million rows per wheel, the user experience offers a cylindrical wheel of just four rows.

> **Note**
>
> Pickers have traditionally been displayed in a different view from the referencing content. For example, date pickers were often presented in a new view when the user tapped on a date field. In iOS 7, Apple's apps have begun to embed pickers within the content of the app, including in tables. Apple's Human Interface Guidelines (HIG) now state that pickers should be inline with the content, without requiring the user to navigate to a different view. This is readily visible in the iOS 7 Calendar app.

Recipe 9-8 Creating the Illusion of a Repeating Cylinder

```
- (NSInteger)numberOfComponentsInPickerView:
    (UIPickerView *)pickerView
{
    return 3; // three columns
}


- (NSInteger)pickerView:(UIPickerView *)pickerView
    numberOfRowsInComponent:(NSInteger)component
{
    return 1000000; // arbitrary and large
}


- (CGFloat)pickerView:(UIPickerView *)pickerView
    rowHeightForComponent:(NSInteger)component
{
    return 120.0f;
}


- (UIView *)pickerView:(UIPickerView *)pickerView
```

```objc
    viewForRow:(NSInteger)row forComponent:(NSInteger)component
    reusingView:(UIView *)view
{

    // Load up the appropriate row image
    NSArray *names = @[@"club", @"diamond", @"heart", @"spade"];
    UIImage *image = [UIImage imageNamed:names[row%4]];

    // Create an image view if one was not supplied
    UIImageView *imageView = (UIImageView *) view;
    imageView.image = image;
    if (!imageView)
        imageView = [[UIImageView alloc] initWithImage:image];

    return imageView;
}


- (void)pickerView:(UIPickerView *)pickerView
    didSelectRow:(NSInteger)row inComponent:(NSInteger)component
{

    // Respond to selection by setting the view controller's title
    NSArray *names = @[@"C", @"D", @"H", @"S"];
    self.title = [NSString stringWithFormat:@"%@•%@•%@",
                  names[[pickerView selectedRowInComponent:0] % 4],
                  names[[pickerView selectedRowInComponent:1] % 4],
                  names[[pickerView selectedRowInComponent:2] % 4]];
}


- (void)viewDidAppear:(BOOL)animated
{
    [super viewDidAppear:animated];

    // Set random selections as the view appears
    [picker selectRow:50000 + (rand() % 4) inComponent:0 animated:YES];
    [picker selectRow:50000 + (rand() % 4) inComponent:1 animated:YES];
    [picker selectRow:50000 + (rand() % 4) inComponent:2 animated:YES];
}


- (void)loadView
{
    self.view = [[UIView alloc] init];
    self.view.backgroundColor = [UIColor whiteColor];

    // Create the picker and center it
    picker = [[UIPickerView alloc] initWithFrame:CGRectZero];
    [self.view addSubview:picker];
    PREPCONSTRAINTS(picker);
    CENTER_VIEW_H(self.view, picker);
```

```
CENTER_VIEW_V(self.view, picker);

// Initialize the picker properties
picker.delegate = self;
picker.dataSource = self;
picker.showsSelectionIndicator = YES;
}
```

Get This Recipe's Code

To find this recipe's full sample project, point your browser to https://github.com/erica/iOS-7-Cookbook and go to the folder for Chapter 9.

Using `UIDatePicker`

Sometimes you want to ask a user to enter date information. Apple supplies a tidy subclass of `UIPickerView` to handle several kinds of date and time entry. Figure 9-11 shows the four built-in styles of `UIDatePicker`s you can choose from—for selecting a time, selecting a date, selecting a combination of the two, and a countdown timer.

Creating the Date Picker

Lay out a date picker exactly as you would a `UIPickerView`. The geometry is identical. After that, things get much, much easier. You need not set a delegate or define data source methods. You do not have to declare any protocols. Just assign a date picker mode. Choose from `UIDatePickerModeTime`, `UIDatePickerModeDate`, `UIDatePickerModeDateAndTime`, and `UIDatePickerModeCountDownTimer`:

```
[datePicker setDate:[NSDate date]]; // set date
datePicker.datePickerMode = UIDatePickerModeDateAndTime; // set style
```

Optionally, add a target for when the selection changes (`UIControlEventValueChanged`) and create the callback method for the target-action pair.

Here are a few properties you'll want to take advantage of in the `UIDatePicker` class:

- `date`—Set the date property to initialize the picker or to retrieve the information set by the user as he or she manipulates the wheels.

- `maximumDate` and `minimumDate`—These properties set the bounds for date and time picking. Assign each one a standard `NSDate`. With these, you can constrain your user to pick a date from next year rather than just enter a date and then check whether it falls within an accepted time frame.

- **minuteInterval**—Sometimes you want to use 5-, 10-, 15-, or 30-minute intervals on your selections, such as for applications used to set appointments. Use the minuteInterval property to specify that value. Whatever number you pass, it has to be evenly divisible into 60.

- **countDownDuration**—Use this property to set the maximum available value for a countdown timer. You can go as high as 23 hours and 59 minutes (that is, 86,399 seconds).

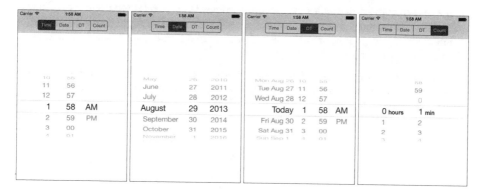

Figure 9-11   The iPhone offers four stock date picker models. Use the datePickerMode property to select the picker you want to use in your application.

Summary

This chapter introduces iOS tables, both simple and complex. You've seen all the basic iOS table features—from simple tables, to edits, to reordering and undo. You've also learned about a variety of advanced elements—from indexed alphabetic listings, to refresh controls, to picker views. The skills covered in this chapter enable you to build a wealth of table-based applications for the iPhone, iPad, and iPod touch. Here are some key points to take away from this chapter:

- When it comes to understanding tables, make sure you know the difference between data sources and delegate methods. Data sources fill up your tables with meaningful content. Delegate methods respond to user interactions.

- UITableViewControllers simplify applications built around a central UITableView. Do not hesitate to use UITableView instances directly, however, if your application requires them—especially in popovers or with split view controllers. Just make sure to explicitly support the UITableViewDelegate and UITableViewDataSource protocols when needed.

- Index controls provide a great way to navigate quickly through large ordered lists. Take advantage of their power when working with tables that would otherwise become unnavigable. Stylistically, it's best to avoid index controls when working with grouped tables.

- Dive into edits. Giving the user control over the table data is easy to do, and your code can be reused over many projects. Don't hesitate to design for undo support from the start. Even if you think you may not need undo at first, you might change your mind later.

- It's easy to convert flat tables into sectioned ones. Don't hesitate to use the predicate approach introduced in this chapter to create sections from simple arrays. Sectioned tables allow you to present data in a more structured fashion, with index support and easy search integration.

- Date pickers are highly specialized and very good at what they do: soliciting your users for dates and times. Picker views provide a less-specialized solution but require more work on your end.

10

Collection Views

Introduced in iOS 6, collection views present organized grids that lay out cells. These collections go well beyond standard table views and their vertically scrolling lists of cells. Collection views use many of the same concepts as tables but provide more power and more flexibility. With collection views, you create side-scrolling lists, grids, one-of-a-kind layouts like circles, and more. Plus, this class offers integrated visual effects through layout specifications and lots of great features like snapping into place after scrolling.

As with tables, you can add an enormous range of implementation details to collection views. This chapter introduces you to the basics: to the collection view, its client sources, its special-purpose controller, and its cells. You'll read about how to develop standard and customized collections, how to start adding special effects to your presentations, and how to take advantage of the built-in animation support to create the most effective interaction possible.

Keep in mind that collection views are more powerful than any single chapter can properly cover. This chapter offers fundamental collection view concepts. From here, how you hone your collection view knowledge and experience is up to you.

Collection Views Versus Tables

`UICollectionView` instances present an ordered collection of data items. Like table views, collections are made up of cells, headers, and footers powered by data sources and delegates. Unlike tables, collections introduce a layout—a class that specifies how items are placed onscreen. Layouts organize the location of each cell, so items appear exactly where needed.

Table 10-1 compares these two layout families. As you see, each family offers a core view class and a prebuilt controller class. These classes rely on a data source that feeds cells on demand and provides other content information. They use a delegate to respond to user interactions.

There are also several fundamental differences, starting with the humble index path. Both classes are organized by section as their primary grouping, and each section contains indexed individual cells. Because collection views can scroll either direction, vertical or horizontal, terminology has changed. Table views use sections and rows; collection views use sections and items. The `NSIndexPath` class was updated in iOS 6 as well to reflect this scheme.

Collection views introduce a new kind of content called "decoration" views, which provide visual enhancements like backdrops. This class understands that cells and scrolling are just the starting point. You can customize the entire look to create coherent presentations using any metaphor you can imagine. Collection views also rethink headers and footers, transforming them into supplementary views with a little more API flexibility than those found in tables.

Table 10-1 **Collection Views Versus Tables**

Item	Collection Views	Tables
Primary class	`UICollectionView`	`UITableView`
Controller	`UICollectionViewController`	`UITableViewController`
Contents	Cells, supplementary views (for example, headers and footers), decoration views (backdrops and visual adornments)	Cells, headers, and footers
User-directed reloading	Flow updates in real time to match current data. Refresh controls in limited situations.	Refresh controls (`UIRefreshControl`)
Programmatic reloading	`reloadData`	`reloadData`
Reusable cells	`UICollectionViewCell` (`dequeueReusableCellWithReuseIdentifier:forIndexPath:`)	`UITableViewCell` (`dequeueReusableCellWithIdentifier:forIndexPath:`)
Registration	Register class or XIB for cell, supplementary, or decoration view reuse	Register class or XIB for cell reuse
Headers and footers	`UICollectionReusableView`	`UITableViewHeaderFooterView`
Layout	`UICollectionViewLayout` and `UICollectionViewFlowLayout`	Not applicable
Data source	`UICollectionViewDataSource`	`UITableViewDataSource`
Delegation	`UICollectionViewDelegate`	`UITableViewDelegate`
Layout delegation	`UICollectionViewDelegateFlowLayout`	Not applicable
Indexing	Sections and items	Sections and rows
Scrolling directions	Horizontal or vertical	Vertical
Visual effects	Set up via custom layouts	Not applicable

Practical Implementation Differences

Expect a few practical differences between building table views and collection views. Collection views are less tolerant of lazy data loading. As a rule, when you create a collection view, make sure the data source that powers that view is fully prepared to go—even if it's prepared with a minimal or empty set of cells as you load data elsewhere in your application.

You cannot wait until your initialization or `loadView` or `viewDidLoad` methods to prepare content. Get content ready and going first, whether in your application delegate or before you instantiate and add your collection view or push a new child collection view controller. If your data is not ready to go, your app will crash; this is not the user experience you should be aiming toward.

Make sure you fully establish your collection view's layout object before presenting the collection. As you'll see in recipes in this chapter, you set up all layout details, including the scroll direction and any properties that don't rely on delegate callbacks. Only then do you create and initialize your collection view, as shown here:

```
MyCollectionController *mcc = [[MyCollectionController alloc]
    initWithCollectionViewLayout:layout];
```

Passing a `nil` layout produces an exception.

You are not limited to a single layout for the life of the collection view. The `collection-ViewLayout` property provides direct access to the layout of the collection. Setting this property updates the layout immediately, without animation. iOS 7 provides a simple method to animate the transition between multiple layouts:

```
- (void)setCollectionViewLayout:(UICollectionViewLayout *)layout
    animated:(BOOL)animated completion:(void (^)(BOOL finished))completion
```

With iOS 7, Apple also introduced a mechanism for creating complex, interactive transitions. Although beyond the scope of this book, more information is available in the `UICollectionView` Class Reference available at Apple's iOS Developer Center or in Xcode's iOS 7 docset.

Establishing Collection Views

As with tables, collections come in two flavors: views and prebuilt controllers. You either build an individual collection view instance and add it to a presentation or use a `UICollectionViewController` object that conveniently offers a view controller prepopulated with a collection view. The controller automatically sets the view's data source delegate to itself and declares both protocols. Embed the collection view controller as a child of any container (such as a navigation controller, tab bar controller, split view controller, page view controller, and so on) or present it on its own.

> **Note**
>
> Like table views, collection views have `delegate` and `dataSource` properties. The `UICollectionViewFlowLayout` class expects the collection view's delegate to also adopt the `UICollectionViewDelegateFlowLayout` protocol. Your collection view controller can implement the appropriate methods of all three protocols.

Controllers

To build a controller, first create and set up a layout object and then allocate the new instance and initialize it with the prepared layout:

```
UICollectionViewFlowLayout *layout =
    [[UICollectionViewFlowLayout alloc] init];
layout.scrollDirection = UICollectionViewScrollDirectionHorizontal;

MyCollectionController *mcc = [[MyCollectionController alloc]
    initWithCollectionViewLayout:layout];
```

This snippet uses a collection view flow layout in its default form, only setting the scroll direction. As you'll see through this chapter, you can do a lot more with layouts. Typically, you set additional properties or subclass system-supplied layouts and add your own behavior.

As a rule, you use the `UICollectionViewFlowLayout` class. It's the layout workhorse for collection views. Use it to build any basic presentation. In its default form, each section automatically wraps items to fit the screen, and you can specify how much space appears between sections, between lines, between items, and so forth. It's insanely customizable, as you'll see in the next section, which details many tweaks you can apply to flow layouts.

The parent class `UICollectionViewLayout` offers an abstract base class for subclassing (which you mostly avoid; nearly every time, you'll want to subclass the flow layout version instead) and isn't meant for direct use.

> **Note**
>
> When looking at subclassing layouts, refer to `UICollectionViewLayout`. The parent of the `UICollectionViewFlowLayout` class, its documentation provides the canonical list of customizable methods.

Views

To create a collection view for embedding into another view (without using a `UICollectionViewController`), establish a layout, create the collection view using the layout, and set the data source and delegate. The flow layout delegate utilizes the object you set as the collection view's delegate property:

```
UICollectionViewFlowLayout *layout =
    [[UICollectionViewFlowLayout alloc] init];
layout.scrollDirection = UICollectionViewScrollDirectionHorizontal;

collectionView = [[UICollectionView alloc] initWithFrame:CGRectZero
    collectionViewLayout:layout];
collectionView.dataSource = self;
collectionView.delegate = self;
```

Data Sources and Delegates

View controllers coordinating collection views declare UICollectionViewDataSource and UICollectionViewDelegate. Unlike with table views, when using a flow layout, a third protocol is also declared, UICollectionViewDelegateFlowLayout.

The delegate flow layout protocol coordinates layout information with your collection's layout instance through a series of callbacks. Your collection view's delegate adopts this protocol—that is, you do not have to specify a third collection view property like delegateFlowLayout.

As with table views, the data source provides section and item information and returns cells and other collection view items on demand. The delegate handles user interactions and provides meaningful responses to user changes. The flow layout delegate introduces section-by-section layout details and is, for the most part, completely optional. You'll read about flow layouts and their delegate callbacks in the next section.

Flow Layouts

Flow layouts provided by the UICollectionViewFlowLayout class create organized grid presentations in an application. They provide built-in properties that you edit directly or establish via delegate callbacks. These properties specify how the flow sets itself up to place items onscreen. In its most basic form, the layout properties provide you with a geometric vocabulary, where you talk about row spacing, indentation, and item-to-item margins.

Scroll Direction

The scrollDirection property controls whether sections are lined up horizontally (UICollectionViewScrollDirectionHorizontal) or vertically (UICollectionViewScroll-DirectionVertical). Figure 10-1 demonstrates otherwise identical layouts with horizontal (left) and vertical (right) flows. The members of each grouped section wrap to available space, based on the current flow. Because there is more vertical space than horizontal space in the iPhone portrait presentation, section groups are longer and thinner in the horizontal flow than in the vertical flow.

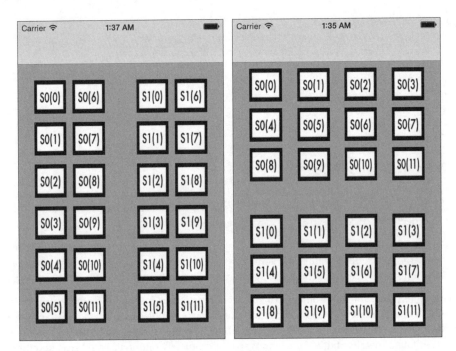

Figure 10-1   Horizontal (left) and vertical (right) flows determine a collection view's overall scrolling direction. The left image scrolls left–right. The right image scrolls up–down. For each example, a flow layout automatically handles wrapping duties at the end of each line. There are 6 items per line in the left image and 4 per line on the right. Each section includes 12 items.

Item Size and Line Spacing

Use the `itemSize` property to specify the default size for each onscreen item, like the small squares in Figure 10-1. The `minimumLineSpacing` and `minimumInteritemSpacing` properties specify how much space you need wrapped between objects within each section. Line spacing always goes between each line in the direction of flow. For example, line spacing refers to the space between S0(0) and S0(6) in Figure 10-1 (left) or between S0(0) and S0(4) in Figure 10-1 (right). Item spacing is orthogonal (at right angles) to lines, specifying the gap to leave between each consecutive item, such as between S0(0) and S0(1) and between S0(1) and S0(2).

Figure 10-2 shows these properties in action, in this case using a vertical flow. The left figure shows consistent spacing of 10 points. The middle figure expands line spacing to 50 points. This space appears between lines of items, where the flow wraps from one line to the next. The right figure expands item spacing to 30 points. Item spaces appear along each row, adding spacers between each object.

As with many new layout items introduced in iOS 6 and later, these settings are requests. Specifically, the spacing may exceed whatever value you specify, but the layout tries to respect the minimums you assign.

You can set the mentioned layout properties directly to assign default values applied across an entire collection. You can also use flow layout delegate callback methods to specify values from code. Setting these values at runtime offers far more nuance than the default settings, as they are applied on a section-by-section and item-by-item basis rather than globally. The following methods handle item size and minimum spacing:

- `collectionView:layout:sizeForItemAtIndexPath:`—Corresponds to the `itemSize` property, on an item-by-item basis.

- `collectionView:layout:minimumLineSpacingForSectionAtIndex:`—Corresponds to the `minimumLineSpacing` property but controls it on a section-by-section basis.

- `collectionView:layout:minimumInteritemSpacingForSectionAtIndex:`— Corresponds to the `minimumInteritemSpacing` property, again on a section-by-section basis.

Of these, the first method for item sizes offers the adaptation most typically used in iOS development. It enables you to build collections whose items, unlike those shown in Figure 10-2, vary in dimension. Figure 10-4, which follows later in this chapter, shows a flow layout that adjusts itself to multisized contents.

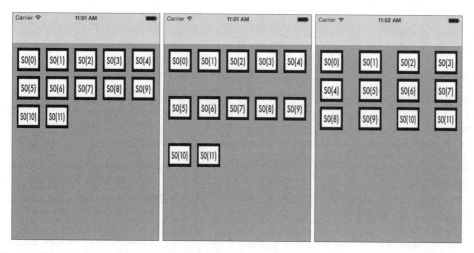

Figure 10-2   Minimum line and inter-item spacing control how items are wrapped within each section. Item sizes specify the dimensions for each cell. The left image uses default spacing. The center image increases line spacing to 50 points. The right image increases inter-item spacing to 30 points.

Header and Footer Sizing

The `headerReferenceSize` and `footerReferenceSize` properties define how wide or how high header and footer items should be. Notice the difference between the extents for these items in Figure 10-3 in the top two and bottom two screen shots. The horizontal flow at the top uses 60-point-wide spacing for these two items. The vertical flow at the bottom uses 30-point-high spacing. Although you supply a full `CGSize` to these properties, the layout uses only one field at any time, based on the flow direction. For horizontal flow, it's the width field; for vertical flow, it's the height.

Here are the two callbacks used to generate the Figure 10-3 layouts. They return complete size structures even though only one field is used at any time. If the delegate does not implement these methods, the flow layout object uses the property values above:

```
- (CGSize) collectionView:(UICollectionView *)collectionView
    layout:(UICollectionViewLayout *)collectionViewLayout
    referenceSizeForHeaderInSection:(NSInteger)section
{
    return CGSizeMake(60.0f, 30.0f);
}

- (CGSize) collectionView:(UICollectionView *)collectionView
    layout:(UICollectionViewLayout *)collectionViewLayout
    referenceSizeForFooterInSection:(NSInteger)section
{
    return CGSizeMake(60.0f, 30.0f);
}
```

Insets

The two minimum spacing properties define how each in-section item relates to other items within a section. In contrast, the `sectionInset` property describes how the outer edges of a section add padding. This padding affects how sections relate to their optional headers and footers and how sections move apart from each other in general.

Edge insets consist of a set of *{top, left, bottom, right}* values. Figure 10-3 shows how this works with collection views. Each shot in Figure 10-3 presents a flow using the same edge insets of 50 points at the top, 30 points at the bottom, and 10 points left and right:

```
UIEdgeInsetsMake(50.0f, 10.0f, 30.0f, 10.0f)
```

The top screens show a horizontal flow and the bottom screens a vertical flow. In each case, you see how the insets affect layout. The insets pad the content items from their enclosing container. In the horizontal flow, the content items adjust vertically from the top of the collection view to allow for the top spacing and horizontally from the header and footer. In the vertical flow, the padding of the content items happens below the header and above the footer. Similarly, the left and right spacing are incorporated between the edges of the collection view and the contained items.

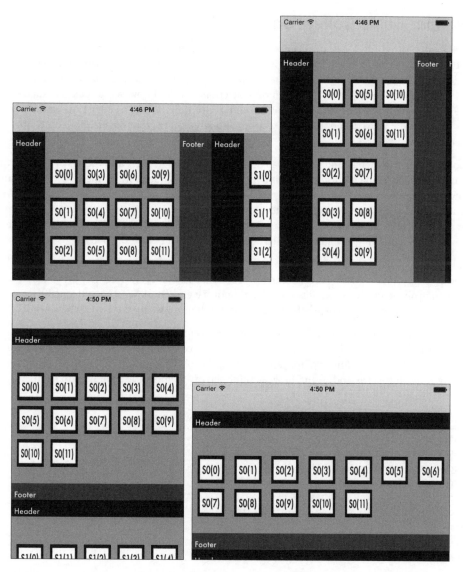

Figure 10-3   Section insets control the space that leads up to and away from a section's items. The top images show a horizontal flow and the bottom images a vertical flow. All images use a top spacing of 50 points and a bottom spacing of 30 points, along with 10-point left and right spacing.

Recipe: Basic Collection View Flows

Recipe 10-1 introduces a basic collection view controller implementation, with support for optional headers and footers. This recipe implements the essential data source and delegate methods you need for a simple grid-based flow layout. Apple provides a number of properties to configure responses for the common collection view and flow layout delegate methods. Use these provided properties and simple modification of the source to adjust the number of sections to be viewed, the items per section, and any other layout details that control the overall flow.

Boolean properties determine whether a collection view uses headers and footers. The size can be configured by implementing the first two reference size requests in Recipe 10-1. You'll find these two methods, one each for header and footer, just after the Flow Layout pragma mark. Returning a 0 size to the header or footer flow delegate method tells the collection view to omit those features for the section in question. When you return any other size, the collection view moves on to requesting the supplementary views for either a header or footer.

Make sure to register all cell and supplementary view classes before using them in your data source. Recipe 10-1 registers its classes in its viewDidLoad method. Once they are registered, you can dequeue instances on demand. You do not have to check whether a dequeuing request returns a usable instance. The methods create and initialize instances for you when needed.

We encourage you to dive into the sample code for Recipe 10-1 and tweak each layout value and callback (which was done to create the figures you've already seen in this section) to see how they affect overall flow and appearance. Recipe 10-1 offers a great jumping-off point for testing collection views and seeing how each property influences the final presentation.

Recipe 10-1   **Basic Collection View Controller with Flow Layout**

```
@interface TestBedViewController : UICollectionViewController
// Layout and collection view configuration
@property (nonatomic, assign) BOOL useHeaders;
@property (nonatomic, assign) BOOL useFooters;
@property (nonatomic, assign) NSInteger numberOfSections;
@property (nonatomic, assign) NSInteger itemsInSection;
@end

@implementation TestBedViewController

#pragma mark Flow Layout
- (CGSize)collectionView:(UICollectionView *)collectionView
    layout:(UICollectionViewLayout *)collectionViewLayout
    referenceSizeForHeaderInSection:(NSInteger)section
{
    return self.useHeaders ? CGSizeMake(60.0f, 30.0f) : CGSizeZero;
}
```

```objc
- (CGSize)collectionView:(UICollectionView *)collectionView
  layout:(UICollectionViewLayout *)collectionViewLayout
  referenceSizeForFooterInSection:(NSInteger)section
{
    return self.useFooters ? CGSizeMake(60.0f, 30.0f) : CGSizeZero;
}


#pragma mark Data Source
// Number of sections total
- (NSInteger)numberOfSectionsInCollectionView:
    (UICollectionView *)collectionView
{
    return self.numberOfSections;
}


// Number of items per section
- (NSInteger)collectionView:(UICollectionView *)collectionView
    numberOfItemsInSection:(NSInteger)section
{
    return self.itemsInSection;
}


// Dequeue and prepare a cell
- (UICollectionViewCell *)collectionView:
    (UICollectionView *)aCollectionView
    cellForItemAtIndexPath:(NSIndexPath *)indexPath
{
    UICollectionViewCell *cell = [self.collectionView
        dequeueReusableCellWithReuseIdentifier:@"cell"
        forIndexPath:indexPath];

    cell.backgroundColor = [UIColor whiteColor];
    cell.selectedBackgroundView =
        [[UIView alloc] initWithFrame:CGRectZero];
    cell.selectedBackgroundView.backgroundColor =
        [[UIColor blackColor] colorWithAlphaComponent:0.5f];

    return cell;
}


// If using headers and footers, dequeue and prepare a view
- (UICollectionReusableView *)collectionView:
    (UICollectionView *)aCollectionView
    viewForSupplementaryElementOfKind:(NSString *)kind
    atIndexPath:(NSIndexPath *)indexPath
{
    if (kind == UICollectionElementKindSectionHeader)
```

```
    {
        UICollectionReusableView *header = [self.collectionView
            dequeueReusableSupplementaryViewOfKind:
                UICollectionElementKindSectionHeader
            withReuseIdentifier:@"header" forIndexPath:indexPath];
        header.backgroundColor = [UIColor blackColor];
        return header;
    }
    else if (kind == UICollectionElementKindSectionFooter)
    {
        UICollectionReusableView *footer = [self.collectionView
            dequeueReusableSupplementaryViewOfKind:
                UICollectionElementKindSectionFooter
            withReuseIdentifier:@"footer" forIndexPath:indexPath];
        footer.backgroundColor = [UIColor darkGrayColor];
        return footer;
    }
    return nil;
}


#pragma mark Delegate methods
- (void)collectionView:(UICollectionView *)aCollectionView
    didSelectItemAtIndexPath:(NSIndexPath *)indexPath
{
    NSLog(@"Selected %@", indexPath);
}


- (void)collectionView:(UICollectionView *)aCollectionView
    didDeselectItemAtIndexPath:(NSIndexPath *)indexPath
{
    NSLog(@"Deselected %@", indexPath);
}


#pragma mark Setup
- (void)viewDidLoad
{
    [super viewDidLoad];
    // Register any cell and header/footer classes for re-use queues
    [self.collectionView
        registerClass:[UICollectionViewCell class]
        forCellWithReuseIdentifier:@"cell"];
    [self.collectionView
        registerClass:[UICollectionReusableView class]
        forSupplementaryViewOfKind:UICollectionElementKindSectionHeader
        withReuseIdentifier:@"header"];
    [self.collectionView
        registerClass:[UICollectionReusableView class]
```

```
            forSupplementaryViewOfKind:UICollectionElementKindSectionFooter
            withReuseIdentifier:@"footer"];

    self.collectionView.backgroundColor = [UIColor lightGrayColor];

    // Allow users to select/deselect items by tapping
    self.collectionView.allowsMultipleSelection = YES;
}

- (instancetype)initWithCollectionViewLayout:(UICollectionViewLayout *)layout
{
    self = [super initWithCollectionViewLayout:layout];
    if (self)
    {
        // Set some reasonable defaults
        self.useFooters = NO;
        self.useHeaders = NO;
        self.numberOfSections = 1;
        self.itemsInSection = 1;
    }
    return self;
}
@end

// From the application delegate
- (BOOL)application:(UIApplication *)application
    didFinishLaunchingWithOptions:(NSDictionary *)launchOptions
{
    _window = [[UIWindow alloc]
        initWithFrame:[[UIScreen mainScreen] bounds]];
    _window.tintColor = COOKBOOK_PURPLE_COLOR;

    // Create the layout and then pass to our collection VC
    UICollectionViewFlowLayout *layout =
        [[UICollectionViewFlowLayout alloc] init];
    TestBedViewController *tbvc = [[TestBedViewController alloc]
        initWithCollectionViewLayout:layout];
    tbvc.edgesForExtendedLayout = UIRectEdgeNone;

    // Configure layout and collection view properties
    layout.itemSize = CGSizeMake(50.0f, 50.0f);
    layout.sectionInset =
        UIEdgeInsetsMake(10.0, 10.0f, 50.0f, 10.0f);
    layout.scrollDirection =
        UICollectionViewScrollDirectionVertical;
    layout.minimumLineSpacing = 10.0f;
    layout.minimumInteritemSpacing = 10.0f;
```

```
    tbvc.numberOfSections = 10;
    tbvc.itemsInSection = 12;
    tbvc.useHeaders = YES;
    tbvc.useFooters = YES;

    UINavigationController *nav = [[UINavigationController alloc]
        initWithRootViewController:tbvc];
    _window.rootViewController = nav;
    [_window makeKeyAndVisible];
    return YES;
}
```

Get This Recipe's Code

To find this recipe's full sample project, point your browser to https://github.com/erica/
iOS-7-Cookbook and go to the folder for Chapter 10.

Recipe: Custom Cells

Recipe 10-1 creates uniformly sized objects, but there's no reason your collections cannot be
filled with items of any dimension. Flow layouts allow you to create far more varied presentations, as shown in Figure 10-4. Recipe 10-2 adapts its collection view to provide this juiced-up
presentation by creating custom cells. These cells add image views, and the image's size powers
the "size for item at index path" callback to the collection view's data source:

```
- (CGSize) collectionView:(UICollectionView *)collectionView
    layout:(UICollectionViewLayout*)collectionViewLayout
    sizeForItemAtIndexPath:(NSIndexPath *)indexPath
{
    UIImage *image = artDictionary[indexPath];
    return image.size;
}
```

To create custom cells, subclass `UICollectionViewCell` and add any new views to the
cell's `contentView`. This recipe adds a single image view subview and exposes it through an
`imageView` property. When providing cells, the data source adds custom images to the image
view, and the layout delegate specifies their sizes.

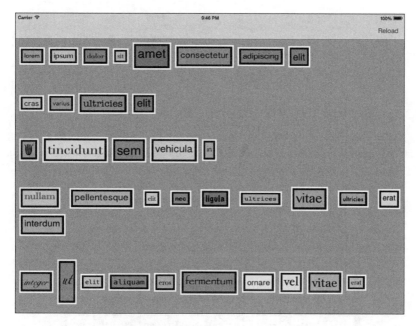

Figure 10-4   Flow layouts work with items that present varying heights and widths, not just basic grids.

Recipe 10-2   **Custom Collection View Cells**

```objc
@interface ImageCell : UICollectionViewCell
@property (nonatomic) UIImageView *imageView;
@end

@implementation ImageCell
- (instancetype)initWithFrame:(CGRect)frame
{
    self = [super initWithFrame:frame];
    if (self)
    {
        _imageView = [[UIImageView alloc] initWithFrame:
            CGRectInset(self.bounds, 4.0f, 4.0f)];
        _imageView.autoresizingMask =
            UIViewAutoresizingFlexibleWidth |
            UIViewAutoresizingFlexibleHeight;
        [self.contentView addSubview:_imageView];
    }
    return self;
}
@end
```

Recipe: Scrolling Horizontal Lists

Collection views offer the ability to create horizontal scrolling lists, a counterpoint to table
views that only scroll vertically. To accomplish this, you need to take a few things into account,
primarily that flow layouts in their default state naturally wrap their sections. Consider Figure
10-5. It shows two collection views, both of which scroll horizontally. The top image consists
of a single section with 100 items; the bottom has 100 sections of a single item each.

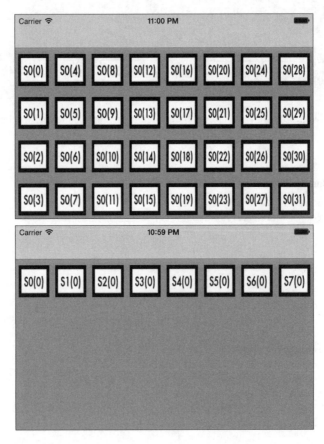

Figure 10-5   Top: A single section with 100 items. Bottom: 100 sections with a single item
each.

You could force the top layout not to wrap by adding large left and right section margins, but getting them to work correctly is messy; the margins depend on both device and orientation. Assigning one item per section is a much easier solution and ensures a single line of items, regardless of size.

Recipe 10-3 creates a horizontally scrolling collection as a standalone view rather than as a view controller. This approach allows the view to be inset as a subview, neatly avoiding the big empty area at the bottom of the screen shown in Figure 10-5 (bottom).

This recipe's `InsetCollectionView` class provides its own data source and exposes its collection view as a read-only property to allow clients to provide delegation. Figure 10-6 shows this recipe in action, providing an embedded horizontally scrolling list.

Recipe 10-8, which appears later in this chapter, introduces a fully customized layout subclass that offers true grid layouts. Recipe 10-3 offers a handy shortcut for using the default flow layout, as shipped. Plus, it demonstrates how to create a collection view outside the context of a prebuilt controller.

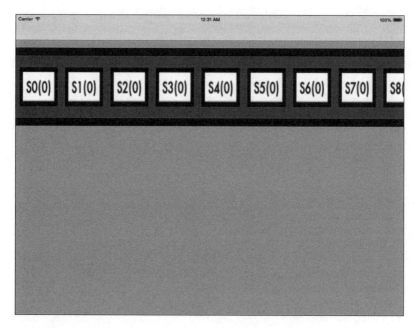

Figure 10-6   Recipe 10-3 creates an embeddable horizontally scrolling collection view.

Recipe 10-3   **Horizontal Scroller Collection View**

```
@interface InsetCollectionView : UIView
    <UICollectionViewDataSource>
@property (strong, readonly) UICollectionView *collectionView;
```

```objc
@end

@implementation InsetCollectionView

// 100 sections of 1 item each
- (NSInteger)numberOfSectionsInCollectionView:
    (UICollectionView *)collectionView
{
    return 100;
}

- (NSInteger)collectionView:(UICollectionView *)collectionView
    numberOfItemsInSection:(NSInteger)section
{
    return 1;
}

// This is a little utility that returns a view showing the
// section and item numbers for an index path
- (UIImageView *)viewForIndexPath:(NSIndexPath *)indexPath
{
    NSString *string = [NSString stringWithFormat:
        @"S%d(%d)", indexPath.section, indexPath.item];
    UIImage *image = blockStringImage(string, 16.0f);
    UIImageView *imageView =
        [[UIImageView alloc] initWithImage:image];
    return imageView;
}

// Return an initialized cell
- (UICollectionViewCell *)collectionView:
        (UICollectionView *)_collectionView
    cellForItemAtIndexPath:(NSIndexPath *)indexPath
{
    UICollectionViewCell *cell = [self.collectionView
        dequeueReusableCellWithReuseIdentifier:@"cell"
        forIndexPath:indexPath];

    cell.backgroundColor = [UIColor whiteColor];
    cell.selectedBackgroundView =
        [[UIView alloc] initWithFrame:CGRectZero];
    cell.selectedBackgroundView.backgroundColor =
        [[UIColor blackColor] colorWithAlphaComponent:0.5f];

    // Show the section and item in a custom subview
    if ([cell viewWithTag:999])
        [[cell viewWithTag:999] removeFromSuperview];
```

```objc
    UIImageView *imageView = [self viewForIndexPath:indexPath];
    imageView.tag = 999;
    [cell.contentView addSubview:imageView];

    return cell;
}

#pragma mark Setup
- (instancetype)initWithFrame:(CGRect)frame
{
    self = [super initWithFrame:frame];
    if (self)
    {
        UICollectionViewFlowLayout *layout =
            [[UICollectionViewFlowLayout alloc] init];
        layout.scrollDirection =
            UICollectionViewScrollDirectionHorizontal;
        layout.sectionInset =
            UIEdgeInsetsMake(40.0f, 10.0f, 40.0f, 10.0f);
        layout.minimumLineSpacing = 10.0f;
        layout.minimumInteritemSpacing = 10.0f;
        layout.itemSize = CGSizeMake(100.0f, 100.0f);

        _collectionView = [[UICollectionView alloc]
            initWithFrame:CGRectZero collectionViewLayout:layout];
        _collectionView.backgroundColor = [UIColor darkGrayColor];
        _collectionView.allowsMultipleSelection = YES;
        _collectionView.dataSource = self;

        [_collectionView registerClass:[UICollectionViewCell
            class] forCellWithReuseIdentifier:@"cell"];
        [self addSubview:_collectionView];

        PREPCONSTRAINTS(_collectionView);
        CONSTRAIN(self, _collectionView,
            @"H:|[_collectionView(>=0)]|");
        CONSTRAIN(self, _collectionView,
            @"V:|-20-[_collectionView(>=0)]-20-|");
    }
    return self;}
@end
```

Get This Recipe's Code

To find this recipe's full sample project, point your browser to https://github.com/erica/iOS-7-Cookbook and go to the folder for Chapter 10.

Recipe: Introducing Interactive Layout Effects

Flow layouts are fully controllable. When subclassing `UICollectionViewFlowLayout`, you gain immediate real-time control over how items are sized and placed onscreen. This provides incredible power to you as a developer, letting you specify item presentation with great delicacy. You can use this power to develop flows that seem to work in three dimensions or ones that break the linear mold and transform columns and rows into circles, piles, Bezier curves, and more.

Customizable layout attributes include standard layout elements (`frame`, `center`, and `size`), transparency (`alpha` and `hidden`), position on the z-axis (`zIndex`), and transform (`transform3d`). You adjust these when the flow layout requests element attributes, as demonstrated in Recipe 10-4.

This recipe creates a flow that zooms items out toward the user in the center of the screen and shrinks them as they move away to the left or right. It calculates how far away each item is from the horizontal center of the screen. It applies its scaling based on a cosine function (that is, one that maxes out as the distance from the center decreases).

Figure 10-7 shows this effect, although it's much better to run Recipe 10-4 yourself and see the changes in action.

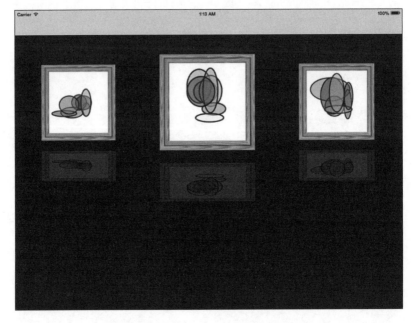

Figure 10-7   The custom layout defined by Recipe 10-4 zooms items as they move toward the horizontal center of the screen.

Recipe 10-4   **Interactive Layout Effects**

```
@interface PunchedLayout : UICollectionViewFlowLayout
@end
@implementation PunchedLayout
{
    CGSize boundsSize;
    CGFloat midX;
}


// Allow the presentation to resize as needed
- (BOOL)shouldInvalidateLayoutForBoundsChange:(CGRect)bounds
{
    return YES;
}


// Calculate the distance from the view center
-(void)prepareLayout
{
    [super prepareLayout];
    boundsSize = self.collectionView.bounds.size;
    midX = boundsSize.width / 2.0f;
}


// Lay out elements
- (NSArray *)layoutAttributesForElementsInRect:(CGRect)rect
{
    // Retrieve the default layout
    NSArray *array = [super layoutAttributesForElementsInRect:rect];
    for (UICollectionViewLayoutAttributes* attributes in array)
    {
        attributes.transform3D = CATransform3DIdentity;
        // Only handle layouts for visible items
        if (!CGRectIntersectsRect(attributes.frame, rect)) continue;

        CGPoint contentOffset = self.collectionView.contentOffset;
        CGPoint itemCenter = CGPointMake(
            attributes.center.x - contentOffset.x,
            attributes.center.y - contentOffset.y);
        CGFloat distance = ABS(midX - itemCenter.x);

        // Normalize the distance and calculate the zoom factor
        CGFloat normalized = distance / midX;
        normalized = MIN(1.0f, normalized);
        CGFloat zoom = cos(normalized * M_PI_4);
```

```
        // Set the transform
        attributes.transform3D =
            CATransform3DMakeScale(zoom, zoom, 1.0f);
    }
    return array;
}
@end
```

Get This Recipe's Code

To find this recipe's full sample project, point your browser to https://github.com/erica/
iOS-7-Cookbook and go to the folder for Chapter 10.

Recipe: Scroll Snapping

Recipe 10-4 focuses user attention at the center of the screen. Why not ensure that the central
object moves to the most optimal position? Accomplish this by implementing a layout method
that snaps to specific boundaries. Recipe 10-5 shows how.

The `targetContentOffsetForProposedContentOffset:` method, which is called during
scrolling, specifies where the scroll would naturally stop. It iterates through all the onscreen
objects, finds the one closest to the view's horizontal center, and adjusts the offset so that the
object's center coincides with the view's.

Recipe 10-5   **Customizing the Target Content Offset**

```
- (CGPoint)targetContentOffsetForProposedContentOffset:
        (CGPoint)proposedContentOffset
    withScrollingVelocity:(CGPoint)velocity
{
    CGFloat offsetAdjustment = CGFLOAT_MAX;

    // Retrieve all onscreen items at the proposed starting point
    CGRect targetRect = CGRectMake(proposedContentOffset.x, 0.0,
        boundsSize.width, boundsSize.height);
    NSArray *array =
        [super layoutAttributesForElementsInRect:targetRect];

    // Determine the proposed center x-coordinate
    CGFloat proposedCenterX = proposedContentOffset.x + midX;

    // Search for the minimum offset adjustment
    for (UICollectionViewLayoutAttributes* layoutAttributes in array)
    {
        CGFloat distance =
```

```
            layoutAttributes.center.x - proposedCenterX;
        if (ABS(distance) < ABS(offsetAdjustment))
            offsetAdjustment = distance;
    }


    CGPoint desiredPoint =
        CGPointMake(proposedContentOffset.x + offsetAdjustment,
            proposedContentOffset.y);

    // Workaround for edge conditions. Hat tip, Nicolas Goles.
    if ((proposedContentOffset.x == 0) ||
        (proposedContentOffset.x >=
            (self.collectionViewContentSize.width -
                boundsSize.width)))
    {
        NSNotification *note = [NSNotification
            notificationWithName:@"PleaseRecenter" object:
                [NSValue valueWithCGPoint:desiredPoint]];
        // Notify view controller of modified desired point
        [[NSNotificationCenter defaultCenter]
            postNotification:note];
        return proposedContentOffset;
    }


    // Offset the content by the minimal amount necessary to center
    return desiredPoint;
}
```

Get This Recipe's Code

To find this recipe's full sample project, point your browser to https://github.com/erica/iOS-7-Cookbook and go to the folder for Chapter 10.

Recipe: Creating a Circle Layout

Circle layouts offer an eye-catching way to arrange views around a central area, as shown in Figure 10-8. Recipe 10-6 is heavily based on Apple's sample code, which was first presented at WWDC 2012. This layout provides an excellent introduction to the way items can animate into place upon creation and deletion.

Recipe 10-6's layout flow uses a fixed content size via the `collectionViewContentSize` method. This prevents collection view scrolling as it creates a layout area with well-understood static geometry. The code further limits its layout to an inset area, calculated in the `prepareLayout` method. The height or width of the screen, whichever is currently smaller, determines the circle's radius. This remains fixed, regardless of device orientation.

The layout calculates each item's position by its index path. This presentation uses a single section, and the order of the item within that section (that is, whether it is the third or fifth item) sets its progress along the circle:

```
CGFloat progress = (float) path.item / (float) numberOfItems;
CGFloat theta = 2.0f * M_PI * progress;
```

You can easily extend this to any shape or path whose progress can be normalized within the range [0.0, 1.0]. For a circle, this goes from 0 to 2 pi. A spiral might go out 3, 4, or even 5 pi. For a Bezier curve, you iterate along whatever control points define the curve and interpolate between them as needed.

Creation and Deletion Animation

Of particular interest in Recipe 10-6 are the methods that specify the initial attributes for newly inserted items and final attributes for newly deleted ones. These properties allow your collection views to animate item creation and deletion from the previous layout to the new layout after those items have been added or removed.

In this recipe, as in Apple's original sample code, new items start off transparent in the center of the circle and fade into view as they move out to their assigned position. Deleted items shrink, fade, and move to the center. When you run the sample code, you'll see these animations take effect.

The documentation for the `initialLayoutAttributesForAppearingItemAtIndexPath` and `finalLayoutAttributesForDisappearingItemAtIndexPath` methods is confusing at best; it implies that these methods are only called on the inserted and deleted items. In reality, the starting and ending attribute requests are called on all items, not just the added and deleted ones. Because of this, Recipe 10-6 sorts items into collections: added index paths and deleted index paths. It limits its custom insertion and deletion attributes to those items.

This mechanism offers a way to animate layout attributes for all items, enabling you to add extra animations as needed. For example, you might animate an object moving from the end of row 3 to the start of row 4 as a new item is inserted into row 3. This approach allows you to animate the cell offscreen to the right of row 3 and then onscreen from the left of row 4 versus the default behavior, which has it move diagonally from its old position to the new one.

Powering the Circle Layout

This recipe makes a number of changes to Apple's original sample. For one thing, Recipe 10-6 uses Add and Delete bar buttons rather than gestures. For another, each view is distinct and identifiable by its color. Instead of deleting "any item" or adding "some item," Recipe 10-6 uses selections. The user chooses an item to focus on. That selection controls which item is deleted (the selected item) or where new items should be added (just after the selected item).

The following deletion code retrieves the currently selected item, deletes it, and selects the next item. Then it enables or disables the Add and Delete buttons, depending on how many items are currently onscreen:

```
- (void)delete
{
    if (!count) return;

    // Decrement the number of onscreen items
    count--;

    // Determine which item to delete
    NSArray *selectedItems =
        [self.collectionView indexPathsForSelectedItems];
    NSInteger itemNumber = selectedItems.count ?
        ((NSIndexPath *)selectedItems[0]).item : 0;


    NSIndexPath *itemPath =
        [NSIndexPath indexPathForItem:itemNumber inSection:0];

    // Perform deletion
    [self.collectionView performBatchUpdates:^{
        [self.collectionView deleteItemsAtIndexPaths:@[itemPath]];
    } completion:^(BOOL done){
        if (count)
            [self.collectionView selectItemAtIndexPath:
                    [NSIndexPath indexPathForItem:
                        MAX(0, itemNumber - 1) inSection:0]
                animated:NO
                scrollPosition:UICollectionViewScrollPositionNone];
        self.navigationItem.rightBarButtonItem.enabled =
            (count > 0);
        self.navigationItem.leftBarButtonItem.enabled =
            (count < (IS_IPAD ? 20 : 8));
    }];
}
```

In the real world, there are very few use cases for adding and deleting interchangeable views, but there are many use cases for views that have meaning. These changes provide a more solid jumping-off point for extending this recipe to practical applications.

The Layout

Figure 10-8 shows the layout that Recipe 10-6 builds. As users add new items, the circle grows more crowded, up to a maximum count of 20 items on the iPad and 8 on the iPhone. You can easily modify these limits in the add and delete methods to match the view sizes for your particular application.

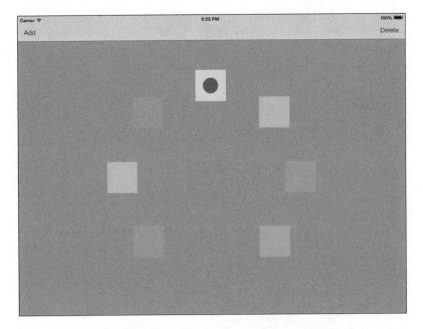

Figure 10-8   This circle layout flow is inspired by sample code provided by Apple and was encouraged by the efforts of developer Greg Hartstein.

Recipe 10-6   **Laying Out Views in a Circle**

```
@implementation CircleLayout
{
    NSInteger numberOfItems;
    CGPoint centerPoint;
    CGFloat radius;

    NSMutableArray *insertedIndexPaths;
    NSMutableArray *deletedIndexPaths;
}

// Calculate and save off the current state
- (void)prepareLayout
{
    [super prepareLayout];
    CGSize size = self.collectionView.frame.size;
    numberOfItems =
        [self.collectionView numberOfItemsInSection:0];
    centerPoint =
        CGPointMake(size.width / 2.0f, size.height / 2.0f);
    radius = MIN(size.width, size.height) / 3.0f;
```

```objc
        insertedIndexPaths = [NSMutableArray array];
        deletedIndexPaths = [NSMutableArray array];
}


// Fix the content size to the frame size
- (CGSize)collectionViewContentSize
{
    return self.collectionView.frame.size;
}


// Calculate position for each item
- (UICollectionViewLayoutAttributes *)
    layoutAttributesForItemAtIndexPath:(NSIndexPath *)path
{
    UICollectionViewLayoutAttributes *attributes =
        [UICollectionViewLayoutAttributes
            layoutAttributesForCellWithIndexPath:path];
    CGFloat progress = (float) path.item / (float) numberOfItems;
    CGFloat theta = 2.0f * M_PI * progress;
    CGFloat xPosition = centerPoint.x + radius * cos(theta);
    CGFloat yPosition = centerPoint.y + radius * sin(theta);
    attributes.size = [self itemSize];
    attributes.center = CGPointMake(xPosition, yPosition);
    return attributes;
}


// Calculate layouts for all items
- (NSArray *)layoutAttributesForElementsInRect:(CGRect)rect
{
    NSMutableArray *attributes = [NSMutableArray array];
    for (NSInteger index = 0; index < numberOfItems; index++)
    {
        NSIndexPath *indexPath =
            [NSIndexPath indexPathForItem:index inSection:0];
        [attributes addObject:
            [self layoutAttributesForItemAtIndexPath:indexPath]];
    }
    return attributes;
}


// Build insertion and deletion collections from updates
- (void)prepareForCollectionViewUpdates:(NSArray *)updates
{
    [super prepareForCollectionViewUpdates:updates];

    for (UICollectionViewUpdateItem* updateItem in updates)
    {
```

```
            if (updateItem.updateAction ==
                    UICollectionUpdateActionInsert)
                [insertedIndexPaths
                    addObject:updateItem.indexPathAfterUpdate];
            else if (updateItem.updateAction ==
                    UICollectionUpdateActionDelete)
                [deletedIndexPaths
                    addObject:updateItem.indexPathBeforeUpdate];
    }
}


// Establish starting attributes for added item
- (UICollectionViewLayoutAttributes *)
    insertionAttributesForItemAtIndexPath:(NSIndexPath *)itemIndexPath
{
    UICollectionViewLayoutAttributes *attributes =
        [self layoutAttributesForItemAtIndexPath:itemIndexPath];
    attributes.alpha = 0.0;
    attributes.center = centerPoint;
    return attributes;
}


// Establish final attributes for deleted item
- (UICollectionViewLayoutAttributes *)
    deletionAttributesForItemAtIndexPath:(NSIndexPath *)itemIndexPath
{
    UICollectionViewLayoutAttributes *attributes =
        [self layoutAttributesForItemAtIndexPath:itemIndexPath];
    attributes.alpha = 0.0;
    attributes.center = centerPoint;
    attributes.transform3D = CATransform3DMakeScale(0.1, 0.1, 1.0);
    return attributes;
}


// Handle insertion animation for all items
- (UICollectionViewLayoutAttributes*)
    initialLayoutAttributesForAppearingItemAtIndexPath:
        (NSIndexPath*)indexPath
{
    return [insertedIndexPaths containsObject:indexPath] ?
        [self insertionAttributesForItemAtIndexPath:indexPath] :
        [super initialLayoutAttributesForAppearingItemAtIndexPath:
            indexPath];
}


// Handle deletion animation for all items
- (UICollectionViewLayoutAttributes*)
```

```
finalLayoutAttributesForDisappearingItemAtIndexPath:
    (NSIndexPath*)indexPath
{
    return [deletedIndexPaths containsObject:indexPath] ?
        [self deletionAttributesForItemAtIndexPath:indexPath] :
        [super finalLayoutAttributesForDisappearingItemAtIndexPath:
            indexPath];
}
@end
```

Get This Recipe's Code

To find this recipe's full sample project, point your browser to https://github.com/erica/iOS-7-Cookbook and go to the folder for Chapter 10.

Recipe: Adding Gestures to Layout

Recipe 10-7 builds on Recipe 10-6, adding interactive gestures that adjust presentation layout. It uses two recognizers, a pinch recognizer and a rotation recognizer, to enable users to scale and rotate the circle of views. These items are set up to recognize simultaneously, so users can pinch and rotate at the same time.

The rotate recognizer uses a slightly more sophisticated approach than the pinch one. Unlike pinch values, rotations are relative. You rotate *by* an amount, not *to* a specific angle. To accommodate this, Recipe 10-7 implements callbacks to handle two states. The first is called as rotations happen, updating the presentation to match each movement. The second resets the rotation baseline as the gesture ends, so the next interaction will take up where the last one left off:

```
- (void)pinch:(UIPinchGestureRecognizer *)pinchRecognizer
{
    CircleLayout *layout =
        (CircleLayout *)self.collectionView.collectionViewLayout;
    [layout scaleTo:pinchRecognizer.scale];
    [layout invalidateLayout];
}


- (void)rotate:(UIRotationGestureRecognizer *)rotationRecognizer
{
    CircleLayout *layout =
        (CircleLayout *)self.collectionView.collectionViewLayout;

    if (rotationRecognizer.state == UIGestureRecognizerStateEnded)
        [layout rotateTo:rotationRecognizer.rotation];
    else
```

```
        [layout rotateBy:rotationRecognizer.rotation];
    [layout invalidateLayout];
}
```

Notice how these callbacks invalidate the layout so that the presentation is updated in real time. This recipe is best tested on-device due to the high graphical load.

Recipe 10-7 calculates the effect of user gestures on the layout by adjusting the view radius (it scales from a minimum of 0.5 to a maximum of 1.3 times the original layout) and the layout's start angle, which is initially at 0 degrees but is adjusted each time the rotation updates. The scaled radius and the adjusted angle value form the basis for the new presentation.

Recipe 10-7   **Adding Gestures to Collection View Layouts**
_____

```
// Intermediate rotation
- (void)rotateBy:(CGFloat)theta
{
    currentRotation = theta;
}


// Final rotation
- (void)rotateTo:(CGFloat)theta
{
    rotation += theta;
    currentRotation = 0.0f;
}


// Scaling
- (void)scaleTo:(CGFloat)factor
{
    scale = factor;
}


// Calculate position for each item
- (UICollectionViewLayoutAttributes *)
    layoutAttributesForItemAtIndexPath:(NSIndexPath *)path
{
    UICollectionViewLayoutAttributes *attributes =
        [UICollectionViewLayoutAttributes
            layoutAttributesForCellWithIndexPath:path];
    CGFloat progress = (float) path.item / (float) numberOfItems;
    CGFloat theta = 2.0f * M_PI * progress;

    // Update the scaling and rotation to match the current gesture
    CGFloat scaledRadius = MIN(MAX(scale, 0.5f), 1.3f) * radius;
    CGFloat rotatedTheta = theta + rotation + currentRotation;
```

```
    // Calculate the new positions
    CGFloat xPosition =
        centerPoint.x + scaledRadius * cos(rotatedTheta);
    CGFloat yPosition =
        centerPoint.y + scaledRadius * sin(rotatedTheta);
    attributes.size = [self itemSize];
    attributes.center = CGPointMake(xPosition, yPosition);
    return attributes;
}
@end
```

> **Get This Recipe's Code**
>
> To find this recipe's full sample project, point your browser to https://github.com/erica/
> iOS-7-Cookbook and go to the folder for Chapter 10.

Recipe: Creating a True Grid Layout

The default flow layout wraps its rows to fit into a scrolling view that moves in just one direction. If you're willing to do the math—there's quite a bit of it, and it's not easy—you can create a custom layout subclass that shows a grid of items that scrolls in *both* directions and doesn't wrap its lines. Figure 10-9 shows such a layout.

Recipe 10-8 fully customizes its layout subclass, overriding `collectionViewContentSize` and `layoutAttributesForItemAtIndexPath:` to manually place each item. This implementation fully respects all spacing requests and delegate callbacks. In contrast, the normal flow layout attempts to fit items in while meeting various minimum values. This layout uses those values exactly but adjusts the underlying scrolling view's content size to precisely match sizing needs.

Recipe 10-8 works by exhaustively calculating each layout element. What it doesn't use, however, is the line-spacing property that describes how to wrap rows. This grid presentation never wraps any rows, so the recipe ignores that entirely.

This recipe also adds a new custom layout property, `alignment`. This property controls whether each grid row aligns at the top, center, or bottom. It accomplishes this by looking at the overall height for an entire row and then optionally offsetting items that are smaller than that height.

Recipe 10-8 includes the entire layout code to give you a sense of how much effort is involved for a complete custom subclass. The trick is, of course, in the details. Test layouts as thoroughly as possible over a wide range of source objects.

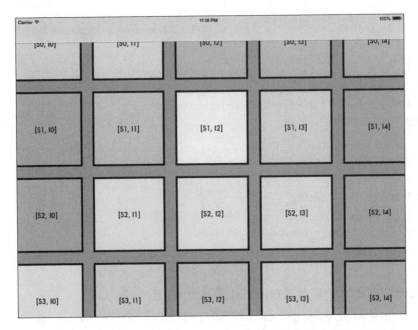

Figure 10-9   This custom layout grid enables users to scroll in both directions.

Recipe 10-8   **Grid Layout Customization**

```
@implementation GridLayout

#pragma mark Items
// Does a delegate provide individual sizing?
- (BOOL)usesIndividualItemSizing
{
    return [self.collectionView.delegate respondsToSelector:
        @selector(collectionView:layout:sizeForItemAtIndexPath:)];
}

// Return cell size for an item
- (CGSize)sizeForItemAtIndexPath:(NSIndexPath *)indexPath
{
    CGSize itemSize = self.itemSize;
    if ([self usesIndividualItemSizing])
        itemSize = [(id <UICollectionViewDelegateFlowLayout>)
            self.collectionView.delegate
                collectionView:self.collectionView
                layout:self sizeForItemAtIndexPath:indexPath];
    return itemSize;
}
```

```
#pragma mark Insets
// Individual insets?
- (BOOL)usesIndividualInsets
{
    return [self.collectionView.delegate respondsToSelector:
        @selector(collectionView:layout:insetForSectionAtIndex:)];
}


// Return insets for section
- (UIEdgeInsets)insetsForSection:(NSInteger)section
{
    UIEdgeInsets insets = self.sectionInset;
    if ([self usesIndividualInsets])
        insets = [(id <UICollectionViewDelegateFlowLayout>)
            self.collectionView.delegate
                collectionView:self.collectionView
                layout:self insetForSectionAtIndex:section];
    return insets;
}


#pragma mark Item Spacing
// Individual item spacing?
- (BOOL)usesIndividualItemSpacing
{
    return [self.collectionView.delegate respondsToSelector:
        @selector(collectionView:layout:
            minimumInteritemSpacingForSectionAtIndex:)];
}


// Return spacing for section
- (CGFloat)itemSpacingForSection:(NSInteger)section
{
    CGFloat spacing = self.minimumInteritemSpacing;
    if ([self usesIndividualItemSpacing])
        spacing = [(id <UICollectionViewDelegateFlowLayout>)
            self.collectionView.delegate
                collectionView:self.collectionView
                layout:self
                minimumInteritemSpacingForSectionAtIndex:section];
    return spacing;
}


#pragma mark Layout Geometry
// Find the tallest subview
- (CGFloat)maxItemHeightForSection:(NSInteger)section
{
    CGFloat maxHeight = 0.0f;
    NSInteger numberOfItems =
```

```
            [self.collectionView numberOfItemsInSection:section];
    for (int i = 0; i < numberOfItems; i++)
    {
        NSIndexPath *indexPath = INDEXPATH(section, i);
        CGSize itemSize = [self sizeForItemAtIndexPath:indexPath];
        maxHeight = MAX(maxHeight, itemSize.height);
    }
    return maxHeight;
}


// "Horizontal" row-based extent from the start of the section to its end
- (CGFloat)fullWidthForSection:(NSInteger)section
{
    UIEdgeInsets insets = [self insetsForSection:section];
    CGFloat horizontalInsetExtent = insets.left + insets.right;
    CGFloat collectiveWidth = horizontalInsetExtent;

    NSInteger numberOfItems =
        [self.collectionView numberOfItemsInSection:section];
    for (int i = 0; i < numberOfItems; i++)
    {
        NSIndexPath *indexPath = INDEXPATH(section, i);
        CGSize itemSize = [self sizeForItemAtIndexPath:indexPath];

        collectiveWidth += itemSize.width;
        collectiveWidth += [self itemSpacingForSection:section];
    }

    // Take back one spacer, n-1 fence post
    collectiveWidth -= [self itemSpacingForSection:section];

    return collectiveWidth;
}


// Bounding size for each section
- (CGSize)fullSizeForSection:(NSInteger)section
{
    CGFloat headerExtent = (self.scrollDirection ==
        UICollectionViewScrollDirectionHorizontal) ?
        self.headerReferenceSize.width :
        self.headerReferenceSize.height;
    CGFloat footerExtent = (self.scrollDirection ==
        UICollectionViewScrollDirectionHorizontal) ?
        self.footerReferenceSize.width :
        self.footerReferenceSize.height;

    UIEdgeInsets insets = [self insetsForSection:section];
    CGFloat verticalInsetExtent = insets.top + insets.bottom;
```

```objc
    CGFloat maxHeight = [self maxItemHeightForSection:section];

    CGFloat fullHeight = headerExtent + footerExtent +
        verticalInsetExtent + maxHeight;
    CGFloat fullWidth = [self fullWidthForSection:section];

    return CGSizeMake(fullWidth, fullHeight);
}


// How far is each item offset within the section
- (CGFloat)horizontalInsetForItemAtIndexPath:(NSIndexPath *)indexPath
{
    UIEdgeInsets insets = [self insetsForSection:indexPath.section];
    CGFloat horizontalOffset = insets.left;
    for (int i = 0; i < indexPath.item; i++)
    {
        CGSize itemSize = [self sizeForItemAtIndexPath:
            INDEXPATH(indexPath.section, i)];
        horizontalOffset += (itemSize.width +
            [self itemSpacingForSection:indexPath.section]);
    }
    return horizontalOffset;
}


// How far is each item down
- (CGFloat)verticalInsetForItemAtIndexPath:(NSIndexPath *)indexPath
{
    CGSize thisItemSize = [self sizeForItemAtIndexPath:indexPath];
    CGFloat verticalOffset = 0.0f;

    // Previous sections
    for (int i = 0; i < indexPath.section; i++)
        verticalOffset += [self fullSizeForSection:i].height;

    // Header
    CGFloat headerExtent = (self.scrollDirection ==
        UICollectionViewScrollDirectionHorizontal) ?
        self.headerReferenceSize.width :
            self.headerReferenceSize.height;
    verticalOffset += headerExtent;

    // Top inset
    UIEdgeInsets insets = [self insetsForSection:indexPath.section];
    verticalOffset += insets.top;

    // Vertical centering
    CGFloat maxHeight =
        [self maxItemHeightForSection:indexPath.section];
```

```
        CGFloat fullHeight = (maxHeight - thisItemSize.height);
        CGFloat midHeight = fullHeight / 2.0f;

        switch (self.alignment)
        {
            case GridRowAlignmentNone:
            case GridRowAlignmentTop:
                break;
            case GridRowAlignmentCenter:
                verticalOffset += midHeight;
                break;
            case GridRowAlignmentBottom:
                verticalOffset += fullHeight;
                break;
            default:
                break;
        }

        return verticalOffset;
}

#pragma mark Layout Attributes
// Provide per-item placement
- (UICollectionViewLayoutAttributes *)layoutAttributesForItemAtIndexPath:
    (NSIndexPath *)indexPath
{
    UICollectionViewLayoutAttributes *attributes =
        [UICollectionViewLayoutAttributes
            layoutAttributesForCellWithIndexPath:indexPath];
    CGSize thisItemSize = [self sizeForItemAtIndexPath:indexPath];

    CGFloat verticalOffset =
        [self verticalInsetForItemAtIndexPath:indexPath];
    CGFloat horizontalOffset =
        [self horizontalInsetForItemAtIndexPath:indexPath];

    if (self.scrollDirection == UICollectionViewScrollDirectionVertical)
        attributes.frame = CGRectMake(horizontalOffset,
            verticalOffset, thisItemSize.width, thisItemSize.height);
    else
        attributes.frame = CGRectMake(verticalOffset,
            horizontalOffset, thisItemSize.width,
            thisItemSize.height);

    return attributes;
}
```

```objc
// Return full extent
- (CGSize)collectionViewContentSize
{
    NSInteger sections = self.collectionView.numberOfSections;

    CGFloat maxWidth = 0.0f;
    CGFloat collectiveHeight = 0.0f;

    for (int i = 0; i < sections; i++)
    {
        CGSize sectionSize = [self fullSizeForSection:i];
        collectiveHeight += sectionSize.height;
        maxWidth = MAX(maxWidth, sectionSize.width);
    }

    if (self.scrollDirection ==
            UICollectionViewScrollDirectionVertical)
        return CGSizeMake(maxWidth, collectiveHeight);
    else
        return CGSizeMake(collectiveHeight, maxWidth);
}

// Provide grid layout attributes
- (NSArray *)layoutAttributesForElementsInRect:(CGRect)rect
{
    NSMutableArray *attributes = [NSMutableArray array];
    for (NSInteger section = 0;
        section < self.collectionView.numberOfSections; section++)
        for (NSInteger item = 0;
            item < [self.collectionView
                numberOfItemsInSection:section];
            item++)
        {
            UICollectionViewLayoutAttributes *layout =
                [self layoutAttributesForItemAtIndexPath:
                    INDEXPATH(section, item)];
            [attributes addObject:layout];
        }
    return attributes;
}

- (BOOL) shouldInvalidateLayoutForBoundsChange:(CGRect)oldBounds
{
    return YES;
}
@end
```

> **Get This Recipe's Code**
>
> To find this recipe's full sample project, point your browser to https://github.com/erica/
> iOS-7-Cookbook and go to the folder for Chapter 10.

Recipe: Custom Item Menus

Collection views support menus like the one shown in Figure 10-10, using a standard tap-and-hold gesture. The menu provides cut, copy, and paste actions by default. These default actions can be filtered out and custom actions added to build a menu like the one shown.

Menu support is provided through three delegate methods on `UICollectionView`:

- `collectionView:shouldShowMenuForItemAtIndexPath:`—Determines whether an item at the specified index path should show a menu.

- `collectionView:canPerformAction:forItemAtIndexPath:withSender:`—Confirms that the delegate can perform the specified action on the item at the index path. This delegate method can be used to filter out unwanted default actions: cut, copy, and paste.

- `collectionView:performAction:forItemAtIndexPath:withSender:`—Tells the delegate to perform the specified action on the item at the index path.

In addition to returning YES for the first two items and handling the action delegate method, your collection view must be able to become a first responder:

```
- (BOOL)canBecomeFirstResponder
{
    return YES;
}
```

Once you carefully meet all these requirements, a menu appears when the user taps and holds on a collection view item.

Double-Tap Alternative

Instead of implementing the long-tap gesture menu provided by `UICollectionView`, Recipe 10-9 creates a custom cell class and adds a double-tap gesture recognizer. When activated, the callback sets the cell as the first responder and presents a standard menu.

Recipe 10-9 shows the relevant details. The cell subclass declares that it can become the first responder, a necessary precondition for presenting menus. It sets the menu items it wants to work with and then adds the `canPerformAction:withSender:` support that confirms each item's appearance. Figure 10-10 displays the menu created by this code.

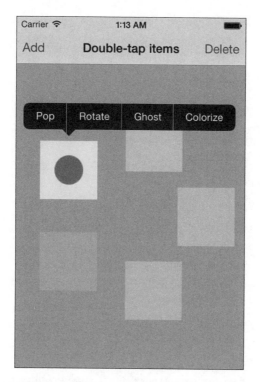

Figure 10-10   These custom item-by-item menus require cells to become the first responder.

Recipe 10-9   **Custom Collection View Cell Menus**

```
- (BOOL) canBecomeFirstResponder
{
    return YES;
}

- (BOOL) canPerformAction: (SEL) action withSender: (id) sender
{
    if (action == @selector(ghostSelf)) return YES;
    if (action == @selector(popSelf)) return YES;
    if (action == @selector(rotateSelf)) return YES;
    if (action == @selector(colorize)) return YES;
    return NO;
}

- (void) tapped: (UIGestureRecognizer *) uigr
{
```

```
    if (uigr.state != UIGestureRecognizerStateRecognized) return;

    [[UIMenuController sharedMenuController] setMenuVisible:NO
        animated:YES];
    [self becomeFirstResponder];

    UIMenuController *menu = [UIMenuController sharedMenuController];
    UIMenuItem *pop = [[UIMenuItem alloc]
        initWithTitle:@"Pop" action:@selector(popSelf)];
    UIMenuItem *rotate = [[UIMenuItem alloc]
        initWithTitle:@"Rotate" action:@selector(rotateSelf)];
    UIMenuItem *ghost = [[UIMenuItem alloc]
        initWithTitle:@"Ghost" action:@selector(ghostSelf)];
    UIMenuItem *colorize = [[UIMenuItem alloc]
        initWithTitle:@"Colorize" action:@selector(colorize)];

    [menu setMenuItems:@[pop, rotate, ghost, colorize]];
    [menu update];
    [menu setTargetRect:self.bounds inView:self];
    [menu setMenuVisible:YES animated:YES];
}
```

Get This Recipe's Code

To find this recipe's full sample project, point your browser to https://github.com/erica/iOS-7-Cookbook and go to the folder for Chapter 10.

Summary

This chapter introduces collection views paired with the powerful flow layout. You've read how to create both basic collection view controllers and their standalone views. You've discovered how to set critical layout properties. You've learned about creating live effect feedback and insertion and deletion dynamic effects. Before moving on to the next chapter, here are a few points to consider about collection views:

- Collection views offer an amazing amount of power without requiring a lot of coding. Most things that are maddening and nearly impossible with table views are now possible with a much more powerful set of APIs.

- This chapter barely touches on header and footer views, and it doesn't use decoration views at all. See the sample code included with this chapter for more details on the fine points of creating custom supplementary view classes.

- Transform-based updates help bring life to your collection view layouts. Don't be afraid to let your interfaces animate to respond to user interactions. At the same time, avoid adding effects simply for the sake of adding effects. A little animation goes a long way.

- Speaking of animations, the same inserted and deleted attribute methods this chapter uses for items are available for supplementary elements. This feature lets you animate the arrival and departure of new sections in your collection.

- On a similar note, integrate gestures meaningfully. If a user isn't likely to discover your long-press or triple-tap add or delete request, skip it. Instead, use pop-ups, menus, floating overlays, or simple buttons to communicate how items can be managed and changed.

- When exploring layout, don't depend on the flow layout documentation. Look instead through the `UICollectionViewLayout` abstract parent class. It details all the core methods you override.

- Finally, always test on devices. The performance of layouts, especially ones that update frequently or use transforms, cannot be represented accurately on the simulator. Device testing, along with Instruments, will better reflect whether you're actually asking too much from your presentation.

11

Documents and Data Sharing

Under iOS, applications can share information and data as well as move control from one application to another, using a variety of system features. Each application has access to a common system pasteboard that enables copying and pasting across apps. The apps can request a number of system-supplied "actions" to apply to a document, such as printing, tweeting, or posting to Facebook. Apps can declare custom URL schemes that can be embedded in text and web pages. This chapter introduces the ways you can integrate documents and data sharing between applications. You'll see how to add these features to your applications and use them smartly to make your app a cooperative citizen of the iOS ecosystem.

Recipe: Working with Uniform Type Identifiers

Uniform Type Identifiers (UTIs) represent a central component of iOS information sharing. You can think of them as the next generation of MIME types. UTIs are strings that identify resource types such as images and text. UTIs specify what kind of information is being used for common data objects. They do this without relying on older indicators, such as file extensions, MIME types, or file-type metadata such as `OSTypes`. UTIs replace these items with a newer and more flexible technology.

UTIs use a reverse-domain-style naming convention. Common Apple-derived identifiers look like this: `public.html` and `public.jpeg`. These refer, respectively, to HTML source text and JPEG images, which are both specialized types of information.

Inheritance plays an important role with UTIs. UTIs use an OO-like system of inheritance, where child UTIs have an "is-a" relationship to parents. Children inherit all attributes of their parents but add further specificity of the kind of data they represent. That's because each UTI can assume a more general or more specific role, as needed. Take the JPEG UTI, for example. A JPEG image (`public.jpeg`) is an image (`public.image`), which is in turn a kind of data (`public.data`), which is a kind of user-viewable (or listenable) content (`public.content`), which is a kind of item (`public.item`), the generic base type for UTIs. This hierarchy is called *conformance*, where child UTIs conform to parent UTIs. For example, the more specific `jpeg` UTI conforms to the more general `image` or `data` UTI.

Figure 11-1 shows part of Apple's basic conformance tree. Any item lower down on the tree must conform to all of its parent data attributes. Declaring a parent UTI implies that you support all of its children. So, an application that can open `public.data` must service text, movies, image files, and more.

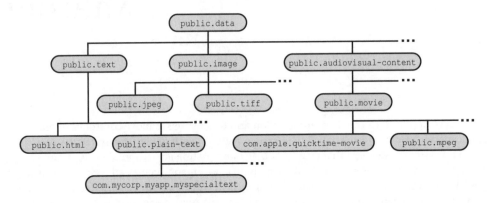

Figure 11-1   Apple's public UTI conformance tree.

UTIs enable multiple inheritance. An item can conform to more than one UTI parent. So, you might imagine a data type that offers both text and image containers, which declares conformance to both.

There is no central registry for UTI items, although each UTI should adhere to conventions. The `public` domain is reserved for iOS-specific types, common to most applications. Apple has generated a complete family hierarchy of public items. Add any third-party company-specific names by using standard reverse domain naming (for example, `com.sadun.myCustomType` and `com.apple.quicktime-movie`).

Determining UTIs from File Extensions

The Mobile Core Services module offers utilities that enable you to retrieve UTI information based on file extensions. Be sure to import the module when using these C-based functions. The following function returns a preferred UTI when passed a path extension string. The preferred identifier is a single UTI string:

```
@import MobileCoreServices;

NSString *preferredUTIForExtension(NSString *ext)
{
    // Request the UTI for the file extension
```

```
    NSString *theUTI = (__bridge_transfer NSString *)
        UTTypeCreatePreferredIdentifierForTag(
            kUTTagClassFilenameExtension,
            (__bridge CFStringRef) ext, NULL);
    return theUTI;
}
```

You can pass a MIME type instead of a file extension to UTTypeCreatePreferredIdentifier-
ForTag() by using kUTTagClassMIMEType as the first argument. This function returns a
preferred UTI for a given MIME type:

```
NSString *preferredUTIForMIMEType(NSString *mime)
{
    // Request the UTI for the MIME type
    NSString *theUTI = (__bridge_transfer NSString *)
        UTTypeCreatePreferredIdentifierForTag(
            kUTTagClassMIMEType,
            (__bridge CFStringRef) mime, NULL);
    return theUTI;
}
```

Together these functions enable you to move from file extensions and MIME types to the UTI
types used for modern file access.

Moving from UTI to Extension or MIME Type

To go the other way, producing a preferred extension or MIME types from a UTI, use
UTTypeCopyPreferredTagWithClass(). The following functions return jpeg and image/
jpeg, respectively, when passed public.jpeg:

```
NSString *extensionForUTI(NSString *aUTI)
{
    CFStringRef theUTI = (__bridge CFStringRef) aUTI;
    CFStringRef results =
        UTTypeCopyPreferredTagWithClass(
            theUTI, kUTTagClassFilenameExtension);
    return (__bridge_transfer NSString *)results;
}
```

```
NSString *mimeTypeForUTI(NSString *aUTI)
{
    CFStringRef theUTI = (__bridge CFStringRef) aUTI;
    CFStringRef results =
        UTTypeCopyPreferredTagWithClass(
            theUTI, kUTTagClassMIMEType);
    return (__bridge_transfer NSString *)results;
}
```

You must work at the leaf level with these functions—at the level that declares the type extensions directly. You cannot reference the parent types. Extensions are declared in property lists, where features like file extensions and default icons are described. So, for example, passing `public.text` or `public.movie` to the extension function returns nil, whereas `public.plain-text` and `public.mpeg` return extensions of `txt` and `mpg`, respectively.

The former items live too high up the conformance tree, providing an abstract type rather than a specific implementation. There's no current API function to look down to find items that descend from a given class that are currently defined for the application. You may want to file an enhancement request at bugreport.apple.com. Surely, all the extensions and MIME types are registered somewhere (otherwise, how would the `UTTypeCopyPreferredTagWithClass()` lookup work in the first place?), so the ability to map extensions to more general UTIs should be possible.

MIME Helper

Although the extension-to-UTI service is exhaustive, returning UTIs for nearly any extension you throw at it, the UTI-to-MIME results are scattershot. You can usually generate a proper MIME representation for any common item; less common ones are rare.

The following lines show an assortment of extensions, their UTIs (retrieved via `preferredUTIForExtension()`), and the MIME types generated from each UTI (via `mimeTypeForUTI()`):

```
xlv: dyn.age81u5d0 / (null)
xlw: com.microsoft.excel.xlw / application/vnd.ms-excel
xm: dyn.age81u5k / (null)
xml: public.xml / application/xml
z: public.z-archive / application/x-compress
zip: public.zip-archive / application/zip
zoo: dyn.age81y55t / (null)
zsh: public.zsh-script / (null)
```

As you can see, there are quite a number of blanks. These functions return `nil` when they cannot find a match. To address this problem, the sample code for this recipe includes an extra `MIMEHelper` class. It defines one function, which returns a MIME type for a supplied extension:

```
NSString *mimeForExtension(NSString *extension);
```

Its extensions and MIME types are sourced from the Apache Software Foundation, which has placed its list in the public domain. Out of the 450 extensions in the sample code for this recipe, iOS returned all 450 UTIs but only 89 MIME types. The Apache list ups this number to 230 recognizable MIME types.

Testing Conformance

You test conformance using the `UTTypeConformsTo()` function. This function takes two arguments: a source UTI and a UTI to compare to. It returns `true` if the first UTI conforms to the second. Use this to test whether a more specific item conforms to a more general one. Test equality using UTTypeEqual(). Here's an example of how you might use conformance testing to determine whether a file path likely points to an image resource:

```
BOOL pathPointsToLikelyUTIMatch(NSString *path, CFStringRef theUTI)
{
    NSString *extension = [path pathExtension];
    NSString *preferredUTI = preferredUTIForExtension(extension);
    return (UTTypeConformsTo(
        (__bridge CFStringRef) preferredUTI, theUTI));
}


BOOL pathPointsToLikelyImage(NSString *path)
{
    return pathPointsToLikelyUTIMatch(path, CFSTR("public.image"));
}


BOOL pathPointsToLikelyAudio(NSString *path)
{
    return pathPointsToLikelyUTIMatch(path, CFSTR("public.audio"));
}
```

Retrieving Conformance Lists

UTTypeCopyDeclaration() offers the most general (and most useful) of all UTI functions in the iOS API. It returns a dictionary that includes the following keys:

- **kUTTypeIdentifierKey**—The UTI name, which you passed to the function (for example, public.mpeg)

- **kUTTypeConformsToKey**—Any parents that the type conforms to (for example, public.mpeg conforms to public.movie)

- **kUTTypeDescriptionKey**—A real-world description of the type in question, if one exists (for example, "MPEG movie")

- **kUTTypeTagSpecificationKey**—A dictionary of equivalent OSTypes (for example, MPG and MPEG), file extensions (mpg, mpeg, mpe, m75, and m15), and MIME types (video/mpeg, video/mpg, video/x-mpeg, and video/x-mpg) for the given UTI

In addition to these common items, you encounter more keys that specify imported and exported UTI declarations (kUTImportedTypeDeclarationsKey and kUTExportedType-DeclarationsKey), icon resources to associate with the UTI (kUTTypeIconFileKey), a URL that points to a page describing the type (kUTTypeReferenceURLKey), and a version key that offers a version string for the UTI (kUTTypeVersionKey).

Use the returned dictionary to ascend through the conformance tree to build an array that represents all the items that a given UTI conforms to. For example, the public.mpeg type conforms to public.movie, public.audiovisual-content, public.data, public.item, and `public.content`. These items are returned as an array from the `conformanceArray` function in Recipe 11-1.

Recipe 11-1 **Testing Conformance**

```
// Build a declaration dictionary for the given type
NSDictionary *utiDictionary(NSString *aUTI)
{
    NSDictionary *dictionary =
        (__bridge_transfer NSDictionary *)
            UTTypeCopyDeclaration((__bridge CFStringRef) aUTI);
    return dictionary;
}


// Return an array where each member is guaranteed unique
// but that preserves the original ordering wherever possible
NSArray *uniqueArray(NSArray *anArray)
{
    NSMutableArray *copiedArray =
        [NSMutableArray arrayWithArray:anArray];

    for (id object in anArray)
    {
        [copiedArray removeObjectIdenticalTo:object];
        [copiedArray addObject:object];
    }

    return copiedArray;
}


// Return an array representing all UTIs that a given UTI conforms to
NSArray *conformanceArray(NSString *aUTI)
{
    NSMutableArray *results =
        [NSMutableArray arrayWithObject:aUTI];
    NSDictionary *dictionary = utiDictionary(aUTI);
    id conforms = [dictionary objectForKey:
        (__bridge NSString *)kUTTypeConformsToKey];

    // No conformance
    if (!conforms) return results;

    // Single conformance
    if ([conforms isKindOfClass:[NSString class]])
    {
        [results addObjectsFromArray:conformanceArray(conforms)];
        return uniqueArray(results);
```

```
    }

    // Iterate through multiple conformance
    if ([conforms isKindOfClass:[NSArray class]])
    {
        for (NSString *eachUTI in (NSArray *) conforms)
            [results addObjectsFromArray:conformanceArray(eachUTI)];
        return uniqueArray(results);
    }

    // Just return the one-item array
    return results;
}
```

Get This Recipe's Code

To find this recipe's full sample project, point your browser to https://github.com/erica/ iOS-7-Cookbook and go to the folder for Chapter 11.

Recipe: Accessing the System Pasteboard

Pasteboards, also known as clipboards on some systems, provide a central OS feature for sharing data across applications. Users can copy data to the pasteboard in one application, switch tasks, and then paste that data into another application. Cut/copy/paste features are similar to those found in most other operating systems. Users can also copy and paste within a single application, when switching between text fields or views, and developers can establish private pasteboards for app-specific data that other apps would not understand.

The `UIPasteboard` class offers access to a shared device pasteboard and its contents. This snippet returns the general system pasteboard, which is appropriate for most general copy/paste use:

```
UIPasteboard *pb = [UIPasteboard generalPasteboard];
```

The system-provided general pasteboard and the find pasteboards are shared across all applications on the device. In addition to the shared system pasteboards, iOS offers both application-specific and custom-named pasteboards that can be used across applications from the same organization with a common team ID in the application portal. Create app-specific pasteboards using `pasteboardWithUniqueName`, which returns an application pasteboard object that persists until the application quits.

Create shared pasteboards using `pasteboardWithName:create:`, which returns a pasteboard with the specified name. The `create` parameter specifies whether the system should create the pasteboard if it does not yet exist. This kind of pasteboard can persist beyond a single application run; set the persistent property to `YES` after creation. Use `removePasteboardWithName:` to destroy a pasteboard and free up the resources it uses.

> **Note**
>
> Prior to iOS 7, custom-named pasteboards could be shared across all applications aware of the pasteboard name, not just applications from the same organization and application group. This has changed in iOS 7, as described in the iOS 7 Release Notes. This change breaks numerous existing applications that relied on publicly sharable custom pasteboards. You now need new methods for sharing between apps. Consider using `openURL` (see Recipe 11-8) or external shared storage.

Storing Data

A pasteboard can store one or more items at a time. Each pasteboard item is represented as a dictionary containing one or more key-value pairs that store the data and the associated type. A single pasteboard item might contain multiple entries to make it more likely that other apps can find a compatible data type. A UTI is commonly used to specify what kind of data is stored. For example, you might find `public.text` (and, more specifically, `public.utf8-plain-text`) to store text data, `public.url` for URL address, and `public.jpeg` for image data. These are among the many common data types used on iOS.

`UIPasteboard` provides methods to work with a single pasteboard item or multiple pasteboard items at a time, including investigating the data types of items as well as getting and setting pasteboard data. Many of the single pasteboard item methods work specifically on the first item in the pasteboard. You can retrieve an array of all available items via the pasteboard's `items` property.

You can set the data and associate a type for the first item in the pasteboard by passing an `NSData` object and a UTI that describes a type the data conforms to:

```
[[UIPasteboard generalPasteboard]
    setData:theData forPasteboardType:theUTI];
```

Alternatively, for property list objects (that is, string, date, array, dictionary, number, or URL), set an `NSValue` via `setValue:forPasteboardType:`. These property list objects are stored internally somewhat differently than their raw-data cousins, giving rise to the method differentiation.

Storing Common Types

Pasteboards are further specialized for several data types, which represent the most commonly used pasteboard items. These are colors (not a property list "value" object), images (also not a property list "value" object), strings, and URLs. The `UIPasteboard` class provides specialized getters and setters to make it easier to handle these items. You can treat each of these as properties of the pasteboard, so you can set and retrieve them using dot notation. What's more, each property has a plural form, allowing you to access those items as arrays of objects.

Pasteboard properties greatly simplify using the system pasteboard for the most common use cases. The property accessors include the following:

- **string**—Sets or retrieves the string of the first pasteboard item
- **strings**—Sets or retrieves an array of all strings on the pasteboard
- **image**—Sets or retrieves the image of the first pasteboard item
- **images**—Sets or retrieves an array of all images on the pasteboard
- **URL**—Sets or retrieves the URL of the first pasteboard item
- **URLs**—Sets or retrieves an array of all URLs on the pasteboard
- **color**—Sets or retrieves the first color on the pasteboard
- **colors**—Sets or retrieves an array of all colors on the pasteboard

Retrieving Data

When using one of the four special classes listed previously, simply use the associated property to retrieve data from the pasteboard. Otherwise, you can fetch data using the `dataForPasteboardType:` method. This method returns the data from the first item in the pasteboard. Any other items in the pasteboard are ignored.

If you need to retrieve all matching data, recover an `itemSetWithPasteboardTypes:` and then iterate through the set to retrieve each dictionary. Recover the data type for each item from the single dictionary key and the data from its value.

Modified pasteboards issue a `UIPasteboardChangedNotification`, which you can listen to via a default `NSNotificationCenter` observer. You can also watch custom pasteboards and listen for their removal via `UIPasteboardRemovedNotification`.

> **Note**
>
> If you want to successfully paste text data to Notes or Mail, use `public.utf8-plain-text` as your UTI of choice when storing information to the pasteboard. Using the `string` or `strings` properties automatically enforces this UTI.

Passively Updating the Pasteboard

iOS's selection and copy interfaces are not, frankly, the most streamlined elements of the operating system. There are times when you want to simplify matters for your user while preparing content that's meant to be shared with other applications.

Consider Recipe 11-2. It enables the user to use a text view to enter and edit text, while automating the process of updating the pasteboard. When the watcher is active (toggled by a simple button tap), the text updates the pasteboard on each edit. This is accomplished by implementing a text view delegate method (`textViewDidChange:`) that responds to edits by automatically assigning changes to the pasteboard (`updatePasteboard`).

This recipe demonstrates the relative simplicity involved in accessing and updating the pasteboard.

Recipe 11-2   **Automatically Copying Text to the Pasteboard**

```
- (void)updatePasteboard
{
    // Copy the text to the pasteboard when the watcher is enabled
    if (enableWatcher)
        [UIPasteboard generalPasteboard].string = textView.text;
}

- (void)textViewDidChange:(UITextView *)textView
{
    // Delegate method calls for an update
    [self updatePasteboard];
}

- (void)toggle:(UIBarButtonItem *)bbi
{
    // switch between standard and auto-copy modes
    enableWatcher = !enableWatcher;
    bbi.title = enableWatcher ? @"Stop Watching" : @"Watch";
}
```

Get This Recipe's Code

To find this recipe's full sample project, point your browser to https://github.com/erica/iOS-7-Cookbook and go to the folder for Chapter 11.

Recipe: Monitoring the Documents Folder

iOS documents aren't trapped in their sandboxes. You can and should share them with your users. Offer users direct control over their documents and access to any material they may have created on-device. A simple `Info.plist` setting enables iTunes to display the contents of a user's Documents folder and enables those users to add and remove material on demand.

At some point in the future, you may use a simple `NSMetadataQuery` monitor to watch your Documents folder and report updates. At this writing, that metadata surveillance is not yet extended beyond iCloud for use with other folders. Code ported from OS X fails to work as expected on iOS. At this writing, there are precisely two available search domains for iOS: the ubiquitous data scope and the ubiquitous documents scope (that is, iCloud and iCloud). Until general functionality arrives in iOS, use kqueue. This older technology provides scalable event notification. With kqueue, you can monitor, add, and clear events. This roughly equates to looking for files being added and deleted, which are the primary kinds of updates you want to react to. Recipe 11-3 presents a kqueue implementation for watching the Documents folder.

Enabling Document File Sharing

To enable file sharing, add an Application Supports iTunes File Sharing key to the application's Info.plist and set its value to YES. You can edit the plist directly or use the Xcode-provided editor. The editor is accessible in the Custom iOS Target Properties of the application target in the Project > Target > Info screen, as shown in Figure 11-2. When working with raw keys and values, this item is called UIFileSharingEnabled. iTunes lists all applications that declare file-sharing support in each device's Apps tab, as shown in Figure 11-3.

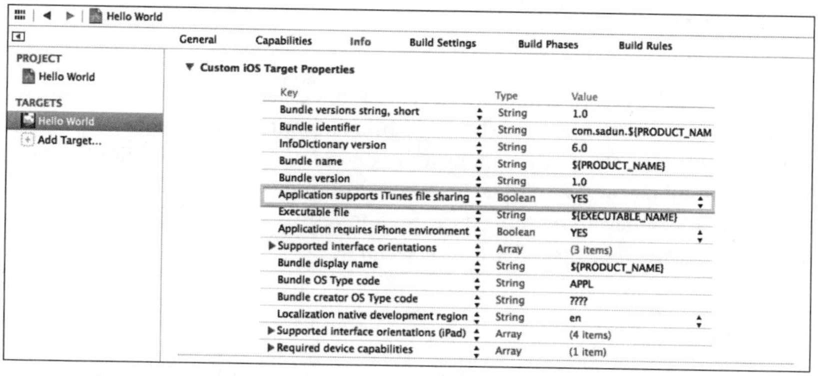

Figure 11-2   Enable Application Supports iTunes File Sharing to allow user access to the Documents folder via iTunes.

User Control

You cannot specify which kinds of items are allowed to be in the Documents folder. Users can add any materials they like, and they can remove any items they want to remove. What they cannot do, however, is navigate through subfolders using the iTunes interface. Notice the Inbox folder in Figure 11-3. This is an artifact left over from application-to-application document sharing, and it should not be there. Users cannot manage that data directly, and you should not leave the subfolder there to confuse them.

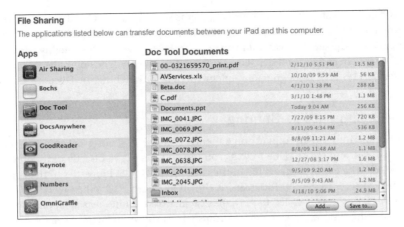

Figure 11-3   Each installed application that declares `UIFileSharingEnabled` is listed in iTunes in the device's Apps tab.

Users cannot delete the Inbox in iTunes the way they can delete other files and folders. Nor should your application write files directly to the Inbox. Respect the Inbox's role, which is to capture any incoming data from other applications. When you implement file-sharing support, always check for an Inbox on resuming active status and process that data to clear out the Inbox and remove it whenever your app launches and resumes. Best practices for handling incoming documents are discussed later in this chapter.

Xcode Access

As a developer, you have access not only to the Documents folder but also to the entire application sandbox. Use the Xcode Organizer (Command-Shift-2) > Devices tab > *Device* > Applications > *Application Name* to browse, upload, and download files to and from the sandbox.

Test basic file sharing by enabling the `UIFileSharingEnabled` property to an application and loading data to your Documents folder. After those files are created, use Xcode and iTunes to inspect, download, and delete them.

Scanning for New Documents

Recipe 11-3 works by requesting `kqueue` notifications in its `beginGeneratingDocument-NotificationsInPath:` method. Here, it retrieves a file descriptor for the path you supply (in this case, the Documents folder) and requests notifications for add and clear events. It adds this functionality to the current run loop, enabling notifications whenever the monitored folder updates.

Upon receiving that callback, it posts a notification (for example, the custom kDocument-Changed, in the kqueueFired method) and continues watching for new events. This all runs in the primary run loop on the main thread, so the GUI can respond and update itself upon receiving the notification.

The following snippet demonstrates how you might use Recipe 11-3's watcher to update a file list in your GUI. Whenever the contents change, an update notification allows the app to refresh those directory contents listings:

```
- (void)scanDocuments
{
    NSString *path = [NSHomeDirectory()
        stringByAppendingPathComponent:@"Documents"];
    items = [[NSFileManager defaultManager]
        contentsOfDirectoryAtPath:path error:nil];
    [self.tableView reloadData];
}


- (void)viewDidLoad
{
    [super viewDidLoad];
    [self.tableView registerClass:[UITableViewCell class]
        forCellReuseIdentifier:@"cell"];
    [self scanDocuments];

    // React to content changes
    [[NSNotificationCenter defaultCenter]
        addObserverForName:kDocumentChanged
        object:nil queue:[NSOperationQueue mainQueue]
        usingBlock:^(NSNotification *notification){
        [self scanDocuments];
      }];

    // Start the watcher
    NSString *path = [NSHomeDirectory()
        stringByAppendingPathComponent:@"Documents"];
    helper = [DocWatchHelper watcherForPath:path];
}
```

Test this recipe by connecting a device to iTunes. Add and remove items using the iTunes App tab interface. The device's onboard file list updates to reflect those changes in real time.

There are some cautions to be aware of when using Recipe 11-3. First, for larger documents, you shouldn't be reading the file immediately after you're notified of their creation. You might want to poll file sizes to determine when data has stopped being written. Second, iTunes File Sharing transfer can, upon occasion, stall. Code accordingly.

Recipe 11-3   **Using a** kqueue **File Monitor**

```objc
#import <fcntl.h>
#import <sys/event.h>

#define kDocumentChanged \
    @"DocumentsFolderContentsDidChangeNotification"

@interface DocWatchHelper : NSObject
@property (strong) NSString *path;
+ (id)watcherForPath:(NSString *)aPath;
@end

@implementation DocWatchHelper
{
    CFFileDescriptorRef kqref;
    CFRunLoopSourceRef  rls;
}

- (void)kqueueFired
{
    int             kq;
    struct kevent   event;
    struct timespec timeout = { 0, 0 };
    int             eventCount;

    kq = CFFileDescriptorGetNativeDescriptor(self->kqref);
    assert(kq >= 0);

    eventCount = kevent(kq, NULL, 0, &event, 1, &timeout);
    assert( (eventCount >= 0) && (eventCount < 2) );

    if (eventCount == 1)
        [[NSNotificationCenter defaultCenter]
            postNotificationName:kDocumentChanged
            object:self];

    CFFileDescriptorEnableCallBacks(self->kqref,
        kCFFileDescriptorReadCallBack);
}

static void KQCallback(CFFileDescriptorRef kqRef,
    CFOptionFlags callBackTypes, void *info)
{
    DocWatchHelper *helper =
        (DocWatchHelper *)(__bridge id)(CFTypeRef) info;
    [helper kqueueFired];
}
```

```objc
- (void)beginGeneratingDocumentNotificationsInPath:
    (NSString *)docPath
{
    int                     dirFD;
    int                     kq;
    int                     retVal;
    struct kevent           eventToAdd;
    CFFileDescriptorContext context =
        { 0, (void *)(__bridge CFTypeRef) self,
            NULL, NULL, NULL };

    dirFD = open([docPath fileSystemRepresentation], O_EVTONLY);
    assert(dirFD >= 0);

    kq = kqueue();
    assert(kq >= 0);

    eventToAdd.ident  = dirFD;
    eventToAdd.filter = EVFILT_VNODE;
    eventToAdd.flags  = EV_ADD | EV_CLEAR;
    eventToAdd.fflags = NOTE_WRITE;
    eventToAdd.data   = 0;
    eventToAdd.udata  = NULL;

    retVal = kevent(kq, &eventToAdd, 1, NULL, 0, NULL);
    assert(retVal == 0);

    self->kqref = CFFileDescriptorCreate(NULL, kq,
        true, KQCallback, &context);
    rls = CFFileDescriptorCreateRunLoopSource(
        NULL, self->kqref, 0);
    assert(rls != NULL);

    CFRunLoopAddSource(CFRunLoopGetCurrent(), rls,
        kCFRunLoopDefaultMode);
    CFRelease(rls);

    CFFileDescriptorEnableCallBacks(self->kqref,
        kCFFileDescriptorReadCallBack);
}

- (void)dealloc
{
    self.path = nil;
    CFRunLoopRemoveSource(CFRunLoopGetCurrent(), rls,
        kCFRunLoopDefaultMode);
    CFFileDescriptorDisableCallBacks(self->kqref,
```

```
        kCFFileDescriptorReadCallBack);
}

+ (id)watcherForPath:(NSString *)aPath
{
    DocWatchHelper *watcher = [[self alloc] init];
    watcher.path = aPath;
    [watcher beginGeneratingDocumentNotificationsInPath:aPath];
    return watcher;
}
@end
```

Get This Recipe's Code

To find this recipe's full sample project, point your browser to https://github.com/erica/
iOS-7-Cookbook and go to the folder for Chapter 11.

Recipe: Activity View Controller

Introduced in iOS 6, the activity view controller integrates data activities into the interface
shown in Figure 11-4. With minimal development cost on your part, this controller enables
your users to copy items to the pasteboard, post to social media, share via e-mail and texting,
and more. Built-in activities include Facebook, Twitter, Weibo, SMS, mail, printing, copying to
pasteboard, assigning data to a contact, and saving to the Camera Roll. iOS 7 adds a new set
of activities, including adding to the Reading List, Flickr, Vimeo, Weibo, and AirDrop. Apps
can define their own custom services as well, which you'll read about later in this section. The
comprehensive list of current activity types includes the following:

- UIActivityTypePostToFacebook

- UIActivityTypePostToTwitter

- UIActivityTypePostToWeibo

- UIActivityTypeMessage

- UIActivityTypeMail

- UIActivityTypePrint

- UIActivityTypeCopyToPasteboard

- UIActivityTypeAssignToContact

- UIActivityTypeSaveToCameraRoll

- UIActivityTypeAddToReadingList

- UIActivityTypePostToFlickr

- `UIActivityTypePostToVimeo`

- `UIActivityTypePostToTencentWeibo`

- `UIActivityTypeAirDrop`

Significantly missing from this list are two important activities: Open in... for sharing documents between applications and Quick Look for previewing files. These two features are discussed later in this chapter, with recipes that show you how to support these features independently and, in the case of Quick Look, integrated with the activity view controller.

Figure 11-4   The `UIActivityViewController` class offers system and custom services.

Presenting the Activity View Controller

How you present the controller varies by device. Show it modally on members of the iPhone family and in a popover on tablets. The `UIBarButtonSystemItemAction` icon provides the perfect way to populate bar buttons linking to this controller.

Best of all, almost no work is required on your end. After users select an activity, the controller handles all further interaction, such as presenting a mail or Twitter composition sheet, adding a picture to the onboard library, or assigning it to a contact.

Activity Item Sources

Recipe 11-4 creates and presents the activity view controller from code. This implementation has its main class adopt the `UIActivityItemSource` protocol and adds `self` to the `items` array passed to the controller:

```
UIActivityViewController *activity =
    [[UIActivityViewController alloc] initWithActivityItems:@[self]
        applicationActivities:nil];
[self presentViewController:activity];
```

The `UIActivityItemSource`—`self` in this case—represents the data that is being acted upon.

The protocol's two mandatory methods supply the item to process (the data that will be used for the activity) and a placeholder for that item. The item corresponds to an object that's appropriate for a given activity type. You can vary which item you return based on the kind of activity that's passed to the callback. For example, you might tweet "I created a great song in *App Name*," but you might send the actual sound file through e-mail.

The placeholder for an item is typically the same data returned as the item unless you have objects that you must process or create. In that case, you can create a placeholder object without real data.

Both callbacks run on the main thread, so keep your data small. If you need to process your data, consider using a provider described in the next section instead.

Optional methods introduced in iOS 7 allow the delegate to configure further options on your data. Delegate methods are provided to return the thumbnail preview image, subject text, and a UTI for the specified activity type. These elements can be used by activity services that support them.

Item Providers

Extending the previous approach, the `UIActivityItemProvider` class conforms to the `UIActivityItemSource` protocol and enables you to delay passing data. It's a type of operation (`NSOperation`) that offers you the flexibility to manipulate data before sharing. For example, you might need to process a large video file before it can be uploaded to a social sharing site, or you might need to subsample some audio from a larger sequence.

Subclass the provider class and implement the `item` method. This takes the place of the `main` method you normally use with operations. Generate the processed data, safe in the knowledge that the method will run asynchronously without blocking your user's interactive experience.

Item Source Callbacks

Recipe 11-4 passes `self` to the controller as part of its `items` array. `self` adopts the source protocol (`<UIActivityItemSource>`), so the controller understands to use callbacks when retrieving data items. The callback methods enable you to vary your data based on each one's intended use. Use the activity types (such as Facebook or Add to Contacts; they're listed earlier in this section) to choose the exact data you want to provide. This is especially important when selecting from resolutions for various uses. When printing, keep your data quality high. When tweeting, a low-res image may do the job instead.

If your data is invariant—that is, you'll be passing the same data to e-mail as you would to Facebook—you can directly supply an array of data items (typically strings, images, and URLs) instead of UIActivityItemSource objects. For example, you could create the controller like this, using a single image:

```
UIActivityViewController *activity = [[UIActivityViewController alloc]
    initWithActivityItems:@[imageView.image]
    applicationActivities:nil];
```

This direct approach is far simpler. Your primary class need not declare the item source protocol; you do not need to implement the extra methods. It's a quick and easy way to manage activities for simple items.

You're not limited to passing single items, either. Include additional elements in the activity items array as needed. The following controller might add its two images to an e-mail or save both to the system Camera Roll, depending on the user's selection:

```
UIImage *secondImage = [UIImage imageNamed:@"Default.png"];
UIActivityViewController *activity = [[UIActivityViewController alloc]
    initWithActivityItems:@[imageView.image, secondImage]
    applicationActivities:nil];
```

Broadening activities to use multiple items enables users to be more efficient while using your app.

Recipe 11-4   The Activity View Controller

```
- (void)presentViewController:
    (UIViewController *)viewControllerToPresent
{
    if (popover) [popover dismissPopoverAnimated:NO];
    if (IS_IPHONE)
    {
        [self presentViewController:viewControllerToPresent
            animated:YES completion:nil];
    }
    else
    {
        popover = [[UIPopoverController alloc]
            initWithContentViewController:viewControllerToPresent];
        popover.delegate = self;
        [popover presentPopoverFromBarButtonItem:
                self.navigationItem.leftBarButtonItem
            permittedArrowDirections:UIPopoverArrowDirectionAny
            animated:YES];
```

```
        }
}

// Popover was dismissed
- (void)popoverControllerDidDismissPopover:
    (UIPopoverController *)aPopoverController
{
    popover = nil;
}

// Return the item to process
- (id)activityViewController:
    (UIActivityViewController *)activityViewController
    itemForActivityType:(NSString *)activityType
{
    return imageView.image;
}

// Return a thumbnail version of that item
- (id)activityViewControllerPlaceholderItem:
    (UIActivityViewController *)activityViewController
{
    return imageView.image;
}

// Create and present the view controller
- (void)action
{
    UIActivityViewController *activity =
        [[UIActivityViewController alloc]
            initWithActivityItems:@[self]
            applicationActivities:nil];
    [self presentViewController:activity];
}
```


Get This Recipe's Code
To find this recipe's full sample project, point your browser to https://github.com/erica/ iOS-7-Cookbook and go to the folder for Chapter 11.

Adding Services

Each app can provide application-specific services by subclassing the `UIActivity` class and passing that activity to the `UIActivityController` on initialization. These custom activities are available in the presented activity view controller alongside the system-provided activities.

When selected, the custom activity presents a view controller allowing the user to interact with the passed data or service in some way, such as entering credentials or manipulating the data.

Listing 11-1 introduces a skeletal `UIActivity` subclass that presents a simple text view. This custom activity is shown in Figure 11-5 as the List Items (Cookbook) option. When this icon is tapped, a custom view controller is presented, displaying a view that lists the items passed to it by the activity controller. It displays each item's class and description. The view controller includes a handler that updates the calling `UIActivity` instance by sending `activityDidFinish:` when the user taps Done.

Adding a way for your activity to complete is important, especially when your controller doesn't have a natural ending point. When your action uploads data to an FTP server, you know when it completes. If it tweets, you know when the status posts. In this example, it's up to the user to determine when this activity finishes. Make sure your view controller contains a weak property pointing back to the activity so that you can send the did-finish method after your work concludes.

The activity class contains a number of mandatory and optional items. You should implement *all* the methods shown in the following list. The methods to support a custom activity include the following:

- `activityType`—Returns a unique string that describes the type of activity. One of this string's counterparts in the system-supplied activities is `UIActivityTypePostToFacebook`. Use a similar naming scheme. This string identifies a particular activity type and what it does. Listing 11-1 returns `@"CustomActivityTypeListItemsAndTypes"`, which describes the activity.

- `activityTitle`—You supply the text you want to show in the activity controller. The custom text in Figure 11-5 was returned by this method. Use active descriptions when describing your custom action. Follow Apple's lead and use, for example, Save to Camera Roll, Print, and Copy. Your title should finish the phrase "I Want to..."—for example, "I Want to Print," "I Want to Copy," or, in this example, "I Want to List Items." Use header case and capitalize each word except for minor ones like *to* or *and*.

- `activityImage`—Returns an image for the controller to use. The controller converts your image to a one-value bitmap. Use simple art on a transparent background to build the contents of your icon image.

- `canPerformWithActivityItems:`—Scans the passed items and decides whether your controller can process them. If so, returns `YES`.

- `prepareWithActivityItems:`—Stores the passed items for later use (here, the passed activity items are assigned to a local instance variable) and performs any necessary preprocessing.

- `activityViewController`—Returns a fully initialized presentable view controller, using the activity items passed earlier. This controller is automatically presented to the user, and he or she can customize options before performing the promised action.

Adding custom activities allows your app to expand its data-handling possibilities while integrating features into a consistent system-supplied interface. It's a powerful iOS feature. The strongest activity choices integrate with system services (such as copying to the pasteboard or saving to the photo album) or provide a connection to off-device APIs, such as Facebook, Twitter, Dropbox, and FTP.

This example, which simply lists items, represents a weak use case. There's no reason the same feature couldn't be provided as a normal in-app screen. When you think *actions*, try to project outside the app. Connect your user's data with sharing and processing features that expand beyond the normal GUI.

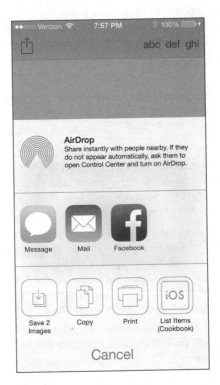

Figure 11-5   Adding your own custom application activities.

Listing 11-1   **Application Activities**

```
// All activities present a view controller. This custom controller
// provides a full-sized text view.
@interface TextViewController : UIViewController
  @property (nonatomic, readonly) UITextView *textView;
  @property (nonatomic, weak) UIActivity *activity;
@end
```

```
@implementation TextViewController

// Make sure you provide a done handler of some kind, such as this
// or an integrated button that finishes and wraps up
- (void)done
{
    [_activity activityDidFinish:YES];
}

// Just a super-basic text view controller
- (instancetype)init
{
    self = [super init];
    if (self)
    {
        _textView = [[UITextView alloc] init];
        _textView.font =
            [UIFont fontWithName:@"Futura" size:16.0f];
        _textView.editable = NO;

        [self.view addSubview:_textView];
        PREPCONSTRAINTS(_textView);
        STRETCH_VIEW(self.view, _textView);

        // Prepare a Done button
        self.navigationItem.rightBarButtonItem =
            BARBUTTON(@"Done", @selector(done));
    }
    return self;
}
@end

// A custom activity subclass to display a list of source items
@interface MyActivity : UIActivity
@end

@implementation MyActivity
{
    NSArray *items;
}

// A unique type name
- (NSString *)activityType
{
    return @"CustomActivityTypeListItemsAndTypes";
}
```

```objc
// The title listed on the controller
- (NSString *)activityTitle
{
    return @"List Items (Cookbook)";
}


// A custom image that says "iOS" with a rounded rect edge
- (UIImage *)activityImage
{
    CGRect rect = CGRectMake(0.0f, 0.0f, 75.0f, 75.0f);
    UIGraphicsBeginImageContext(rect.size);
    rect = CGRectInset(rect, 15.0f, 15.0f);
    UIBezierPath *path = [UIBezierPath
        bezierPathWithRoundedRect:rect cornerRadius:4.0f];
    [path stroke];
    rect = CGRectInset(rect, 0.0f, 10.0f);
    NSMutableParagraphStyle * paragraphStyle =
        [[NSMutableParagraphStyle alloc] init];
    paragraphStyle.lineBreakMode = NSLineBreakByWordWrapping;
    paragraphStyle.alignment = NSTextAlignmentCenter;
    NSDictionary * attributes =
        @{NSParagraphStyleAttributeName : paragraphStyle,
          NSFontAttributeName : [UIFont fontWithName:@"Futura"
              size:18.0f]};
    [@"iOS" drawInRect:rect withAttributes:attributes];
    UIImage *image = UIGraphicsGetImageFromCurrentImageContext();
    UIGraphicsEndImageContext();

    return image;
}


// Specify if you can respond to these items
- (BOOL)canPerformWithActivityItems:(NSArray *)activityItems
{
    return YES;
}


// Store the items locally for later use
- (void)prepareWithActivityItems:(NSArray *)activityItems
{
    items = activityItems;
}


// Return a view controller, in this case one that lists
// its items and their classes
- (UIViewController *)activityViewController
{
```

```
    TextViewController *tvc = [[TextViewController alloc] init];
    tvc.activity = self;
    UITextView *textView = tvc.textView;

    NSMutableString *string = [NSMutableString string];
    for (id item in items)
        [string appendFormat:
            @"%@: %@\n", [item class], [item description]];
    textView.text = string;

    // Make sure to provide some kind of done: handler in
    // your main controller.
    UINavigationController *nav = [[UINavigationController alloc]
        initWithRootViewController:tvc];
    return nav;
}
@end
```

Items and Activities

The activities presented for each item vary by the kind of data you pass. Table 11-1 lists offered activities by source data type on a U.S. phone:

Table 11-1   **Activity Types for Data Types**

Source	Offered Activity
`NSString` String, single or multiple	Message, Mail, Twitter, Facebook, Copy.
`NSAttributedString` Attributed string	Message, Mail, Twitter, Facebook, Copy.
`UIImage` Image, single	Message, Mail, Twitter, Facebook, Save Image, Assign to Contact, Copy, Print.
`UIImage` Image, multiple	Message, Mail, Facebook, Save Images, Copy, Print.
`UIColor` Colors	Copy.
`NSURL` URLs	Message, Mail, Twitter, Facebook, Add to Reading List, Copy. URLs using the `assets-library:` scheme can be used with Facebook. The `mailto:` scheme is valid with Mail activities, and `sms:` works with Message.

Source	Offered Activity
`UIPrintPageRenderer,` `UIPrintFormatter,` and `UIPrintInfo`	Print.
`NSDictionary` Dictionaries	If objects are supported, the activities for those objects. Sadly, the same does not hold true for arrays, which are unsupported.
Unsupported items	For example, `AVAsset`, `NSData`, `NSArray`, `NSDate`, or `NSNumber`: Nothing, a blank view controller.
Various items	Union of all supported types (for example, for string plus image, you get Message, Mail, Twitter, Facebook, Save Image, Assign to Contact, Copy, Print).

These activities may vary based on locale. As you see in the recipes that follow, preview controller support expands beyond these foundation types:

- iOS's Quick Look framework integrates activity controllers into its file previews. The Quick Look–provided activity controller can print and e-mail many kinds of documents. Some document types support other activities as well.

- Document interaction controllers offer "Open in..." features that enable you to share files between applications. The controller adds activities into its "options"-style presentation, combining activities with "Open in..." choices.

Excluding Activities

You can specifically exclude activities by supplying a list of activity types to the `excludedActivityTypes` property:

```
UIActivityViewController *activity =
    [[UIActivityViewController alloc]
        initWithActivityItems:items
        applicationActivities:@[appActivity]];
activity.excludedActivityTypes = @[UIActivityTypeMail];
```

Recipe: The Quick Look Preview Controller

The Quick Look preview controller class enables users to preview many document types. This controller supports text, images, PDF, RTF, iWork files, Microsoft Office documents (Office 97 and later, including DOC, PPT, XLS, and so on), and CSV files. You supply a supported file type, and the Quick Look controller displays it for the user. An integrated system-supplied activity view controller helps share the previewed document, as you can see in Figure 11-6.

Either push or present your preview controllers. The controller adapts to both situations, working with navigation stacks and with modal presentation. Recipe 11-5 demonstrates both approaches.

Figure 11-6   This Quick Look controller is presented modally and shows the screen after the user has tapped the Action button. Quick Look handles a wide range of document types, enabling users to see the file contents before deciding on an action to apply to them.

Implementing Quick Look

Implementing Quick Look requires just a few simple steps:

1. Declare the QLPreviewControllerDataSource protocol in your primary controller class.

2. Implement the numberOfPreviewItemsInPreviewController: and preview-Controller:previewItemAtIndex: data source methods. The first of these methods returns a count of items to preview. The second returns the preview item referred to by the index.

3. Ensure that preview items conform to the QLPreviewItem protocol. This protocol consists of two required properties: a preview title and an item URL. Recipe 11-5 creates a conforming QuickItem class. This class implements an absolutely minimal approach to support the data source.

Once these requirements are met, your code is ready to create a new preview controller, set its data source, and present or push it.

Recipe 11-5   **Quick Look**

```
@interface QuickItem : NSObject <QLPreviewItem>
@property (nonatomic, strong) NSString *path;
@property (readonly) NSString *previewItemTitle;
@property (readonly) NSURL *previewItemURL;
@end

@implementation QuickItem

// Title for preview item
- (NSString *)previewItemTitle
{
    return [_path lastPathComponent];
}

// URL for preview item
- (NSURL *)previewItemURL
{
    return [NSURL fileURLWithPath:_path];
}
@end

#define FILE_PATH   [NSHomeDirectory() \
    stringByAppendingPathComponent:@"Documents/PDFSample.pdf"]

@interface TestBedViewController : UIViewController
    <QLPreviewControllerDataSource>
@end

@implementation TestBedViewController
- (NSInteger)numberOfPreviewItemsInPreviewController:
    (QLPreviewController *)controller
{
    return 1;
}

- (id <QLPreviewItem>)previewController:
        (QLPreviewController *)controller
    previewItemAtIndex:(NSInteger)index;
{
    QuickItem *item = [[QuickItem alloc] init];
    item.path = FILE_PATH;
    return item;
```

```objc
}

// Push onto navigation stack
- (void)push
{
    QLPreviewController *controller =
        [[QLPreviewController alloc] init];
    controller.dataSource = self;
    [self.navigationController
        pushViewController:controller animated:YES];
}

// Use modal presentation
- (void)present
{
    QLPreviewController *controller =
        [[QLPreviewController alloc] init];
    controller.dataSource = self;
    [self presentViewController:controller
        animated:YES completion:nil];
}

- (void)loadView
{
    self.view = [[UIView alloc] init];
    self.view.backgroundColor = [UIColor whiteColor];

    self.navigationItem.rightBarButtonItem =
        BARBUTTON(@"Push", @selector(push));
    self.navigationItem.leftBarButtonItem =
        BARBUTTON(@"Present", @selector(present));
}
@end
```

Get This Recipe's Code

To find this recipe's full sample project, point your browser to https://github.com/erica/iOS-7-Cookbook and go to the folder for Chapter 11.

Recipe: Using the Document Interaction Controller

The UIDocumentInteractionController class enables applications to present interaction options to users, enabling them to use document files in a variety of ways. With this class, users can take advantage of the following:

- iOS application-to-application document sharing (that is, "Open this document in... *some app*")
- Document preview using Quick Look
- Activity controller options such as printing, sharing, and social networking

You've already seen the latter two features in action in the activity view controller earlier in this chapter. In both presentation and behavior, `UIDocumentInteractionController` is actually very similar to `UIActivityViewController`. The document interaction class adds a powerful app-to-app sharing capability.

The controller offers two styles, as shown in Figure 11-7. The "Open in..." style offers only "Open in" choices. The "options" style provides a list of interaction options, including "Open in...," Quick Look, and any supported actions. It's essentially all the good stuff you get from a standard Actions menu, along with "Open in..." extras. You do have to explicitly add Quick Look callbacks, but doing so takes little work.

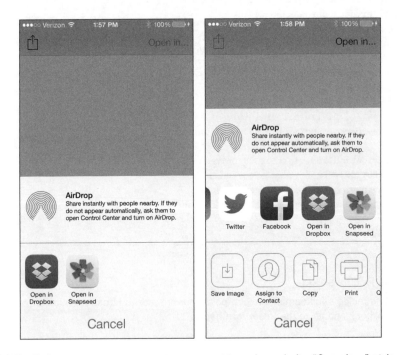

Figure 11-7   The `UIDocumentInteractionController` shown in its "Open in..." style (left) and options style (right).

Creating Document Interaction Controller Instances

Each document interaction controller is specific to a single document file. This file is typically stored in the user's Documents folder, represented by the `fileURL` in this snippet:

```
dic = [UIDocumentInteractionController
    interactionControllerWithURL:fileURL];
```

You supply a local file URL and present the controller using either the "options" variation (basically the Action menu) or the "Open in..." style. Present the Options menu in one of these two styles from a bar button or an onscreen rectangle:

- `presentOptionsMenuFromRect:inView:animated:`

- `presentOptionsMenuFromBarButtonItem:animated:`

- `presentOpenInMenuFromRect:inView:animated:`

- `presentOpenInMenuFromBarButtonItem:animated:`

The iPad uses the bar button or `rect` you pass to present a popover. On the iPhone, the implementation presents a modal controller view. As you would expect, more bookkeeping takes place on the iPad, where users may tap on other bar buttons, may dismiss the popover, and so forth.

Disable each iPad bar button item after presenting its associated controller and re-enable it after dismissal. This is important because you don't want your user to re-tap an in-use bar button and need to handle situations where a different popover needs to take over. Basically, there are a variety of unpleasant scenarios that can happen if you don't carefully monitor which buttons are active and what popover is in play. Recipe 11-6 guards against these scenarios.

Document Interaction Controller Properties

Each document interaction controller offers a number of properties, which can be used in your controller delegate callbacks:

- **URL**—This property enables you to query the controller for the file it is servicing. This is the same URL you pass when creating the controller.

- **UTI**—This property is used to determine which apps can open the document. It uses the system-supplied functions discussed earlier in the chapter to find the most preferred UTI match, based on the filename and metadata. You can override this in code to set the property manually.

- **name**—This property provides the last path component of the URL, offering a quick way to provide a user-interpretable name without having to manually strip the URL yourself.

- **icons**—Use this property to retrieve an icon for the file type that's in play. Applications that declare support for certain file types provide image links in their declaration (as you'll see shortly, in the discussion about declaring file support). These images correspond to the values stored for the kUTTypeIconFileKey key, as mentioned earlier in this chapter.

- **annotation**—This property provides a way to pass custom data along with a file to any application that will open the file. There are no standards for using this property; however, the item must be set to some top-level property list object—namely dictionaries, arrays, data, strings, numbers, and dates. Because there are no community standards, use of this property tends to be minimal except where developers share the information across their own suite of published apps.

Providing Document Quick Look Support

Add Quick Look support to the controller by implementing a trio of delegate callbacks:

```
#pragma mark QuickLook
- (UIViewController *)
     documentInteractionControllerViewControllerForPreview:
         (UIDocumentInteractionController *)controller
{
    return self;
}

- (UIView *)documentInteractionControllerViewForPreview:
    (UIDocumentInteractionController *)controller
{
    return self.view;
}

- (CGRect)documentInteractionControllerRectForPreview:
    (UIDocumentInteractionController *)controller
{
    return self.view.frame;
}
```

These methods declare which view controller will be used to present the preview, which view will host it, and the frame for the preview size. You may have occasional compelling reasons to use a child view controller with limited screen presence on tablets (such as in a split view, with the preview in just one portion), but for the iPhone family, there's almost never any reason not to allow the preview to take over the entire screen.

Checking for the Open Menu

When you use a document interaction controller, the Options menu almost always provides valid menu choices, especially if you implement the Quick Look callbacks. You may or may not, however, have any "Open in..." options to work with. Those options depend on the file data you provide to the controller and the applications users install on their devices.

A no-open-options scenario happens when there are no applications installed on a device that support the file type you are working with. This may be caused by an obscure file type, but more often it occurs because the user has not yet purchased and installed a relevant application. This is a common occurrence when using the iOS simulator.

Always check whether to offer an "Open in..." menu option. Recipe 11-6 performs a rather ugly test to see if external apps will offer themselves as presenters and editors for a given URL. This is what it does: It creates a new temporary controller and attempts to present it. If it succeeds, conforming file destinations exist and are installed on the device. If not, there are no such apps, and any "Open in..." buttons should be disabled.

On the iPad, you must run this check in `viewDidAppear:` or later—that is, after a window has been established. The method immediately dismisses the controller after presentation. Your end user should not notice it, and none of the calls use animation.

This is obviously a rather dreadful implementation, but it has the advantage of testing as you lay out your interface or when you start working with a new file. File an enhancement request at bugreporter.apple.com.

One further caution: Although this test works on primary views (as in Recipe 11-6), it can cause headaches in nonstandard presentations in popovers on the iPad.

> **Note**
>
> You rarely offer users both option and "Open in..." items in the same application. Recipe 11-6 uses the system-supplied Action item icon for the Options menu. You may want to use this in place of "Open in..." text for apps that exclusively use the open style.

Recipe 11-6   Document Interaction Controllers

```objc
@implementation TestBedViewController
{
    NSURL *fileURL;
    UIDocumentInteractionController *dic;
    BOOL canOpen;
}


#pragma mark QuickLook
- (UIViewController *)
    documentInteractionControllerViewControllerForPreview:
        (UIDocumentInteractionController *)controller
{
    return self;
}


- (UIView *)documentInteractionControllerViewForPreview:
    (UIDocumentInteractionController *)controller
{
    return self.view;
```

```
}

- (CGRect)documentInteractionControllerRectForPreview:
    (UIDocumentInteractionController *)controller
{
    return self.view.frame;
}

#pragma mark Options / Open in Menu

// Clean up after dismissing options menu
- (void)documentInteractionControllerDidDismissOptionsMenu:
    (UIDocumentInteractionController *)controller
{
    self.navigationItem.leftBarButtonItem.enabled = YES;
    dic = nil;
}

// Clean up after dismissing open menu
- (void)documentInteractionControllerDidDismissOpenInMenu:
    (UIDocumentInteractionController *)controller
{
    self.navigationItem.rightBarButtonItem.enabled = canOpen;
    dic = nil;
}

// Before presenting a controller, check to see if there's an
// existing one that needs dismissing
- (void)dismissIfNeeded
{
    if (dic)
    {
        [dic dismissMenuAnimated:YES];
        self.navigationItem.rightBarButtonItem.enabled = canOpen;
        self.navigationItem.leftBarButtonItem.enabled = YES;
    }
}

// Present the options menu
- (void)action:(UIBarButtonItem *)bbi
{
    [self dismissIfNeeded];
    dic = [UIDocumentInteractionController
        interactionControllerWithURL:fileURL];
    dic.delegate = self;
    self.navigationItem.leftBarButtonItem.enabled = NO;
    [dic presentOptionsMenuFromBarButtonItem:bbi animated:YES];
```

```
}

// Present the open-in menu
- (void)open:(UIBarButtonItem *)bbi
{
    [self dismissIfNeeded];
    dic = [UIDocumentInteractionController
        interactionControllerWithURL:fileURL];
    dic.delegate = self;
    self.navigationItem.rightBarButtonItem.enabled = NO;
    [dic presentOpenInMenuFromBarButtonItem:bbi animated:YES];
}

#pragma mark Test for Open-ability
- (BOOL)canOpen:(NSURL *)aFileURL
{
    UIDocumentInteractionController *tmp =
        [UIDocumentInteractionController
            interactionControllerWithURL:aFileURL];
    BOOL success =
        [tmp presentOpenInMenuFromRect:CGRectMake(0,0,1,1)
        inView:self.view animated:NO];
    [tmp dismissMenuAnimated:NO];
    return success;
}


- (void)viewDidAppear:(BOOL)animated
{
    [super viewDidAppear:animated];
    // Only enable right button if the file can be opened
    canOpen = [self canOpen:fileURL];
    self.navigationItem.rightBarButtonItem.enabled = canOpen;
}

#pragma mark View management
- (void)loadView
{
    self.view = [[UIView alloc] init];
    self.view.backgroundColor = [UIColor whiteColor];
    self.navigationItem.rightBarButtonItem =
        BARBUTTON(@"Open in...", @selector(open:));
    self.navigationItem.leftBarButtonItem =
        SYSBARBUTTON(UIBarButtonSystemItemAction,
            @selector(action:));

    NSString *filePath = [NSHomeDirectory()
        stringByAppendingPathComponent:@"Documents/DICImage.jpg"];
```

```
        fileURL = [NSURL fileURLWithPath:filePath];
}
@end
```

Get This Recipe's Code

To find this recipe's full sample project, point your browser to https://github.com/erica/iOS-7-Cookbook and go to the folder for Chapter 11.

Recipe: Declaring Document Support

Application documents are not limited to files an application creates or downloads from the Internet. As you discovered in Recipe 11-6, applications may handle certain file types. They may open items passed from other apps. You've already seen document sharing from the sending point of view, using the "open in" controller to export files to other applications. Now it's time to look at it from the receiver's end.

Applications declare their support for certain file types in their `Info.plist` property list. The Launch Services system reads this data and creates the file-to-app associations that the document interaction controller uses.

Although you can edit the property list directly, Xcode offers a simple form as part of the Project > Target > Info screen. Open the Document Types section, which is below the Custom iOS Target Properties. Click + to add a new supported document type. Figure 11-8 shows what this looks like for an app that accepts JPEG image documents.

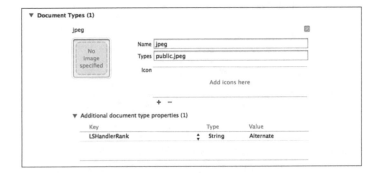

Figure 11-8　Declare supported document types in Xcode's Target > Info screen.

This declaration contains three minimal details:

- **Name**—The name is both required and arbitrary. It should be descriptive of the kind of document in play, but it's also somewhat of an afterthought on iOS. This field makes more sense when used on a Macintosh (it's the "kind" string used by Finder), but it is not optional.

- **One or more UTIs**—Specify one or more UTIs as your types. This example specifies only `public.jpeg`. Add commas between items when listing several items. For example, you might have an `image` document type that opens `public.jpeg`, `public.tiff`, and `public.png`. Enumerate specific types when you need to limit file support. Although declaring `public.image` would cover all three types, it might allow unsupported image styles to be opened as well.

- **Handler rank**—The launch services handler rank describes how the app views itself alongside the competition for handling this file type. Owner says that this is a native app that creates files of this type. Alternate, as in Figure 11-8, offers a secondary viewer. You add the `LSHandlerRank` key manually in the additional document type properties.

You may optionally specify icon files. These are used in OS X as document icons and have minimal overlap with the iOS world. The only case where you might see these icons is in the iTunes Apps tab when you're using the File Sharing section to add and remove items. Icons are typically 320×320 (`UTTypeSize320IconFile`) and 64×64 (`UTTypeSize64IconFile`) and are normally limited to files that your app creates and for which it defines a custom type.

Under the hood, Xcode uses this interactive form to build a `CFBundleDocumentTypes` array in your application's `Info.plist`. The following snippet shows the information from Figure 11-8 in its `Info.plist` form:

```
<key>CFBundleDocumentTypes</key>
<array>
    <dict>
        <key>CFBundleTypeIconFiles</key>
        <array/>
        <key>CFBundleTypeName</key>
        <string>jpg</string>
        <key>LSHandlerRank</key>
        <string>Alternate</string>
        <key>LSItemContentTypes</key>
        <array>
            <string>public.jpeg</string>
        </array>
    </dict>
</array>
```

Creating Custom Document Types

When your application builds new kinds of documents, you should declare them in the Exported UTIs section of the Target > Info editor, which you see in Figure 11-9. This registers support for this file type with the system and identifies you as the owner of that type.

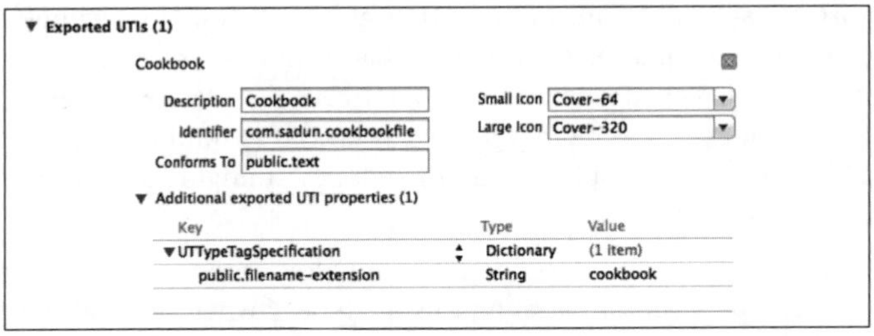

Figure 11-9   Declare custom file types in the Exported UTIs section of the Target > Info editor.

To define the new type, supply a custom UTI (here, com.sadun.cookbookfile), document art (at 64 and 320 sizes), and specify a filename extension that identifies your file type. As with declaring document support, Xcode builds an exported declaration array into your project's Info.plist file. Here is what that material might look like for the declaration shown in Figure 11-9:

```
<key>UTExportedTypeDeclarations</key>
<array>
    <dict>
        <key>UTTypeConformsTo</key>
        <array>
            <string>public.text</string>
        </array>
        <key>UTTypeDescription</key>
        <string>Cookbook</string>
        <key>UTTypeIdentifier</key>
        <string>com.sadun.cookbookfile</string>
        <key>UTTypeSize320IconFile</key>
        <string>Cover-320</string>
        <key>UTTypeSize64IconFile</key>
        <string>Cover-64</string>
        <key>UTTypeTagSpecification</key>
        <dict>
            <key>public.filename-extension</key>
            <string>cookbook</string>
        </dict>
    </dict>
</array>
```

If you add this to your project, your app should open any files with the cookbook extension, using the com.sadun.cookbookfile UTI.

Implementing Document Support

When your application provides document support, you should check for an Inbox folder each time it becomes active:

```
- (void)applicationDidBecomeActive:(UIApplication *)application
{
    // perform inbox test here
}
```

Specifically, see if an Inbox folder has appeared in the Documents folder. If it has, you should move elements out of that Inbox to where they belong, typically in the main Documents directory. After the Inbox has been cleared, delete it. This provides the best user experience, especially in terms of any file sharing through iTunes, where the Inbox and its role may confuse users.

When moving items to Documents, check for name conflicts and use an alternative path name (typically by appending a hyphen followed by a number) to avoid overwriting any existing file. Recipe 11-7 helps find an alternative name for a destination path. It gives up after a thousand attempts. Seriously, none of your users should be hosting that many duplicate document names. If they do, there's something deeply wrong with your overall application design.

Recipe 11-7 walks through the ugly details of scanning for the Inbox and moving files into place. It removes the Inbox after it is emptied. As you can see, any method like this is File Manager–intensive. It primarily involves handling all the error combination possibilities that might pop up throughout the task. Processing the Inbox should run quickly for small file support. If you must handle large files, such as video or audio, make sure to perform this processing on its own operation queue.

If you plan to support `public.data` files (which will open anything), you might want to display those files by using `UIWebView` instances. Refer to Technical Q&A QA1630 (http://developer.apple.com/library/ios/#qa/qa1630) for details about which document types iOS can and cannot display in those views. Web views can present most audio and video assets, as well as Excel, Keynote, Numbers, Pages, PDF, PowerPoint, and Word resources, in addition to simple HTML.

Recipe 11-7   Handling Incoming Documents

```
#define DOCUMENTS_PATH    [NSHomeDirectory() \
    stringByAppendingPathComponent:@"Documents"]
#define INBOX_PATH        [DOCUMENTS_PATH \
    stringByAppendingPathComponent:@"Inbox"]

@implementation InboxHelper
+ (NSString *)findAlternativeNameForPath:(NSString *)path
{
    NSString *ext = path.pathExtension;
    NSString *base = [path stringByDeletingPathExtension];
```

```
    for (int i = 1; i < 999; i++)
    {
        NSString *dest =
            [NSString stringWithFormat:@"%@-%d.%@", base, i, ext];

        // if the file does not yet exist, use this destination path
        if (![[NSFileManager defaultManager]
            fileExistsAtPath:dest])
            return dest;
    }

    NSLog(@"Exhausted possible names for file %@. Bailing.",
        path.lastPathComponent);
    return nil;
}


- (void)checkAndProcessInbox
{
    // Does the Inbox exist? If not, we're done
    BOOL isDir;
    if (![[NSFileManager defaultManager]
        fileExistsAtPath:INBOX_PATH isDirectory:&isDir])
        return;

    NSError *error;
    BOOL success;

    // If the Inbox is not a folder, remove it
    if (!isDir)
    {
        success = [[NSFileManager defaultManager]
            removeItemAtPath:INBOX_PATH error:&error];
        if (!success)
        {
            NSLog(@"Error deleting Inbox file (not directory): %@",
                error.localizedFailureReason);
            return;
        }
    }

    // Retrieve a list of files in the Inbox
    NSArray *fileArray = [[NSFileManager defaultManager]
        contentsOfDirectoryAtPath:INBOX_PATH error:&error];
    if (!fileArray)
    {
        NSLog(@"Error reading contents of Inbox: %@",
```

```
            error.localizedFailureReason);
        return;
    }


    // Remember the number of items
    NSUInteger initialCount = fileArray.count;

    // Iterate through each file, moving it to Documents
    for (NSString *filename in fileArray)
    {
        NSString *source = [INBOX_PATH
            stringByAppendingPathComponent:filename];
        NSString *dest = [DOCUMENTS_PATH
            stringByAppendingPathComponent:filename];

        // Is the file already there?
        BOOL exists =
            [[NSFileManager defaultManager] fileExistsAtPath:dest];
        if (exists) dest = [self findAlternativeNameForPath:dest];
        if (!dest)
        {
            NSLog(@"Error. File name conflict not resolved");
            continue;
        }

        // Move file into place
        success = [[NSFileManager defaultManager]
            moveItemAtPath:source toPath:dest error:&error];
        if (!success)
        {
            NSLog(@"Error moving file from Inbox: %@",
                error.localizedFailureReason);
            continue;
        }
    }

    // Inbox should now be empty
    fileArray = [[NSFileManager defaultManager]
        contentsOfDirectoryAtPath:INBOX_PATH error:&error];
    if (!fileArray)
    {
        NSLog(@"Error reading contents of Inbox: %@",
            error.localizedFailureReason);
        return;
    }
```

```
    if (fileArray.count)
    {
        NSLog(@"Error clearing Inbox. %d items remain",
            fileArray.count);
        return;
    }

    // Remove the inbox
    success = [[NSFileManager defaultManager]
        removeItemAtPath:INBOX_PATH error:&error];
    if (!success)
    {
        NSLog(@"Error removing inbox: %@",
            error.localizedFailureReason);
        return;
    }

    NSLog(@"Moved %d items from the Inbox", initialCount);
}
@end
```

| **Get This Recipe's Code**

To find this recipe's full sample project, point your browser to https://github.com/erica/
iOS-7-Cookbook and go to the folder for Chapter 11.

Recipe: Creating URL-Based Services

Apple's built-in applications offer a variety of services that can be accessed via URL calls. You
can ask Safari to open web pages, open Maps to show a map, or use the `mailto:`-style URL to
start composing a letter in Mail. A URL scheme refers to the first part of the URL that appears
before the colon, such as `http` or `ftp`.

These services work because iOS knows how to match URL schemes to applications. A URL that
starts with `http:` opens in Mobile Safari. The `mailto:` URL always links to Mail. What you
may not know is that you can define your own URL schemes and implement them in your
applications. Not all standard schemes are supported on iOS. For example, the FTP scheme is
not available for use.

Custom schemes enable applications to launch whenever Mobile Safari or another application
opens a URL of that type. For example, if your application registers xyz, `xyz:` links go directly
to your application for handling, where they're passed to the application delegate's URL
opening method. You do not have to add any special coding there. If all you want to do is run
an application, adding the scheme and opening the URL enables cross-application launching.

Handlers extend launching to allow applications to do something with the URL that's been passed to it. They might open a specific data file, retrieve a particular name, display a certain image, or otherwise process information included in the call.

Declaring the Scheme

To declare your URL scheme, edit the URL Types section of the Target > Info editor (see Figure 11-10) and list the URL schemes you will use. The `Info.plist` section created by this declaration looks like this:

```
<key>CFBundleURLTypes</key>
<array>
    <dict>
        <key>CFBundleURLName</key>
        <string>com.sadun.urlSchemeDemonstration</string>
        <key>CFBundleURLSchemes</key>
        <array>
            <string>xyz</string>
        </array>
    </dict>
</array>
```

Figure 11-10   Add custom URL schemes in the URL Types section of the Target > Info editor.

The `CFBundleURLTypes` entry consists of an array of dictionaries that describe the URL types the application can open and handle. Each dictionary is quite simple. Each one contains two keys: a `CFBundleURLName` (which defines an arbitrary identifier) and an array of `CFBundleURLSchemes`.

The schemes array provides a list of prefixes that belong to the abstract name. You can add one scheme or many. This following example declares just one. You might want to prefix your name with an x (for example, `x-sadun-services`). Although the iOS family is not part of any standards organization, an x prefix indicates that this is an unregistered name. A draft specification for `x-callback-url` is under development at http://x-callback-url.com.

A number of informal registries have popped up so iOS developers can share their schemes in central listings. You can discover services you want to use and promote services you offer. Each registry lists services and their URL schemes and describes how other developers can use these services. Some of these registries include http://handleopenurl.com, http://wiki.akosma.com/IPhone_URL_Schemes, and http://applookup.com/Home.

Testing URLs

You can test whether a URL service is available. If the UIApplication's canOpenURL: method returns YES, you are guaranteed that openURL: can launch another application to open that URL:

```
if ([[UIApplication sharedApplication] canOpenURL:aURL])
    [[UIApplication sharedApplication] openURL:aURL];
```

You are not guaranteed that the URL is valid—only that its scheme is registered properly to an existing application.

Adding the Handler Method

To handle URL requests, you implement the URL-specific application delegate method shown in Recipe 11-8. Unfortunately, this method is guaranteed to trigger only when the application is already running. If the app is not running and the app is launched by the URL request, control first goes to the launching methods (will- and did-finish).

You want to ensure that your normal application:didFinishLaunchingWithOptions: method returns YES. This allows control to pass to application:openURL: sourceApplication:annotation:, so the incoming URL can be processed and handled.

Recipe 11-8   **Providing URL Scheme Support**

```
// Called if the app is open or if didFinishLaunchingWithOptions returns YES
- (BOOL)application:(UIApplication *)application
    openURL:(NSURL *)url
    sourceApplication:(NSString *)sourceApplication
    annotation:(id)annotation
{

    NSString *logString = [NSString stringWithFormat:
        @"DID OPEN: URL[%@] App[%@] Annotation[%@]\n",
        url, sourceApplication, annotation];
    tbvc.textView.text =
        [logString stringByAppendingString:tbvc.textView.text];
    return YES;
}


// Make sure to return YES
- (BOOL)application:(UIApplication *)application
    didFinishLaunchingWithOptions:(NSDictionary *)launchOptions
{

    _window = [[UIWindow alloc]
        initWithFrame:[[UIScreen mainScreen] bounds]];
    tbvc = [[TestBedViewController alloc] init];

    UINavigationController *nav = [[UINavigationController alloc]
        initWithRootViewController:tbvc];
```

```
    window.rootViewController = nav;
    [window makeKeyAndVisible];
    return YES;
}
```

Get This Recipe's Code

To find this recipe's full sample project, point your browser to https://github.com/erica/iOS-7-Cookbook and go to the folder for Chapter 11.

Summary

Want to share data across applications and leverage system-supplied actions? This chapter shows you how. You've read about UTIs and how they are used to specify data roles across applications. You've seen how the pasteboard worked and how to share files with iTunes. You've read about monitoring folders and discovered how to implement custom URLs. You've dived deep into the activity view controller and document interaction controller, and you've seen how to add support for everything from printing to copying to previews. Here are a few thoughts to take with you before leaving this chapter:

- You are never limited to the built-in UTIs that Apple provides, but you should follow Apple's lead when you decide to add your own. Be sure to use custom reverse domain naming and add as many details as possible (public URL definition pages, typical icons, and file extensions) in your exported definitions. Precision matters.

- Conformance arrays help you determine what kind of thing you're working with. Knowing that you're working with an image and not, say, a text file or movie, can help you better process the data associated with any file.

- The Documents folder belongs to the user and not to you. Remember that and provide respectful management of that directory.

- When you're looking for one-stop shopping for data sharing, you'll be hard-pressed to find a better solution than an activity view controller. Easy to use, and simple to present, this single controller does the work of an army, integrating your app with iOS's system-supplied services.

- For a lot of reasons, many developers used custom URL schemes in the past, but the document interaction controller often provides a better alternative. Use this controller to provide the app-to-app interaction your users demand and don't be afraid of introducing annotation support to help ease the transition between apps.

- Don't offer an "Open in…" menu option unless there are onboard apps ready to back up that button. The solution you read about in this chapter is crude, but using it is better than dealing with angry, frustrated, or confused users through customer support. Consider providing an alert, backed by this method, that explains when there are no other apps available.

12

A Taste of Core Data

iOS's Core Data framework provides persistent data solutions. Your applications can query and update Core Data's managed data stores. With Core Data, you gain a Cocoa Touch–based object interface that brings relational data management out from SQL queries and into the Objective-C world of iOS development. Core Data delivers the perfect technology to power your table view and collection view instances.

This chapter introduces Core Data. It provides just enough how-to to give you a taste of the technology, offering a jumping-off point for further Core Data learning. By the time you finish reading through this chapter, you'll have seen Core Data for iOS in action and gotten an overview of the technology.

Introducing Core Data

Core Data simplifies the way your applications create and use persisted objects, known as *managed* objects. Until the 3.x SDK, all data management and SQL access were left to a fairly low-level library. It wasn't pretty, and it wasn't easy to use. Since then, Core Data has joined the Cocoa Touch framework family, bringing powerful data management solutions to iOS. Core Data provides a flexible infrastructure, offering tools for working with persistent data stores and generating solutions for the complete object life cycle.

Core Data lives in the *model* portion of the Model–View–Controller (MVC) paradigm. It understands that application-specific data must be defined and controlled outside the application's GUI, even as it powers that interface. Core Data integrates beautifully with table view and collection view instances. Cocoa Touch's fetched-results controller class was designed and built with these kinds of classes in mind. It offers useful properties and methods that support data source and delegate integration.

Entities and Models

Entities live at the top of the Core Data hierarchy. They describe objects stored inside your database. Entities provide the virtual cookie cutters that specify how each data object is created. When you build new objects, entities detail the attributes and relationships that make up each object. Every entity has a name, which Core Data uses to retrieve entity descriptions as your application runs.

You build entities inside model files. Each project that links against the Core Data framework includes one or more model files. These `.xcdatamodeld` files define entities, their attributes, and their relationships.

Building a Model File

Create your model in Xcode by laying out a new data model file. Some iOS templates allow you to include Core Data as part of the project. Otherwise, you create these Xcode model files by selecting File > New > File from the Xcode menu and then choosing iOS, Core Data, Data Model, and Next. Enter a name for your new file (this example uses Person), check the targets for your project, and click Save. Xcode creates and then adds the new model file to your project (for example, `Person.xcdatamodeld`). Click the `xcdatamodeld` file in the File Navigator to open it in the editor window shown in Figure 12-1.

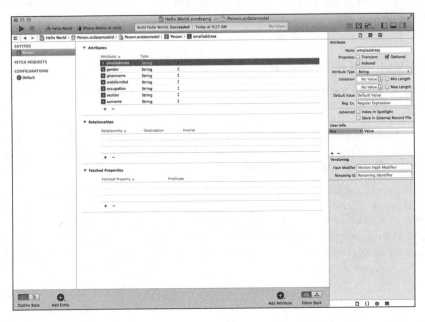

Figure 12-1   Xcode's editor enables you to build managed object definitions for your Core Data applications.

You add new entities (basically classes of objects) to the left list in the editor window by clicking the Add Entity button near the bottom left. Add attributes (essentially instance variables for entities) by clicking the Add Attribute button at the bottom right. Double-click any individual entity or attribute name to change it; use the Type pop-up to set an attribute's type.

Use the center portion of the editor to customize your attributes and relationships. Relationships are the optional ways entities relate to each other in the database. An inspector to the right provides context-specific settings. In Figure 12-1, it's showing details for the Person entity's `emailaddress` attribute.

The Entity editor provides two layout styles. Toggle between the table view and an object graph by tapping the Editor Style buttons at the bottom right of the editor pane.

The detail table style shown in Figure 12-1 provides a list of each entity, attribute, and relationship defined in the model. The object graph offers a grid-based visual presentation of the entities you have defined, allowing you to visualize and edit entity relationships—the way entities relate to each other. For example, a parent can have several children and one spouse. A department may include members, and a manager may serve on several committees.

Attributes and Relationships

Each entity may include attributes, which store information such as a name, a birth date, a designation, and so forth. The Objective-C object that corresponds to an entity expresses properties defined by these attributes.

Each entity may also define relationships, which are links between one object and another. These relationships can be single, using a one-to-one relationship (spouse, employer), or they can be multiple (children, credit card accounts), using a one-to-many relationship. In addition, relationships should be reciprocal, providing an inverse relationship (my child, his parent).

Select an entity to start adding attributes. With the entity selected, tap the Add Attribute button at the bottom right of the editor pane. (Or tap and hold this button to choose either Add Attribute, Add Relationship, or Add Fetched Property.) Each attribute has a name and a data type, just as you would define an instance variable.

Relationships provide pointers to other objects. When working with the Graph editor, you can Control-drag to create them. Arrows represent the relationships between the various kinds of entities in a project.

At the simplest level, you can work with just one entity and without relationships, even though Core Data offers a fully powered relational database. Most iOS applications do not require a high level of sophistication. A flat database with section attributes is all you need to power table views and collection views.

To build the model in Figure 12-1, create a Person entity and add these seven attributes: `emailaddress`, `gender`, `givenname`, `middleinitial`, `occupation`, `surname`, and `section`. Set each type to `String`.

Building Object Classes

After creating your entity definition, save your changes to the data model file. Select an entity in the column on the left and from the Xcode menu, choose Editor > Create NSManagedObject Subclass. Select your data model and the entity (or entities) you intend to manage. Save to your project folder, select the group you want to add the classes to, and click Create. Xcode generates class files from your entity description. Here is what the automatically generated Person class looks like:

```
@interface Person : NSManagedObject

@property (nonatomic, strong) NSString *section;
@property (nonatomic, strong) NSString *emailaddress;
@property (nonatomic, strong) NSString *gender;
@property (nonatomic, strong) NSString *givenname;
@property (nonatomic, strong) NSString *middleinitial;
@property (nonatomic, strong) NSString *occupation;
@property (nonatomic, strong) NSString *surname;

@end


@implementation Person

@dynamic section;
@dynamic emailaddress;
@dynamic gender;
@dynamic givenname;
@dynamic middleinitial;
@dynamic occupation;
@dynamic surname;

@end
```

Each attribute corresponds to a string property. When you use other attribute types, their properties correspond accordingly (for example, NSDate, NSNumber, NSData). If you were to add a one-to-many relationship, you'd see a set. The @dynamic directive creates property accessors at runtime.

Creating Contexts

In Core Data, entities provide descriptions. Objects are actual class instances that you create from entity specifications. These instances all descend from the NSManagedObject class and represent entries in the database.

Core Data objects live within a managed object context. These contexts, which are instances of NSManagedObjectContext, each represent an object space within your application. This chapter uses a single object context, although more complex implementations may be required in your own apps, primarily to support multithreaded Core Data access.

In this single-object-context example, you establish your context as you start up your application and use that context for all object fetch requests from the stored data. The context story begins by loading any models you have created from the application bundle. You do not need to specify any names:

```
// Init the model
NSManagedObjectModel *managedObjectModel =
    [NSManagedObjectModel mergedModelFromBundles:nil];
```

Next, create a store coordinator and connect it to a file (a store) in the app sandbox. The coordinator manages the relationship between the managed object model in your application and a local file. You provide a file URL that specifies where to save the data. This snippet uses NSSQLiteStoreType, which creates a file using the standard SQLite binary format:

```
// Create the store coordinator
NSPersistentStoreCoordinator *persistentStoreCoordinator =
    [[NSPersistentStoreCoordinator alloc]
        initWithManagedObjectModel:managedObjectModel];

// Connect to the data store (on disk)
NSURL *url = [NSURL fileURLWithPath:dataPath];
if (![persistentStoreCoordinator
    addPersistentStoreWithType: NSSQLiteStoreType
    configuration:nil URL:url options:nil error:&error])
{
    NSLog(@"Error creating persistent store coordinator: %@",
        error.localizedFailureReason);
    return;
}
```

Finally, you create the actual context and set a property to the coordinator you just created:

```
// Create a context and assign to the context property
_context = [[NSManagedObjectContext alloc] init];
_context.persistentStoreCoordinator = persistentStoreCoordinator;
```

Adding Data

The NSEntityDescription class enables you to insert new objects into your context. This lets you add new data entries to populate your file. Provide an entity name and the context you're working with:

```
// Create new object
- (NSManagedObject *)newObject
{
```

```
NSManagedObject *object = [NSEntityDescription
    insertNewObjectForEntityForName:_entityName
    inManagedObjectContext:_context];
return object;
}
```

The request returns a new managed object for you to work with. After you receive the new managed object, you customize it however you like and then save the context:

```
// Save
- (BOOL)save
{
    NSError __autoreleasing *error;
    BOOL success;
    if (!(success = [_context save:&error]))
        NSLog(@"Error saving context: %@", error.localizedFailureReason);
    return success;
}
```

A typical call pattern goes like this: Create one or more new objects, set their properties, and save. You could use the above methods to insert a new Person entity in the database as follows:

```
Person *person = (Person *)[dataHelper newObject];
person.givenname = @"Chris";
person.surname = @"Zahn";
person.section = [[person.surname substringFromIndex:0] substringToIndex:1];
person.occupation = @"Editor";
[dataHelper save]
```

Notice that the section property here derives from the surname. In nearly every basic iOS application, you'll want to add a section property to allow Core Data to group entries together by some common connection. The property name does not matter; you pass it as an argument. section is easy to recognize and remember. Advanced users will write a method to provide their grouping criteria instead of hard-coding it as this example does.

This snippet creates a group-by-surname-initial approach. When you want to group by some other property, either iterate through your data to update the property you use for sections or supply a different attribute to your fetch request. This flexibility makes it easy to change from grouping by last initial to grouping by occupation. A section later in this chapter discusses fetch requests and querying your Core Data store.

Don't confuse iOS sections (used for table views and collection views) with sorting, which is another concept you encounter with Core Data. Sections specify groupings within your object collection. Sorting controls how items are ordered within each section.

Examining the Data File

If you run the preceding code in the simulator, you can easily inspect the SQLite file that Core Data creates. Navigate to the simulator folder (~/Library/Application Support/iPhone Simulator/*Firmware*/Applications, where *Firmware* is the current firmware release; for example, 7.0) and then into the folder for the application itself.

Stored in the Documents folder (depending on the URL used to create the persistent store), an SQLite file contains the database representation you've created. The command-line `sqlite3` utility enables you to inspect the contents by performing a `.dump` operation:

```
% sqlite3 Person.sqlite
SQLite version 3.7.13 2012-07-17 17:46:21
Enter ".help" for instructions
Enter SQL statements terminated with a ";"
sqlite> .dump
PRAGMA foreign_keys=OFF;
BEGIN TRANSACTION;
CREATE TABLE ZPERSON ( Z_PK INTEGER PRIMARY KEY, Z_ENT INTEGER, Z_OPT INTEGER,
ZEMAILADDRESS VARCHAR, ZGENDER VARCHAR, ZGIVENNAME VARCHAR, ZMIDDLEINITIAL VARCHAR,
ZOCCUPATION VARCHAR, ZSECTION VARCHAR, ZSURNAME VARCHAR );
INSERT INTO "ZPERSON" VALUES(1,1,1,'ChristopherLRobinson@foomail.com','male','Christop
her','L','Home care aide','C','Robinson');
INSERT INTO "ZPERSON" VALUES(2,1,1,'NicholasJGrant@spambob.com','male','Nicholas','J',
'Steadicam operator','N','Grant');
INSERT INTO "ZPERSON" VALUES(3,1,1,'JosephJTreece@spambob.
com','male','Joseph','J','Shoe machine operator','J','Treece');
INSERT INTO "ZPERSON" VALUES(4,1,1,'HelenEShaffer@dodgit.
com','female','Helen','E','Coin vending and amusement machine servicer
repairer','H','Shaffer');
CREATE TABLE Z_PRIMARYKEY (Z_ENT INTEGER PRIMARY KEY, Z_NAME VARCHAR, Z_SUPER INTEGER,
Z_MAX INTEGER);
INSERT INTO "Z_PRIMARYKEY" VALUES(1,'Person',0,3000);
CREATE TABLE Z_METADATA (Z_VERSION INTEGER PRIMARY KEY, Z_UUID VARCHAR(255), Z_PLIST
BLOB);
INSERT INTO "Z_METADATA" VALUES(1,'85E928DB-1464-4C3B-BCEA-
9277B8817A04',X'62706C6973743030D601020304050607090A0D0E0F5F101E4E5353746F72654D6F646
56C56657273696F6E4964656E746966696572735F101D4E5350657273697374656E63654672616D65776F
726B56657273696F6E5F10194E5353746F72654D6F64656C56657273696F6E4861736865735B4E5353746
F7265547970655F10125F4E534175746F56616374756E4D6C6576656C6C5F10204E5353746F72654D6F64656C
56657273696F6E48617368657356657273696F6EA1085011019AD10B0C56506572736F6E4F1020D261E38
54795D61A5D69048846ECC3DCFEAC4861D9FCD1540A071C875FE89EA95653514C69746551321003081536
56727E93B6B8B9BCBFC6E9F0F200000000000000010100000000000000010000000000000000000000000
000F4');
COMMIT;
sqlite> .quit
%
```

Here you see several SQL table definitions that store the information for each object plus the `insert` commands used to store the instances built in your code. Although you are thoroughly cautioned against directly manipulating the Core Data store with `sqlite3`, it offers a valuable insight into what's going on under the Core Data hood.

Querying the Database

Retrieve objects from the database by performing fetch requests. A fetch request describes your search criteria for selecting objects. It's passed through to Core Data and used to initialize a results object that contains an array of fetched objects that meet those criteria. Here is a sample fetch method that saves the resulting fetched results to a local instance variable (`_fetchedResultsController`) associated with a helper class property:

```
- (void)fetchItemsMatching:(NSString *)searchString
        forAttribute:(NSString *)attribute
        sortingBy:(NSString *)sortAttribute
{
    // Build an entity description
    NSEntityDescription *entity = [NSEntityDescription
        entityForName:_entityName inManagedObjectContext:_context];

    // Init a fetch request
    NSFetchRequest *fetchRequest = [[NSFetchRequest alloc] init];

    fetchRequest.entity = entity;
    [fetchRequest setFetchBatchSize:0];

    // Apply an ascending sort for the items
    NSString *sortKey = sortAttribute ? : _defaultSortAttribute;
    NSSortDescriptor *sortDescriptor = [[NSSortDescriptor alloc]
        initWithKey:sortKey ascending:YES selector:nil];
    NSArray *descriptors = @[sortDescriptor];
    fetchRequest.sortDescriptors = descriptors;

    // Optional setup predicate
    if (searchString && attribute) fetchRequest.predicate =
        [NSPredicate predicateWithFormat:@"%K contains[cd] %@",
            attribute, searchString];

    // Perform the fetch
    NSError __autoreleasing *error;
    _fetchedResultsController = [[NSFetchedResultsController alloc]
        initWithFetchRequest:fetchRequest managedObjectContext:_context
        sectionNameKeyPath:@"section" cacheName:nil];
    if (![_fetchedResultsController performFetch:&error])
        NSLog(@"Error fetching data: %@", error.localizedFailureReason);

}
```

Setting Up the Fetch Request

A fetch request describes how you want to search through data. This process starts by retrieving an entity description for a given entity name. For the Person entity, that name is @"Person". The description specifies what kinds of data you want to search for.

Create a new fetch request, initializing it with the entity description you just retrieved and a batch size. A 0 batch size corresponds to an indefinite request. If you want to limit the number of returned results, set the batch size to a positive number.

Each request must contain at least one sort descriptor. This method sorts in ascending order (ascending:YES), using a sort key. As with the entity name, the sort key is a string (for example, @"surname"). Set the fetch request's sortDescriptors property with an array of descriptors.

Fetch requests use optional predicates to narrow the results to items that match certain rules. When callers supply the appropriate searchString and attribute parameters, this method creates a predicate of the form *attribute contains*[cd] *searchString*.

This form creates a non-case-sensitive text match; the [cd] after contains refers to non-case-sensitive and non-diacritic-sensitive matching. Diacritics are small marks that accompany a letter, such as the dots of an umlaut (¨) or the tilde (~) above a Spanish *n*.

The %@ format includes an item directly in the predicate, such as the search string used here. The %K format specifies an entity attribute. If you fail to use it, the predicate '*surname*' contains[cd] 'u' will always return true because the second letter in surname is *u*. Use %K to match the property, not the name of the property.

For more complex queries, you could assign a compound predicate. Compound predicates allow you to combine simple predicates using standard logical operations such as AND, OR, and NOT. The NSCompoundPredicate class builds compound predicates out of component predicates. You can also skip the compound predicate class and include AND, OR, and NOT notation directly in simple NSPredicate text.

> **Note**
>
> Predicates provide a powerful mechanism to filter and search data. Apple's *Predicate Programming Guide* provides an exhaustive review of creating and using predicates. See https://developer.apple.com/library/ios/DOCUMENTATION/Cocoa/Conceptual/Predicates/predicates.html.

Performing the Fetch

Create a new fetched results controller for each query. Initialize it with the fetch request, the context, and the section name key path. You can always use @"section" and make sure to define a section attribute for the objects; often, the needs are not complex.

The controller also uses a cache name parameter. Caching reduces overhead associated with producing data that's structured with sections and indexes. Multiple fetch requests are ignored when the data has not changed, minimizing the cost associated with fetch requests over the lifetime of an application. The name used for the cache is arbitrary. Either use `nil` to prevent caching or supply a name in the form of a string. This method uses `nil` to avoid errors related to mutating a fetch request.

Finally, perform the fetch. If it is successful, the method returns `true`. If not, it updates the error that you pass by reference, so you can see why the fetch failed.

The fetch is synchronous. When this method returns, you can use the array of objects in the fetched results controller's `fetchedObjects` property right away. Here's an example of using this method to fetch data, where the request searches for surnames matching a text field's string and lists the matching data in a text view:

```
- (void)list
{
    if (!textField.text.length) return;

    [dataHelper fetchItemsMatching:textField.text
        forAttribute:@"surname" sortingBy:@"surname"];
    NSMutableString *string = [NSMutableString string];
    for (Person *person in dataHelper.fetchedResultsController.fetchedObjects)
    {
        NSString *entry = [NSString stringWithFormat: @"%@, %@ %@: %@\n",
            person.surname, person.givenname,
            person.middleinitial, person.occupation];
        [string appendString:entry];
    }
    textView.text = string;
}
```

Removing Objects

Removing objects from a flat database is straightforward: Just tell the context to delete an object and save the results. Here are two methods that delete either one object or all objects from a database:

```
// Delete one object
- (BOOL)deleteObject:(NSManagedObject *)object
{
    [self fetchData];
    if (!_fetchedResultsController.fetchedObjects.count) return NO;
    [_context deleteObject:object];
    return [self save];
}
```

```
// Delete all objects
- (BOOL)clearData
{
    [self fetchData];
    if (!_fetchedResultsController.fetchedObjects.count) return YES;
    for (NSManagedObject *entry in
        _fetchedResultsController.fetchedObjects)
        [_context deleteObject:entry];
    return [self save];
}
```

Working with relationships can prove slightly more difficult than simply removing objects. Core Data ensures internal consistency before writing data out, and it throws an error if it cannot. Some models that use cross-references get complicated. In some data models, you must clear lingering references before the object can safely be removed from the persistent store. If you don't clear the references, objects may point to deleted items and unexpected failure cases.

To avoid this problem, set Core Data delete rules in the data model inspector. Delete rules control how an object responds to an attempted delete. You can Deny delete requests to ensure that a relationship has no connection before allowing object deletion. Nullify resets inverse relationships before deleting an object. Cascade deletes an object plus all its relationships; for example, you could delete an entire department (including its members) all at once with a cascade. No Action ensures that the objects pointed to by a relationship remain unaffected, even if those objects point back to the item that is about to be deleted.

Xcode issues warnings when it detects nonreciprocal relationships. Avoid unbalanced relationships to simplify your code and provide better internal consistency. If you cannot avoid nonreciprocal items, you need to take them into account when you create your delete methods.

Recipe: Using Core Data for a Table Data Source

Core Data on iOS works closely with table views. The NSFetchedResultsController class includes features that simplify the integration of Core Data objects with table data sources. As you can see in the following subsections, many of the fetched results class's properties and methods are designed from the ground up for table support.

Index Path Access

The fetched results class offers object–index path integration in two directions. You can recover objects from a fetched object array using index paths by calling objectAtIndexPath:. You can query for the index path associated with a fetched object by calling indexPathForObject:. These two methods work with both sectioned tables and tables that are flat—that is, that use only a single section for all their data.

Section Key Path

The `sectionNameKeyPath` property links a managed object attribute to section names. This property helps determine which section each managed object belongs to. You can set this property directly at any time, or you can initialize it when you set up your fetched results controller.

Recipe 12-1 uses an attribute named `section` to distinguish sections, although you can use any attribute name for this key path. For this example, this attribute is set to the first character of each object name to assign a managed object to a section. Set the key path to `nil` to produce a flat table without sections.

Section Groups

Recover section subgroups with the controller's `sections` property. This property returns a collection of sections, each of which stores the managed objects whose section attribute maps to the same letter.

Each returned section implements the `NSFetchedResultsSectionInfo` protocol. This protocol ensures that sections can report their `objects` and `numberOfObjects`, their `name`, and an `indexTitle`—that is, the title that appears on the quick reference index optionally shown above and at the right of the table.

Index Titles

The fetched results controller's `sectionIndexTitles` property generates a list of section titles from the sections within the fetched data. For Recipe 12-1, that array includes single-letter titles. The default implementation uses the value of each section key to return a list of all known sections.

Two further instance methods, `sectionIndexTitleForSectionName:` and `sectionForSectionIndexTitle:atIndex:`, provide section title lookup features. The first returns a title for a section name. The second looks up a section via its title. Override these to use section titles that do not match the data stored in the section name key.

Table Readiness

As the properties and methods you've learned about reveal, fetched results instances are table-ready. Recipe 12-1 presents all the standard table methods, adapted to Core Data fetched results. As you can see, each method used for creating and managing sections is tiny. The built-in Core Data access features reduce these methods to one or two lines each. That's because all the work in creating and accessing the sections is handed over directly to Core Data. The call that initializes each fetched data request specifies what data attribute to use for the sections. Core Data then takes over and performs the rest of the work.

Figure 12-2 shows the interface that Recipe 12-1 builds. It offers a full-featured table, complete with section headers and a floating index.

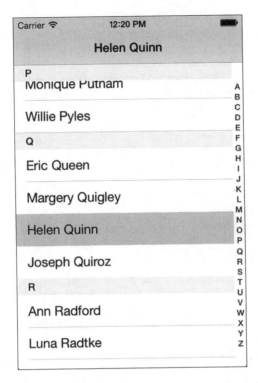

Figure 12-2   Recipe 12-1 creates a full-featured table with an absolute minimum of programming. Core Data powers all these features, from cell contents to section headers to the index.

> **Note**
>
> Reset the simulator or delete the Hello World app from your devices between recipes in this chapter because they all use the same database file (`Person.sqlite`), which will persist in the Documents folder.

Recipe 12-1   **Building a Sectioned Table with Core Data**

```
#pragma mark Data Source
// Number of sections
- (NSInteger)numberOfSectionsInTableView:
        (UITableView *)tableView
{
    return dataHelper.fetchedResultsController.sections.count;
}

// Rows per section
```

```objc
- (NSInteger)tableView:(UITableView *)tableView
        numberOfRowsInSection:(NSInteger)section
{
    id <NSFetchedResultsSectionInfo> sectionInfo =
        dataHelper.fetchedResultsController.sections[section];
    return sectionInfo.numberOfObjects;
}


// Return the title for a given section
- (NSString *)tableView:(UITableView *)aTableView
        titleForHeaderInSection:(NSInteger)section
{

    NSArray *titles = [dataHelper.fetchedResultsController
        sectionIndexTitles];
    if (titles.count <= section)
        return @"Error";
    return titles[section];
}


// Section index titles
- (NSArray *)sectionIndexTitlesForTableView:
        (UITableView *)aTableView
{

    return [dataHelper.fetchedResultsController
        sectionIndexTitles];
}


// Populate a cell for the index path
- (UITableViewCell *)tableView:(UITableView *)tableView
        cellForRowAtIndexPath:(NSIndexPath *)indexPath
{

    UITableViewCell *cell =
        [tableView dequeueReusableCellWithIdentifier:
            @"cell" forIndexPath:indexPath];
    Person *person =
        (Person *)[dataHelper.fetchedResultsController
            objectAtIndexPath:indexPath];
    cell.textLabel.text = person.fullname;

    return cell;
}


#pragma mark Delegate
- (void)tableView:(UITableView *)tableView
        didSelectRowAtIndexPath:(NSIndexPath *)indexPath
{
    // When a row is selected, update title accordingly
```

```
Person *person =
    (Person *)[dataHelper.fetchedResultsController
        objectAtIndexPath:indexPath];
self.title = person.fullname;
}
```

Get This Recipe's Code

To find this recipe's full sample project, point your browser to https://github.com/erica/iOS-7-Cookbook and go to the folder for Chapter 12.

Recipe: Search Tables and Core Data

Core Data stores are designed to work efficiently with `NSPredicates`. Predicates allow you to create fetch requests that select only managed objects that match the predicate's rule or rules. Adding a predicate to a fetch request limits the fetched results to matching objects. Recipe 12-2 takes advantage of the predicates introduced earlier in this chapter to add searching to a table view.

Users may search for entries whose last names match the search string they type. As the text in the search bar at the top of the table changes, the search bar's delegate receives a `searchBar:textDidChange:` callback. In turn, that callback method performs a new fetch, using that string as the basis for searching.

Only a few changes to Recipe 12-1 are required to support search within your table, as shown in Recipe 12-2:

- The `loadView` method adds a search controller; the `viewDidAppear:` method scrolls the search field out of sight.

- The section index expands to include a search icon, and the section for indexing method respects that icon by scrolling the search controller frame into view.

- The search bar delegate methods fetch new results whenever the search field contents change. They submit a new Core Data fetch requests and use those results to populate the table view.

Together, these few changes create a search field–powered table that responds to user-driven queries. As both Recipes 12-1 and 12-2 show, it takes surprisingly little work to make table views work with Core Data.

Recipe 12-2   **Using Fetch Requests with Predicates**

```
// Section index titles plus search
- (NSArray *)sectionIndexTitlesForTableView:
        (UITableView *)aTableView
{
```

```
        if (aTableView == searchController.searchResultsTableView)
            return nil;
        return [[NSArray arrayWithObject:UITableViewIndexSearch]
            arrayByAddingObjectsFromArray:
            [dataHelper.fetchedResultsController sectionIndexTitles]];
}


// Allow scrolling to search bar
- (NSInteger)tableView:(UITableView *)tableView
        sectionForSectionIndexTitle:(NSString *)title
        atIndex:(NSInteger)index
{
    if (title == UITableViewIndexSearch)
    {
        [self.tableView scrollRectToVisible:
            searchController.searchBar.frame animated:NO];
        return -1;
    }
    return [dataHelper.fetchedResultsController.sectionIndexTitles
        indexOfObject:title];
}


// Return a cell specific to the table being shown
- (UITableViewCell *)tableView:(UITableView *)aTableView
        cellForRowAtIndexPath:(NSIndexPath *)indexPath
{
    [aTableView registerClass:[UITableViewCell class]
        forCellReuseIdentifier:@"cell"];
    UITableViewCell *cell =
        [aTableView dequeueReusableCellWithIdentifier:@"cell"
            forIndexPath:indexPath];
    Person *person = [dataHelper.fetchedResultsController
        objectAtIndexPath:indexPath];
    cell.textLabel.text = person.fullname;
    return cell;
}


// Handle cancel by fetching all data
- (void)searchBarCancelButtonClicked:(UISearchBar *)aSearchBar
{
    aSearchBar.text = @"";
    [dataHelper fetchData];
}


// Handle search field update by fetching matching entries
- (void)searchBar:(UISearchBar *)aSearchBar
        textDidChange:(NSString *)searchText
```

```
{
    [dataHelper fetchItemsMatching:aSearchBar.text
        forAttribute:@"surname" sortingBy:nil];
}


// Set up search and Core Data
- (void)loadView
{
    self.view = [[UIView alloc] init];
    self.tableView = [[UITableView alloc] init];
    self.view.backgroundColor = [UIColor whiteColor];

    // Create a search bar
    UISearchBar *searchBar =
        [[UISearchBar alloc] initWithFrame:
            CGRectMake(0.0f, 0.0f, 0.0f, 44.0f)];
    searchBar.autocorrectionType = UITextAutocorrectionTypeNo;
    searchBar.autocapitalizationType = UITextAutocapitalizationTypeNone;
    searchBar.keyboardType = UIKeyboardTypeAlphabet;
    searchBar.delegate = self;
    self.tableView.tableHeaderView = searchBar;

    // Create the search display controller
    searchController = [[UISearchDisplayController alloc]
        initWithSearchBar:searchBar contentsController:self];
    searchController.searchResultsDataSource = self;
    searchController.searchResultsDelegate = self;

    // Establish Core Data
    dataHelper = [[CoreDataHelper alloc] init];
    dataHelper.entityName = @"Person";
    dataHelper.defaultSortAttribute = @"surname";

    // Check for existing data
    BOOL firstRun = !dataHelper.hasStore;

    // Set up Core Data
    [dataHelper setupCoreData];
    if (firstRun)
        [self initializeData];

    [dataHelper fetchData];
    [self.tableView reloadData];
}


// Hide the search bar
- (void)viewDidAppear:(BOOL)animated
```

```
{
    [super viewDidAppear:animated];
    NSIndexPath *path = [NSIndexPath indexPathForRow:0 inSection:0];
    [self.tableView scrollToRowAtIndexPath:path
        atScrollPosition:UITableViewScrollPositionTop animated:NO];
}
```

Get This Recipe's Code

To find this recipe's full sample project, point your browser to https://github.com/erica/iOS-7-Cookbook and go to the folder for Chapter 12.

Recipe: Adding Edits to Core Data Table Views

You've seen how table views integrate well with static data. Now it's time to bring that technology to the next level. Recipe 12-3 demonstrates how to add edits to both the table presentation and the Core Data store that's backing the table.

Much of this recipe should look familiar. Its code is based on the basic edits you read about in Chapter 9, "Creating and Managing Table Views." Users can add new rows by tapping + and delete them by swiping or entering edit mode. All the remaining features, including the search table and the section index, remain in place.

In this recipe, the new data is loaded from a collection of fake contacts, courtesy of fakenamegenerator.com. When users tap +, the app loads a random name into the database from its collection.

You should make a number of adaptations to bring table edits into the Core Data world. Topics you should consider when building your table implementation include undo/redo support, user control limits, and using controller delegation for data updates.

Adding Undo/Redo Support

Core Data simplifies table undo/redo support to an astonishing degree. It provides automatic support for these operations and requires little programming effort. Add this support by assigning an undo manager when you create a Core Data context:

```
_context = [[NSManagedObjectContext alloc] init];
_context.persistentStoreCoordinator = persistentStoreCoordinator;
_context.undoManager = [[NSUndoManager alloc] init];
_context.undoManager.levelsOfUndo = 999;
```

As with all other undo/redo support, your primary controller must become the first responder while it is onscreen. The standard suite of first responder methods includes canBecomeFirstResponder (respond YES), viewDidAppear: (the controller view becomes first responder as soon as it appears), and `viewWillDisappear:` (the controller view resigns first responder as it leaves the screen):

```
- (BOOL)canBecomeFirstResponder
{
    return YES;
}

- (void)viewDidAppear:(BOOL)animated
{
    [super viewDidAppear:animated];
    [self becomeFirstResponder];

    if (dataHelper.numberOfEntities == 0) return;

    // Hide the search bar
    NSIndexPath *path = [NSIndexPath indexPathForRow:0 inSection:0];
    [self.tableView scrollToRowAtIndexPath:path
        atScrollPosition:UITableViewScrollPositionTop animated:NO];
}

- (void)viewWillDisappear:(BOOL)animated
{
    [super viewWillDisappear:animated];
    [self resignFirstResponder];
}
```

Notice that this search bar is scrolled offscreen only if the table contains at least one entry. That workaround was not needed in Recipe 12-2. On a table where users have direct control over the contents by adding and removing entries, it is entirely possible that the table is presented without any data at all.

Creating Undo Transactions

Build your Core Data updates into undo transactions by bracketing them into undo groupings. The `beginUndoGrouping` and `endUndoGrouping` calls appear before and after context updates. Specify an action name that describes the operation that just took place. This action name is primarily used for shake-to-undo support (for example, "Undo delete?"). It also helps document the action you're expressing.

The braces used in the following undo-grouping sample are purely stylistic. You do not need to include them in your code. They are provided to highlight the transactional nature that underlies undo groupings:

```
// Delete request
if (editingStyle == UITableViewCellEditingStyleDelete)
{
    NSManagedObject *object = [dataHelper.fetchedResultsController
```

```
        objectAtIndexPath:indexPath];
    NSUndoManager *manager = dataHelper.context.undoManager;
    [manager beginUndoGrouping];
    [manager setActionName:@"Delete"];
    {
        [dataHelper.context deleteObject:object];
    }
    [manager endUndoGrouping];
    [dataHelper save];
}
```

The three calls (begin, end, and setting the action name) in this snippet ensure that Core Data can reverse its operations. For this minimal effort, your application gains a fully realized undo management system, courtesy of Core Data. Be aware that any undo/redo history will not survive quitting your application. The stack resets each time the app launches.

Rethinking Edits

When working with Core Data–powered tables, Recipe 12-3 doesn't let users reorder rows. That's because its fetch requests sort the data, not users. Recipe 12-3's `tableView:canMoveRowAtIndexPath:` method hard-codes its result to `NO`. Yes, you can work around this by introducing a custom row position attribute. Much of the time you won't want to. Recipe 12-3 shows a common use case.

In a similar vein, make sure you coordinate any database edits to your data sources. With Core Data–driven tables, these changes may come from user requests (swiping, pressing +, and so forth) and also from the undo manager. By subscribing to the fetched results controller as its delegate, you'll know whenever data has updated from undo actions. Use the fetch result delegate callbacks to reload your data whenever data changes occur.

Recipe 12-3   **Adapting Table Edits to Core Data**

```
// Update items in the navigation bar
- (void)setBarButtonItems
{
    // Expire any ongoing operations
    if (dataHelper.context.undoManager.isUndoing ||
        dataHelper.context.undoManager.isRedoing)
    {
        [self performSelector:@selector(setBarButtonItems)
            withObject:nil afterDelay:0.1f];
        return;
    }

    UIBarButtonItem *undo = SYSBARBUTTON_TARGET(
        UIBarButtonSystemItemUndo,
        dataHelper.context.undoManager, @selector(undo)));
```

```
    undo.enabled = dataHelper.context.undoManager.canUndo;
    UIBarButtonItem *redo = SYSBARBUTTON_TARGET(
        UIBarButtonSystemItemRedo,
        dataHelper.context.undoManager, @selector(redo));
    redo.enabled = dataHelper.context.undoManager.canRedo;
    UIBarButtonItem *add = SYSBARBUTTON(
        UIBarButtonSystemItemAdd, @selector(addItem));

    self.navigationItem.leftBarButtonItems = @[add, undo, redo];
}


// Refetch data
- (void)refresh
{
    // If searching, fetch search results, otherwise all data
    if (searchController.searchBar.text)
        [dataHelper fetchItemsMatching:
                searchController.searchBar.text
            forAttribute:@"surname" sortingBy:nil];
    else
        [dataHelper fetchData];
    dataHelper.fetchedResultsController.delegate = self;

    // Reload tables
    [self.tableView reloadData];
    [searchController.searchResultsTableView reloadData];

    // Update bar button items
    [self setBarButtonItems];
}


// Respond to section changes
- (void)controller:(NSFetchedResultsController *)controller
    didChangeSection:(id <NSFetchedResultsSectionInfo>)sectionInfo
        atIndex:(NSUInteger)sectionIndex
        forChangeType:(NSFetchedResultsChangeType)type
{
    if (type == NSFetchedResultsChangeDelete)
        [self.tableView deleteSections:
                [NSIndexSet indexSetWithIndex:sectionIndex]
            withRowAnimation:UITableViewRowAnimationAutomatic];

    if (type == NSFetchedResultsChangeInsert)
        [self.tableView insertSections:
                [NSIndexSet indexSetWithIndex:sectionIndex]
            withRowAnimation:UITableViewRowAnimationAutomatic];
```

```objc
        sectionHeadersAffected = YES;
}


// Respond to item changes
- (void)controller:(NSFetchedResultsController *)controller
        didChangeObject:(id)anObject
        atIndexPath:(NSIndexPath *)indexPath
        forChangeType:(NSFetchedResultsChangeType)type
        newIndexPath:(NSIndexPath *)newIndexPath
{

    UITableView *tableView = self.tableView;

    if (type == NSFetchedResultsChangeInsert)
        [tableView insertRowsAtIndexPaths:@[newIndexPath]
            withRowAnimation:UITableViewRowAnimationAutomatic];

    if (type == NSFetchedResultsChangeDelete)
        [tableView deleteRowsAtIndexPaths:@[indexPath]
            withRowAnimation:UITableViewRowAnimationAutomatic];
}


// Prepare for updates
- (void)controllerWillChangeContent:
        (NSFetchedResultsController *)controller
{

    sectionHeadersAffected = NO;
    [self.tableView beginUpdates];
}


// Apply updates
- (void)controllerDidChangeContent:
        (NSFetchedResultsController *)controller
{

    [self.tableView endUpdates];

    // Update section headers if needed
    if (sectionHeadersAffected)
        [self.tableView reloadSections:
            [NSIndexSet indexSetWithIndexesInRange:
                    NSMakeRange(0, self.tableView.numberOfSections)]
                withRowAnimation:UITableViewRowAnimationNone];

    [self setBarButtonItems];
}
```

```objc
// Only allow editing on the main table
- (BOOL)tableView:(UITableView *)aTableView
        canEditRowAtIndexPath:(NSIndexPath *)indexPath
{
    if (aTableView == searchController.searchResultsTableView) return NO;
    return YES;
}

// No reordering allowed
- (BOOL)tableView:(UITableView *)tableView
        canMoveRowAtIndexPath:(NSIndexPath *)indexPath
{
    return NO;
}

- (void)addItem
{
    // Surround the "add" functionality with undo grouping
    NSUndoManager *manager = dataHelper.context.undoManager;
    [manager beginUndoGrouping];
    {
        Person *person = (Person *)[dataHelper newObject];
        [self setupNewPerson:person];
    }
    [manager endUndoGrouping];
    [manager setActionName:@"Add"];
    [dataHelper save];
}

// Handle deletions
- (void)tableView:(UITableView *)tableView
        commitEditingStyle:(UITableViewCellEditingStyle)editingStyle
        forRowAtIndexPath:(NSIndexPath *)indexPath
{
    // delete request
    if (editingStyle == UITableViewCellEditingStyleDelete)
    {
        NSManagedObject *object = [dataHelper.fetchedResultsController
            objectAtIndexPath:indexPath];
        NSUndoManager *manager = dataHelper.context.undoManager;
        [manager beginUndoGrouping];
        {
            [dataHelper.context deleteObject:object];
        }
        [manager endUndoGrouping];
```

```
        [manager setActionName:@"Delete"];
        [dataHelper save];
    }
}

// Toggle editing mode
- (void)setEditing:(BOOL)isEditing animated:(BOOL)animated
{
    [super setEditing:isEditing animated:animated];
    [self.tableView setEditing:isEditing animated:animated];

    NSIndexPath *path = [self.tableView
        indexPathForSelectedRow];
    if (path)
        [self.tableView deselectRowAtIndexPath:path
            animated:YES];

    [self setBarButtonItems];
}
```

Get This Recipe's Code

To find this recipe's full sample project, point your browser to https://github.com/erica/iOS-7-Cookbook and go to the folder for Chapter 12.

Recipe: A Core Data–Powered Collection View

It takes work to convert Recipe 12-3 from a table to a collection view, but it doesn't take an overwhelming amount. Ditch the search view controller, get rid of the index view, update the edits a little, and switch out the controller class from table to collection. Figure 12-3 shows the results. This collection view displays the same data as the table did, offering selectable cells, edits, and undo/redo support.

The refactoring story begins with the data model. Recipe 12-4 adds a new attribute, a binary data item called `imageData`. The image is built out of each person's first and last name and it's saved in binary format. This extra attribute allows the collection view to present each data entry as a reusable image, sized to fit each name.

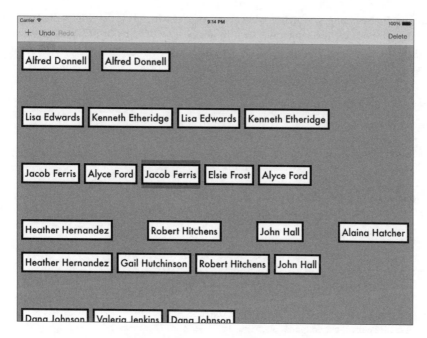

Figure 12-3   Recipe 12-4 builds a collection view powered by Core Data.

The data source methods all update from table view to collection view versions. Some need little work. The section count and items-per-section methods switch to their collection view counterparts, while their internals essentially stay the same.

Others experience a bigger makeover. The cell-for-path method gets a complete refresh as cells are built to present images rather than populate a title with text. Recipe 12-4 does not include the search view controller and the index view and header callbacks. Finally, Recipe 12-4 adds a custom cell size layout method to match each view size to its embedded image size. That layout is an important component in collection views but is not needed in table views.

Edits are affected as well and no longer center around cell animation. Instead of providing deletion support through a table-based commit edits method, Recipe 12-4 adds a standalone deleteItem method that corresponds to the addItem method used in Recipe 12-3.

The bar button on the right that used to switch into and out of edit mode on the table now becomes a Delete button that is activated whenever any item is selected in the collection view. The remaining items in the navigation bar that provide undo and redo support, and the methods that power them, make the jump from tables to collection views unchanged.

Nothing much else changes, which is what you'd expect with MVC development. The Core Data model methods are the same ones used in Recipe 12-3. The UIKit-provided views are stock items. Only the controller part needs or receives updates, which simplifies this refactoring exercise.

Recipe 12-4   **Core Data Collection View**

```
#pragma mark Data Source
// Return the number of sections
- (NSInteger)numberOfSectionsInCollectionView:
        (UICollectionView *)collectionView
{
    if (dataHelper.numberOfEntities == 0) return 0;
    return dataHelper.fetchedResultsController.sections.count;
}


// Return the number of items per section
- (NSInteger)collectionView:(UICollectionView *)collectionView
        numberOfItemsInSection:(NSInteger)section
{
    id <NSFetchedResultsSectionInfo> sectionInfo =
        dataHelper.fetchedResultsController.sections[section];
    return sectionInfo.numberOfObjects;
}


// This method builds images into collection view cells
- (UICollectionViewCell *)collectionView:
        (UICollectionView *) aCollectionView
        cellForItemAtIndexPath:(NSIndexPath *)indexPath
{
    UICollectionViewCell *cell = [self.collectionView
        dequeueReusableCellWithReuseIdentifier:@"cell"
        forIndexPath:indexPath];
    Person *person = [dataHelper.fetchedResultsController
        objectAtIndexPath:indexPath];
    UIImage *image = [UIImage imageWithData:person.imageData];

    cell.backgroundColor = [UIColor clearColor];
    if (![cell.contentView viewWithTag:IMAGEVIEWTAG])
    {
        UIImageView *imageView =
            [[UIImageView alloc] initWithImage:image];
        imageView.tag = IMAGEVIEWTAG;
        [cell.contentView addSubview:imageView];
    }

    UIImageView *imageView =
```

```
    (UIImageView *)[cell.contentView viewWithTag:IMAGEVIEWTAG];
    imageView.frame = CGRectMake(0.0f, 10.0f, image.size.width, image.size.height);
    imageView.image = image;

    cell.selectedBackgroundView = [[UIView alloc] init];
    cell.selectedBackgroundView.backgroundColor =
        [UIColor redColor];

    return cell;
}


// Return the size for layout
- (CGSize)collectionView:(UICollectionView *)collectionView
      layout:(UICollectionViewLayout*)collectionViewLayout
      sizeForItemAtIndexPath:(NSIndexPath *)indexPath
{
    Person *person = [dataHelper.fetchedResultsController
        objectAtIndexPath:indexPath];
    UIImage *image = [UIImage imageWithData:person.imageData];
    return CGSizeMake(image.size.width, image.size.height + 20.0f);
}


#pragma mark Delegate methods
- (void)collectionView:(UICollectionView *)aCollectionView
        didSelectItemAtIndexPath:(NSIndexPath *)indexPath
{
    [self setBarButtonItems];
}


#pragma mark Editing and Undo
- (void)setBarButtonItems
{
    // Delete requires a selected item
    self.navigationItem.rightBarButtonItem.enabled =
        (self.collectionView.indexPathsForSelectedItems.count != 0);

    // Set up undo/redo items
    UIBarButtonItem *undo =
        SYSBARBUTTON_TARGET(UIBarButtonSystemItemUndo,
            self.dataHelper.context.undoManager, @selector(undo));
    undo.enabled = self.dataHelper.context.undoManager.canUndo;
    UIBarButtonItem *redo =
        SYSBARBUTTON_TARGET(UIBarButtonSystemItemRedo,
            self.dataHelper.context.undoManager, @selector(redo));
    redo.enabled = self.dataHelper.context.undoManager.canRedo;
    UIBarButtonItem *add =
        SYSBARBUTTON(UIBarButtonSystemItemAdd, @selector(addItem));
```

```
      self.navigationItem.leftBarButtonItems = @[add, undo, redo];
}


// Refresh the data, update the view
- (void)refresh
{
    [dataHelper fetchData];
    dataHelper.fetchedResultsController.delegate = self;
    [self.collectionView reloadData];
    [self performSelector:@selector(setBarButtonItems)
        withObject:nil afterDelay:0.1f];
}


- (void)controllerDidChangeContent:
        (NSFetchedResultsController *)controller
{
    // Respond to data change from undo controller
    [self refresh];
}


// Add a new item
- (void)addItem
{
    NSUndoManager *manager = dataHelper.context.undoManager;
    [manager beginUndoGrouping];
    {
        Person *person = (Person *)[dataHelper newObject];
        [self setupNewPerson:person];
    }
    [manager endUndoGrouping];
    [manager setActionName:@"Add"];
    [dataHelper save];
    [self refresh];
}


// Delete the selected item
- (void)deleteItem
{
    if (!self.collectionView.indexPathsForSelectedItems.count)
        return;

    NSIndexPath *indexPath =
        self.collectionView.indexPathsForSelectedItems[0];
    NSManagedObject *object =
        [dataHelper.fetchedResultsController
        objectAtIndexPath:indexPath];
```

```
    NSUndoManager *manager = dataHelper.context.undoManager;
    [manager beginUndoGrouping];
    {
        [dataHelper.context deleteObject:object];
    }
    [manager endUndoGrouping];
    [manager setActionName:@"Delete"];
    [dataHelper save];
    [self refresh];
}

#pragma mark Setup
- (void)viewDidLoad
{
    [super viewDidLoad];
    [self.collectionView registerClass:
        [UICollectionViewCell class]
            forCellWithReuseIdentifier:@"cell"];

    self.collectionView.backgroundColor =
        [UIColor lightGrayColor];
    self.collectionView.allowsMultipleSelection = NO;
    self.collectionView.allowsSelection = YES;

    self.navigationItem.leftBarButtonItem =
        SYSBARBUTTON(UIBarButtonSystemItemAdd,
        @selector(addItem));
    self.navigationItem.rightBarButtonItem =
        BARBUTTON(@"Delete", @selector(deleteItem));
    self.navigationItem.rightBarButtonItem.enabled = NO;
}
```

Get This Recipe's Code

To find this recipe's full sample project, point your browser to https://github.com/erica/iOS-7-Cookbook and go to the folder for Chapter 12.

Summary

When you are working with table views and collection views, Core Data provides the perfect backing technology. It offers easy-to-use model support that easily integrates into UIKit data sources. This chapter offers just a taste of Core Data's capabilities. These recipes have shown you how to design and implement basic Core Data support for managed object models. You've read about defining a model and implementing fetch requests. You've seen how to add objects, modify them, delete them, and save them. You've learned about predicates and undo operations. After reading through this chapter, here are a few final thoughts to take away with you:

- If you're not using Core Data with tables and collection views, you're missing out on one of the most elegant ways to populate and control your data.

- When working with Core Data, you're not limited to scrolling views of content. Use Core Data to save any kind of tabular information. It offers a relational database solution that goes well beyond the demands of most applications.

- Always design for undo/redo support. Even if you don't think you'll need it right away, having the work done in advance lets you add features later. We're not big fans of shake-to-undo, but it offers a button-free way to integrate this functionality into otherwise overdesigned interfaces.

- Predicates are one of our favorite SDK features. Spend some time learning how to construct them and use them with all kinds of objects, such as arrays and sets, not just with Core Data.

- iCloud provides a tantalizing match between Core Data and ubiquitous data, extending iOS data to the user's desktop, to each of his or her devices, and to the cloud as a whole. While Core Data integration with iCloud has been panned in the past due to stability and related issues, Apple insists that iOS 7 includes much-needed improvements. Look up `UIManagedDocument` to learn more about iCloud and Core Data integration.

- Core Data's capabilities go way beyond the basic recipes you've seen in this chapter. Check out Tim Isted and Tom Harrington's *Core Data for iOS: Developing Data-Driven Applications for the iPad, iPhone, and iPod touch* (Addison-Wesley Professional) for an in-depth exploration of Core Data and its features.

13

Networking Basics

As Internet-connected devices, the iPhone and its iOS family members are particularly well suited to retrieving remote data and accessing web-based services. Apple has lavished the platform with a solid grounding in all kinds of network computing and its supporting technologies. This chapter surveys basic techniques for network computing, from connectivity testing and web-based downloading to processing the traditional forms of data provided via web services.

Recipe: Checking Your Network Status

Networked applications need a live connection to communicate with the Internet or other nearby devices. Applications should know whether such a connection exists before reaching out to send or retrieve data. Checking the network status lets an application communicate with users and explain why certain functions might be disabled.

Apple has rejected and will continue to reject applications that do not check network status before providing download options to the user. Apple reviewers are trained to check whether you properly notify the user, especially in the case of network errors. Always verify network status and alert the user accordingly.

Apple also may reject applications based on "excessive data usage." If you plan to stream large quantities of data, such as voice or video, in your application, you should test for the current connection type. Provide lower-quality data streams for users on a cell network connection and higher-quality data for users with a Wi-Fi connection. Apple has had little tolerance for applications that place high demands on cell network data. Keep in mind that unlimited data has given way to metered accounts in the United States. You can alienate your users as well as Apple by overusing cell networks.

iOS tests for the following configuration states: some (that is, any kind of) network connection available, Wi-Fi available, and cell service available. No App Store–safe application programming interfaces (APIs) allow the iPhone to test for Bluetooth connectivity at this time (although you can limit your application to run only on Bluetooth-enabled devices), nor can you check whether a user is roaming and utilizing a potentially expensive cellular network before offering data access.

The System Configuration framework offers network-checking functions. Among these, SCNetworkReachabilityCreateWithAddress tests whether an IP address is reachable. Recipe 13-1 shows a simple example of this test in action.

The networkAvailable method determines whether your device has outgoing connectivity, which it defines as having both access and a live connection. This method, based on Apple sample code, returns YES when the network is available and NO otherwise. The flags used here indicate both that the network is reachable (kSCNetworkFlagsReachable) and that no further connection is required (kSCNetworkFlagsConnectionRequired). Other flags you may use are as follows:

- **kSCNetworkReachabilityFlagsIsWWAN**—Tests whether your user is using the carrier's wireless wide area network (WWAN) or local Wi-Fi. When available via WWAN, the network can be reached via EDGE, GPRS, LTE, or another type of cell connection. When using a WWAN connection, you might want to use lightweight versions of your resources (for example, smaller versions of images or lower-bandwidth videos) due to the connection's constricted or costly bandwidth.

- **kSCNetworkReachabilityFlagsConnectionOnTraffic**—Specifies that addresses can be reached with the current network configuration but that a connection must first be established. Any actual traffic will initiate the connection.

- **kSCNetworkReachabilityFlagsIsDirect**—Tells whether the network traffic goes through a gateway or arrives directly.

Evaluating whether connectivity code works, it is best to test on a variety of devices. The iPhone and cell-enabled iPads offer the most options. These devices provide both cell and Wi-Fi support, enabling you to confirm that the network remains reachable when using a cellular WWAN connection.

Test this code by toggling Wi-Fi and cell data off and on in the iPhone's Settings app. A slight delay sometimes occurs when checking for network reachability, so design your applications accordingly. Let the user know what your code is up to during the check.

SCNetworkReachabilityGetFlags is a synchronous call that can block for a long period of time, particularly on Domain Name System (DNS) lookup if there is no connection. Never call this method from your main thread in production code. A long enough delay on the main thread will result in your app being booted by the iOS watchdog.

Use NSOperationQueue to move the blocking call off the main thread. Be sure to push any interaction with the UI back on to the main thread:

```
[[[NSOperationQueue alloc] init] addOperationWithBlock:
 ^{
     // blocking call
     BOOL networkAvailable = [device networkAvailable];

     // UI interaction
     [[NSOperationQueue mainQueue] addOperationWithBlock:^{
```

```
        textView.text = networkAvailable ? @"Yes" : @"No";
    }];
}];
```

Indicate whether your application is using the network by setting the networkActivity-
IndicatorVisible property for the shared application instance. A spinning indicator in the
status bar shows that network activity is in progress.

Recipe 13-1 Testing a Network Connection

```
SCNetworkReachabilityRef reachability;
SCNetworkConnectionFlags connectionFlags;

- (void)pingReachability
{
    if (!reachability)
    {
        BOOL ignoresAdHocWiFi = NO;
        struct sockaddr_in ipAddress;
        bzero(&ipAddress, sizeof(ipAddress));
        ipAddress.sin_len = sizeof(ipAddress);
        ipAddress.sin_family = AF_INET;
        ipAddress.sin_addr.s_addr =
            htonl(ignoresAdHocWiFi ? INADDR_ANY : IN_LINKLOCALNETNUM);

        reachability = SCNetworkReachabilityCreateWithAddress(
            kCFAllocatorDefault, (struct sockaddr *)&ipAddress);
        CFRetain(reachability);
    }

    // Recover reachability flags
    BOOL didRetrieveFlags = SCNetworkReachabilityGetFlags(
        reachability, &connectionFlags);
    if (!didRetrieveFlags)
        NSLog(@"Error. Could not recover network reachability flags");
}

- (BOOL)networkAvailable
{
    [[UIApplication sharedApplication]
        setNetworkActivityIndicatorVisible:YES];
    [self pingReachability];
    BOOL isReachable =
        (connectionFlags & kSCNetworkFlagsReachable) != 0;
    BOOL needsConnection =
        (connectionFlags & kSCNetworkFlagsConnectionRequired) != 0;
    [[UIApplication sharedApplication]
```

```
        setNetworkActivityIndicatorVisible:NO];
    return (isReachable && !needsConnection) ? YES : NO;
}}
```

Get This Recipe's Code

To find this recipe's full sample project, point your browser to https://github.com/erica/iOS-7-Cookbook and go to the folder for Chapter 13.

Scanning for Connectivity Changes

Connectivity state may change while an application is running. Checking once at application launch usually isn't enough for an application that depends on data connections throughout its lifetime. When a network connection is lost or when it can finally be established, your UI should adjust accordingly, such as disabling or enabling a button or alerting the user.

Listing 13-1 addresses this challenge by extending the UIDevice reachability category to monitor network changes. It provides a pair of methods that allow you to schedule and unschedule reachability watchers—observers that notify when the connectivity state changes. It builds a callback that messages a watcher object when that state changes. The monitor is scheduled on the current run loop and runs asynchronously. Upon detecting a change, the callback function triggers.

Listing 13-1's callback function redirects itself to a custom delegate method, reachability-Changed, which must be implemented by its watcher. That watcher object can then query for current network state.

The method that schedules the watcher assigns the delegate as its parameter. Here's a trivial case of how that might be implemented skeletally, using Listing 13-1's implementation. In real-world deployment, you'll want to update the functionality presented in your GUI to match the availability (or lack thereof) of network-only features. Inform your user when connectivity changes and update your interface to mirror the current state. You might want to disable buttons or menu items that depend on network access when that access disappears. Providing an alert of some kind lets the user know why the GUI has updated.

Be prepared for multiple callbacks. Your application will generally receive one callback at a time for each kind of state change (that is, when the cellular data connection is established or released) or when Wi-Fi is established or lost. Your user's connectivity settings (especially remembering and logging in to known Wi-Fi networks) will affect the kind and number of callbacks you may have to handle.

Listing 13-1   **Monitoring Connectivity Changes**

```objc
@protocol ReachabilityWatcher <NSObject>
- (void)reachabilityChanged;
@end


// For each callback, ping the watcher
static void ReachabilityCallback(
    SCNetworkReachabilityRef target,
    SCNetworkConnectionFlags flags, void* info)
{
    @autoreleasepool {
        id watcher = (__bridge id) info;
        if ([watcher respondsToSelector: @selector(reachabilityChanged)])
            [watcher performSelector: @selector(reachabilityChanged)];
    }
}


// Schedule watcher into the run loop
- (BOOL)scheduleReachabilityWatcher:(id <ReachabilityWatcher>)watcher
{
    [self pingReachability];

    SCNetworkReachabilityContext context =
        {0, (__bridge void *)watcher, NULL, NULL, NULL};
    if(SCNetworkReachabilitySetCallback(reachability,
        ReachabilityCallback, &context))
    {
        if (!SCNetworkReachabilityScheduleWithRunLoop(
            reachability, CFRunLoopGetCurrent(),
            kCFRunLoopCommonModes))
        {
            NSLog(@"Error: Could not schedule reachability");
            SCNetworkReachabilitySetCallback(reachability, NULL, NULL);
            return NO;
        }
    }
    else
    {
        NSLog(@"Error: Could not set reachability callback");
        return NO;
    }
    return YES;
}


// Remove the watcher
- (void)unscheduleReachabilityWatcher
```

```
{
    SCNetworkReachabilitySetCallback(reachability, NULL, NULL);
    if (SCNetworkReachabilityUnscheduleFromRunLoop(
        reachability, CFRunLoopGetCurrent(),
        kCFRunLoopCommonModes))
        NSLog(@"Success. Unscheduled reachability");
    else
        NSLog(@"Error: Could not unschedule reachability");

    CFRelease(reachability);
    reachability = nil;
}
```

The URL Loading System

Apple provides a robust stack of APIs for communicating over the network. Each level of the stack is available to you, starting with the BSD Sockets layer at the base, the C-based CoreFoundation layer, and the Objective-C–based Foundation layer. For client-side apps, there is rarely a need to dive deeper than the Foundation layer.

For most applications, your network communication can be provided by the URL Loading System found in the Foundation layer. With this system, you connect, download, and upload data to many services that can be referenced via a URL. This functionality is not limited to HTTP-based services (http and https) but includes support for file transfer protocol (ftp), local file URLs, and data URLs.

The URL Loading System shipped with the initial iOS SDK, NSURLConnection (which is confusingly both the name of the technology as well as the name of the headlining class), provided the heavy network lifting for thousands of apps. This framework was initially built for the Safari browser and then migrated to Foundation.

With iOS 7, Apple radically overhauled NSURLConnection to be even more flexible, configurable, and robust. The new technology, NSURLSession, is a complete replacement that provides substantial improvements to the granularity of configuration, better authentication handling, a more convenient and richer delegate model, and easy access to the new background downloading also introduced in iOS 7. While the old NSURLConnection system is still available, there is no reason not to move to the new NSURLSession technology.

While many classes used in NSURLConnection are maintained in NSURLSession, such as NSURL, NSURLRequest, and NSURLResponse, a new set of classes provide additional support for configuration and the task of downloading or uploading data.

Configuration

Configuration of a session uses an NSURLSessionConfiguration object. Each session uses a separate configuration object, improving on the global configuration provided in the legacy NSURLConnection. You set properties for connection policies, number of connections, cell usage, cache, credentials, and cookie storage. Use one of the class factories to create a configuration and then modify appropriately.

One welcome new property is an explicit resource timeout in addition to the network timeout. The network timeout (timeoutIntervalForRequest), which existed as a request-level configuration in the past, specifies the timeout for the minimum frequency of incoming bytes of data. The new resource timeout (timeoutIntervalForResource) specifies the overall timeout for the entire transfer.

Once the NSURLSessionConfiguration object is configured, pass it to the constructor of your NSURLSession object. A copy of your NSURLSessionConfiguration is stored in the session. While the configuration object is mutable, once it is passed to your session, changes are ignored; make sure your configuration is set appropriately.

Tasks

Each unit of work in a session is defined by an NSURLSessionTask object. Tasks are a close corollary to the original NSURLConnection class, each representing a single network request. A task provides the current state of a request. Once active, you can use a task to cancel, suspend, or resume activity. Much of the connection state that required the implementation of a delegate to access in NSURLConnection are now available as properties on NSURLSessionTask.

NSURLSessionTask is an abstract class with three concrete classes provided for general data transfers, download, and upload functions, as shown in Figure 13-1 (left): NSURLDataTask, NSURLDownloadTask, and NSURLUploadTask. All these tasks support a convenient block-based handler as well as a more flexible delegate-based mechanism for performing and handling the network request.

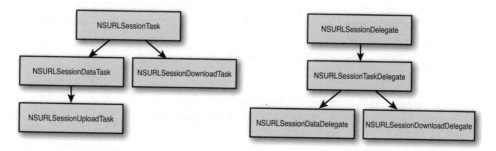

Figure 13-1   A family of session tasks provide the ability to download and upload data (left). An accompanying hierarchy of delegate protocols for the tasks as well as NSURLSession allow for accessing and responding to state changes (right).

The subclasses of NSURLSessionTask provide similar functionality, with a few important differences. Data tasks provide a general-purpose base class, supporting both the sending and receiving of data from memory. Upload tasks are identical to data tasks (they are actually a subclass of NSURLSessionDataTask) but with an additional delegate call for status and the ability to be used in the background transfer functionality (see Recipe 13-5). Download tasks store the incoming data directly to a file and allow the resumption of a cancelled or failed download.

NSURLSession

In the new URL Loading System, sessions maintain the current configuration and serve as the factory for creating tasks. These long-lived objects are intended to be active over multiple network tasks. When creating a session, you can use the class constructors to retrieve the default session or create a custom session. The primary difference is that the default session uses a shared configuration (actually the same shared stack that the legacy NSURLConnection uses), whereas the custom session can be configured with your own customized, private configuration.

NSURLSession also maintains the single delegate that is used for callbacks from the entire stack of session classes, as shown in Figure 13-1 (right). This includes NSURLSessionDelegate, NSURLSessionTaskDelegate, NSURLSessionDataTaskDelegate, NSURLSessionDownloadTaskDelegate, and NSURLSessionUploadTaskDelegate. Delegate usage is addressed further in Recipe 13-3.

When you are done with a session, be sure to invalidate it with invalidateAndCancel, cancelling outstanding tasks immediately, or finishTasksAndInvalidate, which returns and waits for the last task to complete. After the tasks have been cancelled or finished, references to the delegate objects and callbacks will be severed and released. You cannot use a session object again once it's invalidated.

Recipe: Simple Downloads

Many classes provide convenience methods that allow you to request data from the Internet, wait until that data is received, and then move on to the next step in the application. The following snippet is both synchronous and blocking:

```
- (UIImage *)imageFromURLString:(NSString *)urlstring
{
    // This is a blocking call
    return [UIImage imageWithData:[NSData
        dataWithContentsOfURL:[NSURL URLWithString:urlstring]]];
}
```

You will not return from this method until all the data is received. If the connection hangs, so will your app. The iOS system watchdog will summarily terminate your app if it blocks the main thread for too long; it won't just hang forever.

Do not use such convenience methods without moving them to a background thread (as shown in Recipe 13-1).

While these helper methods are quick and easy to use, they lack flexibility and control, such as tracking the progress of the download, suspending the transfer, or setting security credentials. Using NSURLSession is the preferred approach for general downloads with full control and configurability. You can use a series of delegate callbacks or a convenient block-based handler.

Recipe 13-2 focuses on the simpler, block-based approach. On your session, use the NSURLSessionDownloadTask factory method that accepts a completion handler:

```
NSURLSessionDownloadTask *task =
    [session downloadTaskWithRequest:request
        completionHandler:^(NSURL *location,
            NSURLResponse *response,
            NSError *error) { // do something }];
```

When the download finishes, the completion handler is passed the location of the downloaded file, a response object, and an error object. You can then process the downloaded file or move it to a more appropriate location. The initial location of the file is temporary; the file should not be used outside the handler.

Some Internet providers produce a valid web page, even when given a completely bogus URL. The data returned in the response parameter helps you determine when this happens. This parameter points to an NSURLResponse object. It stores information about the data returned by the URL connection. These parameters include expected content length and a suggested filename. If the expected content length is less than zero, that's a good clue that the provider has returned data that does not match up to your expected request:

```
NSLog(@"Response expects %d bytes",
    response.expectedContentLength);
```

Recipe 13-2 allows testing with three predefined URLs. There's one that downloads a short (3 MB) movie, another using a larger (35 MB) movie, and a final fake URL to test errors. The movies are sourced from the Internet Archive (http://archive.org), which provides a wealth of public domain data.

With the large movie, you may wish to allow access only via a non-cellular connection. This can be configured using the NSURLSessionConfiguration object:

```
NSURLSessionConfiguration *configuration =
    [NSURLSessionConfiguration defaultSessionConfiguration];
configuration.allowsCellularAccess = NO;
```

Pass this configuration when creating your NSURLSession:

```
NSURLSession *session =
    [NSURLSession sessionWithConfiguration:configuration];
```

As you can see in Recipe 13-2, NSURLSessionDownloadTask with the completion handler provides no interdownload feedback. Recipe 13-3 addresses this issue by using the somewhat more complex but fully featured delegate mechanism.

Recipe 13-2 **Simple Downloads**

```
// Large Movie (35 MB)
#define LARGE_MOVIE @"http://www.archive.org/download/\
    BettyBoopCartoons/Betty_Boop_More_Pep_1936_512kb.mp4"

// Short movie (3 MB)
#define SMALL_MOVIE @"http://www.archive.org/download/\
    Drive-inSaveFreeTv/Drive-in--SaveFreeTv_512kb.mp4"

// Fake address
#define FAKE_MOVIE \
    @"http://www.idontbelievethisisavalidurlforthisexample.com"

// Current URL to test
#define MOVIE_URL [NSURL URLWithString:LARGE_MOVIE]

// Location to copy the downloaded item
#define FILE_LOCATION [NSHomeDirectory()\
    stringByAppendingString:@"/Documents/Movie.mp4"]

@interface TestBedViewController : UIViewController
@end

@implementation TestBedViewController
{
    BOOL success;
    MPMoviePlayerViewController *player;
}

- (void)playMovie
{
    // Instantiate movie player with location of downloaded file
    player = [[MPMoviePlayerViewController alloc]
        initWithContentURL:[NSURL fileURLWithPath:FILE_LOCATION]];
    [player.moviePlayer setControlStyle: MPMovieControlStyleFullscreen];
    player.moviePlayer.movieSourceType = MPMovieSourceTypeFile;
    player.moviePlayer.allowsAirPlay = YES;
    [player.moviePlayer prepareToPlay];

    // Listen for finish state
    [[NSNotificationCenter defaultCenter] addObserverForName:
            MPMoviePlayerPlaybackDidFinishNotification
```

```
            object:player.moviePlayer queue:[NSOperationQueue mainQueue]
            usingBlock:^(NSNotification *notification)
            {
                [[NSNotificationCenter defaultCenter] removeObserver:self
                    name:MPMoviePlayerPlaybackDidFinishNotification
                    object:nil];
                self.navigationItem.rightBarButtonItem.enabled = YES;
            }];

    [self presentMoviePlayerViewControllerAnimated:player];
}


// Perform an asynchronous download
- (void)downloadMovie:(NSURL *)url
{
    // Turn on network activity indicator
    [UIApplication sharedApplication].networkActivityIndicatorVisible
        = YES;

    NSDate *startDate = [NSDate date];

    // Create a URL request with the URL to the movie
    NSURLRequest *request = [NSURLRequest requestWithURL:url];

    // Create a session configuration
    NSURLSessionConfiguration *configuration =
        [NSURLSessionConfiguration defaultSessionConfiguration];

    // Turn off cellular access for this session
    configuration.allowsCellularAccess = NO;

    // Create a session with the custom configuration
    NSURLSession *session =
        [NSURLSession sessionWithConfiguration:configuration];

    // Create a download task with the block-based convenience
    // handler to fetch the data
    NSURLSessionDownloadTask *task =
        [session downloadTaskWithRequest:request
            completionHandler:^(NSURL *location,
                NSURLResponse *response, NSError *error) {

            // Turn off the network activity indicator
            [UIApplication sharedApplication]
                .networkActivityIndicatorVisible = NO;

            // Upon an error, reset the UI and abort.
```

```objc
            if (error)
            {
                self.navigationItem.rightBarButtonItem.enabled = YES;
                NSLog(@"Failed download.");
                return;
            }

            // Copy temporary file
            [[NSFileManager defaultManager] copyItemAtURL:location
                toURL:[NSURL fileURLWithPath:FILE_LOCATION]
                error:&error];

            NSLog(@"Elapsed time: %0.2f seconds.",
                [[NSDate date] timeIntervalSinceDate:startDate]);

            // Play the movie
            [self playMovie];
        }];

    // Begin the download task
    [task resume];
}

// Respond to the user's request to play movie
- (void)action
{
    self.navigationItem.rightBarButtonItem.enabled = NO;

    // Stop any existing movie playback
    [player.moviePlayer stop];
    player = nil;

    // Remove any existing data
    if ([[NSFileManager defaultManager] fileExistsAtPath:FILE_LOCATION])
    {
        NSError *error;
        if (![[NSFileManager defaultManager]
                removeItemAtPath:FILE_LOCATION error:&error])
            NSLog(@"Error removing existing data: %@",
                error.localizedFailureReason);
    }

    // Fetch the data
    [self downloadMovie:MOVIE_URL];
}

- (void)loadView
```

```
{
    self.view = [[UIView alloc] init];
    self.view.backgroundColor = [UIColor whiteColor];
    self.navigationItem.rightBarButtonItem =
        BARBUTTON(@"Play Movie", @selector(action));
}

@end
```

Get This Recipe's Code

To find this recipe's full sample project, point your browser to https://github.com/erica/iOS-7-Cookbook and go to the folder for Chapter 13.

Recipe: Downloads with Feedback

The block-based factory methods provided by `NSURLSession` create tasks with a convenient completion handler. When a task is completed, you can process your data and move on. While these methods are simple to use, sometimes you may need more interaction during your download or upload. `NSURLSessionDelegate` and its family of subprotocols provide more access and configurability to your tasks. The subprotocols include support for the parent `NSURLSession`-related delegate methods as well as callbacks specific to a general task, data task, or download task.

These delegates provide corresponding data about the progress or state of your session and tasks. Your `NSURLSession` object maintains a single, common delegate object that will respond to any of the session callbacks as well as possible task callbacks. This can seem a bit odd at first but realize that whatever delegate you assign to the `NSURLSession` object is responsible for responding to delegate methods for both the session and corresponding tasks.

To monitor the state of the download task, implement the `URLSession:downloadTask:didWriteData:totalBytesWritten:totalBytesExpectedToWrite:` delegate method. `totalBytesWritten` (number of total bytes transferred) and `totalBytesExpectedToWrite` (expected number of bytes to be transferred) provide ample information to create a progress indicator in your user interface. You can also query the `countOfBytesReceived` and `countOfBytesExpectedToReceive` properties on the download task directly. Note the somewhat confusing use of *written* and *received* in these method signatures; each refers to the bytes transferred, and they should be interchangeable.

By dividing the bytes transferred by those expected to be transferred, you can derive a useful status string and compute a percentage that can be passed to a `UIProgressView`:

```
int64_t kilobytesReceived =
    downloadTask.countOfBytesReceived / 1024;
int64_t kilobytesExpected =
    downloadTask.countOfBytesExpectedToReceive / 1024;
```

```
NSString * statusString = [NSString stringWithFormat:@"%lldk of %lldk",
    kilobytesReceived, kilobytesExpected];
double progress = (double)kReceived / (double)kExpected;
progressLabel.text = statusString;
[progressBarView setProgress:progress animated:YES];
```

In Recipe 13-3, a table provides a list of sizable movie downloads that can be downloaded by tapping on the table view cell. The navigation bar provides the live progress of the download and is updated in real time, as shown in Figure 13-2. At the completion of the download, the video can be viewed. While multiple downloads can be easily supported, the complexities in designing an instructional example while providing status on multiple downloads is a bit egregious. Recipe 13-3 restricts the user to a single download at a time.

Figure 13-2   A table view tracks a list of download tasks and their current progress state.

> **Note**
>
> In iOS 7, Apple introduced NSProgress to provide generalized progress tracking and reporting. In Recipe 13-3, with single file downloads and basic status reporting, little tracking beyond the immediate update of the UI is required. This is easily provided by the download delegate callbacks, making the more robust and complex NSProgress unnecessary. NSProgress excels at tracking the overall state of a group of tasks, including tasks that provide less opportunity and access for tracking, as well as progress to UI elements through Key-value observing (KVO).

Recipe 13-3 **Downloads with Feedback**

```objc
// Helper class to hold information about a movie and its corresponding download
@interface MovieDownload : NSObject
@property (nonatomic, strong) NSURL *movieURL;
@property (nonatomic, strong) NSURLSessionDownloadTask *downloadTask;
@property (nonatomic, readonly) NSString *localPath;
@property (nonatomic, readonly) NSString *movieName;
@property (nonatomic, readonly) NSString *statusString;
@property (nonatomic, readonly) double progress;
- (instancetype)initWithURL:(NSURL *)movieURL
    downloadTask:(NSURLSessionDownloadTask *)downloadTask;
@end

@implementation MovieDownload

- (instancetype)initWithURL:(NSURL *)movieURL
    downloadTask:(NSURLSessionDownloadTask *)downloadTask
{
    self = [super init];
    if (self)
    {
        _movieURL = movieURL;
        _downloadTask = downloadTask;
    }
    return self;
}

// A local file path for copying our temporary file
- (NSString *)localPath
{
    NSString *localPath =
        [NSString stringWithFormat:@"%@/Documents/%@",
            NSHomeDirectory(), [self.movieURL lastPathComponent]];
    return localPath;
}

// Display name in UI
- (NSString *)movieName
{
    return [self.movieURL lastPathComponent];
}

// Status string based on progress from download task
- (NSString *)statusString
{
    int64_t kReceived =
```

```
        self.downloadTask.countOfBytesReceived / 1024;
    int64_t kExpected =
        self.downloadTask.countOfBytesExpectedToReceive / 1024;
    NSString *statusString =
        [NSString stringWithFormat:@"%lldk of %lldk",
            kReceived, kExpected];
    return statusString;
}


// Progress percentage from download task
- (double)progress
{
    double progress = (double)self.downloadTask.countOfBytesReceived /
        (double)self.downloadTask.countOfBytesExpectedToReceive;
    return progress;
}
@end


// Large Movie (35 MB)
#define LARGE_MOVIE @"http://www.archive.org/download/\
    BettyBoopCartoons/Betty_Boop_More_Pep_1936_512kb.mp4"


// Medium movie (8 MB)
#define MEDIUM_MOVIE @"http://www.archive.org/download/\
    mother_goose_little_miss_muffet/\
    mother_goose_little_miss_muffet_512kb.mp4"


// Short movie (3 MB)
#define SMALL_MOVIE @"http://www.archive.org/download/\
    Drive-inSaveFreeTv/Drive-in--SaveFreeTv_512kb.mp4"


@interface TestBedViewController : UITableViewController
    <NSURLSessionDownloadDelegate>
@end


@implementation TestBedViewController
{
    NSMutableArray *movieDownloads;
    NSURLSession *session;
    UIProgressView *progressBarView;
    MPMoviePlayerViewController *player;
    BOOL downloading;
}


#pragma mark - NSURLSessionDownloadDelegate


// Handle download completion from the task
```

```objc
- (void)URLSession:(NSURLSession *)session
    downloadTask:(NSURLSessionDownloadTask *)downloadTask
    didFinishDownloadingToURL:(NSURL *)location
{
    NSInteger index =
        [self movieDownloadIndexForDownloadTask:downloadTask];
    if (index < 0) return;
    MovieDownload *movieDownload = movieDownloads[index];

    // Copy temporary file
    NSError *error;
    [[NSFileManager defaultManager] copyItemAtURL:location
        toURL:[NSURL fileURLWithPath:[movieDownload localPath]]
        error:&error];
}


// Handle task completion
- (void)URLSession:(NSURLSession *)session
    task:(NSURLSessionTask *)task
    didCompleteWithError:(NSError *)error
{
    if (error)
        NSLog(@"Task %@ failed: %@", task, error);

    // Update UI
    [progressBarView setProgress:0 animated:NO];
    self.navigationItem.title = @"";
    downloading = NO;

    // This method is called after didFinishDownloadingToURL
    // Task state is up-to-date and reflects completion.
    [self.tableView reloadData];
}


- (void)URLSession:(NSURLSession *)session
    downloadTask:(NSURLSessionDownloadTask *)downloadTask
    didResumeAtOffset:(int64_t)fileOffset
    expectedTotalBytes:(int64_t)expectedTotalBytes
{
    // Required delegate method
}

// Handle progress update from the task
- (void)URLSession:(NSURLSession *)session
    downloadTask:(NSURLSessionDownloadTask *)downloadTask
    didWriteData:(int64_t)bytesWritten
    totalBytesWritten:(int64_t)totalBytesWritten
```

```
        totalBytesExpectedToWrite:(int64_t)totalBytesExpectedToWrite
{
    NSInteger index =
        [self movieDownloadIndexForDownloadTask:downloadTask];
    if (index < 0) return;
    MovieDownload *movieDownload = movieDownloads[index];

    // Update UI
    [progressBarView setProgress:movieDownload.progress animated:YES];
    self.navigationItem.title = movieDownload.statusString;
}


#pragma mark - UITableViewDatasource

- (NSInteger)numberOfSectionsInTableView:(UITableView *)tableView
{
    NSInteger sectionCount = 1;
    return sectionCount;
}


- (NSInteger)tableView:(UITableView *)tableView
    numberOfRowsInSection:(NSInteger)section
{
    NSInteger rowCount = movieDownloads.count;
    return rowCount;
}


- (UITableViewCell *)tableView:(UITableView *)tableView
    cellForRowAtIndexPath:(NSIndexPath *)indexPath
{
    static NSString *cellIdentifier = @"CellIdentifier";
    UITableViewCell *cell =
        [tableView dequeueReusableCellWithIdentifier:cellIdentifier];
    if (cell == nil)
    {
        cell = [[UITableViewCell alloc]
            initWithStyle:UITableViewCellStyleSubtitle
                reuseIdentifier:cellIdentifier];
    }

    // Reset the cell UI
    cell.selectionStyle = UITableViewCellSelectionStyleDefault;
    cell.textLabel.enabled = YES;
    cell.detailTextLabel.enabled = YES;

    // Set our text label to the file name
    cell.textLabel.text = [movieDownloads[indexPath.row] movieName];
```

```objc
    // Acquire the appropriate download task and check its state
    NSURLSessionDownloadTask *downloadTask =
        [movieDownloads[indexPath.row] downloadTask];
    if (downloadTask.state == NSURLSessionTaskStateCompleted)
    {
        cell.detailTextLabel.text = @"Ready to Play";
    }
    else if (downloadTask.state == NSURLSessionTaskStateRunning)
    {
        cell.detailTextLabel.text = @"Downloading...";
    }
    else if (downloadTask.state == NSURLSessionTaskStateSuspended)
    {
        // If download already in progress, disable suspended cells.
        if (downloading)
        {
            cell.selectionStyle = UITableViewCellSelectionStyleNone;
            [cell.textLabel setEnabled:NO];
            [cell.detailTextLabel setEnabled:NO];
        }

        if (downloadTask.countOfBytesReceived > 0)
        {
            cell.detailTextLabel.text = @"Download Paused";
        }
        else
        {
            cell.detailTextLabel.text = @"Not Started";
        }
    }

    return cell;
}


#pragma mark - UITableViewDelegate

- (void)tableView:(UITableView *)tableView
    didSelectRowAtIndexPath:(NSIndexPath *)indexPath
{
    // Acquire downloadTask and respond to user's selection
    NSURLSessionDownloadTask *downloadTask =
        [movieDownloads[indexPath.row] downloadTask];
    if (downloadTask.state == NSURLSessionTaskStateCompleted)
    {
        // Download is complete.  Play movie.
        NSURL *movieURL =
            [NSURL fileURLWithPath:[movieDownloads[indexPath.row]
```

```
                          localPath]];
            [self playMovieAtURL:movieURL];
    }
    else if (downloadTask.state == NSURLSessionTaskStateSuspended)
    {
        // If suspended and not already downloading, resume transfer.
        if (!downloading)
        {
            [downloadTask resume];
            downloading = YES;
        }
    }
    else if (downloadTask.state == NSURLSessionTaskStateRunning)
    {
        // If already downloading, pause the transfer.
        [downloadTask suspend];
        downloading = NO;
    }
    [tableView deselectRowAtIndexPath:indexPath animated:YES];
    [tableView reloadData];
}


#pragma mark - Movie Download Handling & UI

// Helper method to get index of a movieDownload object from array
- (NSInteger)movieDownloadIndexForDownloadTask:
        (NSURLSessionDownloadTask *)downloadTask
{
    NSInteger foundIndex = -1;
    NSInteger index = 0;
    for (MovieDownload *movieDownload in movieDownloads)
    {
        if (movieDownload.downloadTask == downloadTask)
        {
            foundIndex = index;
            break;
        }
        index++;
    }
    return foundIndex;
}


// Play movie at the provided URL
- (void)playMovieAtURL:(NSURL *)url
{
    // Instantiate movie player with location of downloaded file
    player =
```

```objc
        [[MPMoviePlayerViewController alloc] initWithContentURL:url];
    player.moviePlayer.controlStyle = MPMovieControlStyleFullscreen;
    player.moviePlayer.movieSourceType = MPMovieSourceTypeFile;
    player.moviePlayer.allowsAirPlay = YES;
    [player.moviePlayer prepareToPlay];

    [self presentMoviePlayerViewControllerAnimated:player];
}


// Convenience method to add movieDownload objects to our array
- (void)addMovieDownload:(NSString *)urlString
{
    NSURL * url = [NSURL URLWithString:urlString];
    NSURLRequest *request = [NSURLRequest requestWithURL:url];
    NSURLSessionDownloadTask *downloadTask =
        [session downloadTaskWithRequest:request];

    MovieDownload *movieDownload = [[MovieDownload alloc]
        initWithURL:url downloadTask:downloadTask];
    [movieDownloads addObject:movieDownload];
}


// Reset the UI, session, and tasks
- (void)reset
{
    for (MovieDownload *movieDownload in movieDownloads)
    {
        // Cancel each task
        NSURLSessionDownloadTask *downloadTask =
            movieDownload.downloadTask;
        [downloadTask cancel];

        // Remove any existing data
        if ([[NSFileManager defaultManager]
            fileExistsAtPath:movieDownload.localPath])
        {
            NSError *error;
            if (![[NSFileManager defaultManager]
                removeItemAtPath:movieDownload.localPath
                    error:&error])
                NSLog(@"Error removing existing data: %@",
                    error.localizedFailureReason);
        }
    }

    // Cancel all tasks and invalidate session (releases delegate)
    [session invalidateAndCancel];
```

```objc
    session = nil;

    // Create new configuration / session and set delegate
    NSURLSessionConfiguration *sessionConfiguration =
        [NSURLSessionConfiguration defaultSessionConfiguration];
    session = [NSURLSession
            sessionWithConfiguration:sessionConfiguration
        delegate:self delegateQueue:[NSOperationQueue mainQueue]];

    // Create the MovieDownload objects
    movieDownloads = [[NSMutableArray alloc] init];
    [self addMovieDownload:SMALL_MOVIE];
    [self addMovieDownload:MEDIUM_MOVIE];
    [self addMovieDownload:LARGE_MOVIE];

    // Reset the UI
    [progressBarView setProgress:0 animated:NO];
    self.navigationItem.title = @"";
    downloading = NO;
    [self.tableView reloadData];
}

- (void)viewDidLoad
{
    [super viewDidLoad];
    self.view.backgroundColor = [UIColor whiteColor];
    self.navigationItem.rightBarButtonItem =
        BARBUTTON(@"Reset", @selector(reset));

    // Set up the progress bar in the navigation bar
    progressBarView = [[UIProgressView alloc]
        initWithProgressViewStyle:UIProgressViewStyleBar];
    progressBarView.frame = CGRectMake(0, 0,
        self.navigationController.navigationBar.frame.size.width, 4);
    [self.navigationController.navigationBar
        addSubview:progressBarView];

    [self reset];
}

@end
```

Get This Recipe's Code

To find this recipe's full sample project, point your browser to https://github.com/erica/iOS-7-Cookbook and go to the folder for Chapter 13.

Resuming Downloads

One neat feature of NSURLSessionDownloadTask is support for resuming downloads. If a download fails, you can query the download task for a resume data blob. Connection error callbacks provide this resume data in the [error userInfo] dictionary, with the NSURLSessionDownloadTaskResumeData key. You can also cancel your download task and receive the most current resume data blob via a block handler:

```
[downloadTask cancelByProducingResumeData: ^(NSData *resumeData) {
    // save resume data
  }];
```

When you are ready to resume your download, you can use the session downloadTask-WithResumeData: or downloadTaskWithResumeData:completionHandler:, passing in the saved resume data blob to create a new task that will continue the download near where the previous download task left off.

Recipe: Background Transfers

iOS 7 introduced an amazing feature that has been on many developers' wish lists since the creation and availability of the SDK: the ability to continue and process a download or upload even when the application is in the background. Background transfers require the use of a delegate for event delivery. You can use either the upload or download tasks and their corresponding delegates. Background transfers are also limited to HTTP and HTTPS protocols. They can be created in the foreground or even when the app is already in the background.

In many ways, there is little difference between the creation and handling of an in-process transfer and of an out-of-process transfer. You set up your session and your download task and begin the network transfer.

The key to enabling background transfers is the configuration of your session. Use the backgroundSessionConfiguration: class constructor on NSURLSessionConfiguration, passing a unique identifier string that you will use in the future to reconnect with this session:

```
NSURLSessionConfiguration *configuration =
    [NSURLSessionConfiguration
        backgroundSessionConfiguration:@"CoreiOSBackgroundID"];
configuration.discretionary = YES;

session = [NSURLSession sessionWithConfiguration:configuration
    delegate:self delegateQueue:nil];
```

The discretionary configuration property is available for background transfers to encourage them to occur when a device is plugged into power and on Wi-Fi.

When handling background transfers, this session setup needs to occur when you are establishing your application. If the app is launched after a crash or exit while a background transfer is proceeding, the re-creation of the session with the background ID will reestablish the background session that may be in progress. Delegate method calls will immediately begin firing for tasks associated with that session. You can also call `getTasksWithCompletion-Handler:` to receive all the existing background tasks directly.

If your application remains in the foreground, the progress and completion delegate methods will be called normally, and the transfer will resolve as a normal in-process download. If your application leaves the foreground, the download task will continue. Once completed, your app will be relaunched in the background.

> **Note**
>
> If your application suspends, exits, or even crashes, the background transfer will continue. Background transfers occur in a separate daemon process. The data will be available for your application on its next launch.

In your app delegate, you will implement `application:handleEventsForBackgroundURL-Session:completionHandler:`. If your application is not running and your transfer requires an authorization request or when your tasks complete, your application will be launched in the background, and the application delegate method will be called.

Although your application is running in the background, your application UI is actually fully restored but hidden. You can update your UI based on the data just downloaded. An updated snapshot of your UI will be taken for use in the task switcher. To initiate this snapshot, call the `completionHandler` block passed to the app delegate method when you have finished handling your background tasks and updated your UI.

Recipe 13-4 takes the basic functionality of Recipe 13-2 and expands the download process to allow for background transfers. After the movie download is initiated, exiting or suspending the application will not stop the transfer. When the transfer completes, the movie will be saved and the UI prepared for the next foregrounding of the application. Unfortunately, the background transfer API does not allow you to bring your application into the foreground automatically. However, as shown in Recipe 13-4, it is possible to trigger a local notification.

Testing Background Transfers

To test, begin your download and tap the Home button on the device to suspend your app or use the Exit App button in the navigation bar. This button calls `abort()`, a function that immediately terminates the application. (Don't ever use this function in a production application; it will be rejected in the app review process.)

Immediately relaunching the application after backgrounding or termination should bring up the app with the download still in progress. Following this same process without relaunching allows the transfer to complete in the background. When it is complete, the app is launched in the background, kicking off a local notification and an update of the UI in the task switcher.

Recipe 13-4   **Background Transfers**

```objc
// Notify the user of a background transfer completion
- (void)presentNotification
{
    UILocalNotification *localNotification =
        [[UILocalNotification alloc] init];
    localNotification.alertBody = @"Download Complete!";
    localNotification.alertAction = @"Background Transfer";
    localNotification.soundName = UILocalNotificationDefaultSoundName;
    localNotification.applicationIconBadgeNumber = 1;
    [[UIApplication sharedApplication]
        presentLocalNotificationNow:localNotification];
}


// Reset the application icon badge on activation
- (void)applicationDidBecomeActive:(UIApplication *)application
{
    application.applicationIconBadgeNumber = 0;
}


// Handle the background transfer completion event
- (void)application:(UIApplication *)application
    handleEventsForBackgroundURLSession:(NSString *)identifier
    completionHandler:(void (^)())completionHandler
{
    // Update the UI to make it apparent in the task switcher
    tbvc.view.backgroundColor = [UIColor greenColor];
    tbvc.statusLabel.text = @"BACKGROUND DOWNLOAD COMPLETED!";

    // Present the local notification to the user
    [self presentNotification];

    // Update the task switcher snapshot
    completionHandler();
}
```

Get This Recipe's Code

To find this recipe's full sample project, point your browser to https://github.com/erica/iOS-7-Cookbook and go to the folder for Chapter 13.

Web Services

It is becoming difficult to build an iOS app of any significance these days without interacting with one or more web services. Nearly all data available on the Internet, both public and private, is provided via a web service.

These utilitarian network endpoints generally use HTTP with messages encoded as JSON or XML. The APIs for these services are published publically for many sites. While many require registration to use, a few are still fully accessible. Private enterprise web services are only documented and accessible to those who have the correct authorization.

Apple provides the tools required to download and process most web services with ease. The URL Loading System gets and posts your data, and provided parsers can interpret and generate the messages passed back and forth.

Recipe: Using JSON Serialization

The NSJSONSerialization class is tremendously handy when you're working with JSON-based web services. All you need is a valid JSON container (namely an array or a dictionary) whose components are also valid JSON objects, including strings, numbers, arrays, dictionaries, and NSNull. Test an object's validity with isValidJSONObject, which returns YES if the object can be safely converted to JSON format:

```
// Build a basic JSON object
NSArray *array = @[@"Val1", @"Val2", @"Val3"];
NSDictionary *dict = @{@"Key 1":array,
    @"Key 2":array, @"Key 3":array};

// Convert it to JSON
if ([NSJSONSerialization isValidJSONObject:dict])
{
    NSData *data = [NSJSONSerialization
        dataWithJSONObject:dict options:0 error:nil];
    NSString *result = [[NSString alloc]
        initWithData:data encoding:NSUTF8StringEncoding];
    NSLog(@"Result: %@", result);
}
```

The code from this method produces the following JSON. Notice that dictionary output is not guaranteed to be in alphabetic order:

```
Result: {"Key 2":["Val1","Val2","Val3"],"Key 3":
    ["Val1","Val2","Val3"],"Key 1":["Val1","Val2","Val3"]}
```

Moving from JSON to a conforming object is just as easy. Recipe 13-5 uses JSONObjectWithData:options:error: to convert NSData representing a JSON object into an Objective-C representation. This recipe downloads the current weather forecast from the site http://openweathermap.org, retrieves an array of forecasts for the next seven days from the returned dictionary, and uses it to power a standard table view.

Recipe 13-5 **JSON Data**

```
#define WXFORECAST @"http://api.openweathermap.org/data/2.5/\
    forecast/daily?q=%@&units=Imperial&cnt=7&mode=json"
#define LOCATION @"Fairbanks"

// Return a cell for the index path
- (UITableViewCell *)tableView:(UITableView *)aTableView
    cellForRowAtIndexPath:(NSIndexPath *)indexPath
{
    // Top level dictionary for the forecast data
    NSDictionary *top = [items objectAtIndex:indexPath.row];

    // The date of this forecast under top
    NSString *unixtime = top[@"dt"];

    // The weather dictionary that includes the sky description
    NSDictionary * weather = top[@"weather"][0];

    // The sky description string under weather
    NSString *wxDescription = weather[@"description"];

    // Convert the unixtime to something we can use
    NSDate *wxDate = [NSDate dateWithTimeIntervalSince1970:
        [unixtime doubleValue]];

    UITableViewCell *cell = [self.tableView
        dequeueReusableCellWithIdentifier:@"cell"];
    if (cell == nil)
    {
        cell = [[UITableViewCell alloc]
            initWithStyle:UITableViewCellStyleSubtitle
                reuseIdentifier:@"cell"];
    }
    cell.textLabel.text = wxDescription;
    cell.detailTextLabel.text =
        [dateFormatter stringFromDate:wxDate];
    return cell;
}

#pragma mark - Web Service Download

- (void)loadWebService
{
    self.title = LOCATION;

    // Start the refresh control
    [self.refreshControl beginRefreshing];
```

```
    // Create the URL string based on location
    NSString *urlString =
        [NSString stringWithFormat:WXFORECAST, LOCATION];

    // Set up the session
    NSURLSessionConfiguration * configuration =
        [NSURLSessionConfiguration defaultSessionConfiguration];
    NSURLSession *session =
        [NSURLSession sessionWithConfiguration:configuration];
    NSURLRequest *request =
        [NSURLRequest requestWithURL:[NSURL
            URLWithString:urlString]];

    // Create a data task to transfer the web service endpoint contents
    NSURLSessionDataTask *dataTask =
        [session dataTaskWithRequest:request
            completionHandler:^(NSData *data,
                NSURLResponse *response, NSError *error) {

            // Stop the refresh control
            [self.refreshControl endRefreshing];
            if (error)
            {
                self.title = error.localizedDescription;
                return;
            }

            // Parse the JSON from the data object
            NSDictionary *json = [NSJSONSerialization
                JSONObjectWithData:data options:0 error:nil];

            // Store off the top level array of forecasts
            items = json[@"list"];

            [self.tableView reloadData];
        }];

    // Start the data task
    [dataTask resume];
}
```

Get This Recipe's Code

To find this recipe's full sample project, point your browser to https://github.com/erica/iOS-7-Cookbook and go to the folder for Chapter 13.

Recipe: Converting XML into Trees

While many web services have moved to the simpler JSON format, XML is still a popular and powerful document encoding. iOS's NSXMLParser class scans through XML, creating callbacks as new elements are processed and finished (that is, using the typical logic of a SAX parser). This class is terrific for when you're downloading simple data feeds and want to scrape just a bit or two of relevant information. It might not be so great when you're doing production-type work that relies on error checking, status information, and back-and-forth handshaking.

Recipe 13-6 retrieves the same weather forecast data from http://openweathermap.org as Recipe 13-5 but in XML format. It requests the xml mode rather than the json mode and uses an XML parser to populate its table:

```
#define WXFORECAST \
    @"http://api.openweathermap.org/data/2.5/\
    forecast/daily?q=%@&units=Imperial&cnt=7&mode=xml"
#define LOCATION @"Fairbanks"

- (void)loadWebService
{
    self.title = LOCATION;

    // Start the refresh control
    [self.refreshControl beginRefreshing];

    // Create the URL string based on location
    NSString *urlString =
        [NSString stringWithFormat:WXFORECAST, LOCATION];

    // Set up the session
    NSURLSessionConfiguration * configuration =
        [NSURLSessionConfiguration defaultSessionConfiguration];
    NSURLSession *session =
        [NSURLSession sessionWithConfiguration:configuration];
    NSURLRequest *request =
        [NSURLRequest requestWithURL:[NSURL URLWithString:urlString]];

    // Create a data task to transfer the web service endpoint contents
    NSURLSessionDataTask *dataTask =
        [session dataTaskWithRequest:request
        completionHandler:^(NSData *data, NSURLResponse *response,
            NSError *error) {

        // Stop the refresh control
        [self.refreshControl endRefreshing];
        if (error)
        {
            self.title = error.localizedDescription;
```

```
            return;
        }

        // Create the XML parser
        XMLParser *parser = [[XMLParser alloc] init];

        // Parse the XML from the data object
        root = [parser parseXMLFromData:data];

        // Store off the top level parent of forecasts
        forecastsRoot = [root nodesForKey:@"forecast"][0];

        [self.tableView reloadData];
    }];

    // Start the data task
    [dataTask resume];
}


// Return a cell for the index path
- (UITableViewCell *)tableView:(UITableView *)aTableView
    cellForRowAtIndexPath:(NSIndexPath *)indexPath
{
    TreeNode *forecastRoot = forecastsRoot.children[indexPath.row];
    NSString *day = [forecastRoot attributes][@"day"];
    TreeNode *cloudsNode = [forecastRoot nodeForKey:@"clouds"];
    NSString *wxDescription = [cloudsNode attributes][@"value"];

    UITableViewCell *cell =
        [self.tableView dequeueReusableCellWithIdentifier:@"cell"];
    if (cell == nil)
    {
        cell = [[UITableViewCell alloc]
            initWithStyle:UITableViewCellStyleSubtitle
                reuseIdentifier:@"cell"];
    }
    cell.textLabel.text = wxDescription;
    cell.detailTextLabel.text = day;
    return cell;
}
```

Trees

Using tree data structures is an excellent way to represent XML data. They allow you to create search paths through data so that you can find just the data you're looking for, as long as you can comfortably fit the data into memory. You can retrieve all elements, search for a success value, and so forth. Trees convert text-based XML back into a multidimensional structure.

To bridge the gap between NSXMLParser and tree-based parse results, you can use an NSXMLParser-based helper class to return more standard tree-based data. This requires a simple tree node like the kind shown here:

```
@interface TreeNode : NSObject
@property (nonatomic, weak)     TreeNode        *parent;
@property (nonatomic, strong)   NSMutableArray  *children;
@property (nonatomic, strong)   NSString        *key;
@property (nonatomic, strong)   NSDictionary    *attributes;
@property (nonatomic, strong)   NSString        *leafValue;
@end
```

This node uses double linking to access its parent and its children, allowing two-way traversal in a tree. Only parent-to-child values are retained, allowing the tree to deallocate without being explicitly torn down.

For example, take the following simplified XML snippet from the open http://weathermap.org web service:

```
<time day="2013-12-01">
    <clouds value="sky is clear"/>
</time>
```

This valid XML will be parsed into two TreeNode objects with key values time and clouds. The time node's children array will contain a clouds node. The clouds node will have a time node as a parent. The time node will have an attributes dictionary that includes a day key with the value 2013-12-01. Similarly, the clouds node will have an attributes diction-ary with a value key and a corresponding value sky is clear.

Building a Parse Tree

Recipe 13-6 introduces the XMLParser class. Its job is to build a parse tree as the NSXMLParser class works its way through the XML source. The three standard NSXML routines (start element, finish element, and found characters) read the XML stream and perform a recursive depth-first descent through the tree.

The class adds new nodes when reaching new elements (parser:didStartElement: qualifiedName:attributes:) and adds leaf values when encountering text (parser:foundCharacters:). Because XML allows siblings at the same tree depth, this code uses a stack to keep track of the current path to the tree root. Siblings always pop back to the same parent in parser:didEndElement:, so they are added at the proper level.

After finishing the XML scan, the parseXMLFromData: method returns the root node.

Recipe 13-6   **The** XMLParser **Helper Class**

```objc
@implementation XMLParser
// Parser returns the tree root. Go down
// one node to the real results
- (TreeNode *)parse:(NSXMLParser *)parser
{
    stack = [NSMutableArray array];
    TreeNode *root = [TreeNode treeNode];
    [stack addObject:root];

    [parser setDelegate:self];
    [parser parse];

    // Pop down to real root
    TreeNode *realRoot = [[root children] lastObject];

    // Remove any connections
    root.children = nil;
    root.leafValue = nil;
    root.key = nil;
    realRoot.parent = nil;

    // Return the true root
    return realRoot;
}

- (TreeNode *)parseXMLFromURL:(NSURL *)url
{
    TreeNode *results = nil;
    @autoreleasepool {
        NSXMLParser *parser =
            [[NSXMLParser alloc] initWithContentsOfURL:url];
        results = [self parse:parser];
    }
    return results;
}

- (TreeNode *)parseXMLFromData:(NSData *)data
{
    TreeNode *results = nil;
    @autoreleasepool {
        NSXMLParser *parser =
            [[NSXMLParser alloc] initWithData:data];
        results = [self parse:parser];
    }
    return results;
```

```
}

// Descend to a new element
- (void)parser:(NSXMLParser *)parser
    didStartElement:(NSString *)elementName
    namespaceURI:(NSString *)namespaceURI
    qualifiedName:(NSString *)qName
    attributes:(NSDictionary *)attributeDict
{

    if (qName) elementName = qName;

    TreeNode *leaf = [TreeNode treeNode];
    leaf.parent = [stack lastObject];
    [(NSMutableArray *)[[stack lastObject] children] addObject:leaf];
    leaf.attributes = attributeDict;
    leaf.key = [NSString stringWithString:elementName];
    leaf.leafValue = nil;
    leaf.children = [NSMutableArray array];

    [stack addObject:leaf];
}

// Pop after finishing element
- (void)parser:(NSXMLParser *)parser
    didEndElement:(NSString *)elementName
    namespaceURI:(NSString *)namespaceURI
    qualifiedName:(NSString *)qName
{

    [stack removeLastObject];
}

// Reached a leaf
- (void)parser:(NSXMLParser *)parser
    foundCharacters:(NSString *)string
{
    if (![[stack lastObject] leafValue])
    {
        [[stack lastObject]
            setLeafValue:[NSString stringWithString:string]];
        return;
    }
    [[stack lastObject] setLeafValue:
        [NSString stringWithFormat:@"%@%@",
        [[stack lastObject] leafValue], string]];
}
@end
```

> **Get This Recipe's Code**
>
> To find this recipe's full sample project, point your browser to https://github.com/erica/iOS-7-Cookbook and go to the folder for Chapter 13.

Summary

This chapter introduces basic network-supporting technologies. You have seen how to check for network connectivity, download data, and convert to and from JSON. Here are a few thoughts to take away with you from this chapter:

- A portion of Apple's networking support is provided through low-level C-based routines. If you can find a friendly Objective-C wrapper to simplify your programming work, consider using it. The only drawback occurs when you specifically need tight networking control at the most basic level of your application, which is rare. There are superb resources out there. Just search online for them.

- The NSURLSession-based URL Loading System in iOS 7 provides a powerful new abstraction to downloading and uploading data from the Internet. Take advantage of this new API when possible.

- The background transfer support in iOS 7 can be tremendously useful in providing a responsive and up-to-date user experience. When combined with the new silent push notifications (notifications that do not display alerts but can trigger download activity) and background fetch (a new background mode for frequent background downloads) also introduced in iOS 7, your application can always be current when the user launches.

- The most important lesson about connecting from a device to the network is this: It can fail. Design your apps accordingly. Check for network connectivity, test for aborted downloads, and assume that data may arrive corrupted. Everything else follows from the basic fact that you cannot rely on data to arrive when you want, how you expect it to, and as you requested.

- When working with networking, always think "threaded." Naiveté in your approach to networking and the main thread will likely result in your application being summarily killed. Blocks and queues are your new best friends when it comes to creating positive user experiences in networked applications.

14

Device-Specific Development

Each iOS device represents a meld of unique, shared, momentary, and persistent properties. These properties include the device's current physical orientation, its model name, its battery state, and its access to onboard hardware. This chapter looks at devices—from their build configuration to their active onboard sensors. It provides recipes that return a variety of information items about the unit in use. You'll read about testing for hardware prerequisites at runtime and specifying those prerequisites in the application's Info.plist file. You'll discover how to solicit sensor feedback via Core Motion and subscribe to notifications to create callbacks when sensor states change. You'll read about adding screen mirroring and second-screen output and about soliciting device-specific details for tracking. This chapter covers the hardware, file system, and sensors available on the iPhone, iPad, and iPod touch and helps you programmatically take advantage of those features.

Accessing Basic Device Information

The `UIDevice` class exposes key device-specific properties, including the iPhone, iPad, or iPod touch model being used, the device name, and the OS name and version. It's a one-stop solution for pulling out certain system details. Each method is an instance method, which is called using the `UIDevice` singleton, via `[UIDevice currentDevice]`.

The system information you can retrieve from `UIDevice` includes these items:

- **systemName**—This property returns the name of the operating system currently in use. For current generations of iOS devices, there is only one OS that runs on the platform: iPhone OS. Apple has not yet updated this name to match the general iOS rebranding.

- **systemVersion**—This property lists the firmware version currently installed on the unit: for example, 4.3, 5.1.1, 6.0, 7.0.2, and so on.

- **model**—This property returns a string that describes the platform—namely iPhone, iPad, and iPod touch. Should iOS be extended to new devices, additional strings will describe those models. `localizedModel` provides a localized version of this property.

- **userInterfaceIdiom**—This property represents the interface style used on the current device—either iPhone (for iPhone and iPod touch) or iPad. Other idioms may be introduced as Apple offers additional platform styles.

- **name**—This property presents the iPhone name assigned by the user in iTunes, such as "Joe's iPhone" or "Binky." This name is also used to create the local hostname for the device.

Here are a few examples of these properties in use:

```
UIDevice *device = [UIDevice currentDevice];
NSLog(@"System name: %@", device.systemName);
NSLog(@"Model: %@", device.model);
NSLog(@"Name: %@", device.name);
```

For current iOS releases, you can use the idiom check with a simple Boolean test. Here's an example of how you might implement an iPad check:

```
#define IS_IPAD (UI_USER_INTERFACE_IDIOM() == UIUserInterfaceIdiomPad)
```

Notice the convenience macro provided by UIKit—`UI_USER_INTERFACE_IDIOM()`. It tests for selector conformance and then returns `[[UIDevice currentDevice] userInterfaceIdiom]` if possible, and `UIUserInterfaceIdiomPhone` otherwise. If this test fails, you can currently assume that you're working with an iPhone/iPod touch. If and when Apple releases a new family of devices, you'll need to update your code accordingly for a more nuanced test.

Adding Device Capability Restrictions

An application's Info.plist property list enables you to specify application requirements when you submit applications to the App Store. These restrictions enable you to tell iTunes and the mobile App Store what device features your application needs.

Each iOS unit provides a unique feature set. Some devices offer cameras and GPS capabilities. Others don't. Some have onboard gyros, autofocus, and other powerful options. You specify what features are needed to run your application on a device.

When you include the `UIRequiredDeviceCapabilities` key in your Info.plist file, iTunes and the mobile App Store limit application installation to devices that offer the required capabilities. Provide this list as either an array of strings or a dictionary.

An array specifies each required capability; each item in that array must be present on your device. A dictionary enables you to explicitly require or prohibit a feature. The dictionary keys are the capabilities. The dictionary values set whether the feature must be present (Boolean true) or omitted (Boolean false).

Table 14-1 details the current keys for required device capabilities. Only include those features that your application absolutely requires or cannot support. If your application can provide workarounds, do not add restrictions in this way. Table 14-1 discusses each feature in a positive sense. When using a prohibition rather than a requirement, reverse the meaning—for example, that an autofocus camera or gyro cannot be onboard, or that Game Center access cannot be supported.

Table 14-1 **Required Device Capabilities**

Key	Use
telephony	Application requires the Phone application or uses tel:// URLs.
wifi	Application requires local 802.11-based network access. If iOS must maintain that Wi-Fi connection as the app runs, add `UIRequiresPersistentWiFi` as a top-level property list key.
sms	Application requires the Messages application or uses sms:// URLs.
still-camera	Application requires an onboard still camera and can use the image picker interface to capture photos from that still camera.
auto-focus-camera	Application requires extra focus capabilities for macro photography or especially sharp images for in-image data detection.
front-facing-camera	Application requires a front-facing camera on the device.
camera-flash	Application requires a camera flash feature.
video-camera	Application requires a video-capable camera.
accelerometer	Application requires accelerometer-specific feedback beyond simple `UIViewController` orientation events.
gyroscope	Application requires an onboard gyroscope on the device.
location-services	Application uses Core Location of any kind.
gps	Application uses Core Location and requires the additional accuracy of GPS positioning.
magnetometer	Application uses Core Location and requires heading-related events—that is, the direction of travel. (The magnetometer is the built-in compass.)
gamekit	Application requires Game Center access (iOS 4.1 and later).
microphone	Application uses either built-in microphones or (approved) accessories that provide a microphone.
opengles-1	Application requires OpenGL ES 1.1.

Key	Use
opengles-2	Application requires OpenGL ES 2.0.
armv6	Application is compiled only for the armv6 instruction set (3.1 or later).
armv7	Application is compiled only for the armv7 instruction set (3.1 or later).
peer-peer	Application uses GameKit peer-to-peer connectivity over Bluetooth (3.1 or later).
bluetooth-le	Application requires Bluetooth low-energy support (5.0 and later).

For example, consider an application that offers an option for taking pictures when run on a camera-ready device. If the application otherwise works on pre-camera iPod touch units, do not include the still-camera restriction. Instead, check for camera capability from within the application and present the camera option when appropriate. Adding a still-camera restriction eliminates many early iPod touch (first through third generations) and iPad (first generation) owners from your potential customer pool.

User Permission Descriptions

To protect privacy, the end user must explicitly permit your applications to access calendar data, the camera, contacts, photos, location, and other functionality. To convince the user to opt in, it helps to explain how your application can use this data and describe your reason for accessing it. Assign string values to the following keys at the top level of your Info.plist file:

- NSBluetoothPeripheralUsageDescription
- NSCalendarsUsageDescription
- NSCameraUsageDescription
- NSContactsUsageDescription
- NSLocationUsageDescription
- NSMicrophoneUsageDescription
- NSMotionUsageDescription
- NSPhotoLibraryUsageDescription
- NSRemindersUsageDescription

When iOS prompts your user for resource-specific permission, it displays these strings as part of its standard dialog box.

Other Common Info.plist Keys

Here are a few other common keys you may want to assign in your property list, along with descriptions of what they do:

- **UIFileSharingEnabled (Boolean, defaults to off)**—Enables users to access the contents of your app's Documents folder from iTunes. This folder appears at the top level of your app sandbox.

- **UIAppFonts (array, strings of font names including their extension)**—Specifies custom TTF fonts that you supply in your bundle. When added, you access them using standard UIFont calls.

- **UIApplicationExitsOnSuspend (Boolean, defaults to off)**—Enables your app to terminate rather than move to the background when the user taps the Home button. When this property is enabled, iOS terminates the app and purges it from memory.

- **UIRequiresPersistentWifi (Boolean, defaults to off)**—Instructs iOS to maintain a Wi-Fi connection while the app is active.

- **UIStatusBarHidden (Boolean, defaults to off)**—If enabled, hides the status bar as the app launches.

- **UIStatusBarStyle (string, defaults to UIStatusBarStyleDefault)**—Specifies the style of the status bar at app launch.

Recipe: Checking Device Proximity and Battery States

The UIDevice class offers APIs that enable you to keep track of device characteristics including the states of the battery and proximity sensor. Recipe 14-1 demonstrates how you can enable and query monitoring for these two technologies. Both provide updates in the form of notifications, which you can subscribe to so your application is informed of important updates.

Enabling and Disabling the Proximity Sensor

Proximity is an iPhone-specific feature at this time. The iPod touch and iPad do not offer proximity sensors. Unless you have some pressing reason to hold an iPhone against body parts (or vice versa), using the proximity sensor accomplishes little.

When proximity is enabled, it has one primary task: It detects whether there's a large object right in front of it. If there is, it switches the screen off and sends a general notification. Move the blocking object away, and the screen switches back on. This prevents you from pressing buttons or dialing the phone with your ear when you are on a call. Some poorly designed protective cases keep the iPhone's proximity sensors from working properly.

Siri uses the proximity feature. When you hold the phone up to your ear, it records your query and sends it to be interpreted. Siri's voice interface does not depend on a visual GUI to operate.

Recipe 14-1 demonstrates how to work with proximity sensing on the iPhone. Its code uses the `UIDevice` class to toggle proximity monitoring and subscribes to `UIDeviceProximityStateDidChangeNotification` to catch state changes. The two states are on and off. When the `UIDevice` `proximityState` property returns `YES`, the proximity sensor has been activated.

Monitoring the Battery State

You can programmatically keep track of the battery and charging state. APIs enable you to know the level to which the battery is charged and whether the device is plugged into a charging source. The battery level is a floating-point value that ranges between 1.0 (fully charged) and 0.0 (fully discharged). It provides an approximate discharge level that you can use to query before performing operations that put unusual strain on the device.

For example, you might want to caution your user about performing a large series of mathematical computations and suggest that the user plug in to a power source. You retrieve the battery level via this `UIDevice` call, and the value returned is produced in 5% increments:

```
NSLog(@"Battery level: %0.2f%%",
    [UIDevice currentDevice].batteryLevel * 100);
```

The charge state has four possible values. The unit can be charging (that is, connected to a power source), full, unplugged, and a catchall "unknown." Recover the state by using the `UIDevice` `batteryState` property:

```
NSArray *stateArray = @[
    @"Battery state is unknown",
    @"Battery is not plugged into a charging source",
    @"Battery is charging",
    @"Battery state is full"];

NSLog(@"Battery state: %@",
    stateArray[[UIDevice currentDevice].batteryState]);
```

Don't think of these choices as persistent states. Instead, think of them as momentary reflections of what is actually happening to the device. They are not flags. They are not OR'ed together to form a general battery description. Instead, these values reflect the most recent state change.

You can easily monitor state changes by responding to notifications that the battery state has changed. In this way, you can catch momentary events, such as when the battery finally recharges fully, when the user has plugged in to a power source to recharge, and when the user disconnects from that power source.

To start monitoring, set the `batteryMonitoringEnabled` property to `YES`. During monitoring, the `UIDevice` class produces notifications when the battery state or level changes. Recipe 14-1 subscribes to both notifications. Note that you can also check these values directly, without waiting for notifications. Apple provides no guarantees about the frequency of level change updates, but as you can tell by testing this recipe, they arrive in a fairly regular fashion.

Recipe 14-1   **Monitoring Proximity and Battery**

```objc
// View the current battery level and state
- (void)peekAtBatteryState
{
    NSArray *stateArray = @[@"Battery state is unknown",
                            @"Battery is not plugged into a charging source",
                            @"Battery is charging",
                            @"Battery state is full"];

    NSString *status = [NSString stringWithFormat:
        @"Battery state: %@, Battery level: %0.2f%%",
        stateArray[[UIDevice currentDevice].batteryState],
        [UIDevice currentDevice].batteryLevel * 100];

    NSLog(@"%@", status);
}


// Show whether proximity is being monitored
- (void)updateTitle
{
    self.title = [NSString stringWithFormat:@"Proximity %@",
        [UIDevice currentDevice].proximityMonitoringEnabled ? @"On" : @"Off"];
}


// Toggle proximity monitoring off and on
- (void)toggle:(id)sender
{
    // Determine the current proximity monitoring and toggle it
    BOOL isEnabled = [UIDevice currentDevice].proximityMonitoringEnabled;
    [UIDevice currentDevice].proximityMonitoringEnabled = !isEnabled;
    [self updateTitle];
}


- (void)loadView
{
    self.view = [[UIView alloc] init];

    // Enable toggling and initialize title
    self.navigationItem.rightBarButtonItem =
        BARBUTTON(@"Toggle", @selector(toggle:));
    [self updateTitle];

    // Add proximity state checker
    [[NSNotificationCenter defaultCenter]
        addObserverForName:UIDeviceProximityStateDidChangeNotification
        object:nil queue:[NSOperationQueue mainQueue]
```

```
            usingBlock:^(NSNotification *notification) {
                // Sensor has triggered either on or off
                NSLog(@"The proximity sensor %@",
                    [UIDevice currentDevice].proximityState ?
                    @"will now blank the screen" : @"will now restore the screen");
        }];

        // Enable battery monitoring
        [[UIDevice currentDevice] setBatteryMonitoringEnabled:YES];

        // Add observers for battery state and level changes
        [[NSNotificationCenter defaultCenter]
            addObserverForName:UIDeviceBatteryStateDidChangeNotification
            object:nil queue:[NSOperationQueue mainQueue]
            usingBlock:^(NSNotification *notification) {
                // State has changed
                NSLog(@"Battery State Change");
                [self peekAtBatteryState];
        }];

        [[NSNotificationCenter defaultCenter]
            addObserverForName:UIDeviceBatteryLevelDidChangeNotification
            object:nil queue:[NSOperationQueue mainQueue]
            usingBlock:^(NSNotification *notification) {
                // Level has changed
                NSLog(@"Battery Level Change");
                [self peekAtBatteryState];
        }];
}
```

Get This Recipe's Code

To find this recipe's full sample project, point your browser to https://github.com/erica/iOS-7-Cookbook and go to the folder for Chapter 14.

Detecting Retina Support

In recent years, Apple has converted all but a few lower-cost devices to Retina displays. Pixel density of Retina displays, according to Apple, is high enough that the human eye cannot distinguish individual pixels. Apps shipped with higher-resolution art take advantage of this improved display quality.

The UIScreen class offers an easy way to check whether the current device offers a built-in Retina display. Check the screen scale property, which provides the factor that converts from the logical coordinate space (points, each approximately 1/160 inch) into a device coordinate space (pixels). It is 1.0 for standard displays, so 1 point corresponds to 1 pixel. It is 2.0 for Retina displays (4 pixels per point):

```
- (BOOL) hasRetinaDisplay
{
    return ([UIScreen mainScreen].scale == 2.0f);
}
```

The `UIScreen` class also offers two useful display-size properties. `bounds` returns the screen's bounding rectangle, measured in points. This gives you the full size of the screen, regardless of any onscreen elements such as status bars, navigation bars, or tab bars. The `applicationFrame` property, also measured in points, excludes the status bar, providing the frame for your application's initial window size.

Recipe: Recovering Additional Device Information

Both `sysctl()` and `sysctlbyname()` enable you to retrieve system information. These standard UNIX functions query the operating system about hardware and OS details. You can get a sense of the kind of scope on offer by glancing at the /usr/include/sys/sysctl.h include file on the Macintosh. There you can find an exhaustive list of constants that can be used as parameters to these functions.

These constants enable you to check for core information such as the system's CPU count, the amount of available memory, and more. Recipe 14-2 demonstrates this functionality. It introduces a `UIDevice` category that gathers system information and returns it via a series of method calls.

You might wonder why this category includes a platform method, when the standard `UIDevice` class returns device models on demand. The answer lies in distinguishing different types of units.

An iPhone 3GS's model is simply `iPhone`, as is the model of an iPhone 4S. In contrast, this recipe returns a platform value of `iPhone2,1` for the 3GS, `iPhone4,1` for the iPhone 4S, and `iPhone5,1` for the iPhone 5. This enables you to programmatically differentiate the 3GS unit from a first-generation iPhone (`iPhone1,1`) or iPhone 3G (`iPhone1,2`).

Each model offers distinct built-in capabilities. Knowing exactly which iPhone you're dealing with helps you determine whether that unit likely supports features such as accessibility, GPS, and magnetometers.

Recipe 14-2   **Extending Device Information Gathering**

```
@implementation UIDevice (Hardware)
+ (NSString *)getSysInfoByName:(char *)typeSpecifier
{
    // Recover sysctl information by name
    size_t size;
```

```
    sysctlbyname(typeSpecifier, NULL, &size, NULL, 0);

    char *answer = malloc(size);
    sysctlbyname(typeSpecifier, answer, &size, NULL, 0);

    NSString *results = [NSString stringWithCString:answer
        encoding: NSUTF8StringEncoding];
    free(answer);

    return results;
}

- (NSString *)platform
{
    return [UIDevice getSysInfoByName:"hw.machine"];
}

- (NSUInteger)getSysInfo:(uint)typeSpecifier
{
    size_t size = sizeof(int);
    int results;
    int mib[2] = {CTL_HW, typeSpecifier};
    sysctl(mib, 2, &results, &size, NULL, 0);
    return (NSUInteger) results;
}

- (NSUInteger)busFrequency
{
    return [UIDevice getSysInfo:HW_BUS_FREQ];
}

- (NSUInteger)totalMemory
{
    return [UIDevice getSysInfo:HW_PHYSMEM];
}

- (NSUInteger)userMemory
{
    return [UIDevice getSysInfo:HW_USERMEM];
}

- (NSUInteger)maxSocketBufferSize
{
    return [UIDevice getSysInfo:KIPC_MAXSOCKBUF];
}
@end
```

Core Motion Basics

The Core Motion framework centralizes access to the motion data generated by the iOS hardware. It provides monitoring of three key onboard sensors: the gyroscope, which measures device rotation; the magnetometer, which provides a way to measure compass bearings; and the accelerometer, which detects gravitational changes along three axes. A fourth entry point, called *device motion*, combines all three of these sensors into a single monitoring system.

Core Motion uses raw values from these sensors to create readable measurements, primarily in the form of force vectors. Measurable items include the following properties:

- `attitude`—Device attitude is the device's orientation relative to some frame of reference. The attitude is represented as a triplet of roll, pitch, and yaw angles, each measured in radians.

- `rotationRate`—The rotation rate is the rate at which the device rotates around each of its three axes. The rotation includes x, y, and z angular velocity values, measured in radians per second.

- `gravity`—Gravity is a device's current acceleration vector, as imparted by the normal gravitational field. Gravity is measured in g's, along the x-, y-, and z-axes. Each unit represents the standard gravitational force imparted by Earth (namely 32 feet per second per second, or 9.8 meters per second per second).

- `userAcceleration`—User acceleration is the acceleration vector being imparted by the user. Like `gravity`, user acceleration is measured in g's along the x-, y-, and z-axes. When added together, the user vector and the gravity vector represent the total acceleration imparted to the device.

- `magneticField`—The magnetic field is the vector representing the overall magnetic field values in the device's vicinity. The field is measured in microteslas along the x-, y-, and z-axes. A calibration accuracy is also provided, to inform your application of the field measurements quality.

Testing for Sensors

As you read earlier in this chapter, you can use the application's Info.plist file to require or exclude onboard sensors. You can also test in-app for each kind of sensor support by querying a Core Motion `CMMotionManager` object:

```
if (motionManager.gyroAvailable)
    [motionManager startGyroUpdates];
```

```
if (motionManager.magnetometerAvailable)
    [motionManager startMagnetometerUpdates];

if (motionManager.accelerometerAvailable)
    [motionManager startAccelerometerUpdates];

if (motionManager.deviceMotionAvailable)
    [motionManager startDeviceMotionUpdates];
```

Accessing Sensor Data

Core Motion provides two mechanisms for accessing sensor data. For periodic, passive access to motion data, activate the appropriate sensor (for example, startAccelerometerUpdates) and then access the data from the corresponding motion data property on the CMMotionManager object (accelerometerData).

In cases where polling is not sufficient, you can use a block-based update mechanism that executes a block that you provide for each sensor update (for example, startAccelerometer-UpdatesToQueue:withHandler:). When using the handler methods, be sure to set the update interval for the sensor (accelerometerUpdateInterval). The interval is capped at minimum and maximum values, so if the actual frequency is critical to your app, make sure to check the timestamp associated with the data object passed to the block.

Recipe: Using Acceleration to Locate "Up"

The iPhone and iPad provide three onboard sensors that measure acceleration along the device's perpendicular axes: left/right (X), up/down (Y), and front/back (Z). These values indicate the forces affecting the device, from both gravity and user movement. You can get some neat force feedback by swinging the iPhone around your head (centripetal force) or dropping it from a tall building (freefall). Unfortunately, you might not recover that data after your iPhone becomes an expensive bit of scrap metal.

To monitor accelerometer updates, create a Core Motion manager object, set the interval for updates, and start the manager, passing in a handler block to be processed:

```
motionManager = [[CMMotionManager alloc] init];
motionManager.accelerometerUpdateInterval = 0.005;
if (motionManager.isAccelerometerAvailable)
{
    [motionManager startAccelerometerUpdatesToQueue:
            [NSOperationQueue mainQueue]
        withHandler:^(CMAccelerometerData *accelerometerData,
            NSError *error) {
                // handle the accelerometer update
            }];
}
```

When using Core Motion, always check for the availability of the requested sensor. When started, your handler block receives CMAccelerometerData objects, which you can track and respond to. Each of these objects contains a CMAcceleration structure consisting of floating-point values for the x-, y-, and z-axes, and each value ranges from –1.0 to 1.0.

Recipe 14-3 uses these values to help determine the "up" direction. It calculates the arctangent between the X and Y acceleration vectors and returns the up-offset angle. As new acceleration messages are received, the recipe rotates a UIImageView instance with its picture of an arrow, as shown in Figure 14-1, to point up. The real-time response to user actions ensures that the arrow continues pointing upward, no matter how the user reorients the device.

Figure 14-1   A little math recovers the "up" direction by performing an arctan function using the x and y force vectors. In this example, the arrow always points up, no matter how the user reorients the device.

Recipe 14-3   **Handling Acceleration Events**

```
- (void) loadView
{
    self.view = [[UIView alloc] init];
    self.view.backgroundColor = [UIColor whiteColor];
```

```
arrow = [[UIImageView alloc]
    initWithImage:[UIImage imageNamed:@"arrow"]];
[self.view addSubview:arrow];
PREPCONSTRAINTS(arrow);
CENTER_VIEW(self.view, arrow);

motionManager = [[CMMotionManager alloc] init];
motionManager.accelerometerUpdateInterval = 0.005;
if (motionManager.isAccelerometerAvailable)
{
    [motionManager
        startAccelerometerUpdatesToQueue:
            [NSOperationQueue mainQueue]
        withHandler:
            ^(CMAccelerometerData *accelerometerData,
                NSError *error) {
        CMAcceleration acceleration =
            accelerometerData.acceleration;

        // Determine up from the x and y acceleration components
        float xx = -acceleration.x;
        float yy = acceleration.y;
        float angle = atan2(yy, xx);
        [arrow setTransform:CGAffineTransformMakeRotation(angle)];
    }];
    }
}
```

Get This Recipe's Code

To find this recipe's full sample project, point your browser to https://github.com/erica/iOS-7-Cookbook and go to the folder for Chapter 14.

Working with Basic Orientation

The UIDevice class uses the built-in orientation property to provide the physical orientation of a device. iOS devices support seven possible values for this property:

- **UIDeviceOrientationUnknown**—The orientation is currently unknown.
- **UIDeviceOrientationPortrait**—The home button is down.
- **UIDeviceOrientationPortraitUpsideDown**—The home button is up.
- **UIDeviceOrientationLandscapeLeft**—The home button is to the right.
- **UIDeviceOrientationLandscapeRight**—The home button is to the left.

- **UIDeviceOrientationFaceUp**—The screen is face up.

- **UIDeviceOrientationFaceDown**—The screen is face down.

The device can pass through any or all these orientations during a typical application session. Although orientation is created in concert with the onboard accelerometer, these orientations are not tied in any way to a built-in angular value.

iOS offers two built-in macros to help determine whether a device orientation enumerated value is portrait or landscape: UIDeviceOrientationIsPortrait() and UIDeviceOrientationIsLandscape(). It is convenient to extend the UIDevice class to offer these tests as built-in device properties, as shown in the following snippet:

```
@property (nonatomic, readonly) BOOL isLandscape;
@property (nonatomic, readonly) BOOL isPortrait;

- (BOOL) isLandscape
{
    return UIDeviceOrientationIsLandscape(self.orientation);
}

- (BOOL) isPortrait
{
    return UIDeviceOrientationIsPortrait(self.orientation);
}
```

The orientation property returns zero until the orientation notifications have been initiated with beginGeneratingDeviceOrientationNotifications. Once device orientation notifications are enabled, your code can subscribe directly to device reorientation notifications by adding an observer to catch the ensuing UIDeviceOrientationDidChangeNotification updates. As you would expect, you can finish listening by calling endGeneratingDeviceOrientationNotification.

Calculating Orientation from the Accelerometer

The UIDevice class does not report a proper orientation when applications are first launched. It updates the orientation only after the device has moved into a new position or UIViewController methods kick in.

An application launched in portrait orientation may not read as "portrait" until the user moves the device out of and then back into the proper orientation. This condition exists on the simulator and on the iPhone device and is easily tested. (Radars—tickets filed in Apple's issue tracking system—for this issue have been closed with updates that the features are working as designed.)

For a workaround, consider recovering the angular orientation from the accelerometer via Core Motion. You can then calculate the device angle:

```
float xx = acceleration.x;
float yy = -acceleration.y;
device_angle = M_PI / 2.0f - atan2(yy, xx);

if (device_angle > M_PI)
    device_angle -= 2 * M_PI;
```

Once this is calculated, convert from the accelerometer-based angle to a device orientation. Here's how that might work in code:

```
// Limited to the four portrait/landscape options
- (UIDeviceOrientation)acceleratorBasedOrientation
{
    CGFloat baseAngle = self.orientationAngle;
    if ((baseAngle > -M_PI_4) && (baseAngle < M_PI_4))
        return UIDeviceOrientationPortrait;
    if ((baseAngle < -M_PI_4) && (baseAngle > -3 * M_PI_4))
        return UIDeviceOrientationLandscapeLeft;
    if ((baseAngle > M_PI_4) && (baseAngle < 3 * M_PI_4))
        return UIDeviceOrientationLandscapeRight;
    return UIDeviceOrientationPortraitUpsideDown;
}
```

Be aware that this example looks only at the *x–y* plane, which is where most user interface decisions need to be made. This snippet completely ignores the *z*-axis, meaning that you'll end up with vaguely random results for the face-up and face-down orientations. Adapt this code to provide that nuance if needed.

The UIViewController class's interfaceOrientation instance method reports the orientation of a view controller's interface. Although this is not a substitute for accelerometer readings, many interface layout issues rest on the underlying view orientation rather than device characteristics.

Be aware that, especially on the iPad, a child view controller may use a layout orientation that's distinct from a device orientation. For example, an embedded controller may present a portrait layout within a landscape split view controller. Even so, consider whether your orientation-detection code is satisfiable by the underlying interface orientation. It may be more reliable than device orientation, especially as the application launches. Develop accordingly.

Calculating a Relative Angle

Screen reorientation support means that an interface's relationship to a given device angle must be supported in quarters, one for each possible front-facing screen orientation. As the UIViewController automatically rotates its onscreen view, the math needs to catch up to account for those reorientations.

The following method, which is written for use in a `UIDevice` category, calculates angles so that the angle remains in synchrony with the device orientation. This creates simple offsets from vertical that match the way the GUI is currently presented:

```
- (float)orientationAngleRelativeToOrientation:
    (UIDeviceOrientation)someOrientation
{
    float dOrientation = 0.0f;
    switch (someOrientation)
    {
        case UIDeviceOrientationPortraitUpsideDown:
            {dOrientation = M_PI; break;}
        case UIDeviceOrientationLandscapeLeft:
            {dOrientation = -(M_PI/2.0f); break;}
        case UIDeviceOrientationLandscapeRight:
            {dOrientation = (M_PI/2.0f); break;}
        default: break;
    }

    float adjustedAngle =
        fmod(self.orientationAngle - dOrientation, 2.0f * M_PI);
    if (adjustedAngle > (M_PI + 0.01f))
        adjustedAngle = (adjustedAngle - 2.0f * M_PI);
    return adjustedAngle;
}
```

This method uses a floating-point modulo to retrieve the difference between the actual screen angle and the interface orientation angular offset to return that all-important vertical angular offset.

> **Note**
>
> Beginning with iOS 6, instead of using `shouldAutorotateToInterfaceOrientation:`, use `supportedInterfaceOrientations` on your root view controller and/or your Info.plist file to allow and disallow orientation changes. iOS uses the intersection of these two values to determine whether rotation is allowed.

Recipe: Using Acceleration to Move Onscreen Objects

With a bit of programming, the iPhone's onboard accelerometer can make objects "move" around the screen, responding in real time to the way the user tilts the phone. Recipe 14-4 builds an animated butterfly that users can slide across the screen.

The secret to making this work lies in adding a "physics timer" to the program. Instead of responding directly to changes in acceleration, the way Recipe 14-3 does, the accelerometer handler measures the current forces. It's up to the timer routine to apply those forces to the butterfly over time by changing its frame. Here are some key points to keep in mind:

- As long as the direction of force remains the same, the butterfly accelerates. Its velocity increases, scaled according to the degree of acceleration force in the *x* or *y* direction.

- The `tick` routine, called by the timer, moves the butterfly by adding the velocity vector to the butterfly's origin.

- The butterfly's range is bounded. So when it hits an edge, it stops moving in that direction. This keeps the butterfly onscreen at all times. The `tick` method checks for boundary conditions. For example, if the butterfly hits a vertical edge, it can still move horizontally.

- The butterfly reorients itself so it is always falling "down." This happens through the application of a simple rotation transform in the `tick` method. Be careful when using transforms in addition to frame or center offsets. Always reset the math before applying offsets and then reapply any angular changes. Failing to do so may cause your frames to zoom, shrink, or skew unexpectedly.

Setup and Teardown

The `establishMotionManager` and `shutDownMotionManager` methods in Recipe 14-4 enable your application to start up and shut down the motion manager on demand. These methods are called from the application delegate when the application becomes active and when it suspends:

```
- (void)applicationWillResignActive:(UIApplication *)application
{
    [tbvc shutDownMotionManager];
}


- (void)applicationDidBecomeActive:(UIApplication *)application
{
    [tbvc establishMotionManager];
}
```

These methods provide a clean way to shut down and resume motion services in response to the current application state.

> **Note**
>
> Timers in their natural state do not use a block-based API. If you'd rather use a block than callbacks with your timers, check GitHub to find an implementation that does this.

Recipe 14-4   **Sliding an Onscreen Object Based on Accelerometer Feedback**

```objc
@implementation TestBedViewController

- (void)tick
{
    butterfly.transform = CGAffineTransformIdentity;

    // Move the butterfly according to the current velocity vector
    CGRect rect = CGRectOffset(butterfly.frame, xVelocity, 0.0f);
    if (CGRectContainsRect(self.view.bounds, rect))
        butterfly.frame = rect;

    rect = CGRectOffset(butterfly.frame, 0.0f, yVelocity);
    if (CGRectContainsRect(self.view.bounds, rect))
        butterfly.frame = rect;

    butterfly.transform =
        CGAffineTransformMakeRotation(mostRecentAngle - M_PI_2);
}

- (void)shutDownMotionManager
{
    NSLog(@"Shutting down motion manager");
    [motionManager stopAccelerometerUpdates];
    motionManager = nil;

    [timer invalidate];
    timer = nil;
}

- (void)establishMotionManager
{
    if (motionManager)
        [self shutDownMotionManager];

    NSLog(@"Establishing motion manager");

    // Establish the motion manager
    motionManager = [[CMMotionManager alloc] init];
    if (motionManager.accelerometerAvailable)
        [motionManager
         startAccelerometerUpdatesToQueue:
            [[NSOperationQueue alloc] init]
         withHandler:^(CMAccelerometerData *data, NSError *error)
         {
             // Extract the acceleration components
```

```
        float xx = -data.acceleration.x;
        float yy = data.acceleration.y;
        mostRecentAngle = atan2(yy, xx);

        // Has the direction changed?
        float accelDirX = SIGN(xVelocity) * -1.0f;
        float newDirX = SIGN(xx);
        float accelDirY = SIGN(yVelocity) * -1.0f;
        float newDirY = SIGN(yy);

        // Accelerate. To increase viscosity,
        // lower the additive value
        if (accelDirX == newDirX)
            xAccel = (abs(xAccel) + 0.85f) * SIGN(xAccel);
        if (accelDirY == newDirY)
            yAccel = (abs(yAccel) + 0.85f) * SIGN(yAccel);

        // Apply acceleration changes to the current velocity
        xVelocity = -xAccel * xx;
        yVelocity = -yAccel * yy;
    }];

    // Start the physics timer
    timer = [NSTimer scheduledTimerWithTimeInterval: 0.03f
        target:self selector:@selector(tick)
        userInfo:nil repeats:YES];
}

- (void)initButterfly
{
    CGSize size;

    // Load the animation cells
    NSMutableArray *butterflies = [NSMutableArray array];
    for (int i = 1; i <= 17; i++)
    {
        NSString *fileName =
            [NSString stringWithFormat:@"bf_%d.png", i];
        UIImage *image = [UIImage imageNamed:fileName];
        size = image.size;
        [butterflies addObject:image];
    }

    // Begin the animation
    butterfly = [[UIImageView alloc]
        initWithFrame:(CGRect){.size=size}];
    [butterfly setAnimationImages:butterflies];
```

```
    butterfly.animationDuration = 0.75f;
    [butterfly startAnimating];

    // Set the butterfly's initial speed and acceleration
    xAccel = 2.0f;
    yAccel = 2.0f;
    xVelocity = 0.0f;
    yVelocity = 0.0f;

    // Add the butterfly
    [self.view addSubview:butterfly];
}

- (void)viewDidAppear:(BOOL)animated
{
    [super viewDidAppear:animated];

    // Get our butterfly centered
    butterfly.center = RECTCENTER(self.view.bounds);
}

- (void)loadView
{
    self.view = [[UIView alloc] init];
    self.view.backgroundColor = [UIColor whiteColor];
    [self initButterfly];
}
```

Get This Recipe's Code

To find this recipe's full sample project, point your browser to https://github.com/erica/iOS-7-Cookbook and go to the folder for Chapter 14.

Recipe: Accelerometer-Based Scroll View

Several readers asked that we include a tilt scroller recipe in this edition. A tilt scroller uses a device's built-in accelerometer to control movement around a UIScrollView's content. As the user adjusts the device, the material "falls down" accordingly. Instead of a view being positioned onscreen, the content view scrolls to a new offset.

The challenge in creating this interface lies in determining where the device should have its resting axis. Most people would initially suggest that the display should stabilize when lying on its back, with the z-direction pointed straight up in the air. It turns out that's actually a fairly bad design choice. To use that axis means the screen must actually tilt away from the viewer during navigation. With the device rotated away from view, the user cannot fully see what is happening onscreen, especially when using the device in a seated position and somewhat when looking at the device while standing overhead.

Instead, Recipe 14-5 assumes that the stable position is created by the z-axis pointing at approximately 45 degrees, the natural position at which users hold an iPhone or iPad in their hands. This is halfway between a face-up and a face-forward position. The math in Recipe 14-5 is adjusted accordingly. Tilting back and forward from this slanting position leaves the screen with maximal visibility during adjustments.

The other change in this recipe compared to Recipe 14-4 is the much lower acceleration constant. This enables onscreen movement to happen more slowly, letting users more easily slow down and resume navigation.

Recipe 14-5   **Tilt Scroller**

```
- (void)tick
{
    xOff += xVelocity;
    xOff = MIN(xOff, 1.0f);
    xOff = MAX(xOff, 0.0f);

    yOff += yVelocity;
    yOff = MIN(yOff, 1.0f);
    yOff = MAX(yOff, 0.0f);

    // update the content offset based on the current velocities
    UIScrollView *sv = (UIScrollView *) self.view;
    CGFloat xSize = sv.contentSize.width - sv.frame.size.width;
    CGFloat ySize = sv.contentSize.height - sv.frame.size.height;
    sv.contentOffset = CGPointMake(xOff * xSize, yOff * ySize);
}

- (void) viewDidAppear:(BOOL)animated
{
    [super viewDidAppear:animated];
    NSString *map = @"http://maps.weather.com/images/\
        maps/current/curwx_720x486.jpg";
    NSOperationQueue *queue = [[NSOperationQueue alloc] init];
    [queue addOperationWithBlock:
     ^{
        // Load the weather data
        NSURL *weatherURL = [NSURL URLWithString:map];
        NSData *imageData = [NSData dataWithContentsOfURL:weatherURL];

        // Update the image on the main thread using the main queue
        [[NSOperationQueue mainQueue] addOperationWithBlock:^{
            UIImage *weatherImage = [UIImage imageWithData:imageData];
```

```
UIImageView *imageView =
    [[UIImageView alloc] initWithImage:weatherImage];
CGSize initSize = weatherImage.size;
CGSize destSize = weatherImage.size;

// Ensure that the content size is significantly bigger
// than the screen can show at once
while ((destSize.width < (self.view.frame.size.width * 4)) ||
       (destSize.height < (self.view.frame.size.height * 4)))
{
    destSize.width += initSize.width;
    destSize.height += initSize.height;
}

imageView.frame = (CGRect){.size = destSize};
UIScrollView *sv = (UIScrollView *) self.view;
sv.contentSize = destSize;
[sv addSubview:imageView];

// only allowing accelerometer-based scrolling
scrollView.userInteractionEnabled = NO;

// Activate the accelerometer
[motionManager startAccelerometerUpdatesToQueue:
    [NSOperationQueue mainQueue] withHandler:
        ^(CMAccelerometerData *accelerometerData,
            NSError *error) {

    // extract the acceleration components
    CMAcceleration acceleration =
        accelerometerData.acceleration;
    float xx = -acceleration.x;
    // between face-up and face-forward
    float yy = (acceleration.z + 0.5f) * 2.0f;

    // Has the direction changed?
    float accelDirX = SIGN(xVelocity) * -1.0f;
    float newDirX = SIGN(xx);
    float accelDirY = SIGN(yVelocity) * -1.0f;
    float newDirY = SIGN(yy);

    // Accelerate. To increase viscosity lower the additive value
    if (accelDirX == newDirX)
        xAccel = (abs(xAccel) + 0.005f) * SIGN(xAccel);
    if (accelDirY == newDirY)
        yAccel = (abs(yAccel) + 0.005f) * SIGN(yAccel);
```

```
                    // Apply acceleration changes to the current velocity
                    xVelocity = -xAccel * xx;
                    yVelocity = -yAccel * yy;
                }];

                // Start the physics timer
                [NSTimer scheduledTimerWithTimeInterval:0.03f
                    target:self selector:@selector(tick)
                    userInfo:nil repeats:YES];
            }];
        }];
}
```

Get This Recipe's Code

To find this recipe's full sample project, point your browser to https://github.com/erica/iOS-7-Cookbook and go to the folder for Chapter 14.

Recipe: Retrieving and Using Device Attitude

Imagine an iPad sitting on a desk. There's an image displayed on the iPad, which you can bend over and look at. Now imagine rotating that iPad as it lays flat on the desk, but as the iPad moves, the image appears to stay fixed in place, retaining the same alignment with the world around it. Regardless of how you spin the iPad, the image doesn't "move" with the device as the image view updates to balance the physical movement. That's how Recipe 14-6 works, taking advantage of a device's onboard gyroscope—a necessary requirement to make this recipe work.

The image adjusts however you hold the device. In addition to that flat manipulation, you can pick up the device and orient it in space. If you flip the device and look at it over your head, you see the reversed "bottom" of the image. As you manipulate the device, the image responds to create a virtual still world within that iPad.

Recipe 14-6 shows how to do this with just a few simple geometric transformations. It establishes a motion manager, subscribes to device motion updates, and then applies image transforms based on the roll, pitch, and yaw returned by the motion manager.

Recipe 14-6   **Using Device Motion Updates to Fix an Image in Space**

```
- (void)shutDownMotionManager
{
    NSLog(@"Shutting down motion manager");
    [motionManager stopDeviceMotionUpdates];
    motionManager = nil;
}
```

```
- (void)establishMotionManager
{
    if (motionManager)
        [self shutDownMotionManager];

    NSLog(@"Establishing motion manager");

    // Establish the motion manager
    motionManager = [[CMMotionManager alloc] init];
    if (motionManager.deviceMotionAvailable)
        [motionManager
         startDeviceMotionUpdatesToQueue:
             [NSOperationQueue currentQueue]
         withHandler: ^(CMDeviceMotion *motion, NSError *error) {
             CATransform3D transform;
             transform = CATransform3DMakeRotation(
                 motion.attitude.pitch, 1, 0, 0);
             transform = CATransform3DRotate(transform,
                 motion.attitude.roll, 0, 1, 0);
             transform = CATransform3DRotate(transform,
                 motion.attitude.yaw, 0, 0, 1);
             imageView.layer.transform = transform;
    }];
}
```

Get This Recipe's Code

To find this recipe's full sample project, point your browser to https://github.com/erica/iOS-7-Cookbook and go to the folder for Chapter 14.

Detecting Shakes Using Motion Events

When the iPhone detects a motion event, such as a shake, it passes that event to the current first responder, the primary object in the responder chain. Responders are objects that can handle events. All views and windows are responders, and so is the application object.

The responder chain provides a hierarchy of objects, all of which can respond to events. When an object toward the start of the chain handles an event, that event does not get passed further down. If it cannot handle it, that event can move on to the next responder.

An object may become the first responder by declaring itself to be so, via becomeFirst-Responder. In this snippet, UIViewController ensures that it becomes the first responder whenever its view appears onscreen, and upon disappearing, it resigns the first responder position:

```
- (BOOL) canBecomeFirstResponder {
    return YES;
}

// Become first responder whenever the view appears
- (void) viewDidAppear: (BOOL) animated {
    [super viewDidAppear:animated] ;
    [self becomeFirstResponder] ;
}

// Resign first responder whenever the view disappears
- (void) viewWillDisappear: (BOOL) animated {
    [super viewWillDisappear:animated] ;
    [self resignFirstResponder] ;
}
```

First responders receive all touch and motion events. The motion callbacks mirror UIView touch callback stages. The callback methods are as follows:

- **motionBegan:withEvent:**—This callback indicates the start of a motion event. At this writing, only one kind of motion event is recognized: a shake. This may not hold true in the future, so you might want to check the motion type in your code.

- **motionEnded:withEvent:**—The first responder receives this callback at the end of the motion event.

- **motionCancelled:withEvent:**—As with touches, motions can be cancelled by incoming phone calls and other system events. Apple recommends that you implement all three motion event callbacks (and, similarly, all four touch event callbacks) in production code.

The following snippet shows a pair of motion callback examples:

```
- (void) motionBegan: (UIEventSubtype) motion
    withEvent: (UIEvent *) event {

    // Play a sound whenever a shake motion starts
    if (motion != UIEventSubtypeMotionShake) return;
    [self playSound:startSound] ;
}

- (void) motionEnded: (UIEventSubtype) motion withEvent: (UIEvent *) event
{
    // Play a sound whenever a shake motion ends
    if (motion != UIEventSubtypeMotionShake) return;
    [self playSound:endSound] ;
}
```

If you test this on a device, notice several things. First, from a user perspective, the began and ended events happen almost simultaneously. Playing sounds for both types is overkill. Second, there is a bias toward side-to-side shake detection. The iPhone is better at detecting side-to-side shakes than the front-to-back and up-and-down versions. Finally, Apple's motion implementation uses a slight lockout approach. You cannot generate a new motion event until a second or so after the previous one was processed. This is the same lockout used by shake-to-shuffle and shake-to-undo events.

Recipe: Using External Screens

There are many ways to use external screens. Take the newest iPads, for example. The second-, third-, and fourth-generation models offer built-in screen mirroring. Attach a VGA or HDMI cable, and your content can be shown on external displays and on the built-in screen. Certain devices enable you to mirror screens wirelessly to Apple TV using AirPlay, Apple's proprietary cable-free over-the-air video solution. These mirroring features are extremely handy, but you're not limited to simply copying content from one screen to another in iOS.

The `UIScreen` class enables you to detect and write to external screens independently. You can treat any connected display as a new window and create content for that display separate from any view you show on the primary device screen. You can do this for any wired screen, and with the iPad 2 and later, the iPhone 4S and later, and the iPod touch fifth generation and later, you can do so wirelessly using AirPlay to Apple TV 2 and later. A third-party app called Reflector enables you to mirror your display to Mac or Windows computers using AirPlay.

Geometry is important. Here's why: iOS devices currently include the 320×480 old-style iPhone displays, the 640×960-pixel Retina display units, the 1024×768-pixel iPads, and the 2048×1536-pixel Retina display units. Typical composite/component output is produced at 720×480 pixels (480i and 480p) and VGA at 1024×768 and 1280×720 (720p), and then there's the higher-quality HDMI output as well. Add to this the issues of overscan and other target display limitations, and Video Out quickly becomes a geometric challenge.

Fortunately, Apple has responded to this challenge with some handy real-world adaptations. Instead of trying to create one-to-one correspondences with the output screen and your built-in device screen, you can build content based on the available properties of your output display. You just create a window, populate it, and display it.

If you intend to develop Video Out applications, don't assume that your users are strictly using AirPlay. Many users still connect to monitors and projectors using old-style cable connections. Make sure you have at least one of each type of cable on hand (composite, component, VGA, and HDMI) and an AirPlay-ready iPhone and iPad, so you can thoroughly test on each output configuration. Third-party cables (not branded with Made for iPhone/iPad) won't work, so make sure you purchase Apple-branded items.

Detecting Screens

The `UIScreen` class reports how many screens are connected:

```
#define SCREEN_CONNECTED ([UIScreen screens].count > 1)
```

You know that an external screen is connected whenever this count goes above 1. The first item in the screens array is always your primary device screen.

Each screen can report its `bounds` (that is, its physical dimensions in points) and its screen `scale` (relating the points to pixels). Two standard notifications enable you to observe when screens have been connected to and disconnected from the device:

```
// Register for connect/disconnect notifications
[[NSNotificationCenter defaultCenter]
    addObserver:self selector:@selector(screenDidConnect:)
    name:UIScreenDidConnectNotification object:nil];
[[NSNotificationCenter defaultCenter]
    addObserver:self selector:@selector(screenDidDisconnect:)
    name:UIScreenDidDisconnectNotification object:nil];
```

Connection means *any* kind of connection, whether by cable or via AirPlay. Whenever you receive an update of this type, make sure you count your screens and adjust your user interface to match the new conditions.

It's your responsibility to set up windows whenever new screens are attached and tear them down when detach events occur. Each screen should have its own window to manage content for that output display. Don't hold onto windows upon detaching screens. Let them release and then re-create them when new screens appear.

> **Note**
>
> Mirrored screens are not represented in the `screens` array. Instead, the mirror is stored in the main screen's `mirroredScreen` property. This property is nil when mirroring is disabled, unconnected, or simply not supported by the device's abilities.
>
> Creating a new screen and using it for independent external display always overrides mirroring. So even if a user has enabled mirroring, when your application begins writing to and creating an external display, it takes priority.

Retrieving Screen Resolutions

Each screen provides an `availableModes` property. This is an array of resolution objects ordered from lowest to highest resolution. Each mode has a `size` property that indicates a target pixel-size resolution. Many screens support multiple modes. For example, a VGA display might offer as many as one-half dozen or more different resolutions. The number of supported resolutions varies by hardware. There will always be at least one resolution available, but you should offer choices to users when there are more.

Setting Up Video Out

After retrieving an external screen object from the `[UIScreens screens]` array, query the available modes and select a size to use. As a rule, you can get away with selecting the last mode in the list to always use the highest possible resolution or the first mode for the lowest resolution.

To start a Video Out stream, create a new `UIWindow` and size it to the selected mode. Add a new view to that window for drawing. Then assign the window to the external screen and make it key and visible. This orders the window to display and prepares it for use. After you do that, make the original window key again. This allows the user to continue interacting with the primary screen. Don't skip this step. Nothing makes end users crankier than discovering their expensive device no longer responds to their touches. The following snippet implements all of these necessary steps to set up the secondary screen for use:

```
self.outputWindow = [[UIWindow alloc] initWithFrame:theFrame];
outputWindow.screen = secondaryScreen;
[outputWindow makeKeyAndVisible];
[delegate.view.window makeKeyAndVisible];
```

Adding a Display Link

Display links are a kind of timer that synchronizes drawing to a display's refresh rate. You can adjust this frame refresh time by changing the display link's `frameInterval` property. It defaults to 1. A higher number slows down the refresh rate. Setting it to 2 halves your frame rate. Create the display link when a screen connects to your device. The `UIScreen` class implements a method that returns a display link object for its screen. You specify the target for the display link and a selector to call.

The display link fires on a regular basis, letting you know when to update the Video Out screen. You can adjust the interval up for less of a CPU load, but you get a lower frame rate in return. This is an important trade-off, especially for direct manipulation interfaces that require a high level of CPU response on the device side.

The code in Recipe 14-7 uses common modes for the run loop, providing the least latency. You `invalidate` your display link when you are done with it, removing it from the run loop.

Overscanning Compensation

The `UIScreen` class enables you to compensate for pixel loss at the edge of display screens by assigning a value to the `overscanCompensation` property. The techniques you can assign are described in Apple's documentation; they basically correspond to whether you want to clip content or pad it with black space.

VIDEOkit

Recipe 14-7 introduces VIDEOkit, a basic external screen client. It demonstrates all the features needed to get up and going with wired and wireless external screens. You establish screen monitoring by calling `startupWithDelegate:`. Pass it the primary view controller whose job it will be to create external content.

The internal `init` method starts listening for screen attach and detach events and builds and tears down windows as needed. An informal delegate method (`updateExternalView:`) is called each time the display link fires. It passes a view that lives on the external window that the delegate can draw onto as needed.

In the sample code that accompanies this recipe, the view controller delegate stores a local color value and uses it to color the external display:

```
- (void)updateExternalView:(UIImageView *)aView
{
    aView.backgroundColor = color;
}

- (void)action:(id)sender
{
    color = [UIColor randomColor];
}
```

Each time the action button is pressed, the view controller generates a new color. When VIDEOkit queries the controller to update the external view, it sets this as the background color. You can see the external screen instantly update to a new random color.

> **Note**
>
> Reflector App ($12.99/single license, $54.99/5-computer license, http://reflectorapp.com) provides an excellent debugging companion for AirPlay, offering a no-wires/no-Apple TV solution that works on Mac and Windows computers. It mimics an Apple TV AirPlay receiver, letting you broadcast from iOS direct to your desktop and record that output.

Recipe 14-7   **VIDEOkit**

```
@protocol VIDEOkitDelegate <NSObject>
- (void)updateExternalView:(UIView *)view;
@end

@interface VIDEOkit : NSObject
@property (nonatomic, weak) UIViewController<VIDEOkitDelegate> *delegate;
@property (nonatomic, strong) UIWindow *outputWindow;
@property (nonatomic, strong) CADisplayLink *displayLink;
+ (void)startupWithDelegate:
        (UIViewController<VIDEOkitDelegate> *)aDelegate;
```

```
@end

@implementation VIDEOkit
{
    UIImageView *baseView;
}

- (void)setupExternalScreen
{
    // Check for missing screen
    if (!SCREEN_CONNECTED) return;

    // Set up external screen
    UIScreen *secondaryScreen = [UIScreen screens][1];
    UIScreenMode *screenMode =
        [[secondaryScreen availableModes] lastObject];
    CGRect rect = (CGRect){.size = screenMode.size};
    NSLog(@"Extscreen size: %@", NSStringFromCGSize(rect.size));

    // Create new outputWindow
    self.outputWindow = [[UIWindow alloc] initWithFrame:CGRectZero];
    _outputWindow.screen = secondaryScreen;
    _outputWindow.screen.currentMode = screenMode;
    [_outputWindow makeKeyAndVisible];
    _outputWindow.frame = rect;

    // Add base video view to outputWindow
    baseView = [[UIImageView alloc] initWithFrame:rect];
    baseView.backgroundColor = [UIColor darkGrayColor];
    [_outputWindow addSubview:baseView];

    // Restore primacy of main window
    [_delegate.view.window makeKeyAndVisible];
}

- (void)updateScreen
{
    // Abort if the screen has been disconnected
    if (!SCREEN_CONNECTED && _outputWindow)
        self.outputWindow = nil;

    // (Re)initialize if there's no output window
    if (SCREEN_CONNECTED && !_outputWindow)
        [self setupExternalScreen];

    // Abort if encounter some weird error
    if (!self.outputWindow) return;
```

```
    // Go ahead and update
    SAFE_PERFORM_WITH_ARG(_delegate,
        @selector(updateExternalView:), baseView);
}

- (void)screenDidConnect:(NSNotification *)notification
{
    NSLog(@"Screen connected");
    UIScreen *screen = [[UIScreen screens] lastObject];

    if (_displayLink)
    {
        [_displayLink removeFromRunLoop:[NSRunLoop currentRunLoop]
            forMode:NSRunLoopCommonModes];
        [_displayLink invalidate];
        _displayLink = nil;
    }

    self.displayLink = [screen displayLinkWithTarget:self
        selector:@selector(updateScreen)];
    [_displayLink addToRunLoop:[NSRunLoop currentRunLoop]
        forMode:NSRunLoopCommonModes];
}

- (void)screenDidDisconnect:(NSNotification *)notification
{
    NSLog(@"Screen disconnected.");
    if (_displayLink)
    {
        [_displayLink removeFromRunLoop:[NSRunLoop currentRunLoop]
            forMode:NSRunLoopCommonModes];
        [_displayLink invalidate];
        self.displayLink = nil;
    }
}

- (instancetype)init
{
    self = [super init];
    if (self)
    {
        // Handle output window creation
        if (SCREEN_CONNECTED)
            [self screenDidConnect:nil];

        // Register for connect/disconnect notifications
        [[NSNotificationCenter defaultCenter]
```

```
            addObserver:self selector:@selector(screenDidConnect:)
            name:UIScreenDidConnectNotification object:nil];
        [[NSNotificationCenter defaultCenter] addObserver:self
            selector:@selector(screenDidDisconnect:)
            name:UIScreenDidDisconnectNotification object:nil];
    }
    return self;
}


- (void)dealloc
{
    [self screenDidDisconnect:nil];
}


+ (VIDEOkit *)sharedInstance
{
    static dispatch_once_t predicate;
    static VIDEOkit *sharedInstance = nil;
    dispatch_once(&predicate, ^{
        sharedInstance = [[VIDEOkit alloc] init];
    });
    return sharedInstance;
}


+ (void)startupWithDelegate:
        (UIViewController <VIDEOkitDelegate> *)aDelegate
{
    [[self sharedInstance] setDelegate:aDelegate];
}
@end
```

Get This Recipe's Code

To find this recipe's full sample project, point your browser to https://github.com/erica/iOS-7-Cookbook and go to the folder for Chapter 14.

Tracking Users

Tracking is an unfortunate reality of developer life. Apple deprecated the UIDevice property that provided a unique identifier tied to device hardware. It replaced it with two identifier properties. Use advertisingIdentifier in the ASIdentifierManager class to return a device-specific identifier unique to the current device for advertising purposes. The identifierForVendor property on UIDevice supplies an identifier that's tied to each app vendor. This should return the same unique identifier, regardless of which of your apps is in use. This is *not* a customer ID. The same app on a different device can return a different identifier, as can an app from a different vendor.

These identifiers are built using the new NSUUID class. You can use this class outside the tracking scenario to create UUID strings that are guaranteed to be globally unique. Apple writes, "UUIDs (Universally Unique Identifiers), also known as GUIDs (Globally Unique Identifiers) or IIDs (Interface Identifiers), are 128-bit values. A UUID is made unique over both space and time by combining a value unique to the computer on which it was generated and a value representing the number of 100-nanosecond intervals since October 15, 1582 at 00:00:00."

The UUID class method can generate a new RFC 4122v4 UUID on demand. Use [NSUUID UUID] to return a new instance. (Bonus: It's all in uppercase!) From there, you can retrieve the UUIDString representation or request the bytes directly via getUUIDBytes:.

One More Thing: Checking for Available Disk Space

The NSFileManager class enables you to determine how much space is free on the iPhone and how much space is provided on the device as a whole. Listing 14-1 demonstrates how to check for these values and show the results using a friendly comma-formatted string. The values returned represent the total and free space in bytes.

Listing 14-1   Recovering File System Size and File System Free Size

```
- (void)logFileSystemAttributes
{
    NSFileManager *fm = [NSFileManager defaultManager];
    NSDictionary *fsAttr =
        [fm attributesOfFileSystemForPath:NSHomeDirectory()
            error:nil];

    NSNumberFormatter *numberFormatter =
        [[NSNumberFormatter alloc] init];
    numberFormatter.numberStyle = NSNumberFormatterDecimalStyle;

    NSNumber *fileSystemSize =
        [fsAttr objectForKey:NSFileSystemSize];
    NSLog(@"System space: %@ bytes",
        [numberFormatter stringFromNumber:fileSystemSize]);

    NSNumber *fileSystemFreeSize =
        [fsAttr objectForKey:NSFileSystemFreeSize];
    NSLog(@"System free space: %@ bytes",
        [numberFormatter stringFromNumber:fileSystemFreeSize]);
}
```

Summary

This chapter introduces core ways to interact with an iOS device. You have seen how to recover device info, check the battery state, and subscribe to proximity events. You have learned how to differentiate the iPod touch from the iPhone and iPad and determine which model you're working with. You have discovered the accelerometer and have seen it in use in several examples, from the simple "finding up" to moving onscreen objects and shake detection. You have jumped into Core Motion and learned how to create update blocks to respond to device events in real time. You have also seen how to add external screen support to your applications. Here are a few parting thoughts about the recipes you just encountered:

- Low-level calls can be App Store–friendly. They don't depend on Apple APIs that may change based on the current firmware release. UNIX system calls may seem daunting, but many are fully supported by the iOS device family.

- When submitting to iTunes, use the Info.plist file to specify which device capabilities are required. iTunes uses this list of required capabilities to determine whether an application can be downloaded to a given device and run properly on that device.

- Remember device limitations. You might want to check for free disk space before performing file-intensive work and for battery charge before running the CPU at full steam.

- Dive into Core Motion. The real-time device feedback it provides is the foundation for integrating iOS devices into real-world experiences.

- The iPhone and iPad accelerometer provides a novel way to complement the touch-based interface. Use acceleration data to expand user interactions beyond the "touch here" basics and to introduce tilt-aware feedback.

- Now that AirPlay has cut the cord for external display tethering, you can use Video Out for many more exciting projects than you might have previously imagined. AirPlay and external video screens mean you can transform your iOS device into a remote control for games and utilities that display on big screens and are controlled on small ones.

Accessibility

Accessibility enhancements open up iOS to users with disabilities. General Settings features enable users to magnify (or "zoom") displays, invert colors, and more. For a developer, accessibility enhancement centers on VoiceOver, which enables visually impaired users to "listen" to their GUI. VoiceOver converts an application's visual presentation into an audio description.

Don't confuse VoiceOver with Voice Control, or the Siri assistant. The former is a method for presenting an audio description of a UI and is highly gesture-based. The latter refers to Apple's proprietary voice-recognition technology for hands-free interaction.

This chapter briefly overviews VoiceOver accessibility. You'll read about adding accessibility labels and hints to your applications and testing those features in the simulator and on the iOS device. Accessibility is available and can be tested on third-generation or later devices, including all iPads, the iPhone 3GS and later, and the third-generation iPod touch and later.

Accessibility 101

Create accessibility by adding descriptive attributes to your UI elements. This programming interface is defined by the informal UIAccessibility protocol and consists of a set of properties including labels, hints, and values. Together, they act to supply information to VoiceOver to present an audible presentation of your interface.

Either assign these properties in code or add them through Interface Builder (IB). Listing 15-1 shows how you could set a button's accessibilityHint property. This property describes how this control reacts to a user action. In this example, the button's hint updates when a user types a username into a related text field. The hint changes to match the context of the current UI. Instead of giving a general hint about placing a call, the updated version directly names its target.

Listing 15-1   **Programmatically Updating Accessibility Information**

```
- (BOOL)textField:(UITextField *)textField
        shouldChangeCharactersInRange:(NSRange)range
        replacementString:(NSString *)string
{
    // Catch the change to the username field and update
    // the accessibility hint to mirror that
    NSString *username = textField.text;
    if (username && username.length > 1)
        callbutton.accessibilityHint = [NSString
          stringWithFormat:@"Places a call to %@", username];
    else
        callbutton.accessibilityHint =
            @"Places a call to the person named in the text field.";
    return YES;
}
```

The UIAccessibility protocol includes the following properties:

- **accessibilityTraits**—A set of flags that describe a UI element. These flags specify how items behave or how the interpretive system should treat them. For example, these traits include state, such as selected or enabled, and behavior, such as behaving like a button.

- **accessibilityLabel**—A short phrase or word that describes the view's role or the control's action (for example, Pause or Delete). Labels can be localized.

- **accessibilityHint**—A short phrase that describes what user actions do with this element (for example, Navigates to the home page). Hints can also be localized.

- **accessibilityFrame**—A rectangle specifically for non-view elements, which describes how the object should be represented onscreen. Views use their normal UIView frame property.

- **accessibilityPath**—A UIBezierPath that can be used instead of the accessibility frame for elements that are non-rectangular.

- **accessibilityValue**—The value associated with an object, such as a slider's current level (for example, 75%) or a switch's on/off setting (for example, ON).

Accessibility in IB

The IB Identity Inspector > Accessibility pane (see Figure 15-1) enables you to add accessibility details to UIKit elements in your interface. These fields and the text they contain play different roles in the accessibility picture. There's a one-to-one correlation with the UIAccessibility protocol and the inspector elements presented in IB. As with direct code access, labels identify views; hints describe them. In addition to these fields, you'll find a general Accessibility Enabled check box and a number of Traits check boxes.

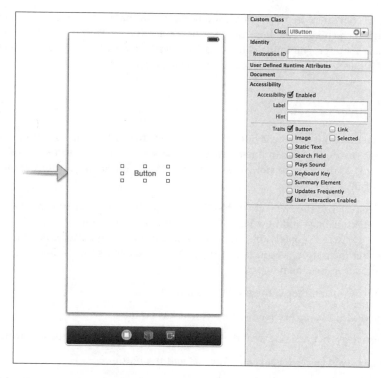

Figure 15-1   IB's Identity Inspector lets you specify object accessibility information.

Enabling Accessibility

The Enabled check box controls whether a UIKit view works with VoiceOver. To declare an element's accessibility support, set the isAccessibilityElement property to YES in code or check the Accessibility Enabled box in IB (see Figure 15-1). This Boolean property allows GUI elements to participate in the accessibility system. By default, all UIControl instances inherit the value YES.

As a rule, enable accessibility unless the view is a container whose subviews need to be accessible. Enable only the items at the most direct level of interaction or presentation. Views that organize other views don't play a meaningful role in the voice presentation. Exclude them.

Table view cells offer a good example of accessibility containers (that is, objects that contain other objects). The rules for table view cells are as follows:

- A table view cell without embedded controls should be accessible.

- A table view cell with embedded controls should not be accessible. Its child controls should be.

Nonaccessible containers are responsible for reporting how many accessible children they contain and which child views those are. See Apple's *Accessibility Programming Guide for iOS* for further details about programming containers for accessibility. Custom container views need to declare and implement the UIAccessibilityContainer protocol.

Traits

Traits characterize UIKit item behaviors. VoiceOver uses these traits while describing interfaces. As Figure 15-1 shows, there are numerous possible traits you can assign to views. Select the traits that apply to the selected view, keeping in mind that you can always update these choices programmatically.

Traits help characterize the elements in your interface to the VoiceOver system. They specify how items behave and how VoiceOver should treat them. You set them via the accessibilityTraits property, by selecting a single flag or OR'ing two or more flags. You can also set them in IB, as you saw in Figure 15-1. These traits vary in how they operate and how VoiceOver uses them.

At the most basic, default level, there's the "no trait" flag:

- **UIAccessibilityTraitNone**—The element has no traits.

There are also flags that describe *what* the user element is. These include the following:

- **UIAccessibilityTraitButton**—The element is a button.
- **UIAccessibilityTraitLink**—The element is a hyperlink.
- **UIAccessibilityTraitStaticText**—The element is unchanging text.
- **UIAccessibilityTraitSearchField**—The element is a search field.
- **UIAccessibilityTraitImage**—The element is a picture.
- **UIAccessibilityTraitKeyboardKey**—The element acts as a keyboard key.
- **UIAccessibilityTraitHeader**—The element is a content header.

Apple's accessibility documents request that you only check one of the following four mutually exclusive items at any time: Button, Link, Static Text, or Search Field. If a button works as a link as well, choose either the button trait or the link trait but not both. You choose which best characterizes how that button is used. At the same time, a button might show an image and play a sound when tapped, and you can freely add those traits.

There are a few basic state flags, which discuss the selection, adjustability, and interactive state of the object:

- **UIAccessibilityTraitSelected**—The element is currently selected, such as in a segmented control or the selected row in a table.
- **UIAccessibilityTraitNotEnabled**—The element is disabled, disallowing user interaction.

- **UIAccessibilityTraitAdjustable**—The element can be set to multiple values, as with a slider or picker. You specify how much each interaction adjusts the current value by implementing the `accessibilityIncrement` and `accessibilityDecrement` methods.

- **UIAccessibilityTraitAllowsDirectInteraction**—The user can touch and interact with the element.

If an element plays a sound when interacted with, there's a flag for that as well:

- **UIAccessibilityTraitPlaysSound**—The element will play a sound when activated.

Finally, a handful of states caution and describe how an element behaves and interacts with the larger world:

- **UIAccessibilityTraitUpdatesFrequently**—The element changes often enough that you won't want to overburden the user with its state changes, such as the readout of a stopwatch.

- **UIAccessibilityTraitStartsMediaSession**—The element begins a media session. Use this to limit VoiceOver interruptions when playing back or recording audio or video.

- **UIAccessibilityTraitSummaryElement**—The element provides summary information when the application starts, such as the current settings or state.

- **UIAccessibilityTraitCausesPageTurn**—The element should automatically turn the page when VoiceOver finishes reading its text.

As Figure 15-1 demonstrates, most of these traits (but not all) can be toggled off or on through the IB Identity Inspector pane. If you need finer-grained control, set the flags in code.

Labels

Set an element's label by assigning its `accessibilityLabel` property. A good label tells the user what an item is, often with a single word. Label an accessible GUI the same way you'd label a button with text. Edit, Delete, and Add all describe what objects do. They're excellent button text and accessibility label text.

But accessibility isn't just about buttons. Feedback, User Photo, and User Name might describe the contents and function of a text view, an image view, and a text label. If an object plays a visual role in your interface, it should play an auditory role in VoiceOver. Here are a few tips for designing your labels:

- **Do not add the view type into the label.** For example, don't use "Delete button," "Feedback text view," or "User Name text field." VoiceOver adds this information automatically, so "Delete button" in the identity pane becomes "Delete button button" in the VoiceOver playback.

- **Capitalize the label but don't add a period.** VoiceOver uses your capitalization to properly inflect the label when it speaks. Adding a period typically causes VoiceOver to end the label with a downward tone, which does not blend well into the object-type that follows. "Delete. button" sounds wrong. "Delete button" does not.

- **Aggregate information.** When working with complex views that function as a single unit, build all the information in that view into a single descriptive label and attach it to that parent view. For example, in a table view cell with several subviews but without individual controls, you might aggregate all the text information into a single label that describes the entire cell.

- **Label only at the lowest interaction level.** When users need to interact with subviews, label at that level. Parent views, whose children are accessible, do not need labels.

- **Localize.** Localizing your accessibility strings opens them up to the widest audience of users.

Hints

Assign the `accessibilityHint` property to set an element's hint. Hints tell users what to expect from interaction. In particular, they describe any nonobvious results. For example, consider an interface where tapping on a name—for example, John Smith—attempts to call that person by telephone. The name itself offers no information about the interaction outcome, so offer a hint telling the user about it—for example, "Places a phone call to this person," or, even better, "Places a phone call to John Smith." Here are tips for building better hints:

- **Use sentence form.** Start with a capital letter and end with a period. Do this even though each hint has a missing, implied subject. For example, in "Clears text in the form," the implied subject is *"This button."* Using sentence format ensures that VoiceOver speaks the hint with proper inflection.

- **Use verbs that describe what the element does, not what the user does.** *"[This text label]* Places a phone call to this person." provides the right context for the user. *"[You will]* Place a phone call to this person." does not.

- **Do not say the name or type of the GUI element.** Avoid hints that refer to the UI item being manipulated. Skip the GUI name (its label, such as "Delete") and type (its class, such as "button"). VoiceOver adds that information where needed, preventing any overly redundant playback, such as the confusing "Delete button *[label]* button *[VoiceOver description]* button *[hint]* removes item from screen." Use the succinct "Removes item from screen." instead.

- **Avoid the action.** Do not describe the action that the user takes. Do not say "Swiping places a phone call to this person" or "Tapping places a phone call to this person." VoiceOver uses its own set of gestures to activate GUI elements. Never refer to gestures directly.

- **Be verbose.** "Places call" does not describe the outcome as well as "Places a call to this person," or, even better, "Places a call to John Smith." A short but thorough explanation better helps the user than one that is so terse that the user has to guess about details. Avoid hints that require the user to listen again before proceeding.

- **Localize.** As with labels, localizing your accessibility hints works with the widest user base.

Testing with the Simulator

The iOS simulator's Accessibility Inspector is designed for testing accessible applications before deploying them to the iOS device. The simulator's inspector simulates VoiceOver interaction with your application, providing immediate visual feedback via a floating pane (there is no actual voice produced) without requiring the use of the VoiceOver gesture interface directly. Because you cannot replicate many VoiceOver gestures with the simulator (such as triple-swipes and sequential hold-then-tap gestures), the inspector focuses on describing interface items rather than responding to VoiceOver gestures.

Enable this feature by opening Settings > General > Accessibility. Switch the Accessibility Inspector to On. The inspector, shown in Figure 15-2, immediately appears. It lists the current settings for the currently selected accessible element.

> **Note**
>
> Unfortunately, Apple's current Xcode 5 development tools do not properly support the simulator's Accessibility Inspector. Apple should remedy this in a future update. The screen shots presented here are edited compositions based on the current presentation in Xcode 5 along with the valid inspector content provided with Xcode 4.6. The fully functional screens should be similar to those provided.

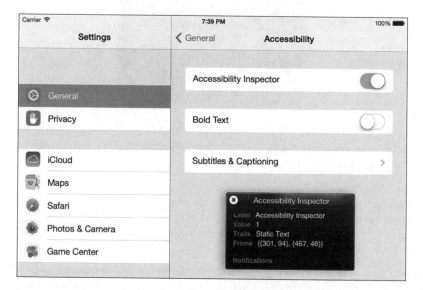

Figure 15-2   The iPad simulator's Accessibility Inspector highlights the currently selected GUI feature, revealing its label, hint, and other accessibility properties.

Know how to enable and disable the inspector: The circled X in the top-left corner of the inspector controls that behavior. Click it once to shrink the inspector to a disabled single line. Click again to restore the inspector to active mode. For the most part, keep the inspector disabled until you actually need to inspect a GUI item. Figure 15-3 shows a button interface as described in the Accessibility Inspector.

Figure 15-3   The Accessibility Inspector reflects the values set either in IB or in code that describe the currently selected item.

Like VoiceOver, the inspector interferes with normal application gestures. It will slow down your work, so use it sparingly (normally when you are ready to test). Launch your application with the inspector disabled but available. Navigate to the screen you want to work with and then enable the inspector.

When you update accessibility hints in code, the inspector updates in real time to match those changes. Activating the inspector allows you to view the current hint as those changes happen, ensuring that the onscreen hints and labels reflect the up-to-date interface.

Broadcasting Updates

Your application should post notifications to let the VoiceOver accessibility system know about onscreen element changes outside direct user interaction:

- When you add or remove a GUI element the `UIAccessibilityLayoutChanged-Notification` gives the VoiceOver accessibility system a heads-up about those changes.

- Applications can post a `UIAccessibilityPageScrolledNotification` after completing a scroll action. The notification's object should contain a description of the new scroll position (for example, "Page 5 of 17" or "Tab 2 of 4").

- When the zoomed frame changes, send a `UIAccessibilityZoomFocusChanged` notification. Include a user dictionary with `type`, `frame`, and `view` parameters. These parameters specify the type of zoom that has taken place, the currently zoomed frame (in screen coordinates), and the view that contains the zoomed frame.

In addition to these change updates, you can broadcast general announcements through the accessibility VoiceOver system. `UIAccessibilityAnnouncementNotification` takes one parameter, a string, which contains an announcement. Use this to notify users when tiny GUI changes take place, or for changes that only briefly appear on screen, or for changes that don't affect the UI directly.

Testing Accessibility on iOS

Testing on the iPhone or iPad is a critical part of accessibility development. The device enables you to work with the actual VoiceOver utility rather than a window-based inspector. You hear what your users will hear and can test your GUI with your fingers and ears rather than with your eyes.

Like the simulator, the iPhone provides a way to enable and disable VoiceOver on-the-fly. Although you can enable VoiceOver in Settings and then test your application with VoiceOver running, you'll find that it's much easier to use a special toggle. The toggle lets you avoid the hassle of navigating out of Settings and over to your application by using VoiceOver gestures. You can switch VoiceOver off, use normal iOS interactions to get your application started, and then switch VoiceOver back on when you're ready to test.

To enable that toggle, follow these steps:

1. Go to the Accessibility settings pane. Navigate to Settings > General > Accessibility.

2. Locate and tap Accessibility Shortcut to display a list of possible accessibility actions for when you triple-click the hardware Home button.

3. Choose VoiceOver to set it as your triple-click action. When it is selected (a check appears to its right), enable and disable VoiceOver by triple-clicking the physical Home button at the bottom of your iOS device. A spoken prompt confirms the current VoiceOver setting.

This VoiceOver toggle offers you the ability to skip many of the laborious details involved in navigating to your application using triple-fingered drags and multistage button clicks. At the same time, you should be conversant with VoiceOver gestures and interactions. Table 15-1 summarizes the VoiceOver gestures that you need to know to test your application.

Take special note of Screen Curtain, which enables you to blank your device display, offering a true test of your application as an audio-based interface. Try the iPhone calculator application with Screen Curtain enabled to gain a true sense of the challenge of using an iPhone application without sight.

Table 15-1   **Common VoiceOver Gestures for Applications**

Task	VoiceOver Equivalent
Toggle VoiceOver	Triple-tap the physical Home button.
Toggle ScreenCurtain	Three-finger triple-tap the screen (that is, tap the screen three times with three fingers).
Toggle VoiceOver speech	Toggle the VoiceOver speech entirely (not just for a single description) by double-tapping the screen with three fingers.
Stop speaking the current item	Double-tap the screen with two fingers. Repeat the gesture to resume speaking. In the home screen, when VoiceOver is not active, this gesture stops and resumes audio playback.
Activate an item (Example: Activate a button)	Method 1: Tap and hold the item with one finger. Tap the screen with another finger. Method 2: Tap the item to select it. Double-tap the screen to activate the button.
Adjust the text insertion point	With an editable text view or field selected, adjust the insertion point by flicking up or down with a single finger. The point may move by characters or by words, depending on how you have set your preferences.
Access the spoken text menu	With an editable text view or field selected, place two fingers on the screen and twist clockwise or counterclockwise. This gesture is properly known as the *rotor*.
Select and deselect text	Set the insertion point and enter text edit mode. Two-finger pinch open and close to select and deselect text.
Type text	Enter text edit mode by selecting a text field or text view and then double-tap the screen. The keyboard appears onscreen. Method 1: Tap and hold a keyboard button with your left pointer finger. Tap somewhere else on the screen with your right pointer finger. This is the best way to use the Delete key repeatedly. Method 2: Tap on a key to select it. Double-tap the screen to type that key.

Task	VoiceOver Equivalent
Move sliders	Select the slider and then flick up or down with a single finger to adjust the slider value.
Scroll up or down one page	Flick three fingers up or down.
Scroll left or right one page	Flick three fingers left or right.
Select and speak an item	Tap the item.
Spell out the selected item one character or word at a time	Flick a single finger up or down. This uses the settings from the spoken text menu.
Move to the next or previous item	Flick a single finger left or right.
Read the entire screen	Two-finger flick upward. This doesn't work as consistently as it should. Alternatively, use the following approach: Flick left repeatedly to the first item in the screen. Read the screen starting from the currently selected item using the two-finger flick-down gesture.
Unlock	Select the Unlock slider. One-finger double-tap the screen.

Speech Synthesis

In iOS 7, Apple added text-to-speech capability, providing another handy tool for both accessibility and other tasks, including navigation and general fun. Use the AVSpeechSynthesizer and AVSpeechUtterance classes to speak any string you would like. This can be handy for long-form speech and provides a greater level of programmatic control than VoiceOver, including voice selection, pitch, rate, and timing. In addition, this functionality is available even when the user is not utilizing Accessibility.

Listing 15-2 demonstrates the utterance of a simple string with the added twist of randomizing the voice from all currently available English-speaking voices. You can easily change this to other languages and locales. Use AVSpeechSynthesisVoice to select a specific language or to iterate through all available voices.

Listing 15-2   **Utilizing Text-to-Speech in iOS 7**

```
- (void)action
{
    // Establish a new utterance
    AVSpeechUtterance *utterance =
        [AVSpeechUtterance speechUtteranceWithString:
            @"Hello there you beautiful world!"];
```

```
    // Slow down the rate
    utterance.rate = AVSpeechUtteranceMinimumSpeechRate +
        (AVSpeechUtteranceMaximumSpeechRate -
            AVSpeechUtteranceMinimumSpeechRate) * 0.2f;

    // Set the language
    utterance.voice = [self anotherVoiceForLanguage:@"en"];

    // Speak
    AVSpeechSynthesizer *synthesizer =
        [[AVSpeechSynthesizer alloc] init];
    [synthesizer speakUtterance:utterance];
}

- (AVSpeechSynthesisVoice *)anotherVoiceForLanguage:
        NSString *)lang
{
    srand(time(NULL));
    NSArray *voices = [AVSpeechSynthesisVoice speechVoices];
    NSMutableArray *voicesForLanguage =
        [[NSMutableArray alloc] init];
    for (AVSpeechSynthesisVoice * voice in voices)
    {
        if ([voice.language hasPrefix:lang])
            [voicesForLanguage addObject:voice];
    }
    NSUInteger voiceIndex =
        rand() % voicesForLanguage.count;
    return voicesForLanguage[voiceIndex];
}
```

Dynamic Type

iOS has long supported accessibility features to adapt apps for a wide range of abilities and limitations. Now, under iOS 7, that philosophy has entered the mainstream of day-to-day app use. Users may adjust display settings throughout all their installed apps that opt in.

A single setting in General > Text Size (see Figure 15-4) globally adjusts reading size—including font weight, line height, and spacing. Younger users with strong eyes can dial back on font sizes, displaying more text on each screen. Older folks with weaker vision can push out bigger font requests with a simple drag.

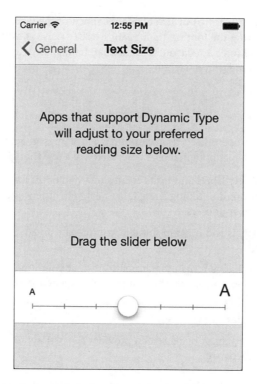

Figure 15-4   Changing text size globally involves a simple slider in the General system preferences in iOS 7.

To use Dynamic Type in your app, you must select fonts via the `preferredFontFor-TextStyle` method and pass in one of the following styles: `UIFontTextStyleHeadline`, `UIFontTextStyleSubheadline`, `UIFontTextStyleBody`, `UIFontTextStyleFootnote`, `UIFontTextStyleCaption1`, or `UIFontTextStyleCaption2`. If you use the preconfigured text styles instead of specifying a font name and size directly, iOS will style and size your fonts appropriately, based on the General settings.

To respond to user changes in text size, add an observer for `UIContentSizeCategoryDidChangeNotification` and update your UI appropriately:

```
UIViewController __weak *weakself = self;
[[NSNotificationCenter defaultCenter]
 addObserverForName:UIContentSizeCategoryDidChangeNotification
 object:nil
 queue:[NSOperationQueue mainQueue]
 usingBlock:^(NSNotification *note) {
     UIViewController *strongSelf = weakself;
     [strongSelf performSelector:@selector(updateLayout)];
}];
```

Using Auto Layout and standard UIKit text elements, much of the work will be handled for you. Generally, resetting the font on the `UILabel` or `UITextView` will invalidate the intrinsic content size and force a re-layout. For manual, frame-based layout, you need to call `setNeedsLayout` to trigger a re-layout.

Summary

When an iOS application opens itself to Accessibility, it becomes an active participant in a wider ecosystem, with a larger potential user base. Here are a few thoughts to take with you:

- Including accessibility labels and hints creates new audiences for your application, just as language localizations do. Adding these takes relatively little work to achieve and offers excellent payoffs to your users.

- Keep the role of labels and hints in mind as you prepare an auditory description of your application in IB.

- Don't be afraid to change hints programmatically. Let your interface descriptions update as your interface does, to provide the best possible experience for visually impaired users.

- iOS's accessibility system is an evolving system. Keep on top of Apple's documentation to find the latest updates and changes.

- Test with Screen Curtain. A blank screen provides the best approximation of the VoiceOver user experience.

Objective-C Literals

Think about how often you type cookie-cutter templates like [NSNumber numberWith-Integer:5] to produce number objects in your code. Perhaps you've defined macros to simplify your coding. Beginning in Xcode 4.4 (and LLVM 4.0), Objective-C literals introduce features that transform awkward constructs such as NSNumber and NSArray creation instances into easy-to-read parsimonious expressions.

Speaking as those who long created/used macro definitions for the NSNumber declarations, we love the way these literals provide more readable, succinct code. These literals save an enormous amount of typing and provide a natural, coherent presentation.

Now, instead of establishing an endless series of those declarations, you can use a simple literal like @5. This number literal is just like the string literals you've used for years. With strings, follow the at sign with a string constant (for example, @"hello"); with numbers, use an at sign followed by a number value. Similar literals simplify the creation and indexing of NSDictionarys and NSArrays.

This new advance squeezes together previously wordy constructs to create simpler, more succinct representations.

Numbers

Through the magic of its LLVM Clang compiler, Xcode's number literals allow you to wrap scalar values like integers and floating-point numbers into object containers. Just add an @ prefix to a scalar. For example, you can transform 2.7182818 to a conforming NSNumber object as follows:

```
NSNumber *eDouble = @2.7182818;
```

This number literal is functionally equivalent to the following:

```
NSNumber *eDouble = [NSNumber numberWithDouble: 2.7182818];
```

The difference is that the compiler takes care of the heavy lifting for you. You don't have to use a class call, and you don't have to write out a full method, brackets and all. Instead, you prefix the number with @ and let Clang do the rest of the work.

Standard suffixes allow you to specify whether a number is a float (F), long (L), longlong (LL), or unsigned (U). Here are some examples of how you would use them. Notice how simple each declaration is, not requiring you to use numerous specialized method calls:

```
NSNumber *two = @2;                     // [NSNumber numberWithInt:2];
NSNumber *twoUnsigned = @2U;            // [NSNumber numberWithUnsignedInt:2U];
NSNumber *twoLong = @2L;                // [NSNumber numberWithLong:2L];
NSNumber *twoLongLong = @2LL;           // [NSNumber numberWithLongLong:2LL];
NSNumber *eDouble = @2.7182818;         // [NSNumber numberWithDouble: 2.7182818];
NSNumber *eFloat = @2.7182818F;         // [NSNumber numberWithFloat: 2.7182818F];
```

Unfortunately, according to the Clang specification, you cannot wrap long double numbers. (Apple's runtime doesn't support long doubles either.) Be aware that the following statement causes the compiler to complain:

```
NSNumber *eLongDouble = @2.7182818L; // Will not compile
```

The Boolean constants @YES and @NO produce number objects equivalent to [NSNumber numberWithBool:YES] and [NSNumber numberWithBool:NO].

Finally, note that @-5 works in Xcode 4.5 and later. You don't have to enclose the value in parentheses.

Boxing

Xcode 4.4 supports only literal scalar constants after the @. If you want to interpret a value and then convert it to a number object, you have to use the traditional method call:

```
NSNumber *two = [NSNumber numberWithInt:(1+1)];
```

Xcode 4.5 introduced boxed expression support, avoiding this awkward approach. *Boxed expressions* are values that are interpreted and then converted to number objects. A boxed expression is enclosed in parentheses, and it tells the compiler to evaluate and then convert to an object. For example:

```
NSNumber *two = @(1+1);
```

and

```
int foo = ...; // some value
NSNumber *another = @(foo);
```

Boxed expressions are not limited to numbers. They work for strings as well. The following assignment evaluates the results of strstr() and forms an NSString from the results (that is, @"World!"):

```
NSString *results = @(strstr("Hello World!", "W"));
```

Enums

When working with boxing, you need to think of other considerations as well. Take enums, for example. Although you might think that you should be able to define an enum and then use it directly, allowing user-defined sequences that start with @ and continue with text could cause issues. Observe the following poorly chosen enum:

```
enum {interface, implementation, protocol};
```

You might imagine that you could create an NSNumber with the value 2 by defining the following:

```
NSNumber *which = @protocol;
```

This would, quite obviously, be bad. Boxing prevents any conflict with current and future @-delimited literals:

```
NSNumber *which = @(protocol); // [NSNumber numberWithInt:2];
```

Container Literals

Container literals add another great language feature to the LLVM Clang compiler. Prior to its addition, you had to create dictionaries and arrays as shown in the following snippet, which creates a three-item array and a three-key dictionary:

```
NSArray *array = [NSArray arrayWithObjects: @"one", @"two", @"three", nil];
NSDictionary *dict = [NSDictionary dictionaryWithObjectsAndKeys:
                        @"value 1", @"key 1",
                        @"value 2", @"key 2",
                        @"value 3", @"key 3",
                        nil];
```

These forms are wordy and require a nil terminator. That's not always a bad thing, but certainly it's a thing that's easy to forget and that's bitten nearly every developer at some point along the line. What's more, the dictionary declaration requires value followed by key. That's the opposite of how most people conceptualize and express dictionary entries, even though the method name indicates the proper order.

Container literals address both concerns by introducing a new, simpler syntax. These examples declare an array and a dictionary with the same contents as the manual example you saw detailed earlier:

```
NSArray *array = @[@"one", @"two", @"three"];
NSDictionary *dict = @{
        @"key 1":@"value 1",
        @"key 2":@"value 2",
        @"key 3":@"value 3"
    };
```

Array literals consist of square brackets with a comma-delimited list of items. Dictionaries are formed with a list enclosed in curly braces, where comma-delimited key/value pairs are associated by colons. In neither case do you need to add a `nil` terminator. Notice that the key/value ordering has switched to a far more sensible key-then-value definition versus the older object-then-key layout.

When evaluated, these expressions produce the same results as the previous two assignments declared with the traditional approach. The standard container rules still apply:

- Don't add keys or values that evaluate to `nil`.
- Make sure that each item is typed as an object pointer.
- Keys must conform to `<NSCopying>`.

Subscripting

Clang introduces container access using standard subscripting, via square brackets. In other words, you can now access an `NSArray` just as you would a C array. You can do the same with an `NSDictionary`, although indexed by key rather than number. Here are a couple examples of doing so, using the array and dictionary declared earlier:

```
NSLog(@"%@", array[1]); // @"two"
NSLog(@"%@", dictionary[@"key 2"]); // @"value 2"
```

But you're not just limited to value look-ups. Using this new syntax, you can also perform assignments for mutable instances. Here's how you might use the new subscripting features in simple assignments:

```
mutableArray[0] = @"first!";
mutableDictionary[@"some key"] = @"new value";
```

You still have to watch out for the index. Reading and writing an index outside the array range raises an exception.

Best of all, you can extend this subscripted behavior to custom classes by implementing support for a few core methods. So, if you want an element of a custom class to offer indexed access, you can provide that support by implementing one or more of the following methods:

- `-(id) objectAtIndexedSubscript: anIndex`
- `-(void) setObject: newValue atIndexedSubscript: anIndex`
- `-(id) objectForKeyedSubscript: aKey`
- `-(void) setObject: newValue forKeyedSubscript: aKey`

You choose whether you want access by order (array-style index) or keyword (dictionary-style key) and whether that access can update values (mutable style). Simply implement the methods you want to support and let the compiler handle the rest for you.

Feature Tests

As a final note, be aware that you can create feature-dependent coding. Just use Clang's `__has_feature` test to see whether literals are available in the current compiler. Feature tests include array literals (`objc_array_literals`), dictionary literals (`objc_dictionary_literals`), object subscripting (`objc_subscripting`), numeric literals (`objc_bool`), and boxed expressions (`objc_boxed_expressions`):

```
#if __has_feature(objc_array_literals)
    // ...
#else
    // ...
#endif
```

Index

E

F

J-K

L

M

N

O

FREE
Online Edition

Your purchase of **The Core iOS Developer's Cookbook** includes access to a free online edition for 45 days through the **Safari Books Online** subscription service. Nearly every Addison-Wesley Professional book is available online through **Safari Books Online**, along with over thousands of books and videos from publishers such as Cisco Press, Exam Cram, IBM Press, O'Reilly Media, Prentice Hall, Que, Sams, and VMware Press.

Safari Books Online is a digital library providing searchable, on-demand access to thousands of technology, digital media, and professional development books and videos from leading publishers. With one monthly or yearly subscription price, you get unlimited access to learning tools and information on topics including mobile app and software development, tips and tricks on using your favorite gadgets, networking, project management, graphic design, and much more.

Activate your FREE Online Edition at
informit.com/safarifree

STEP 1: Enter the coupon code: YOJZGAA.

STEP 2: New Safari users, complete the brief registration form.
Safari subscribers, just log in.

If you have difficulty registering on Safari or accessing the online edition,
please e-mail customer-service@safaribooksonline.com